D0208047

The Routledge Dictionary of
Politics

Now in its third edition, this dictionary is the essential guide to politics; its terminologies, ideologies & institutions. Fully revised and expanded, it includes authoritative and up-to-date information that is invaluable to anyone concerned with politics or current affairs.

It provides:

- Well over 500 extensive definitions
- An understanding of the basics of political thought and theory
- Clear, no-nonsense coverage of complex ideologies and dogmas
- Succinct definitions of highly specialised and technical terms
- Coverage of latest emerginig ideas and terminologies within political thought

David Robertson is Professor of Politics at the University of Oxford and Fellow of St Hugh's College, Oxford.

The Routledge Dictionary of

Politics

David Robertson

THIRD EDITION

Routledge
Taylor & Francis Group

LONDON AND NEW YORK

Third Edition

First published 2002
by Europa Publications
11 New Fetter Lane, London EC4P 4EE

(A member of Taylor & Francis Group)

Paperback edition published by Routledge 2004
11 New Fetter Lane, London EC4P 4EE

Simultaneously published in the USA and Canada
by Routledge
29 West 35th Street, New York, NY 10001

Routledge is an imprint of the Taylor & Francis Group

© 2004 David Robertson

David Robertson has asserted his moral rights to be identified as the
author of this work. All rights reserved. No part of this publication
may be photocopied, recorded, or otherwise reproduced, stored in a
retrieval system or transmitted in any form or by any electronic or
mechanical means, without the prior permissionof the copyright owner.

Typeset by Bibliocraft Ltd, Dundee
Printed and bound in Great Britain by TJ International Limited,
Padstow, Cornwall

All rights reserved. No part of this book may be reprinted or
reproduced or utilised in any form or by any electronic, mechanical,
or other means, now known or hereafter invented, including
photocopying and recording, or in any information storage or
retrieval system, without permission in writing from the publishers.

British Library Cataloguing in Publication Data
A catalogue record for this book is available from the British Library

Library of Congress Cataloging in Publication Data
A catalog record for this book has been requested

ISBN 0–415–323770–0

for Jessica, Oliver and Giles

Preface

This book has been in print for nearly twenty years; this is the third edition. After that time there is, perhaps, only one thing of which I am sure—prefaces get harder to write. Whether this is merely a reflection of the uncertainties and intellectual modesty of middle age or also a reflection of the developments in politics over that time is unclear. Certainly nothing seems as clear about 'modern' politics now as it did in 1984, or even in 1992. Yet politics, perhaps no more than any aspect of social change, is a curious mixture of continuity, change, and repetition. In the 1992 preface I commented on the fact that the first preface had been written when 'Ronald Reagan... was [still] the world's foremost hawk, a true believer in Star Wars, rather than the man who signed the Intermediate Nuclear Forces Treaty'. The current US President is the son of Reagan's successor, and has re-energized Star Wars—and replaced Reagan's old 'Evil Empire' with 'The Axis of Evil'. Plus ça change?

British politics has changed, has it not? In 1992 the Conservative party was still in power, though without Margaret Thatcher. Since then the Labour party has won an unprecedented secure second term. But, as the entries for 'New Labour' and 'Third Way' suggest, the degree of substantive change in British politics may be less well indicated by that fact than by comparing what the Labour Party defeated in 1992 has in common with its victorious descendant of 1997 and 2001. Plus ça change?

But of course things do change, often irreversibly. This third edition reflects change, even if it has to be written with a stronger sense of the unpredictability of politics than its predecessor volumes. It reflects change in the large number of new entries and the much smaller number of entries dropped. It reflects change in the way that most continuing entries have been re-written at least slightly, and a good number significantly. The changes may be more in the way of continuation of the picture of 1992 rather than the sharp discontinuities between 1984 and 1992, but they are real. The whole geo-political story of Central Europe is to point, as is the huge transformation of the old European Community, or the further development of a consensus on economic policy in most advanced economies.

The changes since 1992 have been more incremental than the huge change, the end of the Cold War, that occurred between the first and second edition. But they have given us a world of such groping uncertainty that the need for a book like this is perhaps even greater. I have done my best to capture the crucial ideas and points of this political world, tentative and uncertain as it is both at the international level but also in the domestic politics of all nations.

What has not changed, because it defines the book and has well stood the test of time, is the expository technique. Unlike most such reference works it is single-authored, and consists not of a very large number of brief entries, but of around 500 short essays. This dual technique imposes its own constraints. There is much of technical importance that a reader will not find here—an encyclopedia should be consulted. What he or she will find is one man's attempt both to describe and evaluate many of the most important ideas that shape modern politics. Because this book is fundamentally about ideas. It is not restricted to '-isms', of course. But an important concept, idea, thought, view, ambition, lies behind every entry. People are in the book, relatively rarely, because of something they have stood for over and above their own political careers; events are in the book not because they were suddenly vitally important, but because they shape the way we come to think. So, for example, 11 September 2001 is here not because it was an undoubted tragedy, but because it is a symbol both for an actual problem and, more importantly, a way of thinking about that problem. Mrs Thatcher is in the book, though in many ways only another successful Tory leader, because a senior member of the 'New' Labour Party very recently thought it not only valid, but useful, to address a group of socialists with the message that 'we are all Thatcherite now'. For that matter 'class' might be said to be in the book more because the current 'New Labour' British Prime Minister once thought in intelligible to tell the his electorate that they were 'all middle-class now' as because class actually shapes politics—it clearly does not do so as much as when the first edition was published.

The underlying structure and the analytic approach are much the same as in the first edition. My initial enthusiasm for this project arose because of the countless times I have given students an essay topic and wanted to tell them to look up some key word in the title before starting their reading, to ensure that they got off on the right lines. Later I came to see a wider potential use. All political scientists have to live with the fact that any educated person believes him- or herself to know as much as they do about politics because, after all, we are (as Aristotle tells us) all political animals. Yet there *is* a professional vocabulary (as well as a lot of awful jargon) which is not part of common parlance. Increasingly these words ('charismatic' is an example—we were once told that Bill Clinton is charismatic, and nowadays that Berlusconi is) are expropriated and, too often, misused by the media, becoming a part of general discourse more likely to confuse than inform. And, of course, there are 'facts', 'ideas', 'concepts' about which any serious newspaper reader should be informed but, bluntly, usually is not.

Public policy concerns frequently make such technical terms vitally important, and ignorance of their meaning on the part both of journalists and readers does not facilitate communication or opinion formation. No one should really form a conviction about the federal prospects for Europe if they are unsure about the meaning of federalism. More specifically, unless one understands the distinctions between 'directives', 'direct applicability', 'regulations' and 'direct effect', it is very hard to work out exactly what the European Union is actually doing. (And, by the way, it helps to understand the different roles of the Commission and the Council!) Similarly the language of 'rights' is even more important than it was twenty years ago, but then the United Kingdom had no Human Rights Act, and its court structure was much less amenable to 'judicial review'. These are highly technical areas, as well as highly emotive ones, and clarity helps avoid emotiveness getting in the way of serious policy. Politics as an art (an indefinable art—there is no entry just on 'politics'), and political science as a discipline, are overwhelmingly about words, shades of meaning, ideological linkages neither grammatically nor logically determined. Though she was talking of something else, the poet Elizabeth Jennings has the lines:

> Since clarity suggests simplicity,
> And since the simple thing is here inapt
> We choose obscurities of tongue and touch,
> The darker side of language,
> Hinted at in conversations close to quarrel,
> Conceived within the mind in aftermaths.

This dictionary is meant to penetrate some of the darkness, to reduce obscurity, to make the conversations less quarrelsome.

Some advice may be useful on using this book. Cross references are to be found in most entries, indicated in bold type. These are of two main sorts. The more obvious is where I use, in one entry, a word or concept which has an entry of its own elsewhere, and where a full understanding of the subject of the main entry requires an understanding of the highlighted entry. For example, the entry on Bentham refers to his views on **representative democracy** and the bold type thus indicates that there is a separate entry dealing with this concept. Other cross references are based on the idea that a reader interested in X is likely, independently, to be interested in Y, which has just been mentioned in passing, and should be informed that there is an entry on Y. Despite this, each entry is designed to be as self-contained as possible. Words in the title of an entry, may not correspond exactly to the words a reader has picked up and been curious about, but a little searching around should help. It might be said that the book has been designed and written with one eye to the fact that many people actually *enjoy reading reference books* and thus browsers are an important category of reader.

A book this long in print, after three editions, presents, finally, a tactical question about who the author should thank. Tact makes it imperative to decide whether to thank, truthfully, hundreds of people, or to go for simplicity and ignore them all. With two exceptions I opt for ignoring everyone, at least in public. Paul Kelly, my editor—though he is much grander in the world of publishing now than when he started work on this book—remains that as well, has become almost a co-author, and I continue to grow in my gratitude and respect. Secondly the last preface mentioned a two-year-old who had eaten some of the drafts. She is now 12, and brings me political news. Perhaps I should have emulated her approach. Was not her summary of the first round of the recent French Presidential elections all that needed saying? 'Oh Daddy, someone odd came second and people are crying in Paris.' Perhaps I *have* emulated this approach—certainly I share her judgment of the ephemeral and have sought to follow it in selecting material. Or is it her four-year-old sister who cannot be bothered even to *eat* my work who should be emulated? My love to them, to my wife, and to my three older children to whom this book remains dedicated.

David Robertson,
Oxford,
June 2002

A

Abortion

Abortion is a politically controversial issue in many Western countries, mainly because it clashes with some Christian teachings on the sanctity of life. In the past, by contrast, some communist societies had made abortion so easy that, in the Soviet Union, for example, it was close to being the main method of birth control. It is still extensively, and often compulsorily, practised in the People's Republic of China. The controversy revolves around two issues: the first is one of **natural rights**, of a woman to decide whether she wants to give birth, and of an unborn child to have life; the second concerns the level of church interference in state policies. Although **Roman Catholicism** is often seen as having the most firm teachings against abortion, **anti-clerical** sentiments have usually predominated in Europe, so that even Italy has a fairly liberal abortion policy. Ireland, by contrast, with a tradition of state subservience to the church on matters of private morality, still denies abortion in most circumstances. The legalization of abortion more or less 'on demand' in Britain, in 1968, was relatively uncontroversial, being carried out by a private member's bill, with all parties allowing their members a free vote; subsequent attempts to reverse or substantially modify abortion legislation have been unsuccessful.

It is in the USA that abortion has been the most explosive political issue. Until 1974 there was no federal law on abortion, the issue being treated, as are most matters of private behaviour, as falling under the jurisdiction of the individual states, with consequent variation of policy throughout the country. In 1973 the Supreme Court, in its *Roe v. Wade* decision, ruled that the states could only regulate abortion in limited ways, depending mainly on the stage of pregnancy at which a woman sought an abortion. Arguments over the viability of a foetus have become more problematic since the ruling, as medical science continually lowers the age at which an infant might realistically hope to survive, and consequently also at which the states might seek to intervene. Both the Catholic Church and the increasingly politically-important Protestant **fundamentalist** movements have opposed the *Roe v. Wade* decision ever since, sometimes in violent ways. Anti-abortionists are particularly prominent in **new right** politics, but are present right across the political spectrum.

Candidates for electoral office have increasingly come under pressure to take a public stand on abortion from pressure groups on either side, and some state governments have continued to try to exceed the *Roe v. Wade* limits on state intervention. As the Supreme Court became more conservative over the years, as the result of appointments by more right-wing presidents, the liberal intentions of the Supreme Court's 1973 decision have been increasingly restricted in later rulings, but the basic principle has never been overturned. The issue has become important in the new democratic republics of Eastern Europe, and the **constitutional courts** of countries like Hungary have gone to great pains to find a balance between protecting women's rights and allowing the new governments to interfere without restrictions. Ireland apart, Germany is the only country in which a constitutional court has taken a firm anti-abortion position as a matter of outright principle, but even there abortion is relatively easily obtained. Islamic societies share much the same attitude as that of Christian pressure groups in the West, and abortion is largely banned.

Absolutism

Absolutism describes a political theory which became popular during the 17th century, its main theorists being Bodin (*c.* 1530–96) and **Hobbes**. An absolutist system is one in which there is no limitation on what a legitimate government may legally do, where authority is absolute and unchecked. This is not to say that a legitimate government can do anything whatsoever and get away with it, but rather an assertion that a duly constituted government has a right to absolute authority.

If, as some constitutional experts do, one takes the view that 'the Crown in Parliament' is a single entity, then the United Kingdom has an 'absolute' government. The USA is not absolutist because Congress and the presidency can check each other, and because the constitution prohibits certain executive and legislative acts. The UK has no effective **bill of rights** and no **separation of powers**, and so its government could be described as unlimited and therefore absolutist. However, recent developments, especially the UK's entry into the **European Union**, may have started a process of legal limitation on central government autonomy.

Another approach to absolutism is to ask whether the general ideology or justification to which the government owes its power imposes any limits on the use of that power. One might argue, with **Locke**, that as all rule is based on the consent of the governed, there cannot be unlimited, and therefore absolute, government. Other theories, especially some versions of Hobbesianism, would deny that citizens can regulate government, which must therefore be legitimate and absolutist.

In practice, the reasons for justifying absolutism tend to be fear of the instability that might be caused by having more than one source of authority, or the use of a justifying theory (**theocracy** or **Marxism**, for example), in which rival views cannot be tolerated and some body or group has the absolute right to determine truth. Absolutism does not refer to the content of the laws, which could, in principle, be few and extremely liberal.

Accountability

Accountability in the modern state has two major meanings, which overlap. Firstly there is the standard meaning, common in democracies, that those who exercise power, whether as governments, as elected representatives or as appointed officials, are in a sense stewards and must be able to show that they have exercised their powers and discharged their duties properly. Secondly, accountability may refer to the arrangements made for securing conformity between the values of a delegating body and the person or persons to whom powers and responsibilities are delegated. Thus in the United Kingdom the government is said to be accountable to Parliament in the sense that it must answer questions about its policies and may ultimately be repudiated by Parliament. In 1979, for example, the Labour government headed by James Callaghan was defeated by a majority of one in a vote of no **confidence**, precipitating a general election. In the UK the Parliamentary Commissioner for Administration (popularly known as the **Ombudsman**) is thought to have improved the accountability of the administration by the scrutiny of administrative methods and inquiries into complaints against government departments. Ultimately, of course, governments in democracies are accountable to the people through the mechanism of elections.

Accountability is not confined to democratic forms of government, although it is in democracies that demands for greater accountability are generally heard. Any delegation of power will usually carry with it a requirement to report on how that power is exercised, and any institution seen as having power may be required to justify its operations to a superior authority. Thus it would be possible to speak of a **dictatorship** or of a **totalitarian** regime making the press, the universities or the trade union movement accountable to the government. With an increased interest in **human rights** and **democracy** throughout the world, and especially in the new Eastern European democracies, electorates desire accountability more than ever. It is often linked with the idea of 'transparency' in government, the ability to know exactly what elected officials are doing.

Additional Member System

The concern that systems of **proportional representation** can weaken the links of **representative democracy** between voters and legislators can be allayed by the additional member system, a version of which is used in Germany. Effectively, two sorts of candidates are elected. There are single-member constituencies in which candidates are elected either by a simple plurality system (see **voting systems**), or one of its modifications like the **second ballot** or **alternative vote** system. But in addition a number of parliamentary seats are not allocated to constituencies. These are allotted to parties according to the total number of votes they have received across all the constituencies, and bring their representation nearer to a fair proportion of all votes cast. How proportionate the system is depends on parameters such as the number of additional seats, and how they are allotted. The German system has equal numbers of seats of the two sorts, but a country would be free to set aside only a small number of additional seats, and thus to modify the initial constituency-based results only marginally. As in the example of Germany, it is also possible to set a minimum level of support, perhaps 5%, before a party is awarded seats. Commissions examining the idea of proportional representation for the United Kingdom usually favour some version of the additional member system. Probably the fairest version is to require voters to cast two votes, as in Germany, one for the individual representative which they prefer in their constituency, and one for the **party list** they prefer. This allows a voter to select on both personal grounds for their constituency, and for the overall party list which they prefer—the two votes can thus be split between parties. A version of this system was recommended for use in the United Kingdom in the report of the Independent Commission on the Voting System (the Jenkins Report of 1998).

Administration

This term may be used in a number of senses and the meanings are frequently blurred. It may refer simply to the political part of the **executive** branch and it is frequently so used in the USA, as in 'the Bush administration'; this usage is becoming more common in the United Kingdom. In some countries where a sharper distinction is drawn between politicians and civil servants, the word may describe the **civil service** or **bureaucracy** alone; this is also common usage in the UK. The term also relates to the process of implementing decisions and organizing the government of a country, as in the administration of quasi-governmental agencies, nationalized industries and local authorities.

In recent years both active politicians and political scientists have become concerned with the problem of governmental overload and the inefficiencies which result from an executive which has too many responsibilities. One solution which seemed possible for a time in the UK was **devolution**. A solution attempted under **Thatcherism**, apart from general **privatization**, was to allocate many functions of government to independent administrative agencies directly accountable to parliament.

In the USA the problem has to some extent been tackled by deregulation, which involves strict reviews of government rules and orders, and efforts to reduce or even remove government intervention and control. Other questions which arise in relation to administration are whether the administrative corps is either competent (see **maladministration**) or socially representative enough, and whether the administration can be effectively controlled by the politicians (see **accountability**).

Administrative Courts

Administrative courts comprise a distinct system of courts which exist to implement and develop public as opposed to private law, and which handle disputes in which the state is a party or has an interest. Many English jurists, such as A. V. Dicey (1835–1922), once considered administrative courts inimical to traditional ideas of liberty, assuming that they would apply standards unduly favourable to authority. More recently, however, opinion has tended to favour the establishment of such courts, partly because of the rapid extension of governmental activity (in, for example, the **welfare state**) and partly because a need has been felt for distinct principles of law which can be applied to protect the individual when coming into contact with governmental authority. It is still largely true that the **common law** jurisdictions have less clear and less powerful administrative courts than the **civil law** countries. Nothing exists in the USA or the United Kingdom, for example, with the authority and independence of the French Conseil d'Etat. Indeed, the **administrative law** judges in the USA are often seen, just as Dicey feared, to be clearly under the control of the government departments whose work they are supposed to regulate. In practice the Queen's Bench Division of the High Court has for a long time operated as an administrative court in the UK, specializing in such issues as appeals against the immigration service, and any of the multiplicity of **tribunals**. Nevertheless, the UK has no 'court of first instance' that operates purely for administrative law matters, and the legal rules applied in administrative law cases are developed from common law, rather than being seen as a distinct branch of law. This position is already changing with the implementation of the **Human Rights Act** (1998) and the impact of European ideas about public law coming from both the European Court of Human Rights and the **European Court of Justice**.

Administrative Élites

All countries need some sort of apolitical professional administrative group to carry out the policies proposed by the government and legitimized by the parliament (or whatever bodies carry out these functions). These administrative bodies are generally referred to as a **civil service** or **bureaucracy**, and usually employ a large number of people, although the boundaries of which state functions are seen as carried out by civil servants vary—in France and Germany schoolteachers and the police are included, but in the United Kingdom they are not. Most state employees purely carry out the job of applying government policy, but at the top of each civil service is a small body of highly-educated and talented administrators who do much more than administrate. They advise their political superiors and often have as much influence over the shape of policy as government ministers. This group, the administrative élite, is small, in the UK numbering perhaps only 3,000 out of a civil service of millions.

Although all countries have such a body, the extent to which it is a real élite of talent and training, as compared to the élites in business, education, the media and so on varies enormously, largely as a consequence of both the social status and financial rewards of taking the posts. In the UK and France these higher status civil servants have traditionally been a real élite, the best graduates from the most respected universities. In France, for example, the graduates from the École Nationale d'Administration, called the 'énarques', are socially, intellectually and ultimately financially comparable with the graduates of the Harvard Graduate School of Business Administration in the USA, while in the UK a disproportionate number of entrants into the upper reaches of the civil service still come from the universities of Oxford and Cambridge and, while the considerable financial rewards may not match the highest business salaries, a secure career and privileged position of influence and power is guaranteed. In some countries, however, a public service career is much less attractive. In the USA, for example, very few graduates of the leading universities join the federal or state civil services, partly because the positions with real influence are political appointments, changing with each administration (only about half of all ambassadorships, for example, go to career foreign service officers). In other countries the public esteem of government functionaries is so low that the talented prefer to make their way in the professions or in commerce. In Italy, for example, both the pay and status of the public administration is so poor that incompetence and inertia in public administration continues to be a major cause of the country's political problems (see **Italian Second Republic**). Where senior administrators are less genuinely élite they still exercise great power, but typically in a restrictive way through the insistence on formalities.

In all countries, however, the presence of a small group of powerful and secure civil servants, which may have developed their own set of priorities, can make it very difficult to get a political decision implemented exactly as the government had intended. There are various systems, the French ministerial cabinet or the British political adviser being examples, to try and circumvent such an administrative élite.

Administrative Law

Administrative law is the legal code, or set of rules and precedents, governing relations between the individual citizen and the state. Many such interactions, for example a contractual dispute between the administration and a company supplying it services, naturally fall within ordinary **civil law**, but even in cases like this there may be special rules that would not apply in a conflict between two private companies. The extent to which administrative law is distinct from national civil law, and the mechanisms for handling disputes vary widely (see **administrative courts**). It is important to distinguish between administrative law and constitutional law because the former never deals with the legitimacy of legislation *per se,* but with that of administrative acts carried out under legislation. For this reason the central concept in all administrative law systems is that which is called in England the *ultra vires* doctrine. This is the process whereby a court decides whether or not a bureaucrat or minister is actually empowered to do something for which they claim to have statutory authority. Although it may seem a very obvious and simple question, modern legislation grants so much discretionary power to a government that it can be extremely difficult to decide whether or not the discretion was used as the framers of the legislation intended. The main contrast between European 'code law' countries and the **common law** world in administrative law concerns the extent to which a court will overrule an administrative act because the action itself is thought wrong, excessive or unfair, or will only overrule where it is procedurally improper. At least until recently, common law courts have tended sharply towards the latter position, while code law systems have allowed more substantive judgments. This latter position is likely to emerge in the United Kingdom as a result of the enactment of the **Human Rights Act**.

Affirmative Action

Affirmative action, also referred to as positive and reverse discrimination, describes the deliberate policy of giving preferential treatment to some groups in a society on the grounds that they have hitherto been disadvantaged either by governmental policies or as a result of popular prejudice. It has been used to help ethnic minorities and women (see **feminism**), and it is sometimes suggested that it should be used to help other kinds of minorities, for example **homosexuals** or the handicapped. The idea has been most extensively translated into public policy in the USA, where the executive has encouraged the hiring and advancement of minorities by requiring, *inter alia,* that all organizations which have contracts with the federal government employ a given percentage of people belonging to a minority group. A policy of affirmative action has proved extremely controversial in relation to university and graduate school admissions, and one of the most celebrated constitutional cases of recent years (*Bakke v. Regents of the University of California,* 1978) set limits to the extent to which the policy could be used. Some US Supreme Court decisions of the late 1980s and early 1990s were clearly intended to limit the possibilities for affirmative action. At the same time, European law, especially under the influence of the **European Court of Justice**, was beginning to constrain discrimination, and may lead to a more positive approach along the lines of affirmative action.

Afghan War

After the creation of the independent states of India and Pakistan in 1947, Afghan foreign policy was dominated by close relations with the Soviet Union and tension with Pakistan, the latter caused by territorial disputes over Pashtun tribal lands on Pakistan's north-west frontier. In April 1978 the Afghan dictator Lt-Gen. Muhammad Daud (who had been prime minister between 1953 and 1963, and had overthrown the monarchy, although he was himself a member of the royal family, in 1973) was killed in a military **coup d'état**. The communist People's Democratic Party of Afghanistan took power, but, paradoxically, relations with the Soviet Union became strained as the revolutionary regime became increasingly torn by factional disputes and its inability to suppress the rebellion in the provinces led by the Muslim *Mujahidin* **guerrilla** forces. In December 1979, with the support of Soviet armed forces, the Afghan president, Hafizullah Amin, was killed in a further coup d'état, and replaced by Babrak Karmal.

During the 1980s the civil war between the Afghan army (heavily supported by the Soviet army) and the *Mujahidin* rebels (supported by Pakistan, over whose border they could take refuge, and covertly but massively by the USA, who supplied arms) escalated. The Soviet Union, technically 'invited' to assist the Afghan army by Karmal, quickly became embroiled in what has frequently been described as its equivalent to the USA's **Vietnam War**. As in Vietnam the invading **superpower** was able to control the cities, but lost control of most of the countryside, and especially of the mountainous regions. The tactics applied were very similar, involving search and destroy missions and the emplacement of heavily defended outposts from which the Soviet troops could only venture at great risk.

The war seriously affected relations between the Soviet Union and the USA, making it impossible for President Jimmy Carter to obtain Senate ratification for the **SALT** II treaty, and contributing to a breakdown in the **détente** which had characterized most of the 1970s. The war dragged on in stalemate until 1989 when President Mikhail **Gorbachev** finally withdrew the last Soviet troops. As in Vietnam for the first few years after American withdrawal, the situation remained much the same. The pro-Soviet government, still very heavily dependent on the Soviet Union for supplies, continued to control some areas with their own troops, but had to accept that the various guerrilla bands could defy them throughout most of the provinces. Soviet involvement in the war was deeply unpopular in the Soviet Union, being fought largely by conscripts among whom there were many casualties, but it ended not so much because of popular discontent but because the military and financial drain on the Soviet Union was too great to be continued. Furthermore, the fear of Islamic **fundamentalism** spreading from Iran through Afghanistan and into the southern Soviet republics seemed to subside with the beginnings of moderation in Iranian politics in the late 1980s.

In 1991 the Soviet Union and the USA pledged to stop supplying arms to the combatants in the civil war. Eventually, and after the final demise of the Soviet Union itself, the communist regime in Afghanistan fell in 1992. However, civil war continued, but now between rival factions of the ever disparate *Mujahidin*. Peace of a sort was enforced in 1996, when a Pashtun-dominated Islamic fundamentalist group, the **Taliban**, largely created by Pakistani military intelligence, took control of two-thirds of the country and enforced a repressive version of Islamic law (see **Shari'a**). They were never able to eradicate opposition completely, however, and resistance remained strong in the north. After numerous international condemnations of their conduct, the Taliban were eventually defeated by a combination of US-led bombing raids and troop advances by the disparate *Mujahidin*-based Northern Alliance, following the beginning of the so-called 'War on Terrorism' in October 2001 (the Taliban were sympathetic to the aims of Osama bin Laden, the Islamist militant who was believed to have ordered the attacks on the USA in September from a base in Afghanistan). The broad-based government installed to replace the Taliban brought some peace to the country, although its effectiveness in controlling the whole of Afghanistan remained open to question in 2002.

Agrarian Parties

Agrarian parties are political parties chiefly representing the interests of peasants or, more broadly, the rural sector of society. The extent to which they are important, or whether they even exist, depends mainly on two factors.

One, obviously, is the size of an identifiable peasantry, or the size of the rural relative to the urban population. The other is a matter of social integration: for agrarian parties to be important, the representation of countryside or peasantry must not be integrated with the other major sections of society. Thus a country might possess a sizeable rural population, but have an economic system in which the interests of the voters were predominantly related to their incomes, not to their occupations or location; and in such a country the political system would be unlikely to include an important agrarian party. As agriculture has come to employ a progressively smaller percentage of Western populations, which concurrently become ever more urbanized, this sort of political party has tended either to decline in importance or to broaden its appeal by shifts in its policies. The politics of the **Third Republic** in France were, to a large extent, based on an urban/rural **cleavage** leading to at least semi-agrarian parties. These declined rapidly in the **Fourth Republic** and **Fifth Republic** as the predominantly rural population turned into a predominantly urban one. Similarly, the importance of agrarian parties in Scandinavian party systems, once great, has declined.

In some countries, for example the USA, separate agrarian parties do not exist because loose party structures have permitted the existence of identifiably agrarian wings within parties, developed around other cleavages. (However, in the 1880–1910 period some US states did have specific farmers' parties, and the Democratic Party in the state of Minnesota is still known as the Democratic-Farmer-Labor Party.)

Some commentators think that agrarian parties may return to prominence as less developed economies integrate with highly urbanized economies in organizations like the **European Union**. Several agrarian parties were formed, or revived, in the new multi-party democracies of Eastern Europe, reflecting the larger agricultural labour forces and the relative lack of advanced methods in those countries. Because agrarian interests tend to come into conflict with more general economic policy, for example on questions of tariff levels and **free trade**, the agrarian vote cannot be disregarded by governments. On a global level, the problem of integrating primary producers with the largely tertiary economic sectors of advanced societies is becoming acute, as witnessed by problems in the **GATT** and **World Trade Organization** negotiations.

Aid to the Civil Power

This phrase is used to describe the role of the military in the United Kingdom when called upon by the government to help out in some domestic emergency. Such situations range along a spectrum from entirely peaceful to being close to civil war. At one end can be essentially humanitarian actions, as in providing emergency relief after a natural disaster. Somewhat in-between are the occasional uses of troops when **strikes** stop essential public services such as the ambulance or fire brigade services. A more controversial case, which has sometimes been threatened by the government, would be the sending in of troops to run prisons during a prison officers' strike. The most serious cases, rare in recent history in mainland Britain, are when troops are used to back up **police** in controlling public disorder; the most celebrated example of this was during the General Strike of 1926. These situations are intensely disliked by the military because of the strains of loyalty placed on troops who may be ordered to fire on civilians with whom they have great sympathy. Aid to the civil power differs from **martial law** in that the civilian authorities retain legal control. The troops operate under instruction from civilian officials, most usually a senior police officer, and their conduct is regulated by ordinary civil and criminal law. Thus an officer might, for example, be charged with murder after giving an order to fire when it was later judged that a lesser degree of force would have sufficed. The long-term use of the army to assist in policing Northern Ireland is, in most respects, an example of troops being used in aid of the civil power, though with somewhat more autonomy from civilian instruction than is usual (see **IRA**).

AIDS

Acquired Immune Deficiency Syndrome (AIDS), which is caused by contracting the Human Immunodeficiency Virus (HIV), was first recognized as a major problem in the late 1970s and early 1980s. It has become an important political issue in the USA and, to a lesser extent, in Europe for several reasons. Firstly, if some of the predictions of its likely rate of increase are true, AIDS will present an enormous strain on health service resources within a few years. Not only will the number of cases be very large, but the length of hospital care before eventual death, and the need for extreme caution to avoid infection, makes AIDS patients unusually expensive to treat. Secondly, fear of AIDS has led to demands for very intrusive testing and quarantine measures which are offensive in various degrees to many conceptions of **civil liberties**. All of these factors would apply whatever the cause of the disease. However, because AIDS is primarily a sexually contracted disease, and has disproportionately affected the male **homosexual** community, it has highlighted the ever ambiguous state of tolerance for alternative life styles. While some right-wing elements use the fear of AIDS to attack the legal tolerance of homosexuality, homosexuals themselves argue that governments would have been far more positive in dealing with the crisis were it more common among heterosexuals. Many policies to combat the spread of AIDS, as for example providing free hypodermic needles to drug users and urging the use of condoms, or even providing them to adolescents, immediately trigger deeply held conservative instincts among sectors of society. There is felt to be a pressing need, especially in the USA, for legal enforcement of **civil rights** to those who, being known to be HIV positive or an AIDS sufferer, experience wide ranging **discrimination** at all levels of society, but with most practical significance from institutions such as insurance companies.

In some African countries, South Africa being a particular example, the pervasiveness of infection with HIV is far worse than in the USA and other Western countries, and the proportion of heterosexuals among those infected is far greater. Here, however, the level of treatment and the attempts at prevention are far less, and the social and economic consequences perhaps far worse.

Alienation

Alienation is a very widely, and loosely, used concept, which originates in its modern form with **Marx**, although he took the term from **Hegel**, and a similar usage can be found in **Rousseau**. In modern sociological analysis it has much in common with the Durkheimian concept of **anomie**. It is helpful to take an etymological approach in trying to define this important but sometimes obscure concept. In legal terms 'alienation' means giving up rights in property; analogously, political philosophers have used 'inalienable rights' to mean those rights which cannot be given up, and cannot ever legitimately be taken away. But the derivation, from alien, suggesting something other, foreign, distant, is also helpful.

For Marx, alienation is a condition occurring in pre-socialist societies, where the human nature of man is made other than, alien to, what man is really capable of being. This is also the sense in which Rousseau used it, though his view was that contemporary society had made man other, and more corrupt, than had once been so. Marx had a sophisticated theory of alienation, especially as it occurred in **capitalism**. People could be alienated firstly from their own selves (i.e. from their true nature), secondly from other people (absence of natural **fraternity**), thirdly from their working life (because it was meaningless and involved 'alienating', in a legal sense, their labour for the benefit of others), and fourthly from the product of their labour (because most industrial workers do not have the satisfaction of designing and creating an entire product through the exercise of their skills). All of these are interconnected, and for Marx they all stem from the capitalist productive system, and especially from its practice of **division of labour**.

This stress on human nature, and on the way in which man is turned into a wage slave, without respect for self, fellows or daily work, is much weakened in the later and more economics-oriented work of Marx, but it has continued to be of vital interest and importance in social thought generally. It has often been applied far too loosely so that alienation frequently means no more than unhappiness; but some new applications are obviously legitimate extensions of Marx's usage, as when feminists argue that capitalist society, as part of its generally dehumanizing effect, alienates men from women. However, there are serious objections to the concept of alienation. Firstly, though Marx's writing is often highly persuasive in regard to the existence of the phenomenon, many critics hold that alienation is created by the division of labour endemic to any high-technology economy (perhaps even by the very nature of such economies) rather than by a particular system of property rights; and if this is so, alienation will remain a problem even under fully-developed **communism**. Secondly, the concept of alienation relies on the unprovable idea that a basic or true human nature exists. From a philosophical point of view the concept would be useful only if it could be shown (a) that man really would have certain characteristics under a different system, and (b) that these are in some sense 'natural'. Yet Marxists, and most others who make use of the concept, are strongly opposed to the idea that any basic human nature exists independently of social reality. Despite such problems, the concept retains its vigour and is widely used in social analysis.

Alternative Vote

The alternative vote is probably the simplest of all forms of **proportional representation**, though as a result it is not very proportional. It works by asking each voter to order their preferences among candidates. A candidate receiving a majority of first preferences is elected, giving the same result as under the plurality system (see **voting systems**). If no candidate gains a majority of first preferences, the least successful candidate is eliminated and the second preferences of their supporters allocated and added to the initial totals. If there is still no candidate with a majority of the new sum of first and second preferences, this procedure continues for as many rounds as are required to produce one. This system does help to increase the representation of parties which typically come second in seats where no majority occurs, but large degrees of misrepresentation can still survive. This method is, in fact, a simpler and automatic version of the **second ballot** system, though it is capable of modification in various ways. One sensible modification is to exclude not the candidate with least first preferences, but the candidate with most last preferences. This avoids the anomaly that a candidate who was every voter's second choice, and no voter's first choice, cannot be elected in the ordinary alternative vote system, because they will be eliminated after the first round.

Amendment

An amendment is a change made to a bill, law, constitutional provision or regulation. The process of making such a change is also known as amendment. The provisions of some **constitutions** make constitutional amendment especially difficult, and these are known as entrenched constitutions. In some legal systems certain laws are thought to be of peculiar importance and are similarly protected—for example, laws guaranteeing freedom of speech, freedom of religion or other basic liberties. Where a constitution has been altered or supplemented, the amendments may become almost as important as the original text. This is the case in the USA, where the first ten amendments to the Constitution are collectively known as the **Bill of Rights**. They were ratified in 1791 and have since proved a major instrument for the protection of individual freedom in the USA as well as providing models for other countries. Of particular note because they have passed into the general political vocabulary are the First Amendment, guaranteeing freedom of speech, religion and thought, and the Fifth Amendment, which grants the individual protection against self-incrimination in criminal proceedings. The most important aspect of the Fifth Amendment is its guarantee that no person shall be deprived of life, liberty or property without proper legal process (see **due process**); further guarantees are secured under the Sixth and Fourteenth Amendments. Since 1954 the Fourteenth Amendment of the Constitution has been used by the Supreme Court to promote both procedural and substantive equality in the USA in a way which has also served as a model for other jurisdictions (see **equal protection**).

Where ordinary rather than constitutional laws are concerned, the general assumption is that the stronger the **executive** and the weaker the **legislature**, the less likely are amendments offered in the latter to be successful. Thus in the French **Fifth Republic** it is rare for bills to be changed significantly during their passage through the National Assembly. In Britain, when the government has a working majority, amendments of substance are also rare, although the combined pressure of government back-benchers and opposition parties can sometimes lead to successful amendments.

Amnesty International

Amnesty International is pre-eminent among the many **non-governmental organizations** (NGOs) operating in the field of human rights. It was founded in 1961 by a British lawyer, Peter Benenson (1921–), principally to work for the release of 'prisoners of conscience' and political prisoners, the latter defined by Amnesty to mean those imprisoned for daring to state politically unpopular beliefs, provided they have neither practised nor advocated violence. Its original technique was to encourage the mass writing of letters to such people, in part to bring comfort, but mainly to expose regimes practising such repression to international public opinion. More recently it has broadened both its range of concerns and its strategies, and has built a large and complex organization world-wide.

Amnesty's concerns now cover opposition to the death penalty, all forms of torture, the use of landmines in warfare and the general problems of refugee women and children. It even campaigns against female genital mutilation as a private rather than state practice. Similarly some of its definitions have widened, so that, for example, people imprisoned for homosexuality are now considered as political prisoners.

The original techniques of letter writing and petitions by individual members still continue, but Amnesty's international reputation has been established largely through its research activities. Where possible, teams of experts visit countries and write reports on the behaviour of the state. These reports have always been subject to scrupulous standards of verifiability and accuracy, and are widely recognized as reliable evidence. They have, for example, been relied on by courts dealing with political asylum cases, and in such cases are often regarded as more reliable than analyses by governments. In an attempt to keep itself strictly outside politics, traditionally, Amnesty has not lobbied national governments, but increasingly it lobbies and is taken seriously by international organizations such as the **United Nations (UN)**, the Council of Europe and the **European Union.** This independence means that it has to rely for funding on its very large international membership and general charitable collection, a reliance which has helped it build a large network world-wide. The respect in which Amnesty is held internationally was symbolized by it being awarded the Nobel Peace prize as early as 1977. An example of this respect was the British Law Lords allowing it to act as *amicus curiae* (literally, 'a friend of the court') during hearings related to the attempted extradition to Spain of former Chilean President Augusto Pinochet in 1999.

Anarchism

Anarchism is a political theory based on two propositions: that society does not need government, and that no government is legitimate unless truly, and in detail, consented to by the individuals governed. Its history is long and confused, and the other political attitudes held by anarchists have ranged from far right to far left in the political spectrum. The common denominator of anarchists is an alienation from the existing structures of government and society.

The earliest serious anarchist thinkers were 19th-century writers such as Proudhon (1809–65) and the French theoreticians of **syndicalism**, who began to develop ideas about founding a society without government. However, anarchist elements can be found in many social theorists. One good example is **Marx**, whose doctrine that the **state** will 'wither away' under **communism** has clear affinities with anarchist goals.

Theoretically, anarchism rests on the moral assumption that freedom is an absolute value and that no one should ever be obliged to obey authority without having freely consented to do so. Empirically it rests on a set of assumptions about the possibility of organizing genuine voluntary associations dedicated to co-operative work and mutual aid. These assumptions seem more plausible where no great degree of industrial sophistication is involved, and there has often been a rather idealistic aura of peaceful rurality about anarchist theories.

Despite this there are important connections between anarchist theory and the more general theories recommending **direct democracy** and **industrial democracy**. The sort of commitments to extreme egalitarianism and total liberty that characterize anarchism have been taken over by radical socialist and Marxist groups, or, in more moderate versions, by exponents of industrial democracy. Anarchism of a form has had a re-birth at the beginning of the 21st century as political activists in many Western countries have begun to demonstrate against **globalization** and **capitalism**, often using violent means. Much of the opposition is clearly anarchist in that it does not urge the creation of some rival, perhaps a socialist, economic system, but concentrates entirely negatively on attacking the existing forms. Anarchist groups have been prominent among those involved in sometimes violent protests during several international meetings of government leaders.

Anarcho-Syndicalism (see Syndicalism)

Anomie

Anomie is a sociological concept, originated by **Durkheim**, similar in scope to **Marx's** concept of **alienation**. Anomie is held to be present in a society where normative regulation, the common acceptance of value and rules, is weak, and it consists of feelings of individual isolation, loneliness and meaninglessness that manifest themselves in social disorder. Though there are many technical definitions, both by Durkheim and in later works, the basic meaning of anomie is contained in one of Durkheim's more poetic descriptions: it is 'the malady of infinite aspiration'. What Durkheim meant was that modern industrial society, which sometimes seems to lack any moral or ethical basis beyond **utilitarianism** or arguments based on rational expectation, cannot offer anyone a reason for not doing, or trying to get, anything they want, although ever-growing personal appetites cannot ultimately be satisfied. To

Durkheim this state of affairs was the result of the Industrial Revolution, which broke down the traditional pattern of existence that bound men together closely through deeply accepted cultural norms (see **corporatism**). The concept can be used to explain unrest and dissatisfaction in any sort of social system, though it is often used either loosely or even tautologously (for example, to mean no more than a state of lawlessness, despite the fact that the term is actually intended to explain the lawlessness). One may question the validity of Durkheim's contrast between anomic industrial societies and traditional societies where the malady is absent because all know and accept their role; but the concept of anomie itself, if used with care, can be illuminating.

Anti-Ballistic Missile (ABM) Treaty

As part of the **SALT** I process the USA and the Soviet Union negotiated an agreement severely restricting their entitlement to deploy missile systems intended to defend either centres of population or their own **ICBM** sites by shooting down incoming strategic missiles. This, the Anti-Ballistic Missile Treaty, also restricted the provision of radar systems intended for use with such defensive screens, and limited the testing of new forms of defence against ballistic missiles. The treaty was relatively easy to negotiate because, though both sides had begun to build and deploy such systems, it was widely agreed that any effective defence system against ballistic missiles would certainly be fantastically expensive to develop, and would be of very dubious reliability even if built. It was a classic example of an arms control agreement forbidding something no one really wanted, but which, if one side went ahead and tried to build it, the other would be forced to follow suit. The ABM Treaty was not only adhered to, but neither side even deployed all that they were allowed to. This situation, however, broke down when the US President Ronald Reagan decided to invest in the hugely expensive, and technologically nearly impossible, Strategic Defense Initiative (SDI, popularly known as Star Wars (see also **Son of Star Wars**). It seems, with hindsight, that his decision perhaps had more to do with putting strain on the Soviet economy, even less able to bear the costs of such a scheme, and with forcing the Soviet Union into a negotiating position on reduction of strategic weapons, than with a serious intent to build what many experts thought impossible. The ABM Treaty was, at least, strained by the research into the SDI. Actually to deploy Star Wars weapons would certainly have been a major breach of the agreement, but it was widely interpreted that even testing the components was outlawed.

After the end of the cold war public attention drifted away from ballistic missile defence. Funding was reduced during the Clinton administrations

(1993–2001), and the research focus shifted to more modest systems which could track and destroy a few missiles launched by a terrorist organization or 'rogue state', and responsibility for strategic defence research was transferred from the SDI to the newly-created Ballistic Missile Defence Organization (BMDO). In 2001 the administration of President George W. Bush insisted that such a system be prepared for implementation, and increased funding to the Missile Defense Agency (MDA), as the BMDO was re-named. The Bush presidency encountered severe international criticism, especially from Russia, but made it clear that the USA was prepared unilaterally to abrogate the Treaty, which it regarded as having no further international purpose or importance. A treaty on arms reduction signed by the US and Russian presidents in May 2002 was perceived as having superseded the ABM treaty.

Anti-Clerical

An anti-clerical political outlook is one which is strongly opposed to the churches wielding any direct political influence or power. Anti-clerical parties or politicians have had an important role in most Western societies at one time or another. Nowadays a clerical/anti-clerical **cleavage** still exists in Italy and, to a lesser extent, France. In France, during the period 1870–1958, important sections of the electorate would automatically back certain political parties because they could be relied upon to oppose any clerical influence in politics. As the principal political voice of the Roman Catholic church, the **Mouvement Républicaine Populaire**, ceased to be of influence early in the **Fifth Republic** the distinction became less vital. Other electors (nowadays especially the Christian Democrats in Italy) vote as they do precisely because they feel that churches *should* play a significant role in the state.

In general it has been **Roman Catholicism** that has been the focus of anti-clerical politics, largely because it has historically been associated with conservative values and therefore seen as supporting upper classes. In the Dutch party system, however, anti-clericalism applies to the general opposition to church influence in politics, especially since the development of inter-denominational political groupings (which was itself a sign of the declining influence of the churches in politics and society in general). As the Catholic Church has changed and, particularly in the Third World, been seen as 'revolutionary' and an advocate of **liberation theology**, the traditional basis for anti-clericalism has declined. The general **secularization** of modern society has further reduced concern about religious influence in the state. Thus some political parties (the German Christian Democrats, for example) have become pure conservative parties (see **conservatism**), with religious affiliation playing no role in their support or rejection. However, religious **fundamentalism** has become both stronger and politically more relevant since the 1970s, so there is no guarantee that a form of opposition to religious involvement in politics, such as is already developing in USA, will not become important again. This opposition will probably not deserve the title of anti-clericalism as previously understood, because the fundamentalists' support is based in **populism** rather than, supposedly, the interests of the upper classes.

Anti-Semitism

Anti-Semitism, in political terms the discrimination against or persecution of Jews, is nowadays associated in most people's minds with **Hitler's** Germany. In fact it has a very much longer history, has had some political importance in most Western societies, and is by no means a spent force. The historical origins of anti-Semitism are complex and date back to the Middle Ages and beyond. Most European nations practised some form of discrimination against Jews, more or less intermittently and with varying degrees of clerical approval, for centuries before 19th-century anti-Semites, and later the **National Socialist** party, changed the emphasis of anti-Semitism from religious to racial hatred. To Hitler the Jews constituted an international conspiracy and exercised the real power in all the nations opposed to Germany, whether capitalist or communist.

Modern anti-Semitism is a common element in right-wing political creeds for a largely functional reason: such creeds base much of their appeal on **nationalism** and an ideal of national unity that denies the existence of important conflicts within the **nation**. It is a common feature of societies, from the level of the playground to international relations, to have a group of 'outsiders' against whom others can unite; **racism** often characterizes the selection of this group. In a political system such a group might be blamed for the social ills that might otherwise be attributed to the rulers or the social system. These reflexes can exist in both right-wing and left-wing systems, as evidenced by Nazi and Soviet anti-Semitism. Where a Christian tradition is an important part of the historic national identity, anti-Semitism is a peculiarly, if sadly, apt creed. Thus, for example, American right-wing movements such as the John Birch Society and the Ku Klux Klan have tended to be most popular in parts of the American South where Christian **fundamentalism** is very strong; such movements have never omitted to add anti-Semitism to their anti-black stance, despite the integration of Jews into American society. From the 1980s onwards economic depression and increased **immigration**, particularly from the **Third World** and Eastern and South-Eastern Europe, led to a resurgence in support for **neo-fascism** in Europe; again, anti-Semitism was often a strong element of such political platforms, even though immigration of Jews was minimal. In the new Eastern European party systems, anti-Semitism was a feature of several right-wing nationalist parties. The **Arab–Israeli**

conflict, and anti-**Zionism** in the Arab states and elsewhere, are not primarily anti-Semitic phenomena, but it is hard to determine how much latent anti-Jewish sentiment lies behind the more objective problems of the existence of the State of Israel.

Apartheid

Apartheid was the official doctrine of the South African government, and the ruling National Party (NP), between 1948 and 1991. Meaning 'separateness', it was in practice nothing more than an excuse for domination by the white minority population of blacks and 'coloureds' (see **racism**). The word 'coloured' is used here in the South African legal sense as someone who cannot be classified as black, but is not 'purely' white. Apartheid consisted of a set of legal inequalities. Non-whites were restricted in the areas in which they could live, and had to carry 'passbooks' to prove they were entitled to enter white areas for purposes of work or whatever; this central element of apartheid was officially removed in 1986, when a uniform identity document for all races was introduced. Most publicly and privately provided facilities, from schools and transport to bathing beaches and public toilets, were racially segregated. There was, until 1985, a legal ban on marriage, and indeed extra-marital sexual intercourse, between members of different races. But above all blacks and, until 1983, coloureds, were not allowed to vote in national elections, so that there was absolutely no peaceful political route through which they could work to end apartheid. This naturally encouraged political activists into illegal channels, particularly the African National Congress (ANC) which was banned in the wake of demonstrations against the 'pass laws' in 1960, and remained so until 1990. In 1961 the ANC established a military wing, the **guerrilla** movement Umkhonto we Sizwe (Spear of the Nation).

As was inevitable in such circumstances, a whole set of other inequalities were perpetuated by apartheid even if they were not legally enshrined, so that on all indicators—income, job opportunities, poverty rates, health statistics, educational opportunities and attainment—the black, and to a lesser extent coloured, population was deeply exploited. After defying world opinion, and some economic pressure, throughout the 1970s and 1980s, the NP government accepted the inevitability of change and began to remove the structures of apartheid. The formal legal expression of apartheid was abolished by 1991, and by 1993 multi-party negotiations on constitutional reform had been completed, with the first non-racial elections following in 1994. The NP participated in coalition governments until 1996, since when government membership has reflected the overwhelming black majority among the electorate. It will be several decades, however, before the accrued effects of inequality and racial **discrimination** evaporate.

Apparatchik

Apparatchik, properly speaking, means an employee of the *apparat,* perhaps best translated into English by the use of the modern Marxist term 'state apparatus', that is, any institution involved in the running of the state, whether formally part of the state or not. In the communist countries where the word was used, it meant in practice a member of the communist party who occupied an intermediate position in the bureaucracy. It is the *apparatchiki* who formed the bulk of the **new class** of **Djilas**. The term is sometimes used pejoratively of administrators and bureaucrats who bully those in their power and truckle to their superiors.

Aquinas

St Thomas Aquinas (1225–74) was one of the earliest Western thinkers to merge Aristotelian philosophy into the Christian political and philosophical heritage. Aquinas was primarily a theologian, but his writings had political significance since there was no clear-cut distinction between purely theological and political writing during the Middle Ages, when the Church was a major political and social force.

Like Aristotle, Aquinas regards **civil society**, or the political system, as a natural part of life. For Aquinas man cannot be truly human outside some sort of ordered society, and he conceives of the family as the basic political unit. (Aristotle too starts *The Politics* with an analysis of the domestic economy.) But Aquinas insists that such small units can never provide an ordered and secure social framework, and therefore sees full-scale political societies built up from the family as essential. The main purpose of such societies is to provide a framework within which man can develop his reason and moral sense, and thus come to live well and, specifically, to live as a Christian. On the all-important question of who should rule, Aquinas again follows Aristotle, arguing that though the best form of government, given the unequal reasoning powers of humans, would be a **monarchy** or **aristocracy**, these are too easily corrupted. Hence he too argues for a mixed constitution.

Aquinas's main differences with Aristotle occur where Christian doctrines clash with pagan values. The most important area here is the definition of human nature. For Aquinas there is a crucial difference between the human nature of the Christian, influenced by baptism, and that of the pagan; and for this reason he did not expect that his political theory could be relevant to all people. Now that our culture is fully familiar with classical Greek thought, Thomism (the name for Aquinas's doctrines) is often regarded as superfluous, although much of the political thinking of the Catholic Church even today is based on Thomist principles. Thomism, formulated at a period of increasing monarchial centralization, with its doctrine of mixed government and its stress on reason rather than **authority**, had a radical aspect, and this is one of the reasons why Thomism remains most influential among Catholic clergy of a radical persuasion in areas such as Latin America, where elements in the Church practise **liberation theology**.

Arab–Israeli Conflict

Conflict between Israel and its Arab neighbours started as soon as the **United Nations** gave the State of Israel official existence in 1948. Since then there have been three major wars, in 1956, 1967 and 1973, and a massive military intervention in Lebanon in 1982. More accurately though, there has never been a period of total peace between Israel and its neighbours since 1948, because **guerrilla** attacks by Palestinian groups and Israeli military strikes have been endemic. The original war in 1948 principally involved armed forces from Transjordan (which became Jordan in 1949), although troops from Egypt, Iraq, Lebanon and Syria were also present, fighting a hastily-created Israeli military largely based on the **kibbutz** movement and the irregular armed movement that had been fighting the British (which had held a Mandate to administer Palestine since 1923). Israel extended its borders beyond those fixed by the UN as a result of this war, while the West Bank came under Jordanian control and Jerusalem was partitioned between Arab and Israeli control.

The next war, in 1956, was an invasion by Israeli forces in which they captured the Sinai peninsula and Gaza Strip from Egypt. This war was fought as a result of a secret alliance with Britain and France, who wanted an opportunity to humiliate Egypt to force the country's president, Gamal Abd an-Nasser, to reverse the nationalization of the Suez Canal which had taken place earlier in the year. Israel had withdrawn from all territories occupied by early 1957, and the diplomatic losers of these incidents were clearly Israel, France and Britain, whose prime minister, Anthony Eden, was eventually obliged to resign.

In 1967 Israel was aware of an impending attack by Egypt, to be assisted by Jordan, Iraq and Syria, and won a brilliant and total victory in only six days (consequently the fighting is known as the 'Six-Day War'), largely because they launched a pre-emptive attack on the Arab air forces, effectively removing the ability of Egypt and Jordan to provide air cover for their ground troops. Israel took control of the Sinai peninsula and the Gaza strip from Egypt, the Golan Heights from Syria and, finally, the whole of Jerusalem and the West Bank from Jordan.

The 1973 'Yom Kippur' war, when Israel was attacked by Egypt and Syria, was vastly different. To start with the Egyptians and Syrians achieved tactical surprise, and the attacking Arab forces were much better trained and equipped. The Israelis did finally repulse the attacks, but at great cost, and in a way that showed they could not expect easy victories in the future. The cease-fire was followed by extensive peace negotiations, led by the USA, and finally a formal peace treaty between Israel and Egypt in 1979; this, however, led to Egypt being shunned elsewhere in the Arab world.

The wars were essentially caused by the unwillingness of Israel's neighbours to accept its legitimacy as a state at all, and were only made possible by massive military aid to Israel from the USA and to the Arab states from the Soviet Union. The basic principle of Israel's right to existence and within which borders, together with its treatment of Palestinians in the West Bank and elsewhere, remain the main areas of conflict. It is improbable, however, that any further major wars will be fought between Arabs and Israelis, particularly as the end of the **cold war** and the collapse of the Soviet Union has left US influence in the **Middle East** essentially unchallenged. This was demonstrated when Iraq tried, by attacking Israel with missiles during the **Gulf War**, to raise the anti-Israel standard again, and the Arab members of the US-led United Nations action stayed loyal to the alliance. However, continual conflict with Palestinian movements (see **PLO**), will continue until a lasting settlement of these areas of dispute is achieved. Even the creation of a Palestinian National Authority in 1994, and the restricted independence given to parts of historic Palestine thereafter, has not brought peace. Continuing violence from militant Palestinian Islamist movements, and conflict over the expansion of Jewish settlements in the West Bank, have ensured that a state of tension amounting to near war continues in the area.

Arbitration

Arbitration is a method of conflict resolution which, with more or less formalized mechanisms, occurs in many political and legal spheres. There are two main characteristics to arbitration. The first is that it is a voluntary process under which two parties in conflict agree between themselves to be bound by the judgment of a third party which has no other authority over them; the judgment, however, is not legally binding. The second is that there is usually no clear body of law or set of rules that must apply; the arbitrator is free, subject to any prior agreement with the conflicting parties, to decide on whatever basis of justice is deemed suitable. Arbitration has been used successfully, for example, to decide on disputed borders between Israel and Egypt, where local history was a major part of the arbitrator's decision.

Although lacking a precise legal position, arbitration will often have a recognized place as a pre-legal procedure. For example labour relations laws in several countries make it compulsory for **trade unions** and employers to go to arbitration before a **strike** can be legal, and commercial contracts often require arbitration before either side can sue the other. The political use of arbitration is that it can reduce tension, as well as being speedier and less formal than an orthodox court. Furthermore it is seen as less undignified to go to arbitration than to be legally forced into court, which in areas like labour relations law can be an advantage. The normal structure of an arbitral **tribunal** is to have each side appoint one or more arbitrators of its own choice, and for these two to appoint a neutral chairman, with the consequence that the chairman's view tends to dominate. The same principle applies in the International Court of Justice where, if the bench does not already contain a national from either of the contending countries, extra judges from the countries are appointed. It is through the use of arbitrators that much international private law is being built up, in the absence of a legally enforceable genuine **international law** in commercial matters, and through arbitration that a respect for basic principles in international public law is increasing.

Arendt

Hannah Arendt (1906 –75) was one of the generation of German intellectuals who fled Nazi Germany and took up residence in the USA. When the Nazis took power in 1933 she initially went to live in Paris, until after the German invasion of 1940. Like many of this generation she taught in élite American universities, including the New School for Social Research in New York, along with many other émigré intellectuals. For want of a better label, she has to be characterized as a political theorist, though her major works do not fit easily into the dominant traditions of that field, and some, above all her most controversial book, *Eichmann in Jerusalem* (1963), range far wider than political theory. In part this is because a dominant question throughout her work is precisely what 'the political' is. One of her major concerns was the way traditional political and social thought limited the range of that which is seen as political by an oversimplistic acceptance of the distinction between the **public and private spheres**.

Her own initial intellectual background, predominantly as a German theologian, led her to concentrate on the extensiveness of evil in modern society. For Arendt, modern society and social thought, by disaggregating individuals into different aspects of their being, and by downplaying the central idea of citizenship with its duties to others, has weakened social control against man's potential for evil. To a large extent, she argues, we are encouraged to see each other, and ourselves, as means to ends. The range of influences on her work is huge, and evokes such different thinkers as **Marx** and **Kant.** However, the most striking characteristic of her work is its insistence on looking afresh, and usually very critically, at traditional understandings. Thus one of her most famous works, *The Origins of Totalitarianism* (1951), attacks **Rousseau,** otherwise seen as an exponent of democracy and an icon of the left since the French Revolution, as one of the sources of the 20th century's worst excesses. While many of her contemporaries, equally famous in their time, have not seemed relevant to contemporary social thought, Hannah Arendt's work, whether accepted or denounced, strikes readers as increasingly, rather than decreasingly, of concern.

Aristocracy

Aristotle defined aristocracy, one of his three types of good government (see also **monarchy** and **democracy**), as the rule of the best in the public interest, and opposed it to **oligarchy**, the rule of a few in their own interest. In reality aristocracy has always been the rule of the rich, though often justified by ideologies which argued for the moral and intellectual superiority of the rulers, and which purported to show that the rule of a small hereditary élite was in the public interest. The origins of aristocracies have varied, but two elements are usually present. Firstly, aristocracies usually derive from war leaders who, in return for allegiance and material support from a population, undertake to protect them from violence by other groups. Secondly, aristocracies usually involve a connection to land, so that the descendants of the war-lords continue to hold the estates and the allegiance of the lower orders living on them.

The surviving European aristocracy derives from **feudalism**, in which a monarch granted lands to a nobleman in return for his military support and general obedience. In turn a great noble might grant subordinate lords smaller estates from his own holdings in return for an equivalent allegiance. As the Middle Ages gave way to modernity the nature of aristocracies changed considerably, with the noble titles of earl, count and others being granted for a wide range of support to European monarchs who were actively centralizing their **nations** and ruling in a much more direct and organized way. Many hereditary peerages in Britain date only from the 17th or 18th centuries, or even later, and were more likely to have been given, in reward for a variety of services, to men already rich and landed. The continued, if minor, constitutional role of the House of Lords means that a hereditary aristocracy, rather than just a rich élite, has retained some political power, although legislation passed in 1999 removing the right to a seat in the Lords of all but 92 hereditary peers, pending a definitive reform, eroded this further. In France two orders of nobility evolved, known as the 'sword', the traditional military aristocracy, and the 'robe', granted, for example, to leading civil servants and lawyers. Aristocracies everywhere have diminished in power either through actual revolutions, as in France and Russia, or through the impact of the

Industrial Revolution, as in Britain and Germany, where the rising capitalist **bourgeoisie** and the relative decline of agriculture as a source of wealth have made them largely irrelevant to a modern state. Nevertheless, there remains a self-conscious élite of hereditary aristocrats, often enormously wealthy, throughout Europe, even in countries like France and Italy where the state pays no formal recognition to aristocratic titles at all.

Aristotle

Aristotle (384–322 BC) was a thinker of the classical Greek period whose political theories, like those of **Plato**, set the bounds of political discourse throughout the Middle Ages; his work still exercises a profound influence on modern political and social thought. Aristotle's political ideas are more immediately acceptable to the modern Western mind than Plato's because he comes closer to approving of **democracy**. However, even Aristotle saw **direct democracy** as the least undesirable of existing types of government, rather than as the best obtainable form. Like most Greeks of his period he would have preferred a mixed government with important elements of aristocracy intermixed with popular rule. (In this context it should be remembered that the original meaning of 'aristocracy' is 'the rule of the best', not 'the rule of the well born'.)

An important aspect of Aristotle's thought, which derives from his interest in marine biology, was his use of biological analogies in discussing social life. Following Plato, he took an essentially **functionalist** approach to social and political institutions, believing that political life, being natural, takes certain natural forms, and that individuals therefore have natural and fitting places in society from which it would be both immoral and 'disfunctional' for them to depart. Aristotle's direct impact on European social thought began with his reinterpretation by the late medieval Catholic church and **Aquinas's** development and interpretation of his ideas into the Catholic doctrine of **natural law**, from which our modern inheritance of **natural rights** derives. Aristotelian views appear in contemporary **moral philosophy**, with special emphasis on his concern for education and the training of moral instincts.

Armies

Armies (used here, for convenience, to include military forces of all types) are among the oldest of all organized social institutions, and have a correspondingly long history of political importance. However, this apparently trivial point needs expansion. All societies have had some system for organizing military units for temporary or long-term defensive or offensive operations. Armies in a politically important sense are, with the exception of the Roman legionary army, products of the post-medieval era. As long as a nation relies on temporary, amateur troops, its army cannot be a threat to other social and political institutions (see **citizen soldier**). As soon as a permanent, bureaucratically organized, army comes into being, with its own legitimacy and power base, it becomes a potential contender for control of the state. Thus the Roman legions came to determine who should be emperor quite early in post-Republican times.

The earliest politically important armies in the modern world included the Cromwellian army in 17th-century England and the Napoleonic armies in France. The politicians' fear of the political power of standing armies is exemplified by British and American policies in the 18th and 19th centuries. As late as 1940 the USA kept its military establishment as small as possible. Later, after the huge increase in the size of the military machine during and after the Second World War, Dwight D. Eisenhower (who had been Allied Supreme Commander in 1945), warned the USA, in his farewell address as President, in 1961, of the potential threats posed to democracy by 'the military–industrial complex'. In Britain, the army was kept firmly under the political control of the ruling classes by restricting membership of the officer corps to those who could afford to buy their commissions from the Crown—a system that survived until a series of military blunders in the Crimean War (1853–56) forced a change of policy.

Nowadays armies tend to be of most importance in the politically undeveloped countries of the Third World, where military rule is a common feature. In such countries the army usually has a near-monopoly of bureaucratically efficient and disciplined personnel, often trained in the developed countries. As civil services develop and civilian governments acquire an aura of legitimacy, the fear of military **coups d'état** will diminish and armies will become servants rather than masters of the state.

Since the end of the **cold war**, both Western and Eastern states have begun to rethink their need for military forces, and a rich theoretical debate about the nature of defence forces and the function of armies has developed. Increasingly, military force is being thought of as addressed to new targets, for example international **terrorism** and drug dealing. The development of increasingly sophisticated and expensive high-technology weapons systems tends to conflict with an increased need for large numbers of basically trained infantrymen to carry out peace-keeping and **humanitarian intervention** tasks. The role of national military forces as part of international politics, through the **United Nations** and similar organizations, is becoming more important. The problem for Western military systems is to redefine strategy away from the classic idea of a **nation state** enemy which can be invaded and defeated.

Arms Control

While the idea of disarmament has been around, presumably, since the invention of the **nation state**, arms control is a more recent concept. This is largely because only a technological society can produce weapons sufficiently distinct from civilian uses to be covered by an international agreement. Furthermore the acceptance of the thesis that war is, partially, caused by armaments is itself a relatively modern idea. Although the First and Second International Hague Peace Conferences of 1899 and 1907 made gestures towards the desirability of disarmament and limiting the size of armed forces, the first treaties to specifically control armaments were those of the Washington Conference on the Limitation of Armaments of 1921–22 and the London Naval Treaties of 1930, 1935 and 1936.

Arms control can mean one or more of three things. Quantitative arms control either limits or reduces the size of a nation's military capacity by restricting the number of troops and of weapons in general. Thus the **SALT** I agreement of 1972, which set maximum levels for nuclear missiles between the USA and Soviet Union, was an example of quantitative arms control. Qualitative arms control attempts to ban or restrict entire categories of weapons, without making any limitations on what else a nation might buy or develop to defend itself. The 1987 **Intermediate Nuclear Forces (INF) Treaty**, which banned all ground-launched nuclear missiles with a range of more than 500 kilometres from Europe, is a recent example of such an arrangement. The quantitative/qualitative distinction dates to the **League of Nations'** World Disarmament Conference of 1932–34, when attempts were made to eradicate the most feared weapons of the day, particularly bomber aircraft and submarines.

A third meaning to arms control can best be described as **behavioural**. This involves restrictions not on what a country can own in terms of military hardware, nor on how many soldiers it can put into uniform, but on what it can *do* with its capacity. The restrictions applying in this case govern troop movements, the size of exercises, requirement of notice before military movements occur and similar measures. The idea is to reduce the possibility of war by accident, when one country's apparently belligerent activities are taken to imply a threat to another, which then begins to respond. Consequently such arms control restrictions, best exemplified by the 1986 **Stockholm Declaration**, are usually described as confidence-building measures (CBMs).

Each form of arms control has its own peculiar difficulties, but they all share two general problems. The first is technical. No treaty is of great value unless each party can be sure that the others are keeping to it, and not secretly building forbidden weapons or making covert preparations for an attack. This is known as the verification problem, and has become increasingly fraught with modern weapons technology. Agreement in 1930 in London to restrict the numbers of warships needed no particular verification system, because heavy naval ships were impossible to hide, and normal methods of espionage were enough to keep track of what countries were doing. But verification for a treaty restricting the size of nuclear warheads that can be fitted to a missile is impossible without allowing inspection of each country's missile sites, which is difficult to grant both for reasons of national secrecy and as a matter of sovereignty. The successful arms control agreements of the post-war years have been either those that required little 'intrusive' verification, or where breakthroughs in national attitudes to such modifications of national sovereignty have occurred. The second problem with arms control is that it involves extremely hard bargaining. Most nations will only accept a deal which, in their eyes, increases their national security, and often brings associated benefits. Arms control has little to do with moral stances or international public opinion, and everything to do with saving money without increasing vulnerability or giving up some technological advantage. Such deals, where two countries are both prepared to give up a particular weapon, are rare and are likely to succeed because neither independently had much use for the weapon in the first place. It is not unknown for a country to announce plans to build some weapon entirely in order to have something they do not need to surrender in future negotiations.

The most important arms control agreements of the post-war era have been the SALT (Strategic Arms Limitations Talks) treaties of 1972 and 1979, the 1972 **Anti–Ballistic Missile (ABM) Treaty**, the Intermediate Nuclear Forces (INF) Treaty of 1987, the **Conventional Forces in Europe (CFE) Treaty** of 1990 and the Strategic Arms Reduction Talks (START) treaty of 1991. It was the end of the **cold war** which largely brought an end to arms control negotiations and treaties, because neither **NATO** nor the Warsaw Treaty Organization (see **Warsaw Pact**), while it still existed, could actually afford to deploy as many weapons systems as treaties allowed. Renewed interest in ballistic missile defence on the part of the USA, however, has created the possibility of serious international disharmony over its likely abrogation of the ABM Treaty (see **Son of Star Wars**).

Arms Races

There have been arms races several times in recent history, brought about by military equipment becoming highly dependent on technology. Perhaps the first important arms race was the competition between Britain and Germany at the turn of the century to build bigger and better battleships, the 'Dreadnoughts'. The major arms race since the Second World War has been the competition between the USA and the Soviet Union to build up more powerful nuclear weaponry, especially **ICBMs** (Intercontinental Ballistic Missiles), in the hope of achieving a **first strike** capacity over the enemy. In more recent times the emphasis has shifted to competition for more and more sophisticated and accurate conventional weapons; it was these weapons which gave the US-led forces in the **Gulf War** overwhelming superiority over the Iraqi forces.

The arms race is a central part of **balance of power** theory: any technological advance by one side threatens the other, which then tries to build better weapons, forcing the first mover to improve its weapons, and so on. Often a new stage in the arms race may be launched by a relatively small development; for example, circular error probable (CEP—a measure of ballistic missile accuracy) improvements by the Soviet Union led in the early 1970s to extra investments by the USA, and the development of anti-ballistic missile systems by the USA in the 1960s, although defensive in themselves, were seen as a threat to the balance of power by the Russians, who therefore increased their weapons developments still further.

At a lower level, arms races clearly happen between any group of countries with potential conflicts, one of the best recorded being that between India and Pakistan in the 1970s and 1980s. There is considerable theoretical confusion about arms races: it is unclear, for example, whether actual or merely potential military capacity in one country spurs another to build up its forces. Similarly, many force enhancements seem to come about simply because the available technology makes a new weapon system possible, with no reference to any supposed threat elsewhere. It may be more sensible to see arms races as just one element in the overall **threat assessment** that any nation has to make.

Assembly

An assembly is a collection of people who either directly comprise, or represent, a political or social entity. The common example of a school assembly helps to explain the concept. In this case the entire body of people, pupils and staff, who make up the social group of the school, assemble together to discuss or to hear rules, information or instructions. In a political sense assemblies are decision-making or rule-passing groups. In many cases there is no real difference between an assembly and a **parliament**, house of representatives, chamber of **deputies**, or whatever the local terminology of the political system may be. Whereas the terms parliament and **congress** can be used to refer to both houses of a bicameral system, although the meaning is more often the lower chamber which does most of the legislative work, assembly always means just the lower chamber or the single chamber in a unicameral system (see **second chamber**).

There remains a shade of difference in the implication, however. Because a full assembly (as in the school example) implies that *all* relevant people are present, calling some body an assembly implies less a meeting of representatives, perhaps with freedom of action, than a direct collection of all parties. In the **United Nations**, for example, the General Assembly contains all the member states, in contrast to the Security Council which has only a few members. The **authority** of an assembly is accordingly greater than that of a council or set of representatives. The example of the French National Assembly is to the point: the theory of direct representation of the will of the people, which permeates French democratic thought from **Rousseau** onwards, leads to a preference for thinking that elected members somehow stand in for the physical impossibility of collecting the whole population of France into a true general assembly.

Association

An association is a group of people united to pursue a common cause. The right to associate politically is fundamental to **civil liberties** because without it political activity would be largely ineffective. The rights and capacities of political associations vary considerably from one society to another (see **interest groups**).

On an international level, many countries form associations to advance their mutual interests; the Association of South East Asian Nations (ASEAN), for example, exists to promote co-operation in that region.

Augustine

St Augustine (354–430) was the Bishop of the diocese of Hippo in North Africa, and one of the earliest systematic Christian theologians. He was certainly the first to grapple with the question of what should be the proper relationship between the **state** and the Christian religion. In discussing this he was more aware of the value of pre-Christian political philosophy than any thinker before St Thomas **Aquinas**, and much of his doctrine, where it is not specifically Christian, derives from classical political thought, especially from **Plato** and the Roman orator-writer Cicero. Like his classical forebears, Augustine stresses the 'naturalness' of **civil society**, which he regards as an association of men united by a common set of interests and a common sense of justice. Indeed, for Augustine, justice, which he tends to define in a rather Platonic way as the 'ordering' of people in their proper station and the regularizing of their relations, should be the cornerstone of society. Like many later thinkers he is in fact sceptical about human nature, and believes that this idealized civil society is rather unlikely to occur because of man's innate wickedness. This of course reflects his Christian belief in Original Sin, rather than a view based on observation, as, for example, in the work of **Hobbes**. Nevertheless, Augustine argues that Christians will make better citizens than pagans.

Like Plato, Augustine sees it as the function of the state to enforce a moral code, but being a Christian he interprets this role in a subtly but significantly different way. For Plato, simply doing what is right is what matters. For Augustine, state coercion cannot really create good people because it can only direct their external behaviour, whereas it is the desire to be good that marks out the Christian. Politics, then, is a necessary but negative force. Hence Augustine's distinction between the 'two cities' in his most famous work, *The City of God*. The earthly city is the actual political system in which a person lives; the heavenly city is the metaphysical unity of all true Christians. The political relations between these two remain unclear. Indeed Augustine never does produce any definite theory about the proper relations between the secular and the spiritual powers in society. As a Roman citizen, and one who admired much of the past glory of Rome, he would have found this difficult. Living at a time of political collapse many of his contemporaries believed that the Christianization of the Empire had contributed to its weakness, and Augustine is therefore at pains to demonstrate that a Christian could also be a loyal and effective citizen. Had the power of the centralized Christian church been more assured at the time, and had Augustine not been so keen to use any power, secular if necessary, fighting campaigns against heresy, he might have developed a more satisfactory theory on this matter. However, a more 'satisfactory' theory from the viewpoint of the church would not, in all probability, have been well received at this stage by the political rulers. His thought, including both his positive ideas and his omissions, was to influence relations between church and state for centuries.

Authoritarian Personality

The idea of the authoritarian personality was developed by social psychologists of the **Marxist** inclined Frankfurt School during the late 1930s and 1940s. The original researchers, under the leadership of Max Horkheimer (1895–1973) and Theodor Adorno (1903–69, author of a book called *The Authoritarian Personality*), emigrated to the USA in 1935 to avoid Nazi persecution. The theory attempted to explain the ease with which **totalitarianism** finds support, and with which such regimes manage to recruit into even the most repressive and violent of their institutions. It also has a much wider ranging application, in understanding the working of almost any highly hierarchically structured institution, as, for example, an army, and in explaining the attraction of political movements characterized by their **authoritarianism** and inegalitarianism. The mark of an authoritarian personality is that while such a person enjoys the use of **power** and having obedient underlings, they are also happiest when themself subject to firm authority from someone hierarchically superior who can command unquestioning obedience. There are many roots to this personality syndrome and many ways in which it expresses itself. Perhaps the most crucial is that the personality type suffers from extreme insecurity in any decision-making context and requires absolute clarity and certainty about their obligations as well as their rights. One definition puts it that the authoritarian personality suffers from an 'extreme intolerance of ambiguity'. It is an aspect of personality common to most people, in varying degree, making some susceptible to certain political faiths when the authoritarian aspects predominate unusually.

Authoritarianism

Authoritarianism, rather like **totalitarianism**, is perhaps more of a technical term in political science than one in ordinary political usage. An authoritarian system need not, strictly speaking, be a **dictatorship**, and may well not be totalitarian. The essential element is that it is one in which stern and forceful control is exercised over the population, with no particular concern for their preferences or for public opinion. The justification for the rule may come from any one of a number of ideologies, but it will not be a democratic ideology, and ideas of **natural rights** or **civil liberties** will be rejected in favour of the government's right to rule by command, backed by all the force it needs. It is very much tied to the idea of command and obedience, of inflexible rule, and a denial of the legitimacy of opposition or even counter-argument.

Because it is such a broad term, it is, in a way, 'value-free': it is equally sensible to talk of left and right, of communist, capitalist, even religiously-based, authoritarian governments. (This is also true of totalitarianism.) Neither is it limited to describing political systems or faiths. One of the most influential works ever written on the subject was in social psychology by Theodor Adorno *et al.,* entitled *The **Authoritarian Personality***. It is an attempt to discover the personality traits encouraged by, and found among, those who most readily fit into an authoritarian system. The stress here tends to be on characteristics such as a perfect willingness to obey orders from above, combined with a ruthless intolerance of disobedience from those below, an unquestioning attitude to the justifying ideology, and associated psychological attributes such as 'a low tolerance for ambiguity'. It is unsurprising that psychologists have usually found the personality profile of authoritarianism among the military, though any highly structured profession or society is likely to demonstrate it. The real opposition to authoritarianism is **liberalism**, or even **pluralism**. The term can also be used as an epithet not only to political creeds, but of a particular politician's assumed character or aims. Like all the most useful terms of political analysis, it can be applied to micro politics as well as macro—thus it can be useful to describe certain industrial managements as more or less authoritarian in nature, or indeed methods of organizing class-room behaviour in a primary school, though clearly it would make little sense to see a voluntary organization in such terms.

Authoritarianism as a characteristic of actual modern political regimes is frequently tied to religious **fundamentalism**, and has been apparent in such states as **Taliban** Afghanistan and, to a lesser extent, Pakistan and Saudi Arabia, where Islamic theology has a major impact on political thought. Some of the new East European democracies (see **democratic transition**), especially the less well-developed economically, like Bulgaria and Romania, are sometimes considered to be vulnerable to a resurgence of populist authoritarianism partly because the older population seek comfort from the stresses of capitalist development in the authoritarianism they were accustomed to during the communist period.

Authority

Authority means the right to give an order, which will be obeyed with no question as to that right, or, if not an order, the right to evoke legitimate power in support of a decision. Thus someone may have the authority to instruct soldiers to fire on a crowd, the authority to sign a binding legal document, or the authority to pass a security perimeter or frontier.

In the sociology of politics authority is contrasted with mere **power**; authority is being in a position to give an order that will be obeyed because its **legitimacy** is accepted by those to whom the order is addressed, rather than simply being a command which is backed up by coercion, bribery, persuasion, etc. Exactly what it is that gives authority, and what are the sources of legitimacy in politics, is more complicated. The best thinker on the matter is Max **Weber**. He distinguished, broadly, three kinds of authority. The most relevant to the modern day is 'rational-legal' authority, which stems from an overall social view that a system of power is legitimate because it is justified by a general view that it maximizes efficient running of society. A second vital source of legitimate authority is the 'traditional' mode of 'domination' (to use Weber's own language). This is based on the assumption that citizens learn that there are accepted ways of running a society and that any rule enshrined in the tradition should be obeyed simply because it always has been so obeyed.

Finally, but seldom of relevance today, is the **charismatic** mode of legitimate authority, the idea that a command should be obeyed because of the overwhelming personal attributes of the person who gives the order.

Authority will always be a predominantly legal concept, but its roots are much deeper. A person is often referred to as being 'an authority' on, for example, the poetry of Donne, if they are in an unquestioned position of claiming special knowledge and expertise—authority—on the subject. From this can be developed the political usage, that the ideology of the person or institution in question is formed from a position of superior knowledge and expertise, justifying their authority.

Ayatollahs

Ayatollahs are spiritual leaders of the Shi'ite Muslim minority sect. **Islam** is very much less institutionalized and hierarchically ordered than most Christian denominations, and it is not possible to make a direct equivalent to the role of, for example, a bishop or cardinal. A closer analogy, though still not a good one, is to the rabbi in Judaism. Certainly the stress on religious leadership being in part a matter of excellence in scholarship and learning, and therefore in teaching, is important. Because Islam does not grant to any one person or body a decisive authority over matters of faith, as with the pope in **Roman Catholicism** or the synod in some Protestant churches, there is no clear way in which any particular ayatollah can be seen as either institutionally senior to others, or possessing a special right to lay down correct belief on any matter. Furthermore, the divisions between Sunni and Shi'ite Muslims are at least as important as those between Roman Catholics and Protestants in Christianity. Ayatollahs have political importance because the state, according to Islam, is a religious institution (see **Shari'a**) and should be governed accordingly, and because of their particular role in guiding the Islamic **fundamentalist** movements which have so strongly affected world politics since the 1970s. After the Muslim factions in the Iranian revolution of 1979 gained control over the secular radical wing, and thus over Iran, the ayatollahs came to be the effective government, with Ayatollah Ruhollah Khomeini accepted consensually as the leading spiritual guide, being at first the *de facto* and later the *de jure* head of government. However, his authority was never completely institutionalized, nor even necessarily completely effective. Much of the revolution in Iran, and especially the enforcement of Islamic law and ethics, was carried out under the collective authority of a large number of ayatollahs, especially in their role as members of religious courts, or because they also held posts as members of the Iranian parliament. Divisions did occur among this collective body, and after Khomeini's death in 1989 there was no one who had a personal religious authority in the same way, and therefore no possibility of a routine transfer of power. Ayatollahs will continue to exercise enormous authority both in Iran and among fundamentalist Muslim groups elsewhere, and official political leaders will frequently be able to claim this title, although their actual power will increasingly come from more secular bases. In this context it might be noted that Khomeini's initial authority over his fellow ayatollahs derived more from his long-term political opposition to the Shah, symbolized by his lengthy exile, than from any special position he held in terms of his spiritual distinction.

B

Balance of Power

Balance-of-power theory rests on the idea that peace is more likely where potential combatants are of equal military, and sometimes political or economic, power. In the classic period of balance of power, which ran roughly from the end of the Napoleonic wars to the beginning of the First World War, there were always several countries of roughly equal power, none of which could guarantee to defeat a coalition of the others. The key to the balance of power maintaining international stability was that there were no ideological or other constraints on which powers could join others: any coalition was possible because all the members of the system, principally France, Britain, Russia, Austria and Prussia, had essentially similar internal politics and general ideologies. Thus if any one country became ambitious, or seemed to be enhancing its power, others would shift alliances to redress this potential imbalance. It should be noted that advocates of the balance of power never thought it would prevent war altogether, the intention was more that wars, if they broke out, would be fought in a limited way until the balance was restored. It was the preservation of the system, and of the identity and autonomy of the actors, that was the aim. Thus the problem of the First World War was not that it occurred, but that it was fought in such a way, and for so long, that it destroyed, rather than preserved, the system.

The **cold war**, by dividing countries between capitalist and communist, made this shifting of alliances impossible. To keep the theory alive refinements were made to the theory. Balance was still possible in a two-headed, or **bipolar**, system, mainly because the development of weapons of awesome destruction had led to a 'balance of terror'. **Arms races** become particularly characteristic of bipolar balances of power, as the fluid system of offsetting alliances is removed. The development of blocs of countries around the two **superpowers**, particularly in Eastern and Western Europe, was supported by the introduction of a further refinement, multipolarity. With the collapse of the Soviet empire in Eastern Europe, the diminution of the power of the Soviet Union itself and the possible diminishing role of the USA in the defence of

Western Europe balance-of-power theories are likely to return to favour not only as explanations, but also as prescriptions.

Balkans

The viewing of the Balkans as a region of political instability, corruption, economic and social backwardness, and irreconcilable internal social schisms based on religious or ethnic rivalry, is not a recent one. In the late 19th century it was the Balkans which were, rightly as it turned out, regarded as the powder keg which could ignite Europe; they did, in August 1914. In geopolitical terms the Balkans refers to Albania, Bosnia and Herzegovina, Bulgaria, Croatia, Greece, Macedonia, Romania, Slovenia, and the remainder of the former Yugoslavia, Serbia and Montenegro. It is, indeed, a socially divided region, with Roman Catholic and Orthodox **Christianity**, and **Islam**, all much more powerful as motivating forces than religion is in most of the rest of Europe. There are at least eight major languages spoken in the region. It is a very poor region, not only because it failed to keep up with the technical changes that Europe underwent from the 19th century onwards, but because it suffered even more than other regions that fell under communist domination after 1947. In many ways the Balkans today are in a time warp. Authoritarian control of one political colour or another has been dominant ever since the First World War, and little development of the social or cultural fabric often called **civil society**—thought to be required for liberal democracy—took place until the collapse of the communist bloc in 1989. It remains an area of fierce **nationalism** and cultural enmity, with an alienated and suspicious populace lacking almost all faith in politics of any kind. Polls regularly find a complete lack of trust in political institutions or the State. What all the Balkan countries have in common is a lengthy period of rule by the Ottoman Empire from roughly the 15th century until the end of the 19th century. During this period, when other European countries were slowly developing the institutions and cultures of liberal politics, no intellectual or social progress took place, except among very small Westernized élites. Nor was there industrial change: until at least the 1960s these societies were entirely agrarian-based.

Not surprisingly, there is a tendency today to deny that the Balkans as so portrayed ever existed, to insist that it is a Western conception which covers great diversity and presents a simplistic analysis. Consequently the very label is becoming unfashionable, to be replaced with 'South-East Europe'. Nevertheless, much of the Western conception is well founded; the area has, indeed, given us a classic analytic term in international relations—'balkanization'—to refer to the break-up of an area into small feuding units which makes progress and development extremely difficult.

Ballot

Ballots are votes cast in an election contested by two or more individuals or parties. By extension the *ballot box* is the box into which the votes are put, and *to ballot* denotes the process of voting. There are many different kinds of voting procedure (see **voting systems**). In modern democracies ballots must be cast in secret and an effective and impartial machinery must be established to prevent any tampering with the ballot (see **ballot-rigging**).

Ballot-rigging

Ballot-rigging describes any fraudulent, illicit or underhand interference with the voting procedure, the intention being to falsify the result or to make sure of electoral victory in advance. It used to be common in many countries, but systematic attempts to eliminate corruption have generally been successful in most Western states. In 1960, during the US presidential election, there was a strong suspicion that illegalities had occurred in connection with the ballot in Cook County, Illinois; and Chicago's mayoralty election of 1983 also witnessed attempts to inflate the number of eligible voters by false registrations. Allegations that some voters were prevented from registration in Florida surfaced after the US presidential election in 2000; the dispute surrounding the result of the election in that state made the allegations more significant. Similarly, after the Spanish general election of 1989 a number of irregularities were reported and the court rulings on these results were particularly momentous owing to the narrowness of the socialist party's majority. In Ireland there is a saying 'vote early, vote often', referring to the alleged custom of personation—the illegal casting of the votes of people on the electoral register who have died or moved from the district. (See also **gerrymandering**.)

Baltic States

The three Baltic states, Estonia, Latvia and Lithuania, share a common history of suppressed nationhood, having been largely under either Tsarist or Soviet Russian control since the 18th century. There was one brief period of independent statehood for each of them, between 1920 and 1940, but they put up no real resistance to Soviet annexation in 1940, faced with the alternative of subjection to Hitler's Germany. However, despite concerted attempts by Soviet regimes to destroy separate identities and indigenous culture, all three states managed to keep their languages and culture alive, and were among the first to grasp the opportunities presented by Mikhail **Gorbachev's** policy of **glasnost.** This is perhaps even more remarkable in view of the population movements imposed by the Soviet regimes. Not only did deportation by order of the Soviet government and wartime deaths reduce the total number of Baltic nationals, but Soviet industrialization policies led to huge numbers of Russians moving into these countries.

The opportunity to re-assert their identities came from two sources: the Helsinki Final Act (see **Helsinki process**) of 1975, and enthusiastic support for the liberalizing policies of Gorbachev, in particular the idea of glasnost. By the time of the attempted coup against Gorbachev in 1991, popular feeling was so intense, and Western support so strong, that the collapsing Soviet Union was in no position to oppose their demand for independence. Although these countries have experienced all the problems that the larger and more established Central and Eastern European countries had to go through after their own revolutions in 1989, they have managed the transition to liberal democracy remarkably painlessly—unlike, for example, in the **Balkans**. Each has set up a parliamentary form of government with competitive political parties, written constitutions and human rights protection. They have been especially eager to join Western Europe at the institutional level, and have above all sought to become members of **NATO**, though this as yet unachieved goal has more to do with establishing a Western identity than any actual defence need. Their economies have become modernized relatively rapidly, helped in part by the fact that the Soviet Union had itself relied heavily on them for its own economic needs, and had invested relatively generously. The real key to their political success, however, has been the uniformity of their culture, lacking any serious social, linguistic or religious **cleavages**, itself in part a reflection of the long-maintained covert **nationalism**. It may be significant that, after the Second World War, they continued to have at least *de jure* existence because the Western nations never formally accepted their annexation by the Soviet Union. In this sense, at least, they felt less deserted and more respected than some areas controlled from Moscow.

Behavioural

Behavioural approaches in **political science** became important in post-war America and spread to some university departments in Europe. Technically, a behavioural approach is one that concentrates on explaining overt political or social behaviour in terms of other overt or express phenomena. For example, when considering **voting** the only part of the process which can be subjected to a behavioural study is the actual casting of the vote, which can be observed externally and objectively; the ideology of the voter cannot be studied as here more subjective matters are involved. Other objective factors, such as class, religion, region and age can be taken into consideration when describing the voting process, but individual policy preferences or attitudes to issues are much more difficult to study. More generally, however, behaviouralism has come to mean a rather naïve distinction between the more apparently 'science-like' part of political science, concerned with measuring and statistical analysis, and the more traditional aspects, like **political theory** or political history, or institutional/descriptive studies. These barriers are increasingly tending to break down, partly as a result of a revival in political theory, and partly because the skills and techniques used by behaviouralists are coming to be more widely available and to be used by those with no theoretical preference for a behavioural position in general.

Bentham

Jeremy Bentham (1748–1832) is deservedly known as the founding father of **utilitarianism**, although its seeds can be found in the writings of **Hobbes** and **Hume**. Bentham's work, much of it done in collaboration with James **Mill**, was wide-ranging, covering political and **moral philosophy**, jurisprudence, and even practical topics such as prison reform. In jurisprudence he was an early legal **positivist**; in politics he was associated with **Liberalism**, but his utilitarian position was most fully developed in his political theory and moral philosophy. His general argument was that pain and pleasure were the two driving forces of mankind, and that moral or political values had to be translated into these terms. Treating man as mainly selfish, Bentham argued that the only way to judge political institutions was to discover whether they tended to produce a positive or negative balance of pleasure over pain. Strongly influenced by natural science, he believed that such things should be capable of precise measurement, and he proposed the construction of measuring devices and their application, through what he called the 'felicific calculus', to both constitutional engineering and detailed policy-making. James Mill developed the more purely political aspects of this position into a rather limited defence of **representative democracy** with more or less manhood suffrage. Bentham attached great importance to the political role of the middle class (as, for similar reasons, had **Aristotle**), which he believed less likely to push for policies of extreme self-interest than either the aristocracy or the working class. No separate value was given to any of the now-standard liberal democratic values such as **civil liberties**; indeed, Bentham scornfully dismissed all talk about **natural rights** as 'nonsense on stilts'. Bentham and James Mill represent the coldest and least attractive version of utilitarianism, though in practice their basic position was a radical one, far closer to egalitarian and democratic values than any of the orthodox political creeds of their time.

Bentley

Arthur Bentley (1870–1957) was an influential American political scientist of the inter-war period. Methodologically he was a precursor of the **behavioural** movement of the post-war period, while theoretically he was one of the founders of **pluralism**. His main contribution to the analysis of political systems was his **group theory**. Bentley held that the traditional distinctions drawn in political science between democratic and dictatorial systems were largely superficial. He argued that all political systems really consisted of a number of separate groups competing with one another for influence over policy. The role of the government was essentially that of political broker, responding to the demands and influence of different groups and distributing 'goods' (in the form of policies) in response. In many respects this approach represented a development of ideas expressed by the European school of **élitism**, and resembled modifications of earlier ideas made by people such as **Schumpeter**. Like many theories of its period, Bentley's was largely intended to strip away what he saw as an artificial shell of respectability surrounding democratic theory, many elements within which he regarded as no more than myths.

Bill of Rights

Many **constitutions** have bills of rights, often under different names, protecting certain vital **civil liberties**. The most imitated bills of rights are the 1789 French *Declaration of the Rights of Man and of the Citizen,* which has survived into the constitution of the **Fifth Republic**, and the first ten amendments to the US Constitution ratified in 1791, although the English bill of rights, enacted in 1689 to establish Parliament's sovereignty in relation to the monarchy, is earlier. A typical bill of rights will contain provisions guaranteeing the basic **natural rights**, such as the freedoms of speech, religion and assembly and the right to own property. It will usually also contain a set of more legalistic **civil rights**, including, for example, the right to a fair trial, perhaps by jury and with legal representation, prohibitions on cruel and excessive punishment and protection against double jeopardy (being tried twice for the same offence). Many modern bills of rights may also try to guarantee substantive rights such as those to education or employment; these, however, cannot be fully operational, because while a government can, clearly, be stopped from doing something, it cannot be forced to provide a specific good irrespective of the state of the economic or political situation. The constitutions of the new Eastern European democracies, in particular, contain such 'positive rights', and their **constitutional courts** have often enforced them against governments. Their ability to do this stems from the fact that, whatever else may have been lacking in the communist predecessor states, they all had effective welfare systems.

The effect of a bill of rights depends on other aspects of a country's legal system. In the USA, with its written constitution and powerful independent

Supreme Court, if it is proved to the satisfaction of the courts that the rights of a citizen have been contravened by the implementation of a law, that law is effectively invalidated. Other systems have more of a persuasive or partial effect. So, for example, the Canadian Charter of Rights and Freedoms, incorporated in The Constitution Act, 1982, states that the rights it lists are guaranteed unless legal limits 'can be demonstrably justified in a free and democratic society'. The English bill of rights has virtually no effect, in part because it has little relevance to modern legislation, but more fundamentally because the doctrine of parliamentary supremacy and the absence of a written constitution means that no previous act can constrain a later one. However, the passage of the **Human Rights Act** in 1998 has incorporated into English law the European Convention on Human Rights, with dramatic effects on the English judicial approach to citizens' rights.

Bipolar

In traditional **balance-of-power** theory an international system of fluid alliances exists within a group of perhaps three to five significant, but roughly equal, military powers (see **Congress of Vienna**). Any emergence of superiority by a single power or alliance was supposed to result in a regrouping of the states to restore a balance; this logical arrangement, however, ignores the possible influence of political ideologies within international relations. For most of the post-Second World War period international relations have been dominated by two **superpowers**, the USA and the Soviet Union, dominating more or less formal coalitions of allies. To accommodate this state within balance-of-power theory the idea of bipolarity was developed. Bipolar systems tend to stability, but at the cost of endless **arms races** as each polar group seeks for temporary dominance—hence the cycle of **cold war** and **détente** experienced from 1945 until the last decade of the 20th century. The collapse of Soviet power in the early 1990s potentially rendered the international system extremely unstable, because it has not reverted to the historical form of multipolarity, with several roughly equal power blocks. Instead, bipolarity has been succeeded by what should technically be described as a 'dominant member multipolar system', in which there are several moderately powerful nations and one, the USA, potentially able to dominate any coalition among them. In conventional balance-of-power thinking all the other actors should ally to offset the dominance of the USA; this, of course, is not likely to happen.

Bolshevik

The Bolshevik movement was one branch of the revolutionary movement in pre-1917 Russia. It originated from the split at the Second Congress of the All-

Russian Social Democratic Labour Party (RSDLP), held in 1903 in Brussels and London, when the movement broke into two, the **Mensheviks** ('minority') arguing for a less violent solution to Russia's problems. The Bolsheviks ('majority'), from whom developed the **Communist Party of the Soviet Union (CPSU)**, were led by **Lenin**, who advocated a tightly-controlled revolutionary party. Under his leadership the Bolsheviks developed the doctrine of the necessity for the masses to be led by the communist party (the **vanguard of the proletariat**), and for a more or less lengthy period of centralized state control over the people after a revolution before any democracy could be entertained (the **dictatorship of the proletariat**). When the first revolution of 1917 broke out in Russia, the Bolsheviks (now actually a minority among Social Democrats) were not immediately very powerful, and a moderate line, with which the Mensheviks could accord, was initially taken. However, the Bolsheviks were a far better disciplined and organized group, as well as being more ruthless, and in October 1917 they took power in a **coup d'état**, destroyed the liberals and the Mensheviks, and set about creating the party-controlled and centralized Russian state that lasted until the early 1990s. Thus was produced, especially after **Stalin** took control, **Marxist-Leninism**, the hard-line version of **Marxism** that the Mensheviks then, and many modern Marxist scholars now, see as a repudiation of much that **Marx** himself had argued for.

Bourgeois

In its original French usage the word 'bourgeois' was used to distinguish the upper classes of the cities from either the urban lower orders, or anyone from a rural background, however noble or lowly. As a consequence the **aristocracy**, which has tended to have more influence on social attitudes even after its political demise, made the word a pejorative one, precisely because rich town dwellers were aristocratic society's most serious political, economic and social rivals.

Bourgeois has a series of technical or semi-technical usages. The most important is the **Marxist** use. Here the bourgeoisie is a specific class, those who rose with and helped develop **capitalism** and thus took power from the feudal aristocracy. They were, on the whole, urban, and they were rich, but lacked the initial legitimacy of the aristocracy, and indeed were once a revolutionary force. With some authors, arguably **Marx** himself, the creation of a bourgeoisie is a necessary stage in history: until the bourgeoisie exists and creates the economic and social conditions of capitalism, world historical progress cannot lead on to the ultimate **class** revolution.

Whether derived from the Marxist tradition or otherwise, the identity of this group has been accepted by historians, novelists and journalists since the early

19th century at least. In this more general usage, however, much precision has been lost. For example, in its general usage there is scarcely a more bourgeois figure than the middle-class professional, a doctor or lawyer, with a relatively luxurious life style. Yet in Marxist theory such people, not being owners and controllers of the means of production, are actually marginal in class relations, and are ultimately doomed to be crushed by the true property-owning bourgeoisie just as are the workers. As a brief definition of its position in Marxist thought, the bourgeoisie is a class, partially corresponding with the middle class, or upper-middle class of Anglo-Saxon terminology, whose social attitudes are characterized by **conservatism** and fear of its own potential political insecurity, but is dominant in both running the economy and polity, and in setting standards of decent behaviour. As such it is aped by the petit-bourgeoisie, those who occupy even less secure positions intermediate between the new capitalist ruling class and the traditional manual workers, beset by pretensions and anxieties and bent on an upward social mobility.

Outside a proper Marxist theory the term bourgeois has little or no value. Sociologists have much more precisely-defined categories of the classes, and modern culture lacks the value stock to need the phrase, but it lingers on, almost entirely as a pejorative comment.

Brezhnev

Leonid Brezhnev (1906–82) was the effective leader of the Soviet Union from the fall of **Khrushchev** in 1964 until his death. His fame depends on his being the last ruler of the country in the mode set by **Lenin** and **Stalin**, with complete autocratic power based on manipulation of the **Communist Party of the Soviet Union (CPSU)**. The two leaders of the Soviet Union between his death and the rise of Mikhail **Gorbachev** in 1985, Yuri Andropov and Konstantin Chernenko, were both too weak, physically and politically, and too aware of the impending crisis in Soviet economics and politics, to assume the power Brezhnev had wielded. He was a classic **apparatchik**, too young to have taken part in the revolution itself, but already in the party and the party-controlled state apparatus less than ten years later. Like so many of his cohort, he rose through the party ranks on the coat-tails of a patron, in his case Khrushchev, for whom he first worked in 1938, after proving himself by taking part enthusiastically in Stalin's destruction of the Russian peasantry. His career followed Khrushchev's, including his wartime service as a political commissar, but ultimately he was responsible for engineering Khrushchev's fall.

His rule over the Soviet Union was characterized by complete inertia in industrial and economic matters (his own practical experience was entirely in the agricultural sector), a return to cultural and human rights repression after Khrushchev's mild liberalization, and an aggressive and adventurist foreign policy. Above all he was a **militarist**, increasing defence expenditure by 50% in his first five-year plan, and by even more later. In this context he fought an expensive and ultimately futile **arms race** with the USA, the costs of which the Soviet economy could not bear, and increased the threat of nuclear attack on the Eastern European countries of the **Soviet bloc** by using them as bases for nuclear missiles ranged against European **NATO** countries. He was responsible for Soviet intervention in the Third World, for support of Vietnam (see **Vietnam War**), for invading Afghanistan (see **Afghan War**), and above all for brutally suppressing the Czechoslovakian liberalization movement of 1968. It was after the 1968 intervention that he coined what was to be known as the 'Brezhnev Doctrine', proclaiming that the Soviet Union and other communist countries were entitled to suppress anti-communist movements in other socialist societies because fraternal solidarity overcame any 'bourgeois' doctrines of national sovereignty. His complete refusal to modernize the Soviet economy, or to allow any freedom of expression, led to the economic and social collapse inherited by Gorbachev. His personal indifference to the increasingly widespread corruption of the Soviet élite, including several members of his own family, may have done as much as his economic and foreign policy failures to prepare the Soviet Union for the radical departure from tradition which followed so soon after his death, and indeed opened the cracks which led within a decade to the disintegration of the Union.

Bureaucracy

Bureaucracy, in its most general sense, describes a way of organizing the activities of any institution so that it functions efficiently and impersonally. The major theorist of bureaucracy was Max **Weber**, and most subsequent research and theorizing has closely followed his analysis. For Weber, and most subsequent writers, bureaucracy is characterized by a set of basic organizational principles. The most important are: (1) that office-holders in an institution are placed in a clear hierarchy representing a chain of command; (2) that they are salaried officials whose only reward comes from the salary and not directly from their office; (3) that their authority stems entirely from their role and not from some private status, and that the authority exists only in, and as far as it is needed to carry out, that role; (4) that appointments to bureaucratic positions are determined by tests of professional skill and competence and not for considerations of status or patronage; (5) that strict rules exist on the basis of which bureaucrats make their decisions, so that personal discretion is minimized; and (6) that such institutions collect and collate detailed records and operate on the basis of technical expertise. For Weber bureaucracy, which he saw as a necessary development of the modern world, developed along with the shift from a 'traditional' towards a predominantly 'rational-legal' orientation in all aspects of social life. Institutions as diverse as churches, legal systems and symphony orchestras were becoming bureaucratized, as well as government departments and large-scale industrial concerns. Believing bureaucratic institutions to be uniquely efficient, Weber expected this pattern of organization to become supreme; and because he thought **socialism**, with its planned economy, to be essentially bureaucratic, he expected a form of what we would now call **state capitalism** to become dominant throughout the developed world.

Since Weber's day it has become increasingly clear that this 'ideal' type of bureaucracy seldom exists and is not necessarily more efficient than others when it does. However, Weber's is still the best characterization of how large-scale institutions operate much of the time. The idea that the spread of bureaucracy, leading to a **bureaucratic state**, will produce essentially similar societies regardless of whether they are officially capitalist or communist has been developed by later writers, sometimes as the **convergence thesis**, sometimes as a version of class theory (see **new class**). Some of the implications of this theory, particularly as it affects social mobility, have been tested empirically and found to be approximately valid.

The pejorative sense of 'bureaucracy', describing institutions as full of small-minded time-servers, indifferent to the public and incapable of initiative, was largely ignored by the original theorists of bureaucracy, and indeed refers only to a corrupt manifestation of a useful general principle for organization of efficient goal-oriented human interaction. (See also **civil service**.)

Bureaucratic State

Max **Weber** and many later social theorists argued that political systems would become increasingly similar as they all underwent a process of increasing 'bureaucratization'. According to this theory the especial suitability of bureaucratic forms of administration for running complex and large-scale organizations would make the development of a bureaucratic state essential, regardless of official ideologies. One theory derived from Weber, the **convergence thesis**, claimed that even such apparently opposed systems as the USA and the Soviet Union were growing increasingly alike as bureaucracy took over. Political changes in the 1980s undermined this theory. Not only did the communist economies collapse from inefficiency, to be replaced by attempts at free-market capitalism, but liberal, conservative and even social democrat governments throughout the West set out to 'deregulate' their own economies, reducing the role of the **state** considerably. At the same time, however, the accompanying desire to ensure accountability in public enterprises such as education has led to an increase in bureaucratic monitoring.

Burke

Edmund Burke (1729–97) was a politically controversial writer, a journalist and pamphleteer as well as a member of the British Parliament, from an Irish background, who more than anyone of his generation, and possibly of any other, set the philosophical background for modern British **conservatism**. Two events stimulated him to write brilliant and caustic pieces which are still widely read today. One was the French Revolution. His tract on this, *Reflections on the Revolution in France,* set forth principles of the value of slow and natural political evolution, and the duty to conserve the best (hence *Conservatism*), along with a deep distrust of the capacity of ordinary human intelligence to plan and construct an ideal society. Of his other writings the most important is probably his tract decrying the British war against the American Colonists, for Burke saw a great injustice in the rule of a colony which was denied effective representation. One further work of his is often quoted in modern political theory, a speech, published widely, to the voters in his own constituency of Bristol. This outlined his own views of the duties and rights of an elected representative to parliament. He argued that voters should pick the best candidate available, and then leave them alone. What the representative owes to constituents, according to Burke, is their best judgement, not their obedience. It is, thus, an argument of considerable power against the principal alternative version of **representative democracy**—the idea of **delegation**.

Butskellism

Butskellism was a term coined by British political commentators during the first Conservative government (1951–55) after the Second World War; it merged the names of the previous Labour Chancellor of the Exchequer, Hugh Gaitskell, and that of the Conservative Chancellor, R. A. Butler. The term was intended to indicate the apparent similarity between their attitudes towards economic management and Treasury operations. Until this period it had not been fully apparent that a high degree of consensus existed between the two major parties on the all-important question of economic policy. This had in fact been foreshadowed by the common agreement during the 1939–45 coalition government on post-war economic goals and methods, and was a result of the final conversion of political leaders in all parties to **Keynesian** economic theory. However, 'Butskellism' was a term of abuse for many of the politically engaged, since the 'mixed economy', with government intervention through taxation and manipulation of interest rates, and (on the part of Labour) an acceptance of limited nationalization, was only approved of by the 'moderate' wings of the parties. This was especially true of the **Labour Party**, many of whose members believed Gaitskell had 'sold out' by not relying much more on direct controls, coercive economic planning and widespread nationalization. At the same time the right wing of the **Conservative Party** was dismayed that there was little de-nationalization and no return to the gold standard, and that the government should pursue anything but a totally **laissez-faire** economic policy. Butskellism can fairly be said to have lasted until the Conservative Party's conversion to **monetarism** in the late 1970s. By the time of the 1992 general election both parties had resumed a move towards a similar form of convergence, in fact to the right of Butskellism. This trend accelerated in the late 1990s when the Labour Party, under the leadership of Tony Blair, re-branded itself as **New Labour** and abandoned its historic commitment to nationalization. In fact, Butskellism was an early public awareness of the well-tested theory of party competition leading to ideological convergence. The classic theory predicting this, Anthony **Downs'** *An Economic Theory of Democracy*, was not published until some years after Butskellism was first noted.

C

Cabinet

A cabinet is a small body of senior politicians responsible for directing the administration of a country which has the form of government known as **cabinet government**. Subgroups or **committees** often exist within a cabinet for the direction of specific affairs. An inner cabinet will typically consist of members responsible for the economy, home and foreign affairs, defence and justice, and a war cabinet of members responsible for departments directly involved or affected by a state of war in the country.

In some countries, notably France, and in the Commission of the **European Union**, the term 'cabinet' is also applied to the small group of politicians and civil servants who act as the personal advisers to a minister. A group of advisers to the head of the executive who are not members of the cabinet is sometimes known as the 'kitchen cabinet': the term was apparently first applied to advisers of Andrew Jackson, US president from 1829–37, and more recently to confidants of the former British prime minister, Harold Wilson.

Cabinet Government

A cabinet government system exists where responsibility for directing the policies of a country (see **executive**) lies in the hands of a small group of senior politicians. Cabinet government originated in Britain during the 17th and 18th centuries, where the cabinet developed from the inner core of privy counsellors on whom the monarch relied for advice. As the monarch lost power and party government replaced personal authority, the cabinet came to be formed not from the monarch's most trusted advisers but from the most senior members of the dominant political party.

The essence of cabinet government is that it is collective government by a committee of individuals who are theoretically equal and bound by their collective decisions. Fundamental to the way cabinet government operated in Britain until the early 1960s were the dual notions of **collective responsibility** and secrecy. The proceedings of a cabinet debate were secret and it was not permissible for a minister to publicize personal dissent from any decision of the cabinet and to remain a member of the cabinet thereafter. Collective responsibility also meant that if Parliament wished to remove a government from office it had to remove the whole administration; it could not remove part of it or pick ministers off one by one, although individual ministers have resigned for political and personal reasons.

The concept of cabinet government implies that power and responsibility will be shared equally between all members of the cabinet. In fact the **prime minister**, as chairman of the cabinet and, in most systems which have cabinet governments, the person who appoints the other cabinet ministers, wields a power which is generally seen as superior to that of other members of the cabinet individually and even to that of the cabinet as a whole. In the last few years of Margaret Thatcher's prime ministership, however, it was increasingly felt that the idea of 'first among equals', which restricts prime ministerial power, had been largely abandoned. Her successors in office may have initiated a return to a traditional form of cabinet government, but the dominant force in British politics is now indisputably the prime minister. In the British system of cabinet government, a great deal of decision-making and policy preparation is undertaken not by the full cabinet, but by cabinet **committees** which cover specialized areas of policy; membership of the most important of these committees, particularly the economic committee, is greatly prized among cabinet members. One of the reasons for the prime minister's influence over the cabinet is indeed that he or she is the only member who is likely to be on all the important committees.

Britain's system of cabinet government has been exported to other countries, notably those of the **Commonwealth**. However, the norms and practices of cabinet government may vary considerably from one country to another. When the Labor Party comes to power in Australia, for example, it elects the members of the cabinet, thus denying the prime minister one important source of power and patronage. Although there is a body in the US political system called the cabinet, which consists of the politically appointed heads of departments, it has no decision-making power and exists only to advise the president when the latter wants to be advised.

Capitalism

At its most simple and value-free, the term capitalism is used to describe any economic system where there is a combination of private property, a relatively free and competitive market, and a general assumption that the bulk of the work-force will be engaged in employment by private (non-governmental) employers engaged in producing whatever goods they can sell at a profit. Capitalism has its own **ideology** and economic theory, like all politico-economic systems. The original theory of capitalism was essentially that an entirely free market of small-scale entrepreneurs, hiring individual labourers at the minimum possible cost, would produce the maximum output, at the cheapest possible price given the cost of the other inputs necessary for production. This is often called the 'perfect competition model' of economics. One aspect of this model is to require government neither to own any productive enterprise, nor to regulate or control the economy in any way.

However valid or otherwise this simple model might be, current understanding of capitalism focuses on two ideas; production for profit, and the existence of private property which is only partially controlled by the state. To believers in capitalism (which, with some reservations, means all the major parties of the United Kingdom and USA, most parties in Western Europe and the Old Commonwealth, and, since the downfall of the communist governments between 1989 and 1991, most political movements in Eastern Europe and the former Soviet Union), this form of economic organization provides the greater likelihood of maximizing economic performance and defending political liberty while securing something approaching **equality of opportunity**.

In fact there are no pure capitalist economies, and the functioning of modern economies is more a matter of a sliding scale from minimum to maximum private property and regulation. In many economies, Britain's being a prime example, the government, including local government and other public services, employs so large a proportion of the work-force as to make it impossible not to wield enormous influence. Furthermore, the 19th- and early 20th-century experience of completely unregulated economies led to such disasters, and such inequalities, that regulation has been common even in the USA, which is the country most ideologically committed to capitalism. A particular problem of capitalism is that unregulated industries often become monopolistic, with the resulting need for anti-trust legislation to maintain competitiveness. One of the principal objectives of **Thatcherism** was to increase the extent to which the British economy was capitalist by selling off nationalized industries and public utilities, partly in the hope of increasing the 'capitalist' class by encouraging ordinary people to own shares. In many countries, including the UK, a process is now fashionable in which activities formerly entirely or largely conducted by the state, like education or major health facilities, are now financed and controlled by a mixture of for-profit and state bodies.

Capital Punishment

Although capital punishment has historically been universal, and although the range of crimes for which it has sometimes been seen as suitable is wide, opposition to the death penalty is not as recent as is often imagined. Some

European countries abolished the death penalty, at least temporarily, as early as the late 18th century. Even in the USA, which is today the only Western liberal democracy to execute criminals, some states have very early experience of abolition, or at least restriction, of capital punishment. Michigan and Wisconsin, for example, had abolished judicial execution by the mid-19th century.

Nevertheless, until the second half of the 20th century, most states of all political types felt it legitimate to kill people who broke certain laws, even in peacetime. The most liberal of modern societies often allows capital punishment, at least theoretically, during wartime. After the Second World War, partly as a reaction of revulsion to state terror in general, the penalty was abolished in many European countries. Abolition of the death penalty is now, in fact, a requirement for membership of the Council of Europe. Thus by the early 21st century, about 90 countries had formally relinquished capital punishment, and perhaps another 20 have not executed anyone for so long that they can be considered, in practice, as having done so. In particular, states escaping from long periods of authoritarian rule after 1989 have rapidly moved to make execution illegal, as did South Africa almost immediately after the ending of **apartheid**.

Outside the world of developed and stable liberal democracies, the death penalty is still very widely used, and often not only for crimes against the person; for example, drug related offences continue to attract the penalty in many Asian countries. In some Islamic areas there appears to be a religious basis behind the cultural support for executions (see **Shari'a**) in other areas, such as some Caribbean countries, belief in the deterrent effect of execution continues strongly. To a very large extent opposition to capital punishment is élite-led. Even in Europe, public opinion is often much more favourable to the idea of restoring the penalty than those opposed would expect: in some polls as many as 70% of the British public would like to see the return of execution for some types of murder.

It is against this background that one must consider the outstanding exception to the trend away from relying on the state taking life to enforce its law—the USA. For a few years in the 1970s executions were halted in the USA because of the Supreme Court's uncertainty about the constitutionality of the death penalty. When they finally ruled in its favour, in 1976, many of the states drafted new capital punishment laws so that by the beginning of the 21st century 38 states allowed the penalty, and several hundreds of people had been executed, often despite considerable international public pressure. The enthusiasm for execution is not as widespread in the USA as this figure suggests. Several states which put capital punishment laws back on the statute book after 1976 have never used the sentence. More importantly, extensive use of the penalty is largely restricted to the conservative south. Over two-thirds of all executions since 1976 have been in Texas, Virginia, Missouri, Florida,

Oklahoma and Georgia. In 2001, the Federal Government also returned to the practice, though there are relatively few federal criminal laws to which it can be applied.

Caste

Caste, along with **class** and **status**, is a system for social stratification, whereby social respect and wealth are distributed unequally. The most powerful such stratification is the Hindu caste system which dominates much of Indian life. There are four basic Hindu castes: Brahmin (priests), Raja or Kshatriya (rulers and warriors), Vaishya (artisans) and Shudra (servants). However, the system has greatly expanded to number perhaps over 3,000 castes and subcastes according to location and occupation. In addition, beneath the caste system are the so-called untouchables who perform the most menial tasks. Unlike class and status, however, it is impossible for an individual to alter their caste position, which is fixed by birth, and intercaste marriages are still extremely rare. Somewhat as in medieval Europe, once born into a particular social position, with clearly defined rights and duties, a person is expected to accept this with no ambition for betterment. Caste systems require a very powerful **ideology**, usually of a religious nature, to justify them and keep people, if not content, at least acquiescent. Though such ideological control is never perfect, caste systems work most effectively when those in the lower orders actually believe they deserve to be inferior to others. Thus although there have been attempts by the untouchables in Hindu society to break from tradition, even among this group large numbers accept the inevitability of their fate. Similarly, the widespread belief in racially-segregated societies that blacks were inferior to whites was not only used by whites to justify the oppression of blacks, but was at times accepted as truth by the latter, thus preventing rebellion. Caste systems cannot ultimately sustain themselves once even a moderate degree of education and exposure to alternative beliefs becomes widespread, but, as in India, they can nevertheless be very resistant to change.

Castro

Fidel Castro Ruz (1928–) is arguably the only Marxist dictator to have survived into the 21st century, although he came to power in Cuba as a radical nationalist rather than a Marxist. Castro came from a relatively prosperous background, becoming active in student politics in Cuba and elsewhere in Latin America immediately after the Second World War. He was involved in normal electoral politics before the **coup d'état** which returned Gen. Fulgencio Batista y Zaldívar to power in 1952; although he immediately challenged the new regime, he did so simply by filing a complaint in court that it was unconstitutional. Only after the regime was firmly in power did he launch his revolutionary movement with an attack on a barracks on 26 July 1953. The movement, taking as its name the July 26th Movement, retreated to the mountains where the pro-government forces failed completely to deal with it. Batista gave up, rather than being defeated, leaving Cuba at the end of 1958. Thus, a mere five years of only sporadic violence launched the Castro regime. Certainly at this stage, Castro was no Marxist; he was a radical Cuban nationalist, with egalitarian aims, which led him towards the classic policy of agrarian reform. This, in turn, alienated not only the Cuban upper classes but also the USA, whose corporations had important land interests in Cuba.

To a large extent it was American intransigence which turned Castro towards the then Soviet Union as an ally; moulding Marxist analyses into his own radical nationalist orientation with ease. This alliance, however, entrenched American hostility when Castro gave the Soviet Union permission to site nuclear missiles, which could threaten mainland USA, in Cuba, a move which led to the **Cuban Missile Crisis.** Cuba, in fact, benefited from the **cold war,** because Soviet foreign aid to such a strategically-placed ally made up for the American trade embargo. Soviet funds allowed the development of an extensive **welfare state**, and obviated the need for economic efficiency. Since the collapse of the Soviet Union and the end of the cold war, Castro managed successfully to remain in power into the 21st century while maintaining at least the vestiges of a socialist economy and welfare society. The political power of the émigré Cubans in the USA has meant that US foreign policy still treats Cuba as it has done throughout the cold war. It is unlikely, however, that Cuba will avoid major political change once Castro dies.

Catch-All Parties

Catch-all parties are political parties which have no very clear or specific base in terms of the social and economic characteristics of the people who vote for them—unlike, for example, most socialist parties with their predominantly working-class base, or traditional European Liberal parties recruiting almost entirely from the upper middle-class professional and secular sector. The phenomenon of catch-all parties was first commented on by political scientists in the late 1950s. Their enemies see them as predominantly motivated by he desire to put together as large a voting support as possible in order to maximize their chances of winning elections. Catch-all parties are unlikely to stand far from the centre of political spectrum in which they operate, but may well espouse a set of policies which does not fit in with schematic distinctions between **left** and **right**. In practice these parties have usually been right-of-centre, standing for support of the economic and social status quo, or at least hoping not to have to modify it too much. They have, therefore, had all the more reason to deny any specific **class** orientation, since class politics tends to produce natural majorities of working-class voters who are likely to believe that they will gain by radical change.

Typical of parties often defined as catch-all were the **Gaullist** parties in post-war France, especially during the early years of the **Fifth Republic**, when they could attract voters of all classes and almost all political persuasions by appealing to the desire for a strong and stable government. Similarly the old Italian Christian Democrats managed to attract considerable working-class support, although they were to some extent a moderate conservative party, because they could associate support for traditional conservative and religious values with the defence of democracy, and thus 'catch' almost anyone who felt afraid of radical social change such as might be offered by the communists. It is notable that after the end of the **cold war** and the collapse of both the **Christian Democrats** and the **Italian Communist Party** none of the replacement parties managed to achieve such a catch-all status. To a lesser extent the British **Conservative Party**, which has always relied on a considerable 'cross-class vote' from working-class electors, and the major American parties, which have no overt class basis, might be categorized as catch-all parties. As the class basis of electoral politics continues its general decline, the clear sense of some parties being 'catch-all' and others not becomes less obvious. At the same time some structural aspects of voting, such as religious identity, which helped catch-all parties attract voters, are also declining, forcing all parties to aim at the widest possible voter pool.

Censorship

Censorship is the control of what can be said, written or published in any way, either by formal government authority or by informal powers, and in all senses is an attempt to impose conformity on views and behaviour. Censorship has been the norm in most societies in most historical periods, and exists in at least marginal ways everywhere today. The two principal categories of censorship concern morality and politics. Religious censorship covers both categories. Blasphemy would be regarded as offensive to God and therefore immoral, while heresy is the preaching or following of an alternative interpretation to the prevailing religious doctrine; censorship, and indeed persecution, has been used widely to suppress both, in Christendom particularly during the Middle Ages and Reformation, when church and state functions were much closer. Religious movements are still influential in many countries in maintaining laws which purport to protect public morality, especially where sexual explicitness is involved.

Political censorship through the deliberate concealment of information must have existed in even the earliest political society. It became more significant, however, with the wider availability of the printed word, the ability of more people to read it and the extension of the **franchise**. The development of a **mass media** has inevitably widened the possibilities for censorship. There is one area, national security, where all countries retain powers of censorship, through for example the British **Official Secrets Act** and its D Notice system, although in many instances such powers are used little outside times of national emergency or war. Censorship conflicts with some of the most vital values of **liberal democracy**, such as freedoms of speech and the press, but even the most liberal of states requires some control on what may be published, even if only because, for example, the rights to privacy and to not be libelled, and the need to prevent the dissemination of extreme views such as racial hatred, are also important. Censorship was prevalent under communist rule in the former **Soviet bloc**, where states attempted to control completely all publication. Not only national security matters and political dissent were subject to censorship, but even the simple reporting of basic news, an air disaster for example, was often forbidden. Just as the spread of printing and literacy made censorship politically necessary in non-democratic societies, so communications technology made it ultimately futile. Access to photocopiers and computers led to a flourishing underground press (*samizdat* in Russian), which could be curtailed but never completely suppressed. The rapid creation and increasing use of the internet has made all legal attempts to control broadcasting, even legitimate ones like the suppression of child pornography, virtually impossible in high-tech societies.

Central Banks

All states require a central authority to issue valid currency, set interest rates and exercise supervision over the banking and credit sector of the economy. The institutions carrying out these tasks are usually referred to as central banks, though their powers and the degree of their autonomy from other government institutions vary considerably. The central bank for the United Kingdom, the Bank of England, was a public institution since its nationalization by the post-war Labour government in 1946, and since then had been more firmly under the direct control of the government than most central banks. It was, therefore, ironic that the first significant act of the incoming Labour government of 1997 was to free the Bank of England from government control. The US Federal Reserve System is almost entirely independent of the federal government, and the European Central Bank (ECB) established in 1998 to become the issuing authority for the euro currency is also totally autonomous. The principal activities of central banks include the regulation of the **money supply**, the controlling of inflation and the stabilization of the international value of their currency. Money supply can be influenced either directly or, much more usually, by the central banks setting interest rates on the money they lend to ordinary banks or, in their role as agents for the central government, buying or selling government bonds to increase or reduce the amount of money in circulation. (Government bonds are a mechanism for governments to satisfy their frequent need to borrow large amounts of money.) **Monetarists** subscribe to the theory that controlling the money supply through raising interest rates, and thus restricting credit, is virtually the sole determining factor over inflation rates. Central banks must also loosen control over credit if lack of demand threatens too severe a recession. To achieve currency stability they need to set interest rates such that external investment in their own currency adjusts its value against other currencies to the level they deem suitable.

Because there is considerable common interest among the developed economies in having generally stable and predictable currency exchange rates, central banks tend to co-operate to fix such rates. The European Monetary Union has done this even more efficiently since the introduction of the Euro and the ECB. So if, for example, the value of the US dollar falls too low, the central banks of the major countries will all sell their own currencies and buy dollars to increase its price. In many ways the activities of central banks are an attempt to compensate for the lack of an automatic regulating effect formerly supplied by adherence to the gold standard, when currencies were tied to the sheer market value of the gold that banks had to hold to support their issue of notes and coins. Central banks are inevitably undemocratic, as they will not, unless forced, take note of a government's intentions and desires if these clash with the primary aim of stabilizing the internal and external value of their currency. It is partly for this reason, notwithstanding the new independence of the Bank of England, that British governments have been very dubious about the merits of participating in European Monetary Union and introducing the euro.

Central Europe

Central Europe, sometimes called East–Central Europe, is more of a concept than a geographical term. Consensually, whatever it is called, it includes primarily the 'big three' former communist European countries—Poland, Hungary and what was Czechoslovakia, and is now the Czech Republic and Slovakia. Indeed, 'Central Europe' was more recently known as Eastern Europe when that connoted the European part of the **Soviet bloc**. Conceptually the idea that these and some other smaller nations had something in common other than geographical proximity comes from an earlier designation, now somewhat politically incorrect. Central Europe belongs to the old 'Middle Europe', or the 'Mitteleuropa' of late 19th- and early 20th-century politics. As such it covers the incredibly complex patchwork of national identities, linguistic and religious areas, and interwoven political histories of a large swathe of Europe which has never had any lengthy settled period of established nation states.

The borders of the member states of Central Europe are roughly the ones constructed after the Versailles Peace Treaty of 1919. This treaty was dedicated to the idea of giving national independence to areas nearly always ruled by others, primarily the Austro-Hungarian Empire and the Tsarist Russian Empire. For about 20 years after that settlement these countries existed; however, they rapidly fell a long way from the Versailles ideal of liberal democracies. In fact, the intermingling of nationalities and ethnicities rendered the Versailles dream impossible, as did the lack of social and historical underpinnings for democracy in the region. When the Second World War, which destroyed their independence, ended they were incorporated anew into an empire—the Soviet Empire, from which they escaped, more or less simultaneously, in 1989.

Less so than the **Balkans**, but still importantly, the question for this area is whether it can sustain a **democratic transition**. To a large extent, the hope for such transition depends on the vacuity of the label; that is, it depends on the old traditions of Mitteleuropa declining, and the predominantly ethnic and nationalistic bases for the societies evaporating so that the states rely for legitimacy on technical efficiency and procedural democratic competence— as with Western democracies. The aim of the governments of Central Europe is certainly to lose this special identity. Membership of any Western international organization, but especially **NATO** (which some have already achieved) and the **European Union**, is the ideal, and little effort is being made to create a cohesive regional political voice.

Centralization

Centralization describes the concentration of government and political authority in the capital city and at the national level, as opposed to the sharing of powers and responsibilities between national, regional and local authorities. There has often been a strong correlation between centralization and size, so that power tends to be more narrowly held in smaller polities. More recently, where opposition to the establishment focused in a capital city has led to the development of successful regionally-based political parties, the **devolution** of power to regional assemblies has sometimes occurred. There is a limit to how genuine **decentralization** can be unless the constitution is overtly federal (see **federalism**), because ultimately the national government is responsible for policy and accountable to the electorate for whatever goes wrong. Thus, while the United Kingdom had become, if anything, more centralized during the Thatcher years, as central government curbed the spending and tax collecting powers of local government in order to impose its overall desired social and economic policy, the new decentralization since 1997, with a highly autonomous Scottish Parliament, is only possible because it is a disguised form of federalism. In contrast Wales, which was only granted a weak form of local autonomy, has seen very little relaxation of central control. Some larger countries, for example France, have also historically been highly centralized; however, early in the presidency of François **Mitterrand**, administrative and financial responsibilities were transferred from government-appointed prefects to locally-elected departmental assemblies. Similar attempts to increase the political power of regions have been made elsewhere, especially in Italy. Since the rise of the quasi-separatist Northern League, the Italian regions have become steadily more autonomous.

Charisma

Charisma was originally a theological notion, with the literal meaning of the 'gift of grace', an attribute in the Catholic theology of saints. **Weber** used it to describe one of his three principal types of political **authority**. To Weber charisma was a personal quality of attraction and psychological power capable of inspiring deep political loyalty in large numbers of people. Thus charismatic leaders win sway over their followers for entirely personal reasons rather than because of any specific policies they espouse, or because they are in some way a 'legitimate' ruler, perhaps by virtue of traditional inheritance. It has become somewhat over-worked, with almost any political leader who can project a pleasing personality being credited with this actually very rare capacity to demand unswerving support simply because of their own character. Possible candidates of some plausibility are Gandhi, Nasser and **Hitler**, who do seem to have been able to command support in this way. The inclusion of the latter indicates how much we are talking of personal magnetism rather than moral force. Politically, the great problem with authority is what Weber indicated as the 'routinization of charisma'; that is, one dynamic leader may build a state or party around their own qualities, but after them, who should command, and why should the inheritor be obeyed? It seems that charismatic institutions can only be long-lived if there are also pragmatic or traditional reasons for support, or if these can be developed.

Chicago School

The Chicago School refers to a set of ideas and people focusing on several departments at the University of Chicago from the 1950s onwards. Although the Chicago School is usually taken to refer to economics, it has been influential, and under the same label, in American legal thinking. In economics the Chicago School is **monetarist**, and close to the ideas of its most famous European exponent, **Hayek**, though in the USA it is associated mainly with the names of Milton Friedman (1912–) and George Stigler (1911–91). The essence of the economic theory is that **fiscal policy** should not be used to try to manage demand as a method of economic control. Instead manipulation of the **money supply** should be the only economic strategy, and, more importantly, economic policy should be as non-interventionist as possible. The Chicago School is basically a modernization of the traditional 'perfect competition' model of economics, in which economic equilibrium will automatically arise, over the long term, from the invisible forces of market competition.

In the legal field, the Chicago School refers to an approach in which several areas of law, and above all liability (tort) law, requires an economic cost-efficiency analysis. Thus the damages set by a court for personal injury, to take one example, should be seen as equivalent to insurance policy costs. Similarly breach of contract cases should be analysed in terms of rational expectations. This sort of approach strips civil law of any moral element—damages ought not to reflect social disapproval of breaking promises or doing injury, but aim only at restoring the economic balance that existed before the contractual breach or tort happened. Just as the Chicago School's economists are seen as right wing, its judges and lawyers are also usually on the right.

Chilling Effect

Chilling effect is a term originally devised by American constitutional lawyers to describe the hidden impact a particular law or constitutional doctrine may have, over and above its evident impact in the courts. In other words, the mere knowledge that a **constitutional court** may decide a future case in a certain way either inhibits people from even trying to do something, or in some other way restricts how free they feel to act. For example, a recent change in English **constitutional law**, by which the courts announced that they would look at the parliamentary record to help interpret obscure legislation, has been argued to have a chilling effect on how frank government spokespeople will be in parliamentary debates, lest a future court hold them to their words.

Chilling effects are at their most powerful during any period of legal uncertainty. For example, since the new **Human Rights Act** came into force in October 2000 (May 1999 in Scotland) many British institutions have been anxiously rewriting internal disciplinary procedures. The Act, as yet, remains largely uninterpreted by the courts and may turn out to have wide implications. More generally, the theory of the **judicialization of politics** in some

Western European countries is an example of chilling effect, whereby parliamentarians avoid legislative experiments they would wish to support because of their guesses about how their constitutional court may rule if the legislation is challenged. As such, chilling effects are simply a specific example of a general problem of power, which is that an actor may well exercise power, perhaps even against his will, because of other people's anticipation of his future actions. Where chilling effects become a problem is not where they concern the institutions that it is thought may make the future decisions—there is, after all, nothing improper about a legislator refraining from doing something that he thinks may be unconstitutional. The problem is the unscrupulous use of the argument by those opposed for other reasons to some legislation, compounded by inappropriate timidity on the part of the potential supporter. The chilling effect matters when it becomes an excuse not to do something, because a court is not usually allowed to re-assure people by making a prospective statement that it will not, if asked, find a proposed piece of legislation unconstitutional.

Christian Democracy

Christian democracy was principally a post-Second World War political movement, typified by the Christian democrat parties of Italy, Germany and the French **Fourth Republic**. Christian democratic parties also emerged in Latin America and, more recently, in Eastern Europe—both regions where democracy is less well established, but where religious influence remains strong. Traditional democrat parties are similar in most ways to moderate — conservative parties, such as those of Britain and the Old Commonwealth. They are likely to stand for a moderate social **liberalism**, a mixed economy, an acceptance that there should be basic social welfare provisions, and some degree of commitment to full employment through government economic policies. The adjective 'Christian' now often has little religious significance but derives from historical factors, notably the emergence of these parties in France and Italy from Second World War religious resistance movements linked with the Church. The Italian Christian Democrats were partial exceptions to this statement since they were always closely associated with the Catholic Church in Italy. Opposition to the **Eurocommunist** parties was a mainstay of these parties, and Catholic opposition to communism gave the 'Christian' label a certain utility. The word 'Democracy' serves to identify the parties concerned as being dedicated to the general interest, rather than those of an aristocracy or élite like most pre-war conservative parties. The decline in the importance of religion as a politically motivating factor throughout Europe is progressively reducing the appeal of Christian democracy *per se,* but by now many of the leading parties have become so entrenched that they are unlikely to suffer much electoral damage. The obvious exception to this is the Italian Christian

Democrats, who have completely collapsed—but this has more to do with the Italian reaction to decades of corruption than to the mere decline of religiosity. At the same time religion, where it is politically important, has come to be much more firmly oriented to specific moral issues such as **abortion**, further reducing the broad reach of a religious identity, and therefore its electoral utility.

Christian Socialism

Christian socialism is not an organized movement or a specific ideology or body of doctrine (though there have been groups, for example in the early Labour Party, which adopted the name). It is a broad descriptive term for individuals or groups, or for a general attitude that has appeared from time to time in various European countries. The central argument of Christian socialism is that both **Christianity** and **socialism** share certain basic values, and that Christians should therefore give political expression to their religious beliefs by supporting a certain type of socialism. At the same time, it is argued, Christianity gives socialism a moral basis which is lacking in other versions, such as orthodox **Marxism**. The supposed common values are those associated with equality, communal sharing, peace, brotherhood, an absence of competition and rejection of hierarchy and power.

The Christian aspect of Christian socialism involves a stress on one side of Jesus's teaching and one image of him as a man—as a simple carpenter with a radical message. It often also draws for inspiration on the life of the early Church, which is interpreted as a communal and pacifistic movement. Clearly this view of Christianity, whether historically correct or not, is at odds with the way in which the institutions and theology of the Church developed in later centuries. It may be for this reason that Christian socialism is almost entirely a phenomenon of Protestant Christianity, which was sometimes in intention a return to the values of the early Church. However, there have been political movements within the Catholic Church of a roughly similar liberal-socialist character, for example the **Mouvement Republicaine Populaire** in France and the – clerical radicalism found in modern Latin America and the Netherlands, often under the label of **liberation theology**.

Relations between Christian socialists and other socialists are not always easy, since left-wing socialists, in particular, often more or less Marxist in outlook, tend towards **materialism** and to the overt atheism and antagonism towards religion which occur in **Marx's** writings. If only for this reason, the socialism of Christian socialists is generally moderate and non-revolutionary, close to that of the **Fabians** and/or the British **Labour Party**.

Christianity

The political role of Christianity has varied greatly from nation to nation. It has steadily become less important in most Western democracies, since voters increasingly support political parties on grounds that have little to do with religion. Where it retains some importance in politics, this manifests itself in two main ways. One is the conflict between clerical and **anti–clerical** factions, which used to be fierce in France and is still significant in Italy. The other is the conflict between parties representing different Christian denominations. The denominations are usually Catholic and Protestant, although in some countries, notably the Netherlands, divisions inside Protestantism gave rise to separate political organizations. However, a series of consolidations during the 1970s and 1980s along political lines of parties previously distinguished by denomination, principally between Calvinist and Catholic, is an indication of the decline in religion as a politically motivating factor in Europe. Even where there are no overtly Christian parties, politics and religion may still be linked, and some of these links (for example in the **moral majority** in the USA), may even be getting stronger. Political parties in countries as different as Australia, Canada and Britain still tend to attract specific religious groups. Until recently a majority of Roman Catholics of all classes voted for the Labour Party in Britain, while the Conservative Party has traditionally been popular among Anglicans. In some countries or territories, the most notable example being Northern Ireland, conflicts between Christian sects are the entire basis for political alignment. Usually, however, as in the new Eastern European democracies, Christian politics is right wing, socialism still being the prerogative of the rump communist parties.

Christianity as such is not usually seen as leading to any particular political position, and despite its sheer numbers world-wide, it has relatively little political force, though institutions like the World Council of Churches may on occasion exercise a good deal of influence. Where nominally Christian parties exist, as for example in Germany, they tend over time to become fairly orthodox conservative parties (see **Christian democracy**). The political impact of committed Christians since the late 20th century has been somewhat contradictory, depending on other aspects of the relevant political culture. Thus in Europe, radical pacifist movements have often been led by or heavily influenced by Christian movements, while in the USA the impact of 'born again' Christians has been largely conservative, not only on moral issues, such as **abortion**, but across the range of political issues.

Citizenship

At its core, citizenship is a legal status, although increasingly political theorists are seeking to return the concept to an earlier usage when it was, in their view, much more than that. As a legal status the grant of citizenship gives people rights in the political system they inhabit. At minimum there will be the right to be domiciled in and take part in the political mechanisms of the state, usually through voting. There will also be the status of legal equality with all others and the entitlement to be treated thus in the court—what the American **Bill of Rights** calls **equal protection** and **due process** of the law. In most modern liberal democracies citizenship also ensures the protection of other **human rights** and **civil liberties**, not all of which may be available to people who have the right of abode in the country. With lesser rights than a citizen, a subject is someone who owes loyalty to a political sovereign but has no right to partake in the decision-making processes of the system. A subject may have other rights, particularly the rather diffuse right to be protected by the power he is subject to when abroad, but a subject does not have the right of political participation.

The concept of citizenship comes to us from the Greek democracies and, with somewhat of a change in emphasis, the Roman Republic. For the Greeks a citizen was one of the equal participating élite in a society where the numerical bulk of the population, women, slaves and resident aliens, on whom the prosperity of the society largely depended, had no such right. Neither did they share all of the duties: only a citizen could be expected to take up arms in defence of the society, a distinction usually accepted by modern democracies when applying conscription laws.

Recently there have been attempts to claim that the full conception of citizenship involves a broader duty: concern with the common interest and a sense of communal purpose and values. Thus citizenship is contrasted with a more individualistic orientation where one has no duty other than narrowly-defined legal duties and where the pursuit of self-interest protected by one's rights within the state is fully legitimate and all that can be expected or asked of the citizen. Thus **communitarian** theorists seek to place citizenship in a set of value preferences, rather than making it a purely procedural concept.

Citizen Soldier

The citizen soldier has a significant place in much democratic theory. There is no clear distinction between a citizen soldier and a conscript, and the term is sometimes used to cover the latter, but the full implication of independence and voluntariness found in, for example, the early American state **militias** is lost when the term is broadened to include all soldiers who are not career professionals. The paradigm has for a long time been found in Switzerland, but citizen soldiers have been valued in many other historical contexts for centuries. There are two important characteristics of the citizen soldier, the first of which relates to control of the political system. Citizen soldiers, whose principal activities are in the civilian arena and who only take up arms in an emergency, are likely to be loyal members of a stable, democratic and fairly egalitarian society. They will wish to preserve the existing political system, unless it lacks **legitimacy**, in which case they may refuse to bear arms in its defence. But they will not be interested in overthrowing the system and installing a military **junta** or some political élite, whereas professional **armies**, divorced from the society they defend and holding a monopoly of force, may well come to control the political system against the interests of the mass.

The second characteristic is that a citizen soldiery is much less likely than a professional military machine to tolerate aggressive or adventurist foreign policies: it fights only when it absolutely has to and consequently, it is argued, will only take part in genuinely defensive wars. Whether this is an objective truth is unclear, as under certain conditions whole populations can be aroused to expansionist fury. The French armies of the early revolutionary days were citizen armies in the sense that they were more or less voluntary mass movements of people who had previously been civilian, and they fought with great eagerness to spread their revolution. A general distaste for military life and military thinking arises from a desire to have a society in which the values of the military are minimized. This is linked to the idea, to be found in classical Greece, that it is every full citizen's duty to defend their state, and that to have a purely professional and permanent military organization takes away both the common duty and indeed the chance for ordinary citizens to demonstrate their full commitment to society. In this sense, and it is to be found to some extent in Swiss attitudes, a citizen army reflects egalitarianism and binds society together; everyone has to serve, and the rich cannot, by paying taxes, transmute the burden of their military obligation to some less unpleasant service. Even this, however, has not always been true. The late 19th century French army was notorious for a system which allowed the rich to pay a poor young man to take their son's place in the annual conscription.

Civic Culture

The Civic Culture was the name given to a study based on research carried out in five countries in the early 1960s. It proceeds from the observation that **political cultures** vary considerably in the extent to which they encourage a sense of trust in political authority and facilitate political activity on the part of ordinary citizens. The ideal civic culture would be one in which the political ideas and values of the citizenry were attuned to political equality and participation, and where government was seen as trustworthy and acting in the public interest. This comes close in many ways to the classical Greek notion of the **polis**, and to **Aristotle's** description of man as 'a political animal'. In fact this sense of 'citizen competence' was found to vary considerably, according to factors such as class and education, even within the countries that most nearly approached the ideal of **liberal democracy**. More to the point, Gabriel Almond (b. 1911) and Sidney Verba (b. 1932), the authors of *The Civic Culture*, found that it varied greatly according to the efficacy and stability of the democratic regimes surveyed. It was high in the USA and the United Kingdom, relatively low in Italy, and marginal in Mexico (which was not, at the time, a democracy, but rather a fairly liberal one-party state). However, as actual **political participation** rates are everywhere extremely low, it is unclear that citizens' perceptions of their political competence mean very much.

Civil Defence

Civil defence refers to any systematic attempts or plans by governments to limit civilian casualties and damage to civil property during a war. The first major civil defence programmes were instituted during the late 1930s, when the danger of aerial bombardment of European cities became clear. One important early precaution, in the United Kingdom for example, was the issuing of gas masks to the entire population at the beginning of the Second World War. Although no gas attacks were ever made, the idea that civilian populations could and should be protected against weapons specifically designed for indiscriminate mass killing was established. A parallel development was the extensive building of air-raid shelters in the towns, and it is fairly clear that effective air raid precautions reduced deaths in both Britain and Germany, and the absence of such a programme resulted in a more severe impact in Japan, which was heavily bombed by the USA.

Civil defence, however, is not just a humanitarian activity. It can itself be regarded as a weapon, and certainly has major implications for the military capacity of the country being attacked. Most theorists of air warfare, including those most influential in the Second World War, supported 'strategic' bombing campaigns on the grounds that the direct attacks on the civilian population would destroy morale throughout the enemy's society, and swiftly bring it to capitulate. The more one can protect one's civilians, therefore, the longer one can fight, thus allowing time for direct military or economic superiority to pay off. In fact it is now known from post-war surveys that the Allied bombing offensive did far less damage to German war efforts than had been anticipated, and the morale factor, while perhaps over-emphasized, was the major one.

With the advent of the nuclear age civil defence became a matter of considerable debate, and the Western and Eastern powers acted very differently on the issue. In Britain the official Civil Defence organization was wound down in the 1960s as government expenditure cuts reduced all forms of defence expenditure. Although the USA had originally commissioned an elaborate shelter building programme, and had scheduled air raid practices as late as the Vietnamese war period, it too largely gave up serious efforts at civil defence. The argument in both cases was that there could be no cost effective protection against a counter-city strike by Soviet nuclear weaponry. Civil defence preparations were restricted mainly to protecting government and **administrative élites**, and making plans to control and organize whatever part of the population did manage to survive an attack. Many of those opposed to nuclear weapons view the provision of civil defence as not only useless, but also dangerous to world peace, because civil defence measures suggest survivability, and survivability may encourage nuclear risk-taking.

The policy of the Soviet Union, which had major plans for evacuation and shelter of urban populations, illustrates a general policy difference which permeated all areas of thinking about nuclear war in the West and East. While the USA and the UK basically took the attitude that a nuclear war, if it came, could have no winners, the Soviet Union argued that even such wars can be won. Soviet nuclear weapons strategy was therefore based on a theory of fighting and winning a nuclear war, and a relevant civil defence strategy supported it. Since the virtual removal of any serious threat of superpower nuclear war, civil defence is likely to fade as an issue. However, the experience of the Gulf War has shown fairly clearly that, below the level of nuclear war, extensive civil defence measures, especially against chemical attacks, are still to be taken seriously in likely war zones, and as Western states come to fear the possibility of weapons of mass destruction being deployed by a 'rogue state' or through **terrorism**, it is possible that some from of civil defence may re-emerge.

Civil Disobedience

Civil disobedience is a protest strategy, arguably invented and certainly popularized by Mahatma Gandhi during his campaigns first against 'pass book' laws in South Africa and then against the principle of British rule in India. The idea is to urge large numbers of protesters very publicly to break some specific law, or defy official authority in some clear-cut way. The dual aims are to draw attention to the evil against which the protest is made, and to attempt to force the government into taking extreme action in defending the object or policy protested at. The action thus forced upon the government may be so distasteful to it, or stretch its resources, as eventually to change its attitude. Even if the position of the authorities is not swayed, the dramatic demonstration of intensity of feeling among those who have protested is expected to increase support for the protesters in the population considerably, thus strengthening the campaign.

A vital element of civil disobedience is that campaigns must be non-violent, and indeed, should be as law-abiding as possible in every way, except with regard to the specific law or policy that is being protested at. The reasoning is strictly tactical, and does not follow from any implicit connection between civil disobedience and pacifism. Thus it was essential that the Indian protesters against British rule accept the consequences of their actions and passively submit to imprisonment, making clear the absence of any challenge to the state in general. Similarly, in the 1960s, white Americans campaigning against racial discrimination towards blacks in the southern states would break specific laws, as law-abidingly as possible. Thus they would, for example, attempt to ride in 'Negro Only' rail cars, but would not attempt to evade arrest or avoid punishment. It was particularly important that they did not allow the dominant southern white conservative establishment to hide behind the claim that the protesters were 'un-American', or were radicals whose views need not be taken into account. Later, when the **Vietnam War** was the object of protest, this strategy was crucial. It would have been too easy to brand those who genuinely opposed conscription for what they thought was an immoral war as traitors, and indeed as cowards, had they not attempted to act in due submission to the state apart from their direct actions against conscription. (This does not mean that all, or even most, anti-war protests in this era were in fact law-abiding or peaceful. The movement might have been more successful had they been.)

As early as the mid-1950s similar tactics were tried in the UK against nuclear weapons policies, by the Campaign for Nuclear Disarmament in its first manifestation. A particularly favoured tactic was to attempt to block traffic routes with a 'sit-down', thus disobeying the Traffic Acts, and similar methods have been used in countless student and worker demonstrations and strikes ever since. The most significant recent example in the UK of civil disobedience was the anti-'poll tax' campaign in 1989–91. This, akin to the 'rent strike' some-times used in other contexts, involved the intentional non-payment of the poll tax. It is hard to assess the effectiveness of the campaign because the tax proved generally so unpopular that the government moved to abolish it for fear of electoral disaster. Certainly one of the problems influencing government thinking was that the tax came to be seen as uncollectable.

As far as political theory is concerned, it is entirely unclear whether the concept of peaceful disobedience, or of limited and specific civil disobedience, can be handled inside the general theory of legal and **political obligation**. As long as it is not generally recognized, as it cannot be, that the individual citizen has the right to pick and choose which laws to obey, or for which policies to pay taxes in support of, it is impossible to take account of motivation when dealing with an illegal act. Most would agree that it is not, in principle, very supportive of democratic government for individual policy choices of govern-ments to be overturned because a minority of citizens are prepared to make the cost of enforcing them very high. In fact there are very few clear-cut cases of success attaching to any civil disobedience campaigns, in part because governments have learned not to react too harshly to such protests, and thus the mass waves of sympathy have not followed. It is important not to confuse civil disobedience with the general right, in a democracy, to protest peacefully and in a fully law-abiding way. Such protests may often have much the same impact as is expected of disobedience campaigns, especially in terms of policing them and in the chance of over-reaction by the authorities.

Civil Law

Civil law can have two distinct meanings. One meaning, in Anglo-American usage, refers to the continental European tradition of 'code law', which is often called civil, or even 'civilian', law, as distinct from the **common law** so important in the Anglo-American tradition. The prime distinction is between the gradual accretion of precedents, statutes, rulings and even traditional legal customs which characterizes common law, and the conception, not entirely accurate, of civil law consisting of formal rules deliberately created, codified and passed by a legislative body. In this tradition, which has characterized the entire European legal experience, decisions made by courts in particular cases do not have binding precedential impact on future cases, though *'La Jurisprudence'*, a series of interpretations, may heavily influence the way the code will be read. In the common law system, courts are legitimate makers of law, and law is seen as evolving continually from a distant past; civil law is static, fixed in the form laid down by the legislature. The sources of civil law in this sense are partly the codified law of the Roman Empire, especially as rediscovered by the European universities after the Dark Ages, partly the canon law of the medieval Church, and partly the laws recodified under Napoleon after the French Revolution. (Much of European law is still sometimes described as being the Code Napoléon.) This tradition of civil law exists in certain parts of the common law world where a French presence has been important, notably in the State of Louisiana in the USA and the Province of Québec in Canada, with some vestigial remains in Scottish law. As common law has become increasingly codified, and as courts are seen less and less as legitimate makers of law, the distinction between common law and civil law has narrowed. International **tribunals** whose deliberations have an impact on national legal systems, notably the **European Court of Justice (ECJ)** and, to a lesser extent, the European Court of Human Rights (see also **Human Rights Act**), tend to operate like traditional civil law courts, but the presence of English judges on them has had the effect of diminishing the importance of the old distinctions. Furthermore, a court operating within a developing political system, such as the ECJ, has difficulty in honestly claiming to be interpreting a fixed code. Efforts to produce pan-European legal codes, for example in the law of contract, have turned out to be surprisingly heavily influenced by aspects of English common law, suggesting that the traditional difference may be more of procedure and vocabulary than of substance. The most significant distinction now remaining between the Anglo-American and continental systems probably lies in their respective methods of prosecuting **criminal law** (see **inquisitorial system**). As there is growing disenchantment in Britain with the traditional criminal law mechanism, this distinction may also become less vital. Recent moves to limit access to juries in the United Kingdom certainly point to a declining differentiation.

The term civil law is also used within the common law system, where it denotes a body of law distinct from criminal law. Here civil law concerns contracts, torts, property, taxation and other matters which are not necessarily connected with wrongdoing in the same sense as a criminal action. Such law is concerned less with punishment than with restitution and conflict resolution. Again, however, civil law in this sense can be more or less codified.

Civil Liberties

Civil liberties are freedoms or rights which are thought to be especially valuable in themselves and vital to the functioning of a liberal and democratic society. Emphases vary, but most lists of basic civil liberties will include freedom of speech, freedom of religion and of thought, freedom of movement, freedom of association, the right to a fair trial and freedom of the person. These rights and liberties are essential protections against the arbitrary acts of government and are fundamental to free political association.

In some political systems these freedoms are enshrined in a written document or constitutional code, sometimes known as a **bill of rights**, which is enforced by a special court or constitutional tribunal. In the USA, for example, a powerful body of jurisprudence and legal doctrine has been developed around the first ten amendments to the Constitution—especially the first amendment, the fourth amendment, the **due process** clause of the fifth amendment—and also, more recently, the **equal protection** clause of the fourteenth amendment. In other countries, for example the United Kingdom, civil liberties are simply part of the ordinary law of the land. In the UK, however, the passing of the **Human Rights Act** in 1998 has moved the country a long way towards a more codified version of civil liberties. In many democracies a pressure group exists specifically to protect such liberties; the UK has Liberty (the National Council for Civil Liberties), and the USA, the American Civil Liberties Union.

Even in societies which have good civil liberties records, certain groups—ethnic minorities, for example—may find that some laws operate to their disadvantage, and they may press for greater protection. In the UK there is still concern about the powers of the police to stop, question and detain individuals on suspicion that an offence might have been, or might be about to be, committed because that law has been operated particularly harshly against black citizens. Similarly, there has been continual concern about civil liberties in Northern Ireland, where many normal features of the British legal system have been suspended from time to time and **emergency powers** have been exercised.

Civil liberties and **human rights** are closely related, and all governments pay at least lip service to their importance; but it remains a fact that real political freedom exists in relatively few countries. However, even in countries where the political system is characterized by **dictatorship** or **totalitarianism**, efforts, sometimes no more than token, towards the respect of civil liberties have been made, to satisfy conditions demanded by the rich developed countries for the granting of aid. In time, the pressure exerted by Western governments for improvements in the field of civil liberties may be seen as a crucial factor in the collapse of the communist governments of Eastern Europe and the Soviet Union. In order to enforce civil liberties, these countries have all notably written powerful **constitutional courts** into their new constitutions.

Civil Rights

Civil rights are those rights which are, or which it is argued should be, protected constitutionally or legally as fundamental rights that everyone should enjoy, irrespective of his or her status. They fall essentially into two categories: basic human rights to fair and decent treatment for the individual; and political rights which are seen as vital for a healthy and liberal society, whether or not they are actually desired by many people.

The first category includes the right to legal equality and to equality of treatment and provision, the right to a fair trial and the right to be exempt from unjust or inhuman punishment. The right not to be discriminated against because of one's race, religion or gender, whether by the government or a private agent, as well as protection against arbitrary arrest, a biased jury, police brutality and so on, are seen as basic rights that all should enjoy, and which require constitutional protection in any society.

The more specifically political rights include the right to freedom of speech, to form or join a **trade union**, to worship as one wishes, and to protest in public against government policy. All these are rights taken for granted in a **liberal democracy**.

Naturally these two categories overlap considerably, and it is increasingly argued that they should be extended to cover more 'substantive' rights. Substantive rights—the right to work, for example, or to minimum welfare and education provision—differ from procedural rights (which only guarantee equal treatment) in that they commit society to an absolute standard of provision. It is clearly a breach of a civil right if state education is given to white children and not to black children, or if welfare provisions are given differentially according to the sex of the recipient. In the past it has been considered less obviously a denial of civil rights if no one is provided with free university education, or if unemployment pay is below subsistence level for everyone. However, the development of civil rights theories and of actual civil rights provision has tended to involve a steady extension from procedural equality to guarantees of minimum standards. Some constitutions, for example the Basic Law (Grundgesetz) of Germany, actually list as basic rights things like minimum, or even higher, educational provision rather than restricting the guarantee to fair or unbiased provision of whatever the government decides to make available. This is yet more common in the new democracies of Eastern Europe, where a tradition of extensive welfare provision was built up during the communist years.

Another tendency has been to increase the number of criteria which are not regarded as fair bases for differential treatment. There has, for example, been steady pressure on the US Supreme Court since the 1960s to rule that no policy which distinguishes between people on the basis of sex is constitutional, by analogy with the ruling that any **discrimination** on the basis of race is a denial of civil rights. This is sometimes extended to a ban on discrimination according to sexual orientation, leading, for example, to removal of restrictions on the rights of same sex partners, or the possibility of adoption of children by, or even a form of marriage between, homosexual couples (see **homosexuality**). Another recent development has been the effort to stop private agents, whether corporations or individuals, from acting in a discriminatory manner. In Britain the Race Relations Acts prohibit the private exercise of racial discrimination, for example by a shopkeeper, and in the USA similar measures have been taken in areas such as access to private housing markets. One of the major theoretical problems of civil rights in jurisprudence is the extent to which legal enforcement mechanisms should or can apply only to the State. It is still unclear, for example, whether the United Kingdom's **Human Rights Act** will apply to private organizations as well as to the 'public authorities' it expressly covers. Thus, for example, while the US Supreme Court insisted on police warning arrested persons of their constitutional rights to remain silent and to have a lawyer (known as the Miranda warning, deriving from the

Miranda v. Arizona judgment) as long ago as 1966, studies have shown hundreds of police forces throughout the country ignoring them. Almost all studies of industrial pay in Europe show that women do not, in general, benefit from statutory rights to equal pay. Only complex and powerful enforcement mechanisms can actually guarantee that a *de jure* right becomes a *de facto* one.

Civil Service

The civil service of a country is its public administration, the body of men and women employed by the state to implement policy and apply the laws and regulations made by the **executive** and **legislature**. It usually also includes a small élite group of senior public officers who help the official political leaders to draft laws and translate policies into practical forms. All governments rely on a civil service of some sort, but finding a clear operational definition that distinguishes the public administrators from the politicians is often extremely difficult. The phrase is itself somewhat culture-bound, since it is used and understood mainly in Britain and its ex-colonies, most notable among which, of course, is the USA. There is no equivalent to the concept of civil service in continental Europe; the idea that senior officers of the state are servants of the public, which is one connotation of the English phrase, has no place in the political culture of, say, the French Republic. (Originally, civil servants were simply officers of the Crown who were employed in a non-military capacity.)

In its full sense, 'civil service' is only a meaningful phrase in a democratic society, where it is possible to draw a clear distinction between the politicians, who are elected to office and must face re-election from time to time, and civil servants who are appointed to offices which they will hold, subject to good behaviour, in the same way as any other employed person. A corollary of this is that the civil service itself has no right to issue laws and regulations, or to make policy: they exist only to advise and carry out the instructions of their political masters, and are usually supposed to be non-partisan. In practice these ideals are seldom achieved. Civil services everywhere have a great deal of political power, if only because governments are often totally dependent on their advice, and a combination of time pressure and the technical nature of legislation makes it difficult for politicians to question or check on the advice given by the civil service. In addition, the complexity of human problems for which legislation exists means that quite junior civil servants inevitably have to exercise considerable discretion in dealing with individual cases, whether these be tax matters, welfare payments or local planning permission.

This having been said, in many countries there is little or no pretence that the upper levels of the public administration are non-partisan. In the USA senior appointments are used directly for political patronage. In Italy, the most senior officials belong to one or other of the factions in the Christian Democrat party; and even in Germany, government changes usually involve new appointments in upper-level public administration offices. In the United Kingdom there was some evidence that, in the 1980s, appointments to key civil service posts, especially in the Treasury, were only made if the candidate was seen as a believer in **Thatcherism**. Nevertheless, the idea of a civil service as a politically neutral body, dedicated to the execution of decisions it does not make, remains an influential one.

Civil Society

Civil society was central to the work of some of the most important political thinkers from the 17th century onwards. Among others, **Hobbes, Locke** and even **Hegel** distinguished between the **state** and civil society, that is the organized society over which the state rules. Such a distinction is not entirely valid, since the state is itself part of society. However, we are aware that, as well as institutions bound up with formal authority and political control, there exists a set of interlinked and stable social institutions which have much influence on, or control over, our lives. The distinction, and the consequent importance of civil society as a concept, originates with the **state of nature** theorists, especially Hobbes and Locke. They held that political authority was at least hypothetically dispensable; that is, they argued as though it was possible not to have a state, and they therefore needed a concept to describe the remaining institutions. Civil society, then, is the framework within which those without political authority live their lives—economic relationships, family and kinship structures, religious institutions and so on. It is a purely analytic concept because civil society does not exist independently of political authority, nor vice versa, and, it is generally believed, neither could long continue without the other; therefore, no very clear boundary can be drawn between the two.

The neglect of civil society in recent decades has two main causes. One is the fact that the state itself has been discussed less often, having been replaced, inadequately, by notions like 'the political system'. The other is that the growing trend towards using sociological models in political thinking has tended to efface the barriers between political activity and social activity; both are treated as manifestations of underlying ideological, cultural or even economic patterns. In fact, the question of the interpenetration of state and society in this sense might more sensibly be treated as an empirical question to be solved in each particular case. Perhaps the real use of the concept is to stress that political systems are, morally if not sociologically, secondary to, and ought to be reflections of, direct and sometimes voluntary human relations. Even this point would be denied by some, especially those influenced by the classical

Greek political tradition, who argue that the state creates civil society, rather than itself being appended to the latter.

Class

In one way or another the idea that social class has a vital impact on politics has always been held, and has never been denied by political thinkers of any persuasion. The classical Greek political theorists, for example, were acutely aware of the need for all social classes to fit neatly into their stations in life, and **Aristotle** is often pictured as the champion of a society dominated by the middle class.

Nowadays there are two main approaches to the political relevance of class. One is **Marxist**, while the other is best described as the 'social science' approach to class. For a Marxist, class is fundamental to politics, since historical development is seen as a continuous series of class conflicts culminating in the final class conflict between the **proletariat** and the **bourgeoisie**. As the lowest of social classes, the proletariat cannot be challenged, after their future victory, by some other exploited class (none will exist) and therefore a classless **communism** will be the final form of society. Marxism also produces the simplest and neatest of all class definitions. Classes are defined by their relations to the means of production. Those who at any time 'own and control' the means of economic production (factories, mines, farms, etc.) are the ruling class in any society, and those who do not own them are forced to sell their labour power to those who do. This latter group form the proletariat and are ruled and exploited by the owners and controllers. There are very great difficulties in applying satisfactorily this most simple form of Marxist class analysis, and modern Marxists have devised many subtle and more complex theories to take account of empirical and theoretical problems. For example, most of the comfortably off people who would normally be regarded as middle or upper middle class do not actually own anything except a house and a car, and most 'means of production', such as factories, are owned by publicly-traded companies of which the bulk of shares are legally owned by institutions like pension funds, which may even belong to trade unions. For this reason there has been a tendency to concentrate on the 'control' element of the definition, but even this ignores the role of government.

The alternative treatment of class, which is to be found in the works of non-Marxist sociologists and political scientists, is stronger on empirical observation than theoretical formulation. Typically, a social scientist will use a notion of class which combines elements of social **status** (often based on unproved assumptions about the comparative social respect given to different occupations), wealth and income, and structural aspects of the economic location of individuals. These definitions of class are made for one overwhelmingly important reason—that quite simple distinctions drawn between occupations lead to categories that do seem to correlate highly with political and social beliefs and actions. Research into voting behaviour, for example, used to employ a simple two-class model. Those who earn their living in non-manual jobs (typically defined as the middle class) do in fact vote for the **right** wing parties much more often than for the **left**, while manual workers (the working class) vote more frequently for the left. Although class-voting models in political science are now more sophisticated, their basis is still occupational ranking. Such models of social structure may be more or less complicated, and may correspond more or less successfully to actual social and political behaviour. There are many difficulties inherent in these models too. For example, in countries with a sizeable agricultural sector, it is very hard to fit farmers and farm labourers into a class model. (Though this aspect is accepted in Marxist models as well.) Another typical problem is in assessing the class position of married women, whether they work or not.

A particular problem, both theoretical and empirical, is whether or not class has to be a conscious matter. Is it enough to categorize an individual by external facts about them, or does their own sense of what they are matter? Taking this into consideration leads to endless complications. For example, in the United Kingdom a surprisingly large minority of people whose jobs would put them at the top of the class scale actually report thinking of themselves as working class, while many skilled manual workers claim middle class status. At the theoretical level there has always been a problem of what Marxists call **false consciousness**—people holding beliefs and attitudes which seem to fit with an economic and social position which aids those actually above them on the class ladder.

However difficult it may be to construct class models, whether Marxist or otherwise, the brute facts of politics require them. Though not all parties have a class base, most do at least to some extent, and all societies have political parties whose appeal is based on representing the interests of fairly clear socio-economic groups. Some political parties (notably conservative parties but also some liberal parties) claim as part of their ideology to be classless or to regard class as irrelevant, but this does not necessarily mean that their voting support, or their policies, are any less class oriented. It is, nevertheless, a mistake simply to interpret evidence that people with specific and precise economic interests support one party rather than another as evidence of class politics; this may be no more than evidence that rational income–party connections are easily made. Class has to be a deeply structured factor, if it exists at all. As **Weber** said, class is about the way economic positions affect long-term life chances. Whatever subtle theoretical distinctions and empirical variances are shown, the existence of something that is more akin to class than to status or **caste** seems evident in most Western societies: not only the level, but the source, predictability and security of income and wealth holdings are connected closely to matters such as educational chances, consumption and saving habits, access to jobs and religious behaviour. Even accent and dress style correlate deeply with economic position in Western society. (See also **new class**.)

Cleavage

Cleavage, or 'social cleavage', is a vital concept in much political science analysis, especially in relation to voting behaviour or the formation and working of party systems. It designates a division between groups within a society, based on some more or less fixed attribute: one can have cleavages along lines of **class**, religion, language, race or even, conceivably, sex. The patterns of social cleavages, their interrelationship, salience, number and nature, used to determine the battle lines of competitive politics and generally influence the stability and functioning of the political system. To a large extent this sort of patterning is still crucial, despite an overall tendency towards dealignment in many societies. In origin at least, most political parties represent a given side as defined by one or more cleavage lines, and are likely to be opposed by parties representing the other side or sides. If the politics of a society are based on certain kinds of cleavage patterns, political life is likely to be more violent, and government less competent, than if other cleavages dominate. For example, racial or religious cleavages, if at all strong, are much harder to manage by bargaining and compromise than class cleavages, because they tend to produce absolute demands. The interrelationship between cleavages can also be vitally important. If they reinforce each other, so that two people who are opposed along one cleavage are likely also to be opposed along a second, the temperature of political conflict is likely to be high. Where one finds 'cross-cutting' cleavages—where, for example, opponents on religious issues are likely to find themselves on the same side when the issue is language—intense conflict may well be avoided. One reason why the politics of language in Belgium causes such stress, and parliamentary instability, is that the Flemish–Walloon cleavage largely coincides with Catholic-**anti-clerical** and economic cleavages. By contrast, Italy's survival during the extremely difficult post-war years may have been due partly to the fact that the vital class cleavage in the country did not correspond very closely to the religious–secular cleavage. The Catholic ruling party, the Christian Democrats (see **Christian democracy**), attracted many working-class votes that would probably otherwise have gone to the communists or socialists, while many middle-class voters who rebelled against clerical control in politics were led to vote for left-wing parties. The decline of one of these cleavages, religion, contributed to the collapse of the Italian party system in the early 1990s; the resulting unstable party coalitions are due to the absence of a well-structured cleavage system.

The sheer number of cleavages within any society has a lot to do with whether it has a **multi-party system**, and thus is likely to be governed by possibly unstable coalitions, or a two- or three-party system which may be more likely to produce stable one-party governments. If any pattern exists in the development of cleavages it is probably towards simplification, in particular through a reduction in the importance of secondary cleavages. The Netherlands, for example, used to have a Roman Catholic party and not one, but two, Protestant parties, which in 1980 merged to form a single Christian party. In addition, other parties in the Netherlands have consolidated along conventional class and issue lines, illustrating the declining importance of religious cleavage.

Many cleavage patterns are essentially involuntary: a person is white, or has been baptized and brought up Catholic or speaks a specific language by virtue of birth, not as a matter of opinion or values. This is well demonstrated by the example of Northern Ireland, split by a religious cleavage, where one cannot escape the conflict by being an atheist—it will still be asked whether one is a Catholic atheist or a Protestant atheist. Furthermore, research shows that there is nothing in the specific theological differences between the two denominations which accounts for the hostility between the groups. The most enduring cleavages are deeply historical in origin, closely bound with the development of nationhood, and often outlive subsequent historical development. In the USA, the North–South cleavage dates from before the Civil War (1861–65), even though there are no longer any good economic reasons for people to see their lives much affected by this particular distinction.

Coalition

Coalitions are groupings of rival political units in the face of a common enemy; they occur in situations where protection from that enemy, or the furtherance of some shared goal, overrides differences and potential conflicts between the members of the coalition. Coalitions usually occur in modern parliaments when no single political party can muster a majority of votes. Two or more parties, who have enough elected members between them to form a majority, may then be able to agree on a common programme that does not require too many drastic compromises with their individual policies, and can proceed to form a government.

Coalitions vary in their stability, their life expectancy, and in the way power is distributed within them (which may or may not be related to the relative sizes of the parties involved). Some coalitions are so long established, and so obviously essential if the aspirations of either party are to be realized, that they virtually comprise a new party in its own right. Thus the only hope of being in government for the Liberal Democrats in the UK, the National Party in

Australia or the Free Democrats in Germany are alliances they can form. In the case of Australia the National Party's alliance with the Liberals is, consequently, virtually indestructible. However, political change can break up what seem almost totally united alliances. From 1969 to 1982 West Germany was ruled by a coalition of Social Democrats and Free Democrats which many commentators thought indissoluble. Nevertheless, the Free Democrats ended the alliance, and Germany was then ruled by a coalition of Christian Democrats and Free Democrats. In part this demonstrates the counter-intuitive power that a very small party such as the Free Democrats could wield: as it was the only possible partner for two other parties, neither of which were likely to want to coalesce with the other, that small party was able to dominate politics. Only when a second small party, the Greens, became electorally successful enough to be an alternative coalition partner on the left, in 1998, did the Social Democrats return to power. Indeed, it is this disproportionate power of small political entities that is often used as the principal argument against **proportional representation**.

Coalitions can occur in any political situation involving several rival forces which are in fairly close agreement on essentials. Sometimes they are only intended to be short-lived, or even concerned with a single issue: voting in the multi-party assembly of the French **Fourth Republic** always involved the creation of an *ad hoc* majority of deputies who were agreed only on supporting a particular bill; and despite the two-party system the same situation prevails in the US Congress. Though often accused of leading to unstable governments, coalitions are in fact more likely to be the result of political instability than its cause, and occur wherever several political forces, whether because of electoral rules or some other mechanisms, exist in a rough equilibrium. Traditionally Britain has only resorted to coalition governments in time of war or severe economic crisis, but this is largely because the electoral machinery seldom produces a parliament in which no single party has a majority. When this has occurred, as in the last years of the 1974–79 Labour government, a coalition has been created in fact if not in name.

Coalitions are of equal importance in international relations, especially in defence policy. Few major wars for the last three centuries have actually been fought between two countries (the Franco–Prussian War being an unusual counter-example), instead, they have been coalition wars. In this context there can be either *ad hoc* coalitions, forged by the crisis of a war where naturally opposed partners have to co-operate to defeat a common enemy, the Second World War coalition between the United Kingdom, the Soviet Union and the USA being a good example, or long-standing arrangements made in peacetime between countries with common aims against a common group of enemies, the post-war opposition between **NATO** and the now defunct **Warsaw Pact** being an obvious example. Interestingly, in both domestic and international contexts the main restriction of coalition formation is ideological: if any subset of actors can form a coalition only on specific, precise and short-term issues, coalitions will be short-lived, unstable and unpredictable. In international relations, for example, the traditional **balance-of-power** theory relies precisely on the notion that there are no ideological barriers to any coalition forming. In extreme cases of domestic politics one can find the same 'open texture' to coalition potential. In both domestic and foreign affairs, however, such openness is unusual, and the range of possible coalitions is much diminished. **Coalition theory**, the study of the formation of coalitions, has been the study of one of the more successful political science theoretical efforts since the 1950s, and powerful predictive theories, based in part on **game theory**, have been derived and tested.

Coalition Theory

Coalition theory, much of which developed from **game theory**, is part of the quasi-mathematical rational choice tradition in political science which attempts to construct predictive theories to explain political activity. There are two principal domains of political activity to which coalition theories have been applied: the forming of a government by a coalition of minority parties in a parliament, and the forming of military and diplomatic alliances between states. However, the advocates of coalition theory would claim that it ought to apply to any situation where more than two actors face potential conflicts of interest, and thus co-operation between two or more against one or more opponents is rationally useful. They would further argue that at least the general form of a successful theory would apply to any sample, whether it dealt with a coalition of small firms against a potentially monopolistic rival, a coalition of parties to form a government or a coalition of schoolchildren against the playground bully.

In the example of government formation coalition theories have been quite successful, especially when applied to party systems where the number and sizes of parties, as well as the ideological spectrum of the nation's politics, leaves no obvious coalition grouping. One of the two principal rules to emerge from early work in this sphere was that the most likely coalition to form will be what is called a 'minimum-winning' coalition. In a parliament where 70 seats are needed to form a government, and there are four parties (A–D), running from left to right of an ideological spectrum, A having 50 seats, B 40 seats, C 20 seats and D 10 seats, it is more likely that a two–party coalition of A and B will form than a three–party coalition of B, C and D. What will almost certainly *not* form is a coalition of all four, because such a government would have 50 more seats than it needed and, as a party loses potential benefits the greater the number of other parties with which it has to share the value of being in government, there is seldom a good reason to form an over-large coalition. The other principal rule is of 'ideological connectedness'. Parties will try to co-operate with others nearest to their own political values. Thus one of the minimum-winning coalitions in the example above would be between A and C, but C is not ideologically the closest possible partner for A.

In other examples different factors emerge, such as problems arising from the provision of collective goods and, in the international arena, from the general theory of the **balance of power**.

Cohabitation

Cohabitation was the term used to describe the period between 1986 and 1988 when a socialist French president, François **Mitterrand**, and a centre-right coalition headed by prime minister Jacques Chirac, together formed the government of France The prospect of a president facing a strong and hostile parliamentary majority was thought to be especially problematic because of the constitutional ambiguity in the role and power of the **prime minister**. Mitterrand was not constitutionally required to select a prime minister from the majority coalition in the National Assembly, but an appointee from his own party would have found it extremely difficult to govern. The alternative was a centre-right prime minister (a **Gaullist** in the case of Chirac) who might be able to guarantee to pass legislation through the assembly, but could be presented with an impasse if presidential powers were used regularly to block the implementation of that legislation. Furthermore, all previous **Fifth Republic** prime ministers had been very much subordinate to the presidents, liable to be freely dismissed and in practice having little influence over the selection of ministers. This first experience of divided party control over the executive in France had been much feared as likely to cause instability. In fact French politics managed perfectly well, and there have been similar periods since.

French constitutional experts had long dreaded this situation arising, and what happened was that a very uneasy truce was worked out in which the centre-right government would not try to repeal much of its socialist predecessor's work, and would accept that Mitterrand had a supremacy in certain areas traditionally viewed as in the president's prerogative. This was made easier than it might have been because Mitterrand had himself always been more right wing in his defence policy than most of his party, and because the economic problems of France in the mid-1980s tended to dictate policy in that area. Nevertheless, although the two elements of the government succeeded in working together without too much strain, it was a period of relative inactivity and, had the cohabitation had to continue much longer, problems would have arisen. Once Mitterrand had been re-elected president in 1988 he called a general election, and the French electorate, still in the mood that had re-elected him, returned a sufficient number of left-wing members to the assembly for him to form a coalition government under a socialist prime minister, although this still included some ministers from the centrist Union pour la Démocratie Française. Ironically, Mitterrand had campaigned in the late 1970s to shorten the presidential term to five years to avoid the problem of cohabitation, but made no effort to carry out this promise in the first decade of his presidency. The shortening of the presidential term was finally achieved during a later period of cohabitation, which involved the conservative Chirac as president and a socialist prime minister, Lionel Jospin, in 2000. Thus Chirac's second presidential term, to which he was elected in 2002, was scheduled to last only until 2007.

This is not a problem unique to France. It can arise in any political system where a **president** with real political power is elected at a different time, or separately, from the parliament. In the USA, for example, it is not at all unusual for the party of a president not to enjoy a majority in Congress. For example, following the elections of 2000, while the Republican George W. Bush won control of the presidency (albeit on a minority of votes cast), the Democrats improved their position in both the Senate and House of Representatives, ultimately gaining control of the former.

Cold War

Nothing so demonstrates the impermanence of political life than the history of the cold war. As a concept, cold war gained popularity shortly after the last 'hot' or 'shooting' war to involve all the major powers, the Second World War. It describes a state of extreme hostility between the **superpowers**, associated with **arms races**, diplomatic conflict, and hostile measures of every kind short of overt military action. The cold war started, at the latest, in 1947 with the Berlin Blockade, and remained intense until the middle 1960s, with incidents such as the **Cuban missile crisis** and the building of the Berlin Wall. From the late 1960s **détente** grew, or at least became more fashionable, but the threat of a return to the cold war remained. Some commentators talk of a 'second cold war' beginning roughly with the election of President Reagan in 1980; certainly for a few years in the 1980s arms races took on more energy, defence budgets increased, and diplomatic conflict between the superpowers in many areas of the world intensified. However, from 1985, with **Gorbachev's** rise to power in the Soviet Union, and Reagan's need to curb defence spending to ease the US budgetary crisis, what can now be seen as an inexorable process of winding down this institutionalized, but essentially irrational, conflict began. As reform in the Soviet Union and Eastern Europe accelerated, the economic capacity of the **Warsaw Pact** to compete militarily with **NATO** declined, as

did the political willingness of non-Soviet Warsaw Pact members to participate. At this time, urgent arms control negotiations covering nuclear weapons
(**Intermediate Nuclear Forces** and Strategic Arms Reduction Talks) and
Conventional Forces in Europe, were increasingly clearly in the economic
interests of all countries. However, there can be little doubt that it was
Gorbachev's shifts in foreign policy, usually demonstrated by arms control
concessions, that spelled the long-term end of the cold war. What immediately
ended it, however, were the revolutions in Eastern Europe, so that the conflict
changed from one between two blocs to a conflict between NATO and the
Soviet Union alone. If a single piece of evidence is needed that the cold war
finally has ended (there had been failed promises of this every time the détente
cycle 'warmed'), it was the support which the Soviet government gave to the
UN-sponsored, but American-led, Gulf War against Iraq. Alternatively, the
Soviet Union having to accept that its troops should leave the eastern portion
of the now unified German state might be taken as the symbolic ending of the
purely military aspect of the cold war. The fact that the cold war ended
essentially by accident is fitting—it began that way. Since the 1970s historians
of the period have stressed the way in which mutual misunderstandings and
disappointments between the Soviet Union and the USA about what should
be done with post-war Europe grew into a structured opposition that neither
side had ever intended.

Like most such concepts, 'cold war' can only be valid if some 'natural'
alternative exists; and it is arguably unclear that relations between the major
powers have been any worse during the supposed cold war period than has
usually been the case in many past periods following destructive wars. What
gave the cold war its impetus, and what had usually been missing in the past,
was the deeply felt ideological conflict between the East and West. It is because
of this that some commentators, almost entirely in the USA, want to see the
cold war as a real war which their 'way of life' won. In truth, serious analysts on
both sides of the **iron curtain** had, for years, argued both that neither side had
any real intention of attacking the other, and also that neither side had the
capacity to do so. Nor is it the case that only the Soviet Union lost its
hegemony over its junior alliance partners. The intensification of the cold
war in the early 1980s was met with very deep opposition among Western
European publics, and crucial dissension inside NATO's own governing
councils over the perceived trend towards a return to isolationism in the
USA. There was pressure for Europe to be left to fend for itself, a denouncing
of European NATO members for failing to spend enough on defence (the
'burden-sharing' argument) to such an extent that NATO's lack of ability to
fight a defensive war almost matched the Warsaw Pact's inability and unwillingness to fight an offensive one. The cold war *is* over, but this no more
guarantees peace in Europe than the cold war itself ever really threatened a hot

war. Indeed, one consequence of the end of Soviet domination of Eastern Europe has been the series of conflicts in the former Yugoslavia, making the end of the cold war more dangerous than the cold war itself usually was. What has happened is that the natural and inevitable conflicts in such a complex continent, ones that were frozen by the artificial 'East–West' cold war, have returned, and Europe has become as unstable as at any time since 1914. The cold war had two, contradictory, effects: it paralysed international relations outside of Europe so that regional conflicts became mere instances of a European conflict and were artificially heightened; but at the same time it did impose an order and stability in Europe itself.

Collective Goods

A collective good is one which, if it is to be provided for anyone in a society (or indeed in any institution), has to be provided for every member; it cannot be restricted to a given group, even if members of that group are the only ones who pay for it. The benefits of military defence, for example, could hardly be restricted to citizens willing to pay a special defence tax; and, similarly, clean air programmes give protection against pollution to everyone, not only those who have voted for them. Some collective goods could, in principle, be selective. In the 19th century, for example, London fire brigades were private companies which would put out fires only in premises displaying a sign showing that fees due had been paid. The growth of private security companies in Western cities is, in a sense, the private and therefore selective provision of what would normally be seen as a public good. When the state provides the services, however, it becomes impossible to be selective in this way. Those uninsured against fire present too much of a risk to others not to be looked after, just as the general need to prevent crime makes it undesirable to arrest burglars of some, but not all, premises. At a lower institutional level, **trade unions** have always recognized that the wage rises they secure will be enjoyed by all the workers in the industry concerned, and not just by members of the trade union; this is, indeed, the justification offered for the closed shop—that without one, some workers will get the benefit of union action without themselves having to incur the risks associated with some union activities, and without having to pay union subscriptions.

Collective goods are important because they come as near as possible to being genuine examples of the **common good** or the **public interest**. They also involve a paradox that has long interested political theorists and economists, and has some real political relevance. It would appear that if a policy is in someone's interest, it must also be in their interest to fight for it, or to pay their share of the cost of getting it. Yet it can easily be demonstrated that this is by no means always so. If some people are in a position to procure a common good, and need it badly enough, they will provide it even if only for themselves. But as it *is* common, everyone can enjoy it; so it is actually in the interest of such others not to pay their share. The financial contributions made by member nations of **NATO** have been a case in point. The smaller nations seldom paid their share of the costs; they knew that the USA needed NATO, and that it could, and if necessary would, provide an adequate defence for Europe even when it had to pay more than its 'fair' share. One reason for the end of the **cold war** was a growing sense in the USA that it did not need to protect a Europe unwilling to contribute sufficiently to its own defence, leading to an increasing interest in **isolationism**. Such a defence had been believed to be a common good for all the Western European nations, and advantage was regularly taken of the fact. Many other practical examples could be given of this paradox, which illustrates in political terms the proverbial strength of the weak. In common parlance the problem is often referred to as 'the free rider problem'.

Collective Responsibility

Collective responsibility is a constitutional doctrine more or less peculiar to the Westminster (British) model of government, and of decreasing reality even in the United Kingdom. It means that decisions taken by a collective executive, such as the British **cabinet**, are collective responsibilities: anyone involved in making the decision is expected to support it without reservation in public, and generally to act as though they were themself solely responsible for the decision. This is supposed to apply even where the individual in question has always opposed the decision and actually voted against it: as long as they are not prepared to resign from the decision-making body, they must accept the consequences along with the majority.

In recent years this doctrine has been increasingly disregarded in Britain. On a few crucial issues, notably constitutional questions such as membership of the **European Union**, some prime ministers have allowed cabinet members to campaign publicly against decisions taken by the cabinet of which they were, and remained, members. In the 1960s the conventions of British **cabinet government** began to change. Individual ministers felt freer than before to reveal the substance of what had occurred in cabinet; and this movement towards a more open style of cabinet government culminated in the publication by a former cabinet minister, Richard Crossman, of a detailed set of diaries which revealed cabinet proceedings and many of the aspects of government previously supposed to be confidential. Crossman's diaries have been followed by a number of political memoirs covering cabinet proceedings, providing their writers with a means of distancing, or even disassociating, themselves from earlier cabinet decisions. More immediately damaging is the tendency for cabinet members to leak details of cabinet debate, allowing them effectively, if not overtly, to disclaim responsibility for the subsequent decisions arrived at. A semblance of collective responsibility is needed, however, as long as a cabinet wants to rely on tight party discipline in parliamentary votes. It is clearly absurd to discipline a back-bench MP for voting against a government policy if several members of that government are publicly known to oppose it.

Similarly, by the late 1970s the doctrine of collective responsibility had been modified by the willingness of cabinets to accept defeats on legislative measures in the House of Commons without feeling obliged to resign; such defeats were now assumed not to be votes of no **confidence** in the government as a whole.

Collectivism

Collectivism can be, and often has been, given a complicated theoretical meaning or meanings, but its normal use today is rather simple. Theoretically, and the main work comes from the tradition of **anarchism**, a collective is any group of co-operating individuals who may produce or own goods together, but which does not exercise coercive force on its members, and thus is not a state or political system. Such voluntary associations are not, however, just groups of individuals who retain their own shares and are tied by no bonds other than individual self-interest, for collectivism is used as a theoretical counter to rational individualism, as well as against statism or state socialism.

In practice collectivism has tended to take a much weaker meaning, so that a society is collectivist if it departs in any important way at all from a **laissez-faire** liberalism in terms of duties, obligations, property rights and economic management. Under this weak sense it is common to describe Britain as a collectivist society, or at least as having collectivist tendencies, since the mixed economy and **welfare state** involve an acceptance of collective responsibilities and rights of the individual against the collectivity (for welfare) which are, nevertheless, not sensibly characterized as socialist. In some ways the notion of 'the collectivity' is useful in political discourse, because we need a way of referring to the sum of the members of a society, against whom one may wish to assert a right, or to whom one may wish to claim a duty lies, without wishing to involve the notion of the state. As 'society' itself is an abstraction clearly not capable of rights and obligations, the idea of the 'collective' can play an analytic role.

Collectivization

Collectivization refers to the wholesale and drastic reorganization of the agricultural sector of Soviet society carried out principally by **Stalin** shortly after the death of **Lenin**, at the Communist Party conference of 1923, though much of it was not achieved until he launched his series of five-year plans in

1929. How to organize agriculture in the new, supposedly communist, Soviet state had always been a difficult problem for two related reasons. First, according to **Marx**, the revolution was not supposed to happen until a country was thoroughly industrialized and would therefore have a rather small and dependent peasantry. Consequently the peasantry, as a category, fits badly into the class analysis of Marxism, which posits two, and only two, mutually opposed classes. Secondly, in order to achieve the **Bolshevik** revolution, Lenin had had to lean heavily on the support of the peasantry, in the absence of a large industrial proletariat, yet peasants in Russia, as is almost a universal truth of sociology, were extremely conservative. Their only interest in the revolution had been to gain legal control of the land they had often farmed as tenants, or to gain land from redistribution of large semi-feudal estates. This tendency had been exacerbated by the relaxation of communist economic rules that Lenin had been forced into in the **New Economic Policy**, which had considerably increased the size of the class known as Kulaks, rich peasants with considerable land holdings. Because of the general inadequacy of the industrial base there was not enough money to buy for the urban proletariat the foodstuffs hoarded by the agricultural sector. In any case, the large-scale ownership of private property, and the straightforward profit motivation of the peasantry, were embarrassing in a newly-created communist society.

Stalin's answer was to create vast collective farms, on which the agricultural workers would be employed in much the same way as industrial workers were employed in the state-controlled and centrally-planned factories of the industrial sphere. Other benefits were expected from increasing returns to scale, as high levels of mechanization were seen as economically more suitable than on small-scale private farms. The peasantry in general, and the Kulaks most of all, resented and opposed this appropriation of 'their' land, and the forced change of status from individual owners (and often employers) to mere wage labourers, but Stalin and the party, helped by the Red Army, used all necessary violence to overcome the objections. Massive deportations to other parts of the Union, and the murder of, in some estimates as many as six million, Kulaks and peasants produced an entirely transformed agriculture.

There can be no doubt that the overall results of this policy were catastrophic; agricultural yields fell, despite later efforts by **Khrushchev** to humanize and moderate the system. The Soviet Union, in most recent years, depended on Western agricultural surpluses for as much as 40% of its grain requirements. Some steps were taken to reintroduce a private incentive, by allowing peasants on collective farms to control small plots of land themselves and sell their produce on a free market, but no immediate solution to the agricultural problems became apparent even after the period of **perestroika** and the fundamental reorganization of what used to be the Soviet Union. It should be noted, however, that part of the agricultural problem has always been one of distribution rather than production: in any year a large proportion of production rots in the fields because it cannot be harvested, or in storehouses because it cannot be distributed. Furthermore, the problem of matching agricultural production with both the needs of consumers and the livelihood of farmers is endemic to all economies, and is shown especially in the wasteful subsidies paid to farmers in both the USA and European Union. Historically, collectivization is one of the two great sins attributable to the Stalinist period, the other being the great purges. While the policy was clearly brutal and inhumane, it has to be seen against the pressing need rapidly to industrialize a desperately backward country. In total utilitarian terms it remains to be proven that the experience of the Russian agricultural sector has ever been anything but appalling, and it is certainly not proved that collectivization as a purely technical answer to mass food production is any less sensible than most other methods.

Colonialism

Colonialism is the holding and ownership of colonies, or the treating of another country as though it was in fact a colony. Indeed recently the concept has been extended to refer to 'internal' colonialism, where the capital or economically dominant part of a country treats a distant region just as it might a genuinely foreign colony. For true colonialism to exist two conditions are necessary. The land held as a colony must have no real political independence from the 'mother country', but also the relationship must be one of forthright exploitation. The entire reason for having colonies is to increase the wealth and welfare of the colonial power, either by extracting resources, material or labour from the colony more cheaply than they could be bought on a free market, or by ensuring a market for one's own goods at advantageous rates. In this way a set of colonies may be rather different from an empire. The far flung lands that constitute an empire may be integrated equally in economic and political terms with the original homeland, the motive for imperial expansion being the spreading of a way of life or of a political design, or merely the distancing of external borders, and thus military danger, from the heartland. To some extent this demonstrates a change in meaning of 'colony'. The original colonies were new settlements by Greek city states, where over-population led to a need for expansion. Expansion was not, principally, at the cost of an indigenous population in the new territory, and the relationship between the parent city and the colony was neither exploitative nor one of political dominance.

In practice there are no pure examples either of colonialism, or of this non-exploitative version of **imperialism**. Colonial government has often been justified, sincerely or otherwise, as an attempt to spread 'civilization' to socially underdeveloped societies, and few empires have not rested, fundamentally, on the economic advantage to producers and merchants in the imperial centre of captive markets and resources on the periphery. Britain's Colonial Office, for example, was largely staffed with those who believed that they were both exporting decent values and assisting the development of underprivileged natives. Nevertheless, the essence of colonialism as a concept, and especially in modern pejorative usage, is the idea of deliberate exploitation of another country and its inhabitants. Thus the earliest colonies of the modern world, the British colonies in India or North America, for example, were set up by trading companies operating under royal warrants, with the express intention of making a profit. The earliest colonies of which we have much evidence are probably those set up all over the Mediterranean basin by the Greek city states from around 600 BC. Nothing was seen to be wrong or undesirable about the policy of colonialism at a time when the general indigenous populations of the parent countries themselves were allowed no political involvement, and the idea that colonialism was politically unacceptable arose only with the development of internal democracy in the home countries. In fact the absolute illegitimacy of colonialism is a later 20th-century phenomenon. One of the war aims that was expressed by Germany in both world wars was the achievement of colonial territory on a par with Britain's, and few found the demand in principle wrong, but rather objected simply to having to give up their own colonies or national independence. Not until the creation of the **League of Nations** between the wars, and its successor, the **United Nations**, did it become commonly accepted that only a mandate from the international community to govern in the long-term interests of the colony itself could justify a developed land owning and controlling a less developed one. It is still, of course, often alleged that the essence of colonialism characterizes the relations between former colonial powers and the newly independent states, and indeed between the industrially developed powers and the underdeveloped countries of the **Third World**. This modern objection to colonialism rests on the acceptance of the ethnically based **nation state**, for otherwise there is no *a priori* reason why London or Paris have less right to rule India or Algeria than they have to rule Manchester or Lyons. The French, particularly, tried to make this a justification. They argued that their colonies, especially in Algeria, were simply departments of the French State that happened to be separated physically from mainland France, and several far flung territories continue to constitute parts of metropolitan France.

COMECON

COMECON is the standard way of referring to the Council for Mutual Economic Assistance (CMEA) which, until June 1991, functioned as the Union of Soviet Socialist Republic's and Eastern Europe's equivalent to the European Economic Community (see **European Union**). Alternatively, it can be regarded as the economic equivalent to the **Warsaw Pact**. The dominance which the Soviet Union had over COMECON made this latter analogy perhaps the more appropriate. It was founded by **Stalin** in 1949, and he initially used it mainly as a weapon in his attempt to bring Yugoslavia to heel by economic boycott. The original members were Albania, Bulgaria, Czechoslovakia, the German Democratic Republic, Hungary, Poland, Romania and the Soviet Union; Mongolia, Cuba and Vietnam joined in 1962, 1972 and 1978 respectively. Albania ceased to be a member in 1962 as part of its general severing of relations with the Soviet Union after forming too close a link with China at the time when the Sino–Soviet split began to emerge.

After Stalin COMECON came to be seen as a useful way of countering the increasing integration, especially through the EC and EFTA, of the Western European economies, and above all, as a way of enforcing supranational planning in the interest of the Soviet Union. Little developed in practice until the early 1960s when, despite opposition from some members, a general Eastern European regional plan was enforced at the Soviet Union's insistence. The basis of this plan was to concentrate industrial production in East Germany and Czechoslovakia, while Romania and Bulgaria were to remain essentially agricultural. However, in reality economic development, and particularly the plans for industrial development in East Germany and Czechoslovakia, did little more than accept what would inevitably have happened. The member nations were crucially dependent on trade with the West, and required Western credits to provide their liquidity, as is demonstrated by Poland's huge debts to Western banks.

COMECON was probably less popular with its members even than was the Warsaw Pact and, rightly or otherwise, there came into being a widespread belief in Eastern Europe that it functioned to cream off the best of industrial production, especially in East Germany, for export to the Soviet Union. In addition, as with Cuban membership, it was used partly as a tool of Soviet propaganda and as support for Third World countries whose membership in an international communist movement was of less interest to Eastern Europe than to the Soviet Union. COMECON had no role to play with the collapse of Soviet **hegemony** in Eastern Europe, and with applications not only from former European COMECON members but also from the newly-independent republics of the former Soviet Union itself for membership in pan-European bodies, the organization was wound up in June 1991. Nevertheless, the economies of former COMECON members in Europe are still closely tied together and geographical reasons, if no others, may still lead to the creation of some successor organization, or at least to a recognition that the former members occupy a 'single economic space'. In particular the dependence of many Eastern European economies on cheap energy supplies from Russia is a physical fact that cannot be ignored.

Command Economies

Both in the old Soviet Union and in the East European Soviet satellite countries, economies were structured according to a quasi-Marxist doctrine of 'state socialism'. The hallmark of this was that no form of free market was permitted except at the periphery of economic life (see also **New Economic Policy**. Instead of a process of entrepreneurial competition guided roughly by consumer demand, a rigid and highly-detailed economic plan was imposed on nationalized monopoly production and distribution units. Central economic planning calculated exactly how much of every commodity needed to be produced, both consumer commodities and all intervening production factors. Together with detailed manpower planning, this allowed the political state to command the economy. Wages and prices were kept artificially very low, with workers' income being purely a notional exchange mechanism. With no convertibility into outside currencies, and almost no importation of consumer goods, there was no need to set wages at any internationally comparable level. Furthermore, incentives for economic activity, if provided at all, were as likely to be in kind—better housing, holiday privileges and so on—as in wage or salary terms. As the state provided complete and very extensive, if low quality, health and social insurance, and retirement pensions, there was also no need to save, and no need to set wages to allow for private savings to fund capital investment.

The result was an economy which could be used to satisfy politically-set targets with no need to ensure any balance between state and private consumption preferences; no need to trim political targets according to availability of capital derived from individuals or from external sources; and no need to reward scarce skills by incentives. The economic planners could determine exactly what they thought was needed and arrange for its production and distribution. Taxation was unimportant as a source of government income, so there were no public expenditure/income restraints on state planning. This allowed, for example, for the concentration of as much as 25% of gross national product (or net material product, to use the Soviet terminology) on defence costs in the last days of the Soviet system. The problems were twofold: the only incentives were negative, for example punishment for inadequate performance; and the economic system ran at a very low level of productivity. However, because production targets had to be met, no matter how shoddy the quality, enormous effort, much of it essentially illegal, went into grabbing production resources to make these nominal targets. Secondly, when the state desired to please ordinary people by putting extra resources into consumer production, there was virtually no way of assessing what products of which range and quality should be provided.

Central planning may have been an adequate means of working out what needed to be produced in order to build tanks and aircraft, because the military constitutes a well-informed and demanding customer able to communicate its needs. Ordinary consumers, however, with no competitive market-driven producers to choose from, had no way of signalling exactly what they wanted; indeed, consumer preference was not only unknown, but essentially non-existent, because it requires knowledge of alternatives among which to have preferences.

Nevertheless, centrally-controlled economies worked well in producing major investment in infrastructure; what destroyed them were the increasingly important inefficiencies of the system and its inability to satisfy consumers increasingly aware, in part through the power of the **mass media** of the standard of living available in the West.

Committees

Even the most informal social organization will often have a committee to run its detailed affairs, where the general membership does not have the time or inclination to do so. In more serious political and business parlance, committees are technically groups of members of some deliberative or decision-making body. They are charged with carrying out preparatory or investigatory work on some issue, or with dealing with matters of detail under broad lines agreed by the whole body. The main justification for committee work is that detailed discussion can best be handled by a small number of people, and also that committee members have more expertise, and more time, to dedicate to specific topics than other members of the main body. As the institution of which a committee is a subordinate part will usually have a much wider remit than the scope given to any one committee, this allows for a division of labour and task specialization which would otherwise be impossible.

A consequence of this delegation of responsibility is that committees *per se* cannot make binding decisions, but can only make recommendations to the main body, or report their conclusions. In practice committees often wield very considerable power precisely because members of the main body, a parliament for example, or the governing council of a trade union or a board of directors, are much less well-informed, and have much less time in which to consider a matter, than the specialist committee. Consequently there is a general tendency for committee advice to be taken, often with little debate. Probably the most influential and famous political committees are the specialist subject committees of the US Congress. In many areas these committees are the effective **legislatures**, with the full Senate or House of Representatives being in a position to do no more than endorse the committee resolutions. In these cases, and many other political examples, no legislation or initiative that is not favoured by a majority of the committee can hope even to be reported on to the full legislative body, the committee simply refusing to act on it at all.

Often committees exercise their power not so much against the parent body, but against another committee. For example, proposals from a substantive committee, say the building committee of a college, will be referred from the full governing body back to the finance committee for a test of feasibility. Unless the finance committee agrees, it is unlikely that the full body will accept a building committee recommendation. The power of a committee is generally greater if it represents a small proportion of the size of the full body. Consequently the **cabinet** committees in Britain are relatively powerless because their members, perhaps five ministers, already represent nearly a quarter of the full body, and are usually people whose voices could not have been ignored whether or not they were on the committee. Thus committee membership is often a way of acknowledging the prior political or institutional authority of a subgroup, rather than originating their power.

One particular type of committee, frequently known as a 'steering committee', is often of particular power. Such a committee is charged with preparing the agenda for the main body, and with deciding the rules of debate and timing, and who should be invited to speak to a matter. Again, with a powerful chairman, such a committee can often manipulate arrangements effectively to stifle issues, or to push them through the main debating assembly with little chance for the opposition to make their case or lobby support.

Because of the specific rules of debate and discussion adopted by some parliaments, including the US Congress and the British House of Commons, there has also developed a procedural device by which the entire assembly turns itself into a committee, known as the 'Committee of the Whole House', but in such cases it no longer remains a committee in any substantive sense.

Common Good

The term common good describes a goal or an object of policy that is in the interests of everyone in a society. It is related to such terms as **public interest**, **general will** and, in a more complex way, to **collective goods**. The greatest difficulty in its application arises from the fact that there are very few things which are equally beneficial, and imply equal cost, to all members of a society. A typical example, though one by no means unproblematic in itself, would be the avoidance of industrial pollution, or the provision of military defence. The concept may have more utility in a comparative concept. A politician claiming to work for the common good, rather than for some sectional interest, even when that interest is quite legitimate, may gain more credence. In fact there is no logical reason why this should be so. It is perfectly possible that the provision of something, such as national parks, is indeed a matter of the common good, but that the cost of so doing is unfair in comparison with the interests of a special group, hill farmers perhaps, who would lose economic rights.

Common Law

Common law is the name usually given to the main system of laws and legal practices in England and Wales, most of North America, and other countries that were once part of the British Empire. It is the legal system that developed after the Norman conquest of England, based initially on judicial interpretation of local customs, on judicial and royal decisions in important cases, and on the rare acts of formal legislation contained in royal statutes. The essence of common law is that it relies on the development of legal principles as they are laid down in judicial rulings in particular cases. These rulings are themselves usually developments or reinterpretations of earlier decisions in cases held to be 'binding precedents'. The idea is one of slow growth and development, of a legal system created by the judges themselves during the actual judicial process. This is usually contrasted with the **civil law** system, in which law is deliberately laid down as a complete, codified system by means of legislation. Through much of English legal history the common law was supplemented by another system, equity, in which cases were decided directly on the basis of moral justice; it was introduced because common law, restricted in its scope by previous cases, and by the small number of 'writs' under which one could bring actions, was seen as too limited to give unfailing justice. As the range of common law expanded, and equity itself became more and more rule-bound, the two became merged during the 19th century.

In the 20th century an increasing commitment to democratic ideals made the idea of autonomous judge-made law seem improper. This, and the massive legislation required by the modern state, have much diminished the independent creativity of the judiciary. In the early 1960s, for example, the House of Lords announced, in effect, that no judge could contemplate creating a new criminal offence. However, large areas of English law, especially the laws of contract and of tort, are not codified, and principles can only be discovered by identifying significant precedents. In these and other areas there is still considerable scope for judges to develop law without waiting for parliament to legislate. Furthermore, to interpret the meaning of statute law often involves highly creative judicial work, and the real impact of a statute may depend more on what judges have said in a case which concerned it than on parliament's original intention. The law of real property in the United Kingdom, for example, was intended to be codified by the 1925 Law of Property Act and some subsequent minor acts. To a large extent it is, except that what Clause 9, Section ii, Para B of the Act actually means requires reading several dozen cases where the House of Lords has 'interpreted' it. The common law in other countries has diverged to some extent from English common law, but reference is often made to the decisions of English courts in awkward cases. This is true of the USA as well as countries such as Australia. In fact the process is now two way, with English courts not infrequently citing Australian or American decisions. This has led to the hope that some sort of international common law may emerge. Much incentive towards this is given by the increasing importance of cases, often going to arbitration rather than law, where complex international dealings involving several countries require a uniform solution. Thus 'private' **international law**, vastly important in commercial cases, can only really develop as a form of common law, there being no relevant statute-making body.

Commonwealth

Commonwealth is a historic term in political theory, used by writers of very different political persuasion to refer to their ideal state. It has also been used in the title of the voluntary association of states, the Commonwealth of Nations, which gradually emerged during the first half of the 20th century to replace the British Empire as former colonies achieved self-government and became independent, and in that of the Commonwealth of Independent States set up as an attempt to preserve some unity and co-operation among the former republics of the Soviet Union. It probably derives from the Greek concept of 'oikumene' (living together). Poland and Lithuania formed a Commonwealth in 1569 to protect themselves against threats from the Russian state of Muscovy to the east, the Turkish Ottoman Empire to the south and Sweden to the north, but the usual early example is the English Commonwealth under the Cromwells from the execution of Charles I until the restoration of Charles II. The contemporary political theorist Thomas **Hobbes** used the term to mean that there existed some common 'weal' or values which rational people would co-operate to defend. Four of the earliest US states (Kentucky, Massachusetts, Pennsylvania and Virginia) use the word Commonwealth in their titles; like the English Commonwealth, this was an attempt to find a description of a political system that did not rest on any notion of a monarch legitimately 'owning' the country, but allowed for considerable power to be wielded by a central sovereign institution, whether that be vested in an individual or an assembly.

The modern Commonwealth of Nations can be subdivided into two very general types of countries: the 'Old Commonwealth' refers to those territories which were settled rather than conquered, had all become independent by the First World War, and are predominantly European in origin, such as Canada, Australia and New Zealand; the 'New Commonwealth' countries are those, such as India, Jamaica, Kenya, Malaysia and Nigeria, which have gained their independence since the Second World War, often after a political and even armed struggle. The Commonwealth has never been more than a loose linkage between member states, with no central authority, virtually no civil service, and no general policies or founding treaty (the closest to this is the 1971 Declaration of Commonwealth Principles). It never became an economic unity or an organized military alliance, though British politicians had tried to develop it in both those ways from the end of the 19th century. Even the unity given to it by the fact that the British monarch is its head means little, as several members are **republics**. With the entry of the United Kingdom into the **European Union** its political and economic ties to its former colonies became further weakened, although the Commonwealth remains the biggest international association after the **United Nations**. During the late 1980s quite serious conflicts arose between a majority of members of the Commonwealth and the United Kingdom over the latter's lack of enthusiasm for political and economic sanctions against South Africa over that country's **apartheid** policies, with the consequence that British leadership of the association is much less secure than previously. Ironically this may actually increase the vibrancy of the Commonwealth as a multinational association. Increasingly the Commonwealth uses threatened or actual suspensions from its proceedings to censure members whose internal affairs, it considers, require reforms: since, the late 1980s, Fiji, Nigeria, Pakistan and Zimbabwe have suffered such suspensions.

Communalism

A society characterized by communalism is one in which **ethnicity**, **language group**, religion or other identification largely circumscribes the entire life of the subculture in question. In such a society people will not only marry, reside, speak, and carry out their entire private life inside their subculture, but this pattern may be transposed onto social, economic and political institutions. Separate wings of, for example, political parties and trade unions entirely committed to one subculture are likely to exist, as in the linguistically-defined Belgian party system. States may provide for separate education and broadcasting structures to mirror the subcultures, as in the Netherlands where the structures are defined by religion. Even where the structures are not formally divided in this way, a society with a high degree of communalism will consist of duplication of private organizations, such as separate football leagues and youth clubs. While it is true that political life is always influenced by group identities (see **cleavage**), communalism refers to an extreme form of such political ties. In such a society politics, especially at the electoral level, cannot hope to produce generalized public interest policies, because to a large extent the individual voters do not see themselves as part of a nation-wide public, but rather as members of a particular social group with only a coincidental neighbour relationship to other citizens. Where there is no clear geographical element to communalism within a nation a serious problem of ensuring **representative democracy** exists. Unless separate elections are held for voters registered according to whatever is the distinguishing group character-istic, only **proportional representation** can resolve this.

Commune

Commune has several meanings in politics. The more clear-cut and technical usage is found in Western Europe, where it usually describes the most basic level of **local government**, roughly equivalent to a British parish or local district council, or an American township. Its more theoretically significant usage is as a description of left-wing or radical experiments in communal living. During the late 1960s in particular, many young radicals and 'drop-outs' formed collective organizations in which a few people lived together and shared everything in an ideal form of communism, with no property rights and a total commitment to one another's welfare. The phrase 'hippy communes' came into common use to describe one form taken by this experiment in collective living. Many communes were modelled on the Israeli **kibbutz**, with which they share a respectable philosophical ancestry in writers such as **Rousseau** and other exponents of **direct democracy** or **participatory democracy**, who advocated small, sharing, communal forms of social orga-nization.

The phrase 'The Commune' refers to the revolutionary authority set up in Paris after the Franco–Prussian War of 1870–71 and suppressed by the 'Versailles' government of Thiers with the assistance of the Prussian conquer-ors. Karl **Marx** and later writers of the left have regarded The Commune as foreshadowing modern revolutionary movements.

Communism

Communism can mean one of two things: a theoretical ideal found in the writings of **Marx**, or the actual governing principles of the self-described communist states in the modern world. When used, for example, in the communist parties of France, Italy, Britain, etc., it has typically referred to a combination of **Marxist** ideals and support for the communist governments. Clearly the collapse of the **Communist Party of the Soviet Union (CPSU)** in 1991, hitherto the leading party, had severe repercussions on communist parties elsewhere. As far as Marxist theory goes, communism is a slightly shadowy state in which private property has been abolished, equality reigns, and the state has 'withered away' because all men live in harmony and co-operation, without classes or any social divisions requiring the exercise of authority. Most post-Marxist writers, and especially the leaders of the October Revolution of 1917 in Russia, have believed that there had to be an intermediary phase between the overthrow of **capitalism** and the full realization of communism. This phase is variously described, often as **socialism**, but also as the period in which it will be necessary to exercise the **dictatorship of the proletariat** or where the communist party will have to act as the **vanguard of the proletariat**. This idea was strengthened by the **Bolsheviks** in 1917 largely because they could not pretend that their revolution, unlike the earlier one of that year, was a popular revolution at all. Because it was so clearly a **coup d'état** or putsch, elements in Marxism which seemed to legitimize the rule of the mass by the enlightened few were highlighted. This intermediate phase is, roughly speaking, where the leaders of the Soviet Union, before **Gorbachev**, and its then Eastern European allies would have located themselves.

When used as a description of the former societies of the Soviet Union and Eastern Europe, or, adding yet another complexity, the continuing ones of China and its Asian communist allies, the term indicates a set of political practices that may not, necessarily, have very much to do with the Marxist theory of communism. Communism in this second sense is a system where there is little or no private ownership of major property, this being replaced with state-owned and -run enterprises, and where the communist party rules, non-democratically, both in its own right and through its control, *de facto*, of the official state administration. Values of equality and social co-operation are stressed, as opposed to individual self-seeking or betterment. The economy will be entirely a planned one, with no serious element of competition, although, especially in agriculture, this is often relaxed in minor ways. A characteristic feature of communism as we have seen it develop is an inequality based on position in the ruling party, but a genuine equality, and a very thorough social welfare system, throughout the mass of the population.

Other aspects of a communist state are incidentals, more or less present in different societies. Thus the communist attitude to religion, something scorned by Marxist theory, has varied from hostility in the Soviet Union to a major role for **Roman Catholicism** in Poland, and the extent of **industrial democracy** varied from Yugoslavia's famous experiments to a minimum in East Germany. From the mid-1950s there was an increasingly bitter conflict between the Eastern European and the Chinese brands of communism, first with the development of **Mao Zedong's** communist views. The reason for this, apart from purely nationalistic territorial conflicts, was that the Chinese communists were, originally, much less prepared to use the techniques, and the associated professional hierarchies, of modern Western industrial production. So while, to take one example, the Soviet Union continued to make steel in huge industrial plants, giving great authority to professional engineers and planning the overall production of steel in a centralized and authoritative way (see **command economies**), the Chinese encouraged all their communes to build their own small-scale steel plants, and treated professional engineers as undemocratic examples of **class** status. The Soviet Union remained quite strongly hierarchical, even if the criteria for hierarchy differed from the societies of capitalism, being based on party or professional rank rather than inherited wealth, but the Chinese communists, at least under Mao, worked for a much more total equality. During the **cultural revolution** this rose to a height in which anyone occupying a professional or technocratic job was in danger of being sent to work as a peasant, or, if less fortunate, for **thought reform**. The only generalizations possible about communism as an actual political and social system are that communist regimes are totally controlled by an undemocratic party, abolish most inequalities arising from economic differences, for most citizens, and practise a high degree of economic planning with an extensive welfare state but very little freedom of expression.

The collapse of communism in the Soviet Union and Eastern Europe is a judgement on the failure of one institutional attempt to realize an ideal that retains great emotional, and respectable, theoretical power. The notion that it is possible and desirable for people to live in a non-competitive, non-author-itarian, property-less state of brotherhood and equality has no more been disproved by events than has any other ideal. Most Western admirers of Soviet communism have been cut off from their own Marxist colleagues since the obvious distortion of these ideals by **Stalin**: from the 1940s, at the latest, Western Marxists regarded communist regimes as examples of **state capital-ism**, not of communism.

Communist Party of the Soviet Union (CPSU)

CPSU are the initials by which the former Communist Party of the Soviet Union is often known. Until the revolutionary changes initiated by **Gorba-chev** from the late 1980s, the party completely controlled political and social life in the Soviet Union. About 10% of the population were members, membership being much prized and by no means automatic. In some sectors, the army for example, as many as 75% would be party members. The principal means by which the party exercised control was through what was called the **Nomenclatura**, which was simply a list of jobs which had to be filled by party members, and concerning which the party was given a deciding voice in appointments. As a result nearly all of the most important managerial, admin-istrative and intellectual jobs were filled by loyal party members. (As a further result of this, such positions would continue to be filled by those who at least had been members, whatever their current profession, for a long time after the fall of the CPSU from power in 1991.) In addition the party organized much of social life, controlled the trade unions, and had the sole right to put up candidates in elections. However, because of the sheer size of the party, the degree of organized and uniform control it exercised was sometimes questionable, although its command over education and the media helped it to prevent any serious and widespread doubts about its legitimacy. Senior party members gained many privileges, such as access to imported goods and better educational opportunities for their children, providing yet another incentive for membership. The party was always careful to make sure that it could check the power of potential rivals. This was especially true of the armed forces, each unit of which had, in addition to the military commander, a political officer from the party who shared command. At the end of the party's period of dominance the number of political officers in the Soviet military was bigger than the whole of Britain's Army of the Rhine (i.e. over 55,000).

Once these monopoly powers were taken away, mainly by the **glasnost** doctrine, the gates were opened for Soviet citizens to demonstrate their feelings, which were more often indifference than loathing, but which made retention of control impossible. The tentacles which the CPSU spread into Soviet society were so complex that untangling its influence will take decades. For example, the party owned a huge proportion of the entire real estate of the Soviet Union, because legal ownership of land was forbidden to individuals and most institutions. A major problem for any successor organization will be that, though there is no legal reason why it cannot compete electorally under a system of **pluralism**, it is impossible to imagine what it could stand for, given that its *raison d'être* was specifically the need to lead the people during the period of the **dictatorship of the proletariat**. Despite this, 'reformed' communist parties under that or a similar name continue to be politically viable not only in the former Soviet Union and some parts of Eastern Europe, but also in Italy. They vary in their programme, but tend towards the sort of state-intervention socialism of the social-democratic parties of the 1950s and 1960s.

Communitarianism

Communitarianism is a relatively recent development in political theory, largely of American origin. It was formulated mainly from a right-wing perspective by those dissatisfied with **liberal democracy**. In Europe, and particularly the United Kingdom, it has been more attractive to those on the centre left who wish to replace **social democracy** and its discredited economic theories. There are many varieties of communitarian thought, some complex and calling for highly experimental social re-ordering; some challenging economic theory at its roots by denying that economic actors necessarily act rationally and by insisting that a desire to act in accordance with social norms is as powerful and common as a desire to maximize utility (see **rational choice theory**). What they all have in common is a rejection of the core principle of **liberalism**, which can be taken to mean that each individual is the sole legitimate decision maker in what counts as good for himself. Liberal capitalism and **liberal democracy** wish to maximize the actor's ability to pursue his own goals and endow him with rights for this purpose. Communitarians, in contrast, see the community through tradition and history, socializing people into its moral values, and see actors as most content when they live out the values of this community and assist in its development. Communitarians, in their own language, wish to stress the duties of the citizen as much as the rights.

There is, of course, nothing new at all about communitarianism. It is **Conservatism** of the hue associated with **Burke**, common in European social thought after the French Revolution. However well-intentioned some of its proponents may be, there is no way of disguising the fact that communitarian theory, by denying the primacy of the individual's rights, involves or implies imposing some metaphysical entity, now called the community but indistinguishable from the state above the individual.

The attractions of communitarianism increase with the belief that modern liberal democracies are becoming impossible to govern as the pursuit of individual preferences makes the social order weak and produces increasingly difficult problems of collective action. Thus in Europe the attraction is seen by those whose aim was formerly a socialist utopia (however vague and far into the future), but who are now forced to rely on capitalist market economics. The attraction to communitarianism in the USA is largely because there has never been an orthodox European-style brand of conservatism; US conservatives have simply been liberal capitalists with less concern for the victims of the system than other liberals. It is no accident that **Roman Catholicism** is influential in communitarianism, both in that many of its ideas come from Catholic social philosophy and many of its leading thinkers are Catholic intellectuals.

Community

The word community has a variety of political uses. It can be an ideal, evoking a political order characterized by warm, fraternal and caring social relations of an almost family-like nature. In this usage it resembles the idea of **fraternity**, one of the three parts of the French revolutionary slogan, along with *liberté* and *egalité*. It can be a purely descriptive term merely referring to the informal relations of people who live in some sort of a group, rather than to any formal political system or state they may set up to run their society. It may refer, however, to a small self-supporting group where this previous distinction is not seen as valid. Political theory has often concerned itself with the idea of community in this latter sense, where all members of the society share values so closely that neither a separation between individual and state, nor the enforcement of collective obligations, is necessary. The traditional model of such a community is an extended family, or sometimes a tribal grouping in a pre-state society. Here, it is argued, an identification of the good of the individual with the good of the group is complete (see **common good**). Where positions of authority or **divisions of labour** and responsibility have to exist, they are non-contentious and even 'natural'. This idealized view of a community is found as early as **Plato** and **Aristotle**, and is still powerful today with thinkers like **Marcuse** and many supporters of movements such as the Greens. In most social science uses community is an empirical concept describing a collectivity of individuals who share many values and life experiences, and can be expected to act with some degree of consensus and co-operation in political matters.

Community Power

Community power studies were popular among academics, especially in North America, during the 1950s and late 1960s. Because **power** is not only conceptually elusive but empirically hard to study on the national level, it was felt that it could best be investigated in narrower contexts. As a result, a series of studies were conducted into the distribution of power and influence in individual towns and cities. Most of the studies were carried out to test or develop pluralist theories of power and democracy (see **pluralism**). The results suggested that the communities were not fully democratic, but were dominated by élite groups which controlled different areas of policy. However, most of the studies went on to claim that the various élites functioned separately, without the overlapping that might have given one or more of them a wider-ranging power. The studies were subjected to considerable criticism, largely of a methodological nature, since no obviously correct methodology existed to discover who was influential, or why. Even more disappointing was the fact that it did not really prove possible to extrapolate from studies of local communities to form a picture of power at the national level.

The utility of the studies was even less clear outside the USA. The federal nature of US politics, and the absence of welfare state regulations, did make it sensible to find out who, for example, might be responsible for building a new hospital, or, given the decentralization of education, to enquire into the influence of Parent–Teacher Associations as **pressure groups**. In countries such as Britain, where most such decisions are either taken or very strongly influenced and closely regulated by central government, there is rather less to study. Very few such studies have been carried out in recent years, and it is doubtful whether they will again be seen as a solution to problems involved in studying power in Western Europe. However, the idea that local studies can help in making generalized analysis of an equally unclear centre has already shown itself to be promising in the emerging democracies of Eastern Europe (see **democratic transition**).

Comparative Government

Comparative government (or comparative politics) is one of the main branches of the academic study of politics. The essence of comparative government as a study is to compare the ways in which different societies cope with various problems, the role of the political structures involved being of particular interest. The aim is to develop an understanding of how different institutional mechanisms work within their contexts, and, more ambitiously, to develop general hypotheses concerning government. A typical examination paper in comparative government will ask whether the French or American presidencies enjoy the most power, or ask for a comparison of the roles of the legislatures in Britain and Germany.

Though comparative government is nowadays usually clearly differentiated from **political theory**, this is a recent and probably unfortunate development. **Aristotle**, who is normally thought of as a political theorist, certainly also carried out a comparative study of the political systems known to him, though unfortunately his collection of nearly 200 city state constitutions has not survived. Later theorists, such as Jean Bodin (1530–96), argued for comparative political analysis in the hope that it would reveal universally valid rules and values.

In studies of comparative government, progress has been made in some areas. For example, the effect of different electoral systems on the party system is fairly well understood from wide-ranging comparisons, and predictive theories have been developed which work quite well in relationship to **coalition** membership in **multi-party systems**. The main problem for comparative government as a science is that it lacks a generally-agreed theoretical framework that would identify what the principal tasks of a political system are, and thereby locate the institutions or structures that should be compared. In other words it is hard to know what comparisons are worthwhile or sensible; and as a result, researchers have tended either to stick to obvious comparisons within a limited range, or to rely on less-than commonly-accepted theories, usually borrowed from other approaches, such as **functionalism**. More recently, the **rational choice theory** approach common in other areas of political science has been used quite successfully in comparative government, sometimes under the label of 'The New Institutionalism'. This in part owes its success to a shift towards the study of policy formulation and outcome, which allows for a greater unity of national experiences.

Another problem is that a fruitful comparison of two societies involves a very deep knowledge of their history, culture and languages in order to understand the data and avoid inappropriate comparisons between institutions which are only superficially similar. Many university courses are not really comparative at all, but simply entail the separate study of several foreign countries. At the opposite pole are some texts and courses which deny entirely the need for knowledge in depth and involve comparisons of institutions from all the 190-odd independent nations of the world. Somewhere between these positions progress has been, and will doubtless continue to be, made. One trend that shows great promise is to study problems common to all societies of a particular type, for example environmental pollution in tertiary economies, and the mechanisms these countries use to solve them. The increasing international or multi-national nature of problems and responses promises to make for much sounder and more fruitful comparisons.

Comte

Auguste Comte (1798–1857) was the founder of sociology and the originator of the concept of **positivism** in the social sciences, at least in the sense that he invented both words and was the first more or less academic writer to construct a 'science of society'. Many of his ideas were in fact derived from the early French socialist thinker Saint-Simon, whose secretary he had been.

Comte divided sociology into two disciplines. One, concerned with the structure of societies and the relationships between their constituent elements, he called Social Statics; the other, Social Dynamics, dealt with the development and progress of social forms. It was Comte's Social Dynamics that made most impact in their time, but their interest today lies in the fact that they are utterly at variance with the sociological canon that we take for granted. To Comte the only possible sources of progress or social change were changes in human thought, whereas not only Marxists but most other modern sociologists would give economic factors, or environmental determinants of some kind, an extremely important role. Comte believed he had identified three stages of social development, along with three corresponding modes of thought. During the 'Theological Age' man was quite unable to understand his environment, lacked any conception of causality, and saw every event as the result of divine intervention. In the second, 'Metaphysical Age', man did begin to try to explain the nature of the world, but in a necessarily 'unscientific' way, since the entire intellectual apparatus of modern science (especially the idea of empirically testing hypotheses) was missing. (Comte's analysis here ignores the fact that as early as the 13th century, for example, Roger Bacon was developing a philosophy of science in which experimental method was crucial.) Finally, in Comte's own lifetime, the 'Positivistic' or 'Scientific Age' had arrived, and everything could eventually be understood and explained scientifically. Sociology, as the latest and most far-reaching of all sciences, characterized the age. Society could now be properly planned, and institutions consciously devised or retained and modified to serve specific functions. In this belief Comte is not far removed from the advocates of 'scientific socialism', except that he rejected **materialism** for intellectual determinism and was also more than a little conservative once he got down to details. For example, he attached enormous importance to the family, as conservatives have always done; but unlike earlier conservative thinkers he held that it could now be seen as a rationally functional element in a planned society. Similarly, he attached great importance to religion as a source of social stability; but having dismissed theology as an irrational manifestation belonging to the first age of society, he tried to promote a scientific 'religion of humanity' which functioned like, and indeed resembled in its ritual, orthodox Catholicism without God.

Though it is easy to deride Comte now, the breadth of his vision, his erudition and his developmental approach were quite new, and established once and for all the idea that large-scale theoretical explanations of society were possible. Elements of Comtian thought can be traced to later writers who retain a serious academic standing, notably **Pareto** and **Weber**.

Confederacy

A confederacy, or confederation, is a political system originating in an agreement made between several independent entities that wish to retain a high degree of autonomy. The idea of confederalism is usually contrasted with that of **federalism**, which also involves independent entities but in which the central authority has a considerable degree of power which may be capable of expansion, for example through interpretation of the federal constitution. In a confederacy, by contrast, certain specified powers are surrendered by the component units to the central government, and all other powers remain with the original states. Probably the best known example was the Confederate States of America, 'the Confederacy', formed by the Southern states that seceded from the USA. The name, and the organizing principle, were deliberately chosen to emphasize the difference between the Confederacy and the United States, where the growth of federal power was felt by Southerners to threaten their institutions, above all slavery. The subsequent Civil War resulted in the destruction of the Confederacy. In origin the USA was a confederacy: the Constitution of 1787, written after the American War of Independence, deliberately chose a full federation, partly because of the experience of the weakness of confederal government during the war.

Confederacies need not be confined to the nation-state level: in Britain the major pressure group for business interests is the CBI, the Confederation of British Industry, so called because it is an amalgam of separate interests. One theory of importance when dealing with the federal/confederal choice is that confederacies allow for the disproportionate influence of the larger members, while federations can more easily control any drive to such dominance. This has become important recently in the debate about what, if any, form of **political union** should be developed in the **European Union**.

Conference on Security and Co-operation in Europe (see Organization for Security and Co-operation in Europe)

Confessional Parties

Confessional parties, mainly to be found in Europe and Latin America, are political parties whose members and, to a lesser extent, voters belong to a specific religious denomination. Even where the identities of political parties are not so firmly and objectively tied to questions of religious identity, religion can still be a major element in voter choice, but the idea of a confessional party is restricted to those political movements where the appeal is intentionally to voters with a specific commitment to an overall religious creed, and not simply policy attitudes that correlate with aspects of religious beliefs. The principal role of such parties is to support policies specifically in the interest of, or influenced by, their faith. There are two main types of confessional party. One, often known as a clerical party, exists in a political system where there is a high degree of religious uniformity among those who subscribe to a religious belief at all, but where there is also an **anti-clerical** political movement which is opposed to the influence of any religious body on national politics. A good example comes from the old Italian party system, where the confessional party was the Christian Democrat Party, founded in 1943 as the successor to the pre-fascist Popular Party by groups allied to **Roman Catholicism** and funded, initially, directly by the **papacy**. Its **anti-clerical** opponent was the Italian Communist Party, and its aim, originally at least, was to preserve Italy as a Christian nation, with policy in many areas deliberately set to conform to the church's views.

An alternative version of a confessional party is where a society is split by religious identities, so that political parties evolve to support a particular religious community against both a potentially secular state, and against parties

107

promoting a rival religious community. Until the 1970s the Dutch political system was characterized by this form of rival confessional parties, the Catholic People's Party, and two protestant parties, the Anti-Revolutionary Party and the Christian Historical Union. In that year the three parties formed a federation, the Christian Democratic Appeal (CDA), to counter the erosion of support which each had experienced since the 1960s, and in 1980 the separate parties were abolished altogether in favour of the CDA. Because of the **secularization** of society in many countries, and particularly in Europe, during the second half of the 20th century, confessional parties have either lost their voting support, or been forced to broaden their appeal.

Confidence

In countries where the **executive** is responsible to a **legislature** rather than elected for a fixed term (as in the USA), the support of the legislature is necessary to sustain a government in office. Such support may be tested by a formal vote of no confidence (see **accountability**). If the vote goes against the government, it will usually be required to resign; and then one of two consequences will follow. Either there will be an attempt to form a new government which can command the support of the legislature (a course which is particularly likely where no party has an overall majority), or the legislature will be dissolved and new elections held to ascertain the views of the electorate.

In the United Kingdom, where a strict system of party discipline prevails, it used to be believed that any major defeat sustained by a government in the House of Commons should be treated as a vote of no confidence. Since the 1970s this view has been substantially modified, and governments have come to believe that they may be defeated in the House of Commons without necessarily resigning or even placing the measure before Parliament again in order to reverse their defeat. In some countries, matters are organized in such a way that votes of no confidence are difficult for the government to lose; this is the case in Fifth Republic France, where it represents a response to the pre-1958 situation in which stable government became the exception rather than the rule. Similarly, the German Basic Law (Grundgesetz) constrains the power of the motion of confidence by requiring a positive vote; the motion has to nominate a successor government rather than merely require the resignation of the existing one. Motions of no confidence can be used in any organization which has a voting body, as, for example, the board of directors of a company, or a company shareholders' meeting. In such cases the impact is usually moral, making it hard for the relevant office holders to carry on rather than legally impossible.

Confidence-Building Measures
(see Stockholm Declaration)

Congress

In general terms a congress is a meeting of representatives or officials for debate and discussion. More specifically the term is used to refer to the **legislature** of the USA, which consists of a 435-member House of Representatives (the 'lower' House) and a 100-member Senate. Members of the House of Representatives are elected every two years; members of the Senate are elected for six years, a third of the Senators coming up for re-election in rotation every two years. Although all of these people are strictly speaking members of Congress, it is customary to refer only to members of the lower house as Congressmen or Congresswomen; members of the Senate (see **second chamber**) are referred to as Senators.

In India the main political party involved in the struggle for independence from the British Empire was the Congress Party; it dominated Indian political life from independence in 1947 until the 1980s, and remained the largest party, despite various splits. Various sub-national organizations call themselves congresses, such as the American Federation of Labor and Congress of Industrial Organizations (AFL-CIO) and the Trades Union Congress (TUC), the major **trade union** organizations in the USA and the United Kingdom respectively.

Congress of Vienna

The Congress of Vienna took place at the end of the Napoleonic wars and established the classic **balance-of-power** system in Europe. It is often used as a model or reference point in international relations when efforts are made to predict the system likely to follow the **bipolar** cold war. The Congress met in 1814 and concluded in June 1815 (the fact that Napoleon's second attempt to defeat the allies after his return from exile ended at the Battle of Waterloo in the same month does not seem to have affected the proceedings, in which France was partially included). The decisions were effectively taken by the four leading members of the anti-Napoleon coalition, Britain, Austria, Prussia and Russia. Among the immediate consequences were the creation of: a new united Kingdom of the Netherlands (which included Belgium and Luxembourg); a loosely structured German Confederation of 39 Germanic states under the domination of Prussia; and the restoration of 'legitimate' monarchies in many of the places Napoleon had conquered. Major alterations were made to various state boundaries, especially to the benefit of Austria and Prussia. In essence the European system of states was set by this congress and was to last with only minor modifications until destroyed by the First World

War. Parallel to the Congress of Vienna itself was a process known as the 'Congress System', in which the leading powers tried to organize themselves to control European international politics by a series of diplomatic meetings rather like modern summit meetings. Only five meetings were held before the system finally collapsed in 1825. It failed partly because of conflicts about how far the powers would go in interfering within the domestic politics of countries threatened by revolution, but even more because Britain was determined to distance itself from Europe and enter a period of deliberate **isolationism**. However just the Vienna settlement was, or was not, it achieved a longer peace in Europe, punctuated only by Prussia's wars with Austria in 1866 and France in 1870–71, than had previously obtained in European history. The aspirations of peoples and territories which were ignored in the border settlements at Vienna, however, were major problems at the next great peace conference, resulting in the treaties of Versailles and others in 1919–20, and some lasting implications were still perceptible in Eastern Europe in the 1990s.

Consensual

Consensual simply means 'in agreement', but it refers essentially to a process of agreement reached by an effort to find deep underlying compatibility between different viewpoints, rather than pragmatic and possibly temporary coincidence of separate ends. In claiming that there is a consensus in a society or group about something there are really two points being asserted. Firstly, the agreement is not merely a practical decision by groups or individuals who do not really agree at all, but who see a tactical necessity to vote in the same way. Rather the issues have been debated, the sources of initial disagreement explored, and a solution that everyone can accept, indeed believe in, has been reached. Secondly, it is being suggested that this agreement is both deep-rooted and long-term; the issues will not become controversial again, at least for a reasonable period. This is, obviously, an optimistic, even idealistic, definition, but it adequately explains the hopes expressed by those who seek consensus in situations of political conflict. An example in the United Kingdom is the political consensus on the value of the National Health Service (NHS), where there is overwhelming support for the free provision of basic services to the entire population. However, this sort of definition has shortcomings, because consensus is not merely a matter of head counting. There are issues where an overwhelming majority agree with a policy, but where the minority opposition is so intense and deep-rooted that it would be absurd to claim that a consensus existed. In the UK two examples would be the use of capital punishment and the retention of nuclear weapons. In both cases there are strong, and long-term, majorities on one side of the argument, but absolutely no consensus across the nation as a whole. In the case of the NHS outright abolition would be seen by nearly everyone as a totally unacceptable proposal, whereas with capital punishment and nuclear weapons it is ultimately impossible to compromise. Therefore pure consensus may rarely exist, but there are objective examples which serve as useful political benchmarks.

Consent

Many political theories, in attempting to answer the central question 'Why should anyone obey the government?', fall back on the idea that this obligation is based on an implicit or explicit consent to the exercise of **authority** by the government or state in question. The belief that man is 'by nature' free and independent has led some political thinkers to argue that a free individual cannot be obliged to obey any ruler without freely wishing, willing or agreeing to do so. This sort of doctrine, perhaps best represented by the 17th-century English political philosopher John **Locke**, is usually associated with **social contract** theories. These picture society as set up deliberately by independent individuals who come to see that their own interests are best served by collaboration, and who therefore freely give up some of their independence to a government so that it can function for their benefit. Clearly, given this position, the right of a government to pass laws and coerce citizens can only stem from the citizens having given their willing consent to obey. However, the theory, though admirable, is riddled with problems which political theorists are still trying to solve. To start with, in reality the average citizen is never given a chance to consent or withhold consent, although one might argue that the voluntary acceptance of citizenship when someone is naturalized is such an event. There is, too, the argument that if the government is either looking after your interests, or doing what is 'right', it does not seem to make much difference whether you have consented or not. Locke himself had to stretch his definition of 'consent' so far in order to make his theory work logically that it ceased to have quite the force it might seem to carry. He introduced the notion of 'tacit consent' by which anyone who takes advantage of the laws of a society by travelling on the state's highways, for example, must be seen to have consented. Modern versions of this sort of consent argue that voting in an election, and thus availing oneself of a power that would not automatically be available, is to consent, even if one's preferred party loses. Nevertheless, the idea that obligation can be incurred only through consent remains very attractive, and is still a powerful force in democratic or liberal political theory.

Conservatism

Conservatism is a political theory which is peculiarly difficult to define because one aspect of conservative thought is its rejection of explicit **ideology** and its preference for **pragmatism** in political matters. It is also difficult to define because different societies and generations do not necessarily seek to preserve the same things. Although some elements common to conservative values can be traced back to the early history of political thought, conservatism as a distinctive political creed emerged in the 18th century, when it became necessary to present arguments against the rationalist thinkers of the European **Enlightenment**, the **utopianism** they hoped to create, and the radical forces unleashed by the French Revolution. In Britain Edmund **Burke** published his classic work *Reflections on the Revolution in France*, which emphasized the importance of traditions, institutions and evolutionary change as opposed to abstract ideas, individualism and artificially designed political systems. In France Joseph de Maistre provided a more reactionary version of conservatism in essays which defended established authority against revolutionary ideas; he emphasized the need for order and the importance of the specific national traits in a given political system.

Conservatives do not necessarily oppose change in itself, but they are sceptical about attempts to fashion a perfect society in accordance with some pre-existing model. They also tend to believe that man is flawed by weaknesses that make certain ideal goals illusory, although not all of the major conservative thinkers relate this view to the Christian notion of Original Sin. They regard their support for tradition as reflecting their humility in the face of the experience of earlier generations—an experience which they believe to be crystallized in institutions.

At the level of political practice a number of conservative parties exist in the political systems of Western Europe and the Commonwealth. In continental Europe the parties which share conservative values have typically not called themselves conservative. Most have preferred to use terms like **Christian Democrat**, or, as with the attempt to re-create the now defunct Italian Christian Democratic Party, the 'People's Party'. In France **Gaullism**, as the main conservative force, has used conservatism's call to national unity and patriotism both in its labels and in much of its electoral appeal. Conservatism is as much a matter of personal outlook and reaction as a particular creed: it makes sense, therefore, to talk about the conservative wing in a **socialist** party, for example, stressing the importance of experience, socialist tradition, respect for organizational continuity and so on.

Conservative Party

The modern British Conservative Party is the product of several different historical strands of ideology and party organization. In an important sense the Conservatives have never had an ideology in the sense of a programmatic theory of governance—indeed they have often campaigned on a stand of sheer

pragmatism. It is a descendant of the land-owning Tory party which was in competition with the party of the rising middle class, the Whigs (later the **Liberal Party**). The Tory party had received support from the Liberal Unionists, a group which had split from the Liberal Party as it opposed home rule for Ireland, since 1886, and the two formally merged in 1912 becoming the Conservative and Unionist Party, which remains the official title. Despite its aristocratic and rich industrialist background, the Conservative Party was in fact the first to organize on a mass basis to attract those newly-enfranchised by the parliamentary reform acts of the last third of the 19th century, and has always managed to attract a sizeable share of the working-class vote.

It has combined a patriotic outlook and support for the status quo with an acceptance of an extended **welfare state**. It has always placed a strong value on the ownership of property, while accepting since 1945 the existence of a mixed economy. After 1945 the party became, in turns, imperialist under Winston Churchill and Anthony Eden, 'high' Tory with considerable leanings towards practical social-welfare provision under Harold Macmillan and Sir Alec Douglas-Home, and technocratically **Keynesian** and Europeanist under Edward Heath. However, two distinct factions emerged in the party from the early 1970s. One of them, which dominated the Conservative Party under the leadership of Margaret Thatcher, from 1975–90, advocated, and to a large extent carried out, a reversal of many of the initiatives undertaken by governments since 1945 and the introduction of a more vigorous (**monetarist**) form of market economy (see **Thatcherism**). To that extent it had much in common with classical 19th-century **Liberalism**. The other faction invoked the Disraelian tradition of one nation and sought to preserve the Conservative Party's tradition of social concern and pragmatic solutions to political issues. Briefly at the beginning of the 1990s, under John Major, it seemed that this other, and earlier, tradition of conservatism (see **managerial capitalism**) might become dominant once more. However, the electoral defeats of 1997 and 2001 were each followed by the election of a leader who adhered much more closely to the Thatcherite legacy. Sympathizers of the two schools of thought were sometimes labelled 'dry' and 'wet'.

By any standards the party has been enormously successful electorally. Between the end of the Second World War and 1997 it was out of office for only 17 years and won four consecutive general elections between 1979 and 1992. While this record was a result as much of the distorting effect of Britain's simple plurality **voting system** and the inability of the left to cohere, it also suggests there is something in the pragmatism of the Conservatives that appeals to the British electorate. Whether this electoral dominance can ever be reborn after the crushing defeats by **New Labour** in 1997 and 2001 must be in doubt. The Conservatives found themselves in opposition to an equally pragmatic party, and one, furthermore, which had clearly captured the middle ground of politics—in part because of right-wing dominance of the Conservatives since John Major's resignation as leader. The election in 2001 as Conservative leader of a little known right-wing anti-Europeanist, Iain Duncan Smith, rather than the highly experienced and nationally popular moderate candidate, Kenneth Clarke, did not suggest that the party would be recapturing the centre ground of British politics in the near future.

Consociational Democracy

The example of consociational democracy best known to political scientists is the Netherlands, although there are several other examples of the system in world politics. The essence of consociational democracy is recognition that, in deeply-divided societies, straightforward majoritarian democracy cannot work. This is because deeply entrenched minorities living in a state of actual or potential hostility with an equally cohesive majority cannot trust the results of majoritarian decision making. In the Netherlands, until perhaps the late 1970s, the very deep religious **cleavage** between Protestant and Roman Catholic communities remaining from the historical formation of the Dutch state, combined with a secular sector which objected to any clerical influence in politics, made normal democracy difficult. As a result of this, a system which the Dutch themselves called 'pillarization' developed. Accordingly, whole sectors of society, especially education and the media, were triplicate: the state guaranteed the fair provision of schools, and even universities, separately for each faith community and for the secular world. Similarly, a complex set of **coalition** arrangements ensured that all three pillars were always represented in government, and further steps ensured parity of representation of the two religious communities in public services.

The religious cleavages in the Netherlands have become unimportant because of **secularization**, but, nevertheless, vestiges of the system remain. Other examples, even if not so labelled, can be recognized. The idea of power-sharing in Northern Ireland, for example, is essentially a matter of consociational democracy: there could be no hope for peace in Northern Ireland under single-religion governments supported and elected by a numerical majority of the population. Religion—because it tends to be the most intense of human conflicts—is the most frequent cause of consociationalism, as, for example, for many years in Indonesia under President Suharto.

In practice, consociationalism can be the solution wherever there are entrenched and hostile communities. Perhaps the best way of thinking of it is as a form of non-geographic federalism. The problem is that the very act of separately representing and providing for these different ethnic, religious or other minority cultures risks entrenching them in the social conscience, thus delaying or preventing the growth of a tolerant multicultural society. Tolerance can be the only long-term solution, because even the most intricate of consociational systems relies ultimately on the preparedness of the majority to have less of its own way than it could force by sheer weight of numbers. Anything that breaks down this forbearance threatens destruction to society and makes the position of a vulnerable minority worse than it might have been had earlier steps to break down the hostility been enforced.

Constitution

A constitution consists of a set of rights, powers and procedures that regulate the relationships between public authorities in any state, and between the public authorities and individual citizens. Most countries have a written constitution or basic document which defines these relationships (the United Kingdom is the most notable example of a country without such a constitutional code, while Israel and New Zealand have only recently introduced basic constitutional laws). But all written constitutions have to be supplemented in practice from other sources. The words in any document will need to be interpreted, and constitutional practice may well be amended over time. Thus judicial decisions, custom, convention and even authoritative textbooks may provide guidance and regulation, and may therefore be said to be a part of a country's constitution.

It is possible to classify constitutions in a number of different ways: according to whether they are federal (Australia, the USA) or unitary (the United Kingdom, France); according to whether they exhibit a **separation of powers** (as in the USA) or a fusion of powers (as in the UK); or according to whether they employ some device for **judicial review** (as in Germany) or have a special procedure for repealing constitutional laws; and particularly according to how difficult it is to amend the constitution.

One-party states often issue elaborate constitutions allegedly guaranteeing basic freedoms (see **civil liberties**); the Soviet constitutions of 1936 and 1977 purported to provide for civil liberties but did not in reality circumscribe governmental power in any effective manner.

Constitutional Control

The idea of constitutional control relates to the ability of a political system to work within the confines set by its constitution, and to the ability of the guardians of the constitution to apply it to those who hold power. In the USA the **Watergate** affair, which resulted in the impeachment of President Nixon in August 1974, became a constitutional issue because of the way the chief executive interpreted his powers, and because he resorted to political manoeuvres which seemed contrary to the spirit of the constitution. Nixon's resignation reaffirmed the efficacy of the US constitution and marked the decline of the so-called 'imperial presidency'.

Constitutional control may be exerted in a number of ways, but the most common method in countries with a written constitution is to provide for a **constitutional court** or council (in the USA the Supreme Court) which is supposed to ensure that political institutions conform to constitutional norms. Such bodies can vary enormously as to their effectiveness depending on the political context. The French Conseil Constitutionel was not foreseen as being at all powerful by the authors of the Fifth Republic's constitution, but has become so since the early 1980s, largely just by the determination of its members. It is notable that all of the new democracies in Eastern Europe and the former Soviet Union have written constitutional courts, often very powerful ones, into their new constitutions. In this they are much influenced by Germany which successfully sought, in 1949, to offset its undemocratic past with a written constitution interpreted by a strong constitutional court.

Constitutional Courts

Any written constitution, and some unwritten constitutions, can be seen as a set of rules giving the answers to two questions. The first question concerns the distribution of **power** and **authority** across political institutions, essentially 'which body can do what?'. The second question, though not such an obvious one, is 'what sorts of things can any institution of the state do?' In other words, are there restrictions on state authority to protect various individuals' rights? Given the inevitability of these questions, there is a logical necessity for some entity to act as guardian of these restrictions—to police the boundaries of authority between institutions and to protect the rights of the individual against intrusive action. These entities are what we mean by constitutional courts, although they may not always be called by either word in that phrase.

In some traditions of state authority, France and the United Kingdom being, for different reasons, examples, there has been a tendency to deny that constitutional courts are either necessary or desirable. In such countries the **parliament** is seen as supreme over the constitution itself—the constitution simply refers to a set of conventions largely obeyed, which support the ultimate authority of the parliament. This approach, which goes hand in hand with denouncing any **judicialization of politics**, is only manageable if the system stays purely one of supreme parliamentary sovereignty. Any restrictions introduce the need for the boundary policeman described above. Thus, when the constitution to the French **Fifth Republic** sought to limit the powers of parliament, and strengthen the **executive**, it was found necessary to include a constitutional court, the Conseil Constitutionel (even if it was originally intended to be weak and limited in its scope). Similarly, when the lengthy demand for a **bill of rights** in the UK produced the 1998 **Human Rights Act**, (and as soon as pressure for **devolution** had resulted in the establishment of a parliament in Scotland, where the legal system has differences to that in the rest of the UK), the ultimate court of appeal, the Law Lords (in the House of Lords) began to adopt the role of a constitutional court, though not in name.

There is considerable professional literature on constitutional courts, both in political science and public law, and much of the debate is highly technical. The important questions concern how the court receives its instructions. There are two basic routes. In one instance, some actors, usually a mix of parliamentarians and leaders of the executive, may be entitled to send new legislation to the court before it goes into operation for an *a priori* ruling on whether it is compatible with the constitution. Alternatively, real litigants before ordinary courts may be allowed to challenge the constitutionality of legislation pertaining to their case in a concrete manner. Very different answers, and very different developing constitutional theories, tend to stem from these different modes. Some courts have only one route or the other, some have both; and there are alternative mechanisms for 'seizing' the court with issues, resulting in yet further different traditions of constitutional interpretation.

Constitutional courts have become both more numerous and, collectively and individually, much more powerful in the last 30 years or so, especially in Europe. They depend to some extent on the political acceptability of their decisions to other state actors, and rather more on public legitimacy. Increasingly, they are vitally important political actors in their own rights, sometimes rivalling parliaments, because of the **chilling effect** of their decisions, and leading to a judicialization of politics.

Constitutional Law

Constitutional law refers to the part of a legal system and legal tradition which is directly concerned with interpreting and applying the fundamental rules that define and delimit the powers, rights and duties of governments, other organs of the state, and the citizens. In some cases constitutional law is based on the interpretation of a fixed, binding and usually written formal **constitution**. The constitution of the USA is the most important example of this, because it is highly concrete and absolutely binding, and because it provides for an agency, the Supreme Court, empowered to rule on the constitutionality of the way in which any other element, even the president, has behaved. However, the US constitution is relatively short (even with its 26 Amendments), the clauses often opaque, and is, in any case, more than 200 years old. Precisely because of these factors there is a huge body of constitutional law interpreting and expanding the original document, mainly based on decisions by the courts. Other important formal constitutional codes include those of Australia, Canada and Germany, though in the last case the binding rules are technically only called the 'Basic Law' (Grundgesetz), because at the time of its inception Germany was divided and the authors did not wish to appear to accept the permanence of the division by creating a constitution only for one half of the country.

It is not, of course, necessary to have a single written constitutional document in order to have constitutional law. Indeed, any stable political system must have a set of basic and defining laws or conventions. In Britain, though there is neither a formal constitution nor a court specifically concerned with constitutional matters, there are clear legal rules and practices restricting the actions of political institutions, granting rights and enforcing duties. *Habeas corpus*, for example, is as much a constitutional law as its rough equivalent in the **due process** clauses of the US constitution. There is, in fact, no clear line between constitutional law and ordinary law. The 1964 Police Act, which governs the structure, rights and duties of Britain's police forces, and also the controls over them, could, for example, be regarded in certain contexts as belonging to constitutional law; and so could the annual Mutiny Acts which, until 1879, were necessary to give legal standing to the armed forces (and to an extent their successors, the five-yearly Army Acts and Army and Air Force Acts). Other bodies of law can be seen as at least proto-constitutional law, in particular much of the law deriving from interpretations of the Treaty of Rome by the **European Court of Justice**. The Scotland Act of 1998, which established a quasi-federal structure for policy making, comes as close as anything in British experience to a written constitution.

Containment

Containment is or was (the correct tense to use is unclear) the official US foreign policy doctrine, from 1947 onwards, on how the USA should react to the expansion of international communist influence. The idea, originating with President Truman's approach to problems in the unstable context of immediate post-war Europe, was that America should seek to contain communism within the territorial boundaries it had achieved as a result of the Second World War. Initially this meant the military defence of Western Europe, and of American allies such as Turkey and Greece which were under severe threat in the Mediterranean. As such it represented not the aggressive and even arrogant policy revisionists have tended to paint it as, but a more moderate policy, given a considerable feeling in parts of both America and Britain that communism should be fought directly and ousted from Eastern Europe.

Commentators often cite the **Korean War** as the first major act of the containment policy, though it is unclear why a **United Nations** police action against massive and direct military invasion from North Korea need be justified under such a doctrine at all. If Korea was an example of containment, then it is again evidence of the moderation of the policy, given the way both Presidents Truman and Eisenhower avoided the temptation to push further in their actions against communist China.

Containment became a more aggressive policy when, as a result of a belief that communism had a natural tendency to spread over borders and infect neighbouring countries (the domino theory), the Americans invested military support in protecting South Vietnam from internal and external communist pressure. The **Vietnam War** indeed demonstrated one of the major logical problems in containment, which was its inability to distinguish between aggression by the existing communist societies of the early post-war world, and the indigenous development of apparently similar movements elsewhere. Vietnam apart, containment has mainly been a matter of foreign aid, especially in the **Marshall Plan**, and indirect military aid in the form of weapons credits and training help.

The policy of **détente** of the late 1960s and 1970s might have been seen as bringing an end to containment, or at least a recognition that there could never be anything more than a struggle between the Soviet Union and the USA to impart a world view on nations that might very well have ideas of their own. However, the apparent weakening of détente, as well as the increasing success of Soviet propaganda and aid programmes in the **Third World**, and especially in Latin America and Africa, saw the return of containment as a popular idea in the USA during what has often been called the second **cold war** in the early 1980s. With the collapse of Soviet domination in Eastern Europe, and of communism virtually throughout the former **Soviet bloc**, it is unclear whether containment will have any policy relevance in the future. This is partly because the doctrine never has been applied rigorously to Chinese communism.

The USA, through a combination of bad luck, poor judgement and lack of choice has too often tended to support regimes of extremely unpleasant character against the populations of the countries in question under the name of containment, thus bringing into disrepute a policy which, in general terms, was probably the inevitable consequence of abandoning **isolationism**. With hindsight, it was not inevitable that the USA's 'world policeman' role should have required the belief in a single centre of evil spreading its tentacles everywhere, and whatever international enemies may be identified in the future, no such simplistic building of *cordons sanitaires* is likely to re-emerge. However, there are always tendencies in US political thinking to oversimplify international politics, and there are some signs that a similar process is at work in their identification of world **terrorism** as essentially mono-causal and tied to fundamentalist Islam.

Conventional Arms

Conventional war is war waged only with non-nuclear weaponry, though the definition sometimes also excludes any form of chemical or biological weapons. The concept involves ambiguities and even possible dangers, since it makes the distinction between two ways of creating explosions the main criterion of escalation in warfare. In particular, the distinction invests what are often called 'battlefield' nuclear weapons—small-yield nuclear shells and short-range missiles—with a symbolic significance: because they are nuclear rather than 'conventional', they might be felt to entitle an enemy to respond with more powerful nuclear missiles, even though the 'battlefield' weapons might have had hardly more impact than a heavy 'conventional' bombing raid. Some modern conventional weapons, for example air-fuel explosion bombs, are actually more devastating than an equivalent small nuclear weapon, but if the distinction between conventional and nuclear were regarded as crucial, a heavy attack on a civilian population by conventional bombers would not entitle the defenders to use nuclear weapons in defence. It is unlikely that the distinction is regarded as a vital one by professional military thinkers, though it is of considerable political relevance; some anti-nuclear politicians would advocate the maintenance of massive conventional military strength as an alternative. It is publicly acknowledged that NATO planning was based on the use of low-yield, 'battlefield' nuclear weapons within the first few days of any conflict with the **Warsaw Pact**, principally because of the apparent conventional superiority of the Eastern bloc from the late 1960s until its collapse in the wake of the anti-communist revolutions at the end of the 1980s. But this was never taken to imply that the Western powers would be prepared to launch a major strategic nuclear **first strike**. Nevertheless, the perhaps arbitrary conventional–nuclear distinction is now deeply rooted in the strategic and political vocabulary. As the likelihood of major nuclear war declined, far more careful thinking was carried out about conventional weapons. One result, enshrined partly in the **Conventional Forces in Europe (CFE)** negotiations and treaty was to try to distinguish between offensive and defensive conventional weapons and tactics, and this distinction, theoretically even more difficult, is likely to take the place of the conventional–nuclear dichotomy as of most vital concern.

Conventional Forces in Europe (CFE) Treaty

Discussions about imposing limitations, and preferably reductions, on troop levels and some limits on specified **conventional arms** began in Vienna in

1973. Called, in the West, the Mutual and Balanced Force Reductions Talks (MBFR), these were initially aimed at reducing troop levels to 700,000 army personnel (and 900,000 army and air force combined) on each side. All **Warsaw Pact** countries participated in the talks, as did all **NATO** countries with the exception of France, Iceland, Portugal and Spain. However there was never very much chance of success, because the Western interpretation of 'mutual and balanced' involved a much greater sacrifice on the part of the Warsaw Pact, whose main strength at this time was simply their greater troop strength. The talks were politically useful to various members of the two blocs for their own reasons, so they continued for 15 years, finally being ended only in 1988 because the new world climate had produced a much more hopeful alternative. This alternative, which came to be known as the Conventional Forces in Europe talks, began in late 1987 and rapidly developed some basic guidelines. Firstly they were to cover the whole of Europe 'from the Atlantic to the Urals'. Secondly they were to delimit not only troop strengths, and those quite strictly, but also weapon types. Limits were to be placed on tanks, armoured fighting vehicles, artillery and combat helicopters. There were inevitable definitional problems, for example how heavy did an armoured vehicle have to be before it became a tank? There were also problems about the share of force cuts which should come from each national contingent of the blocs, and about verification inspections and timetables. All of these were dealt with in a considerable spirit of co-operation, but the negotiations were continually outpaced by external political events. Essentially what happened was that the troop levels and deployments agreed upon, very roughly a reduction of 30%, were actually considerably higher than the individual preferences of both sides, and complicated by separate agreements within the Warsaw Pacts for the removal of Soviet troops from the territories of other former **Soviet bloc** countries. The treaty was signed in late 1990, a very short time for so complex a document, but even so history had overtaken it because the Warsaw Pact had already collapsed, Germany had been reunited and little more than a year later the Soviet Union itself was dissolved.

Convergence Thesis

This is the name given to the argument, first formally developed by political scientists in the 1950s but foreshadowed by **Weber** and others much earlier, that **socialist** and **capitalist** societies would inexorably grow more and more alike. The reasons for this prediction vary, but they all have to do with a theory of **bureaucracy** and assumptions about the kind of organization needed to ensure rational policies and efficient decision-making. The basic idea is that planning is paramount in modern societies, and that all forms of planning and administrative control are, whatever their supposed ideological complexion, essentially the same. The Russian Revolution and its supposedly radical **dictatorship of the proletariat** led to monolithic administrative and policy control by the **communist party**, while in the West efficient and powerful **civil services** have developed and close control is exercised over the everyday activities of businessmen, workers and others. The imperatives of planning, and the responses of bureaucrats and planners charged with achieving particular goals, are seen as transcending overt ideological differences between the two societies. The thesis has its points, but probably ignores the crucial difference between bureaucracies which are, and those which are not, subject to electoral power. It has, however, been very influential, and is a useful corrective to the belief that the means we use to achieve goals must be less important than the goals themselves. In its original application, contrasting US and Soviet models, the theory has simply proved to be wrong, because however much planning and state power may have grown in capitalism, it ultimately became necessary for the Soviet-style economies to be abandoned and replaced with market economies. In fact, during the decade that led up to this economic revolution in Soviet and Eastern European societies major efforts were also made in Western societies to 'roll back' the bureaucratic and state influence in their economies by deregulation and **privatization** of state-owned industries.

Convertibility

Convertibility is the arrangement under which the currency of one nation can be freely sold, usually at prices determined by the market, for another currency. As it is almost never the case that a currency cannot be sold for another in any way whatsoever (including the illegal, black market), convertibility really means free convertibility. Convertibility has come to be a particular problem for the post-communist economies of Eastern Europe and the former Soviet Union. The rouble and other Eastern European currencies were not subject to market forces, governments fixing their external prices at quite absurdly artificial prices. The rouble, for example, was officially valued at one pound sterling when its black market value was not even one-hundredth of that. Non-convertibility was more than merely setting an absurd price, however; it also involved refusing to exchange roubles, zlotys and so on for other currencies. Thus if a foreign government or company produced a cheque for one million roubles and asked for US dollars or French francs in return, even at the state-fixed price, they would be refused. The communist countries were more than happy to sell their currencies, indeed tourists were forced to buy a minimum amount, but would not buy it back again. This had two effects. Firstly no country outside the communist bloc was prepared to accept payment for goods or services in the currencies of the bloc, because the money was worthless. Secondly all analyses of the communist economies were massively inaccurate because figures for the level of bank deposits or government expenditure were essentially meaningless. An example of this that used to be crucial in the **cold war** was the difficulty of assessing how much the Soviet Union was spending on defence. The USA used a technique of working out how much an American manufacturer would charge, in dollars, to build, for example, a Soviet T-80 tank, because the rouble values expressed in Soviet figures were meaningless.

Until these former communist countries allow their currencies to be valued on the international currency markets, and accept the financial discipline that Western countries are subject to when their currencies lose or gain value, they will not be able to participate properly in international trade. Until that time they have to pay for imports either in foreign currency, which the new economies find hard to earn, or by a process of bartering their own goods for Western goods. However, though convertibility is a major step to take, and could lead to the established values of the currencies collapsing, most of the old Eastern European economies have accepted it. Those who have not fully done so, like Romania, already had economies so weak as to make this issue relatively unimportant.

Non-convertibility must not be confused with fixed exchange rates which are settled by economic forces. For some time after the Second World War many currencies, notably the pound sterling, were sold only at fixed rates. However the pound was kept to the government's agreed values by buying and selling of sterling carried out by the Bank of England, rather than by a formal pegging of the currency. Indeed the United Kingdom did not accept full market control over the value of the pound until the government decided to allow the pound to float in June 1972. When the UK joined the Exchange Rate Mechanism (ERM) of the European Monetary System in October 1990 it was moving back towards currency control, but only in dealings with other ERM participants. However, this process has been overtaken by the creation of the single currency, the euro, for most European Union members, against which the pound floats freely.

Co-operative

Co-operatives were initially organizations either of agricultural producers (mainly in continental Europe) or of workers which produced or retailed goods at minimum cost by cutting out intermediaries, and redistributed any operating profit to members. In Britain the co-operative movement started in the industrial north. Robert Owen based his model village around a cotton mill at New Lanark, in Scotland, along co-operative lines, and from it developed an early version of socialism. The foundation of the Rochdale Equitable Pioneers in 1844 was an attempt to introduce the principles of an equitable and communal economic system within the boundaries of a **capitalist** society, and the co-operative movement rapidly became very popular, rising from 15,000 members in 1851 to over 400,000 in 1875. A manufacturing and wholesale division, the Co-operative Wholesale Society, was established in 1864, and annual congresses of members followed soon after. In 1917 the Co-operative Congress agreed to organize as a political party and field parliamentary candidates, although it quickly became very closely identified with the **Labour Party**. Although both retail and wholesale divisions of the Co-operative Union still exist, and are important commercially in some areas of the country, it is no longer able to produce a financial incentive to membership any greater than the general attraction of reduced prices in any large supermarket, and has long ceased to have any general social or political importance (although the Co-operative Party continues to sponsor Labour and Co-operative candidates at elections in the United Kingdom).

The idea of co-operative organizations producing fairer prices by mutual co-operation remains common everywhere in the world. Most US universities, for example, have large shops organized on such principles and where profit is distributed as a dividend to members, and the wholesale distribution of agricultural produce in both Italy and France is often handled by farmers' co-operatives. Any enterprise founded by a group of workers regarding themselves as equal, whether as an original initiative or to take over a collapsed company, is likely to be called a co-operative.

Corporatism

Corporatism has at least two distinct meanings. Historically it has designated a form of social organization in which corporations, non-government bodies with great authority over the lives and professional activities of their members, have played an intermediary role between public and state. In origin this goes back to the medieval pluralism in which the great trade guilds or corporations controlled the activities of craftsmen and traders; at the height of their power the guilds represented a third force in society along with the church and the nobility.

Although the Industrial Revolution killed off this form of social organization, it reappeared at the beginning of the 20th century as a theoretical concept in the work of Emile **Durkheim**. It also found a political expression, more façade than reality, in the institutions of **fascism** in the 1930s and 1940s. **Franco's** corporatist design for Spanish society was the longest lived and perhaps most genuine, although **Mussolini's** Italy also had serious corporatist elements. In its 20th-century version the theory suggested that people engaged in a particular trade—employers as well as workers—had more in common with one another than with people of the same **class** or **status** who worked in other trades. In Spain and Italy legislative assemblies and councils of state were therefore organized around such trade corporations rather than around geographic constituencies and the 'capricious' functioning of competitive elections. The convenience of corporatist theory from a fascist point of view was evident: it by-passed both class conflict and democratic elections. Durkheim had had rather different aspirations, looking to the corporations to introduce the moral training and social discipline needed to overcome modern **anomie**, since he regarded the state as too distant and emotionally neutral to be able to solve these problems.

The alternative modern meaning of corporatism (the increasing tendency for the state to work in close co-operation with major business corporations and **trade unions**) is usually distinguished from the older meaning by being labelled **neo-corporatism**.

Coup d'Etat

Coup d'état describes the sudden and violent overthrow of a government, almost invariably by the military or with the help of the military. A coup d'état tends to occur during a period of social instability and political uncertainty, and is usually the work of right-wing elements determined to impose a social discipline and political order that is felt to be missing. It is distinguished from a **revolution**, which usually implies a major change in the social structure or political order. However, the prevailing atmosphere which can precede a coup can be the same one which would allow a revolution to succeed, as was seen in the Soviet Union in 1991.

Coups d'état replace only the ruling group, without necessarily altering the social context in which they rule. Sometimes the makers of the coup d'état return power to the politicians after a fairly short period, when they believe that their aims of stabilizing and ordering the political system have been achieved. This was true, for example, of the Greek **junta** and of various coups d'état in Africa and Latin America. More frequently, an initial promise to do so is reneged on. The sociological conditions in which a successful coup d'état is possible are fairly specific, combining a widespread acceptance of the basic social order with great distrust of the ruling political groups. The tendency of the military to be involved in coups d'état stems from their virtual monopoly of coercive means and the way in which they are often seen as apolitical or even 'above politics'. In less developed societies the military are also likely to have a near monopoly of technological and organizational skills.

Coups need to be distinguished from 'putsches', as well as from revolutions. A coup is carried out by people and bodies which were already part of the power structure, such as army officers, disaffected members of the cabinet or senior civil servants. A putsch is carried out by a small group of leaders, with some degree of mass following, from outside the existing power establishment. There are few famous examples among putsches, but Hitler's abortive putsch in Munich in 1923, and perhaps Mussolini's march on Rome, would qualify as such. It will succeed only if the body of the existing administration, police and military have lost confidence in their official leaders and are prepared to accept the outsiders as replacements without, however, accepting a genuinely revolutionary change in society. In this sense the Bolshevik take-over of Russia in October 1917 may more properly be called a putsch than either a revolution or a coup d'état.

Court of Justice of the European Communities (see European Court of Justice)

Criminal Law

Criminal law describes the part of a legal system which deals with illegal actions, performed by citizens against other citizens or against the state, which are so serious, or so associated with moral turpitude, as to warrant punishment by the state rather than a **civil law** judgment involving the resolution of a conflict or some kind of restitution. The state usually monopolizes the right to carry out prosecutions under criminal law, though some systems, of which the English **common law** is the most important, still include residual private rights to prosecute individuals for breaking the law. In all cases the state has a monopoly of the right to inflict criminal punishment. Criminal law is now increasingly used to enforce the performance of duties in highly regulated spheres such as industrial safety or pollution legislation, or in cases where civil action by an individual to protect their rights is unlikely to be effective. The result has been a blurring of the previously quite sharp distinction between criminal and civil actions. The most important development in criminal law is the increasing pressure to produce some form of international criminal law to deal with, *inter alia*, hostage taking and terrorism, as well as war crimes. The statute of an International Criminal Law has been completed by the UN but is opposed by the USA, without whose membership it would be very weak.

Cuban Missile Crisis

The Cuban missile crisis occurred in 1962 when the Soviet Union, under the leadership of **Khrushchev**, attempted to gain an advantage in the **cold war** by placing medium-range nuclear missiles in Cuba, which under **Castro** had gradually moved into an alliance with the **Soviet bloc**. The missiles would have threatened the American mainland—Cuba is only 90 miles (145 kilometres) from Florida, and constituted an escalation in international tension. In Soviet eyes, however, the placement of such missiles merely redressed an imbalance caused by the USA having similar weapons on the Soviet periphery, most notably in Turkey. John F. Kennedy, the president of the USA, risked international opprobrium and even nuclear conflict by insisting on their removal, and used the US Navy to enforce a blockade of all Soviet ships trying to approach Cuba. Some analysts think that this was the nearest the world has come to a global war since 1945. In the event the Soviet Union gave in under the threat, and this retreat finally swung the Soviet military against Khrushchev, enabling his enemies in the **politburo** to oust him from power a year later. The political significance of the crisis was considerable; among other things it demonstrated the way in which a US president can ignore the other elected branches of government and commit US forces in a major conflict situation. Despite legislation such as the 1973 **War Powers Act**, the US Congress had not been asked to approve military action against an enemy in advance of that action for the entire time period between the Second World War and the **Gulf War** against Iraq in 1991.

Cultural Revolution

Cultural revolution is part of the post-Marx development of **Marxist** theory, most importantly with Chinese communism under the guidance of **Mao Zedong**. The general idea of cultural revolution is as a corrective to the materialistic assumption that some commentators claim to find in Marx, that only physical or legal restraints have to be changed to liberate the **proletariat**. A cultural revolution is a revolution in thought, in ideology, or, more comprehensively, in culture. What might now be called 'mind sets' have to be changed. People have to drop the attitudes, expectations, intellectual orientations of bourgeois society, and these have to be changed separately from the change in, say, the ownership of property.

With some thinkers in this tradition, notably the Italian Communist Party under **Gramsci's** influence, the stress is on getting the cultural revolution first, as the only hope towards persuading electorates to allow the legal and property revolution. Building a true socialist or communist consciousness, however, is seen to be a major and very long-term task by leaders in post-revolutionary societies, because the attitudes of capitalist or feudal society have been shown to linger on long after the political death of these structures.

It was because of this problem that Mao, in the late 1960s, authorized his Red Guards, revolutionary youth, to investigate, punish, humiliate and force into political re-education (see **thought reform**) large numbers of the Chinese élite. The victims were accused of wishing to create a new class system, or of desiring privilege and generally setting themselves apart from the masses in a counter-revolutionary manner. The theoretical problem inside Marxism of the idea of a cultural revolution is that it implies an autonomy of thought from socio-economic structure, which does not fit well with the general thesis that thought and attitude are superstructural, dependent on the economic substructure. Ultimately the cultural revolution in China did great harm, and after Mao's death thousands of desperately needed experts and professionals had to be rehabilitated to help drag China back on to a more orthodox path towards social and economic development.

D

Dahl

Robert Dahl (b. 1915) is probably one of the best known of all the talented and energetic political scientists who appeared on the American academic scene shortly after the Second World War and effected a great development of the discipline that has influenced its practice throughout the Western world. His work covers both political theory and empirical political research, but he is best known as the most important of the **pluralist** writers on democratic theory. The pluralist school recast the definitions of democracy to make it more realistically applicable to the Western political systems. He produced one of the shortest, clearest, and most original of all these restatements of democracy, *A Preface to Democratic Theory*, in which he developed his idea of **polyarchy**. The essence of this approach is that democracy is assured as long as no group or sector influences all or a broad range of issue areas, and that 'intense' minorities have their concerns respected. He also carried out one of the earliest of the **community power** studies, in which he demonstrated, at least to his own satisfaction, that the American city of New Haven satisfied his own theory of democracy. There are few fields of political science he has not touched, and although he has often been criticized by those less convinced of the value of Western political systems, his ideas have not been seriously challenged within mainstream political science.

De Facto

De facto rule or power simply means that, as it happens, a certain group, class, nation or whatever is in a position to control and order some political system. It does not necessarily mean that the rulers are illegitimate, but its principal use is as a contrast with *de jure* power. *De jure* power means that, according to some legal or political theory, a particular group is entitled to give, with **legitimacy**, orders of some type. Again, the actual coincidence depends on the theory one chooses to apply. To take an extreme example, someone might hold that Britain had *de jure* authority over a long-lost colony, or that England only had *de facto* power over Scotland and Wales, depending on the choice of ideologies.

The importance of the conceptual distinction is that it allows a distinction between the actual chance of someone in authority being obeyed (which might be a matter of the number of available machine guns), and the way in which the right to be obeyed is justified, or seen as justifiable by any chosen audience. For example, until the official creation of the state of Zimbabwe, the United Kingdom had had *de jure* authority in what used to be known as Southern Rhodesia, although in fact the society had been controlled by white Rhodesians in revolt against the UK government from 1965 until the creation of Zimbabwe. The distinction has considerable practical effects in the world order, because most countries would have refused to recognize the *de facto* government of that country, and would have assisted in applying what the UK took to be the legal order, as it was the *de jure* ruler.

International law tends to operate by its own version of the common law rule of adverse possession, so that after enough time has passed, de facto rulers come to be seen as having established their own legitimacy. The distinction is probably coming to be much more important in lay discussion than in legal analysis. A common usage would be to answer a question about who makes rules in a community by answering, 'Well, *de facto* it's "x", though *de jure* it's "y"'. Alternatively, *de facto* authority can be identified as meaning the sovereign power in some context where no one has previously had any control. Thus the statement 'The German Federal Bank is the *de facto* monetary authority for Europe', if uttered before the start of the euro, might have recognized an important fact without implying either illegitimacy or the passing from power of some other authority.

De Gaulle

General Charles de Gaulle (1890–1970) was one of the leaders of French resistance to Hitler in the Second World War, and President of the **Fifth Republic** (1959–69). He gave his name not only to a French political party but also to a whole tradition in post-war French politics that still exercises a very important influence. As a colonel in the French army during the 1930s, de Gaulle was a somewhat unpopular figure who advocated modern doctrines of armoured warfare that were largely ignored. He was the senior French soldier to oppose the **Vichy** regime after the fall of France in 1940, and for much of the war headed a French government-in-exile in London. When the Allies liberated France in 1944, de Gaulle became for a while the head of the French government, but his ideas for a strong presidential government were rejected by both politicians and the public, and he retired from political life. In 1958 the crises in the **Fourth Republic**, especially those connected with the Algerian war, led to a widespread demand for him to take power. He accepted, becoming the last prime minister of the Fourth Republic and then the first president of the Fifth Republic. Brought to power in 1958 as a man acceptable to the army, and to be trusted to maintain the status quo because of his vision of French glory, he solved the Algerian crisis only by what was seen as a worse betrayal even than Dien Bien Phu, the defeat in 1954 that ended French involvement in Indo-China. He simply accepted all the Algerian nationalists' demands, and gave them independence within four years of taking office. He led the party (see **Gaullism**) that had fought for his ideas during the 1950s (under a variety of names), and was a highly autocratic ruler of France until he resigned after a referendum defeat in 1969. However, his political position had by then been crystallized into a political ideology supported by his party, and one of his ex-prime ministers, Georges Pompidou, won the resulting presidential election. In modern French politics for much of the time since 1945 there has been a clear ideological position usually identified as Gaullism, which to a large extent represents a development of 'the General's' views; although Gaullist politicians still exist, their views now resembles other brands of modern European **conservatism**, though with more emphasis on national independence. Initially unpopular with the French 'political classes' because of his autocratic manner, his reputation is being reassessed because of the way his successors, especially Valéry Giscard d'Estaing and François **Mitterrand**, have actually extended the presidential domain to the extent of being described as 'royalist' in their style. De Gaulle's main substantive achievements were the re-creation of French independence in foreign and military affairs, and an initial interpretation of the constitution of the Fifth Republic which massively reduced the power of parliament in favour of the executive. Although his party remains enormously influential, the drift of the French centre-right away from pure Gaullism has continued under the incumbent president Jacques Chirac.

De Tocqueville

Alexis de Tocqueville (1805–59) was a French aristocrat who, while in some ways regretting the passing of the Ancien Régime as a result of the French Revolution, nevertheless became one of the most sympathetic and acute observers of Western democratic movements during the 19th century. His two great works were *The Ancien Régime*, a study of the social and political forces at work in France immediately before the Revolution, and *Democracy in America*. The former is still a valuable contemporary document for historians, but de Tocqueville was too close, chronologically and emotionally, to be capable of the sustained value-free analysis that might have made it a first-class work of political science. However, after he visited America in 1830, and despite the fact that he was there for only eight months and visited only a few eastern-seaboard states, he produced a massive, detailed and analytically brilliant study which can still be read today for its insights into the operation of American political culture. It is quite common for modern American political scientists and sociologists to attempt their own version of his American study, invariably finding much that is still true. In this work he also develops a political and social theory about the consequences of mass democracy that is similar in many ways to **Durkheim's** much later thinking. His principal concern was to demonstrate that some aspects of the traditional European **aristocracy** had been beneficial, and that their absence in modern democracy raised dangers to the very values of democracy itself. Formal political equality, without actual economic equality, put the masses in the hands of those whose wealth gave them power, but who lacked the aristocracy's *noblesse oblige* sense of duty towards those whom they ruled. De Tocqueville also feared the vulnerability of the masses to demagogic manipulation, and regretted the absence of the countervailing influence of some aspects of the feudal world order. In this context he was close to the thinking of British liberals, such as John Stuart **Mill**, on whom his influence can clearly be seen. His observations were often acute, for example seeing that America was becoming an increasingly litigious society, where not only inter-personal conflicts but also general political questions rapidly became entangled with the legal system. His predictions were also extremely perceptive. He was convinced that the USA would become one of the leading world powers (which was hardly obvious in 1830), and even foretold that its great opponent would be Russia. Ultimately he approved of American democracy much more than he deprecated it. He was perhaps the first real political sociologist in that he sought to explain American culture in terms of its social and economic conditions and its political culture.

Decentralization

Decentralization denotes a process or situation in which powers and respon-sibilities are transferred from a central authority to other, usually more local, organs. The term can be employed in relation to the political decision-making process, to the distribution of powers between elected authorities and to the organization of the **bureaucracy**. Most federal systems of government, for example Germany, Australia and the USA, exhibit a considerable degree of decentralization, although they may also (as a result) possess overlapping authorities. It can simply mean that detailed decisions are made by local representatives of central powers, though always within policy guidelines, and probably funding arrangements, dictated by the centre. In this way, for example, it is unclear that Germany really is a federation, rather than just a very highly decentralized unitary state, because much of the power of the Land governments is to decide on the detailed application of federal government outline legislation. The term, in any case, refers essentially to reform inside a system, rather than being a description of a system from its outset. As a policy, decentralization appeals particularly to centrist parties in Europe, and is beginning to seem rather dated as the liberal consensus of the 1960s and 1970s declines in importance. In others, however, notably Italy, strains in central government and doubts of its competence have actually re-invigorated decentralist trends. As national unity in many countries comes under pressure from regional or subcultural identities, formerly completely unitary countries like the United Kingdom have allowed major devolutionary changes. (See also **centralization, federalism**.)

Decree

A decree is a legal rule or regulation, having all the power of parliamentary legislation, but issued directly by a minister or department of state under direct authority granted either by a **constitution** or enabling legislation. They are a particular feature of continental European constitutional law, particularly in France. The constitution of the French **Fifth Republic** was intended to limit parliamentary power, and thus the ability to make binding law in many areas had to be transferred to the administrative branch of government. This is a rather wider transfer of power away from an elected body than is to be found in **common law** systems. Although **parliamentary government** in the United Kingdom often allows ministers to add details to legislation, these have to be presented to Parliament, which could alter them; the French National Assembly, in contrast, does not have the power to query a minister about decrees.

The real difference is one of subjective tone. Decree carries with it the suggestion of autocratic power, suggesting a superior administrative or governmental judgment which is not to be challenged by the public. There is a stronger sense than with the law that the people have decided, however indirectly, to bind themselves to some behaviour out of their own concern for the common good. However intangible they may be, these subjective distinctions are important, not only in indicating differences in perspectives on regulatory power between the European **civil law** and Anglo-American common law systems, but also in explaining why European attitudes to governmental power, especially in France and Italy, often involve seeing the state as a hostile and disinterested body. However, problems of parliamentary instability, or difficulties in getting parliamentary majorities make some recourse to decrees inevitable at times. Italy, again, is an example of a country forced at times to rely heavily on such governmental instruments, as are several of the new East European democracies, notably Romania.

Defensive Defence

As popular fears of Soviet aggression against Western Europe declined during the 1980s, and the difficulty in rebutting anti-nuclear attitudes increased correspondingly, there was a series of efforts to devise defence policies which would be cheaper, less potentially aggressive or destabilizing, and would not depend on nuclear weapons. The general principle was that the **Warsaw Pact** should not be seen as having territorially expansionist policies of its own, but instead to be motivated largely by an insecurity worsened by fears of Western aggressive potential as exemplified by current **NATO** policies. The plans, none of which were ever accepted by NATO defence departments, varied enormously in detail, but were taken very seriously by some parties, especially the Social Democratic Party of Germany (SPD) and important elements of the British Labour Party. All the plans had the same common core, which was to construct a military posture which would be physically incapable of advancing into Eastern Europe, or indeed of attacking it by any means. At the same time the plans argued for extensive use of lightly-armed reserves so that both the cost and the symbolic threat of large heavily-armed standing armies would be reduced. During the early part of the **Gorbachev** period of **détente** the idea of defensive defence was picked up by the Soviet military as a bargaining counter in arms control negotiations. The Soviet Union made great diplomatic play with proposed military reforms which, by making it less likely that the Warsaw Pact armies could or would themselves advance westwards, put pressure on NATO to adopt similar policies. Ultimately, the speed of the collapse of the Soviet military economy and of Soviet control in Eastern Europe overtook these more modest plans. They could have been extremely influential, however, as Western fears of defence expenditure had already led to a pressing need for conventional defence reductions, as manifested in the **Conventional Forces in Europe (CFE) Treaty** of 1990.

Deficit

All countries are prone to have deficits on any one of a number of financial accounts at any time. However since the early 1980s the deficit, specifically the gap between public expenditure and government revenues, has been a particular problem in the USA. This deficit grew extremely rapidly under President Ronald Reagan because he combined a huge increase in defence expenditure with major tax cuts in his first two years of office. In the 1992/93 financial year the deficit was estimated at $350 billion, this being over 5% of US gross domestic product (GDP). The deficit has become a persistent political sore, because the only two ways of dealing with it, a cut in federal expenditure or a major increase in taxes (see **fiscal policy**), are both too politically sensitive for politicians to consider. US political culture has always been 'tax-sensitive', despite the fact that, at least in federal terms, Americans pay less tax than most citizens of Western democracies. At the same time efforts to reduce the deficit from the mid-1980s trimmed most avoidable expenditure off the budget, and left very few fully-funded programmes which could be cut without major political repercussions. The end of the **cold war** seemed to present an opportunity to reduce the deficit by cutting military expenditure, but even apart from right-wing political pressure to preserve such budget items, there was less to cut than the liberals in Congress had always assumed.

Part of the expenditure problem is that several extremely expensive social welfare programmes, including Medicare, pensions and unemployment benefit, were badly designed from the outset and have huge actuarial cost overruns. However, they are regarded as entitlement programmes which cannot be cut more than marginally. Budgetary deficits are a major constraint on national economic development, because they have to be financed through borrowing, forcing interest rates up both for business and for the general population. For the USA it has been made even worse because, at the same time, the balance of external trade has also been seriously in deficit. Until a president can be elected on an increased taxation policy, which would run against the whole tradition of US politics, there is not likely to be a fundamental solution. Attempts to solve the problem such as the Gramm-Rudman legislation can make only a minor impression. Ironically the deficit could be cleared in a few years if the burden to the US taxpayer was increased by bringing taxes on petrol and luxury goods up to the European average. The US deficit is likely to grow again in the early 21st century with the election of President George W. Bush who has many of the same policies as Reagan. As his presidency is also particularly needful of defence expenditure following the 2001 terrorist attacks, deficit reduction is extremely unlikely.

Delegation

Delegation of power in political discourse has two rather different usages. The first is the idea that a body, a parliament most typically, with constitutional authority to make law may delegate some part of this power to others. Usually this involves the parliament passing a law which sets the major aims and outline shape of a legislative programme. Rather than try to deal with the details, which themselves may have to be altered frequently to accord with changing circumstances, they may delegate responsibility to make regulations under the act to a **civil service** body, a minister, or even an independent agency (in this context, see **legislative veto**). The body to which power is thus delegated usually has to pass only rather formal tests of the validity of the subsequent rules and regulations, though these may be more easily challenged in courts or elsewhere than originating legislation. In the United Kingdom it is not unusual for a court to hold that a certain measure of, for example, a minister of state taken under the authority of power-delegating legislation is *ultra vires*, exceeding what Parliament had intended. It is, however, impossible to attack an act of the originating body, Parliament, as *ultra vires*, because the British constitution knows no limit to parliamentary power. Only a moderate alteration in this situation has been brought about by the 1998 **Human Rights Act**.

It is also possible to delegate much more broadly, to give to an agency essentially unfettered discretion to make regulations in a specific area, even though the body is unelected and legally not responsible to the delegating authority. In this sense, for example, the US Federal Reserve can be seen as exercising the delegated authority of Congress, even though the latter is not entitled even to set guidelines for the Federal Reserve's monetary policy.

The secondary meaning of delegation is almost the opposite of the above. A delegate is one who is selected to represent a body or group, but unlike a fully free representative, as in the theory of representation of **Burke**, is not at liberty to vote according to their own will. Although not as firmly bound as someone seen as mandated to vote in a particular way, a delegate is expected to carry out broad instructions and to refrain from independent policy-making.

Democracy

Democracy is the most valued and also perhaps the vaguest of political concepts in the modern world. Political systems as diverse as the USA, various one-party states in Africa and communist states all describe themselves as democracies. Indeed, it is characteristic of this vagueness that when a UNESCO conference on democracy was held in 1950, more than 50 nations, representing a full range of political systems, each insisted that they were (and sometimes that *only* they were) a democracy.

The word 'democracy' is derived from two ancient Greek words: *demos* ('the people') and *kratos* ('strength'). By itself democracy means little more than that, in some undefined sense, political power is ultimately in the hands of the whole adult population, and that no smaller group has the right to rule. Democracy only takes on a more useful meaning when qualified by one of the other words with which it is associated, for example **liberal democracy**, **representative democracy**, **participatory democracy** or **direct democracy**.

Those who seek to justify the title 'democracy' for a society where power is clearly in the hands of one section of the population (for example, in many Third World or communist countries) mean something rather different. The claim is not really that the people rule, but that they are ruled in their own interests. Defenders of the system operating in the Soviet Union before the changes initiated by Mikhail **Gorbachev**, for example, claimed that until economic and social progress has been made, and a true 'socialist man' created by education, that is until the masses have lost their **false consciousness**, democratic procedures would be worse than useless. Their argument was that people cannot be left to choose their own leaders, or make their own political choices, until their vision is genuinely free of distortion and they can identify their real needs. This version of democracy has a close connection with the theory of positive **liberty**.

One way of making sense of this diversity of usages is to suggest that a claim to being democratic is, in a sense, a 'negative' claim. That is, a democratic society is one that will not accept the right of any élite to rule except when it can justify itself in terms of mass approval or especial emergency. For example, a claim to rule simply because one was of superior birth, race, religious perception or intellectual power would be negated by the demand for democracy. Democracy is, almost inevitably, negative in this sense, because its basic principle, the right of a majority over any minority, is not capable of justification as a good in itself.

Democratic Centralism

Democratic centralism is the doctrine, espoused by **Lenin**, according to which the **Communist Party of the Soviet Union (CPSU)**, and most other communist parties, was traditionally run. It lays down that conflicting opinions and views should be freely expressed and widely discussed at all levels of the party hierarchy, and that the central committee should take them into account when making any decision, but once a decision has been made, the policy must be unquestioningly accepted and carried out by all party members. Accordingly, the CPSU was organized on strict hierarchical lines, but with considerable control over the committees at each level by the one directly above, thus allowing very little upward flow of views and opinions to take place, while the 'centralist' aspect of the doctrine is fully utilized. Were the freedom to argue fully before the policy decision a reality, there would in fact be relatively little difference between democratic centralist communist parties and such organizations as the British Conservative Party, where policy is ultimately made by a party leadership which expects to be loyally supported by all rank-and-file members. The authority of the CPSU was justified in terms of its own ideology by the need for a **dictatorship of the proletariat** to build communism.

It was in the early days of the party, and especially under Lenin just after the 1917 Revolution, that central control of the party was particularly problematic, and hence from this time that the linking of the two values, democratic participation with central command authority, dates. Democratic centralism's proven inability to allow the filtering of opinions up, as well as down, the hierarchy, eventually contributed to the downfall of the CPSU. Mikhail

Gorbachev's policy of **glasnost** opened the prospect of an alternative version of **democracy** to the people of the Soviet Union, and when a group of 'hardliners' attempted to reimpose the traditions of democratic centralism in August 1991, not only they, but also the CPSU itself, were promptly rejected.

Democratic Party

The US Democratic Party's origins are as an opposition to the dominant **Federalist** party in the early days after the adoption of the US Constitution. Confusingly, at that time it was called the Republican Party, later the Democratic-Republican Party, before taking its present name under Andrew Jackson in 1828. Jackson represented a **populist** political force opposed to the centralizing élitist views of the followers of Thomas Jefferson, who favoured much stronger federal control at the expense of the autonomy of the individual states. To this day the Democratic Party stresses states' rights more strongly than the **Republican Party**. This, and factors such as it still being more populist and less influenced by the intellectual and financial élites of the East Coast, explains why it is so hard to characterize in the political language of Europe. On most issues, and in a very broad sense, the Democrats are to the **left** of the Republicans, or, in the American usage, are more 'liberal'. At least since the Second World War, it has been the party of blacks, of organized labour, and has usually attracted the votes of the **civil liberties** oriented and more egalitarian members of the upper middle class as well. However in the past, and still at times today, the anti-federalist stance has forced them to take up distinctly **reactionary** policies. The classic historical example of this was in the Civil War, where the bulk of the Democrats opposed the use of force to bring the seceding Southern states back into the Union, a policy, which later became an outright war against slavery, which was advocated by the Republican Party. A long-term consequence of this was that the Southern wing of the Democratic Party was often more conservative in Congress than most Republicans, especially on **civil rights** issues. Even today this tendency is still present, and Republican presidents often owe their legislative successes to *ad hoc* coalitions of Southern Democrats with members of their own party. At the same time the more liberal wing of the Democrats, mainly elected from Northern cities, tends to combine with Republicans from the north and west to put their own legislation through. The Democrats had a majority in the House of Representatives for nearly the whole of the second half of the 20th century, because their populism and **welfarism** made them more naturally the party of the less-affluent majority of the population. They often controlled the Senate as well, but usually only with a very small majority. However, the rise of the Republicans in previously 'safe' Democratic states in the south in the 1990s enabled the Republicans to hold majorities in both chambers of Congress during the presidency of the Democrat, Bill Clinton. Conversely when it comes to the presidency the very different nature of the issues, where capacity for economic management is seen to be more naturally a talent of those who come from the rich corporate sector of American life, and where foreign policy used to be seen as requiring a more aristocratic background, the Democrats were less successful. Prior to Clinton's election they had held the presidency for only 19 years between 1945 and 1992.

Changing social and demographic patterns eventually forced the Democratic Party itself to change. Organized labour covers only a small fraction of the working population; the mass **immigration** flows that were the other base of its power in the cities are over; and Republicans were increasingly doing well in the South, previously almost a Democrat monopoly. Having been very unsure of itself and of what it stood for in recent years, the party tried to compete with the Republicans on their own ground of economic management. It was the promise of Clinton in 1992 to get America back to work after years of increasing unemployment and recession, and to guarantee broader access to health provision, that restored the presidency to the Democratic Party, after 12 years of Reagan and Bush administrations, with a strengthened hold on Congress (subsequently lost). The defeat of Clinton's Democrat successor by the Republican George W. Bush, son of a previous president, was so marginal, and so controversial, as to give no indication of the long-term future for the party.

Democratic Transitions

Democratic transition refers to the experience of many countries in the last decades of the 20th century as they moved from some form of non-democratic government to liberal democracy, often very quickly. Until Portugal overthrew the Salazar regime and set up a political system based on free elections in 1974/75 there had been no sudden (indeed, revolutionary) appearance of a modern liberal democracy. At about the same time, Greece overthrew the Colonels' regime, and Spain, on the death of **Franco**, also set up a democracy, a constitutional monarchy like those found in northern Europe. Until this time the West experienced democracy as something that developed slowly over decades, if not centuries, as traditional ruling classes gradually broadened the franchise and retreated from overt power. Alternatively, it had been the rather disappointing experience of post-Versailles states in central Europe.

In 1989 a clutch of almost overnight democracies again occurred when, on the collapse of the old **Soviet bloc**, Poland, Czechoslovakia, Hungary, Romania and some other countries replaced Communist party rule with parliamentary democracy in the space of a few months. The questions for political science are, first, are there common factors in these apparently successful transitions, and secondly, how were such rapid transitions possible when there appeared to be little or no cultural experience or preparedness for democracy? The mere fact that such questions were asked indicates that democracy had come to seem a rare and delicate plant requiring careful nurturing. The answer seems to be that in a world where existing stable democracies exist as models, the creation of a new one when an existing authoritarian system can no longer successfully repress its people, is a matter of rational calculating. Although the stories of transitions differ in detail, they have one thing in common. Various potential leadership groups, often including remnants of the old order, come together and agree on institutions which satisfy a sort of 'second best' rule of politics. The second best solution is limited government where no group can wield dictatorial power. In a situation of extreme uncertainty, where the only certainty is that repression has ceased to work, the second best becomes everyone's rational choice. Whether, however, such purely rationally supported institutions can continue for long, and can survive shocks and, particularly, economic challenges is another question. It seems likely that the conditions for maintaining and developing democracy may be very different from, and harder to achieve than, the conditions for creating it. It is for this reason that so much attention is now being paid to the idea of **civil society**.

Dependency Theory

Dependency theory was a popular radical critique of Western capitalist nations in their relations with the **Third World** during the 1960s and 1970s, and still has its advocates. It derives from a theory of economic imperialism, and is also used as a critique of foreign aid programmes. The basic idea is that major capitalist powers like the USA and leading members of the **European Union** have not really given up their powers of **colonialism**, but in fact exercise enormous political control over Latin American, African and Asian countries. However, they do this now by the use of economic pressure and by exploiting their superior market position to extract unfair advantage in international trade. The theory holds that as most of the finance for industrial and agricultural development in the Third World has to come from the money markets in the developed capitalist states, that development is tied to the economic interests of the West.

The theory is even taken by some to the point that outright foreign aid gifts are suspect, because the funding is simply used to develop Third World economies in such a way that they remain totally dependent on markets in the **First World**. While it is clear that economic power is vital, and that the Western investors will try to maximize their advantage, it is far from clear that poor and over-populated countries have any alternative, at least in the short term, to exploiting their primary products for the Western market. There is, after all, nothing fixed about the terms of trade in primary goods. Oil may have once been a matter for exploitation and political control by the First World; it is now clearly a weapon of considerable power in the hands of the oil states against their former exploiters. Nevertheless, the theory, by pointing out how irrelevant formal political control may be, does help to show how long-lasting are the chains of empire as they were cast during the great development of colonial economic exploitation by the European powers in the 19th century. Combined with the spread of multinational companies outside the control of any Western governments, companies which frequently do control the raw resources of poor countries, the general notion of economic dependency cannot be ignored. During the 1980s, however, it became clear that the Western money markets which had financed Third World development had been seriously damaged by their policies. Instead of the loans to such countries being exploitatively advantageous to New York, London, Paris and so on, widespread inability to repay debts, combined with a greater self-confidence on the part of the debtors, led to billions of dollars being wiped off stock market values in the Western banking sector and the very existence of certain institutions being threatened.

Deputies

Deputies are elected members of a legislative assembly. The term is not normally applied to British members of Parliament, but is used in connection with members of the French, German and Italian legislatures. A legislature member regarded as a deputy has an obligation to echo the views of those voters responsible for his election; in other words, a **delegation** has taken place. The opposite view, that an elected member should be able to speak and vote according to their own convictions, stems from **Burke**. In practice there is no obvious difference in behaviour between deputies and legislators working under other titles.

The term 'deputy' is sometimes used to refer to a person who is a surrogate for a leader or fills their place when necessary. Thus most political parties have deputy leaders. Technically a deputy is someone who acts in place of a decision-maker when the latter is absent or unable to carry out their duties, and is 'deputed' to carry out that person's will. The prefix 'vice-', as in the vice-president of the USA, generally has a similar usage.

Deregulation

Deregulation is closely related, both theoretically and practically, to **privatization**, as common characteristics of economic policy change in the last quarter of the 20th century. There have always been many regulated industries, even in the most ideologically **laissez-faire** capitalist economies like that of the USA. Governments have tended to regulate the number of firms in certain economic areas, or at least the conditions for entry and have even more frequently controlled their activities. Such regulation has stemmed from a fear that uncontrolled competition would be against the public interest and has often proved popular with firms inside regulated zones, owing to reduced competitive pressures. Thus transport, both by air and long-distance coach companies, has frequently been regulated. Routes could not be operated without licences, and the number of companies allowed to compete on a route has usually been restricted. Largely as a part of the return to popularity of free market economic theory from the 1970s onwards, governments have removed or reduced such regulations. The hope has always been that competition would turn out to be safe and produce lower fares, tariffs or other changes without notable reductions in quality of service.

As many of the most regulated areas were also controlled by state monopolies, particularly in energy production and communications, the first step was in fact privatization. However, governments could not allow private monopolies to take the place of state monopolies, so the introduction of competition has gone hand in hand with deregulation. There have been some notable disasters of deregulation, particularly the savings and loan services in the USA in the 1980s. It is perhaps surprising that there have not been more, because the instinct to regulate such areas was well based in fears for the public interest. Other areas though, especially France's deregulation of the broadcast media, or the United Kingdom's deregulation of inter-city coach services should clearly never have been subject to regulation in the first place.

Détente

From the 1960s the word 'détente' crept into our political vocabulary to signify a foreign policy process mainly concerned with an easing of tension between the Soviet Union and the USA. At any particular time the content of policies meant to increase détente varied widely. Very roughly, any policy which involves self-interested economic co-operation, or steps towards reduction in the level of armaments, is likely to qualify as an example of détente. In many ways the apparent existence of a new and softer relationship between the two **superpowers** had more to do with a tendency to use the extreme hostility of the **cold war** of periods in the 1950s and 1960s as a benchmark than with any real reduction in conflict between Western and Eastern states. Most historians would suggest that the process of détente after 1945 has been cyclical, and that the period which first produced the label, during the Nixon and Carter US administrations, was sharply reversed in the early Reagan years. It is common to see the period after **Gorbachev** came to power in the Soviet Union as the second détente. However, there had been earlier periods of relaxation of tension under Khrushchev, and perhaps immediately after Stalin's death in 1953.

The country where détente was both most politically important, and perhaps most real, was Germany, where the Ostpolitik identified with Willy Brandt represented a genuine *rapprochement* between the Soviet Union and West Germany, which took place about 20 years before the collapse of Soviet power in Europe and the unification of the German states.

Deterrence

Deterrence is a concept much used by defence strategists and military planners and their political allies. Literally, deterrence refers to the capacity to protect oneself from attack by another nation by being able to threaten terrible, or at least unacceptable, reprisals. Deterrence, however, has come into its own in the often bizarre world of nuclear **strategy**, and highly sophisticated theories have been developed around the concept. Political leaders of both the Western and Eastern powers have argued, ever since 1945, that their countries need nuclear weapons, or at least very strong conventional forces (see **conventional arms**), so that peace can be maintained. The argument is that as long as a potential enemy knows that any attack by them would cost them dear, no attack will be made. In terms of nuclear capacity a host of other concepts become involved in the detailed working out of this essentially simple notion, especially those of **mutual assured destruction**, **second strike capacity**, pre-emptive strikes, **massive retaliation** and **flexible response**. Perhaps the most significant point is that military capacity does now seem to be justified everywhere in terms of the need to deter others, rather than of having an offensive capacity.

The problem with deterrence is that it is ultimately a matter of comparative psychology: one can never know what will deter a potential enemy, only what would deter oneself. Recent military activity, such as the British recapture of the Falkland Islands from Argentina, or the United Nations-sponsored **Gulf War** against Iraq, ought not to have been necessary because, rationally, the aggressors must have known that their opponents possessed superior military power. In both cases what went wrong was that the aggressors calculated that others would not use those powers. It would certainly appear that nuclear deterrence, where the sheer level of destruction that might follow an act of aggression would be too high to allow even the slightest risk of miscalculating an opponent's reaction, is more effective. In neither of the above examples was there any serious threat of using nuclear forces.

Devolution

Devolution is the process of transferring power from central government to a lower or regional level; among the reasons given for doing so are that it will increase the efficiency of government and meet demands from special sections of the community for a degree of control over their own affairs. The word gained great currency in the United Kingdom in the late 1970s, when proposals were made to establish separate assemblies for Scotland and Wales, each with a range of powers over its own internal affairs. However, a referendum held on the proposals revealed that the majority of voters in Wales were opposed to any such transfer of powers. In Scotland, a majority of those who voted were in favour of the proposals, but this represented less than the 40% of the total electorate which had been stipulated, and the proposed legislation was therefore abandoned. Serious devolution was not to come until the very end of the 20th century, when the 1997 Labour government gave Scotland its own parliament with restricted powers, and gave Wales an assembly with what amounted to glorified local government authority. The Welsh demonstrated hardly more enthusiasm for devolution in the second referendum than in the first, but the Scots were clearly eager for a measure of independence from London.

The question had arisen much earlier in the 20th century when the Irish issue had led to calls for 'home rule all round'. The establishment in 1921 of a separate parliament for Ulster with considerable powers over domestic matters was controversial because the administration was accused of discriminating against the Roman Catholic community. The devolved Ulster parliament was abolished in 1973, and numerous efforts to re-establish it on a power-sharing basis failed. Although Northern Ireland has again had a power sharing assembly since the late 1990s, it is severely hampered by the still irreconcilable differences between the Catholic and Protestant communities. Like **decentralization**, devolution has tended to be attractive to centrist parties which doubt their ability to win and hold power at the central level for long, and campaign for constitutional reform on issues outside the normal ambit of debate between major right- and left-wing parties.

Dialectical Materialism

Dialectical materialism, which is sometimes abbreviated as 'diamat', is a shorthand description of **Marxist** theory officially propagated in the Soviet Union, and developed in particular by **Engels**. It stresses the two main methodological points of Marx's own writings. The first was an insistence on a version of the logical form known as dialectical argument, which Marx had taken over and modified from Hegel. The second was the assumption that the world is entirely **materialist**, that is, the argument that ideas, beliefs, religious creeds and so on all stem from the material conditions of life, and are not independent causative factors in society. The dialectic, as a mode of argument, used by Greek philosophers such as Socrates and **Plato**, claims that change in the world comes about through a process of conflict between opposed movements. For example, there is a particular mode of production which is dominant in an economy. This might be peasant agriculture. A new mode begins to develop, urban industrial manufacture, which is contradictory in needs and demands to the earlier mode. The clash between these produces a new third mode, in this case a revolution which results in the abolition of private property, which in turn becomes dominant. This tripartite process consists of a 'thesis', contrasted to a rival 'antithesis', with the two submerged in the resulting 'synthesis', and is the form that all historical progression, in ideas, the economy, the class struggle, world power relations and so on takes. For Hegel, the modern initiator of the form of argument, the dialectic took place in the realm of ideas and spirit, whereas for Marx, who claimed to have 'stood Hegel on his head', the real progress takes place at the material or physical level, and ideas grow out of this 'substructural' dialectic process. The material level is the economy, characterized at any one time by a particular set of modes and means of production.

Dictatorship

Dictatorship is a form of government in which one person has sole and complete political power. In antiquity, a temporary dictator was often appointed as an emergency measure by states which were normally organized in some other fashion. The Roman Republic appointed dictators during military crises (the term actually originates from this practice), and the ancient Greek city states sometimes gave supreme law-making powers to individuals, for example Solon in 594–93 BC, when civic unity was seriously threatened.

In the modern world many dictators have come to power as leaders of mass movements, and have ruled through their control of such movements or through political parties that have acquired a monopoly of power. Dictators also frequently emerge from the armed forces when a military **junta** takes over after a **coup d'état**. An important distinction should be made between the dictator who exercises personal power based on their own popularity or control of coercive institutions, and the apparently dictatorial leader who is in reality largely a figure-head or no more than the 'first among equals' within a ruling clique. Often the term is used in a debased way to describe someone who does have enormous personal influence, even though they are acting within the legal restrictions of a democracy. **Hitler**, **Mussolini** and **Stalin** were real dictators, whereas more recent leaders of the Soviet Union, who have owed their eminence to their position within the party hierarchy and have had to contend with the rest of the **politburo**, have probably not managed to become dictators. Of other modern leaders, General **Franco** was certainly a powerful ruler in his own right to the end of his life, while General **de Gaulle** came close to being a popularly-appointed 'crisis' dictator on the Roman model. Populist leaders ruling through parliaments completely controlled by their parties, which have often practised electoral fraud, have been common in some parts of the former Soviet Union since its fragmentation; many of these have come close to being dictators, at least for short periods.

Dictatorship of the Proletariat

This is one of the concepts taken from **Marx's** writings by the early leaders of the **Bolshevik** wing of the All-Russian Social Democratic Labour Party (later the **Communist Party of the Soviet Union**), especially by **Lenin**, and used to justify the dominant role of the Communist Party in the state. According to the developed **Marxist-Leninist** doctrine, immediately after the revolutionary overthrow of **capitalism** there will be an intermediate period during which the party, as the **vanguard of the proletariat**, will have to exercise political and economic control in a 'dictatorship of the proletariat'. This undemocratic and inegalitarian state of affairs is unavoidable because the transition from capitalism to true socialism is impossible until the necessary conditions have been created. These conditions are partly economic, depending on the level of capitalist development that has been reached, but more important is the creation of 'Socialist Man'. This entails the development of a true socialist consciousness among the masses. Until they come to grasp the true ideology, it is pointless to entrust political and social decisions to them, since they will still be suffering the **alienation** and ideological distortion that life in a capitalist society produces (see **false consciousness**). Ultimately, when a true socialist understanding has been developed, not only will the party's supreme power be unnecessary, but indeed the whole state will 'wither away', leaving a peaceful co-operative society. Until then democracy could only hold back this development; in fact selfishness and conflict would be rife unless kept down by forceful central control on the part of those who, having been admitted to the party, are known to have a proper understanding of scientific socialism. While there are theoretical difficulties in accepting this idea, it should not be taken as mere cynical pretence. In many areas of Soviet life it was possible to see serious attempts to build such a socialist man, for example in the ordinary criminal law and, above all, the educational system. Nevertheless, it is true that the doctrine was especially useful to the Bolsheviks in 1917 when they worked to turn the mass revolution of February into their own creation. It is generally accepted that Lenin's October Revolution lacked any real popular support and was more of a **coup d'état** or putsch. Hence it was necessary to find a way of explaining how a true popular **Marxist** revolution could, nevertheless, be deemed to have occurred. With the fall of communist governments in Eastern Europe and the Soviet Union, and the acceptance of pluralism, any remaining supporters of the concept have been marginalized. Communist parties in most other countries have long had to drop the idea in order to compete in democratic elections.

Diplomacy

The idea of 'diplomacy' is used in a variety of rather vague ways in political language, all deriving from the techniques and styles developed by European foreign affairs representatives during the 18th century, though, of course, diplomacy as behaviour and political strategy is as old as politics. Technically the diplomatic corps consists of all the men and women professionally engaged in representing the interests of their countries abroad. This activity varies from the gathering of information and evaluation of the politics of the host country, via the direct protection of the legal interests of any fellow nationals who are in trouble in that country (the consular function) to international negotiations and the delivery of special messages to the host government. Diplomacy has come to mean something slightly apart from this, however. It has come to describe an entire method of resolving international conflicts which, though very often referred to in the media, is rather hard precisely to define. At a simple level diplomacy covers anything short of military action, and indeed it is often alleged that 'diplomacy' has failed when countries do engage in outright fighting. The broadness of the concept is demonstrated by some of the ways in which subcategories of diplomacy have had to be invented to describe more precisely what goes on when diplomacy is resorted to. Thus one reads of 'personal diplomacy', when a particular national leader tries to sort out an international problem on the basis of their own personal relations with, and understanding of, other national leaders. A subcategory even of this is the notion of 'shuttle' diplomacy, engaged in almost exclusively by the USA when an influential or important foreign affairs spokesman will travel backwards and forwards between hostile states trying to find grounds for compromise between opponents on the basis of building up a personal connection and understanding with both sides.

Alternatively one reads of 'diplomatic channels', for the delivery of ideas or the collection of information, which essentially means using the diplomatic corps for its proper function, and indeed actually stands in contrast to the amateurishness involved in 'personal' diplomacy. In as much as there is a further real content to the notion of 'diplomacy' *per se* it comes from the idea that diplomats are professional experts in negotiation and information transmission in the international arena. Here it is felt that particular techniques and training are necessary to ensure that no personal emotion or style should colour the message, that two diplomats of different nations have more in common, and are better able to treat the matters they discuss objectively and unemotionally than are two ordinary politicians. As foreign policy is increasingly made, in all countries, directly by the heads of the **executive**, and as international conferences increasingly depend on direct confrontation between senior politicians, it might be thought that diplomacy as a special technique, and the diplomatic corps as professional experts both in the making and execution of foreign policy, are going out of date. There is probably considerable truth in this. It was noteworthy that a British cabinet 'think tank' report on the foreign service urged its radical cutting, and the replacement of most functions by ordinary civil servants who were technical experts in the area in question. No action was taken on this report, but it caused considerable public debate. In the USA the tendency for foreign policy to be taken out of the State Department and into the White House has not attenuated over the years.

One development that has strengthened the idea of diplomacy as a special endeavour has been the growth of importance of transnational bodies, the **European Union (EU)** in particular, which have no direct capacity to use force, but do represent a huge potential power. Thus the presence of EU negotiators in recent conflicts like the **Gulf War** or the Yugoslavian crisis has been a vitally important example of purely diplomatic activity. The international crisis following the terrorist attacks in the USA in 2001 again demonstrated both the importance of the EU and the highly personal nature of diplomacy as consisting of face-to-face meetings between heads of state. In particular the clear personal empathy between Tony Blair, as prime minister of the UK and both President Bush of the USA and President Putin of Russia became crucial.

Direct Democracy

Direct democracy is to be contrasted with **representative democracy**, much as the respective titles suggest. According to the theory of direct democracy, all concerned citizens must directly participate in the making of decisions and the passing of laws, and this function can neither be delegated to others, nor can it be carried out by others chosen to represent the interests of the many. The inspiration for this system of democratic politics comes from classical Greek **democracy**, especially as it is understood, sometimes, to have worked in 5th century Athens. The earliest, and still most influential, exponent in the modern world is Jean Jacques **Rousseau**, particularly in *The Social Contract*.

The arguments given for the advantage of direct instead of representative democracy are varied. Foremost is the idea that only a genuine majority of the population can make a law which really maximizes the democratic nature of rule, and representative government can only very seldom be seen as fully applying the majority principle. Other arguments are equally important. To Rousseau, for example, direct democracy is necessary for true freedom, because one is only free when obeying a law which oneself has 'willed'. As, according to Rousseau, one cannot delegate one's will, it follows that no law in the making of which one has not directly shared can be obeyed without a loss of freedom. A somewhat similar argument is that direct involvement in politics, listening to and joining in debate and voting, has an educative influence. People are seen as coming to understand their own and others' needs more clearly, and to grow in personality and morality through direct participation in decision-making and law-creating. This idea is shared by some theorists of representative democracy, such as John Stuart **Mill**, who emphasize the importance of local politics because such political activity comes nearer to direct democracy. At a less elevated level demands for direct democracy often arise out of a sheer mistrust of putting power in the hands of a few, often because of a feeling that hierarchy, even if it is supposed to be representative, inevitably becomes corrupt. It is not necessarily the case that advocates of direct democracy as a legislative process also insist on full and equal participation in decision-making at the stage of executing policy—indeed Rousseau clearly sees the **executive** as separate from the mass meeting of all citizens that legislates. However, the only arenas where direct democracy is at all widely practised, for example colleges or clubs, usually do not have a clear distinction between legislating and executing.

The problems are fairly obvious. If all citizens are to share fully in decision-making, the society must be very small indeed. Classical Athens could only manage to employ the system because, at its height, the free adult male citizenry probably numbered no more than 20,000, and because most people seldom took up their rights. A second major technical problem is that, unless the society is to be very simple, and operate at a very low technology level, the time consumed in policy-making would prohibit all those who had to work full time from any serious use of their rights to participate. No political system today comes anywhere near operating direct democracy at the national level, nor has one ever done so. At times, local government may have approached this system (the Town Meetings of early New England states are the best example, while newly-democratic Hungary introduced measures for regular consultation at the local level, although the low participation rate in most parts of the democratic process suggested that there was no great enthusiasm for them). However, the cry for direct democracy is being increasingly heard, and increasingly answered, in the running of institutions. Universities, political parties and to some extent industrial plants (see **industrial democracy**) are subject to the demands for such governance, as part of the more general value attached to participation throughout the developed world.

Directed Democracy

Directed democracy, also called guided democracy, is a term sometimes used to justify the absence of anything remotely resembling Western **representative democracy** in developing countries. It was first formulated in the 1960s by the Pakistani leader Ayub Khan, who ruled with the support of the army. It is in many ways analogous to the Marxist concept of the leading role of the communist party during the transitional period known as the **dictatorship of the proletariat**. It rests fundamentally on the argument that the people in a newly-independent Third World country cannot be allowed full participation in electoral politics because they are in no position to make rational political choices. For practical reasons such as lack of general education (if not mass illiteracy) and poor communications, and also because of possible ideological hangovers from colonial times, it may be feared that the people could be easily led astray by reactionary elements. Alternatively they might demand far more in the way of economic benefits than their country could afford, especially at a time when sacrifices might well be needed to build up heavy industry and to create a capital base for the later consumer industry. The idea of directed democracy does allow for some participation: people may join the one permitted party, or it may even be the case that other parties are allowed to exist and to have views on policy, provided they refrain from challenging the decisions ultimately taken in the public interest by 'those who know best'. Some of the European communist states, notably what was the German Democratic Republic (East Germany), were never technically one-party states, for example, but were governed by a permanent coalition dominated by the Communist Party. The stated intention in most directed democracies is that eventually, as barriers to rational participation diminish and economic conditions improve, the people will be 'guided' into a democracy that can function effectively. Though the terminology is seldom used nowadays, most military regimes make very similar claims to justify their rule.

Directive

Directives are, generally, orders given by an authority to a subordinate branch of an organization, instructing the lower branch to carry out some task. Such directives set goals and outline procedures, but leave the details to the agency or division responsible. In current language a directive is likely to refer to a pronouncement of the Commission of the **European Union (EU)**. Directives have been issued in many areas, including pollution control, workers' rights and control over the road haulage industry. In EU law the Commission has the right to issue directives to member states, instructing them to pass legislation to achieve the required end, but the directive does not affect the laws of the countries to which it is addressed until that legislation is passed (whereas an EU **regulation** is directly applicable without any need for national legislation). However, the **European Court of Justice (ECJ)**, impatient at national governments which do nothing about issues where a directive would be unpopular, has begun to develop the argument of 'direct effect'; directives which are sufficiently clear and specific may in fact generate rights and duties inside the legal system of a member state, even if that country's government has passed no specific legislation. Thus, in a hypothetical case, a directive instructing governments to ensure that no one should be subject to more than some specified level of lead poisoning from car exhausts might enable a British citizen to sue the government if they are systematically subject to much higher levels because the government has done nothing to institute the aims of the directive. The problem is that it is virtually impossible to predict whether or not a directive will be deemed by the ECJ to have this characteristic of direct effectiveness. As the debate on **federalism** in Europe continues there may be increasing pressure to reduce the applicability of the direct effect doctrine because it seems to undermine national **sovereignty**.

Discrimination

Discrimination in politics refers to the singling out—usually for unfavourable treatment—of certain groups which are defined by such characteristics as race, language, gender or religion. As a practice it is endemic in most societies; but during the 20th century, especially in the aftermath of the Nazi Holocaust, most democracies made serious efforts to combat it through legislation and judicial decisions. Reverse or positive discrimination (see **affirmative action**) has sometimes been adopted, and it has been suggested that in some circumstances (for example in the hiring of academics in the USA) it actually became be an advantage to be a member of a hitherto disadvantaged group.

In non-democratic societies official discrimination is still common. In Iran under the Khomeini regime, for example, many people were executed simply for belonging to faiths other than the Shi'ite form of Islam. In South Africa the systematic incorporation of racial discrimination into the laws of a state with a tradition of Christian and Western political values made it an object of widespread suspicion and dislike, and the ultimate abolition of **apartheid** was to a large extent a reaction to this international opprobrium. It is an open question whether the state can do much to prevent *de facto* discrimination in private economic and social relations, because the legal and administrative machinery has to be very complex, and discrimination can be extremely difficult to prove. Where such control has been tried, notably in the USA, it has only been partially successful.

Dissent

While dissent obviously means disagreement, its political usage usually means a strongly held opposition on moral grounds by a forceful minority against an important law, or influential idea, equally strongly supported by the majority. Dissent is often applied to issues like a state's foreign or military policy, or to issues traditionally seen as evoking moral outrage such as **abortion**, capital punishment or interference with religious freedom. Alternatively dissent may be towards the entire basis of a state and how it operates, in which case dissenters do not accept the basic **legitimacy** of the state. The noun 'dissenter' has a long history in political theory, probably originally meaning someone who opposes a religious orthodoxy, and came to be applied to, among others, opponents of the regime in totalitarian societies such as the former Soviet Union.

Divine Right

The divine right of kings to rule their realms was a vital political and theological doctrine in medieval Europe, and political theorists as late as Bodin (1530–96) and Hooker (1554–1600) were more or less committed to the doctrine. To some extent it lay behind the Royalist position during the English Civil War, and was finally killed off largely because of the victory of the Parliamentary forces in that war. The argument, which was useful both to the churches and to **monarchies**, developed as a result of the mutual need of the spiritual forces in European society and the monarchial dynasties for a concordat on their relative positions. In return for the ideological defence given them by the Church's imprimatur, kings were expected to defend and support the Roman Catholic Church and its doctrine with physical force, and to leave the regulation of religion and morals entirely to the Pope and his bishops.

The doctrine derived from various theological sources and political occasions, but it is not particularly unusual, in as much as some connection between the right to political power and a religious role is anthropologically common. Indeed, the precedent for the medieval European version stems originally from the dual rule of the early Roman emperors as both gods and rulers, while the combination of tribal chief with archpriesthood is a more general example of this political need for a spiritual backing. Only after defeat in the Second World War did the Japanese emperor abdicate his status as a god. The problem is simply that there is a very restricted number of ways in which one can justify the right of one person to rule over others, and in entirely non-secular societies, with a united and powerful church wielding vital symbols of eternal life or damnation, no ideological claim exists other than one tied to God's purposes for man. It is notable that the first commonly-accepted political theories to use some other form of justification arose in England after the Reformation and the Civil War had made any appeal to such united and powerful religious symbols more dangerous than useful. Until the Reformation few would have doubted that there were two spheres of influence in a society, the religious power and the secular, and that the secular only gained its authority because it was needed to back up the Church, to create the environment in which man could lead a good life. This, the best-argued version of the doctrine, was set out most fully in St **Augustine's** *City of God*.

Division of Labour

Division of labour is the system under which both economic production and other, especially administrative or policy-making, tasks are handled in all modern societies. It is a system contrasted to craftsmanship or to generalized political and social leadership, and it involves the splitting up and distribution of different parts of any job among several people. In a modern manufacturing enterprise, for example, not only the manufacture of a car, but even of a simple object like a pen, may be subdivided into hundreds of very minor tasks, done repetitively by many people, over and over again, with none of them actually being responsible for creating the whole unit. Many social theorists, but especially **Durkheim** and **Marx**, the latter notably in his theory of **alienation**, have attached great importance to the division of labour as a causal factor in social development. Although the division of labour is the corner-stone of modern economic productivity, it is held to have a seriously deleterious impact on human self-confidence and inter-personal relations by such theorists. (Though in fact Durkheim also thought it to be crucial for social solidarity.) In other theories, however, it is seen as a necessary aspect of development and modernization, and in its political coverage is almost a definitional element of theories of **political development** and political modernization. In fact the division of productive tasks seems to have been integral to all known societies, though in primitive societies the distribution of tasks was often on a gender basis. The very earliest of Western political theory assumed automatically that anything larger than a tiny subsistence economy would require specific tasks to be carried out full time by particular individuals, and the theories of both **Plato** and **Aristotle** rest much on this form of organization.

Djilas

Milovan Djilas (1911–95) was born in Montenegro and from an early age was a senior member of the **politburo** of the Yugoslav communist party, fighting with it from 1940 when it was an underground organization. He became a minister in Tito's communist government at the time Tito was managing so successfully to develop Yugoslavia's independent position *vis-à-vis* Moscow. However, Djilas represented just too well the spirit of autonomy inside the liberal communism of Tito's Yugoslavia, and began to be a serious critic of communist governments—and was imprisoned for most of the period 1956–66. His most important work by far is his book, published in 1953, *The New Class*. Here he argues that the sort of **Bolshevik** revolution carried out in the name of the people by an authoritarian Leninist party, either that of Russia in 1917, or like the communist governments set up by the Soviet Union in Eastern Europe after the Second World War, had a fatal flaw. Instead of producing a classless society, the ultimate goal of communism, by abolishing private property, they had instead developed a **new class** system, every bit as exploitative and undemocratic as those of the past. The new class consisted of the party officials, the managers of the nationalized industries, and those bureaucrats whom the rapidly growing state planning and administrative machinery had come to require. These people, and especially the ones near the top of the tree, were the only ones in the communist states to have any power. They used the repressive forces of the state, especially the secret police, to ensure total obedience, and their control over education and media to secure much more acquiescence to their version of a ruling ideology than had any previous state. At the same time they enjoyed a standard of living vastly higher than ordinary members of society, and were able to pass on this privilege to their children. Even though they could not legally own much more than any ordinary citizen, access to high quality education and easy entrance to prestige jobs guaranteed their children the same status that they possessed themselves, and denied it to others. Most of his analysis was entirely correct, and would be accepted by modern Western analysts. It was the public perception of this that fuelled much of the revolutionary fervour which brought down the East European communist societies in 1989–91. Even then, for example in East Germany, the public was shocked when the full extent of privilege enjoyed by the party rulers became clear.

Djilas' particular prescriptions for solving the problems, which involve a great extension of participation and **direct democracy**, which had been more extensively practised in Yugoslavia then elsewhere may, however, be less easily accepted. Orthodox Soviet communists, and some Western Marxists, have refused to accept that these privileges, even if true, constitute a class, on the largely definitional grounds that only outright ownership of the means of production make a society class-based. It is arguable that there is a dangerous loss of theoretical precision in treating any privileged stratum as a class. Djilas did not give up being a Marxist, and should not be read as saying that a classless communist society is impossible, nor, perhaps, even denying its ultimate inevitability. Rather he was doing no more than extending with hindsight and more experience the criticisms that many of Lenin's contemporaries had made.

Doomsday

The idea of a doomsday machine is an intellectual exercise in modern strategic thinking used to clarify certain points in nuclear war theory. The ideal doomsday machine would be a super-bomb triggered to go off automatically if the country which built it was to suffer a serious nuclear attack. As the name is meant to imply, the destruction caused by this bomb would be so total that the aggressor nation would be eliminated totally (as would all others). The point is to take **mutual assured destruction** to its logical conclusion, because a doomsday machine would make it impossible for any nation ever to risk triggering nuclear war.

Although manifestly absurd (though not technologically impossible), the concept acts as a limiting factor in **deterrence** theory. Some proposals that have been seriously made approach these limits. An example is a suggestion of how to control the US Navy's strategic nuclear submarine fleet. The technical problems of communication with an under-sea fleet, especially after a possible attack that may have wiped out the national command and control centres, have always worried planners. One suggestion was that a continuous signal should be transmitted to these submarines, on the cessation of which their captains should automatically launch an attack on the enemy (which was, in the context of the development of the idea, the Soviet Union). This, by making retaliation quite automatic, would have the doomsday effect. The phrase was made popular by the film *Dr Strangelove*, a biting satire on nuclear strategy.

Doves (see Hawks and Doves)

Downs

Anthony Downs (1930–) was an American political scientist in the 1950s (he has since left academic life and become a millionaire), who was responsible for starting an entirely new line of research in politics with just one book, *An Economic Theory of Democracy*. At a time when most empirical research was influenced by sociology and psychology, this argued for the use of models and assumptions drawn from economics in analysing political behaviour. The difference is far from trivial. Downs' approach, which came to be known as the **rational choice theory**, is based on taking 'political man' as a creature who seeks to achieve maximum satisfaction through choices based on rational calculation—just as 'economic man' does. This contrasts sharply with approaches that play down the role of rationality in favour of a political model of human behaviour much closer to the psychologist's stimulus response view of man. Downs showed that much of the behaviour of voters and political parties in Western democracies could be explained very satisfactorily by a few simple assumptions of this rational choice sort. Subsequent work, mainly in the USA and Britain, has considerably developed the theory, and has produced formulations which even have a certain predictive value. There are several reasons for this drive to make political science more like economics, not least being the fact that economics is the most successful and highly-developed of the social sciences, or at least was seen as such before the **Keynesian** monopoly of economic theory collapsed in the 1970s. Furthermore, many political scientists have disliked the patronizing attitude implicit in the assumption that mass political behaviour is a-rational, if not positively irrational. Perhaps most important of all, the Anglo-American tradition of political theory from **Hobbes** to **utilitarianism** and beyond has mainly been based on an assumption of human rationality. Turning empirical research and empirical theory in this direction offers the best chance of uniting the two main traditions in political science, divided since the **behavioural** revolution which at one time seemed likely to lead to the demise of **political theory**. Unlike most political theory, Downsian models have repeatedly been tested in research on European and American politics with considerable success. Indeed the rational choice analysis he pioneered has become almost totally accepted as a paradigm for explaining much of political science.

Due Process

Due process involves a guarantee that an individual who is accused of a crime or faced with legal action will have the opportunity to see that the charges or claims against them are determined by proper legal procedures, without bias, and in open court. The notion of due process may be assimilated to that of procedural fairness, and in the United Kingdom it is implemented by the judiciary who have, since the 1960s, done much to extend the scope of the doctrine in administrative cases (see **administrative courts**).

In the USA due process is a constitutional right available against both the federal and state governments, although the extent to which state governments were subject to the doctrine was not fully settled until the 1950s. Exactly what specific rights are entailed by due process is not necessarily clear in any particular case. Perhaps the best summary definition was given by the US Supreme Court judge, Benjamin Cardozo, who claimed that due process involved whatever was necessary to 'any concept of ordered liberty'. At a minimum it would involve, for example, the right to legal representation, but this right might not always extend to having a lawyer paid for by the state for those too poor to afford one, or a right to challenge the composition of a jury, but not necessarily to exclude jurors on any particular ground. Most Western legal systems have some equivalent to the idea of due process—in Britain it would probably be called 'natural justice'—but nowhere outside the USA has it been so powerful a political challenge to authorities. However, developments in Europe under the influence of the European Court of Human Rights sometimes approach the US standard.

Durkheim

Emile Durkheim (1858–1917), along with **Marx** and **Weber**, was one of the great founding fathers of modern social science. He took as his main task the explanation of the changes that overcame societies with the development of the Industrial Revolution and the change from traditional or feudal society to the sort of liberal **capitalism** current in most developed countries today. His work covered an enormous range, encompassing sociological theory, research methodology, and empirical observation. Apart from Marxists, it is probable that the vast majority of modern sociologists would see at least something of Durkheim in their own intellectual approach. Although he wrote little that was directly and obviously about politics, most of what he has to say is suffused with political importance. Methodologically his position was that individual motivations and feelings were irrelevant to the social scientist, because society was something with a real existence of its own, over and above the individual members who were largely formed by the social structure. Thus social facts were to be explained by other social facts, not by investigating individual human experiences.

A good example of this was his classic study of suicide in which suicide rates in various areas were explained by, *inter alia,* the rates of affiliation to different religions. Thus a highly personal act, self-slaughter, was turned into social fact, and explained in a structural manner. Perhaps his most important work, as far as political implications go, was his study of the breakdown of social regulation and normative order in modern capitalist societies characterized by a high degree of **division of labour**. This led both to his investigation of **anomie** (with important similarities to Marx's idea of **alienation**), and to the development of a theory of **corporatist** politics which was taken over and misused by later **fascist** dictatorships. He is probably the most important precursor of **functionalist** social theory, which enjoyed a great influence in post-war social science, and he has stamped modern French social science deeply with his views and methodology. There are probably few main line sociologists nowadays influenced by Durkheim rather than his rival Max Weber, but Durkheim's influence is felt increasingly strongly in cultural studies.

E

Effectiveness of Government

The question of the effectiveness of government has come to worry many Western governments. Many observers, frequently conservative politicians, claim that the modern **state** is in a parlous condition as a result of what some writers have termed 'governmental overload'. This is said to have resulted from government intervention in areas of social and economic life where it is unable to make any real impact on the substantive problems; the negative by-products include increasing public expenditure and the arousal of a widespread popular cynicism at unfulfilled expectations. In the USA the 'Great Society' years, 1964–68, under President Lyndon B. Johnson, saw a major expansion of the federal government's role in social policy, but this was followed by a reaction based on the observation that poverty seemed as pervasive as ever and some problems (for example crime) even seemed to have become more acute. The resulting mood of scepticism about the role of the federal government (see **neo-conservatism**) led to an unwillingness to spend public money without good evidence that it would make a measurable difference to the problem involved. From desire for visible effectiveness of government comes reluctance to embark on attempts to resolve problems in difficult policy areas, such as social and health matters, and preference that responsibility for these be transferred to agencies and organizations beyond direct government control. Meanwhile, foreign policy problems which seemed to offer a highly visible and positive result over a predictable time period came to be accepted with some eagerness. This broad distinction between the approaches towards two entirely different policy areas illustrates the general dislike for incrementalism, the gradual introduction of minor adjustments to policy with their results continuously monitored, and the favouring of ambitious, wide-ranging total solutions to a problem. However the world-wide acceptance of the limitations of state action which came about when European Socialist parties largely abandoned **social democracy** in favour of something like the UK's **New Labour** or **Third Way** policies has made all governments more modest in their aims and expectations. Furthermore the enthusiasm for foreign policy has abated with the late 20th century's experience of Western governments finding external commitments deeply entangling.

Egalitarianism

Egalitarianism is the doctrine that all citizens of a state should be accorded exactly equal rights and privileges. However, there are many conflicting interpretations of what this commitment means in practice. Three major strands of thought can usefully be identified. Firstly, egalitarianism certainly means that all political rights should be the same for all adult human beings. In terms of access to politics, the suffrage and equality before the law, no social, religious, ethnic or other criterion should be allowed to produce inequality. This is the minimum definition of egalitarianism, and is accepted in theory, and usually in practice, in most Western democracies and many other types of state. Secondly, egalitarianism may also be held to involve **equality of opportunity**, which implies that, regardless of the socio-economic situation into which someone is born, they will have the same chance as everybody else to develop their talents and acquire qualifications, and that when they apply for jobs their case will be considered entirely on the basis of such talents and qualifications, rather than, for example, on the type of school attended or their parents' social status. This requires, at the very least, an educational and social welfare system which will train and provide for the less-advantaged so that they can really compete on equal terms with those from more favourable backgrounds. While no modern state can be said actually to achieve this goal, many seriously attempt to do so, and all would probably pay lip service to the idea. Increasingly governments committed to equality of opportunity plans are finding their strategies thwarted not by non-compliance by institutions, but by a lack of enthusiasm for advanced education on the part of those the governments seek to help. Thirdly, the most stringent version of egalitarianism would require not just equal opportunities, but actual equality in material welfare and, perhaps, political weight. Such total equality is not regarded as even theoretically possible, let alone desirable, by most states. In communist societies, where it had been accepted as an aim, it invariably became conspicuously absent (see **new class**). Most non-Marxist thinkers argue that such an equality could only be attained by extensive loss of liberty, and would be economically inefficient since it would provide no material incentives to effort.

Election

An election is a method of choosing among candidates for some post or office, and elections have become the only fully respectable method for selecting political leaders and governors throughout the world. Even a country which is universally known to be a **dictatorship** or **military regime** will frequently use fraudulent elections to disguise their actual mechanisms for political selection.

Elections can be carried out by a wide variety of techniques. Votes can be given to individuals, as in most national elections, to collective entities (for example national delegations to the **United Nations**) or to institutional units (for example **trade union** branches). The **voting** procedure may be secret, public or even recorded and published, as in many legislative assemblies. Votes may be counted according to any one of a dozen or more methods ranging from varieties of pure **proportional representation** to the simplest 'first-past-the-post' plurality system (see **voting systems**). All that elections have in common is that they are a method of selecting one or more candidates for office from a wider field by aggregating the individual preferences and counting them. Historically, elections have been only one among many methods of selection, and they became the totally dominant method only in the 20th century. There is no necessary connection between elections and **democracy**, for even monarchies have been elective, and the selection of leaders in one-party states involves election, though the effective electorate is likely to consist of a handful of leading party figures, even if their choice is then submitted to a confirming 'popular' election. In fact elections will occur whenever selection does not depend on the will of a single person, force, or some special concept of **legitimacy**.

Electoral College

An electoral college is a group of people who have been specially appointed, nominated or elected in order that they should hold an election for a political office. It thus constitutes a way of making election to some significant position of power indirect rather than direct. The most important example of a modern electoral college is perhaps that which elects the American president. Lists of electors tied to particular presidential and vice-presidential candidatures appear on the ballot paper, and once the votes have been counted the list with the most votes on a simple plurality basis takes all that state's electoral college votes. The candidates with a majority in the electoral college become president and vice-president respectively. If no candidature has an overall majority in the electoral college the House of Representatives then votes, by state, to determine who is to become president, and the Senate, voting as individuals, elects the vice-president. So complete is the domination of US politics by the **Democratic Party** and the **Republican Party** that the most any third-party candidate, such as Ralph Nader or Ross Perot, is likely to achieve is to deprive both principal candidates of a majority in the election and thus force the election into the House: however, it is rare for such candidates even to win any seats in the college.

The states are not equally represented in the US electoral college. Each state is allocated the same number of electors as it has members of the House of Representatives, plus two (although the District of Columbia, with no House representation, receives three electoral college votes, and Delaware and North Dakota, with one House seat, receive only two electoral college votes). Thus a state with two House members would get four votes and a state with 30 House members would get 32 votes. This system of course tends to under-represent the more populous and over-represent the less populous states. The US electoral college never meets as a body, since the electors of each state assemble at their own state capital and cast their votes there.

Criticism of the electoral college surfaces regularly in the USA, and two major arguments are frequently levelled against it. Firstly, because it was devised as a method of protecting the presidency from the excesses of popular government, it has come to seem anachronistically undemocratic. For this reason many liberals in the USA are in favour of direct election of the president, while many conservatives, who argue that the founding fathers of the US Constitution stressed the country's being a **republic**, while not mentioning democracy *per se*, are anxious to retain the college. Secondly, the fact that the votes are distributed on a winner-take-all basis means that the candidature which wins a large state such as California or Texas by the slenderest of margins will gain an enormous advantage, since it will collect all the electoral college votes for that state. There is certainly an element of suspicion of **direct democracy** in the system, and it does to some extent distort the popular vote. Indeed, it is possible for the electoral college to consist of electors favouring a candidature which was not favoured by a majority, or indeed even a plurality, of voters in the election to the college itself. It is not unusual for a presidential candidate with a lead of only a few per cent in the total vote to collect an overwhelming number of electoral college votes. Most Americans were themselves only vaguely conscious of the role of the electoral college until the debate surrounding the election of President George W. Bush in 2001. This firmly brought home the counter-majoritarian impact the electoral college can have, and that part of the constitution is now seriously in doubt.

In the United Kingdom an electoral college featured in the controversial reform of the **Labour Party's** method of electing its leader. Prior to 1981 the leader was elected by the votes of the parliamentary Labour Party alone; then, as a result of a concerted movement to give the extra-parliamentary elements in the Labour Party greater control over policy, it was agreed that trade unions and constituency parties should also participate in leadership elections. The electoral college was expected to give the predominant voice to members of parliament (MPs), but in fact the special conference called to set up the new machinery voted for a system which gave MPs 30% of the electoral college vote, the trade unions 40% and the constituency parties the remaining 30%. The method was first used to elect a new leader, Neil Kinnock, in 1983, since when there has been further argument that the party should move to a more direct method of election. Electoral colleges, not necessarily under that name, have been common; until 1962, for example, the French president was so elected. As political cultures move further towards the idea that only mass participation in decision-making is really acceptable, such devices for restricting popular influence on choice are likely to decline. The **Conservative Party** later moved to a form of election not dissimilar to an electoral college because the full membership can only vote on the referred candidates of the parliamentary party.

Electoral Systems (see Voting Systems)

Élitism

Élitism (or élitist theory) is a rather loose term used to describe a variety of political theories. What all the theories have in common is the conviction that every political system, whatever its official **ideology**, is in fact ruled by a political élite or élites. The originators of modern élitist theory were two late 19th-century Italian social scientists, **Pareto** and Mosca. (Which of the two devised the élitist theory was the subject of an argument between the two men themselves that was continued by later commentators.) In showing that all societies must be governed by élites, Pareto and Mosca intended to destroy the belief in **Marxism** that there could one day be a classless society with complete political equality; ironically, writers with a Marxist perspective subsequently used much the same model to dismiss the democratic pretensions of Western liberal societies. Whereas Pareto treated contemporary democracy as a complete sham, Mosca changed his position over time, eventually accepting that democracy was possible in the form of a system in which competing élites submitted to being chosen or rejected by electors. However, he never moved far from his main position, summed up in his statement that a parliamentary representative was not someone the people had elected, but someone whose friends had arranged for him to be elected.

Élitist theories were developed further in the early 20th century by several thinkers, notably **Schumpeter** and one of Mosca's disciples, Roberto Michels. Setting out his **iron law of oligarchy**, Michels tried to show that even the Social Democratic Party of Germany (SPD), the oldest socialist party in Europe, was inherently undemocratic, and bound to betray its working-class members. In the 1930s Schumpeter mapped out what was to become, with **Dahl** and others, the **pluralist** model. He reinterpreted democracy as nothing more than a system in which rival élites of party leaders vied for power through elections; but, far from condemning this state of affairs, he insisted that ordinary people could not, and indeed should not, have any more say in politics than this power of electoral choice. (Much later **Downs**, in his rational choice model of party politics, tried to show that this did not affect the democratic nature of Western politics.) From the left, many commentators have attempted to show that Western democracies are indeed governed by power élites, or élites based on a ruling class, and are thoroughly undemocratic; but such commentators of course retain their conviction that an abolition of capitalism will lead to political equality.

The various élite theorists share no common ground when attempting to explain the inevitability of élites. Pareto had a complicated psychological theory, linked with a pessimistic view of the human capacity to exercise reason in social life; Mosca and Michels relied heavily on a theory about the nature of organization and **bureaucracy** quite similar to **Weber's**; Schumpeter believed the masses were bound to suffer from the hysteria associated with crowd psychology; and the list could be extended. There is no general agreement among political scientists about the factual accuracy of élite theories or the desirability of the situation they describe. There are, though, few who would care to deny that there is at least some evidence for the existence of élites, if only the relatively sanitized version developed by pluralists, and the less far-reaching claims of writers like Michels in his classic *Political Parties* find considerable support from much later and less biased research.

Emergency Powers

Emergency powers are special powers granted to a government or executive agency which allow normal legislative procedures and/or judicial remedies to be by-passed or suspended. In democracies such emergency powers are usually strictly controlled by the **legislature** and are permitted only for the duration of the emergency. Although the primary association of emergency powers legislation is with wartime, or a national security crisis of similar dimensions, governments in fact retain some such powers for domestic crises. Indeed Edward Heath's Conservative government of 1970–74 declared five states of emergency to deal with industrial unrest, and an Act of 1976 makes permanent provision for the use of the armed forces to undertake work of national importance if, for example, those who would normally carry out such work are involved in an industrial dispute or strike.

Northern Ireland's internal conflicts have generated additional emergency legislation which gives the government power to proscribe organizations and exclude individuals from the United Kingdom. (Although the ultimate power, that of suspending rule from Belfast and administering the province directly from London cannot properly be regarded as an emergency power in this sense.) In France, emergency powers may be exercised under Article 16 of the 1958 constitution (see **Fifth Republic**) by the president, although the president must consult the prime minister, the presidents of the Senate and the National Assembly, and the Constitutional Council before declaring a state of emergency. These powers were in fact used only once, during the period April to September 1961, at the time of the Algerian War of Independence, and this caused considerable political controversy, especially over the powers which parliament might continue to exercise. In the USA emergency powers can, and have, been taken; although the US constitution makes no reference to such emergency powers, President Abraham Lincoln suspended the right of *habeas corpus* during the Civil War, and President Franklin Roosevelt interned Japanese-Americans during the Second World War, and in neither case was any problem incurred with the legislature or courts.

In non-democratic countries emergency powers are frequently referred to as states of siege, and all civil liberties are suspended; one of many examples is the period following the military coup in Chile in 1973.

Engels

Friedrich Engels (1820–95) was the son of a prosperous German industrialist whose business interests extended to cotton mills in Manchester, where Engels spent 20 years of his life and witnessed conditions that greatly influenced his loathing for capitalism. Although attracted in his youth to the rather vague romantic radicalism of the Young Hegelians, he realized the vital importance of economics and began to think of history and philosophy in terms of **materialism** somewhat earlier than the man who later became his lifelong friend, Karl **Marx**. Indeed, Engels introduced Marx to many of the ideas that the latter made so thoroughly his own. So Engels was not only the great popularizer of **Marxism**, but should also be recognized as the originator of much that has entered the Marxist canon. In particular, Engels was a first-class empirical observer, and documents such as *The Condition of the Working Class in England* contain brilliant analyses. The most popular and earliest of the great Marxist writings, *The Communist Manifesto*, was drafted by Engels and only revised by Marx. A theoretically more complex work attacking the rest of the Hegelian movement, *The German Ideology*, which is the backbone of Marxist views on social consciousness, was written by Marx and Engels jointly. Late in his life, mostly after Marx's death in 1883, Engels became closely involved with the Social Democratic Party of Germany (SPD) and fought a bitter campaign against the **revisionism** of its reformist wing. His attack in 1878 on the intellectual leader of that faction, Eugen Dühring, entitled simply *Anti-Dühring*, became perhaps the most important vehicle through which Marxism as a doctrine reached the next generation of young socialists, which included the leaders of the Russian Revolution. Engels had himself been actively involved in revolutionary activities in 1848, the great year of European revolutions, and throughout his life was associated with working-class movements and émigré revolutionary cadres. His intellectual interests were prodigious, and his writings spanned a large number of intellectual disciplines, though Marxists have always considered his greatest service to socialism to be his editing of Marx's last great work, *Das Kapital*.

Enlightenment

The Enlightenment is a conventional label in the history of ideas used to cover a set of theories and attitudes developing just before and after the French Revolution, though some would date the Enlightenment as occupying the whole period from the middle of the 17th century to the end of the 18th. Its political importance stems from the way it has influenced most subsequent political thought, partly in terms of its actual content, but as much simply by destroying earlier political assumptions that had reigned throughout the early and medieval periods of European political history. Although the Enlightenment was a broad movement involving many strands of thought, it is associated particularly with writers like **Rousseau**, Diderot and the other authors of the French *Encyclopedia* ,and, in Britain, with **Hume**, and, stretching the definition slightly, with **Hobbes** and **Locke**.

The Enlightenment creed stressed the possibility of man's own intellect planning a society on rational grounds, and denied, therefore, the traditional authority of Kings and the Church. Freedom, especially of thought, and co-operative human behaviour were the high points of the philosophy, which was, on the whole, optimistic about human nature where the prevailing, religiously-derived, notion of man was pessimistic, accepting the Christian doctrine of Original Sin. In many ways Enlightenment social thought was developed on an analogy with physical science, seeking almost mathematically perfect designs for society. The major importance was, indeed, the rejection of received authority, especially that of the Church, rather than any particular specific doctrine.

Some have thought Rousseau to be responsible for the French Revolution, because he argued that men could be, were originally, but were not now, free, and that this freedom, possible only in an egalitarian society, could be grasped by modern man if only the chains of traditional expectation could be thrown off. In contrast to the conservative doctrines that were developed by, for example, **Burke** in opposition to this movement, the Enlightenment put great emphasis on the power of independent human thought, and may well be seen as the precursor of modern **liberalism** and **socialism**, especially in writers like John Stuart **Mill** and others in the tradition of **utilitarianism**. A later Enlightenment thinker, **Kant**, summed up the entire spirit of the movement with his motto, the title of an article he wrote, *Sapere Aude* ('Dare to Know'). Kant, **Hegel** and **Marx** followed the more continental aspect of the theories originating in Rousseau that have led to the contemporary European socialist position, while James **Mill**, **Bentham** and J. S. Mill developed Hume's British version of the position into **liberalism**. There was, however, an important reaction to the challenges and threats of the Enlightenment, found in Britain with the moderate **conservatism** of Burke, but in Europe in a more sinister, more reactionary trend of thought among those such as De Maistre, and, innocently, among social theorists like **Durkheim** that may be seen as a precursor position to **fascism**. The modern radical intellectual movement originating in France, often described as '**post-modernism**' has in fact taken the Enlightenment as its great enemy, regarding it as a prime example of hubris.

Entryism

Entryism was an acquisition into political vocabulary in the 1970s, though it covered a far from new phenomenon. It referred then to the attempts by members of extreme political movements to join, and take control of, more moderate and established political parties. In Britain in the late 1970s and 1980s some people believed that far-left political activists had 'entered' constituency Labour Parties, in the hope of winning control of the local party executives and thus influencing candidate selection and policy formulation at the annual party conferences. The waves of expulsions from the **Labour Party** of members of, for example, the Militant Tendency in the 1980s and early 1990s would seem to support this thesis. The phenomenon is not limited to an attempted take-over of the moderate left by the extreme left. In the United Kingdom, allegations have been made that some Conservative, and even some Liberal, constituency parties have sometimes come under the influence of 'entryists' from the far right. As a political tactic it is as old as politics.

Environmentalism

Environmentalism started to emerge as a distinct political concern in Western politics during the 1960s and 1970s; since then the movement has developed considerably towards the establishment of a coherent political force, and is widely regarded as a legitimate alternative to all the traditional political parties. Broadly, environmentalism refers to a political stance in which economic growth is regarded as much less important than the protection of standards often referred to as 'the quality of life'. In practice environmentalists tend to be in favour of pollution controls, even if these reduce economic productivity, and, in general, opposed to the development of new extractive industries, nuclear power and large-scale industrial expansion. Several European countries now have well-organized environmentalist parties, often referred to or titled Green, which regularly attain as much as 5% of the vote at general elections and, where the **voting system** allows, achieve minor representation in legislative chambers. For example, Die Grünen (the German Green party, founded in 1980) maintained a particularly high profile in the 1980s and, at Länder (state) level has even shared power with the Social Democratic Party of Germany (SPD). In the United Kingdom the Green Party (founded as the Ecology Party in 1973, changing its name in 1985) has never won any but the most minor elections, largely due to the first-past-the-post system; nevertheless, at the 1989 elections to the European Parliament, the party was the beneficiary of one of the British electorate's periodic 'protest' votes, gaining 15% of the vote and outpolling the traditional third party, the Liberal Democrats, before returning to figures of 1%–2% in opinion polls. In Eastern Europe, environmentalist groups were at the forefront of opposition to the crumbling communist regimes, and the subsequent revelations of widespread pollution on an even greater scale than realized previously confirmed the potential force of single issue politics when the need is sufficiently great. So great was opposition to the environmental damage done by these regimes that some of the successor states have written environmental rights into their constitutions.

Although a concern for environmentalist values in itself hardly constitutes an organized set of policies for governing a society, many other policies which have a psychological rather than logical link to the central concern are espoused. Thus policies like **industrial democracy**, liberalization of laws on private morality, and often a considerable degree of **pacifism**, are associated politically with the main ecological-protection thrust (see **green socialism**). At its most fervent, environmentalism becomes a considered economic-technological policy of opposition to economic growth and commitment to a much simpler and less materially-affluent socio-economic system, through well-argued fears of depletion of world resources. However, since the 1980s parties across the political spectrum, perhaps alerted equally by the growing popularity of environmental groupings and the warnings of long-term ecological damage from scientists, have adopted 'green' policies. For the environmentalist parties, the result of this, together with the reluctance of the vast majority of those in modern developed societies to voluntarily accept a decline in material wealth, will probably be that they never achieve any considerable degree of political power in their own right. At the turn of the century environmentalism even developed its own political extreme, closely allied by anarchist movements, who took, often violent, direct action against world economic leaders at several G-8 summits. (See also **new social movements**.)

Equal Protection

Equal protection is a term which describes the idea that the legal system should protect all citizens from arbitrary discrimination and guarantee them equal rights. Initially it seemed that this idea was very similar to the guarantees of procedural fairness and **due process** offered in many societies. In the 20th century, however, a distinction was increasingly made between, on the one hand, equal protection and simple procedural fairness, which offer a formal equality that may mean little where wealth, education and similar factors are unequal, and, on the other hand, substantive equal protection. In the USA in particular, the idea of equal protection became extended from a procedural guarantee to a fuller conception of equality, albeit in a limited and restricted field.

This guarantee is contained in the equal protection clause of the Fourteenth Amendment—an amendment which was passed in 1868 to protect all citizens (and especially former slaves) against the abridgement of their rights by state governments. Since the innovative era of Chief Justice Earl Warren (1953–69), the US Supreme Court has used this constitutional provision to eliminate various forms of racial discrimination and to promote its own view of constitutionally mandated standards in such areas as criminal law and desegregation (see **judicial review**). It was, for example, the equal protection clause that led to the desegregation of schools in the famous case of *Brown v Board of Education of Topeka* (1954), and which has been behind most court-led anti-discrimination actions—the equal protection clause has even led to the redrawing of constituency boundaries for congressional elections. Positive attempts to redress the effects of discriminations through, for example, **affirmative action**, have been most common in the USA. While other countries do have vestiges of such ideas, even major civil rights statements such as the European Convention on Human Rights (see **Human Rights Act**) tend to stress the procedural due process style of argument rather than the more substantively demanding equal protection approach. Despite this caveat, the programme of **Third Way** governments such as that in the United Kingdom from 1997, has concentrated strongly on anti-discrimination legislation which in some cases exceeds in its reach even the strongest US court decisions.

Equality of Opportunity

Increasingly, in most Western countries, during the 20th century it became accepted that individuals should not be impeded in their careers by such factors as their race, religion or sex. However, while Napoleon advocated the reform of French institutions by making career advancement dependent on skills and performance alone (see **egalitarianism**), in the United Kingdom, for example, recruitment for senior positions in the **civil service** was overwhelmingly from arts graduates from Oxford and Cambridge Universities, and printers' **trade unions** effectively barred entry to the trade to those without a suitable family connection, in both instances until well into the second half of the 20th century. In the 1960s sensitivity to various forms of discrimination became especially strong in both the USA and the UK, and such concerns were reflected from the outset in the Treaty of Rome establishing the European Economic Community, and have subsequently been taken seriously by both the European Commission and the European Court of Justice. In the 1960s and 1970s, Race Relations and Equal Pay Acts were passed making certain forms of racial and sex discrimination illegal. At the end of the century, these were strengthened further, and new legislation protecting the rights, for example, of the disabled, was introduced widely. In the USA the concept of equality of opportunity has become so accepted that all commercial and industrial firms, as well as public institutions, have to ensure that they can prove a good performance on appointments and promotions; indeed, steps have been taken to introduce **affirmative action** as a measure to redress previous inequalities. Meanwhile, in the UK, the issue of discrimination against women, and indeed against, for example, **homosexual** minorities, has been less central to political debate. Even this limitation is waning as industrial tribunals increasingly take a stronger and more assertive role in protecting women's rights, and the courts take notice of issues of sexual identity and orientation.

Escalation

Escalation is a term used in modern military **strategy**, especially nuclear war theory, which indicates an increasing violence or force in the response of a protagonist towards its enemy. Thus a war might start with purely conventional weapons (see **conventional arms**), and when one side finds itself doing badly, it might 'escalate' by using battlefield, or **tactical nuclear weapons**. At this point the other side might move to the same stage, or even to the use of major strategic nuclear weapons, thus 'escalating' the war further. The concept is very much based on the image of a ladder, with rungs representing different levels of force. Most strategic thought is concentrated on minimizing the 'escalating' tendencies of any particular policy, which has led to great emphasis being put on **flexible response**, as a replacement of the old idea of **massive retaliation**.

Established Church

Established churches are religious denominations which are given special legal rights and protection by the **state**, but are also to some extent controlled by the state. The usual example taken is the established church in England, which is the Anglican church, formally called the Church of England. The very fact that this title tells nothing at all about its theology or organization (it is, in fact, strictly speaking, Catholic and Episcopalian) but concentrates entirely on the geographical/political identity demonstrates the nature of established churches quite clearly. The state is directly involved in running the Church of England, with appointments to bishoprics being made by the prime minister, with the monarch officially the head of the church, and with legislation from the General Synod (for example, introducing women priests in 1992) requiring enactment by parliament and the monarch.

These facts have a perfectly natural political explanation arising from the political context of the Church of England's foundation in Tudor England and the subsequent Civil War and revolution of 1688, which led to a firm belief that religious orthodoxy was necessary for political stability, a point accepted by political theorists as different as **Hobbes** and **Rousseau**. However, the establishment of a religion has equally been seen as highly illiberal, and was one of the first things to be forbidden by the US Constitution, in the First Amendment (1791). This was quite probably influenced by **Locke's** *Letter on Toleration* (1689); the English philosopher's liberal principles and opposition to strong state power were generally influential in the drafting of the constitution.

Most codes of civil rights today mention freedom of religious persuasion, and while the establishment of one church does not preclude others, it can be seen as unduly favouring one denomination over others. Certainly a strong minority of priests and lay people in the Church of England feel uneasy and would prefer the Church to be disestablished, as it was in Scotland (in 1689), Ireland (1869) and Wales (1920). It may be quite unconnected, but much research in the sociology of religion has begun to show that competitive churches do better at fending off secularization than do established and therefore non-competitive religious institutions. England is by no means alone in having an established church—the Scandinavian countries have established Lutheranism, and indeed ministers there are actually paid by the state as civil servants, while orthodox Christianity of all denominations has a semi-established place in Germany, where the state assists them by levying a (voluntary) tax on their congregations. In practice it is not the formally established churches which now exert any important political influence, but those, whether the Roman Catholic Church in Italy, or versions of Islamic religion in, for example, Pakistan or Iran, that have a direct mass support with political overtones (see **theocracy**).

Ethnicity

Ethnicity refers to a sometimes rather complex combination of racial, cultural and historical characteristics by which human groups are sometimes divided into separate, and probably hostile, political families. At its simplest the idea is exemplified by racial groupings where skin colour alone is the separating characteristic. At its more refined one may be dealing with the sort of 'ethnic politics' as where, for example, Welsh or Scottish nationalists feel ethnically separated from the 'English' rulers, as they may see them, of their lands. Almost anything can be used to set up 'ethnic' divisions, though, after skin colour, the two most common, by far, are religion and language (see **language groups**). Although racial political divisions have always been vital where they exist, it is probably only in the post-war decades that other forms of ethnic politics have become commonly important, though this is not to say that the actual divisions have not been long established and of personal importance. It is important not to confuse fully blown ethnic politics with the mere existence of a voting cleavage based on, for example language, where linguistic differences raise concrete policy issues. There are, for example, crucial ethnicity problems in Belgium and Canada (mainly language conflicts, but with associated religious splits), Britain (historical-cultural divisions sometimes fought around language politics but also with religious connections and stemming from English domination over formerly independent areas), and remnants of such divisions in Scandinavian countries (mainly language again), to mention just a very small sample.

Ethnicity raises the whole socio-political question of national identity, which is why ethnic politics are often at their most virulent and important in **Third World** and other countries whose geographical definition owes, often, far more to European empire-builders than to any ethnic homogeneity. It was precisely such problems which led to conflict in Yugoslavia and the former Soviet Union in the early 1990s once the power of communism, which had maintained artificial boundaries, collapsed. It is useful to distinguish between the politics of ethnicity in advanced democratic societies, where it is somewhat of a luxury, given the overall strength of national identity and the relative importance of other basic political issues related to organizing a productive economy, and in countries in the Third World and post-communist bloc, where ethnic divisions may be absolutely central to the problems of organizing a working political system. However the re-emergence of racially based ethnic conflict between the still unassimilated Asian communities in Britain, or North African communities in France suggest the likely longevity of ethnic politics even in the most economically advanced liberal democracies. What may give ethnic politics an extra urgency is the increasing linkage of ethnic identity amongst immigration-based groups in countries like the UK with international radical political movements organized around versions of Islamic fundamentalism. (See also **nationalism**.)

Ethnocentrism

Ethnocentrism is a problem arising in much comparative research in the social sciences, and in any study that involves more than one social culture. The problem is one of the researcher, probably unknowingly, reading meanings into the activities of those he is studying that are foreign to them, and which cannot really be their motivation. Another way of putting this is to say that the standards by which we judge and decide are heavily culture bound, and may not be interchangeable between social contexts. One example that is often cited is the tendency of some racial groups to perform badly on standard IQ tests, not because they are in fact innately less intelligent than other races, but because the sorts of questions asked, and the imaginary problems set, have little or no meaning inside their subculture.

While an ethnocentric approach is probably always undesirable, there is in fact a difference between the perhaps inevitable failure to grasp properly the meaning of an action in a foreign culture, and the deliberate use of standards of evaluation from one's own context. An example of this has often been the study of political development. In much of the earlier **behavioural** research on political development the progress of a political system was often judged in terms of its approximation to an ideal type of 'developed' system, when what counted as being 'developed' meant simply 'being like America'. Because, for example, it is usual in technocratic Western societies to expect professional and administrative decisions and appointments to be made on 'universalistic' or 'achievement' grounds, societies where familial relations and emotional links were more important were judged less developed. While there may be a possibility of arguing for the superiority of standards from one's own culture, it is necessary at least to realize that this is a value argument, and not, ethnocentrically, to see one's standards as somehow universal. Similarly concepts cannot be expected automatically to translate between political cultures, and thus the very activity of comparative research, which involves at a minimum the possibility of taxonomy, involves the danger of ethnocentrism.

For example, two institutions can appear to be equivalent, two pressure groups say, and would be judged, ethnocentrically, to be examples of the same political phenomenon. It might, however, be that in one country the emotional symbolism of what is in another a mere pressure group transforms its legitimacy in the foreign culture. To study the French Army in the late Third Republic on the assumption that armies were the same sort of institutions in France, the USA and the UK would, were the judgement made by an Englishman, involve a serious ethnocentric mistake.

In a less technical context, ethnocentrism is akin to **racism**, being the assumption of the innate superiority of one's own culture and society.

Eurocommunism

Eurocommunism was the moderate version of **communism** espoused by some communist parties in Western European democracies, particularly from the late 1960s. The two most important parties to pursue this line were the Italian and Spanish communist parties. The root of the development lay in the need of communist parties in Western democracies to compete electorally with socialist and conservative parties if they were ever to gain political power as a result of an election. During the inter-war years communist parties either hardly existed or managed only barely to survive because they were closely associated with revolutionary politics, and with the **Stalinism** of the Soviet Union. During the Second World War communist parties in France and Italy came to be more respectable because they were deeply involved in opposition to **fascism** and in the resistance movements against German occupation. Nevertheless, after the war they were still seen, on the whole, as anti-democratic, even if they fought elections. The doctrines of the **dictatorship of the proletariat** and the need to transform capitalist society totally and immediately, as well as their close connection to the Soviet Union, which had by this time become the main **cold war** threat to Western Europe, meant that the French and Italian communist parties were effectively excluded from the main arena of democratic politics.

Slowly the Italian Communist Party (PCI) broke away from this position, principally under the leadership of Enrico Berlinguer, and followed the theoretical doctrines developed by **Gramsci** while in a fascist prison. The essence of the new Italian communism was to accept democracy as the only way in which the long-term aim, the transformation of Italian society to communism, could be achieved. In its turn this required at least a temporary acceptance of a mixed economy, where capitalism would still have an important role, and overall a belief in the sort of **gradualism** that used to be preached by the English **Fabian** movement. In more practical terms it meant an acceptance of the need for Italy to remain in **NATO**, and a general move away from automatic support for the Soviet Union in preference for backing European institutions like the **European Union**. The move certainly helped the PCI, which became the principal opposition party to the Christian

Democrat-led coalition governments; indeed, for three years in the late 1970s, a period known as the 'historic compromise', the Christian Democrats relied upon support from the communists). How much Eurocommunism was really a purely Italian phenomenon is still hard to tell. The Spanish Communist Party, only free to practise overt politics after the death of **Franco**, shared much of the creed but had lost most of its support by the end of the 1980s, while the **Parti Communiste Français**, which suffered a steady electoral decline from the mid-1970s onwards, remained much more staunchly orthodox, even Stalinist. So broad was the social backing for the PCI, and so moderate many of its policies, that it was sometimes doubted whether the 'Communist' part of their labels was really very important. Indeed, faced with the disintegration of communism in Eastern Europe, the party acknowledged this by changing its name to the Partito Democratica della Sinistra (Democratic Party of the Left) in 1991. If anything it has increased its hold on the left of Italian politics with the disenchantment that followed the failure of the so-called **Second Italian Republic** to improve much on the old. Like many of the discredited remnants of communist parties in Eastern Europe, it is likely that the Western European communists will seek to re-establish themselves as social democratic parties, but as **social democracy** itself is increasingly seen as outdated, to be replaced by some form of **Third Way**, their long-term survival and significance may depend on remaining nearer to their earlier political form.

European Court of Justice (ECJ)

The Court of Justice of the **European Union (EU)**, popularly referred to as the European Court of Justice, is the judicial branch of the EU, charged with ruling on the legality of actions by the Commission, Council of Ministers and Parliament. It also rules on the validity of laws and regulations passed by national governments in areas where these conflict with EU law, and, to a lesser extent, on the legality of actions concerning individual citizens of the member states. Its jurisdiction is complex, and often involves hearing appeals from national courts. Each of the three original European communities, the European Economic Community, the European Coal and Steel Community and the European Atomic Energy Community (Euratom), recognized the need for a body impartially to interpret its rules, and from its beginning the Court of Justice was busy. It was the administrative amalgamation of the three communities in 1967 that gave the Court its real impetus. The Court has a total of 19 members, usually comprising one judge from every member nation, plus an additional judge from one of the larger nations, and six advocates general. Although there are six chambers, or panels of judges, important cases are invariably heard by the full court. There are two features of the Court's structure and practice that are unfamiliar in the **common law** world. The first is that judgments are always unanimous, in the sense that just one opinion is issued, though no one can know what the voting was in chambers. The second is the role of the advocates general, who review the arguments of the parties and issue their own opinion before the judges consider the matter. The judges are not bound to follow, or even to take note of, the advocate generals' opinions, but they are clearly very influential. Because there is no right of appeal against a decision of the Court of Justice, this prior opinion acts almost like, for example, a judgment of the English Court of Appeal prior to an ultimate appeal to the House of Lords.

The two most important types of cases coming to the Court are those where the European Commission acts against a member government for alleged breach of some EU **regulation** or **directive**, or where one member state sues another claiming to have suffered damage as a result of failure to comply with EU law. However, individuals do have a way of involving the Court in their disputes. If a citizen is suing their government, or a citizen of their own or another state, and the case involves interpretation of an EC ruling, they may ask their national court to refer the matter to the Court of Justice. Ordinary courts have the discretion to grant or refuse such a request, but if the case goes to the highest appeal court in the country, that court must make such a reference. This route, known as the 'Article 177 Procedure' is becoming increasingly common. (Technically, Article 177 of the Treaty of Rome has become Article 234 of the Treaty of Amsterdam, but it is so well known by its original numbering that it is best to continue referring to it that way, as many legal text books have done.) National court systems vary in the extent they welcome this intervention in their own processes; it certainly illustrates the supremacy of EU law over national law. Some, Italy and Germany particularly, have welcomed the extra appeal route, while France tried for a long time to avoid it, but now all national court systems recognize the binding force of Court of Justice rulings.

The Court of Justice is often likened to the US Supreme Court in its early days, when it played a vital role in building the authority of the federal government over the individual states. There is no doubt that the Court is very 'European minded' and will try hard to find in favour of a wide interpretation of a decision or treaty clause which furthers integration. It is also anxious to broaden the range of matters which it considers, and aspects of the Treaty of Rome dealing with **civil liberties** and other non-economic matters are taken very seriously. One interesting feature of the relations between the Court and other bodies is that the court has, of itself, only very weak powers of enforcement. Nevertheless, although some countries have been reluctant to comply on certain issues, the Court has never yet been openly defied. The ECJ has undoubtedly strengthened the grip of European legislation over member states in a series of wide ranging interpretations of treaty and other European legislation, as well as by inventing doctrines whole-sale. What is remarkable is that there has been very little effective resistance to this by national courts, without whose co-operation little could have been done.

European Union

The European Union (EU) is the most recent name of an organization of Western European states. It started life as the European Economic Community (EEC) in 1957. From there it became the European Community in 1967. The differences between the two older stages and the new EU are considerable, and they grow continually through a series of treaties replacing or adding to the agreements contained in the original 1957 Treaty of Rome. The first step was the ratification in 1987 of the Single European Act creating, by 1992, a 'single European market'. This act modified the extent to which single countries could veto European legislation; increased marginally the powers of the European Parliament; increased regional aid; and adopted measures of social policy through the 'Social Charter', which came into effect in the 1990s. The next step was the greatest yet taken, when the member states ratified the Maastricht Treaty of 1993, which also brought about the name change. Although Maastricht entailed many things, including the inception of a move towards common foreign-affairs and military policy, it is famous above all for launching monetary union.

EMU (economic and monetary union) was the move that finally trans-formed the European Communities into something previously unknown in world history. The member states gave up independent control of monetary policy, and indeed stopped having their own monetary system at all, putting total control into the hands of a politically independent European Central Bank: 1999 saw the onset of the single European currency and the end of national monetary policy for those members able and willing to meet stringent economic criteria. Some countries wished to join and failed to meet the conditions, while the UK, probably capable of meeting the conditions, refused to join. By 2002 the last vestiges of independent European national monetary systems had gone when national currency units were all replaced by the 'euro'.

By contrast, the next phase after Maastricht, the 1997 Treaty of Amsterdam, was less dramatic but still vitally important. This treaty further developed the institutions of the Union in order to increase democratic accountability and reduce the possibility of individual states going their own way. The great problem for the EU in the 21st century is one of growth. There is considerable pressure to allow the countries of the democratic transition in Eastern Europe to join, but apart from the notable difference in their economies, there is obviously a serious question as to whether the spectacular success of the EU in turning itself into a completely new form of transnational political entity can continue if it becomes too large. The other problem is the variation in aim and preferred speed of development, with some countries; notably Germany and occasionally France, being eager to produce a fully fledged federal united states of Europe, while others still wish to maintain considerable national autonomy.

Eurosceptic

Eurosceptic became journalistic shorthand for a range of political opinions in the United Kingdom during the last decade of the 20th century. Obviously it applied to the UK's relations with the **European Union (EU)**, and obviously it indicated people who were less than totally convinced that further and deeper integration of the British political and economic system with those of other EU member states was desirable. Beyond that, further precision is impossible. The range of meaning varied enormously, even amongst politicians who were prepared to accept the label; as many with opinions indistinguishable from those who accepted it, hotly denounced it, this came to be even more of a problem. There are few better examples of the cheapening of political analysis in the mass media than the widespread use of this simplistic term.

The term was very largely, though not exclusively, applied to **Conservative Party** politicians, in part because many of them found it a useful rallying cry and a powerful if blunt way of discrediting their opponents inside the party. There had been a long history of Conservative doubts about the suitability of European integration as a policy for the United Kingdom, although it was, of course, a Conservative administration, that of Ted Heath (1970–74) that took Britain into the then European Economic Community (EEC) in 1972. Throughout the years of the Conservative administrations of 1979–92, government policy waxed and waned over how close an integration the UK was prepared to accept. The leader for most of that period, Margaret Thatcher, objected to much of the EU's development based on the dual beliefs that the EU was not as wedded to the free market as she was, and important areas of national decision-making autonomy were at risk. After Thatcher's forced resignation as prime minister, her successor, John Major, had to contend with ever deepening and more acrimonious rifts in his party over Europe. It was at this time that the label of Eurosceptic was coined. The main problem with the term is that many of those who were so labelled were not simply sceptical about the benefits of European integration—that could be a rational policy of caution even for those ideologically wedded to ultimately high degrees of integration. In truth, many of the Eurosceptics were out and out euro-loathers, unprepared to accept anything more than a loose trading-bloc arrangement. However, it has become politically impossible to actually oppose UK membership completely, except for those on the very far right of the party.

Thus Eurosceptics covered a range of opinion from covert opposition to those who simply felt cautious. The issue itself almost lost independent meaning because it did indeed become a rallying cry for those who wanted a hard-right **laissez-faire** economic policy allied to minimum welfare, and a rejection of many of the symbols of pluralist and liberal society. There was, for example, a very high statistical correlation between homophobic attitudes, anti-immigrant orientation, preferences for capital punishment and lengthy prison sentences, tax-cutting, welfare minimalism and euroscepticism. By the beginning of the 21st century, the majority of the remaining parliamentary Conservative Party, after two electoral defeats, were Eurosceptic. In part they clung to this position because of a probably mistaken belief that it was the only policy on which they could win votes. At this stage some degree of authenticity had re-entered the term because of the centrality of one technical issue: whether or not Britain should fully join the EU's Economic and Monetary Union and relinquish its separate currency in favour of the euro.

Executive

The 18th-century French political theorist **Montesquieu** divided the political system into three distinct elements: the **legislature**, the **judiciary** and the executive. Each branch performed a different function and, in Montesquieu's view, ought to be kept separate from the other branches of **government** (see **separation of powers**). The executive is defined as the part of a governmental system which takes decisions and enforces the state's will, as opposed to making laws, although modern political systems in fact allow their executives to legislate. In countries like France the executive has whole areas reserved where it, not the legislature, passes binding decrees. In all parts of the world, the executive has a good deal of influence over what statutes the legislature will effectively be free to pass.

In the United Kingdom members of the executive are recruited from Parliament, whereas in the USA and France no one may be simultaneously a member of the government and of the legislature. In many systems the term 'executive' covers both the elected political and the non-elected bureaucratic parts of government. There are various types of executive, but the most important in modern democratic systems are **presidential government**, quasi-presidential, as in France, and **cabinet government**. There is ambiguity, theoretical as well as empirical, as to how extensive the executive is—should it be used to refer only to the political heads of the state apparatus, does it include for example, the civil service? Oddly it is perhaps best defined negatively—the executive is that part of the organized and official political system which is not the legislature and is not the judiciary.

Existentialism

The existentialist tradition has influenced European political thinkers in various ways since at least the 18th century. Its most recent significant manifestation is in French political thought, with the existentialism of Jean-Paul Sartre (1905–80) and Albert Camus (1913–60). It is unclear whether there are any specific doctrines in existentialism that actually have a direct political consequence, and the philosophy is, in any case, one that Anglo-American culture always found difficult and obscure. Most probably, the political influence of existentialism has more to do with the milieu of left-wing café society, or, as in Camus's case, radical anti-colonialism, in which it was espoused than with such logical connections as one might find normally between a philosophical tradition and a political doctrine. Sartre himself was for some time a follower of **Marxism** as well as existentialism, and his political positions derived rather more obviously from this. The nearest one could safely come to describing the politics of existentialism is to suggest that the philosophy speaks to those who see modern societies as dominated by bureaucrats, characterized by **alienation** and dehumanization, and to those who would wish to destroy these aspects of state power. Indeed a general distaste for organized power, an opposition to being forced to choose between limited alternatives in terms of organized left- and right-wing parties, and a feeling that individual autonomy and creativity are being destroyed by politicians runs through Sartre's work. Especially in his famous four-volume novel of French life from the Spanish Civil War to the fall of France in 1940, *The Roads to Freedom* (1945–49), Sartre certainly paints a perceptive emotional analysis of the corruption of the French **Third Republic**, and it may well be that it is in the not strictly philosophical literature that the political theory is to be found. This would apply equally to other modern existentialists, especially Camus, who had grown up in French Algeria and developed a hatred for the colonial mentality. In the end there is little more than a politics of despair and a fear of power to be found as theoretical doctrine in the existentialist works. One might well link this political reaction to the politics of Kafka's *The Trial*. This is not to deny the genuine influence on many in political circles, especially among fringe left-wing groups and militant students, and many serious critics of political theory might well wish to claim a more clear-cut political consequence for existentialism. What would probably not be denied is that its days of influence have been, at least temporarily, over since the 1960s, largely to be replaced by more recent French radical philosophy in the guise of various versions of **post-modernism**.

F

Fabians

The Fabian Society (which takes its name from the Roman general, Quintus Fabius Maximus 'Cunctator', famous for his tactics of delay) was set up in 1884 by a group of left-wing intellectuals in England, and was one of the groups that joined together around the end of that century to organize the **Labour Party**. Its predominant position has always been one of advocating peaceful political progress towards **socialism**, through electoral and constitutional politics (see **gradualism**). Today there is little to distinguish Fabianism from general **social democracy** within the Labour Party, but in the earlier part of the 20th century it was far more important, representing a powerful non-revolutionary analysis of the need for, and pathways to, socialism, when the alternatives were either pure trade-union politics, or extreme militancy. As orthodox social democracy has lost its grip on Labour party thinking with the development of '**New Labour**' and the growth of ideas associated with the **Third Way**, Fabianism may, ironically, return to salience as a legitimate alternative view of the party, taking the place of the 'hard' left, itself forever discredited.

No specific doctrines could be said to underlie Fabianism over any length of time—it does not, for example, have any particular overall analysis of the shape of the economy in a socialist country, for it is not an ideologically organized group. In its early days intellectuals such as George Bernard Shaw and Sidney and Beatrice Webb, were members, and it was partly the Webbs' disappointment with the actions of the post-1917 communist governments in the Soviet Union that held the Fabians to their gradualist position. Today the membership is very similar, with a considerable sprinkling of senior academics and writers. It has very little influence in the contemporary Labour Party, although its constant production of highly regarded policy-discussion papers gives it the status of a semi-official 'think-tank' for those disenchanted with both the party leadership and the traditional left.

Falangism

The original 'Falange' was the Spanish **fascist** movement, Falange Española, which helped to bring General. Francisco **Franco** to power in the Spanish

Civil War, but subsequently became a declining influence within the Franco regime. Subsequent movements of a similar nature have either adopted, or been christened with, the label 'falangist': the most important being the Christian Falange in Lebanon.

Like **populism**, which it resembles in some respects, it is difficult to give a tight definition to a falangist movement. Essentially, the term denoted a social and political movement in which historical traditions and ideas of national character or destiny are coupled to right-wing and **authoritarian** practices for running a state. The most important of these traditional elements is undoubtedly the Church. Not only is the Christian Falange in the Lebanon clearly Church-based, but the acquiescence and at times enthusiastic, support of the Roman Catholic hierarchy in Spain was vital to Franco's success. The movement is populist in as much as it aims for cross-class support, in which the religious and national identities are claimed to be vastly more important than mere differences in economic status. However, while populism can be said to be working-class in origin, and most probably based on organized labour, a falange rests more on the middle class, looking to the working class for support, but also relying on institutions, especially the Church, for its authority, and lacks the minimum degree of economic redistribution to be found in populism and some forms of fascism. Falangism, consequently, is considered likely to diminish as a political force as secularization reduces the influence of organized religion throughout the world.

False Consciousness

False consciousness is a concept that comes from the theory of **ideology**, and especially from arguments on this subject within **Marxism**. It refers to a state in which people's beliefs, values or preferences are seen as 'false', that is, artificially created by their culture or society. For example, a conflict between trade unions inside a work-force might be seen as a false consciousness on the grounds that workers 'ought' to realize that unity in the face of capitalists is in the 'true interests' of all workers. Similarly, affluent workers who see a government that might increase their taxes to pay for welfare benefits to the less affluent as less in their interest than one which might reduce taxes would also be suffering from a false consciousness, because they 'ought' to realize that ultimately all workers are exploited by capitalist society. A 'true consciousness' would have them supporting their less affluent fellow workers. Clearly it is an evaluative concept, and one that requires a very powerful theory to support it. Otherwise we can all describe anything someone else wants as a 'false' interest. Nevertheless, there are clear examples of people suffering false consciousness, believing that some policy will help them when it will not, or holding values and attitudes that one can easily trace to ideological conditioning or media manipulation. There is a need, as with all concepts in this area, to establish ground rules for using the arguments, which can otherwise turn into a powerful myth to uphold totalitarian or other undemocratic governments (see **dictatorship of the proletariat**). As with similar ideas, for example **alienation**, it is assumed that there exists an essential human nature that is discoverable whatever the apparent characteristics. It is historically similar to ideas in traditional Catholic political theory, for example in **Aquinas** or **Augustine**, where the thesis that man has fallen from a state of grace justified hieratical authority. The idea is that, uncontaminated by external forces, unfallen people would perceive society correctly, and neither be the tools of the exploiters nor be able to exploit, because a potential exploiter would not be able to disguise from himself what he was doing. It is this general distortion which gives false consciousness its power. An example might be the acceptance both by factory owners and workers that minimal pay rates and high job insecurity were necessary for the economy to flourish. The theory, shared by both sides, justifies to everyone both exploiting and being exploited. Only where the exploiters actually do realize that matters might be organized otherwise but continue to maintain the economic theory in question, does a 'false' consciousness become a 'mendacious' consciousness.

Fanon

Frantz Fanon (1925–61) was born and initially educated in one of France's overseas possessions, Martinique, and ended his political life in what was then another, Algeria. In between, he was a psychiatrist, practising as such in Algeria in 1956 when he resigned and joined the outlawed Front de Libération Nationale (FLN), which conducted a successful guerrilla war against French colonialism. His work became, even during his lifetime, a major source of inspiration and doctrine for anti-colonial and anti-racist movements world-wide, and continued to influence radical movements, particularly in Africa, into the 21st century. His best-known book, *The Wretched of the Earth* also achieved significant literary acclaim, a rare accolade for a work of political protest. The essence of Fanon's work was to take many currents of radical thought in post-war France and apply them, first to the anti-colonial struggle, and secondly to racism generally. Thus, he combined radical psychiatry with **Marxism** and even traces of **existentialism**, to produce a synthesis which allowed an analysis of oppression outside the constraints of orthodox Marxist thought, limited, as it often is, to the developed capitalist economy. It is a relatively short leap from producing such an analysis of the plight of oppressed colonial populations to applying it to the situation of racial minorities inside developed economies, and it is probable that Fanon has been just as influential amongst radical black American movements as in Africa itself. Like many such highly synthetic approaches Fanon's theoretical perspective is as much rhetoric and call for action as it is analysis. Indeed it is hard, at first glance, to see how one can combine Jungian psychiatry with Marxism, and orthodox Marxists are no more impressed with his work than are orthodox psychiatrists. Much of Fanon's appeal lies in his rejection of other, that is Western, analytic frameworks. By insisting that theory can only be developed in the context of struggle, advocates of his work are freed from the necessity to debate with other intellectual structures. The other characteristic which puts Fanon beyond the pale to many is his overt justification of violence in political struggles. He did, however, have a considerable predictive streak, and much of the less admirable side of post-colonialist African political experience is depicted in his work. Fanon's work remains influential, though largely at the rhetorical or emotional level.

Fascism

The term fascism is derived from the *fasces* of ancient Rome, a bundle of rods with a projecting axe symbolizing unity and authority, which was adopted by Benito **Mussolini** for his new Italian political movement in the 1920s. The other important fascist parties created in the years between the First and Second World Wars were those led by Adolf **Hitler** in Germany and General Francisco **Franco** in Spain. Fascist governments were also installed in much of central Europe before and during the Second World War. As the full name of Hitler's party (the National Socialist German Workers' Party) suggests, some appeal to working-class solidarity, of a largely **populist** nature, was common to most fascist movements. (The creator of the British Union of Fascists, Oswald Mosley, had been a junior minister in a Labour government.)

There is no coherent body of political doctrine that can be attributed to fascism because all fascist movements were opportunistic, and depended on demagogic exploitation of local fears and hatreds to whip up public support. The most common themes were **nationalism**, often expressed in essentially racist tones as a way of building national unity in the face of class divisions, anti-**communism** and a hatred and contempt for democracy—even if its institutions had been used to gain power. This latter view was usually linked to a well-developed theme of the need for firm leadership, the appeal being to the strong man (*Duce* in Italian, *Führer* in German and *Caudillo* in Spanish) who would solve a country's problems as long as he was given loyal and unquestioning obedience. Post-war outbreaks of fascism have been few, and unsuccessful, and the tendency to assume that any right-wing group, especially if it has nationalistic overtones, is fascist is a debasement of political vocabulary (see **neo-fascism** and **new right**).

Fascism was almost certainly a unique response to a particular historical context, and as a label the word has very little place in our contemporary set of political categories. However, in the mouths of modern radicals a fascist is simply anyone whom they think is fairly right-wing. It has also come to be applied to anyone of extreme views, especially if verbal or physical violence is used by such a person as a political weapon. Hence one sometimes hears references to 'the fascism of the left' as well as to that of the right.

Federalism

Originally federation indicated a loose alliance or union of states for limited purposes, usually military or commercial; and as such it could hardly be distinguished from **confederacy**. In the 18th century, however, the newly-independent American colonies developed a model of federal government which combined a strong role for the central or national authority with a degree of independence for the hitherto autonomous states. 'Federalism' is now used to describe such a form of government, in which power is constitutionally divided between different authorities in such a way that each exercises responsibility for a particular set of functions and maintains its own institutions to discharge those functions. In a federal system each authority therefore has **sovereignty** within its own sphere of responsibilities, because the powers which it exercises are not delegated to it by some other authority.

Federalism is often seen as a complex and cumbersome method of government because it involves a number of potentially overlapping jurisdictions and the maintenance of similar institutions at each level of administration; in the USA, for example, the presidency and Congress have equivalents in every state in a governor and state legislature. Federation is typically used in heterogeneous societies where it is thought necessary to allow distinct areas as much political autonomy as possible. Switzerland, with its different linguistic and religious groupings, is an example that has a history of federal association going back to the 13th century, although the modern Swiss Federation dates from 1874. In the late 1980s and early 1990s, as progress was made towards economic and **political union** in the **European Union**, very different interpretations were put upon federalism. Most member governments saw it as a system for allowing policy-making to take place at the national level wherever appropriate, while the British government in particular saw it as indicating **centralization** (see also **subsidiarity**).

The federal model was much favoured by British governments in the process of decolonization because it allowed small entities to be linked together for defence and foreign policy, and because it seemed an efficient way to protect minorities. Malaya acquired a federal constitution in 1948; Northern and Southern Rhodesia, and Nyasaland were federated in 1953; and the West Indies Federation was created in 1958. Many of these federations have not survived because some of the component parts wanted complete control over their own affairs; and the existence of a federal constitution did not prevent civil war and general political instability in Nigeria.

Size is also a major factor in determining whether a federal constitution is appropriate, since large areas are obviously more difficult to govern effectively from a single centre. Canada, Australia, India and the USA nowadays need federal constitutions, although Indian federalism is unusual in that the states were redefined after the creation of the federal constitution, as much for reasons of sheer size as because of their original political creation, in the same way that the Soviet Union was originally and necessarily federal and its largest successor state, the Russian Federation, is in the process of recreating highly devolved regionalism.

The precise balance of power between the central and local authorities in federal systems will vary between different federations and over time within a particular system. In the USA, for example, powers not originally granted to the federal government (among them the power to impose a federal income tax) have been acquired by constitutional amendment. Less formal methods have also been used to alter the federal–state balance. The courts have on occasion changed their interpretation of the proper spheres of activity of the federal and state authorities, as they did over reapportionment of congressional seats and criminal procedure in the USA in the 1960s; the increasing dependence of the states on the federal government for financial aid has in many ways enabled the federal government to influence policies which are nominally within the control of the state government. Some formally federal systems operate rather more like a unitary system with an uncommon degree of **delegation**. Germany is a federal republic, but in many areas the states act as agents for the central government, administering nationally-determined legislation; in some subjects, such as education, policing and land use, states decide their own policies but the politics of the national government tend to dominate all else.

Two constitutional features are found in most federal systems. There will frequently be an upper house or senate (see **second chambers**) where the states are represented in their own right and equally, as opposed to the representation proportionate to population allocated in the lower house; and there will usually be an enhanced role for the courts since the judiciary is normally required to adjudicate in disputes between the central and local authorities (see **judicial review**). Federalism always remains a possibility for a unitary state when regional, perhaps partially ethnic, divisions become too fraught for a single central authority ; thus the United Kingdom may be *en route* to federalism in granting varying degrees of autonomy to Wales and Scotland. There is no historical example, however, of a federal state being turned peacefully and successfully into a unitary one.

Federalists

'Federalist' may be used as a general term for those who favour a federal system of government (see **federalism**). More narrowly the term refers to an American political faction or party which emerged at the beginning of the Republic's history and advocated a strong national government for the USA. Its main strength lay in the North, and its emphasis on the need for commercial expansion made it the natural party of the trading and manufacturing classes. Its opponents advocated a weaker role for the national government *vis-à-vis* the states, and were supported by agricultural interests. The Federalist Party was dominant during the administrations of George Washington and John Adams (1789–1801), but after Thomas Jefferson's election to the presidency in 1800, the Federalists declined, and the party ceased to be important.

Feminism

The modern feminist movement stems from the middle of the 1960s in North America, and perhaps a little later in Europe, although important political feminist activities (for example, the Suffragette movement in Britain and the League of Woman Voters in the US) long pre-date the contemporary phenomenon. There is no single political doctrine of feminism *per se*, and the various groups and currents of thought among feminists are often in bitter disagreement. Basically the movement seeks equal political and social rights for women as compared with men. The main common theoretical assumption which is shared by all branches of the movement is that there has been an historical tradition of male exploitation of women, stemming originally from the sexual differences which led to a division of labour, as, for example, in child-rearing practices.

The actual policies pursued by feminists vary from the legalistic, in demanding **equality of opportunity** and a ceasing of sexual **discrimination** in, for example, employment policies and wage rates, through demands for facilities such as free day-nurseries to remove disadvantages to women in the job market, ultimately to demands for **affirmative action** or positive discrimination. Feminist issues are generally best promoted by relevant **pressure groups**, although there are women's political parties in Colombia and Iceland, the latter having received over 10% of the votes cast in a general election. Although female politicians have become increasingly prominent, the number of women in the national legislature of most countries is massively disproportionate to their share of the population. Feminism has tended to be left-wing in general orientation, if only because it is attacking what it sees as an established power relationship. However, there are major theoretical problems because of the way that sexual political divisions fit very badly with the class divisions around which the left tends to develop its thought. As a reform movement feminism has been rather successful in a short period, with equal-rights legislation being passed in many countries. Feminist positions, amounting sometimes almost to separate subdisciplines, are now found in many academic subjects. Thus 'feminist political theory' is a recognized specialism within political theory, as is feminist literary criticism, and even feminist legal thought in their respective faculties. Much of the real strength of these intellectual positions comes from redressing the way women's thinking and perspectives have been ignored in the historical development of these subjects.

Feudalism

Feudalism, which has a precise (though very complicated) meaning when used by historians to describe the Western system of land ownership and government in the medieval period, has come to be attributed to a wide variety of modern socio-political systems which have almost nothing in common with genuine feudalism. In **Marxism**, feudalism was regarded as the precursor of **capitalism**. Crudely, feudalism was the basic form of social organization that had arisen in Europe out of the shattered remnants of the old Roman Empire by the ninth century, and which reached its peak, in England anyway, after the Norman invasion of the 11th century. It was founded on the principle that the king, or some other overlord, had rights over land that he could grant to his followers in return for services, originally military, on the basis of an oath of loyalty. At its extreme the king was actually held to own all or most of the land. The one to whom estates were granted could in turn grant what might be thought of as a sub-lease to his followers on similar terms. The whole edifice of feudalism was a complex of two-way obligations, firmly set in an unquestioned set of statuses, rather than being based on contractual rights or more vague notions of citizenship or nationality. While there was no pretence of equality of rights and obligations, and no general sense of what would now be called 'social mobility' (one's position in the social order being more or less fixed at birth), the justifying ideology was one of reciprocation of loyalty.

Modern examples as varied as Latin American *Latifundia* (huge estates privately owned by absentee landlords and worked by ruthlessly exploited day-labour peasants) and Japanese industrial enterprises have been described as feudal. With the former the apparent connection is of a backward or 'medieval' system; in fact the Latin American peasant is far more oppressed than the medieval serf. The latter comparison arises simply because some Japanese firms tend to provide homes and social lives for their workers, and because Japanese society is characterized by an unusually sharp sense of **status** deference; it would be a mistake to regard the similarity as more than a coincidence. There are almost certainly no genuine feudal systems in the contemporary world; not only has the idea of legal ownership of property completely changed, but also the organization of a modern state cannot survive purely on the basis of personal loyalties and obligations.

Fifth Republic

The Fifth Republic is the present political system of France. It came into being in 1958, when mutinies by the French Army in Algeria proved too much for the weak government of the **Fourth Republic** and forced the president, René Coty, to invite General Charles **de Gaulle** to take office as prime minister. De Gaulle made it a condition of his acceptance that he be empowered to write a new constitution and submit it to the public in a referendum. He was elected president in December, taking office in January 1959. De Gaulle's analysis was that the troubles of the **Third Republic**, as well as the Fourth, had stemmed from strong and undisciplined National Assemblies with a cumbersome multi-party system, and the constitution he designed was close to the one he had advocated for the immediate post-war Fourth Republic, with very strong presidential powers (see **presidential government**) and a much weakened **legislature**. This was approved by an overwhelming majority of the electorate.

There is no doubt that the Fifth Republic has been the most successful French regime since Napoleonic times, although there are still fierce arguments about the extent to which this is the result of constitutional engineering, the General's charismatic authority, the popularity of **Gaullism** (his party dominated government coalitions from 1958–81) or a coincidental upsurge of economic prosperity. (From the mid-1950s France enjoyed almost continual economic prosperity for some 30 years, known, indeed, to the French as the '*Trente Glorieuse*'.) Politics in the Fifth Republic have certainly been more stable than in preceding regimes, and the peaceful transfer of power to the socialists in 1981 is in certain respects unique in French history. Even more important as a test was France's experience of **cohabitation** from 1986–88 when there was a socialist president but a conservative majority in the legislature and a Gaullist prime minister and government. So easily did this go that subsequent periods of cohabitation—France had another, with a conservative President and socialist prime minister at the beginning of the 21st century—go almost unremarked. Although such divisions of political power are common in systems with elected presidents, and very regular in the USA, it had been feared that even the strong Fifth Republic might founder under the strain. Coming after nearly 90 years of **immobilisme** and 10 years in which the life expectancy of a government was measured in weeks rather than months, the Fifth Republic has come to be seen by the French as constituting a radical change in the very nature of French political life. François Mitterrand, France's first socialist president, and himself a past member of Fourth Republican governments, who had attacked the Fifth Republic's transfer of power away from the legislature for years, happily accepted the powers and authority of the presidency and failed to consider a reform he had previously urged, to shorten presidential terms from seven to five years, until the end of his own second presidential term was in sight (a constitutional amendment to this effect was eventually approved in 2000, and Jacques Chirac began his second term in the presidency, of five years' duration, following his re-election to the post in May 2002). It is, perhaps, the ability of the system to function during a prolonged period of economic decline and public collapse of confidence, such as happened at the end of the 20th century, that most underlines the permanence and stability of the Republic.

First Strike

The use of nuclear weaponry to attack an enemy which has not already launched such an attack would be known as a first strike, and was eschewed, officially at least, by NATO forces at the strategic level, though not at the tactical level. Soviet military doctrine traditionally did not place restrictions on the **escalation** process, so a nuclear first strike was more likely from this direction.

One form of attack would be a pre-emptive strike, which can be launched with either nuclear or conventional weapons, aimed against some specific feature of another power's potential or actual military capacity. The intention is to prevent the other power from using that specific weapon or capacity. It was sometimes argued in the late 1950s and early 1960s, for example, that the USA should launch a pre-emptive strike against Chinese research establishments to stop them developing nuclear weaponry. Israel carried out what they claimed to be such a pre-emptive strike against Iraqi nuclear reactors in 1980, but using conventional forces. Although they are in fact unprovoked first strikes, they are seen by those who launch them as essentially defensive measures. For most of the period of nuclear rivalry between the USA and the Soviet Union neither side had the capacity to launch a first strike which could destroy enough of the other's **second strike capacity** to make it a rational option, though there was a period in the early 1980s when some American analysts feared the Soviet Union might have such a force level.

First World

First World is used less, but is no less useful as a term, than the commonly found **Third World**, which describes the underdeveloped nations of Africa, Asia and Latin America. The First World consists of the Western European and North American countries which experienced the Industrial Revolution, plus Japan, Australia and New Zealand: in effect, the advanced industrial powers of the period before the First World War. The Second World used to refer to the communist bloc, much of it by now as industrialized as the First World, but on the basis of a different blueprint for economic organization. Membership of the Third World is therefore defined more by the dates at which political independence was achieved and economic growth started than by the actual level of economic development, although in much of the Third World this is in fact extremely low. The classification is very crude, and throws up many anomalies. Can Argentina, for example, be classified as a Third World country when it has much the same level of economic development as New Zealand, and was politically independent earlier? Did Russia move from being a First World nation to the Second World simply because of its political change in 1917, and did it move back again in 1991? Like all simple classifications in politics or political science, this one needs to be used very cautiously, but it is certainly a convenient portmanteau term. In an era when **globalization** has become enormously important, perhaps even more in analysis and theory than in reality, it may be that categorizations such as this will come to have even less utility than in the past.

Fiscal Policy

Fiscal policy is one of the two major weapons governments have for controlling the economy, the other being monetary policy. Though they are interlinked, it is possible to separate them analytically, especially if monetary policy is defined primarily as controlling the **money supply**. Fiscal policy concerns the government's revenue raising and expenditure plans, and operates primarily by raising and lowering tax rates and increasing or decreasing public expenditure to control the size of the government **deficit** or surplus. Because taxes actually exist primarily to pay for expenditure, and expenditure is carried out primarily to produce public goods, fiscal policy often conflicts with the primary aims of government but, equally, even if a government has no intention of controlling the aggregate economy, and has no overt fiscal policy, it cannot avoid having a *de facto* one. During the 20th century attitudes to the use of fiscal policy, and beliefs about the primary aim of such policy, have varied. Until the economics of **Keynesianism** became dominant in Western governments after the Second World War, the primary aim of fiscal policy was to produce balanced budgets, to ensure that government revenue raised by taxation more or less exactly balanced government expenditure. Keynesian economics, which is primarily fiscal, argued instead that deficits should be intentionally created at times of economic depression. If the government receives less in tax than it needs it has to finance expenditure in part by borrowing, which injects new demand into the economy, hopefully increasing consumption and reviving production and therefore employment. If the economy gets over heated and inflation starts to rise, taxes should be increased. This has two effects: higher taxes mean less spending power, lower demand and thus less inflation. At the same time the borrowing needed to cover government expenditure declines, thus reducing injection of consumption power into the economy and bringing demand yet further down. Because predictions of what is going to happen in the economy never turn out to be entirely correct, fiscal policy can easily go adrift, and by the mid-1970s economists and government policy-makers moved steadily away from fiscal policy as a primary tool of economic management in favour of **monetarist** policies. However, member states of the **European Union** who have entered the single currency now no longer have the freedom to set interest rates independently, which some believe may force a return to fiscal policy for economic fine tuning. In practice many other countries, notably the United States of America, have never had political control over interest rates, but neither have they made extensive use of fiscal policy. Where it is important is in situations like the United Kingdom in the late 1990s and early 2000s, where the government intentionally followed the rather old conception of fiscal orthodoxy and refused to allow public expenditure to rise above the income from tax or to increase revenue from direct taxation.

Flexible Response

Flexible response is a strategic doctrine which holds that, in a serious war situation, a whole range of possible defensive and offensive strategies should be available, so that **escalation** need not proceed too rapidly. It is principally opposed to the doctrine of **massive retaliation** that was the mainstay of US defence thinking at the beginning of the nuclear age. The main point of the doctrine is that a country or alliance should be able to meet an attack with increasing but highly specific degrees of force, working gradually up, if necessary, by clear stages to an all-out missile attack against cities. The doctrine calls for subtle targeting and accurate weapons-delivery systems to avoid the need for massive retaliation. It has, nevertheless, been criticized on the grounds that the flexibility simply makes more credible, and therefore more likely, an outbreak of nuclear war. Though the period of **superpower** nuclear stalemate has ended, the doctrine itself may become even more important, because of the need of major powers to maintain the widest possible array of military capacities in order to respond appropriately to any level of crisis, such as the need to intervene in contexts such as the **Gulf War**. This idea returned to importance early in the 21st century when the US publicly refused to promise that it would never use nuclear weapons against non-nuclear armed states. This was in the context of the 'war against terrorism' which followed the attacks on the US of 11 September 2001; the entire notion of such a war underlines the need for maximum flexibility and sophistication in armed response to all forms of threat.

Force Majeure

Force majeure is a phrase which indicates that a given political outcome is dependent on the exercise of irresistible force rather than on consent, agreement or legal process. Thus a strike could be settled by *force majeure* if a government sent troops into a factory to stop it rather than attempting to negotiate with the strikers. A government which had no claim to legitimacy or popular support, but simply depended on repression, would be said to rule by *force majeure*. Such a situation may be deemed to have existed in Poland following the suppression of the independent trade union Solidarity in December 1981 and the subsequent imposition of martial law. The annexation of Kuwait as the 19th Iraqi province, had it succeeded, would have been a classic example of *force majeure*. One implication is that those affected are absolved from any responsibility to oppose the new arrangements because of the sheer impossibility of so doing.

Foucault

Michel Foucault (1926–84) is, of all the post-modernist intellectuals, the one who has had most impact on political science and sociology. (Labels here are always difficult, and it is entirely possible that Foucault would himself have denied that he was a post-modernist, just as he denied while alive various other labels; none the less, if one inspected the reading list of any university course in the politics of **post-modernism**, his work would be the most cited.) Though his work had a very broad range, and his educational formation was very wide, Foucault was essentially a psychologist by training, and indeed his original stance was amongst those teaching what was known as 'antipsychiatry'. As such he developed a passionate concern for victims of oppressive situations, but especially those he considered ill-served by the main, Marxist, alternative to Western social thought. Thus his efforts were concentrated on women, homosexuals and victims of colonialism, rather than the working class, as in **Marxism**. However, his principal interest from an early stage was in the subjects of the criminal justice system, and the first of his books to have a major impact on orthodox Western social science was a study of punishment, especially of imprisonment. This main work, published in 1975, was not his first important publication, but earlier ones which were subsequently to come to be seen as important, were not taken up until his thought became well recognized via the 1975 work. Other studies covered the social understanding of insanity, and more generally the nature and role of medicine in modern society. All of these have a common theme—the many ways in which **power** and **authority** are established and enforced outside either the official activities of the state, or the better recognized power systems of the capitalist economy. It was the medical expert as wielder of power rather than as the bringer of care and mercy which fascinated Foucault, just as he traced the establishment and justification of prison from apparently benevolent motives. His doctrine can be summarized in a phrase—knowledge is power, because it is the claim to knowledge which gives authority to so many role bearers inside and outside the state structure. At the same time, as a member of the postmodern school, the very idea of knowledge and its claim to authority was, for Foucault, highly contestable. Exactly how long-lasting his influence on political science will be is hard to tell. While Foucault himself would not have regretted the difficulty in systemizing his ideas, only that which can be systemized can have a wide-ranging and long-lasting impact as an analytic tool to be used by routine social science.

Fourth Republic

The French Fourth Republic came into being in 1946 after the newly-liberated French electorate resoundingly rejected a continuation of the **Third Republic**, which had been in abeyance since the German victory of 1940 and the setting up of the collaborationist **Vichy** regime. The Fourth Republic was never popular, and never enjoyed the support of a clear majority of the electorate. Designing a new republic after liberation in 1944 was not easy: the first proposals for a new constitution were rejected in a referendum, and the second draft, which became the Fourth Republic, actually differed very little from the discredited Third Republic. Although this draft was given a majority vote in a further referendum, nearly 30% of the electorate abstained (mainly under orders from the Communist Party) and the final vote in favour was actually smaller than the minority which had approved the first draft. The main reason for this outcome was that the leaders of the traditional parties who had governed France before 1940 had no wish for their parties and themselves to lose power, and feared the effects of a strong presidency and a unicameral legislature without the conservative blocking-function of an upper house. The result was a political system no more stable than the previous Republic, with over 20 governments in its 12-year lifetime, many lasting weeks rather than months or years.

In some ways the Fourth Republic did, admittedly, have greater problems than its predecessor. There were overt anti-system parties on both the left and the right. On the left the **Parti Communiste Français (PCF)** regularly won nearly a quarter of the votes in elections, at a time when it was much dominated by Moscow and quite unprepared to accept the legitimacy of the Republic. **Gaullism**, on the right, had backed a very different constitutional plan, not only opposed the Fourth Republic publicly but intrigued against it in private, ultimately bearing a considerable degree of guilt for the Army mutiny in Algeria which overthrew the government, and finally also the constitution. Indeed, the specific political problems that caused the Fourth Republic so much trouble and led to its collapse were the problems of decolonization, the first being the loss of French Indo-China to a **guerrilla** movement, the area then becoming North Vietnam. Given that the much more stable and power- ful USA lost its own **Vietnam War**, the size of the task for a weakened immediate post-war European nation can be appreciated. The second and fatal problem was in North Africa, where France was reluctant to let Algeria become an independent Arab state. Algeria is somewhat misunderstood out- side France, because to the French it was not, in fact, a colony, but an integral part of metropolitan France, with a huge number of white French residents. This fact, combined with the bitterness of the French army, determined to recover their prestige after the disasters of 1940, and what they saw as a political betrayal in Indo-China in 1954, suggests that few governments could have hoped to resolve the problem. To set against these hardly-surprising failures, one should note the extremely rapid industrialization and economic recovery, influenced largely by the entirely new Commissariat Général du Plan, set up by the Republic, and its vital role in creating the European Communities (now the **European Union**). The Republic was ill served by its parliamentarians, and by the numerous centre, centre-right and centre-left governments that ruled it in much the same squabbling fashion that had made the Third Republic a disaster of **immobilisme**. However, at no time has the French parliament been held in greater respect by either the French or foreign analysts, and the contrasting political stability of the **Fifth Republic** is often said to follow **de Gaulle's** emasculation of the National Assembly and his contempt for political parties.

Franchise

The franchise is another name for the eligibility to vote. Conditions attached to such ability have varied both over time and within countries. In the United Kingdom the franchise was gradually extended during the 19th century until in 1918 all men could vote, regardless of whether or not they were property holders. In 1918 also, some women obtained the vote and all women were allowed to vote by 1928. The age of voting has generally been reduced in Western democracies so that it is now 18 years in both the United Kingdom and the USA; only Switzerland and Liechtenstein for long held out against extending the franchise to women (until 1971 and 1984 respectively).

Some countries place severe residence, nationality and citizenship restrictions on the franchise. In the UK people deemed to be represented directly elsewhere may not be allowed to vote; peers, for example, cannot vote in elections for representatives to the House of Commons—they can, however, vote in elections to the European Parliament. Criminals serving sentences of more than a year and inmates of mental institutions are disbarred from voting in the UK.

Franco

Francisco Franco y Bahamonde (1892–1975) was a Spanish army officer, the youngest general in Europe, when he joined a group of officers in rebellion against the short-lived Second Republic in 1936. During the course of the ensuing Spanish Civil War (1936–39) he rose to pre-eminence among the senior officers of the nationalist army, and was made head both of the army and of the provisional government. His success in these roles, and also his ability to unify the disparate elements, made him the supreme power in Spain once the nationalists had won the Civil War. He ruled Spain as an absolute dictator, as head of state, as prime minister (until 1973), as head of the only legal political party and as supreme commander of the armed forces until his death.

Although he took increasingly less interest in most detailed policies, his ruthless use of well-picked subordinates and his skilful control of mass support allowed him to remain virtually unchallenged, and ensured that his ideology prevailed. He was more or less committed to a **corporatism** in the style of **Mussolini**, though much closer both to the Roman Catholic Church and the military which became major supporting institutions to his rule as *Caudillo*.

Over the nearly 40 years of his rule he changed somewhat both the actual policies and the justifying ideology of his system, allowing Spain slowly to modernize economically and, to a lesser extent, to liberalize socially. There was never a clear theory or ideology, never a substantive 'Francoism', but always a firm adherence to a conservative, religious, anti-communist and authoritarian orientation, with the ultimate appeal being to a glorious Spanish past sanctified

by the sacrifices of the Civil War. Largely because of Franco's own preparations, Spain moved easily into a constitutional liberal monarchy on his death,
although there were initially a number of attempts at **coups d'état** in his name
which he would almost certainly have rejected were he alive.

Fraternity

Fraternity (the better translation of the French *fraternité*, the original political
occurrence, would be simply 'brotherhood') was one of the three slogans of
the French Revolution and subsequent regimes. Although the other two
values (*liberté*—see **freedom** and *égalité*—see **egalitarianism**) are enshrined
in the ideologies of most Western states, fraternity is seldom referenced. Instead
the idea of brotherhood, with its implications of communal life and mutual
support and respect, has been found largely in the propaganda and ideology of
communist societies, or in the left-wing internationalist movements. It is a
value less clear perhaps than the other two, and certainly less commented on
and written about in political theory or philosophy. The main reason for its
relative exclusion is probably that, while equality and liberty are essentially
negative rights, in that they deny the government or others the right to do
certain things, or at least place burdens on the state, for example in achieving
equality, brotherhood actually demands positive actions from ordinary people.
This is not to suggest, cynically, that such a call would fail, but rather that
the structure of Western states, and the overall nature of their ideologies, is
geared away from such values and towards an individualism and rational self-
satisfaction that fits ill with such demands. As a revolutionary cry it was
splendid, but as a practical value in the French regimes that followed the
revolution it was harder to achieve. A modern version might be thought to be
the contemporary cry for a return to 'community' as a political value, itself a
consequence of the perceived failure of straightforward rational self interest as a
political doctrine.

Free Trade

Free trade is an international economic system in which no country sets tariff
barriers or other import controls against products from others, and in which
each country has an equal right to sell its own goods in those other countries in
the same terms as indigenous producers. There has probably never been a time
when total free trade existed since the development of **nation states**, and
indeed not all nations have always had internal free trade between regions. In
practice alliances of nations have allowed varying degrees of freedom of trade
among themselves and put up collective barriers against other countries. Such

an alliance is often termed a customs union. The most important example today is in the **European Union** (**EU**), where there are no customs barriers or tariffs that allow discrimination between producers from different member states, and where a common tariff is imposed on third-party states. As an example of just how hard it is actually to guarantee equal treatment of foreign and domestic producers, even when tariffs are theoretically absent, one has only to see the case load of the **European Court of Justice**, the EU's judicial branch, which is largely taken up by complaints that *de facto* discrimination is being practised.

The economic arguments for free trade are complex. In general the economic theory known as the 'theory of comparative advantage' states that the global economic product will be maximized by entirely open international trade competition. However, in the short- or medium-term, it can often be to the interests of some industry or economic sector in a country for it to be protected. Protection may even be in the whole national interest, though this is less likely. Typically the question of international tariff levels to be applied is a matter of political conflict inside a country, as with the intermittent conflict between capital-intensive and labour-intensive industry over tariff levels in the USA. Whether free trade is a 'left' or 'right' wing issue in a country can also vary from time to time, according to the sorts of political values that might be protected by an economic protection policy. During the late 19th century in Britain, for example, it was common for Conservatives to want to use tariff barriers to protect trade between members of the Empire, with the **laissez-faire** Liberals the advocates of free trade. During the 1970s and early 1980s the left wing of the Labour Party, disenchanted with the European Communities (the precursor of the EU) which they saw as essentially capitalist and against the interests of the worker, urged that the only solution to employment problems in Britain was to protect domestic producers with high tariff walls. Largely for personal reasons, US President Ronald Reagan during the early and mid-1980s was a passionate supporter of free trade. **Liberalism**, however, is the political creed which has traditionally been most closely associated with freedom in trade.

Whatever the abstract economic theory, the imposition or not of tariff barriers will always be inherently political, and their consequences will always be as important in the domestic and international political arenas as in the economic. In recent years free trade has become an issue in the developed/less developed world conflict because of barriers, especially relating to agricultural exports, that make it particularly hard for **Third World** countries to earn foreign currency. Because of this the Uruguay round of **GATT** negotiations which ended in the early 1990s, became politically divisive, with most of the world arranged against the EU, whose Common Agricultural Policy is one of the toughest barriers to free trade ever to be imposed; failure in these talks would threaten a trade war, with punitive tariffs imposed by some countries on imports from certain other countries. The successor organization to GATT, the **World Trade Organization** has already been the stage both for **Third World** versus **First World** conflict, and for conflict between the USA and the European bloc, the former regarding the EU as a prime example of the error of non-free trade economics.

Freedom

Liberté (freedom) was, along with brotherhood (see **fraternity**) and equality, one of the great rallying cries of the French Revolution, and it has been, in one guise or another, an unarguable value of most societies ever since. Inevitably there are dozens of versions of freedom as a supreme political virtue. At its most basic, the demand for freedom is the claim that every human has the right to do exactly what they want to do, at any time, provided only that they do not infringe the equal right of every other individual to a similar freedom. There are very few arguments positively to prove this doctrine, because, like equality, it is usually taken as an obvious **natural right**, the infringements of which require justification.

There are three major aspects of freedom which have been politically important. Historically the earliest has not been a notion of individual freedom, but of national freedom as endless nations have sought to throw off foreign domination; even today the 'wars of national liberation' are still with us, notably in Eastern Europe, and the idea of a 'free people' is still a vital coin in political currency. This ideal, of course, says nothing at all about the political and social ties to be found inside the liberated state. The second most important strand historically has been the fight for individualistic, 'legal', freedom, originally the demands of the rising economic bourgeoisie for equal political rights and economic **laissez-faire** against the feudal aristocracies. This was the essential meaning of *liberté* to the French revolutionaries. Developing from this has been the demand for **civil liberties**, for specified basic freedoms that are held to be essential to the chance for man as an individual and for mankind generally to develop and progress. Hence come demands for freedom of assembly, of association, of speech and of religious practice. Within the inevitable limits of imperfection, the basic human freedoms of this sort are available in Western democracies, although economic freedom is often held to have been severely limited in the last few decades by the need for state involvement in controlling the economy. The third broad current in discussions of freedom has come from **socialism**. It is here held that freedom consists not only in legal permission to do or be something, but in the possibility of so doing. Thus, for example, some socialists would argue that we have very little freedom of expression in modern democracies, because while there is no legal censorship, the media is dominated by capitalist enterprises, or the state, and thus rival, radical, views are prevented from being expressed. Any socio-economic barrier to the carrying out of desires is thus held to be an infringement on freedom, with the obvious inference that there can be no liberty without equality. Much of the clash between these second and third meanings of political freedom relates to deep philosophical divisions in the debate often described as being between the 'positive' and 'negative' conceptions of **liberty**.

Functionalism

Functionalism, along with its related theories of **structural functionalism** and **systems theory**, has been one of the most influential of all social science theories, not only in political science and sociology, but in anthropology (where it originated) and several cognate disciplines. Associated with **Durkheim**, functionalism is an attempt to construct a way of comparing both the structures and the operations of all social systems by finding necessary elements common to any stable social system. Much of its origin depends on analogies with biological systems, and in just the way that a biologist might study the role of some physiological aspect, some set of cells, in the maintenance of life, functionalists have tried to understand what are the necessary 'functions' that must be carried out in any political system if it is to cope with its environment and achieve its goals, and to locate the 'structures' (political parties, socializing agencies like churches, etc.) which facilitate the functioning. The theory, which played a considerable part in the **political development** researches of the post-war years, has never been uncontroversial. In particular it has been accused, because of its stress on understanding the sources of stability in political systems, of innate conservatism. However, although perhaps less prominent than in the immediate post-war decades, it is by no means dead as a theoretical perspective, and may well be the only large-scale theory social scientists have with which to challenge the thinking of **Marxism** on its own level. In fact the main cause of decline in the acceptance of functionalism has been the rise to prominence of **rational choice theory** which, by making the individual actor all important, took the concentration away from the structures. An increasing awareness that institutions cannot be ignored has caused many social scientists to return in practice to a form of functionalism, though usually without accepting the partially discredited label.

Fundamentalism

Religious fundamentalism has become a journalistic code word for describing the political excesses of movements whose identity is defined by strict adherence to a religious belief. The word 'fundamentalism' has therefore taken on an almost entirely pejorative tone when its actual meaning is just that some people take the basic elements of their creed very literally. **Islam**, of renewed political importance since the Iranian revolution, has probably most often been qualified by this adjective, with world-wide concern that Islamist fundamentalism could spread throughout the **Middle East**. The reason this particular creed has been picked out is that strict adherence to Islamic belief clashes more intensely with the political culture of Western society than does a firm commitment to most branches of **Christianity**, and thus seems regressive in a world where most advanced economies are at least influenced by the values of the latter. This clash was originally felt particularly keenly over Iran, because the Iranians rebelled against a modernizing autocracy; a return to traditional Islamic beliefs coincided with a rejection of most of what the country had formally been asking the West for. So on issues such as the criminal code, the rights of women, and freedoms of religion, political activity and speech, a 'fundamentalist' religious approach conflicted with the secular values of most Western societies. This position was raised to its ultimate in Afghanistan at the turn of the century, making it the obvious target when the 11 September atrocity of 2001 caused the USA to embark on a 'war against terrorism', where the main source of **terrorism** was seen as this Islamist fundamentalist movement. (See also **jihad** and **shari'a**.)

In a similar way certain Protestant Christian denominations which have become politically important in America are often tagged 'fundamentalist' because they too affront the liberal consensus that dominates the political classes in America. Opposition to **abortion**, a stress on strict sexual ethics, pressure to de-secularize the state by allowing prayer in schools, and all the trappings of Nonconformist (but often, also of Roman Catholic) belief have come to present a threat to politicians, traditionally of greatest strength in the South and Midwest. There seems little to be gained by using a word like fundamentalism to describe a clash of values. Its attraction stems from the way that 'un'-fundamental attitudes, stripped of their own original religious origin, have come to seem, to their holders, more natural, and somehow to possess greater **value freedom**. What has to be noted is that fundamentalist sects have been far more successful in mobilizing their believers than have those sects, of any religion, which have rather moved with the times and reduced their demands and prohibitions on their congregations. (See also **secularization**.)

G

Game Theory

Game theory is an application of mathematical reasoning to problems of conflict and collaboration between rational self-interested actors. Developed in the 1940s by Austrian mathematicians von Neumann and Morgenstern, it has been applied to many problems in political science, strategic theory, and even moral philosophy. To some extent it has been used practically by defence planners, and has applications within economics. The essence of all game theory applications is to analyse the interaction between strategies which actors, intent on maximizing their welfare, are bound to take, or likely to take, given certain levels of information.

The most crucial distinction is probably between two basic sorts of game, a distinction that so neatly summarizes a recurrent quality of real life politics that the terminology has entered ordinary political discourse. This is the distinction between zero sum games and non-zero sum. Simply, one might say that a conflict between, for example, an employer and a trade union is zero sum if there is a fixed amount of profit that the firm can make, which cannot be increased by co-operation between them, or, perhaps, that a conflict between university departments for finance is zero sum if there is no chance that the departments can do anything to increase the total university budget. The technical quality of a zero sum game is that the gains to one player (we assume for convenience that this is a two player game) exactly balance the loss to the other. A non-zero sum version of these examples would allow the total amount available for division to be increased by co-operation between the players— profits might actually go up given good labour relations, or the university budget might be increased by an Education Ministry impressed by altruistic university departments, and so on. Most political situations are probably not in fact zero sum, but most are 'played' by their actors as though they were.

By examining the likely choice of strategies of independent players it is often possible to show not only what the outcome will most likely be, but where apparently rational interest-maximizing choices, if taken by independent actors, will produce a sub-optimal pay-off for both! This is characterized by the most famous of the simple game analyses in game theory, the Prisoner's

Dilemma. One assumes that two prisoners are held in separate cells, accused of a crime they committed together. To each is made the offer of turning state's evidence against the other, or remaining silent. If a prisoner gives evidence against the other, implicating themself, they will receive a minor prison sentence; if they stay silent, but are convicted on their partner's evidence, they will get a major sentence. But if both remain silent, there being no other evidence, they will both be acquitted. What do they choose? Social psychology experiments have given empirical confirmation of the theoretical prediction that they will both confess, rather than trust the other to co-operate and remain silent. Thus a sub-optimal result arrives, in the absence of malice, out of rational calculation.

One point about the prisoner's dilemma game, and it has many real political applications, is that the results depend crucially on the surrounding context, which changes the effective pay-off matrix. Suppose, for example, that both the accused are members of a criminal gang which ruthlessly punishes informers, once they are let out of prison. In this context the prediction changes. The more complicated the game, and to model any important political situation obviously requires vastly more complicated games, the more unexpected become the predictions, but also the more uncertain. One general result is to show how little our major political actions depend ultimately on rational choice, or how limited is the possibility of rationality, even on major issues, given likely information levels.

Game theory is one branch of a whole development of **public choice theories** that are said to shed increasing light on social interaction, and they occupy a curious half-way house between being **moral philosophy** and purely neutral predictive theory. However, the great promise they once showed has not been realized, largely because of the difficulty of building sufficiently accurate empirical assumptions into the models. Where they do work, for example in predicting coalition formation in multi-party governments, the results are often intuitively obvious in any case. It is not so much that game theory does not adequately model rational strategy but that institutional restraints force actors to behave, at best, with what has come to be known as 'bounded rationality'.

GATT

The General Agreement on Tariffs and Trade (GATT), which was signed at Geneva in 1947 and operated as a **United Nations** specialized agency, was part of a series of attempts to reform the international economy after the Second World War, starting with the Bretton Woods agreement of 1944. The main aim of GATT was progressively to reduce tariffs in all signatory countries towards an ultimate state of world-wide **free trade**. A series of 'rounds' of negotiations steadily reduced tariffs on manufacturing products, so that by the end of the seventh round, known as the Tokyo round, in 1979 the international average tariff on imports of manufactured goods was less than 5%. However, the remaining tariffs, on agricultural produce and on textiles, not only remained high, but were of particular concern to the **Third World** developing countries who needed to export these products to the developed economies of the **First World** to earn hard currency and to counterbalance their own imports of manufactured goods. Agricultural tariffs were politically extremely sensitive because the two biggest markets for export of cheap food by Third World economies (and some developed but agriculturally-intensive economies like New Zealand) are the **European Union (EU)** and the USA. In both these areas long-term and politically entrenched policies, the Common Agricultural Policy in the EU and the tradition of farm subsidies dating from the 1930s depression in the USA, protect domestic farmers from competition. The last round of GATT negotiations, which started in Uruguay in 1986, had still not made real progress in reducing these tariffs by the early 1990s, and even threatened to break down completely leading to a trade war. The problem remained to bedevil the early years of its successor organization, the **World Trade Organization (WTO)** at the turn of the century. It will always be unpopular domestically for the governments of EU countries and the USA to support cuts in their own systems of agricultural protection, and it is unclear what progress can be made in this area. Naturally this leads to a more or less justified claim by the Third World that the leading economies were all in favour of free trade when it was in their own interest, but indifferent to it as soon as it threatened to harm their own producers. Rivalries between some First World economies, notably the USA and the EU, are now played out at in the WTO, with a good deal of rather cynical coalition-building with particularly convenient producer countries.

Gaullism

Gaullism is a post-war French political movement originated by General Charles **de Gaulle**, but by no means limited to his own views, or parties founded by him. It nowadays represents perhaps the major conservative force in French politics. There have been several Gaullist parties, the names of which change from time to time, starting with the party de Gaulle founded at the end of the Second World War, the RPF; the current version, the Rassemblement pour la République (RPR), is headed by Jacques Chirac. The prime ministership of Chirac in the mid-1980s, under a socialist president, François **Mitterrand**, whose presidential term overlapped parliamentary elections which the right had won (a period known as **cohabitation**) demonstrated the flexibility of Gaullist politics, as well as the strength of the constitution. Chirac was still the leading figure in French politics, this time as president, cohabiting with a socialist prime minister, at the beginning of the 21st century. The extent to which he was any longer a Gaullist in anything but name remains unclear.

As an overall movement, Gaullism has no particularly distinctive ideology, except its adherence to some of the views that were dear to de Gaulle. Of these the most significant is a belief in the importance of a strong centralized state, with a powerful **executive** and without France's traditional burden of a powerful but anarchic parliament, which had weakened and made ineffective all governments during the Third and Fourth Republics. This had been de Gaulle's aim at the beginning of the **Fourth Republic**, and it was what he created in the **Fifth Republic**. Even this, though, is by no means new as an ideal in French politics, being a re-interpretation of the **Jacobin** tradition. The other vital element of de Gaulle's thinking accepted by modern Gaullism is the importance of French national independence and a suspicion of internationalist movements. Thus de Gaulle partially withdrew France from **NATO**, and the Gaullists remain lukewarm towards France's membership of the **European Union**. This position went hand-in-hand with a stress on France's own military forces: de Gaulle created a nuclear deterrence force, and the Gaullist parties have always been determined to keep up such independent military strength. Even these policies, however, except perhaps the attitude to Europe, may be seen as essentially French rather than Gaullist, because the socialist Mitterrand, president from 1981–95, kept faith with them. Representing what France essentially *is*, though, is exactly how the party would describe itself.

De Gaulle himself had a more complicated political philosophy built round a distinction he drew between 'Noble' and 'Base' politics. Noble politics, which he felt he practised as president, had to do with uniting the nation and leading it in crucial areas of the public interest, being a non-partisan activity. Indeed, de Gaulle derided political parties as divisive and often corrupt, and his personal relations with his own political parties (they never, in fact, had 'party' in their titles) were always distant and aloof. In contrast, base politics were the politics of haggling and compromise on private or sectional interests, which he felt were best left to others, especially parliament, in the day-to-day running of society. Politically, the Gaullists are now a fairly orthodox conservative party, with a predictable support among the middle and upper classes, the religious, the older, and, often, women. Originally it had been an ideologically diverse movement, united above all by a commitment to de Gaulle as a national saviour, and to the need to fight for the stability of the Fifth Republic. With de Gaulle dead and the Republic safely entrenched it has narrowed its ideological and voting base, but remains well organized and politically the main opposition to the united French left, particularly when working in alliance with other centre-right groupings.

Gender Gap

Social scientists suspect that there are a variety of gender gaps. In general, these all refer to a situation where women are supposed to hold beliefs or attitudes, or to engage in some form of socio-political activity, at a different rate or in a different manner than men. The classic example is the long-held theory that women are more politically conservative than men, at least as measured by their tendency to vote for conservative parties more frequently than do men. In the United Kingdom it has been a widely held belief that women are in this sense more conservative than men, at least from the late 1920s when all women were enfranchised on the same terms as men. The theory has more generally been held to be true across Western Europe for much of the post-1945 period. One needs to distinguish between a general and long-term tendency, and a particular difference in voting between men and women in any one election. The latter case can easily come about because of rational differences in the expected utility of victory for one rather than another candidate or party, when an issue on which men and women can be expected to have pragmatically different interests is vital. The gender gap usually suggests a more deeply rooted pattern of ideological preference, based on highly socialized differences in outlook. There is very little hard evidence that such a gender gap continues to be important in Western politics. If it ever existed the progress towards women's equality has almost certainly destroyed whatever deferential attitudes may have formed the basis of such a gender gap.

In particular another gender gap, the long assumed difference in religious adherence—such that women throughout the Christian world have traditionally attended church much more frequently than men—has been thought to underlie a political gender gap. This argument is based on the assumption that at least some forms of religion, notably Roman Catholicism, are inherently more conservative than secular attitudes. Women attend religious services more, so are conditioned to be more conservative, and a religious gender gap produces a political gender gap. However, as **secularization** has progressed, and fewer people go to church, we must assume that this underlying mechanism is dismantling.

General Will

The general will is a political concept that originated, in its most detailed form, with Jean Jacques **Rousseau** in his *Social Contract* although similar ideas have always existed in political thought. For Rousseau the general will meant the collective decision of all the people in a state when they tried to consider only what was good for the whole society rather than what they wanted as individuals. He contrasts the general will with 'the will of all', which is merely an aggregation of the separate desires of selfishly-oriented individuals. Rousseau believed that the supreme political value, **liberty**, could only be assured when each man only had to obey those laws he himself created and accepted. It was his theory that, if a society could be organized so that it was ruled by the general will, by this collective view of what was best for all, then in a fundamental way everyone would be free, because no one could oppose such a decision, and would therefore only be bound to do what he believed in. Hence would follow total **freedom**, but without anarchy or licence.

Clearly much depends in such a theory on the design of the society and the state, in order that the general will, if indeed it exists, can emerge. Much of Rousseau's profounder social theory is addressed to the question of how to get such an organization. The first vital part was a commitment to small-scale societies with full political participation in all decisions by every citizen. While not particularly accurate historically, Rousseau's admiration for the classic Greek city state, and for some small and apparently participatory contemporary societies, such as Geneva, led him to believe that it was possible under such conditions for sectional interests and political self-seeking to be banished, and for the motivation to decide only in the public interest to be victorious, thus achieving the rule by general will. He was aware that much would be needed sociologically before this could happen, advocating, for example, a high degree of economic equality, a great emphasis on collective activities and a ban on parties or cliques. Although few today are quite happy either with the slightly metaphysical undertones of the general will, or the feasibility of organizing small face-to-face societies with total political participation, his ideas are still the motivation for much of the interest in **participatory democracy** or **direct democracy**. The general will as a doctrine relates to similar concerns that have become, if anything, more rather than less popular recently, such as the **common good** and the **public interest**, which remain both matters of common political parlance, and topics of fierce academic debate in political theory. The crucial analytic power of the concept remains valid: it forces us to consider to what extent any political disagreement stems only from arbitrary, and probably inegalitarian, distinctions between citizens, rather than from deep-seated and genuine value differences.

Geopolitics

The term geopolitics was coined at the end of the 19th century by a Swedish geographer, popularized by a British geographer, Halford Mackinder, early in the 20th century, and became notorious during the 1930s when it was used by Nazi strategists in Germany. Not surprisingly it fell out of use for some time after the Second World War, but returned with a rather different meaning in the 1980s and subsequently remained in use. Originally it was an essentially deterministic concept, suggesting that the developments of international politics were largely determined by geographical factors such as land and resource distribution, sea and waterways and so on. Mackinder popularized his concept of 'The Heartland Thesis' by which powers at the centre of large land masses were bound to dominate the politics of their region unless peripheral powers actively coalesced and fought against them. The idea thus proved attractive to many in Nazi Germany, arguing that the country represented the relevant heartland of the Eurasian land mass. Such a theory not only seemed to justify German aggression as somehow or other natural, but it also justified it on the grounds that the peripheral countries would inevitably join forces against Germany—it was a version of the long-held German fear of being overcome by surrounding alliances.

With the rebirth of the idea of Geopolitics, its meaning has become little more than international strategy, an acknowledgement of the physically determined strategic needs and problems of major powers, with little or none of the deterministic undertones of its past usage. Nevertheless, even this more innocent usage does then act as some sort of justification for internationally unpopular policies. The USA's use of the idea has lead to a justification, for example, of strategic missile forces, (and now, of strategic missile defences) on the grounds of America's 'geopolitical' position. Similarly, the concept has been used to defend military policy options internally—from the United Kingdom's 'need' for a strong navy to America's 'need' for a military structure capable of fighting two major wars at once. These and other examples can seem to be easily defended by reference to 'geopolitical necessity'.

Gerrymandering

Gerrymandering is the deliberate drawing of electoral districts or constituencies—whether at the national or local level—in such a way as to secure a partisan advantage and to distort the outcome of the election. The term is of American origin and derives from the name of Elbridge Gerry who, as Governor of Massachusetts, in 1811 created abnormally shaped constituencies which looked like salamanders.

It is probable that all democratic systems indulge in some kind of gerrymandering, but in most political systems opportunities for the worst excesses are reduced by placing the electoral districting or redistributing process in the hands of neutral officials. The machinery varies from country to country, but however hard most systems have tried there is almost always a point at which political self-interest can still enter the constituency drawing arrangements. In the United Kingdom the task of redrawing constituencies is performed by the Boundary Commissioners, although there are still opportunities for the government in power to affect the timing of the implementation of any report. Thus in 1970 the Labour Home Secretary James Callaghan was thought to have delayed implementation of the Commissioners' recommendations, fearing that redistribution would aid the Conservatives and harm Labour.

In the USA since 1962 the courts have played an increasingly important role in ensuring that congressional, state and local districts are of equal or nearly equal size, although the standards for estimating this 'equality' have varied considerably (see also **judicial review**, **equal protection**). The move towards a strict interpretation of the 'one man one vote' injunction of the constitution also reflected an appreciation of the fact that, under the existing pre-1962 practice, urban areas were under-represented by comparison with rural ones and that hence many urban-based minorities (especially blacks and Hispanics) might be unfairly treated in the legislature. However, despite the decisive moves of the Supreme Court, it would be a mistake to see the gerrymandered district as having disappeared from American political life. Each reapportionment exercise is permeated by partisan manoeuvring, and the simple elimination of numerical inequalities between constituencies has not prevented the construction (often with the aid of very sophisticated computer techniques) of constituency units designed to favour one party over another. Gerrymandering is particularly a problem for countries using the simple plurality (or 'first past the post') electoral systems, both because constituency boundaries matter much more, and because this electoral system involves so much distortion in the 'votes-to-seats' equation anyway. Drawing electoral boundaries, and more generally, designing the nature of a geographically based representative system remains a crucial mechanism for constitutional design. Few other topics have been as controversial, for example, in the development of the post-1989 democracies in Eastern Europe.

Glasnost

To further his attempts, as leader of the Soviet Union from 1985, to reform, liberalize and modernize his country, Mikhail **Gorbachev** introduced two key policies, glasnost and **perestroika**. Glasnost was the more immediately, and probably the most, vital of the two. Actually intended to mean something more like the English word 'publicity', glasnost came to mean an opening of discussion, a freeing of all the constraints on expression, whether in journalism, literature or the arts, that **Stalin** and his heirs had imposed on the Soviet Union. Above all it involved freedom of the press, freedom to criticize and freedom of forms of activity, like religious worship, which had for so long been denied. Glasnost was not immediately and smoothly implemented, and the further away a community was from Moscow the less likely the authorities were to heed the reforms. Nevertheless, it very rapidly took effect and indeed various laws were repealed to ensure its survival. The initiation of glasnost was quite intentional, because Gorbachev thought that he could use the glare of publicity, with journals free to criticize the inefficient state-run enterprises, to help enforce perestroika, the restructuring of society. In the event glasnost may have been the enemy of perestroika because open publicity did more to highlight the initial failures of perestroika than to enthuse people in its cause. With the collapse of the Soviet Union after the abortive **coup d'état** of 1991 even glasnost has lost its significance, as a total freedom of expression and speech forced itself on the unwilling bureaucracy.

Globalization

There are few social science concepts quite as popular in the media at the beginning of the 21st century than that of globalization. While popular concepts are often hollow, this one, however, is undoubtedly vitally important. At its core the idea of globalization refers to the way in which economic relations now transcend national boundaries. Large corporations exist in several different countries, making components in several others, selling in many, raising finance in still others. This, of course, has long been known, and the problem of the so-called '**multinationals**' has concerned both politicians and political scientists for nearly a generation. Globalization, however, refers to a much more fundamental interconnectedness. Whole national economies are now intimately linked; a slow-down in a manufacturing industry in one area can have very rapid and often very 'logically distant' impacts thousands of miles away in several quite different sectors. In some ways it is rather like the phenomenon physicists and mathematicians have noted about the instability of supposedly deterministic systems. Proverbially it is said that a butterfly flapping its wings in India can cause a rain storm in Delaware. Globalization can, and has, meant that the collapse of a Japanese bank that over-lent on the basis of over-priced land values in Tokyo can cause the unemployment of car-factory workers in Wales.

Were globalization to mean only this, it would be important, but no more than a shift in scale with what we have experienced before. There is more, however; the very nature of the modern economy, dependent above all on information production and dissemination, has made national boundaries largely irrelevant. This has its mirrors in institutional and legal frameworks. The near impossibility of states controlling pornography on the World Wide Web, for example, is a distasteful example of globalization. Globalization would still be merely a description of economic interdependence were it not for two further factors. One is the rapid development of transnational institutions. There are now over 25,000 non-governmental organizations of an international character, when a century ago there were only a handful. Doctrines of national sovereignty are breaking down and even long-derided political institutions like the UN are beginning to have real authority. Parallel to this is a breakdown of national identity amongst the educated professional élite who run the international economic and political institutions. A new stage in world history seems to be developing. We tend to forget that the nation state is relatively new and that not long ago people felt themselves to be members of much wider communities; similarly the only difference between the international economy of the past, unregulated by states, was the impact of distance. Now that communications and distribution technology have largely made distance irrelevant, states again become unimportant as regulators, and less obviously the focus of identity or ambition.

Gorbachev

Mikhail Sergeyivich Gorbachev was, among many things, the last leader of the Soviet Union, and, more than anyone else, responsible for the abolition of that post and that nation. He was born in the Russian Caucasus in 1931 and followed what had become, for his generation, a standard path for Soviet politicians. He had the obligatory experience of manual work as a machine operator on a collective farm, and indeed was educated at Stavropol Agricultural Institute, but also, more significantly, at Moscow State University where he graduated in law. He rapidly moved into party work, and held a series of posts in district, regional and national party organizations, rising in step with his mentor, Yuri Andropov, Soviet leader between 1982 and 1984. When Andropov died Gorbachev was a potential successor as leader, having joined the Politburo at the unusually young age of 49 in 1980. He had to wait through the brief reign of a more conservative and older leader, Konstantin Chernenko, but finally became General Secretary of the **Communist Party of the Soviet Union (CPSU)** in 1985, giving him *de facto* power, and official head of state, as Chairman of the Presidium of the Supreme Soviet, in 1988.

Gorbachev was, without doubt, passionately convinced of the need for widespread reform in the Soviet Union, and was driven by an acceptance of the appalling state of the Soviet economy. In particular he realized that the Soviet Union's combative foreign and defence policy was far beyond the economy's capacity. He accepted too that existing work habits and industrial socialization had to be changed, incentives for work introduced, and the paralysing weight of party bureaucracy lifted. These matters he tried to change with his policies of **glasnost**, **perestroika** and the fresh approach symbolized by the **new thinking** in foreign affairs. But he was only a reformer. At no stage did he seriously doubt **communism**, the role of the party, or the need for powerful and direct state control. Each of his reforms, for example the introduction of very limited democracy inside the **single-party system**, simply increased the demand for more, without materially affecting the social and economic conditions of the ordinary system. Gorbachev's rule, from 1985 until his resignation on 26 December 1991 after the creation of a Common-wealth of Independent States (CIS) which embraced 11 of the 15 former Soviet republics, was a classic demonstration of the argument that a repressive regime cannot relax slightly: there is no half-way house between effective **totalitarianism** and genuine freedom. His commitment to the communist party did not waver even after the attempted **coup d'état** against him in August 1991. It will never be clear how much of the change in the last years of the Soviet Union was really to his credit, because many argue that any leader, faced with the economic and foreign policy situation of 1985, would have had to act in much the same way. What is clear is that he was never in control either of political forces or of strategy during those last years. His demise came because actual conditions worsened to the point that Soviet citizens were looking back on the **Brezhnev** era as 'the golden years', because he could not persuade people desperate for some improvement in their material welfare to accept the sacrifices necessary to achieve success for his reforms and, perhaps above all, because he was loyal to the party which the mass of the population had come to fear. However, that party never accepted that he was essentially faithful to them, and he has had no part to play in the renewed political success of the mildly reformed Communist Party in opposition.

Government

The term 'government' is a general one used to describe both the body that has authority in a given unit—whether national, regional or local—and the whole constitutional system. There are many different forms of government, such as **democracy**, autocracy and **dictatorship**. The first systematic study and classification of the methods of government was probably that undertaken by **Aristotle**, and since that time political scientists have been involved in distinguishing the different features of government and politics. The word plays a variety of roles in political language; the simple distinction between 'the government' and 'government' in a sentence like 'Government/the govern-ment discriminates against gays' is a good example. One version implicates a current ruling group, the other asserts that any ruling group will discriminate. In fact, to refer to 'the government' is only a common feature of English and English-derived political systems—in American English, for example, the word would be **'administration'**, and no precise translation is easily available for European polities. In the latter, the 'government' would be no more than the political ministry; the more general sense of government is subsumed under the concept of 'The State', itself hardly used in Anglo-American analysis. The origin of the usage which, like so much in political theory stems from classical Greek political thought, has to do with steering a ship, so is not, *ab origine*, about coercive force but based on an analogy with navigation and technical expertise.

Gradualism

Gradualism is, very broadly, a version of **socialism** which denies the need for revolution, and argues instead that the ordinary and 'slow' means of competitive democratic politics can, in time, produce the needed changes in social and economic organization (see **parliamentary socialism**). Thus gradualism is the creed of parties espousing **social democracy**, and of all socialist and communist parties which are prepared to compete against liberals and conservatives in normal elections. The Italian Communist Party, with a long tradition of democratic participation, eventually reorganized itself as a mass social democratic party in 1991, and changed its name to the Democratic Party of the Left, in what might be seen as a logical conclusion of its gradualism. The **Fabians** represented the voice of intellectual gradualists in the early British Labour Party. These approaches would be despised as 'selling out' socialism or being **revisionist** by revolutionary communist and extreme-left parties, which would have included the **Parti Communiste Français** until at least the 1960s.

Theoretically the difference hinges on arguments about the possibility of teaching the public to want socialism by example, by minor changes when a socialist government can get elected, as against forcibly creating a socialist society as soon as power can be won, peacefully or otherwise, and producing immediately the sort of state that people 'ought' to want (see **dictatorship of the proletariat**). The concept of gradualism has become somewhat redundant with the collapse of Soviet communism in the Soviet Union and Eastern Europe, so clearly is it now in the ascendant as the chosen path towards socialism. It still has a theoretical value, however, as it raises the question of whether a society could ever transform itself markedly without a violent break from its past. To those who opposed a gradualist approach, it seemed very clear that the gradualist shrank from the violence, physical or otherwise, of rapid transition because they were still too committed to the values of the society to be overthrown.

Gramsci

Antonio Gramsci (1891–1937) was the founder of the Italian Communist Party, after it split from the Italian Socialist Party in 1921. When the party had to go underground during the fascist period, Gramsci underwent a long term of imprisonment, and died in prison. During this period, however, he laid the foundation for the specifically Italian brand of communist tactics and thought which later, under the post-war Republic, allowed the party to attract the largest support of any Western European communist party. His major work in this area, the *Prison Notebooks*, are the source for much of this inspiration and indeed for the whole **Eurocommunism** movement.

Although Gramsci never dropped the theoretical basis of **communism**, remaining always committed to the doctrine of historical **materialism**, he did drop the insistence on a violent proletarian revolution. He made a distinction between tactics for the socializing of a state between the 'tactics of siege' and the 'tactics of movement'. The former was the traditional notion of building class consciousness inside a working-class ideological ghetto, ignoring all reformist movements, and waiting (as though besieged by an enemy) until the final moment of the 'true revolutionary situation'. This, the working doctrine for example of the French Communist Party, and the one that had been forced on the Russian **Bolsheviks** by their situation and the nature of the Tsarist regime, he felt was quite out of place in Italy. Instead he wished to adopt a much more flexible approach by which the communist movement would seek to ally with progressive forces, and seek to win to its cause those members of the **bourgeoisie** who had no long-term reason to support the capitalist state. At the same time the party should try, by its allies in the media and educational structures, to propagandize the whole society, to win a willing acceptance of communism, rather than try to enforce it by a **dictatorship of the proletariat**. This flexible and non-violent tradition of Italian communism enabled the party to advocate the 'Historical Compromise', by which it hoped to join the ruling Christian Democrats in power. An interesting point about Gramsci's work is that he gave a theoretical justification for **gradualism** which clearly was not subject to the usual criticism that gradualists, in the end, were merely bourgeois reformers. The collapse of the old party system in Italy after 1992, initially seemed to doom all forms of Italian communism. However disenchantment with the centre left governments of the 1990s led to something of an electoral reprieve for the reformed Italian communists. They now cling even more strongly to Gramscian analysis as the only way to seem relevant in the post-cold war new Republic and the 21st century.

Green (see Environmentalism)

Green Socialism

Green socialism is a name sometimes given to ecological or environmental political parties and movements. The term more broadly refers to the concatenation of liberal and socialist values, often attractive to middle-class radicals, which do not form a major part of the class interests of traditional working-class left-wing groups, whose attitudes to cherished values like racial tolerance or freedom of speech are not necessarily very different from those of orthodox right-wing movements. Rather than a concentration on the entirely pragmatic and materialist improvement of living conditions, green socialism is likely to be concerned with more abstract values, but as **environmentalism** becomes more and more important in the policies of all political parties, it is unclear what future green socialism has. When ecological concerns were largely disregarded, a green, or green socialist, party could draw support simply because they urged that such issues should be on the political agenda. Now that this basic point is recognized, the vital question of how to deal with the issues comes to the front, inevitably involving ideological disputes between major political parties. Thus the important question for a voter whose primary concern is the environment becomes one of whether, for example, capitalist or socialist policies are likely best to guarantee success in a commonly accepted endeavour. As such the green socialist movement has probably served its overt purpose. There was, however, always an element in the movement which sought for a much more radical change in society, in which ecological awareness was just the most useful point of discussion. What may give the Green movement more political hope is the essential collapse of the old left-wing reliance on **social democracy** as a political creed. In a world where political competition is largely between more or less liberal versions of moderate conservativism and where the orthodox left and right share almost identical economic policies, the Greens might have a hope of offering a genuine alternative. The main problem is whether they ought to accept coalition with traditional parties as a road to power and influence. Where they have done this, notably in Germany, they have tended to have little influence but had to share the collective blame for failure of traditional policies.

Grotius

Hugo Grotius (1583-1645) was a Dutch lawyer, though he spent much of his life in exile in France. He is often regarded as the founder of **international law** and, indeed, of theoretical work in international relations. Even today lawyers and political scientists refer to 'the Grotian World System' to char-acterize commonly held beliefs about the nature of **states** and the proper relations between them. Writing at a time when religion was still seen as the primary source of law, and in the early part of the development of **nation states**, Grotius attempted to argue for the existence of a **natural law** governing inter-state relations. Natural law was not religious, but based on deep human instincts; indeed, Grotius held that even God could not change natural law. The argument amounts to the claim that rational and well-intentioned statesmen would always see the correct solution to an international conflict, and thus that the absence of a world authority or international government does not make the existence of binding international law impossible. His most famous work, *On the Law of War and Peace* (usually referred to by its Latin title *De iure belli ac pacis*), published in 1625, expounds this doctrine in considerable detail, and includes the first serious effort to create a theory of the **just war** outside theological writing. His theories are a complex mixture of appeals to enlightened self-interest and a belief in essential altruism. Thus his first and overriding principle of international law, *pacta sunt servanda* (promises must be kept), is based mainly on the idea that we will all see that it is in our interest to keep promises and abide by treaties, because otherwise the world will be too chaotic for our own survival. His just war theory is surprisingly modern, insisting that only defensive wars (or, less modern, retaliatory wars) can ever be justified. Although the philosophical basis of his arguments often appear quaint today, most of his ideas are now enshrined in public international law, and his work is still cited in international tribunals. Given the increased salience of international tribunals of one form and another, and a growing public acceptance that states are bound by some form of international law, Grotius' ideas are possibly more important than at any time since he wrote. It is unfortunate for his reputation that he did not on the whole support what would now be known as **'humanitarian intervention'**.

Group Theory

Group theory, in political science, is largely associated with **Bentley** and, in various reformulations, with writers on **pluralism**. The central argument is that societies consist of a large number of social, ethnic or economic groups, more or less well-organized, in political competition with each other to put pressure on the government into producing the policies favourable to the relevant group. Versions of this theory can either claim that it is entirely compatible with the aims of democracy, and that group representation satisfies democratic norms, as well as being empirically realistic, or can alternatively be used to argue that all societies have the same true structure, whatever their surface ideology and characteristics. Other branches of political science have taken the nature and multiplicity of groups as vital elements in determining political stability or indeed the liberalness or otherwise of the society.

Guerrilla

Originally guerrillas were unorthodox soldiers fighting behind enemy lines, challenging conventional forces with harassing actions, and never allowing themselves to be forced into a pitched battle where the conventional superiority would defeat them. The word is of Spanish origin, dating from the Napoleonic Peninsular wars, when some Spanish partisans kept up such unconventional combat. Still in this original sense, the heyday of guerrilla warfare was in the Second World War and, after, in Asia. **Mao Zedong's** peasant armies, when fighting the better equipped Nationalist forces in China, resorted to such techniques, and, indeed, Mao wrote what is still probably the definitive textbook. Thereafter independence movements elsewhere in Asia, especially in Malaya and what was then French Indo-China, used the tactics to try to force out colonial powers. In Malaya the British army managed to develop counter-guerrilla tactics which worked effectively, but Ho Chi Minh's guerrillas ultimately defeated the French colonial forces, leading to the creation of North Vietnam. Subsequently guerrilla warfare contributed to the defeat of the US forces in the **Vietnam War**, though it should be noted that the more conventionally organized North Vietnam Army was the force that actually inflicted serious harm on US forces.

Since the 1960s the phrase 'guerrilla groups' has taken on another meaning, to cover the so-called 'urban-terrorists', for example extreme left-wing groups like the Red Army Faction and the Baader-Meinhoff gang in West Germany, and similar violent opponents of the regimes in Italy and Japan. The tactics are analogous in as much as they consist of sniping and harassment raids against the state power, rather than the building of a conventional revolutionary under-ground intended to fight a pitched battle against police and army. Part of the theory of guerrilla warfare was always to try to force the conventional enemy into repressive actions which would cause those exerting the repression to lose the support of the general population. Although it took a long time for the lessons to be learned, the professional military in most Western countries have developed very powerful anti-guerrilla techniques. Many senior officers in the British and American armies have become converts to the idea that countering guerrilla warfare tactics is the prime professional activity, an argument made all the more powerful with the diminution of traditional military activities with the ending of the **cold war**. Such approaches have come even more to the fore since the launching of the USA's 'war on terrorism' after the atrocity of 11 September, as can be seen by the huge reliance on 'special forces' rather than conventional infantry in, *inter alia*, the Afghanistan campaign.

Gulf War

Iraq invaded Kuwait in August 1990, and this event led to the first major **United Nations (UN)** military campaign since the **Korean War** of the early 1950s. Although the UN Security Council unanimously, and within hours of the invasion, passed Resolution No. 660, calling for the immediate and unconditional withdrawal of Iraqi forces, it was not until November that it authorized, in Resolution No. 678, the multinational force, which had by then been largely assembled (as allowed in Article 51 of the UN Charter), to use 'all necessary means' to liberate Kuwait and to restore peace to the region. Meanwhile, within days of the original military reaction, the USA dispatched a light force to defend Saudi Arabia, which was feared to be under threat of invasion by Iraqi troops stationed on the Kuwaiti border, at the request of the Saudi government. Pressure from Western members of the UN Security Council led to the swift imposition of economic sanctions involving an international embargo on all trade with Iraq (thus forcing the suspension of Iraq's economic lifeline, its oil exports), except for medical and humanitarian relief supplies.

There were several politically sensitive issues with which the UN-sponsored allied powers had to contend. The USA, which was always the clear leader of the campaign to liberate Kuwait, was anxious to broaden the basis of the coalition so that Iraq could not present itself as a Third World power being bullied by the capitalist West. This was extremely successful, because several Arab nations, most importantly Egypt and Syria (which did not even have diplomatic relations with the USA at the time), joined up, as did some, but not all, NATO members. During the autumn and early winter the allied nations built up their forces in Saudi Arabia, especially the USA which committed 430,000 ground troops, 1,300 fighter and support aircraft, 2,000 tanks and 55 warships. (The British contribution, though much smaller in absolute numbers, represented 50% of the armoured and air assets of the British Army of the Rhine.) Although the then Soviet Union was not prepared to dispatch forces, it was generally supportive of the Western members in the Security Council, and certainly made it clear that this **Middle East** crisis was not going to become a **cold war** issue. It took some time for the USA and other allies to persuade the Security Council to move from sanctions to an outright ultimatum, and to authorize the use of force. At the end of November they finally agreed unanimously to authorize the use of military force if Iraq failed to withdraw completely from Kuwait, and to agree to the payment of compensation to Kuwait, by 15 January 1991.

There was also a domestic political battle for the US president, George Bush, in persuading an increasingly **isolationist** USA to allow him to fight. Although those opposed invoked the fears of another **Vietnam War**, and there was much criticism in the Senate, ultimately he gained the necessary authority.

As the ultimatum drew near there was considerable scepticism as to whether the US-led coalition forces would, or even could, take effective military action. Much was made of the apparent size and technical competence of the Iraqi forces, particularly the Revolutionary Guard. Iraq had, after all, fought the **Iran–Iraq War** to a standstill over eight years of battles as bloody as anything since the First World War. It was doubted by many, most importantly by the

Iraqis, that the West really had the courage to go to war. (Bush's problems in persuading the American electorate to let him wage war contributed to Iraq's fatal misperception on this matter.)

When war came, suddenly and within hours of the ultimatum deadline, it must have been obvious immediately to the Iraqis that they had made a serious mistake about the nature of the allied war plans. The allies, mainly the USA, but with significant help from the UK, launched the biggest strategic air bombardment ever seen, without putting a single ground soldier at risk. For nearly a month military and civilian infrastructure targets were systematically destroyed with the loss of only a handful of allied air force personnel. Superior allied technology rendered Iraqi targets almost defenceless. Meanwhile Iraq retaliated with numerous *Scud* missile attacks into Saudi Arabia and, in a futile attempt to sway Arab support for the allies, Israel. There was much speculation over Iraq's capability and intention to arm these missiles with chemical, or even nuclear, warheads, but in the event all the missiles were conventionally armed. The morale and fighting capacity of the Iraqi army was so destroyed that when the inevitable counter invasion, the 'land war', started it lasted only 100 hours, during which much of the Iraqi ground forces were destroyed, captured, surrendered or driven back over their own border. True to the terms of the UN mandate, the allies, on Bush's insistence, refused to invade Iraq itself to complete the destruction of Iraqi military power, a decision which later came to be questioned when the regime of Saddam Hussain survived. The real aim of the USA, and probably the British, had always been transparent—to destroy Iraq's war-making capacity, and to terminate the dictatorship of Saddam Hussain. These unofficial war aims were not accomplished. Much of the Iraqi army survived by fleeing, or troops had never been committed in the first place, and Hussain easily put down rebellions against him by Shi'ite Muslims in the south of Iraq and by Kurds in the north. The UN appeared to be unable to force Hussain to dismantle entirely his nuclear weapons programme, and Iraq almost certainly remained a serious potential threat to stability in the Middle East. In this latter sense it was a massive affirmation that, with the cold war over, the UN really could be a powerful agent for peace, and that aggressive military force could be stopped by collective action. Nonetheless by the beginning of the 21st century Saddam Hussain was regarded as one of the great enemies of the USA, and President George W. Bush's 'war on terrorism' seemed likely to escalate into renewed Western involvement with Iraq.

H

Hawks and Doves

Hawks, and their opposites, doves, came into prominence in the USA during the **Vietnam War**. Hawks were those who favoured tough military activities and a generally forceful solution to problems. Doves were those who took a gentle, conciliatory or pacifistic stance on any issue. Hawks, for example, would be in favour of President Nixon's bombing of Cambodia in 1971, and might oppose arms-control negotiations unless sure that the USA would gain an advantage. Since then the word 'hawk' has expanded its range to refer to any tough approach to almost any problem. One might be, or be seen as, hawkish, if one supported Israel against the **PLO**, but, to take another example, the stringent regulation of picket lines in industrial disputes could be hawkish. Although it often has overtones of conservative or right-wing political views, the emphasis is more on the use of force and coercion rather than diplomacy and negotiation. Thus a left-wing pressure group might have its hawks and doves, in terms of preparedness to participate in demonstrations or street confrontations with authority. Although the terminology was notably absent in the USA during the often fierce debates as to whether or not to go to war over Iraq's invasion of Kuwait, it gained renewed currency with regard to the Middle East peace process in the 1990s and received some use from commentators on the USA's 'war on terrorism' launched in the aftermath of the atrocity perpetrated on the USA in September 2001.

Hayek

Friedrich von Hayek (1899–1992), though born and educated in Vienna, spent most of his career in London (he became a naturalized British citizen in 1936) and Chicago. In Chicago he was one of the founders of the **Chicago School**. Primarily an economic theorist, his work was highly influenced by his **libertarian** approach towards politics, especially in his first major work, *The Road to Serfdom* (1944), in which he attacked proposals for post-war economic planning as being akin to **totalitarianism**. His attitude to planning, and indeed most of his economic theory, derived from a more general position he held on the question of social science. He scorned the social sciences, including much of economics, on the simplistic ground that human behaviour and interaction was too complex for human understanding. (It is said that his contempt for most economists gave him very mixed feelings about accepting the Nobel Prize for economics in 1974.) He believed that prediction and forecasting were impossible in economics, and developed this into an attack on all forms of government planning. According to Hayek only the market, comprising the experience and ideas of millions of actors, could set prices and production levels efficiently, and government intervention was bound to distort this market decision-making process. In fact his opposition to planning was more a matter of political principle, because he saw it as an unjustified interference with individual **freedom**. He had an extremely low opinion of politicians, and this also influenced his belief that **government** should have no economic regulatory powers, because otherwise they would try to bribe the electorate before elections, producing inflation. Planning, however, was defined extremely broadly, so government was to be forbidden all social welfare roles as well as regulatory economic powers. All other institutions that threatened to distort the pure unfettered working of the market were equally anathema, especially the **trade unions**, which he described as 'monopolists of labour'.

In technical economics he was one of the earliest advocates of **monetarism**. Later, in 1979 he argued for a squeeze on the **money supply** so intense that it would end inflation completely, even accepting that this might require 20% inflation for a period. This combination of monetarism and pessimism about politicians led to his most extreme suggestion, in the mid-1970s, that money should be 'denationalized', that is, there ought to be competing public and private currencies. Although he was largely ignored by economists and politicians for most of his career, he became extremely influential in the 1970s and 1980s, when his ideas found favour with the Reagan Administration in the USA and, above all, with the **Thatcherite** wing of the British Conservative Party. This influence in the United Kingdom came about largely through the activity of the Institute of Economic Affairs, which he had persuaded an early supporter to set up in 1957, and which became a think-tank for the Conservative right soon after. He continues to be taken seriously as a political theorist, in part because of the collapse of the previous main alternative for centrist political thought, the doctrines of **social democracy**.

Head of Government

The term 'head of government' refers to the person—whether designated prime minister or president or chancellor—who is formally appointed to head a **government**. Usually this person will be the leading member of his or her party, although sometimes a compromise figure may be asked to form a coalition.

Within the **European Union (EU)** the heads of government of the member countries gather at summit meetings for general reviews of EU business, or for specially convened summits for extraordinary and emergency topics. Until 1974 these meetings were arranged on an *ad hoc* basis, but in that year the custom was formalized with the establishment of the European Council. Between 1974 and 1986 the European Council met three times a year, and from 1986 onwards twice a year. It is to be distinguished from the two executive institutions of the EU: the Council of Ministers, which consists of ministerial representatives from the governments of the member states; and the European Commission, which is regarded as both the supranational and administrative arm of the executive.

Head of State

The head of state is the person who exercises a number of formal and ceremonial powers and responsibilities, such as receiving visiting monarchs and other heads of state, and accepting the accreditation of ambassadors. Usually the head of state will have some residual, almost referee-like, political powers—such as the appointment of a **head of government** or **prime minister**. In political systems which retain a **monarchy** it is the monarch who is the obvious head of state. In others it is a **president**, whose political powers may vary considerably. In some countries, such as Israel the degree of real political power is very limited except when, as occurs quite frequently in Italy for example, coalition formation requires the exercise of discretion in relation to the selection of a prime minister likely to be able to form a government capable of commanding the support of the **parliament**. It is because of this that Italy, following the French model set by the **Fifth Republic**, is debating increasing the powers of the president. In some systems the roles of chief executive—with real political power—and head of state are merged, and this is obviously the case in the USA. In other political systems, notably France in the Fifth Republic, there is an ambiguity surrounding the role of the president, whose powers and responsibilities may vary according to particular political circumstances and the personality of the incumbent. There is no tidy pattern to the structure of states and governments, and the roles of their heads can be very complex. This headship need not even be held by one person: the Yugoslavian presidency after the death of Tito, for example, operated as a collective body of eight members with its leadership rotating among them, while the Israelis experimented, largely unsuccessfully, with alternating the prime ministership between two party leaders.

Hegel

Georg Wilhelm Friedrich Hegel (1770–1831) may well be the most influential philosopher and political theorist Germany has produced, with the possible exception of **Kant**. He follows in a European tradition influenced by **Rousseau** and having important connections with **Plato** and the Classical Greek philosophers. His influence, though often of a tenuous nature, is undeniable across an enormous range of modern social thought, but especially in **Marxism**, even though he would not himself have been in any way a Marxist. No one could reduce the subtleties of Hegel's thought to a dictionary definition. The only approach is to identify a few of his most influential ideas. To start, he argued that human civilization was the story of intellectual and moral progress, and that this was not accidental but the working out of a rational spirit in human perception. This is one of the ways in which he influences Marxists, who also believe in human progress, although they would attach much more importance to material or technological change, while Hegel saw the real source and description of progress as lying in our collective intellectual development. Secondly, his detailed account of change and development, the 'dialectical argument', has been taken over by Marxists (see **dialectical materialism**), but also by many other schools of thought. The dialectic, to Hegel, is the process in which any given social or intellectual state contains an essential contradiction. This contradiction forces a conflict (of ideas to Hegel, of interests to others). As a result we must see human history as a series of conflicts where a 'thesis' (the original state or idea) conflicts with an 'antithesis' to produce a result, the 'synthesis'. But the synthesis itself must contain an internal contradiction, and on we go again. Although such ideas usually seem extremely metaphysical, Hegel's writing is often down-to-earth and illustrative, and shows how useful a dialectical approach can be. In practical terms his major importance is as a precursor of **Marx**; but Marx radically changed Hegel's perspective, by taking material rather than intellectual matters to be crucial. Hegel tended to believe that the **state** was the most important aspect of politics, and much of his more directly political argument was concerned with the development of the state. For Hegel the state, the way we organize our politics and our systems of social coercion, demonstrated our degree of rationality; so the state was the best measure of human progress. He raises so many issues that most subsequent political theories can be related to his work. Apart from Marxism, the most obvious is the work of another German social thinker, of more vital relevance to mainstream academic thought, Max **Weber**.

Hegemony

Hegemony, which essentially means the domination or rule of one actor over others, is mainly a concept in international relations, used both by academics and professionals. Its origin is in Greek historical thought but the concept, and indeed the specific word, has occurred frequently in the history of political thought, in a variety of intellectual traditions. At one level it is a relatively simple idea—a hegemony occurs when one country, for example the USA in the West during the **cold war**, is massively dominant over other actors in the relevant sphere—members of **NATO**, in this case. However, hegemony becomes more complex when one asks about the nature of this dominion, because hegemony cannot rest simply on force, or even on an implied capacity to do great harm to any challenger. Rather, a system is hegemonic when the domination of one actor is taken for granted and unchallenged by those over whom it holds sway. At the least this requires that other actors, not only the hegemon itself, put pressure on any challenger from within the sphere. The extent to which the Soviet Union was hegemonic with respect to Eastern Europe during the cold war, is demonstrated more by what happened to Czechoslovakia in 1968 than Hungary in 1956. In the latter case Hungary's attempt to liberalize its economic and political system was stopped by a brutal invasion of Soviet forces. But in 1968 the Soviet Union orchestrated what came to be known as 'the fraternal invasion', because the forces that entered Czechoslovakia came from several of the Eastern European states, not only the Soviet Union.

The major route to hegemony is to arrange that the other actors in the system, or their élites at least, share an ideology with the hegemon, so that its considerable, actual power is enhanced by the fact that most actors think that what is in the hegemon's interest is in theirs as well—certainly if no obvious alternative arrangement seems even remotely plausible. Thus, returning to the example of the USA and Western Europe, the single major source of the USA's hegemonic status was probably Europe's early dependence on development funds under the **Marshall Plan** in 1947 and its later dependence on the dollar as an international currency, rather than the US nuclear weaponry.

Helsinki Process

The Helsinki process is a portmanteau way of referring both to the original 'Helsinki' conference (some sessions of which were actually conducted in Geneva) of 1973–75, which led to the Helsinki Final Act covering European security, economic and **human rights** affairs, and to the subsequent conferences and agreements arising from the first meetings. The most important part of the Helsinki process has been the increasing institutionalization of the body it set up, the Conference on Security and Co-operation in Europe (CSCE, renamed the **Organization for Security and Co-operation in Europe—OSCE**—in December 1994), which has had a secretariat based in Prague since 1991. The inspiration for the Helsinki process was the short period of **détente** between the Soviet Union and the USA which started with the successful negotiations of the **SALT** I treaties in 1972. Its particular political importance was that it involved every European state (Albania eventually joined in 1991, and several of the newly-independent countries of the former Soviet Union and Yugoslavia were also admitted), and also included the USA and Canada as countries inextricably involved in European security. After 15 years of little practical achievement the initiatives of the Helsinki process suddenly assumed much greater importance at the beginning of the 1990s after the collapse of communism effectively left the whole of Europe with a single ruling **ideology**—some version of liberal capitalism. For example, the OSCE became involved in cease-fire and human rights monitoring in the Yugoslav conflicts, and there has been speculation that, because of its pan-European membership, the organization was better placed to intervene in European emergencies than either **NATO** or the **European Union**.

Hitler

Adolf Hitler (1889–1945) was the political and military leader of Germany from 1933 to his death at the end of the Second World War. He had been a junior corporal in the First World War, a failed artist, and was a rootless but emotionally and intellectually powerful man who took control of a set of movements of the German right in the early and middle 1920s. In the chaotic conditions of the **Weimar Republic** his party, offering a violent and aggressive assertion of nationalism, populism and racism (see **fascism**), and bearing the nowadays self-contradictory title of 'National-Socialist German Working Man's Party', was one apparent answer. Hitler ruthlessly used any phobia he could find in the German population, especially **anti-Semitism**, to build up an emotional support for his party against the apparent threat of the communists, with whom his paramilitary party fought in street demonstrations in German cities. Ultimately he came to power as a result of ordinary electoral politics, helped tacitly by the right-wing president, Paul von Hindenburg (1847–1934), and managed to get himself appointed leader, 'Führer', of Germany for life. Once in legal power he and his party took over all aspects of German life, controlling totally the military and police powers, and much of industry, as well as the whole of civil government. There were no elections allowed in Germany during his rule. His aim was the creation of the 'Thousand Year Reich', a new German state that he hoped would cover most of Europe, and which did, during much of the Second World War, very nearly achieve this.

Hitler was responsible for initiating a movement of fanatical and violent aggression through Europe which took the combined force of the British

Empire, the Soviet Union and the USA to overcome. As far as political science is concerned, Hitler poses two enormous questions. Firstly, how does a movement like his take over a major civilized nation, and secondly, how can one describe the **totalitarianism** he represented, or even begin to make such a political system comprehensible, inside the usual terms of the social sciences? There are no totally satisfactory accounts of Hitler or his impact, but inevitably parallels are drawn between him and **Stalin** and with later dictators such as Idi Amin of Uganda, Saddam Hussein of Iraq or Pol Pot of Cambodia as examples of huge and evilly-used political power. There seems to be an inexplicable tendency for single individuals to wield enormous and catastrophic power at odd times in history, and this (witness, for example, the Roman Emperor Caligula) is not a recent phenomenon. The nearest to an explanation to be offered involves the idea of **charisma**, but much more mundane considerations, such as control over well disciplined and ruthless security forces and the cunning exploitation of tribal or ethnic hatreds, are equally important. At the beginning of the 21st century there appears to be no diminution in public fascination with Hitler and his regime, with new studies often winning large sales, appearing almost monthly.

Hobbes

Thomas Hobbes (1588–1679) is perhaps the most important English political theorist. Potential rivals for such a title, such as John **Locke**, have rough counterparts in other theoretical traditions, but Hobbes may be unique. He wrote during the time of the Commonwealth and the Restoration, and his whole political theory is deeply influenced by the English Civil War. His most famous book, *Leviathan*, tries to present a blueprint for a social system which would be stable and minimize the dangers of anarchy and lawlessness, which Hobbes thought threatened all societies. He is one of the earliest users of the **social contract** approach, and its associated concept of the **state of nature**. His thought is very complicated, and can only be summarized at great risk of misleading, but the central point is a very deep distrust of human nature, which he held to be fixed and unchangeable. To Hobbes all men, left to themselves, were predatory, greedy, cruel and frightened of others. Thus he argues that only the toughest and most draconian of states, with supreme power (held in this model by a sovereign), can possibly hold them under control and allow the development of civilized life. Above all he is concerned to remove all sources of competing political **authority** in the state. There are no rules governing what the sovereign can do to a citizen, because to have such rules would imply some qualification to the absolute duty to obey. If such a limitation existed, there would be a problem in defining who would make judgments on alleged infringements. If it were a court, that would set up a rival authority. Similarly he insists that his sovereign have the right to rule on religious truth, because to allow a church to do that might again set up challenges to authority. Although it can make dreary reading, the development of his argument is subtle and powerful, and Hobbesian ideas permeate many thinkers who would not accept the label. His intellectual commitment was to produce a true 'science' of politics, and he was particularly influenced by the developing mathematical sciences of his day, trying to produce a social science with the same logical certainty. There are still many puzzles about what Hobbes really meant, despite the thousands of studies written on him, and his own beliefs about religion, and the extent to which he felt men could be moral in the right circumstances, are deeply unclear. The toughness of his arguments and their often unpalatable conclusions denied him political favour in his own days, but his theories are still debated, and often seen to be relevant, especially in the study of international relations.

Homosexuality

Since the 1960s, when moral codes were relaxing everywhere in the West in favour of the 'permissive' society, the political implications of homosexuality have become increasingly prominent. The word 'gay' is often used when discussing homosexuality in a political context, and can refer to either male or female homosexuality, although it is frequently restricted to the former. **Discrimination** against homosexuals, and encroachment on their **civil rights** by a heterosexual majority, much of which regards their own sexuality as 'normal', are perhaps the major concerns of this element of the population, usually estimated as not less than 10%, and possibly much more. Politically the gay movement has perhaps now reached maturity, with the continuing crisis of **AIDS**, ensuring its progress. Not only has almost every Western jurisdiction removed any legal ban on homosexuality *per se*, but there has been remarkable progress in ending legal discrimination against gays.

The real problems facing a successful gay political movement are of two quite different types. Practically, it is still a brave politician, certainly as far as the United Kingdom and USA are concerned, who will admit to being homosexual if their political base is on the right. Until recently such an admission would lead rapidly to the end of a political career. This is not the same as saying that it is not known that significant proportions of major legislative assemblies are homosexual. However, this reticence makes it very hard for the gay movement to be politically effective by lobbying orthodox politicians. The other problem is that of the political character of homosexuality itself. Clearly there is a powerful civil rights argument to be made in favour of equal treatment before the law and even of **affirmative action** to redress past discrimination, but there seem to be no issues which are specifically gay-issues as opposed to the interests of all cultural groups. Sexual orientation does not correlate with any ideological attitudes, although only those who live in a more **radical** counter-culture will find it easy publicly to admit their homosexuality. Consequently, and somewhat to its detriment, any gay movement is likely to be perceived as generally radical, which not only loses any support it might get from non-radicals, but makes it even harder for homosexuals in established and often conservative professions to 'come out' and support the politics of the gay movement.

Hostages

Taking hostages to force an opponent to give up something they desire has been a major method of war-fighting since the beginning of armed conflict. Throughout most of history it has been seen as entirely acceptable, and was well controlled by the early rules of warfare and chivalry. Hostages came to particular prominence in international politics at the time of the Islamic revolution in Iran when, in November 1979, revolutionary forces seized the US embassy and imprisoned its staff, holding them hostage against American intervention in internal Iranian affairs. They were only released in January 1981, and although it is unclear that the USA did anything to please the Iranian revolutionary council as a result of their holding hostages, the general idea that it might be useful to capture Westerners, and especially US citizens, became widespread among militant groups in the **Middle East**.

From that time on, and certainly until 1991, the taking of hostages became a widely-used tactic by revolutionary groups in the Middle East, especially in Lebanon, usually to protest against Israeli policy and more generally as a weapon by **fundamentalist** Islamist groups opposed to Western interference in the region. Dozens of Western citizens were captured and held in primitive, sometimes barbaric, conditions for periods running from months to more than five years by various groups. Several hostages died in captivity, and some were deliberately and semi-publicly 'executed'. Though most hostages were US citizens, nationals of several other Western countries were captured at one time or another. Policy towards the hostage takers varied: France was prepared to make deals to get their citizens released; the USA made no overt deals but was widely suspected of covert arrangements to buy the release of some; while the United Kingdom stuck firmly to a policy of not even negotiating, on the grounds that giving any success to the Islamic groups would only encourage them in their tactics.

The political situation changed, however, with the USA and other Western powers becoming less automatically supportive of Israel, and, especially after the **Gulf War**, with a general recognition that there could be a negotiated general settlement in the Middle East, the futility of holding hostages became apparent even to the hostage takers. Particularly important was the increasing moderation of Iran after the death of the leader of their Islamic revolution, **Ayatollah** Khomeini, because that country had, officially or otherwise, been the supporter and sometimes financier of the captors. In addition Syria, newly acceptable to Western powers after its support for the UN-sponsored and US-led Gulf War campaign, applied pressure that it was especially qualified to do as the major Arab power controlling Lebanon. After the lengthy saga of hostage taking, and occasional releases, most of the remaining hostages were released within a few months in the second half of 1991. It is difficult to see what any party gained from the entire process, but the internal politics of the USA was seriously affected from time to time as the world's greatest military power was seen to be totally ineffectual, and even tainted by dubious and disastrous tactics such as the Iran-Contra affair, when arms were secretly (and illegally) sold to Iran, to encourage that country to use its influence over the hostage takers to release Americans held captive, and then the profits were used to fund (again illegally) the Contra **guerrillas** then fighting in Nicaragua. There seems no reason why the tactic of hostage taking should not reappear in the future. To the extent that smaller and less internationalized groups have continued taking hostages—whom they usually kill—it seems the motivations are as much frustration and anger as strategy.

Human Rights

Human rights, one of a family of concepts like **civil rights** or **civil liberties**, or **natural rights**, are those rights and privileges held to belong to any person, regardless of any provision that may or may not exist for them in their legal system, simply because, as a human being, there are certain things which they may not be forbidden by any government. Exactly what the list of these rights is, or why we are entitled to them, varies from thinker to thinker. Since the Second World War there have been several quasi-official listings, among which the most prominent are probably the United Nations Declaration of Human Rights, and the European Convention for the Protection of Human Rights and Fundamental Freedoms. Of these, the latter is actually partially enforceable, because it forms the legal basis for the European Court of Human Rights (which operates under the aegis of the Council of Europe, in Strasbourg), to which citizens of subscribing nations may bring cases against their own governments. Since the passing, in 1998, of the **Human Rights Act** these entitlements have become fully integrated into English law. Typical elements on any list of basic human rights will be, for example, the right to freedom of speech, religion, the right to family life, the right to fair trial procedures in criminal cases, the right to be protected against inhumane punishment, the right to political liberty, and so on. Philosophically all these lists and institutions derive from a long-developed notion of **natural law** or natural rights, but the modern applications can often be quite mundane, if still important. As examples, cases to the European Court of Human Rights have varied from complaints against court-martial procedures in European armies, through restrictions on press freedom in English cases arising from contempt of court orders, to the validity of corporal punishment in Scottish schools and the access to lawyers of German suspected terrorists. Human rights are aspects of the permanent fight of citizens against the power of the **state**, and are to be found, expressed in a variety of ways, as a working part of most legal systems and most political theories. As world political and economic systems become more integrated some sort of consensus may be developing about what rights exist that no government may deny. Such a consensus has some real force, because powerful and rich states like the USA or the leading European states are increasingly making foreign or military aid, or treaty negotiations, conditional on progress being made on human rights by the prospective recipient country. The **Helsinki** agreements on European security specifically require human rights standards as part of the development of military security agreements. Such conceptions of rights however, continue to be 'negative' in that they forbid governments to do things, rather than positive, requiring governments to achieve goals like full employment.

Human Rights Act

The 1998 Human Rights Act (HRA) in the United Kingdom came into full force in October 2000 and was one of the constitutional reforms initiated by the 1997–2001 Labour Government. It was the result of years of pressure from Human Rights activists and judges to do something about the fact that the UK, almost alone amongst European democracies, had no formal bill of rights and no effective court protection for individuals against potential legislative inroads into internationally respected rights. What protection the English public law system provided was only against improper administrative action; as long as the Executive could point to legislative support for its actions, it could not be held to account. A number of solutions were available including the calling of a constitutional convention to draft and implement a brand new purpose-built English Bill of Rights. The Government chose instead to take an effectively incremental approach. Ever since the inception of the Council of Europe's European Convention on Human Rights (ECHR), the UK government had been a signatory and subject to the jurisdiction of the European Court of Human Rights. However these rights could not be relied on in the UK's own courts—they only ensured that, having failed at all levels of appeal inside the UK legal system, a citizen could sue the government before the ECHR. Such a process was very expensive, very slow, and only of use for well-supported litigants making symbolic points. The Human Rights Act makes the European Convention part of UK law, so that those deprived of one of rights by UK legislation can ask an ordinary court to protect them.

The actual working of the HRA is complex, and as yet little tested. The overwhelming problem, which was not solved, is that British constitutional doctrine makes Parliament sovereign. Although there might have been strong public support for the idea, the Government (and indeed the opposition) were not prepared to go all the way and allow a court to overrule Parliament and actually annul a law as unconstitutional. The most an English court can do if it is unable to interpret an offending law to make it compatible with the European Convention rights, is to issue a declaration that the law in question offends these rights. If the court makes this decision, however, it is still required to uphold the law against the plaintiff. There is provision in the HRA for the government to use a 'fast-track' reform system to amend any law against which a declaration is issued. So far this has not happened. If governments regularly do amend such offending laws, the HRA will have achieved a sort of compromise between the protection of rights and parliamentary sovereignty.

Hume

David Hume (1711–76) was a philosopher and political thinker of the Scottish part of the **Enlightenment**. Although he is principally famous as a philosopher, his importance as a political thinker is still considerable and, perhaps, too often disregarded. As a philosopher he was noted for his defence of empiricism, and his resoundingly common-sense approach spread over to his political theory. In some ways he can be seen as a precursor of two vital movements in social thought: the creation of a **utilitarian** approach to political and social philosophy; and the instigation of a 'value-free' political science based on the building up of scientific generalizations from observing actual social behaviour rather than one based on deductions from any notion of innate norms or moral truths. His major political ideas are found in a section of his principal work, *A Treatise of Human Nature*, and a collection of essays on political topics. A good example of his approach to political questions comes from his treatment of property law. Hume does not argue that any particular set of laws about rights to property have any special rectitude, but simply that, in order to have an organized and efficient social system, there must be some set of fixed rules. Thus for him **natural law** is a highly pragmatic set of rules fitting particular circumstances. Similarly he provides a defence for the existence of an aristocracy (which would hardly be accepted today) not on some special, even 'divine' right of the landed gentry, but simply in terms of the likely commitment to social stability and sensible long-term policy-making of those with a permanent, but self-interested, reason to wish for the best return on their investments. His essay on 'The Balance of Power' remains one of the clearest expositions of what later became both a major theory in international relations and an actual practice of governments.

Humanitarian Intervention

Humanitarian intervention is a concept developed in the last decade of the 20th century and made possible only by the end of the **cold war**. It means the use of force by one or more foreign powers to intervene in a country whose population is experiencing great suffering, to facilitate non-military aid that could otherwise not be delivered. The source of the suffering may be civil war, extensive insurgency against a government, or total state collapse. Either way the problem is that deliverers of aid, for instance food and medical services, could not safely go about their relief work unless protected by some independent military presence. This meaning can be extended to cover situations where a total collapse of law and order leaves no functioning state to intervene in a genocidal attempt by any group or tribe. The point about humanitarian intervention is that it is justified only by appeal to high moral principles and is intentionally limited in its aim. It is not, for example, the same as intervening on one side or other in a civil war, with the aim of determining the winner. The humanitarian intervention does not, in itself, seek to solve the underlying political and power struggles that have led to the disaster, only to create safe havens and safe supply routes, safe refugee centres and so on.

The reason humanitarian intervention is so limited in aim is that the world system has not as yet completely given up the idea of national sovereignty, which otherwise precludes forcible intervention in the affairs of a state by outside military and civil institutions. During the cold war it would have been impossible to maintain that such an intervening force was genuinely politically neutral and of limited intent, because whichever countries contributed forces would inevitably have been associated with one or other **superpower**. Even now there is always great suspicion about the genuine neutrality of such forces, and Russia often has to be placated before it will readily accept any intervention which includes US or **NATO** contingents.

I

ICBM

ICBM stands for Intercontinental Ballistic Missile—the immensely powerful, long-range nuclear weapons systems, against which there is currently no effective defence, providing, during the **cold war**, perhaps the most important element of the nuclear balance between the Soviet Union and the USA. There is a broad distinction between SLBMs (submarine-launched ballistic missiles, such as the US Polaris and Trident missiles) and land-based systems. Much of the effort in the **SALT** and Strategic Arms Reduction Talks (START) negotiations has involved trying to reduce the number of ICBM systems. The START treaty signed in July 1991, for example, was to reduce the number of warheads carried by these missiles, world-wide, by around 30%. However, both **superpowers** already sought lower force levels, principally for economic reasons, and the subsequent collapse of the Soviet Union appeared to render the **deterrence** factor of ICBMs largely redundant, as no other country has a true ICBM capacity. The issue re-emerged in 2001, however, when US President George W. Bush announced that the USA would withdraw from all anti-nuclear treaties, including START, which would preclude the development of a system of National Missile Defence (aimed at protecting the USA against ICBMs, launched either in error or by a hostile state, see **Son of Star Wars**).

Ideology

Ideology is a difficult, but frequently-used, concept in the social sciences, and one that has endless submeanings in both academic and everyday discussion. The simplest definition is probably given by a translation of the German word *Weltanschauung*, which is often used as though intertranslatable with 'ideology'. This translation would render 'ideology' as 'world-view', the overall perception one has of what the world, especially the social world, consists of and how it works. An ideology, and most students of ideology would want to say that we all had one, though often without realizing it, is a complete and self-consistent set of attitudes, moral views, empirical beliefs and even rules of logical discourse and scientific testing. However, ideologies, which tell us what we should or do want, and how to achieve these goals, are often held to be highly relative, and even purely subjective. Thus a 15th-century bishop, 19th-century mill owner and 20th-century Russian soldier are all expected to see the world in crucially different ways that might not ever be capable of reconciliation. Not only would they all have different values, they would have different and incompatible explanations for why they valued what they valued.

In the **Marxist** and **Hegelian** traditions of social thought these 'world-views' are supposed to be related to one's social, and particularly to one's class, position. In this version, factory owners and factory workers actually understand their society in quite different ways, although it is also held that the ideology of the ruling class of any society permeates into those of all other classes. Very simply, capitalists will see their profit as the necessary and valid return to their investment of money and effort, while their workers *would* see it as an unfair result of exploitation, unless they have been ideologically manipulated into accepting the owner's own views, and into acquiescing into a **false consciousness**, which leads to an erroneous vision of the capitalist's version of reality as inevitable and true. There are major theoretical problems with such a full version of the idea of ideology, especially the obvious questions about why one world-view, rather than another, should be given more credence. There are also many much weaker versions of the word 'ideology' current in both real political argument and academic political discourse. Often an ideology means nothing more than a particular set of beliefs and values, with no specific view about which set is correct, nor any special theory on how they come about. Some modern social scientists of the **behavioural** tradition would even wish to deny that ideologies are commonly-found phenomena at all, believing instead that only a minority of the population have coherent and logically-consistent views on the full range of social matters. Even if this is true, it remains possible that human perception is so deeply socially influenced that communication between different socio-economic cultures is always difficult and can never be perfect.

Immigration

Demographic movements of people have occurred throughout history, sometimes on a vast scale and over very great distances, but before the development of the **nation state** only warfare and conquest could exert any control over the phenomenon. From perhaps the 17th century, however, immigration was the process whereby citizens of 'older', usually European countries, moved to newly-developing and underpopulated countries, mainly in North America and Australasia. Although immigration controls were occasionally imposed, for most of the period to 1945 relatively free immigration was not only allowed but encouraged by the host countries who needed to increase their populations rapidly in order to develop their economies and exploit their territory. In the USA the waves of immigration have been of great importance socially and politically. As early as the 1920s politicians were attacking the tendency for everyone to be a 'hyphenated-American'; they were referring to the way US citizens described themselves as, for example, Italo-American, German-American or Irish-American. Nevertheless, by the middle of the 20th century less than half the US population was second generation American. Similar examples can be found elsewhere: for example, only Athens itself has a larger urban Greek population than Melbourne in Australia.

The golden days of immigrants being welcomed ended sometime during the 1950s, as population and labour levels reached and exceeded optimum levels. It was then that a different type of immigration came to prominence. It was no longer the movement of, often highly skilled, populations from old European societies. Immigration became, instead, the movement of largely unskilled and uneducated peasants from the Third World, especially from ex-colonies to the former **colonialist** European countries, and to a much lesser extent to the North American/Australasian world. The latter, having achieved their population goals, closed immigration down to a trickle. The former colonial powers, above all France and the United Kingdom, started the post-war period with a perceived obligation to the populations of their former possessions. They also hoped to replace the colonial bonds with some more tenuous relationship, through the British Commonwealth and the informal gatherings of the Francophone countries, which would help retain their world power status, and thus extending citizenship to their former colonial subjects seemed politically rational. At the same time there was a need for cheap labour in the immediately post-war economies. This was felt elsewhere, West Germany being the best example. But in these non-colonial countries immigration tended to mean a short-term importation of labour from poorer countries, Italy and Turkey in Germany's case, which did not involve any right of permanent residence.

Before long the presence of alien cultures, languages and religions began to irritate the British, and the slowing of economic growth also meant that the need to import cheap labour declined. By the early 1960s race riots began to break out, the government started to introduce severe restrictions on immigration, which itself became an emotive political issue. It took somewhat longer in France, but by the end of the 1970s France too had begun to find its ex-colonial citizens politically embarrassing. By the early 1990s immigration had, indeed, become more politically explosive in France, and also in Germany, than it ever had been in the UK, where a consensus among the major parties managed to strangle the more overtly **racist** anti-immigration political movements (see **neo-fascism**).

The USA, for all its fears and though it has restricted immigration, continues to be much more generous to peoples it sees as oppressed, and large numbers of Asians and Hispanics have been allowed to settle, and have become vital members of US society, in the last 20 years. Western Europe, on the other hand, has meanwhile placed severe constraints on immigration. In the 1990s the problem was re-emerging in a novel guise, with significant demands for immigration from Eastern Europe and the former Soviet Union of people seeking the riches and opportunities of developed capitalist societies. So seriously is this taken as a threat that discussions have even been held as to the possibility of using **NATO**-dedicated troops for the purpose of policing immigration. One problem emerging at the end of the 20th century was to distinguish would-be immigrants, especially those referred to as 'economic immigrants', from asylum seekers fleeing persecution. Because most Western nations have obligations under **international law** to accept asylum seekers, some individuals wishing to evade their increasingly strict immigration controls seek to pass themselves off as refugees from persecution. The relative numbers of these 'genuine' and 'bogus' asylum seekers and the process for dealing with their applications to remain in the country have developed into major political issues in a number of Western European countries.

Immobilisme

Immobilisme is a French term, especially applied to the politics of the **Third Republic** (1870–1940) and the **Fourth Republic** (1946–58). Under these systems France had no strong central executive government. Instead all power was vested in the National Assembly, from and by which governments and prime ministers were elected. Because of the multiple divisions in French society, and the complex multi-party system that emerged from these **cleavages** (greatly encouraged in the Fourth Republic by a **proportional representation** voting system), cabinets were extremely unstable coalitions. At times the life of governments was measured only in days, and few lasted more than a year. In consequence, especially as fellow members of the same coalitions were often in deep disagreement about policies, no coherent and lasting set of governmental priorities and policies could be developed. The consequence was that very little was ever achieved as a result of government initiative. Hence the system came to be seen as 'immobile', as incapable of doing anything to adapt France to changing socio-economic trends. In fact, in many ways the Fourth Republic did adapt quickly, with rapid economic growth rates and increasing affluence. This, however, was almost entirely due to the efficiency and power of the administrative civil service, who came to be undisputed masters of the departments of state, no political minister remaining long enough to take control. Certainly almost nothing of value came from the politicians themselves, many of whom, on both the **left** and **right**, were in any case mortal enemies of the regimes. Thus such a political system has come to be called '*immobiliste*', referring above all to the absence of democratically inspired political leadership. Most commentators would see contemporary Italy in the same light, even after the fall of the 'First Republic', and it is arguable that, though for different reasons, the enervation of the Eisenhower presidency combined with a hostile Congress produced an '*immobiliste*' government in the USA during the 1950s. Though with no precise referent outside France, the term remains both vivid and useful.

Imperialism

Imperialism is the policy or goal of extending the power and rule of a government beyond the boundaries of its original state, and taking into one political unit other nations or lands. There are variations in the extent to which the imperial power assumes administrative and political control for the states that make up the empire; some retain degrees of independence and identity, while others are subsumed entirely into the institutions of the imperial state. Neither is it necessary that an empire has any specific form of central government, though there must be one central and ultimately overwhelming force, otherwise it is more likely to be an alliance, league or loose federation. The British Empire at its height was a constitutional monarchy, but Queen Victoria had lost most of the power of the previous English monarchs, and the Empire was essentially a parliamentary one.

In fact, though there have been many empires in world history, few have lasted as long as the modern **nation states** of Europe, and most have collapsed either because of political disunity at the centre, or because of the enormous difficulty of exercising central rule over long distances and against the instincts for local autonomy that always spring up. The motives for creating an empire vary greatly, but imperialism in itself should not be confused with **colonialism**, which is a specific form and motive for holding political control beyond national boundaries. A crucial aspect of imperialism, and one of the best aids to categorization, is the way in which imperial citizenship is handled. If only citizens or subjects of the original 'homeland' can be seen as citizens of the empire, and the rest of the inhabitants are no more than subject peoples with no hope of political power or legal protection, the empire is likely to veer towards the principally exploitative version that is better thought of as colonialism. On the other hand, and the later Roman Empire may be the best example, citizenship, with its legal rights and duties, may be extended to the entire population, or some part of the population, of the whole empire, rather than just the descendants of the nation that built it. In this case the empire is more in the nature of a supranational state which, given the artificiality of many national borders, need be no less legitimate than any nation-state. Despite this, 'imperialism' in modern political language is nearly always used pejoratively, suggesting an illegitimate desire to extend one's power or authority for reasons of self aggrandizement, as, for example, when Richard Nixon was dubbed an 'imperial' president for seeking to take over powers that belonged to the US Congress.

Industrial Democracy

Industrial democracy, or industrial participation, embraces a wide range of alternatives and is espoused in a surprisingly wide range of ideological positions. Essentially, all variants aim to break down the line-of-command hierarchy which characterizes modern industry, and in particular to remove the class/power distinction between work-force and management. The motivation for such plans can be the elimination of work **alienation**, a desire to link the interests of the work-force more clearly with those of the industry or company, the increase of overall human freedom, or more far-reaching intentions to restructure either just the economy or the whole polity on egalitarian and democratic lines. Just as the motives vary considerably in ambition, so do the techniques suggested. At the lowest level of ambition, industrial democracy may mean nothing more than profit-sharing schemes, or an encouragement and facilitation to workers owning shares. It may imply, instead, trade-union representation on boards of directors, as is the case in Germany, and as was planned for the United Kingdom by the Bullock Report (1976). Some firms are entirely owned by the work-force, and have management decisions made by meetings of the worker-owners, though these are rare and have seldom proved successful in capitalist societies; however, a hierarchical management structure generally proves essential in an enterprise of any size.

The full-blooded theory of industrial democracy, however, is an entire rival theory both to **capitalism** and to **communism's** system of state ownership. Developed by such thinkers as, in Britain, G. D. Cole (1889–1959), it imagines the replacement of ordinary **representative democracy** with **direct democracy**, not only in the community but in the individual factories and firms. In these workplaces the workers would be entirely independent and would make all decisions of production, pricing and sales, as well as salaries, themselves. The firms would only loosely be grouped in representative bodies, and there would be no more state control of the economy than of any other aspect of life. The problems of co-ordination raised by such theories are legion, and the approach really belongs within the theory of **anarchism**.

With the radical transformations of the structure of employment in the Post-industrial Western economies, especially the growth of part time work and

237

consultancy arrangements, the core ideas of worker participation and industrial democracy may no longer have anything to which they can be applied.

Initiative

The initiative is a method whereby a group of citizens can put a legislative proposal before the electorate directly for determination in a **referendum**. The proposal may be to enact a new law, to repeal an existing law or to amend a constitution. It became popular in the USA during the late 19th century when criticisms were voiced of the party machines in the USA, and is also important in Switzerland. The initiative thus appeared a way of by-passing the parties which controlled the legislatures of the states, and proved successful as a method of obtaining progressive reforms. About one-third of the US states retain the procedure, but it can not be applied to federal legislation as Article I of the US Constitution prevents Congress from delegating its legislative powers. California, which has become the leader in the use of citizen initiatives, has had unhappy experience, on matters like taxes and the regulation of motor insurance, when the electorate has imposed a law that has been economically disastrous to implement.

Inquisitorial System

The inquisitorial system of **criminal law** is common everywhere in the **civil law** world. It describes the mode of trial in criminal cases where the court, either a single judge or a bench of judges and assessors, seeks directly to ascertain the truth of the charges brought. The court will interrogate witnesses, call for evidence, perhaps require the counsel for prosecution and defence to answer certain points or make certain arguments, and will not be satisfied until it believes it has itself found out all that can be found out about the case. In contrast, the mode of criminal trial in the **common law** systems is known as the accusatorial system. Here the jury has the job only of deciding between the cases put forward by the prosecution and the defence, on the terms they choose to present. The judge has only the duty of seeing a fair trial, of ensuring that the rules of evidence are obeyed, and summing up impartially to the jury. Thus in the latter case no pretence is made that the whole intricate truth will be found out, but only that the prosecution will do its best to convict, and the defence to acquit, and that the better arguments will prevail. For this reason, in an attempt to ensure fairness, it is necessary for the prosecution in the accusatory system to have very powerful cases to acquire a conviction, whereas this is not necessary in the inquisitorial system. Consequently there has grown up a misleading simplification that a defendant is 'innocent until proved guilty' under common law (which is, roughly, true), and 'guilty until proved innocent' (which is not true) in the civil law world. What is true is that the latter, while probably the more efficient, gives the court, and thus the state, far more power in the trial procedure. Thus the common law situation where a jury deliberately acquits an obviously guilty person to show disapproval for the law broken could not happen under the inquisitorial system. Furthermore, the keenness of a prosecutor, and the police, to produce the 'better argument' can lead to a conviction being secured with unreliable, or even false, evidence. Occasionally there have been demands for the English system to be modified in the direction of inquisitorial justice because of such failures in the common law trial system, and indeed the Scottish criminal law system does have elements of this. The point has recently been made that situations where one country tries citizens of another for international terrorism, as with the trial (conducted in the Netherlands under Scottish law) of two Libyan citizens accused of the destruction in 1988 of an airliner over Scotland, require an inquisitorial system to allay international public doubts about the prosecutions.

Institutional Racism

Institutional racism as a term entered everyday political and journalistic language in the United Kingdom at the beginning of the 21st century. It was used by a public inquiry into police mishandling of the investigation into the murder, allegedly by white youths, of a black youth. The report claimed that the investigating police force were 'institutionally racist'; by this was meant not that individual police officers were racist, but that there was a culture of racism which the police force had inadequate mechanisms for combating. Although this conclusion was sternly refuted by many, several chief police officers of other forces bravely admitted publicly that they thought their own forces equally guilty of such institutionalized tolerance for racist attitudes. Since then the concept has been applied to several other public institutions in the UK, including both the Crown Prosecution Service and aspects of the National Health Service.

The introduction of the concept is important for two different interacting reasons. First, there had been a tendency to say of the police that some degree of racism was inevitable, because they were bound to reflect the attitudes of the part of society from which junior officers were predominantly recruited, that is, the white, urban working class. Acceptance of the institutional character of this racism makes the point that, especially for services like the police, although also more generally, there is a public duty to transcend the limitations of recruitment bases. Secondly, it involved accepting that public institutions should be aware that a minority of aggressive bigots can make the entire atmosphere of an institution intolerant, even when the other officers do not necessarily expound racist attitudes. In order to remove this perception from the public consciousness, the police service has determined to adopt a firm disciplinary approach to any expression of racism and to instigate a deliberate programme, such as US military services have operated for years, of sensitization to race issues.

Intelligence Services

It seems likely that all nations have both intelligence and security services of a more or less secret nature. The principal organization in the Soviet Union was the Committee for State Security (KGB), which grew out of **Lenin's** original internal secret police, the Cheka. In 1991, after the KGB had played a major role in the abortive coup attempt against President **Gorbachev**, the organization was dismantled; it seemed likely that its previous paramilitary and intelligence functions would be assumed, in greatly reduced form, by the newly-independent republics of the former Soviet Union. The USA, which had almost no intelligence gathering machinery before the Second World War, developed rapidly the Central Intelligence Agency (CIA), modelled on the British services. It also has many other intelligence analysis organizations, especially the Defense Intelligence Agency (DIA). In the USA, as in most Western countries, the external intelligence and internal security or counter-intelligence operations are divided between different organizations to minimize the risk to democratic institutions of covert forces. So in America the Federal Bureau of Investigations (FBI) is responsible for internal security, although it has been suggested that the CIA has breached this restriction from time to time. The United Kingdom operates two principal services. The Security Service (sometimes called MI5), in co-operation with the Special Branch of the ordinary police is responsible directly to the prime minister for internal security. The UK's external intelligence-gathering activities are the responsibility of the Secret Intelligence Service (SIS, sometimes called MI6), which operates mainly under Foreign Office control. Among other major examples, France has the Direction Générale de la Sécurité Extérieure (DGSE) and a host of internal security organizations, Germany the Bundesnachrichtendienst (BND), and Israel what is arguably the most efficient intelligence service in the world, Mossad. Increasingly there is pressure for such agencies to be restrained by some sort of legislative control because of the danger of executive action in secret. The US Senate has established an intelligence oversight committee which alone can authorize some CIA activities.

Traditional espionage activities have very largely been superseded by electronic intelligence gathering, from radio frequency intercepting. Far more important in real terms than the CIA and MI6 are the US National Security Agency (NSA) and the British Government Communications Headquarters (GCHQ). These, combined with satellite reconnaissance, have been crucial for defence analysis and planning required during the nuclear age. Whether this form of high-technology espionage is as effective against low-technology threats such as international terrorism can be doubted. The allied intervention in Afghanistan in 2002 clearly suffered from a lack of traditional 'human intelligence'.

Intelligence-gathering is not necessarily a hostile act, because the balance of power, and the credibility of deterrent forces, paradoxically requires that potential enemies should know quite a lot about each other's capacity. The end of the **cold war** has not led, as might be expected, to a massive reduction in the work of such agencies, but rather to a change of focus, with terrorism and drug-related crime, along with industrial espionage, taking over from the traditional military intelligence focus.

Interest Groups

Interest groups are associations formed to promote a sectional interest in the political system. Thus **trade unions**, professional associations, employers' organizations and motoring organizations are usually referred to as interest groups. The term has a degree of overlap with **pressure groups** and voluntary organizations, although it is frequently restricted to groups which have organized to promote, advance or defend some common interest—most often of an occupational kind.

A variety of tactics may be used to pursue the aims of the group. Thus trade unionists may threaten to withdraw their labour and to strike, while professional groups typically try to advance their cause by more indirect methods, such as contact with government bureaucrats, propaganda and publicity. Interest groups have been seen by such 20th-century writers as **Bentley** and David B. Truman as a key element in understanding the political system, and interest groups are often described in terms of the motor or input side of government. Many interest groups therefore develop close, even formal, ties with political parties. Thus Britain's trade unions and the Labour Party are constitutionally linked—although in that case the unions existed prior to the Labour Party and were responsible for its establishment. Similarly, close links may exist between interest groups and the bureaucracy or the executive generally. In the USA the 'military–industrial complex' has shown, with its Pentagon links, a high level of political co-operation and interaction, as has the National Union of Farmers with the Department of Agriculture.

Interest groups with fewer overt powers of sanction or persuasion often resort to such direct action as mass rallies, marches and demonstrations; intensive publicity and lobbying may also be used to advance their cause. In most Western societies a whole new profession of political lobbyists has grown up to facilitate interest group contact with either parliamentarians, members of the government or the civil service. The British parliamentary **lobby**, for example, is thought to have expanded tenfold during the years of Margaret Thatcher's prime ministership (1979–90), with similar developments both in European capitals and in Brussels, the latter to lobby the **European Union's** authorities. Much sociological research has been conducted since the 1980s into a phenomenon usually called '**New Social Movements**', more widespread and participatory forms of group politics which are sometimes seen as threatening the legitimacy of orthodox parties.

Internal Colonialism

Internal colonialism is a concept with quite a long history, having been used as early as the late 19th century in reference to Russia. However, like many social science ideas it has notably changed its meaning over time. Originally it was a pre-Marxist way of describing economic relations between affluent urban and impoverished rural sectors. It then came to refer to persistent economic inequalities between the central or core parts of a state and its peripheral regions. Since the 1960s, this latter meaning has been tightened so as to make the idea of such disparities, if they satisfy certain conditions, much more like a colonial relationship between a rich mother country and its colonies. The change in meaning came about when it was realized that quite often underdeveloped peripheral regions differ from a country's heartland in more than simply aggregate wealth. There are essentially two types of differences that mark out internal colonialism from straightforward geographical inequality of economic conditions.

First is the nature of the economy of the poor regions. Just as colonies tend to develop mainly export-orientated and often basic extractive industries, so do some undeveloped regions. Just as colonies tend not to be able to develop the economic underpinnings for a broad-based investment economy but specialize in serving the economic needs of the exploiting country, so too do some regions of otherwise rich nations. Secondly, the cultural and ethnic differences between colonies and their governing state is often mirrored inside a country that practises internal colonialism. There may well be differences in educational attainment and style of education, but these are also apparent in other markers of ethnic differentiation like language and religion. In general, the social status of the inhabitants of the poorer regions marks them out as different from those of the rich core. All these factors together may indeed induce a further similarity, which is that just as real colonies develop independence movements, internal colonies often adopt the politics of autonomy, demand, and indeed occasionally attempt to gain, independence.

It is thought by proponents of the idea that the concept of internal colonialism applies quite widely in modern, developed economies. The problem is that rather than finding a genuine pattern, which can be usefully likened to colonialism, they seem to be doing little more than noting an interesting analogy. Furthermore, the direction of causality is unclear. Do such regions become culturally differentiated because of the internal migration of those who can compete with the inhabitants of the centre? Is the stress on ethnic differentiation largely a compensating drive to make up for the economic disparities?

International Law

International law is usually divided into public international law and private international law. The former consists of the generally understood rules governing the relations between states (see **Grotius**), as well as an enormous mass of treaty-based specific regulations. Thus it covers both fundamental questions, such as the right to go to war (see **just war**), how citizens of neutral countries should be treated, the laws against genocide and the code for treating prisoners of war, as well as the regulations on international air traffic control, the law of the sea bed, extradition of criminals and so on. International law in this sense is administered by a host of agencies, the most famous, though not the most effective, being the International Court of Justice (ICJ) at The Hague (see **war crimes tribunals**), a **United Nations** organization. Legal theorists still debate whether or not international law really is **law** in the full sense, because there exists no mechanism for enforcing judgments. Despite the fact that major powers do, from time to time, ignore rulings of the ICJ, as the USA did in the judgment of *Nicaragua v. USA* which condemned the mining of Nicaraguan ports by the USA in 1984, most international law is obeyed nearly all the time, and clearly affects governmental decisions.

In the late 1990s, following the organization of tribunals to hear cases regarding war crimes in specific conflicts, efforts were made to create a permanent International Criminal Court. A statute detailing the process towards the establishment of such a tribunal (with competence to try suspects on charges of genocide, crimes against humanity and war crimes) was signed in Rome in July 1998, and was scheduled to enter into force in July 2002 (although many considered that the refusal of some important states, including the USA, to become party to the new Court might affect its practical authority).

Private international law, which is of growing significance, is the body of rules and **arbitration** agreements covering contractual arrangements between non-governmental bodies from different countries. Although there is no single international court with jurisdiction in private international law, the increasing interdependence of the world economy, and the economic importance of

multinational firms makes it very much in the interest of such bodies to co-operate in international arbitration, so that the actual effectiveness of private international law may be greater than the formally institutionalized public international law. The importance of international law actually varies from country to country according to whether their internal doctrine of law is 'monist' or not. If it is, a treaty signed by a country may give its own citizens direct rights; in 'dualist' countries, international law has to be directly incorporated by parliamentary action before it can be cited before domestic courts.

International Monetary Fund (IMF)

The IMF is a specialist agency of the **United Nations**, set up after the Second World War mainly as a result of bilateral agreement between the USA and the UK at the Bretton Woods conference of 1944. It was intended to be a means of producing stable international economic relations and, above all, a stable international currency and set of exchange rates. In a sense it was a replacement for the old gold standard which had been abandoned almost everywhere by 1931. The trouble with the gold standard, under which all currencies had to be directly backed by equivalent amounts of gold held by central banks, was that although it produced stability of currencies, its effect was automatic and often very harsh. Thus a country with a balance of payments difficulty would find its unemployment rate increasing in an uncontrollable fashion. In addition, as the supply of gold was not variable by direct political decision, an essentially arbitrary physical restriction was placed on the amount of money available in the world, reducing the possibility of economic growth. Yet when the gold standard was abandoned, anarchy reigned in the international money markets, with instant devaluations or revaluations, and great instability, which itself acted as a restraint on international trade and economic development.

What was needed, it was felt, was a form of international currency which could support national currencies, reduce uncertainty and bring stability, but which would not be automatic in the way gold was. Thus it was vital that the IMF should allow a country undergoing a balance of payments problem to be much more moderate in its internal economic regulatory moves than had been possible in the past. Essentially the IMF worked like a supranational central bank, with member countries paying in an initial deposit (part of this still had to be in gold), and then being allowed to draw out more than they had put in, as a debt to the Fund, when in balance of payments or currency crises. These debts had to be repaid, usually within five years, and rates of interest, varying with the amount borrowed, had to be paid. The arrangement allowed a country to pay its international debts without having to impose internal deflationary controls to reduce demand, and thus possibly increase unemployment. In addition, the total funds in the international economic system could be increased by the Fund simply announcing that each share held by member countries was increased by a certain percentage, as has happened on several occasions to meet the permanent pressure for increased international liquidity.

If the IMF system was to avoid the anarchy of the period after the abandonment of the gold standard, however, its automatic control had to be replaced with some form of international political authority. Thus the IMF was given the power to impose economic policy restrictions on member countries wishing to borrow large amounts, and these controls, which have often been imposed, usually take the form of requirements to reduce inflation, especially by cuts in government expenditure and tax increases. The IMF restrictions on credit have often been seen by left-wing parties, and even by sections of cabinets which have borrowed, as involving undue interference with more socialist-oriented economic policies, and have thus been blamed for preventing the growth of welfare state policies in nations with economic problems. Originally it was also intended that no member state should be able to devalue its currency without consultation with the Fund, but this has never been observed, partly because devaluation decisions are usually taken in great urgency and secrecy.

It would probably be agreed by economists that the IMF has not been the great breakthrough in terms of international economic management that was hoped for, although it has certainly produced stability without the harshly automatic consequences of the gold standard. Probably its greatest drawback has been its failure to expand international liquidity to meet demand. In part this comes from the initial unwillingness of the USA at Bretton Woods to agree to the British idea that member nations who were enjoying a long-term and strong balance of payments advantage should be required to increase imports, thus easing the debt problem for the rest of the world. As the USA was in such a position from 1944 until at least the mid-1950s, this was not surprising. The absence of this restriction, however, has allowed countries like Germany and Japan to benefit from their economic strength without regard to the impact it was having on the rest of the international economy.

As the IMF is inevitably linked to capitalist economic systems and theory, it was spurned by most members of **COMECON**. Since the collapse of the Soviet economic system, however, most former Soviet republics and Eastern European countries have become members of the IMF, even though the economies in question will not be in a fit state to benefit or help for years. Increasingly, since the mid-1970s, the IMF has become much less important to Europe as the **European Union (EU)** developed its own monetary control system, The completion of the union of currencies with the creation of the new euro for most EU countries has created a huge economic unit, 'Euroland', within which the IMF can not hope to have much influence.

International Socialism

Socialist and communist doctrines have always had, as an important element, the idea of the international brotherhood of the working classes, in part because the nation state has been seen as a prop exploited by capitalists. In addition, the revolutionary years of the 19th and early 20th century seemed to require world-wide revolution rather than what **Stalin** was to call 'socialism in one country'. Consequently there have been numerous attempts to set up international co-operative organizations of the separate national socialist, communist and revolutionary groups. The two most important have been the Second and Third Internationals, the latter also known as the Comintern. (The First International was created in 1864 by **Marx**, inspired by *The Communist Manifesto*, which he and **Engels** had been asked to write on behalf of a German émigré workers' group in 1848. Largely because Marx tried to dominate it, and because of disputes with anarchists and syndicalists, it was so ineffective that it was dissolved in 1876.) The Second International was formed in Paris in 1889, and though weakened by the First World War (when socialist parties who had sworn to oppose capitalist wars all rallied to their respective governments), it was reformed in 1923 and still survives (see **Socialist International**). This International was reformist and social democratic in nature, and had nothing to do with revolutionary doctrines. It has had no appreciable effect on either international or domestic policies, and, indeed, given its ideological nature, has no obvious role to play. Part of the reason for its uselessness is that from 1919 it had a serious and much more powerfully radical rival in the Third International.

The Third International was founded at **Lenin's** instigation by the newly victorious **Bolshevik** government in Moscow to organize and control communist parties throughout Europe. Indeed, the formation of the two most important Western communist parties, in France and Italy, stems directly from splits in their respective socialist parties, who were members of the Second International: in both cases the hard-core revolutionary Marxist elements left to join Lenin's Comintern. This body exercised the same autocratic centralized discipline over the foreign members of the International, under the label of **democratic centralism**, as the Central Committee of the Soviet Communist Party did over its subordinate bodies. Its deliberate revolutionary and Moscow-inspired temper probably did more to prevent serious united left-wing governments from coming to power in inter-war Europe than anything else. Electorates and the Second International parties could not trust members of the Third International to take proper care of national interests, and the Third International rejected any reformist road to socialism. It had to be abolished by Stalin in 1943 to placate his liberal democratic wartime allies, and has never been replaced by anything equivalent. There had, briefly, been an attempt by

Trotsky, by then in exile, to create a Fourth International in the 1930s to unite all left-wing parties in an anti-fascist **popular front**. This, however, came to nothing, in part because the Third International itself gave orders in the mid-1930s to forget ideological purity in the face of Soviet fears of a German invasion, and to link up with other left parties. An example of how strong was the control of the Soviet Union over the members of the Third International is the way in which the French Communist Party would not oppose German invasion of France, nor join the resistance, until Hitler's invasion of the Soviet Union in 1941 broke the non-aggression pact between Germany and that country.

IRA

The acronym IRA tends to be applied rather loosely to various interconnected organizations which oppose, both violently and politically, continued British **sovereignty** over Northern Ireland. The long tradition of 'troubles' concerning British–Irish relations is among the strongest examples of religious **cleavage**, with very long-lasting resentments over British/Protestant domination of Irish Catholics. The Irish Republican Army itself grew into an undercover paramilitary, or **guerrilla**, organization after the abortive Easter Rising of 1916 against British rule, but with ties to the political organization Sinn Féin ('We Ourselves') founded in 1905. From then onward, and particularly during the years 1918–22, Sinn Féin and the IRA were major forces in bringing about the creation, and British recognition of, the Irish Free State firstly, in 1922, with dominion status, then with full sovereignty, from 1937, within the **Commonwealth**, and ultimately becoming the Republic of Ireland in 1949. Indeed, the British government was forced to create a special **paramilitary force**, the 'Black and Tans', to contain the IRA during this period. After the agreement over the Irish Free State in 1922 civil war erupted among the nationalists between those prepared to accept the agreement, which involved the partition of Ireland, with six northern and predominantly Protestant counties remaining under full British jurisdiction, and the IRA which insisted on full Irish unity. The IRA was defeated in 1923 by the Free State army, commanded by Michael Collins, a former IRA leader. From the 1930s until the early 1960s the IRA mounted a sporadic campaign of violence against the settlement, mainly on the British mainland but also in Ireland, leading to the Free State declaring it illegal in 1939.

From the early 1960s the IRA shifted its emphasis from the campaign of violence to one for **civil rights**, and specifically against anti-Catholic **discrimination** in Northern Ireland. However, this moderation was unacceptable to some elements who split from the main body, henceforth to be known as the 'Official IRA', and created the 'Provisional IRA', often referred to as the

'Provos', in 1969. In 1972 the Official IRA abandoned its campaign of violence, leaving only its parallel political wing, 'Official Sinn Féin', which changed its name to The Workers' Party in 1978 and has since campaigned for a democratic, socialist and united Irish state. Meanwhile the Provisional IRA, and its parallel political wing Sinn Féin, became the more prominent element of Irish nationalism, particularly in Northern Ireland. The Provisional IRA has frequently struck against military and civilian targets, using guerrilla and **terrorist** tactics, principally in Northern Ireland but also on the British mainland. Several prominent politicians and public figures have been assassinated. Sinn Féin has recorded moderate successes in elections to local councils, and has also had candidates elected to the House of Commons, although its members of parliament have always refused to take their seats; its degree of support for the Provisional IRA's campaign of violence has varied, leading to further splits in the organization. The nationalist movement as a whole, but especially the Provisional IRA, has been supported financially and in other ways by the Irish community in North America. The Provisional IRA has also had connections with various international terrorist organizations. Both Sinn Féin and the IRA have increasingly stressed their autonomy from each other, especially since the Belfast Agreement (informally known as the Good Friday Agreement) of 1998 which made possible limited independent government for Northern Ireland on the basis of free elections. In particular Sinn Féin insists that, as it cannot control the IRA, its political opportunities should not be affected by any failure of the IRA to carry it its part of those agreements. The acts of weapons-abandonment carried out in accordance with these agreements by the Provisional IRA in the early 2000s served to throw into greater relief the continuing armed struggle of further splinter groups such as the 'Real IRA'.

Iran–Iraq War

The Iran–Iraq War began when Iraq attacked Iran in 1980 and, after a lengthy period of attrition warfare with fluctuating fortunes, was stopped by a cease-fire in 1988, finally ending in 1990 when Iraq, attempting to gain advantage during the **Gulf War**, accepted the territorial boundaries which had existed at the beginning of the war. The formal *casus belli* was Iraqi claims to territory that would have increased its ability to control northern Persian Gulf waters, and especially the part known as the Shatt al-Arab, vital for entry to oil exporting ports in both countries. In fact the war was fought, on both sides, more as a test of which country should become the dominant regional power. Saddam Hussein, Iraq's president, had always sought to be the leader of a revolutionary pan-Arab movement, which threatened the national basis of other countries of the **Middle East**. While Iran is not, strictly speaking, an Arab nation at all, the religious complexities of **Islam** made a clash between the two states inevitable. The Iranian revolution which put the **Ayatollah** Khomeini in power in Iran was a Shi'ite **fundamentalist** movement, while the Iraqi regime was dominated by the Sunni sect (although Shi'a Muslims are actually in the majority in that country as well). Therefore Iran's call for Muslim unity threatened Hussain's control of his people, and was also an alternative to his own, originally more secular, call for Arab unity.

The war was deeply anachronistic, resembling the mass infantry trench warfare of the First World War (1914–18), but combined with some elements of modern high-technology warfare. Certainly it was brutal, and while no reliable figures exist, estimates of casualties of perhaps a million on each side are entirely plausible. Although Iran had, under the former regime of the Shah, by far the best equipped and most modern army in the Middle East, the subsequent break with its supplier, the USA, rapidly degraded Iranian forces. Saddam Hussain had built up a less technical army which was, nevertheless, by the end of the war, one of the biggest military machines in the world. Just as in the First World War, the conflict became a stalemate almost from its beginning, and the total amount of land gained or lost was never great. The war had enormous consequences for international oil trade and for confusing, and exposing the inadequacies of, the foreign policies of the USA, the Soviet Union, the European Communities and the whole of the Gulf region. There were also several violations of the embargoes on supplying materials of potential military application to both sides. In general the Western nations tended to favour Iraq, particularly because of fear of Islamic fundamentalism sweeping the region, and even more so after Iran started to threaten general shipping in the Persian Gulf, but just over two years after the cease-fire they were themselves taking up arms against the regime of Saddam Hussain in the Gulf War.

Iron Curtain

The iron curtain was a much used term which referred to the outer limits of the Soviet Union's sphere of control, behind which secrecy often made it difficult for the West to obtain reliable information, from the immediate post-war years until the collapse of Soviet **hegemony** in Eastern Europe in the late 1980s. It is normally attributed to Winston Churchill, the British prime minister during the Second World War, but was in fact used as early as 1920 and, prophetically, by the Nazi Joseph Goebbels, to describe the Soviet dominance over Eastern and South-Eastern Europe which would follow a German surrender. The concept was also partly geographic, delimiting the actual frontiers of Soviet dominated Eastern Europe, but just as much metaphorical, because other countries, with no geographical continuity, like Cuba or North Korea, came to be described as 'behind the iron curtain'. The geographical meaning was dominant because it did describe a very real situation where extensive border fortifications were erected, the most notorious being the Berlin Wall, to keep the citizens of communist countries in, rather than to keep aliens out. The idea was extended later by references to the 'bamboo curtain' to describe a similar self-imposed isolation by the People's Republic of China.

Iron Law of Oligarchy

Roberto Michels (1876–1936), one of the pioneers of political sociology, used the phrase 'iron law of oligarchy' in his study of the internal politics of the Social Democratic Party of Germany (SPD), *Political Parties*. It is part of his general thesis that all organized groups, whether states, political parties, trade unions or whatever, are inherently undemocratic. His argument is that organization is necessary for any effective action in society, that organization inevitably requires bureaucracy, and that bureaucracies equally inevitably concentrate power in the hands of a few at the top of a hierarchy. The reasons he gives for these assertions are multiple and not always compatible, but the general theory is powerful. Briefly, only those at the top of a bureaucracy have the information and control of internal communications and funds that effective propaganda requires. As a result any organization, even the SPD, the earliest effective socialist party in Europe and externally dedicated to democracy, equality and freedom, will not exhibit these characteristics itself. Much of Michels' thesis is simply a development of **Weber's** more general account of bureaucracy, but Michels also thinks that the inevitability of **oligarchy** inside all parties means that democracy in the political system as a whole is thereby made impossible to attain. A similar analysis, if slightly less pessimistic, is found in Robert Mackenzie's *British Political Parties*, which is still the leading textbook on its subject. It is, however, questionable whether an oligarchic leadership must necessarily stray from the preferred path of the mass members, or whether internal democracy in political parties is necessary for external democracy in the system. As long as voters can choose freely between teams of united politicians, it may in fact be an advantage that the parties should be internally oligarchic, if only to ensure the unity necessary before a voter can make a rational choice.

Irredentism

Irredentism referred originally to an Italian political movement of the late 19th century, but has come to be a general label for a common political manifestation. The word is derived from the phrase *Italia irredenta* (literally unredeemed

Italy), a slogan for the return to Italian control of lands they thought of as naturally Italian and lost to Italian rule by the past aggression of their neighbours. Parts of Austria, for example, had once been Italian states, as had Nice and parts of south-eastern France, and in the new spirit of Italian unity the demand for the integration of the whole Italian linguistic region was politically emotive (see **language groups**). The Italian movement collapsed after Italy was forced into an alliance, in 1881, with two of its previous enemies, Germany and Austria, but it gave its name to any similar situation where the return to their rightful home of long-lost lands becomes a rallying cry. The French policy of *revanche*, the retaking of the territories of Alsace and Lorraine lost in the Franco–Prussian war, which was so vital a force in French politics during the early Third Republic, could be described as 'irredentist', as could Hitler's demands for the Third Reich to control German-speaking Czechoslovakia, or, for that matter any long-standing territorial claims based on a largely linguistic claim to national sovereignty. With the collapse of communism in Eastern Europe and the Soviet Union from 1989 onwards, there was a danger of rampant irredentism taking hold, as it was largely only Soviet domination that had preserved stability in a region with few clearly-defined linguistic boundaries.

Islam

Islam is the religion of the followers of the Prophet Muhammad (*c.* 570–632), who are usually called Muslims, but it also has a geographical application. The Islamic world is very large and expanding: a 2001 estimate put it at perhaps 1,200 million people, containing Arabs, Turks, Persians, Indo-Pakistanis, Indonesia-Malayans, West Africans and Afro-Caribbeans spread, of course, over even more political frontiers. Theoretically there is no divide between the Islamic state and faith, because, according to Islam, the state is a religious institution, guided by the Prophet's words in the Koran, and is expected to legislate by the moral and practical precepts therein. Indeed, rather more than Christianity, Islam is a complete socio-economic and political theory, although, naturally, much developed and modified over the centuries. One example of this is in economics, where there is a strong belief in equality which leads, in theory at least, to the forbidding of usury (a doctrine the Roman Catholic church gave up even in theory in the Middle Ages). Another is that the theoretical equality of all Muslims (or at least all Muslim men) has prevented anything like the creation of an élite of institutionalized clergy; while individual spiritual leaders (see **ayatollahs**) have held great power, they have done so on the basis of their own talents, reputation or, in **Weber's** over-used phrase, for once properly relevant, **charisma**.

Islam has been a major force in world politics since the 7th century. The Ottoman Empire, founded in the 14th century, reached its peak in the 16th century, controlling territories far into Europe, Africa and Asia. By the middle of the 19th century it had been reduced to a colonial status as a result of European expansionism, and was dissolved after the First World War. Since the Second World War, however, Islamic power, and the desire to create a truly Islamic state, has been resurgent in several **Middle East** and Asian countries, causing no little trouble on the world scene. Libya, under the militant leader Colonel Muammar al-Qaddafi (b. 1942), was the first state to make Islam into a 20th-century revolutionary creed, partly in an effort to unify the whole Arab world against Israel and its Western allies. At roughly the same time Pakistan, which had been split off from the rest of the Indian sub-continent in 1947 specifically to make a home for Muslims, began to take this position as well. There is an increasing tendency to replace Westernized law, especially in criminal and family law areas, with the Koranic, or **Shari'a**, law; some punishments under this system, including amputations and stonings, are regarded as barbaric in the West. Some moves have even been made to operate the economy as closely as possible on Islamic lines.

An example of the power of Islam was the sudden and shattering overthrow of the Iranian state by militant and right-wing Muslim political groups, and its subsequent violently coercive rule under the direction of Muslim holy men. The ability of this state to survive an eight-year long war with Iraq, a secular Arab state, testifies to the ideological and popular strength of the Islamic revolution. Another example was the fear of dissension among Muslims in the Asian republics of the Soviet Union, causing the latter to invade Muslim Afghanistan in 1979. The Soviet occupying force of over 100,000 troops was frustrated by the Muslim **guerrillas**, the *Mujahidin*, in what became their equivalent of the USA's **Vietnam War**. Ultimately, as in Vietnam, the **superpower** had to withdraw, leaving most of Afghanistan in the hands of the Islamic forces (see **Afghan War**).

It is possible that Islam may grow to be as powerful an international political creed as either **communism** or **capitalism** have been. Certainly it is equally hostile to both, and represents, as well as a legitimate avenue for the expression of aspirations for self rule, a destabilizing force in world politics. However, it would be a mistake to treat Islam as a unified body; in particular, the split between Sunni and Shi'a Muslims is potentially as weakening as that between Catholics and Protestants was to Christianity as a world power in the Reformation period. It is notable that while a large majority, probably 80%, of the world's Muslims are Sunni (followers of *Sunna*, the way of Muhammad), in Iran Shi'ites (who pay particular allegiance to 'Ali, the cousin of Muhammad) are dominant, and are also in the majority in Iraq, although political and economic power is largely monopolized by the Sunni.

The presumed involvement of extreme Islamist groups (see **fundamental-ism**) in the attacks perpetrated on the USA in September 2001, together with the role of Islamist organizations in the **Arab-Israeli conflict** and the often-misunderstood Islamic concept of **Jihad** led many in the West to believe Islam to be particularly susceptible to exploitation by those seeking to use **terrorism** as a political tool. While this is a misrepresentation of the religion (mainstream Muslim opinion repeatedly condemns such violent acts as '11 September') it can be stated that strict adherence to Islamic beliefs clashes more resonantly with Western political and cultural norms than would similar commitments to other major world religions.

Isolationism

Isolationism is a foreign policy strategy in which a nation announces that it has absolutely no interest in international affairs, nor in the affairs of other nations, as long as they do not affect any vital interest of its own; this implies a neutrality in most possible conflicts. The most famous example is the foreign policy of the USA during much of the 19th century and in the inter-war period of the 20th century, where isolationism as regards any part of the globe other than the western hemisphere was a corollary of the **Monroe Doctrine** enunciated in 1823.

In practice the USA only followed isolationism when it was in its interest, and became heavily involved in Asian affairs, as well as finding the definition of 'western hemisphere' extensive enough to include both Hawaii and the Philippines. Isolationism was at its most effective in the USA during the inter-war years, keeping the country out of the League of Nations and preventing it from becoming involved in the Second World War until attacked by Japan at the end of 1941. Whatever the balance of advantages to the USA may have been, the policy was disastrous for Europe, where the rise of the dictators was helped by their confidence in American neutrality. Although isolationism is still attractive to many Americans, the Truman Doctrine of 1947, when the USA pledged to help all peoples fighting for freedom against 'armed minorities or outside pressure', spelled the end even to a pretence of isolationism, which would, in any case, be incompatible with its obligations under the **United Nations (UN)** Charter. Certainly isolationist tendencies, though still present, have not stopped presidents from the first to the second Bush administrations involving the US closely with European affairs.

In effect, of course, isolationism is practised by most small powers most of the time, and only becomes an obviously deliberate strategy where a real choice is available. When Britain was still powerful there sometimes existed a strong isolationist element under the title of 'little Englanders', who wished to give up imperial responsibilities and concentrate effort on protecting the direct interests of the homeland itself. Where there is an apparent choice nowadays, the complexity of international politics and the geographical spread and intermixing of alliances, particularly in a nuclear context, makes isolationism scarcely feasible. Furthermore, the increasing role of the UN, offering for the first time a real possibility of collective security, increases both the practical and moral incentives for countries to be fully engaged in world politics, as was demonstrated by the 1991 **Gulf War**, and by the active involvement by the European Union in Eastern European affairs, and more broadly, in world foreign policy.

Italian Second Republic

Technically there is no Italian Second Republic. The current constitution of Italy is their first republican constitution, promulgated in 1948 after the overthrow of the fascist state previously led by **Mussolini**. The document was amended in April 1993, however, during the course of a massive investigation by the Italian magistracy (known as *mani pulite*—clean hands) which revealed corruption, largely through the granting of building and other contracts in return for contributions to party funds, so widespread that all the major parties at very high official levels were clearly implicated. The extent of the political change caused by the investigation and the consequent trials and constitutional amendments so transformed Italian expectations of politics, and to a lesser extent their practices, that many journalists took to describing the post-1993 political system as the 'Second Republic', and the phrase has entered the terminology of political science. The idea that Italy is now living under a second constitution arises from the sense that the changes were so extreme as to amount to a peaceful revolution. A further root of the political changes was the end of the **cold war**, and thereby the disappearance of much of the rationale of the dominance of the Christian Democrat Party (DC), which had been in control of every government from the beginning of the Republic, and which kept the Italian Communist Party (PCI) out of government despite its roughly similar level of voting support. With the removal of cold war fears and the consequent unlocking of voters from these traditional orientations, other political tendencies, especially the regional and semi-separatist Northern League were able to gain real support.

In a series of referendums, voters opted for a radical change in the electoral system, owing to disillusion with the endless succession of DC-led, but highly fragile, coalitions and the rampant inefficiency and corruption of the public-service sector. Italy had suffered from an extreme form of the multi-party system caused by its near perfect proportional electoral system. The new elections, first used in 1994, moved sharply—though not completely—towards an Anglo-American style plurality system. Much of the idea that there is a

Second Republic was based on the hope that such institutional reform would transpose the party system into something like the two-party or two-block system found in, for example, France or the United Kingdom. In fact, the changes in government stability, while undeniable, have not been that great, while the list of parties represented is smaller, though not much smaller, than in the past. Indeed, the two most notable changes, somewhat longer-lasting governments and the fact that the parties form two electoral coalitions of the centre-left and centre-right, have come about for other reasons. The first is that the collapse of the DC and the PCI has allowed their replacement with slightly more orthodox centrist parties of the left and right, although these new parties are not highly disciplined. The more important fact may be the almost complete decimation of the old–style party leaders, and indeed parliamentary deputies, through their arrests and investigations for corruption. The politicians of the Second Republic are to a very large extent either completely new figures, or the few figures from the pre-1993 era able to demonstrate a clean record. There is no doubt among observers that the necessary constitutional and institutional reforms have not yet been extensive enough to produce genuinely effective, responsive, and honest government in Italy. Unfortunately, there are signs that both the public and the political classes are now tired of change, and they would prefer to consolidate the reforms that have occurred rather than pressing for more.

J

Jacobins

The Jacobins were a revolutionary group during the French Revolution of 1789 onwards, and their principal fight was for the creation of a single national parliament, democratically expressing the will of the people and solely symbolizing the **sovereignty** of the state. Revolutionary leaders, such as Lenin, who have ruled through centrally-imposed decision, as they maintain for the good of the populace, have also been described as Jacobin. Its modern use, especially in French politics, derives from this early concern with central authority, the objection to what was called *pouvoirs intermédiaires*, the feudal idea of a hierarchy of levels of authority, with legitimate foci of power and citizen-loyalty between the individual and the state. In its modern guise this becomes an insistence that all important decisions be made centrally in a state, and that only the official central government should in any way express sovereignty or be seen as entitled to legitimacy and loyalty. Thus politicians in France who are regarded as Jacobin deny the need for semi-autonomous regional governments, and would also oppose any **delegation** of decision-making power to other national institutions. France is, in fact, notable for its degree of **centralization** of policy-making, as much on minor as on major issues. Thus decisions as trivial as the renaming of a tiny commune, or as important, but elsewhere non-standardized, as which textbooks should be used in schools, are entirely controlled from Paris. It is interesting that this Jacobin position cuts across ordinary party ideological gulfs. The two most Jacobin parties in recent French orthodox politics have been from the extreme left and right of orthodox politics: the **Parti Communiste Français (PCF)** and from **Gaullism**, the Rassemblement pour la République (RPR). Both insisted on the primacy of central government, while the **Parti Socialiste** and, to much the same extent, the centre-right, were committed to regionalism and decentralization. There is no reason why the label Jacobin should not be used of politicians in other countries, but it has its particular importance in France simply because the Jacobins were so successful for so very long, to the almost total exclusion of real local government even until the late 20th century.

Jihad

Jihad is one of the few Muslim concepts well-known to non-Muslim Westerners, and it is very largely misunderstood to the detriment of Islamic societies. Jihad did originally have a core meaning of religious war against non-believers, part of a general conception that **Islam** should be expansionist and aim at the complete suppression of non-Islamic societies. This was entirely parallel, and approximately chronologically simultaneous, to similar views about the necessity for Christianity to expand to cover the world, frequently by unashamed use of war and aggression. Under conditions where Muslims live in non-Muslim societies which persecute them and prevent their fulfilling religious duties, Jihad still probably requires, or at least justifies, violent resistance, but even then only if declared as a duty by a legitimate Muslim leader. Certainly Jihad has been declared from time to time, against British and Italian rule during their colonial periods, for example, and by Afghan rebels against Soviet authority in the last quarter of the 20th century. Increasingly, though, Jihad is seen as a sense of personal moral duty to conquer sin in one's own life, or, because it is primarily a collective concept, to overcome evil in society.

The attraction to political rebels of the idea of Jihad has come from the teaching that a person who dies in the course of prosecuting Jihad is absolved of all sin and immediately enters heaven. It was for this reason that Islamic radicals from the Iranian revolution, and even more those in the Israeli–Palestinian conflict, have stressed the original violent and expansionist conception of Jihad. One restrictive aspect of the doctrine is that it is supposed to be impermissible for Jihad to be declared against another Muslim society—though in fact Iran's leaders did claim their war against Iraq was blessed by the idea of Jihad. Likewise, Christianity always attempted to distinguish between the lesser legitimacy of war against another Christian nation than that against a non-believing nation. Taken literally as a duty on all Islamic societies to prosecute aggressive war against all infidel societies, Jihad could never be central to the foreign policy of any modern Islamic state and will always be, at best, a rallying point for ideological extremists. It must be said that there is considerable debate within Islamic society about the true meaning of the term, and one which is deeply dependent on the particular sect of Islam the believer adheres. Beyond doubt there is no general aggressive meaning held by modern Islamic political leaders as an inescapable duty.

Judicial Review

Judicial review is a method whereby a superior judicial body may decide whether an **executive** or legislative action is constitutional or in any way illegal. It is most frequently used when a court decides that an act of the

legislature is unconstitutional and hence void, as in the USA where the Supreme Court has, over the past 200 years, declared invalid some significant acts of Congress as well as pronounced unconstitutional certain congressional procedures, such as the **legislative veto**. For example, a large portion of President Franklin Roosevelt's **New Deal** legislation was ruled unconstitutional by the Supreme Court in an orgy of judicial review, which led it into a major confrontation with the President. Judicial review was not, however, written into the Constitution of the USA, but was inferred from its provisions in a major case of 1803—*Marbury v. Madison*—in which the Supreme Court took the view that its own interpretation of the Constitution should take precedence over other interpretations, including the views of the popularly-elected legislature.

Judicial review need not always be as dramatic as in the USA. The more common form of judicial review—which is found in almost all countries where the **judiciary** enjoys some independence—involves the application by the judges of their own standards and values, their understanding of the constitution and their interpretation of the law, to the acts promulgated by the legislature or committed by the executive. Sometimes this process will simply produce a pattern of statutory interpretation which was not necessarily envisaged by the legislature or the executive; sometimes it will result in an actual conflict between the judiciary and the other elements in the system. It is therefore a mistake to see the existence of judicial review as being confined to those countries with written constitutions and countries which recognize the practice. Rather, judicial review is a feature of any system in which the judges can control legislative and executive acts by reference to broad constitutional, political and legal principles.

Judicial review has a highly technical meaning in modern English law, relating to a mechanism to bring administrative action before the courts; since the passing of the **Human Rights Act** 1998 a limited version of American-style judicial review has also been possible in the United Kingdom.

Judicialization of Politics

Over the last 20 years political scientists have become much more aware of the importance of **constitutional courts** in politics. In part this is because they have objectively become more important in some countries (for example, in France), in part because there are more of them, (essentially in countries experiencing **democratic transition**), but also because the study of courts was neglected for far too long by European political scientists. One consequence of this new attention has been the observation of a phenomenon often described as the judicialization of politics. This does not refer to the actual power or actions of the constitutional courts of these countries, so much as to an incidental effect. As constitutional courts have become active, often striking down legislation as unconstitutional, there has, it is claimed, been a change in legislative behaviour. The idea is that parliamentarians have become increasingly aware that wielding a parliamentary majority may not be enough to put desired legislation in place. They must now be aware of the possibility that the courts can annul their statutes. This is particularly a concern in countries such as France and Germany where a minority of legislators, having lost the vote in the chamber, may refer an act before it has come into operation to the constitutional court. Thus, the opposition frequently has a second chance to achieve in the courts what it was unable to do in parliament. As a result, politicians have become very much more aware of constitutional issues and cite these during their debates on legislation. Rather than risk having new legislation struck down, governments try to predict what objections constitutional courts might make and avoid them by careful drafting. In the same way, oppositions attempt to have amendments accepted by the government by disguising them as motions to reduce the risk of the legislation falling foul of the courts. Hence politics becomes 'judicialized'. Some commentators seem to regard this as an unfortunate consequence of the rise of judicial power, referring often to the **chilling effect** on legislative preferences. Alternatively, it might be seen as a desirable fact that elected politicians take more care to behave in a constitutional manner.

The problem, if it is one, applies particularly where this form of judicial review of an act before it comes into operation, known as *a priori* and abstract review, occurs. In the USA, where the Supreme Court has always been powerful, critics seldom claim to have noticed a judicialization in Congressional behaviour. However, as in all **common law** jurisdictions with **judicial review**, the US courts may only take note of the Constitution after legislation is in place and in the context of a genuine piece of litigation.

Judiciary

The judiciary is the body of judges in a constitutional system. The powers and role of the judiciary varies from country to country, but there will always be some, albeit indirect, significance both in the methods used by judges to interpret the law and in the *ex cathedra* statements of individual judges. The scope for judicial influence in the policy-making process will be greatest where there is a written constitution with ambiguous provisions and, as in the USA, the institution of **judicial review**. However, even in systems such as the British legal system where the judges are traditionally reticent about their law-making as opposed to law-finding functions, there may be great scope for judicial policy-making and for judicial intervention in the political arena. Thus in the United Kingdom in the 1960s the field of **administrative law** was elaborated by a series of judicial initiatives, and the courts have found themselves in conflict with governments of both parties over the interpretation of statutes.

The recruitment pattern of the judiciary is of political interest because it has frequently been assumed by critics that the law has an individualistic and conservative bias which, when combined with a socially unrepresentative judiciary, militates against collectivist policies. For this reason early experiments with extended welfare provision in Britain—for example by the Liberal governments of the early 20th century—provided that **tribunals** rather than the ordinary courts should resolve disputes about such matters as workers' compensation and old-age pensions. For a period lasting up to the 1950s attempts were made by Parliament to protect some statutes from judicial intervention by excluding any appeal from statutory tribunals to the ordinary court system. However, in a series of decisions, of which the Anisminic case is the most important (Anisminic was a company trading in Egypt which claimed compensation for losses incurred as a result of unrest in Egypt), the courts found ways around these procedures to maintain their ultimate right to supervise all quasi-judicial activity.

In some legal systems (for example in England and Wales) recruitment to the higher judiciary is almost entirely from the litigating branch of the legal profession (the bar); the bar's near monopoly on such appointments was demonstrated by their relatively successful fight against initiatives by the Thatcher government (1979–90) to make judicial selection more open. In other systems, especially in Europe, the judiciary is a career for which lawyers opt at the very beginning of their professional practice. In some jurisdictions—mainly a number of states within the USA—judges are elected, though seldom by a process which approximates to the partisan conflict of ordinary political elections. Nevertheless, judges in such jurisdictions can lose their seats if their decisions anger the public, as was demonstrated in 1987 when the Chief Justice of the California Supreme Court, Rose Bird, lost her seat because her liberal decisions in matters like the death penalty were not in keeping with public attitudes.

Because of the danger of corruption and undue or improper influence on the judiciary, most democracies make it difficult to remove judges, although where they are elected (or, as in California, appointed and then submitted for election or ratification) they may be subjected to **recall** and are therefore also subjected to direct political constraints. A more common term than 'the judiciary' in continental European countries is 'the magistracy'.

Junta

Junta is the Spanish word for a council or board, but its general use in politics, for which the full Spanish phrase would be *junta militar*, is 'military government'. **Military regimes** come in several forms, and the particular form for which junta is shorthand has most frequently been found in Latin American countries. Such a junta is usually composed of several officers, of essentially equal political rank, drawn from all the armed services. The resulting government is direct military government by the whole military machine, balancing the interests of the various services according to their relative power inside the military apparatus. A junta usually will not be dominated by any one person, though this is not invariably true (for example in Chile after the coup against Salvador Allende, the junta was dominated by General Augusto Pinochet), and thus the presidency, or whatever it is called, can often change hands frequently as rivalries between the services and between members of the junta fluctuate. In contrast is the form of military government more commonly found outside Latin America, where a dictator uses the military to retain power, but probably governs mainly through civilian institutions, rather than acting simply as *primus inter pares* among a group of officers. Thus in Pakistan, which was governed by generals for most of the 1960s and 1970s, there was never a junta, but rather a series of strong men for whom the military forces were no more than tools.

Just War

The theory of when it is just to fight a war, and how to fight justly, comes principally from medieval Christian thought and from the great development of international law that followed, especially in the works of **Grotius** and Samuel Pufendorf (1632–94). Public interest in just war theory declined considerably in the 20th century with the growing realization of the horror of total war. This emotional reaction not only led to a spread of semi-pacifism, but also to the position that war could not be just, and had to be renounced by all civilized nations as an instrument of policy. The theory of just war has in recent years been of great interest to some professional military organizations, because of increasing unwillingness by professional officer corps to abandon a more civilian sense of doing only what satisfies their conscience. Largely as a result of the American involvement in the **Vietnam War** the topic has come to be of increasing interest again, as public debate increased on all defence matters in Western societies.

The traditional argument on just war (and modern versions have so far added very little indeed to the well worked-out theory of the past) distinguishes two questions. Usually referred to by their associated Latin tags, the distinctions are between *jus ad bellum* and *jus in bello*. The first raises the question of when it is just or right to go to war, the second considers what methods may be used in warfare. To simplify enormously, most arguments on the justice of going to war at all boil down to the idea that only defensive war is just, though one might claim justly to go to war in defence of a weak third party, and to not be limited only to defending one's own territorial integrity. It was this notion of defence of a weak victim that was used in the **United Nations (UN)** to justify the **Gulf War** against Iraq, although the original theory had not contemplated an international organization as having the right to fight. In fact one aspect of just war theory refers specifically to the notion of 'a competent authority', which has hitherto always been taken to mean a nation state. The point is not irrelevant, because on it depends the question of whether organizations such as the **PLO** or the **IRA** are entitled to see themselves as fighting a war, rather than being merely terrorists or criminals. In contrast, arguments over what warlike actions are permissible have been more heated, less consensual, but probably more influential. At least since the beginning of the 20th century, and in most countries increasingly so, most soldiers and politicians have made serious efforts to limit the barbarity of war, through mechanisms like the Geneva Conventions. During the early stages of the conflict between the UN and Iraq the language and concepts of just war theory were prominent in public debate, and much care was taken by the governments contributing to the UN effort to insist that the doctrines of just war were being observed, particularly in view of the known capacity of the Iraqi forces to use reviled means such as gas and chemical weapons. Acts of atrocity, though they have happened often enough, have not always gone without punishment, and would be more frequent and worse were it not for a general attempt to abide by *jus in bello*, even when a combatant could not realistically claim *jus ad bellum*.

A basic doctrine that runs through both halves of the theory of just warfare is the idea of proportionality, which roughly means that an action taken must not cause suffering vastly out of proportion to the harm suffered from the attacker. Thus, for example, even defence of one's own land might be unjust were the reaction to the invasion of some arid and useless border land with little strategic value to be the destruction of an enemy city with a nuclear missile. While there are strong arguments that the USA was behaving justly in going to war in Vietnam to protect the weak state of South Vietnam from aggression on the part of China-backed North Vietnam, there can be little doubt that the search and destroy missions, or declarations of huge portions of the country as free-fire zones, were disproportional to the military utility and constituted a breach of *jus in bello*.

In the context of nuclear warfare it is very difficult to see how the theory can be developed in any useful way, but such a conclusion should not lightly be accepted, if only because of the effect on morale, and thus the effect on the credibility of **deterrence**. Equally difficult, in a completely different way, is the application of just war theory to international terrorism, whether one is considering the actions of terrorists or of the attacked nation states.

Justice

Justice is a fundamental value of political science, forming the main preoccupation of both **Plato's** *Republic* and **Aristotle's** *Politics*. It can most conveniently be divided into two aspects, procedural justice, and substantive, or 'social', justice. Procedural justice is considerably the easier to deal with, involving as it does, relatively technical questions such as **due process**, fair trial and equality before the law. Substantive justice refers to the overall fairness of a society in its division of rewards and burdens. Such divisions can be made on the basis of social efficiency (for example, incentive payments), merit, desert, need or several other criteria. The principal meaning of 'social' justice is probably a matter of giving to people what they are 'entitled to' or 'need' (the concepts are not identical) in terms of basic social rights, food, clothing, housing, etc., and thereafter distributing any surplus in a fair and equitable way. Although it is clearly a matter of great importance, 'justice' as a political value can really be analysed no further than to say that it requires a 'fair' distribution of goods. It is, in fact, often described as 'distributive' justice, and the criteria which count as 'fair' depend on previous ideological judgments. In this sense Plato and Aristotle were using the word translated as 'justice' to connote a much broader summation of the good in political life. An increasingly important application of the political sense of justice has been in the international arena, where the disparity in wealth between, for example, the **Third World** and the **First World**, is treated as a failure of justice.

K

Kant

Immanuel Kant (1724–1804) was a German philosopher of enormous influence in every area of philosophical, political and moral thought. In political terms he is especially important as a writer in the **Enlightenment** tradition and as a successor to **Rousseau** and an influence on **Hegel**. No very specific political doctrine can be derived from Kant, but without his intellectual groundbreaking many modern political philosophies, including not only **Marxism** but also **existentialism**, would be poorer. In his own times, and in terms of his own orientation, we should probably see Kant as a liberal, but the complexity and power of his thought is relevant to a far wider range of theories.

Two of Kant's arguments are especially significant. One is that all moral and political judgements should be 'universal', that is, made according to general moral or policy rules rather than solely with regard to the particulars of an individual case. This is the element of **liberalism**, supporting as it does the idea of the rule of law. Another is that he was acutely aware of the way our concepts and categories determine our social thought, and even the categories into which we distinguish the world. This suggestion that our social perception is not autonomous observation of what actually exists in absolute terms, but is conditioned by what we *think* exists, has deeply influenced the development of the theory of **ideology**, especially Marx's reinterpretation of Hegel and the thinking of Marxists such as **Mannheim**. Kant wrote relatively little on practical politics, but a major exception is his essay on international relations (IR), *Perpetual Peace* (1795). In this he argues for a form of international society, and introduces for the first time the idea that international justice requires a more or less democratic form of government inside each participating society. It remains extremely influential in the rather small body of theoretical works concerning international relations. Indeed a major tenet of modern IR theory, that democracies do not make war on each other, can be traced directly to this essay.

Keynesianism

John Maynard Keynes (1883–1946) was a British economist who was closely involved with practical politics in the 1920s and 1930s, especially with the Liberal Party and their senior political leaders both at the Versailles Peace Conference and later during the inter-war slump. In his economic works, particularly his classical *General Theory of Employment, Interest and Money* (1936), he advocated a theory of how governments could control and manipulate the economy to avoid the worst of slumps and inflationary booms. This involved the idea of using budget deficits or surpluses to counter cyclical trends in the economy by pumping money into the economy during a slump, thus increasing purchasing power and raising demand, or raising taxes during an inflationary period in order to take excess demand out of the economy. During the 1930s and 1940s these ideas rather slowly became accepted in government circles through much of the Western world, eventually forming the basis of government policy in post-war economic debate. For example, even the highly conservative US President Richard Nixon announced, in 1972, that he was a Keynesian.

The main features of Keynes' theory were commitments to full employment and stable currency, and above all the idea that economic performance was controllable without recourse to socialist methods of **nationalization** and direct state control of economic decisions. Instead governments could leave all detailed decisions in the hands of individual firms, and operate through setting tax levels and interest rates to 'fine tune' the overall economy. Until the late 1970s this was a more or less consensual policy among most important political parties and the vast majority of professional economists. Thereafter the ideas came under more and more pressure from 'right-wing' alternatives, especially **monetarism** associated with American economic theorists like Milton Friedman of the **Chicago School**, which, by the late 1980s, gained a dominance in Western societies equivalent to Keynesianism's earlier sway. There are very few professional economists who would now identify themselves as Keynesian, and fewer politicians. The extent to which his doctrines are actually contradicted by the dominant monetarist school is, however, unclear.

Khrushchev

Nikita Sergeyevich Khrushchev was the first overall leader of the Soviet Union to have risen entirely within the ranks of the organized party apparatus (see **Communist Party of the Soviet Union**), being of the generation after the original leaders who had organized the machinery of the state. Having fought, as a young man, with the Red Army in the Civil War that followed the Revolution, he rose rapidly in the party, serving as regional First Secretary in Moscow from 1936 and in Ukraine during and after the Second World War. As he managed not only to survive the **Stalin** purges, but even to be trusted by Stalin in the late 1940s to reorganize agricultural production, he must have been a very safe and orthodox **apparatchik**. His rise to overall command after Stalin's death was delayed by the introduction of collective leadership, as a result of a fear of another period of **Stalinism**, though he had risen to hold one of the two most important posts, First Secretary of the party, within six months of Stalin's death. Only in 1958, in the wake of a failed attempt to oust him, did he collect enough power to have himself appointed Chairman of the Council of Ministers (premier and effectively head of state), finally removing rivals such as Nikolai Bulganin and Georgy Malenkov. His supremacy lasted for only six years, being himself ousted in 1964.

Khrushchev had, in part, come to power as an agricultural specialist, and tried to reorganize the party to give more freedom and influence to agricultural interests, so the continued failure of the agricultural sector was a personal failure. This was by no means his only reverse, however. He attempted a complicated balancing act in which investment demands, military as well as agricultural, were supported and an attempt to increase the consumer production side of industry, to win public support, was also made. These mutually conflicting demands could not be satisfied, and he gradually lost the support of all the sectors that had helped put him in power. Nevertheless, it was almost certainly his foreign-policy failures that finally cost him his position. The most notorious of these was his entanglement of the Soviet Union in the **Cuban missile crisis**, against the advice of the military, who held him responsible for their embarrassing inability to frighten the USA because he had failed to back them earlier in their demands for weapons development, and had, indeed, presided over the biggest reduction of Soviet military power by any leader until **Gorbachev**. At much the same time his intransigence towards **Mao Zedong's** China brought fears of a Sino–Soviet war. On his removal the Soviet Union reverted, briefly, to a collective leadership, with Aleksei Kosygin and Leonid **Brezhnev** holding the posts of prime minister and First Secretary, respectively. Yet again the First Secretary triumphed, with Brezhnev rapidly becoming the sole ruler. The agricultural system was put back into the orthodox party model, consumer investment decreased, and a major arms programme started. Khrushchev had, however, presided over a slight liberalization of Soviet society, and had never attempted Stalinist tactics. However, tolerant though he may have been internally, he had fiercely crushed any moves towards liberalization in Eastern Europe, especially in Poland and in the draconian crushing of the 1956 Hungarian uprising.

Kibbutz

The kibbutz movement developed in Palestine during the 1930s as part of the Jewish struggle to establish a Jewish state and homeland, and became a vital part of Israel's early agricultural expansion after the state was established. Originally simply an agricultural settlement, on virgin and usually inhospitable territory, more recently the typical kibbutz has also engaged in industrial production. The kibbutz movement is highly 'communal' in orientation, with all work being rationally planned and shared, and with little or no private property, the profits of the enterprise being used communally. Many kibbutzim adopt other policies that contrast sharply with life in capitalist societies. A particular example of this is the communal rearing of children, intended not only to free most women for productive work along with the men, but also deliberately to create a spirit and psychology of communalism, and to reduce individualism. As perhaps the only successful examples of **communes** in the West the kibbutzim have been a source of inspiration for many Western intellectuals, though in contemporary Israel itself they are not necessarily admired. The kibbutz movement has produced a disproportionate number of the more dedicated and successful soldiers in the Israeli Defence Forces (largely because self-defence was so crucial during the years before the creation of the state of Israel, and because even today these settlements are prime targets for attack by Israel's enemies) and also of those in prominent political and trade-union positions. The economic importance of the Kibbutz movement is no longer very great, and successor generations of the Kibbutzim have tended to move to cities and to ordinary professional and industrial lives, despite efforts by the governments to reinforce the communities.

Korean War

The Korean peninsula had been dominated to a greater or lesser extent by China for 2,000 years, and particularly between the 13th and 19th centuries, after which, following a short period of independence, it was annexed by Japan in 1910. After the Japanese defeat at the end of the Second World War, Korea was partitioned into areas under Soviet and US military control along the 38th parallel. Attempts to agree on a democratic unification failed, and two separate states were set up, the Republic of Korea in the South after elections which were held in early 1948, and shortly after the Democratic People's Republic of Korea under Soviet influence in the North. US forces were withdrawn from the Republic of Korea in 1949 and in June 1950 Northern troops invaded the South. At US instigation the **United Nations (UN)** Security Council ordered a withdrawal, and asked member nations to provide troops to enforce its edict. The USA immediately acted and sent its first troops into South Korea at the end of June.

The initial results were devastating for the USA and the UN. The first US troops to arrive, all taken from comfortable posts as occupation troops in Japan, were undertrained, unwilling and ill-equipped, and were soundly beaten by the North Koreans who not only captured the South Korean capital of Seoul, but nearly drove the UN forces out of the country. Reinforcements from the USA, coupled with contingents from several other UN members, including the United Kingdom, Canada, France and Turkey, landed at Inchon in September and forced the North Koreans well back into their own territory. At this stage a disastrous political conflict took place between the US government and the UN commander in Korea, the US war hero General Douglas MacArthur. Fiercely anti-communist, MacArthur insisted on driving north, with the intention of destroying the North Korean state. In so doing he came to seem threatening to the newly-installed communist government of the People's Republic of China (PRC), which immediately sent huge, if also ill-equipped, peasant armies to the aid of the North Koreans. The combined communist forces succeeded again in driving the UN forces south, in vicious battles that caused the USA to suffer more casualties than the **Vietnam War** was to do later. MacArthur was relieved of his command, and the UN finally regained some of its ground, pushing the communist forces back to the original frontier on the 38th parallel.

Peace negotiations started in July 1951, although fighting continued until an armistice agreement was reached in July 1953. No peace treaty has ever been signed between any of the combatants, and the North/South Korean border remained a site of armed tension. However, some progress was made towards an eventual peace treaty, and indeed reunification of the two Koreas, in the early 1990s, including a reduction in the number of US forces stationed in South Korea. Further progress in the late 1990s and early 2000s failed to bring about a treaty, although the two states appeared less likely to resume open hostilities than at any time since the war's conclusion.

The Korean War was deeply unpopular with the US public, who saw no reason why they should be engaged in a campaign that had no obvious connection to their national interest. In a complex way the military experience in Korea was to do the US military great harm 15 years later in Vietnam. The military felt they had been defeated, or at the best only scored a draw in Korea, and this seriously affected morale and planning in Vietnam. But the war had even more far reaching consequences. Though there is little direct evidence that the Soviet Union planned or approved of North Korea's actions, they supported their war effort as a way of competing with the USA. More than anything else this Soviet involvement convinced US policy-makers of the need for a firm military stand against 'International Communism', and led to the **arms races** and confrontations in Europe, Asia and Latin America (see **Cuban missile crisis**) that characterized the **cold war** for the next 35 years. One further consequence should be noted. The unpopularity of the war, and the cost of the **conventional arms** hardware and tactics it involved, convinced President Dwight Eisenhower, who came to office towards the end of the war, that US military policy should be primarily nuclear, with all the inevitable development of nuclear **strategy** and hardware that followed. North Korea remains to this day one of the states identified by the USA as a threat to world security, and the US military presence in the south, while reduced, remains numerically significant.

L

Labour Party

The original title of the Labour Party, the Labour Representation Committee (LRC), makes clear what the party was originally about. It existed to get representatives elected to parliament as direct spokespeople for the interests of the industrial working class, but not as advocates of **socialism** *per se*. The LRC was founded, in 1900, by co-operation between existing working-class political movements, particularly the Independent Labour Party (ILP), middle-class socialists (the **Fabians**) and the **trade union** movement. At the 1906 general election, 30 of the LRC's 51 candidates were elected, demonstrating the movement's real potential, and it subsequently adopted the name the Labour Party. It began to gain respectability and, during the First World War, several leading members had government posts in Lloyd George's post-1916 cabinet. It became more overtly socialist when it adopted a new constitution in 1918 which called, among other things, for 'the common ownership of production, distribution and exchange' (Clause IV). Labour's first taste of power was as a minority government, with Ramsay MacDonald as prime minister, for the first 10 months of 1924, but it was easily beaten by the **Conservative Party** in a general election at the end of that period. It again formed a minority government in 1929 when it was the largest party after that year's election, and struggled on until 1931. The world-wide slump forced it to adopt increasingly conservative measures and the cabinet split when the more **left**-wing members refused to support these. Although the ensuing 'National Government' was a grand coalition led by the Labour leader, MacDonald, and went into the election as a single entity, the rump of the Labour Party held the party machinery and gained 52 seats. These events were bitterly hated by the Labour Party, who ever afterwards saw MacDonald as a traitor.

Labour did not gain power again until 1945, at the end of the Second World War, when for the first time it gained an overall majority—and a large one too. The 1945–51 Labour governments, with Clement Attlee as prime minister, essentially created the modern **welfare state** and nationalized several major industries. The almost inevitable austerity of this post-war period, however, led to the return of the Conservatives, who then presided over a post-war boom that kept them in power until 1964. During this period Labour went through a period of fierce internal debate over how socialist they should be, culminating in victory for the moderates under Hugh Gaitskell, and then Harold Wilson, who became prime minister from 1964–70. This period of Labour administration was very different from the post-war government, and introduced Labour as a technocratic party sharing a wide consensus with the Conservatives and committed to managing a mixed economy alongside a welfare state. Labour returned to power again after two general elections held in 1974, at first as a minority and then with a small majority; James Callaghan succeeded Wilson as prime minister in 1976, and after by-election losses and parliamentary defections Labour again found itself as a minority government, and was forced to rely on the **Liberal Party** for support through the 'Lib-Lab pact', which lasted from March 1977 to May 1978. During this period the behaviour of the trade unions, in contributing to inflation by demanding large wage increases and through frequent damaging **strikes** (including those in the 'winter of discontent' of 1978/79), and their dominant role in Labour Party policy and administrative affairs, may have contributed to the onset of a long-term decline in the party's popularity. Its defeat in 1979, and replacement by a more determinedly right-wing Conservative government under Margaret Thatcher, renewed the party debate over ideological principles. In 1981 several prominent moderates left the party to form the Social Democratic Party (SDP), and the Labour Party manifesto for the 1983 general election, while the left was temporarily dominant under the leadership of Michael Foot, has been described as 'the longest suicide note in history'. The Conservatives duly won a landslide victory, with Labour only just holding on to second place, in terms of votes cast, from the new SDP which campaigned in alliance with the Liberal Party. For the next eight years Neil Kinnock, who had himself come to prominence in the party as a left-winger, fought a lengthy battle to return the party to a more managerial, 'Wilsonite', mixed-economy position. Although the Conservatives won another large majority at the 1987 general election, Labour did appear to be well on the way towards assuming a position in the centre of the political spectrum. At the 1992 general election, however, despite **opinion poll** predictions of a Labour victory, the Conservatives were returned to office for a fourth consecutive term, even though with a much reduced majority. Kinnock promptly announced his resignation as party leader and was succeeded by John Smith. After Smith's early death in 1994 the party was taken over by Tony Blair, leader along with several others (of whom the future Chancellor of the Exchequer, Gordon Brown, was pre-eminent) of a reformist group. This group succeeded in remaking the party, indeed in effectively (though unofficially) renaming it as '**New Labour**'. The new party, which dropped even its symbolic Clause IV commitment to nationalization, became a purely centrist party, committed to most free-market principles and to monetarism. It won the 1997 and 2001 elections easily, expounding a rather vague doctrine of the **Third Way** meant to replace even **social democracy** from its past ideological commitments.

The British Labour Party has always had the problem of its close links to the trade-union movement, to which it owes its birth. Although these have provided it with most of its funds and much of its membership, they have also tied the party to often unpopular positions on industrial relations and in general acted as a restraint on the party developing policies that could be advantageous electorally. Part of what made Blair's reformulation possible was the decline in power of the trade unions following Thatcherite reform in employment law under the preceding Conservative governments.

Many other countries have labour parties, some of which pre-date the British Labour Party. All of these parties follow socialist or social democratic paths, and many also have links with their countries' trade-union movements. Australia, Norway and Sweden are examples of countries with powerful labour parties.

Laissez-faire

Laissez-faire is the doctrine that the government of a state should have no control at all over economic matters. It is especially associated with 19th-century **Liberalism**, but is by no means absent from the modern world. In origin it was a liberal opposition to traditional, semi-feudal, monopolistic patterns in which the state involved itself in direct control of aspects of the economy for general purposes of policy. It later came to signify opposition to any governmental infringement on the absolute freedom of contract, because it was believed that maximal economic performance was possible only where the market forces of supply and demand were allowed to find their own balance, under which conditions everyone, whether entrepreneur or unskilled worker, would be better off. Thus controls, even minimum-wage laws or restrictions on child labour hours, were seen as unacceptable infringements on total economic freedom. The political theory of laissez-faire was buttressed by adherence to the early versions of technical economic theory, the 'perfect competition' theories of writers like David Ricardo (1772–1823) and Alfred Marshall (1842–1924), who tried to show that an economy consisting of many equally-small units of production would automatically work to maximize social value. For a long time the common law doctrines of contract also operated to support this position, despite the fact that both legal and effective monopolies were distorting the perfect competition model, and inequalities of bargaining power, especially between workers and employers, were reducing the theoretical fairness of laissez-faire policies. Although it was claimed that laissez-faire required a total independence of the economy and the political system, it was in fact dependent on political support for established power relations. Nevertheless, advocates of laissez-faire economic policies are still occasionally influential in policy-making in modern societies, and there are certain connections between this doctrine and other conservative economic policies, especially **monetarism**.

Rather weak and modified versions of laissez-faire economic philosophy have been behind the policies of recent conservative governments, notably the Thatcher governments in the United Kingdom and the administrations of Reagan and the elder and younger Bush in the USA. Essentially identical policies were followed by '**New Labour**' after its election in 1997, including their granting independence to the Bank of England. One reason why these and similar governments cannot return entirely to laissez-faire is that the old theories relied on the external control of the gold standard to regulate currency values, which was abandoned by most countries in the early 1930s. Modern versions of automatic currency control, the process culminating in the **European Union's** Economic and Monetary Union, have perhaps nudged European economies a little further back to this economic theoretical ideal.

Language Groups

Language groups are often of vital importance in politics. It is not just that which language one speaks, or is forced to speak for social advancement, is of great practical significance, but, even more, that the recognition of a language is a major aspect of the legitimization of a culture and history. Very frequently, where language is politically relevant, one language group is an ethnic minority suppressed by what they see as an alien conqueror or oppressing élite. In such places having to speak the language of the rulers is not just a practical difficulty, but a violently-charged symbol of unfreedom. In many cases languages will turn out to be correlated with other social symbols, of which religion and **ethnicity** are the most potent. As a result, language groups can become important centres for the focusing of revolutionary, or at least protest, politics in modern societies, often keeping alive **cleavages** which might otherwise have died away. After class and religion (with which they are, in any case, often interdefined), linguistic cleavages are the most important source of conflict in modern politics. Belgium, Romania, Spain, the United Kingdom and the former Soviet and Yugoslav republics are particular examples, among European nations alone, where political movements or conflicts are based mainly on language groups. In the **Third World** the situation is even more complex because language may be a vital element in the attempt to construct a national unity out of a political system that is really only the result of imperialist map-makers. Unity can, indeed, sometimes only be hoped for by getting agreement to common use of a foreign, formerly imperialist, language, as with the Indian need to operate in English because of the multiplicity of local languages.

Language probably has its deep political significance because of the way in which our thoughts, stock of concepts, and very self-image are reflected by language and restricted by it. Thus it is more rational, perhaps, to define political culture around language than most other cleavage patterns, and this may account for the virulence of language-group politics. In modern societies, however, linguistic politics are sometimes deeply resented by residents of the relevant language area who have accepted political assimilation with the speakers of the dominant tongue, and who regard adherence to the indigenous language as atavistic or even merely nostalgic.

Law

Law is any system of widely recognized and compulsory regulations that govern the behaviour of citizens or political actors, either between each other, or between actor and some overall power or authority. Within the complexities of the theory of law it may be generally accepted that there are two broad schools of thought. On the one hand there is the **positive law** tradition, particularly strong in American and English legal thinking, in which all law is seen as positive, as direct commands from someone or something able to enforce them. This school, represented in the United Kingdom by the works of H. L. A. Hart (1907–92), tends to differentiate sharply between law and morality, and to treat any command from a *de jure* power as lawful and legally binding, whatever its character. It also seeks to deny the status of 'law' to non-enforceable rules, such as those otherwise recognized as making up the body of conventions and expectations known as 'international' law. On the other hand there is what is often referred to as the **natural law** school, which is dominant in continental Europe and which sees law as somehow representing binding obligations arising from a prior moral sphere, to which the actual positive laws merely give effect (or ought to). Other basic characteristics of law, for example, whether or not they must always be universal in character, what authorities in a society may promulgate them or when, if ever, they may legitimately be denied, are bound up with these broader theoretical problems. Until relatively recently the positive law tradition was dominant in American and English legal thinking, and most common among practitioners of law, if not theorists, everywhere, but this position is increasingly challenged, especially by writers in the new liberal tradition following **Rawls** and **Nozick**. Law, rather like democracy, acts as a powerful symbolic restraint in political argument: few would ever dare admit that their actions were illegal but good, rather they would attempt to justify them by criticizing the validity of the laws they were breaking. The reason is the same in both cases; in the modern world there are no justifiable appeals to anything but majority opinion, so the impersonal regulation of life by rules set out, ultimately by the majority, is the only acceptable arbiter. The difficulty in practice is that no known set of legal rules can actually abolish the role of purely discretionary decisions by those appointed to administer law; indeed, the major theoretical debate between 'positivist' legal theorists, such as Hart, and the Dworkinian school is precisely about the nature of this discretion.

Law and Order

Law and order refers to a state of society in which there is a regular process of criminal and civil law and in which certain agencies, such as the **police**, are responsible for maintaining domestic tranquillity. Law and order is generally seen by most conservatives and many liberals as the basic requirement of a state, since without these conditions **civil society**, political freedom and **civil liberties** are impossible. Law and order in common parlance has also come to mean the provision of a strong police force and a concern with reducing crime and vandalism. As such, law and order may become an election issue in democracies concerned with rising crime rates. George Wallace campaigned for the US presidency as the candidate of the American Independent Party in 1968, emphasizing concern for law and order. **Conservative Party** campaigns in the United Kingdom have often laid considerable stress on this theme. So important do politicians regard this issue electorally that even Labour governments seek to appear, in Tony Blair's words, 'tough on crime and tough on the causes of crime'.

Leadership

Leadership is a quality which in theory signifies the ability of a person or a group of people to persuade others to act by inspiring them and making them believe that a proposed course of action is the correct one.

Political leadership is generally thought to be a desirable property, except when a leader becomes too conscious of his or her position and refuses to acknowledge their **accountability** to the rank and file of their party or to the electorate. Leadership may, in certain romantic or **fascist** philosophies, take on a special role, but in normal democratic politics it is seen as a routine feature of the political process.

Sometimes the ruling élite of a party may be known as its leadership (see **élitism**). In the Soviet Union, for example, the Communist Party stressed its 'collective leadership' as a basic principle of government in contrast to the

Stalinist period when one-man leadership was the order of the day. In many countries—especially newly independent countries with a recent history of nationalist struggle—the leader is seen as the embodiment of the people and the nation, as with Dr Hastings Banda of Malawi. However, leadership in **Third World** countries is often difficult to sustain over a long period of time in the absence of durable political institutions and economic progress.

League of Nations

In January 1918, nine months after the USA had entered the First World War, its president, Woodrow Wilson, made it clear, in his 'Fourteen Points', that he wanted a new order to world politics, the abandonment of the **balance-of-power** system and the introduction of some form of international association to provide collective security. The League of Nations, ratified by the signatories to the Versailles Peace Treaty in 1919 and instituted in 1920, was this new association. Ironically the main reason it failed was that the USA's membership was blocked by the Senate. With the USA thus entering an **isolationist** period the hope that the League would be able to enforce its decisions on aggressive member states depended on the European powers, which effectively meant on the United Kingdom and France, because the primary problems were caused by the other two powers, Germany and Italy. Germany in fact withdrew from the League in 1933 as soon as **Hitler** came to power and Italy withdrew in 1937 two years after the League had declared it the aggressor in its invasion of Abyssinia (Ethiopia); the Soviet Union was expelled in 1939 after its invasion of Finland.

Because the League had no military force it attempted to wield power by economic sanctions, although these were never effectively applied. Had France and the UK seriously wished to support the League's peacemaking efforts they could probably have done so. But during the 1930s the UK was preoccupied with its policy of appeasement towards the **dictatorships**, and **Third Republic** France was internally too divided and weak to engage in a forceful foreign policy. Nevertheless, the League had some successes: its judicial branch, the Permanent Court of International Justice, was rather more effective and respected than its successor, the **United Nations'** International Court of Justice, and its International Labour Organization was surprisingly effective in improving working conditions throughout the League's membership, and survived the transition from League of Nations to United Nations. The League was formally dissolved in 1946 to make way for its successor, the UN, which until relatively recently was no more successful, despite not suffering from US refusal to participate.

Left

The term left, or left-wing, to signify socialist or radical political tendencies dates as a symbol from the days immediately preceding the French Revolution. At this stage the French Estates-General (roughly equivalent to a **parliament**) was so ordered that those supporting the king and the traditional social structure sat on the right of the assembly, and their opponents sat on the left. In fact the association of 'left' or 'left-handedness' with those less than totally orthodox is a much deeper element of European culture—the left hand has always been connected with the supernatural or with the socially unacceptable. (The 'bend sinister', a left-slanting line on a heraldic device, indicated a nobleman born out of wedlock.) Left, and **right**, its obvious opponent, are frequently used, but ultimately empty, slogan-words in modern politics. The most that can be safely said is that those on the 'left' wish to change things, and to do this in the direction of more equality and less tradition than those on the right. The whole idea of the left/right dichotomy assumes that political life can be put into a one-dimensional framework. In Western political terms a 'left-wing' position has come to signify belief in state intervention in society and the economy to enhance the political and economic liberty and equality of the people, in contrast to the right which emphasizes the ability of individuals to secure their most favourable conditions. However, in the old communist societies, 'left' in Western eyes, the labels were reversed, limiting the consistent application of the term to radical opposition to an establishment.

Legislative Veto

The legislative veto is a legal device adopted by the US **Congress** to give itself the power to control the behaviour of the vitally important regulatory agencies which govern so many areas of US policy-making. It is often seen by the **executive** as a trick to get round the constitutional **separation of powers** which forbids the legislative branch to exercise direct control over the execution and application of laws.

The technique involves writing into any legislation which sets up or grants general powers to agencies the right of Congress to pass, by resolution, a motion forbidding the agency to go ahead with any particular policy or regulation that Congress does not favour. The important point is that resolutions of Congress, unlike acts, are not subject to presidential veto. In this way Congress can try to by-pass the president's control over the executive side of government. Although they were first used in the 1930s, legislative-veto provisions proliferated in the 1970s as part of the general resurgence of congressional power *vis-à-vis* the presidency.

Many argued over the constitutionality of this technique, and in 1983 the Supreme Court, in *Immigration and Naturalization Service v. Chadha*, heard a case

277

in which a specific decision not to deport an allegedly illegal immigrant had been overruled by the House of Representatives using a congressional veto provision written into the INS authorizing legislation. The ruling was that once Congress had made a general grant of delegated authority, it had no further right to interfere with its execution, unless it chose to invoke the full regular legislative process. Further cases are needed fully to clarify the situation, and Congress continued to pass legislation which contains legislative veto provisions, in the hope that the rulings will not be effective in enforcing this aspect of the separation of powers.

Legislatures

The legislature is the official rule-making body of a political system, as opposed to the institutions charged with applying the rules, or with judging those alleged to have broken them. There is an entirely erroneous tendency to equate legislatures with elected **parliaments**, but there is no theoretical reason why, even as an ideal, the legislative function should be carried out by such a body, unless a prior commitment has been made to democracy as the source of legitimate rule making. The essence of the distinction lies in the **separation of powers**, so that a non-democratic state might still have a legislative body.

Usually, however, it is an elected chamber, parliament or **assembly** which is referred to as a legislature, though the entities so identified, the US Congress or the British Houses of Parliament, for example, are not usually pure legislative bodies, having some residual control over the **executive**. As a vast amount of the material that serves to lay down binding and legally enforceable rules in any modern society does not originate in, and may hardly have been seen by the parliament or legislative body, but is instead created by the executive under relatively light legislative powers of overview, the distinction is rapidly losing an empirical referent. Some systems, notably **Fifth Republic** France and post-war Italy, provide directly for law-making by the executive—**decrees** rather than laws, with no legislative overview at all. Nevertheless, the idea of the legislative function, even when there is no single body that uniquely serves the function, is an important conceptual distinction.

Legitimacy

Legitimacy is both a normative and an empirical concept in political science. Normatively, to ask whether a political system is legitimate or not is to ask whether the state, or government, is entitled to be obeyed. As such the idea of legitimacy is connected with the legal concepts of *de jure* and *de facto* power. Whatever the accepted grounds of **political obligation** may be, legitimacy refers to these. Its more interesting application, however, may be in the empirical usage, especially in **political sociology**. Here the concentration is principally on how any given political system comes to be seen as 'legitimate' by a majority of its citizens. Why do most citizens of the USA and the People's Republic of China see their government as entitled to require their obedience when, presumably, people are much the same in both countries but the policies and structures of the state are very different? This is the question addressed by those who study legitimacy as an empirical fact rather than a philosophical problem. As well as being a major question in such research, the bases of legitimacy, a categorization of systemical grounds for obedience that actually work, can provide most useful rules for grouping different sorts of political systems. Many of the classifications of political systems found in the modern study of **comparative government** rely on typologies based on the various grounds of political legitimacy. (These, incidentally, nearly all derive in one way or another from the pioneering work of Max **Weber**.) Thus democracies tend to argue for their legitimacy in terms of giving voters what they immediately want, while other political systems may offer general principles to support their right to command. Socialist states may focus on the ultimate benefit to workers, right-wing **juntas** on some sense of traditional national identity. In recent social science considerable attention has been paid to a so called 'crisis of legitimacy', by which is meant the increasing difficulty Western states have in justifying themselves, because their only appeal is to utilitarian socio-economic rewards which they are incapable of sustaining.

Lenin

Vladimir Ilyich Lenin (1870–1924, originally named Ulyanov) was, like his younger revolutionary colleague **Trotsky**, a revolutionary before he was a **Marxist**, both chronologically and intellectually. Probably his lifelong passion for revolution, and his total dedication to politics and nothing else, stemmed from the execution of his brother for complicity in the assassination of Tsar Alexander III in 1886. In 1894 Lenin was imprisoned, and then exiled to Siberia until 1900. The following year he left Russia for Europe, and was to spend the years until 1917, except for a period from 1905–08, there, helping to organize, and then take over, the rather heterogeneous collection of émigré Russian left-wing movements that made up the All-Russian Social Democratic Labour Party (RSDLP). He rejected the view of many that Russia was too underdeveloped economically to undergo a full Marxist revolution that would lead to socialism, and finally managed to win a majority, the **Bolshevik** wing, of the RSDLP to his side, to form the Bolshevik party; those opposed to Lenin's radical approach became known as the **Mensheviks**. Lenin, though accepting much of Marx's philosophy, added two vital ingredients to make up what became the official doctrine of the Soviet Union, under the label of **Marxist–Leninism**.

The first point, which caused conflict not only with the Mensheviks but also with other equally radical Marxists, such as Trotsky and Rosa **Luxemburg**, was a very strong stress on the need for an organized, full-time professional revolutionary cadre. This was not just a tactical issue; Lenin never accepted that the Russian masses could be allowed much say in the revolution or its aftermath, and continually stressed the need for élite leadership and highly authoritarian control of the party central committee (see **vanguard of the proletariat**). This later became the official doctrine of **democratic centralism**, and is held by many to have paved the way for the totalitarian rule of **Stalin** and later periods. It is significant that Lenin was quite open in insisting that this leadership should come from the left-wing bourgeois intellectuals, and never allowed workers' movements like trade unions any important role. Left to themselves, he argued, the masses could not rise beyond a 'trade union' mentality, could never really throw off the chains of **capitalism**.

The second point, again contested by Trotsky, was that, knowing the Russian industrial proletariat was too small and too new to carry out a successful revolution itself, he advocated an alliance with the peasantry, despite their traditional conservatism. What he then expected to happen, and which did in fact start to happen under his rule after the October 1917 revolution, was that the Soviet state itself, denying democracy and industrial participation, would complete the process of industrialization until, at a later, perhaps much later, date, full **communism** would be possible. He expected, in other words, that the revolution would stop short of the full change of society. When, in October 1917, he staged a **coup d'état** against the moderate and moderate-left government that had taken power after the Abdication of Tsar Nicholas II, he lost little time in abolishing all other parties, even though it would have been possible to create a broadly based left-wing government with the participation of the Mensheviks. Because of the rigours of the last stages of the First World War, followed rapidly by the civil war between the 'White' and 'Red' armies, the Russian economy nearly collapsed and Lenin had to accept a considerable weakening of the early socialist economics, in the **New Economic Policy**.

Lenin died in 1924 and the ensuing in-fighting among the Soviet leaders led ultimately to **Stalinism**. Lenin, more than any other single man, could have changed the nature of Russian communism, but his real talents lay as a tactician, rather than as a strategist or ideologue. Nevertheless, at least two of his many writings continue to be of vital influence to communist intellectuals. The first, the essay *What Is To Be Done?* (1902), set the blueprint for democratic centralism. The second, *Imperialism: the Highest Stage of Capitalism*, offered an explanation of why Marx's economic predictions that capitalism would collapse through its own internal contradictions had not held, and why, as a result, the revolution could not be a spontaneous rising of the real proletariat, but had to be managed and created by the vanguard party.

Leninism

Leninism is that part of the doctrine of Soviet **communism**, and to a lesser extent part of the official ideology of Western communist parties, that altered **Marxism** to fit the perceptions of organized communist movements. It consists mainly of a justification for a strong, authoritarian and essentially undemocratic party as necessary for socialist revolution. Leninism claims that the ordinary industrial proletariat cannot of themselves become revolutionary, cannot perceive their true interests, and must be led by intellectual revolutionaries—the **vanguard of the proletariat**. While **Lenin** himself believed this strongly, his position was relative to the historical conditions of Russia in the early decades of this century, and to the period of massive imperial control of the **Third World** by Western nations, and was probably never intended to be a permanent doctrine. Nevertheless, communist and extreme left movements today can be usefully characterized by whether they adopt a Leninist version of Marxism (see **Marxist-Leninism**), or some other. The two most usual alternatives to Leninism are **Trotskyism** and **Maoism**.

Liberal Democracy

Liberal democracy, which is what most developed Western nations would claim to practise, is actually a combination of two values which do not necessarily go together logically. As far as the democracy aspect is concerned, liberal democracy is a form of **representative democracy**. Thus the usual system is the election by the whole electorate of a small number of representatives, probably organized in political parties, who form a legislative assembly. The majority of this assembly makes the law, and may, in parliamentary systems like those of the United Kingdom, Canada, Australasia, India and others derived from the Westminster model select some among themselves to form the **executive**. It is thus a rather indirect form of majority rule. The liberal aspect refers to a set of traditional values, drawn from the basic stock of **civil rights** and **natural rights**, which are seen as central to the political culture, and may indeed be enshrined in a constitution and protected by the courts. However, social research has often shown that a majority of the electorate of Western democracies are, under certain conditions, hostile to certain of these rights, for example aspects of the **due process** of law. Thus the empirical will of the majority may conflict with the vital system values. As a result liberal democracy cannot be a full-blooded majoritarian system.

Furthermore, because those elected to the assembly are usually seen as unbound representatives, as argued by **Burke**, rather than as bound delegates, legislative assemblies often thwart the desires of those who elect them. A classic example in the UK is the question of capital punishment. Ever since its abolition in 1967 there has been a strong majority of the population in favour of its return, yet several times votes in the House of Commons have rejected the policy by sizeable majorities of the representatives. Similarly certain rules developed by the US Supreme Court to protect the rights of those accused in criminal trials are seen by a majority of citizens as hampering the police in dealing with the crime problem, yet the unelected court, in what claims to be a democracy, can and has prevented the popular will. Liberal democracy can be seen as the answer to the traditional fear, as expressed by **de Tocqueville** and John Stuart **Mill**, of the **tyranny of the majority**—that unhampered major-itarian democracy could be more dangerous to liberal values than many ordinary tyrannies.

Liberal Party

The British Liberal Party, and its successor since 1988 the Liberal Democrats, are the political descendants of the 18th and early 19th century Whigs, the party which originally stood for the industrial and commercial middle class against the rural upper class who supported the Tory party. It was also, *de facto*, the party of the working class, and championed social reform, particularly in the governments they formed between 1905 and 1922 (as part of a coalition government from 1915). The Liberals could not, however, hold on to the working-class vote once the **Labour Party** had become sufficiently organized and had won credibility by forming a government in 1924. They very rapidly slipped from being a potential ruling party to being a very small centre party, at least in terms of seats in Parliament. The Liberals and their successors never won more than 23 seats in the House of Commons in any general election between those of 1935 and 1992, and on four separate occasions that number fell as low as six. A system of **proportional representation**, for which they have tirelessly campaigned, would have given them many more seats as they have frequently gained around 20% of votes cast, and there are indications that their electoral support would be higher were it not that people see a vote for the party as wasted, given the impossibility of the party doing well. As a party of the centre in an essentially **two-party system** they were inevitably squeezed by the two class-related parties. However, it could be argued that in the general elections of 1997 and 2001 this hindrance became a help. The popular desire to oust the ruling Conservatives in 1997, and to keep them out of office in 2001, saw a significant increase in **tactical voting** whereby the Liberal Democrats attracted voters from Labour in constituencies where the latter's chance of defeating the Conservatives was slight. Thus, in 1997 the Liberal Democrats increased their representation in Parliament from 20 to 46, despite their share of total votes cast actually decreasing, compared with the election of 1992. The party won 52 seats, with 18.3% of the popular vote, in 2001.

Despite the long history of the Liberal Party it would be a mistake to see any real ideological continuity over the years. The modern Liberal Democrats, and the Liberal Party that immediately preceded it, have been in many ways more **radical**, especially on constitutional reform, than the Labour Party, and they retain virtually nothing of the **bourgeois** individual ethic with which they competed against the Tory party in the earlier days (see **Liberalism**). The Liberals have become essentially a party of middle-class professionals (although their electoral support tends to be spread equally across all classes), radical in their own way (they were more consistently committed to the **unilateralist** Campaign for Nuclear Disarmament than the Labour Party, for example), but essentially supportive of a free-market, Europe-oriented economy, as long as their policy embraces such concerns as **environmentalism** and civil liberties. The Liberal Party merged, in 1988, with the Social Democratic Party (SDP) after the two parties had worked in alliance since 1981. In the early 1980s the benefit of additional support from the SDP, essentially a splinter group from the Labour Party, although it also drew support and members for the **Conservative Party** and indeed the Liberal Party itself, had promised to give the centre in British politics sufficient strength to break the two-party system (alliance politicians spoke frequently of 'breaking the mould of British politics'). The collapse of this hope after the 1987 general election was accounted for in both parties by their lack of unity, and the subsequent merger created a new party the identity of which was overwhelmingly that of the old Liberal Party. A minority of dissenting Social Democrats pledged to continue in an independent SDP, but were of no electoral significance by the time of the 1992 general election. The major shift to the centre of the Labour Party from the mid-1990s increasingly made plausible the claim of the Liberal Democrats to be the UK's radical party, and its increased parliamentary representation from 1997 led to optimism that its influence in British politics may continue to strengthen.

Liberalism

Liberalism can mean either a particular party creed in a particular time period, especially the late 19th century (the hey-day of Liberalism), or a general social and political attitude and orientation. Historically Liberalism was a middle-class or **bourgeois** movement for freedom from remaining feudal and monarchial control, and was associated, *inter alia*, with **freedoms** both legalistic, such as the economic theory of **laissez-faire**, and individual. From this position of supporting basic **civil liberties** or **human rights**, liberalism has developed a modern political creed in which the independence of the ordinary citizen against any powerful body, whether the state or, for example, organized labour, is taken as vital. Modern liberal parties, and they exist in most democratic states, although not necessarily under that title, tend to argue that traditionally-organized class politics, with an apparently insoluble conflict between **capitalism** and some form of **socialism** or **Marxism**, is misplaced, and that a greater concentration on the talents, capacities and needs of actual individuals rather than systems of social composites is possible and desirable. Liberalism is one of the best reasons for doubting the suitability of the standard **left/right** model of politics because it contains both the commitment to equality by the left and to approval of individual human effort and freedom by the right. In this sense it is often seen as being in the middle of the political spectrum, but most Liberals would argue that, far from being 'centre' or 'moderate', they are in fact **radical**, wishing to change much in society. Their opposition to class politics is illustrated by the example of recent British general elections, in which the **Liberal Party**/Liberal Democrats have gained almost exactly the same percentage from *all* social classes. A similar pattern tends to be found in most other Western countries.

Liberation Theology

During the 1970s some Roman Catholic theologians began to respond to the poverty and political oppression of mass populations in the **Third World** by developing doctrines on the mission of the Church in these countries. Though the focus was on Latin America, where the largest part of **Roman Catholicism's** world congregation is to be found, and though many of the leaders of the movement were Latin American priests and bishops, leading theologians in Europe, especially in Germany and the Netherlands, were also influential. Exactly what a supporter of liberation theology actually believes which is different from traditional theology is not easy to discern, though the political views of its adherents are easier to trace. The starting point, with which no Christian can disagree, is that Christ's message is a message of liberation, but the liberation to be found in the Christian Bible and its derived teaching is liberation from sin, so that mankind can be truly free to develop spiritually towards God. Liberation theologians argue that such spiritual liberation is only possible where people are physically, politically and economically free. Only when freedom from hunger and oppression have been guaranteed can Christians hope to have the spiritual energy to free themselves from sin. This view in itself poses some problems for orthodox theology, in part because of the Christian tradition of martyrs, those who either despite, or even through, their worldly suffering were able to achieve a state of moral purity. Nevertheless, it might be generally accepted that for most of us it is unrealistic to expect spiritual growth when living in a cardboard shack outside some Latin American city ruled by a corrupt and violent **oligarchy**. Thus the general political thrust, that the Church should use all its efforts, material, political and doctrinal, to bring about social justice, jargonistically called 'the preferential option for the poor', is not in itself a heretical position, however embarrassing it may be for a Church traditionally on good terms with the exploiting classes. The real problem comes when, advocating social justice, liberation theologians turn to what they sometimes openly admit to be a Marxist analysis of **class** and poverty. There is no way to avoid the fact that **Marxism** is a materialistic theory, and overtly treats religion as an ideological phenomenon ('the opium of the people' in Marx's own words), a consequence of **alienation**. Thus, according to the most orthodox of theologians, beliefs incompatible with basic Christian doctrine are incorporated into liberation theology. Priests may legitimately put effort into achieving social justice (by non-violent means), but can never see it as their primary role, cannot act in ways dictated by an anti-religious theory, and above all cannot disregard the priority of personal moral salvation or believe it to be incompatible with any socio-political structure whatsoever.

Libertarianism

Libertarianism is primarily an American political theory, though it has adherents in Western Europe. At its simplest it is an extreme form of **Liberalism** lacking most of the moral overtones of traditional Liberalism. A libertarian believes that radical individual freedom and complete self-reliance is the most desirable of political states, and should be used as the yardstick against which to judge actual social systems and their restrictions on freedom. Libertarianism is not anarchism, mainly because it accepts the need for a state, whereas anarchism propounds regulation by peer-group or other non-state pressure and libertarians want individuals to be genuinely free and independent, not simply free from a coercive state. Anarchism often imagines high degrees of voluntary collectivism—libertarians imagine any collective action as purely contractual and based on coincidence of sheer self-interest.

The libertarian believes in something usually called a 'minimal state' where only a very few crucial matters need to be, or morally can be, dealt with by the state, and the state's power to coerce financial or other contributions towards such provision is severely limited. Probably the only services easily accepted as suitable for the state are internal and external security provision—the police and the army. Even emergency-service provision like that of fire brigades is often seen as something best left to private insurance. Absolutely no intervention in an individual's free choice on the ground that it is in his interest could be accepted—libertarians commonly criticize legislation restricting the use of drugs, for example. Needless to say, no tax-based provision of welfare services can be countenanced by a libertarian, to whom the sanctity of private property is the core value. The starting point for libertarian thought is the idea that there is no way of legitimizing the rule of one person over another except by his consent, and that such consent must be specifically limited to situations where it is in the objective interest of the consenter to accept very specific orders from the ruler.

Liberty

Liberty (or **freedom**) is often divided by political theorists into two types, for analytic clarity. Negative liberty refers essentially to 'absence of external constraints' (see **state of nature**). Thus, as long as there is no law or social practice preventing me from doing something, or forcing me into some course of action, I can be seen as free in that respect. This is the idea of liberty most commonly found in modern Western democratic societies and in classical **liberalism**. The emphasis is on what other people might do to stop me carrying out my will. But what I choose to do is taken as outside the bounds of the concept. If I choose to be a drug addict, I am either free or not depending on what society does to stop me buying my preferred drugs. Often, though not invariably, this will be linked to the idea that the political system is only entitled to infringe on someone's freedom when it is preventing actions that would hurt another person, and that what an individual does to themselves is their own business. This concept of liberty is the basic one found in English social thought from **Hobbes** and **Locke** through **utilitarianism** and onwards.

The more continental European tradition of liberty, often referred to as positive liberty, has its roots originally in classical Greek thought, and later, in European Idealist philosophy like that of **Hegel** or **Kant**. More recently it has been found particularly in some **Marxist** thinkers, especially those like **Marcuse**. The stress here is on actual internal freedom of choice, rather than, as in the English liberal tradition, external constraints on putting a choice into action. Basically the argument rests on the idea that the essential human nature will produce rational and good choices. But this inner human nature can be warped by social forces and ideological manipulation so that the individual does not realize what they truly want, and makes false choices. Ultimately it goes back to the Platonic doctrine that no one can ever freely choose what is wrong, and that evil is a fault in understanding, not a weakness of will. In the hands of later theorists it becomes the doctrine that society, especially capitalist society, alienates people from their true nature, and produces apparent needs and desires which are convenient for the rulers of that sort of society. Sometimes the doctrine has obvious sense: those addicted to dangerous drugs can, perhaps, be said to be unfree in pursuing their desires. But often the theory depends on a specially privileged position by which those who are ideologically sound are allowed to stipulate what other people would really want if only they realized it existed. Thus the argument is used, for example, to question election results in modern democracies, on the grounds that the working class would actually vote for socialist parties if they had not been 'tampered' with by the media, and are suffering a lack of 'positive' freedom in voting because of their deluded notions.

Neither positive nor negative liberty concepts are as simple as these accounts, and it is unlikely that any single political thinker will hold entirely to any one. But the distinction is an important one, identifying as it does a long-term conflict within Anglo-European social thought, and relating to real arguments in modern political positions.

Limited War

Limited war, an idea found in modern strategic thought, implies that the war in question should not spread to involve the **superpowers** in an all-out nuclear confrontation. However, within these limits there are enormous variations. Thus both the **Arab–Israeli conflicts** and the Argentine–British conflict in the South Atlantic are limited wars. Similarly the **Gulf War** against Iraq would be described as a limited war, despite the role played by the USA, the high technology weaponry used by the UN-sponsored alliance and the number of participating countries. In the first of these examples the entire existence of a nation state was in question, while in the others no actual threat to continued national independence was really posed to any of the combatant nations. The first war to which the term was applied was the **Korean War**, because not only did the USA not use nuclear weapons, but the war resulted only in the restoration of the status quo before North Korea's invasion. In fact the concept is largely based on a distinction only relevant since the Second World War: the idea that wars should not be fought to the point of extinguishing the enemy has been the norm throughout history. Whether 'limited war' doctrine has any part to play in 21st-century conflict, dominated as it may be by unequal fighting between nation states and international terrorist groups, as in the US intervention in Afghanistan in 2001, is unclear.

Lobby

Lobby can function either as a verb or noun in political discourse, and as the latter has two quite distinct meanings; in all meanings the word derives from the 'lobbies' in parliament or congress where politicians meet after votes to discuss affairs. As a verb, 'to lobby' means to apply pressure, present arguments or other incentives to try to make a political decision-maker favour one's position. It can be used either in an institutional setting, where a representative of a **pressure group** may lobby a parliamentarian, minister, or civil servant to further the group's interest. It may also be used among equals, where, for example, one member of a committee, interested in a forthcoming issue, may lobby fellow members to seek their support, or even where the executive assistants of the US president may attempt to lobby congressmen to seek their vote on some impending legislation.

As a noun the word refers to established institutional arrangements for such transmission of information and pressure on issues. There is, in the USA, for example, an official register of lobbyists, whose full-time occupation it is to represent the arguments of their clients, whether they be the armaments industry or some fund-starved university, to the federal government. Lobbyists have become increasingly important in Western government everywhere. The parliamentary lobbying profession in the United Kingdom, for example, is thought to have increased tenfold in the 1980s. Who is lobbied depends on the structure of power in a society, so that in most European governments (and in the **European Union**) the targets of the lobbyists tend to be civil servants and ministers, while in the USA and other countries with weak party discipline elected legislators are assiduously courted by professional lobbyists.

In the UK, uniquely, the noun 'lobby' has an additional meaning, referring to the established and accredited group of media correspondents who are made privy to government secrets as a means for ministers to communicate discreetly with the public. They are often given highly confidential briefings on the understanding that they will exercise very great discretion in what they print and in concealing their source of information.

Local Government

Local government is a system of administration for small political units—towns, counties and rural districts, for example. It operates within a larger governmental framework but, unlike the relationship between state governments and the federal government within a federal system (see **federalism**), the powers of the local government usually derive from **delegation** by the national or central government. The powers of local government bodies, which are traditionally democratically elected, vary both between countries and within individual states over a period of time. They generally extend over such matters as local environmental health, refuse collection, parks and recreation, traffic regulation and matters to do with town and country planning applications. However, in unitary states the degree of real power over sensitive areas of policy, such as education, may be limited. In France before the election as president of François Mitterrand the government appointed prefects who possessed the power of financial veto over the mayoral decisions in the provinces, and it is unclear how far-reaching the subsequent reform of prefectoral power has been. In Italy the nationally-appointed prefects still retain great discretion over decisions by the communes. In Britain the powers and responsibilities of local government have become especially controversial since the 1970s because of Conservative governments' desire to keep an overall control of public expenditure at all levels. The Conservative government of Edward Heath introduced major reforms of the local government system in the period 1972–74, and the governments of Margaret Thatcher made further amendments, in particular by abolishing the Greater London Council and six other metropolitan authorities, and by imposing ever tighter controls on how much money local authorities may spend, or indeed raise. This development culminated in the short-lived attempt to impose a wholly new structure of local government financing, the community charge (or 'poll tax').

In many countries local government has been seen as both a training-ground for politicians with national ambitions, and as an arena in which ordinary citizens can have a more real involvement in politics than is possible at the national level. Some theorists, such as John Stuart **Mill**, were convinced that experience in local government was essential for developing a real political competence in the population, and thus crucially underscored democracy.

Locke

John Locke (1632–1704) may be one of the most famous political theorists in the Anglo-American world not so much because of the quality of his thought, as for his impact on world events, since many of his ideas were taken as models by the founding fathers of the US Constitution. Like his great rival Thomas **Hobbes**, though slightly later, he was writing against the background of the English Civil War, and his own political connections were vital to the development of his political theory. Hobbes and Locke used much the same theoretical methodology: the discussion of a hypothetical **state of nature** and the idea of a **social contract** or compact to get out of this state into **civil society**. He was very much in the **natural law** tradition but, unlike Hobbes, his perception of natural law was much more orthodox. The main aim in his theories, set out in the *First and Second Treatises on Civil Government*, was to draw a blueprint for a political system in which the government would be severely limited in its role, and subject to control and even abolition by the citizenry were it to exceed the tight bounds he put on it. As with **Rousseau** later, he argued that **sovereignty** lay with the people, not with a monarch, and that governments had their authority only because the citizens consented to their rule to achieve specific benefits. Only the need for a greater protection of certain natural rights could be a good reason for consenting to leave the total liberty of a state of nature for membership of a state where some liberty would be lost, and hence endowing the state with authority.

At the same time, because he feared the growth of executive power, he insisted on a **separation of powers** between the **legislature**, the representative of the people's sovereignty, and the **executive**. Although he hinted at the further separation of the judicial system from the executive, this model of the separation of powers and of government acting in a trust capacity to achieve limited objectives went to the hearts of the newly-independent American politicians in the Constitutional Convention (as did similar arguments by **Montesquieu**, though his were later than Locke's), and his influence is beyond doubt. Though his theory is, in its end result, an encapsulation of many modern liberal values, Locke himself was neither a democrat nor an advocate of equality. Indeed the principal value he wished the political system to preserve was the right to private property, which he defends with an odd but ingenious theological argument. He is quite clear in the *Second Treatise* that he does not expect the ordinary people to play any role in the running of the state, and his famous reliance on free consent to create authority in fact ends up, by sleight of hand, as being very much less liberal than it seems. Politically he was on what would pass as the left-wing of the period: his family had fought for Parliament in the Civil War, and his patron, the Earl of Shaftesbury, was implicated in an attempted revolution against the restored monarchy. Some critics, indeed, regard the *Second Treatise* as, in part, an attempted justification of Shaftesbury's position, and he certainly was unusual in writing into his theory a defence of the need occasionally to rebel against government. But the left-wing position of his day can more easily be seen as the intellectual support for the rise of the bourgeoisie, and his advocacy is indeed for the form of government and ideas on property particularly convivial to the development of **laissez-faire** economies. Probably his better intellectual work was as a philosopher, and in that capacity he is studied today almost as much as he is analysed as a political theorist.

Luxemburg, Rosa

Rosa Luxemburg's reputation and ideas still play a vital, if controversial, role in modern **Marxism**. She was involved in the **Bolshevik** movement and the development of Marxism into an active revolutionary movement and creed from the beginning, helped build a post-war attempt at revolution in Germany, in 1918, and was murdered by soldiers when the uprising was crushed. Her real importance, apart from as a romantic martyr symbol, was that she repeatedly criticized **Lenin** and his Russian version of **communism**, especially after their coming to power in 1917. Although in many ways she was a perfectly orthodox Marxist, stressing the inevitability of a proletarian revolution, she was seen very much as an advocate of much greater democracy, both in the movement itself, and in the post-revolutionary regime. For this reason she was a great inspiration to most non-Soviet communist and Marxist movements. In particular the Social Democratic Party of Germany (SPD), which was until the early 1960s defiantly Marxist in theory, was infused with her spirit, because it seemed a way of being non-revolutionary, democratic, and yet still true to Marxism. While debates about what 'true' Marxism is are necessarily sterile, it does tend to be forgotten that she was only one of many leaders of the communist movement in the early part of this century who had disagreements with Lenin, and she was, nevertheless, an economic determinist who co-operated in a violent revolution. An example of how her importance probably is more symbolic than theoretical is that another anti-Lenin Marxist revolutionary, **Trotsky**, completely ignored her while she was alive. Only years after her death, when founding a Fourth International (see **international socialism**), did he suddenly 'discover' their similarity of position, because his Fourth International was itself an attempt to weld together all the dissident Marxists, for many of whom she had become a patron saint.

M

Machiavelli

Niccolo Machiavelli (1469–1527) was a Florentine diplomat and civil servant whose writing included not only political theory but also plays. He is famous more for attitudes somewhat unfairly associated with him than for anything that he really wrote. The work of Machiavelli's most often quoted is *The Prince*, dedicated to Machiavelli's patron, Duke Lorenzo di Piero de' Medici. It is a short analysis of how to rule an Italian city state successfully in the late middle ages. He also, however, wrote a much more solid study of early Italian political history, *The Discourses on the First Ten Books of Livy*, which sets out Machiavelli's commitment to republicanism (although he believed that a single ruler was necessary to found or reform states). In both works he presents a tough and practical view of politics, in which questions of how to use **power** to achieve desired ends, by the use of any and every technique and resource available, are seen as vastly more important than moral or philosophical questions about the desirability of such strategies. He is also sometimes seen as the first writer in political science, meaning an attempt to work out basic empirical rules of political life and to construct a 'non-normative' account of the political system, as opposed to clearly normative and evaluative political philosophy.

His name has been lent, through 'Machiavellianism', to any highly manipulative and cynical political activity of a self-seeking nature, especially when totally devoid of general principles. This is actually most unfair to a man dedicated to the welfare of his native city state, and whose other works are an outstanding plea for Italian unity, which aim was indeed the inspiration of *The Prince* itself. However, as a label for a common phenomenon in political life it is very useful.

Majority System

A simple majority system is one in which a full arithmetic majority of votes (50% + 1) is required before an act or rule can be passed, a decision implemented, a candidate elected, or a motion accepted. As such, majority systems can exist in committees, legislatures, electorates and anywhere where some process of vote counting is required to elect or confirm a candidate or motion. Majority vote has a hallowed, if theoretically insecure, position in democratic belief, resting on the argument that a decision accorded to by more people than oppose it is politically legitimate. In practice there are very few fully-fledged majority systems, and the logic of majority voting is seldom fully applied or thought out in decision-making arenas.

There are a host of theoretical problems—does a majority involve, for example, all those entitled to vote, or only those who appear and cast a vote? Further problems occur when one considers whether or not a majority vote really represents a positive preference, or simply a relative preference for one rather than another of a set of unpopular alternatives. This has always been a major objection to the use of the **referendum** as a decision-making device, and is particularly troublesome with elections to office, when either a complicated set of rules, several ballots, or both, become necessary to ensure that the winner is actually preferred to all alternatives by a majority of voters (see **proportional representation**). Nevertheless, the idea of majority rule is firmly entrenched in political attitudes. Among varieties of the system one of the most important is the qualified majority, that is, a requirement that a fixed proportion other than 50% + 1 of an electorate support an issue or candidate for a valid result. Thus constitutional amendments both in political systems and other organizations often require a two-thirds vote for passage. When a referendum was held in Scotland in 1979 on **devolution**, the legislation authorizing it required not only a majority of votes cast to be in favour, but also that those votes had to represent at least 40% of all those entitled to vote. In fact a majority of those voting did favour devolution, but due to a large number of abstentions the 40% threshold was not reached. The logic for majoritarian systems other than a simple majority is, therefore, slightly hazy; if 50% + 1 is not sacrosanct, then why fix on any other figure, specifically, short of absolute unanimity? (See also **voting systems**.) In practice, politicians with a majority, however slender, have no hesitation on relying on majority rule, as was seen at the end of the 20th century in several cases where tiny majorities in referendums upheld support for **European Union** treaties.

Maladministration

Maladministration refers to actions of the **civil service**, government ministers, **local government** officers or anyone with legal authority to make decisions affecting the public where those actions are corrupt or otherwise illegal. Where a decision is massively incompetent and individuals can show that they have suffered serious personal hurt the issue of maladministration may arise, but mere incompetence generally would not be treated as maladministration. The typical issue in a case of maladministration is likely to be what **common law** calls an *ultra vires* action, that is, an official has made a decision they did not have the legal power to make. Versions of this can come about where an official, although entitled to use their discretion to make a decision, took account of matters that ought to have been disregarded or ignored vital evidence. Maladministration is dealt with in various ways in different jurisdictions. The two most usual are through special **administrative courts,** or by the use of some version of the **ombudsman** system. An accusation of maladministration can have very serious consequences for a government, particularly where, as in the United Kingdom, there is a doctrine of ministerial **responsibility**, in theory making a minister liable to have to resign for the actions of a civil servant they may know nothing about.

Mandate

Mandates are typically claimed by successful parties in national elections even when they have actually gained only a smallish plurality of votes. The claim is that if a party, or a candidate, has stood for election on a particular set of policies, then, having won election, a 'mandate' from the people has been gained to implement those policies. Thus governments often claim that they are 'mandated' to carry out some action even if there is no good reason to believe that the policy in question had very much to do with their electoral victory. The original meaning is where some body, perhaps a constituency division of a political party or a trade-union branch, on being required to send a representative to a national conference, gives the chosen representative binding instructions to argue or vote in a fixed way on some particular issue. The question of mandating a representative is a vital one in democratic theory. One view holds that those who elect a representative are entitled to mandate them to cast specific votes so as directly to represent the majority view in the selecting body. An alternative to this is the theory of **delegation**, most forcefully put by Edmund **Burke**, that selecting a representative (who may in fact be an authorized candidate at a subsequent public election, perhaps as a member of parliament) is a matter of choosing the best person one can find, and then trusting that person's judgement on issues that arise. Questions of whether a mandate does or could exist, how much anyone is bound by it, and when an election result would certify such a mandate are hotly-contested matters of modern arguments about democracy both in parliaments and parties. In Britain the doctrine of the mandate has another, more or less constitutional, role, relating to the powers of the House of Lords. It is often held that the Lords ought not to vote down legislation coming from the House of Commons if it relates to a specific promise made in the government's previous electoral **manifesto**.

Legally a mandate is a grant of authority to someone to do something specific as the agent of a body entitled to do that act itself. After the First World

War the **League of Nations** created mandates transferring administrative controls over colonial territories of the defeated German and Turkish empires to certain of the victorious powers. The mandate was to govern the territories in the best interests of their populations, with independence as the eventual aim. A similar system exists in the trustee system of the **United Nations**.

Manifesto

Manifestos are usually taken to be the official statements of intended policy issued by political parties at the beginning of election campaigns. In fact manifesto can have a broader meaning, covering all statements of political intent or even a call for support in a revolutionary situation, as with *The Communist Manifesto* written by **Marx** and **Engels** in 1848. Manifestos vary enormously in length, style and political importance, but virtually every political **party** in every democratic system issues some equivalent to a manifesto before every election. They can be politically quite irrelevant, neither read by anyone nor influencing elected party members, as with the 'platforms' issued by the US political parties. These are lengthy documents negotiated by **committee** at the nominating conventions for presidential candidates, which often have important symbolic interest to party activists, but are of no consequence whatever. In some systems, notably the Italian system today, and the French **Fourth Republic**, manifestos were important bargaining tools for coalition building: a party could insist that if they were to join a coalition it must accept a specific policy on the grounds that the policy was in their manifesto. These can even reach the level of a 'common programme', as with the arrangement between the French socialists and communists in the late 1970s. It is usually thought that the breakdown over this common programme delayed the socialists' electoral victory until 1980.

In the United Kingdom manifestos have become largely standardized since the 1960s, taking the form of small booklets of about 15,000–20,000 words, although recently they have become increasingly glossily produced, and created by a party committee. In the past the Conservative Party manifesto was often just the party leader's personal address to the electorate. In the Labour Party the manifesto has always been vital because it has reflected the conflict in the party over different electoral strategies. The policies carried out by governments have not followed closely the promises made in manifestos, even though manifesto commitments are taken seriously by many party members. In part they represent a way for back-benchers to retain some control over their own government's behaviour. They also have a constitutional role in the UK. It is widely accepted that the House of Lords (see **second chamber**) ought not to interfere seriously with government legislation if it stems from a policy that was enshrined in the party's election manifesto; a manifesto has been submitted to the electorate, whereas the House of Lords is an unelected body.

Mannheim

Karl Mannheim (1893–1947) was a German sociologist and theorist who, both before and after the Second World War, developed some of the most pene-trating ideas on the problem of **ideology** in society yet to be published. Although there are **Marxist** overtones to his theoretical writing, he was not a Marxist in any orthodox sense, and provides us with the only powerful non-Marxist analysis of the social conditioning of thought, and the consequences for political life of socio-economically derived ideologies. His classic work, *Ideology and Utopia*, distinguishes with great care the various ways in which all people suffer from viewing the world through categories, values and assump-tions that owe more to their own location in the socio-economic system than from any really clear observation of reality. It is part of Mannheim's corrective to Marxism that he insists that all those with clear socio-economic interests are liable to a distortion in the way they see the world and understand, for example, the workings of the economy. Thus there cannot be some especially privileged **class**, as some Marxists want to regard the proletariat, who perceive things truly while the bourgeoisie are blinkered by **false consciousness**. He does, however, grant to one sector of society a greater chance to see clearly. These are what he calls the 'free-floating intelligentsia', who, because they have no clear economic interest, being neither workers in the proper Marxist sense, nor capitalists, can hope to synthesize the conflicting world pictures of the two opposing classes. It was this social group on whom Mannheim placed his trust for the creation of a new and peaceful Europe after the Second World War. Not only has the intelligentsia come to be more and more influential in post-war countries in both Eastern and Western Europe, but they also fit very badly into most orthodox Marxist class analyses. The declining acceptance of Marx-ism amongst modern social scientists has not removed the need for a theory of ideology, making Mannheim even more potentially influential.

Mao Zedong

Mao Zedong (1893–1976) can best be characterized with an aphorism that suits well his own literary style, unusually erudite among modern communist leaders. He is the man who ruled a quarter of the world's population for a quarter of a century. The son of a peasant farmer, he discovered **Marxism** while in Beijing (having already broken with Chinese tradition in disobeying his father and leaving the peasant life). Mao was one of the founders of the Chinese Communist Party (CCP), in 1921, and from then until the setting up of the People's Republic of China in 1949 he was fully engaged in revolutionary and military activities. He proved a great guerrilla leader and military tactician, fighting successively the established Chinese authorities, the Japanese, and the nationalists of Chiang Kai-shek. He was Chairman of the CCP from 1935 until his death in 1976, and became Chinese head of state in 1949. His most important contribution was the radical rethinking of **Marxist-Leninism** to suit the overwhelmingly agricultural and traditionalist societies of Asia, and his insistence on finding his revolutionary élite from the peasantry rather than the urban proletariat. This alone, and his success in achieving the theoretical goal, would have made him a master tactician of Marxism. However, he went much further in his thought, continually trying to make a communist regime much less dependent on the bureaucratic élite of the party than any other leader in power (as opposed to the outsiders like Rosa **Luxemburg** or the later **Trotsky**). In a series of radical attacks on the institutionalized 'cadres' of the party and state he fought, often alone among his élite, a battle to keep close contacts with the actual aspirations of Chinese peasant life. Classically educated himself (he was a poet of considerable distinction), he tended to express his ideas in the idiom of classical Chinese tradition rather than the jargon of Marxist-Leninism, and indeed **Stalin**, among others, felt that he either actually did not know, or did not wish to know, very much about the 'scientific socialism' of the orthodox canon. Certainly he appears to have used Marxism simply as a handy weapon to fight the encrusted tradition of Chinese feudalism.

Three of his great campaigns against institutionalized and undemocratic party élitism are characteristic. In 1956, when the communist world was rocked by the Hungarian uprising, and when its repercussions were met with extra repression in Eastern Europe, Mao reacted in quite the opposite way. Launching a campaign he called 'The Hundred Flowers', he urged the Chinese actively to criticize the shortcomings of party leaders, insisting that any injustices must be brought to light, and that no party that was vulnerable to such attacks deserved to rule. The campaign was brought to a rapid halt, demonstrating what was little realized in the West at the time, that Mao had far from perfect control over his own party leaders, and was often without a majority in the **politburo**. A few years later he ignored the arguments of technicians and economists and tried to rush China's economic development, to build true communism, in a massive and short term plan. Typical of this (he called it The Great Leap Forward) was his plan to push Chinese steel production to 30 million tons a year by urging the building of thousands of tiny 'backyard' steel furnaces. As with most of his economic plans, it was a disaster, completely ignoring the need for massive capital injection and large plants with increasing returns to scale. Again it was stopped short, after little more than a year, by pressure from his fellow leaders.

The final push by Mao to stop the development of a new party-based ruling middle class was the **cultural revolution**. This he launched in 1965, fearing, quite correctly, that he was losing all control of the party. The movement urged the forming of radical 'Red Guards' who would go into the countryside and raise what was very nearly a populist revolution against the communist state. His commitment to the peasant life was so strong, and his dislike of the whole principle of division of labour was so great, that he tried to force all technocrats, students and party bureaucrats to be made to work in the countryside along with the peasants and to give up not only their privileges, but also their technical authority. Thousands were killed, and hundreds of thousands forced to give up their specialities, confess their **revisionism**, and do penance. Though the cultural revolution only lasted, at its height, for a year, it did massive damage to China's economic and technical development. After Mao's death most of those associated with this movement were purged as thousands of much needed technicians streamed back to the cities, discipline was restored in the universities, and the post-Mao leadership struggled to return China to a more orthodox approach to socio-economic modernization. His political thought, neatly expressed in a small book called, officially, *The Thoughts of Chairman Mao*, and, more popularly, *The Little Red Book*, became the unofficial bible not only in China, but world-wide. His insistence on Chinese autonomy was in part responsible for the widening gulf between the Soviet Union and China which led, especially after the rapprochement between the USA and the People's Republic in the 1970s, to a serious ideological split in the communist world. Mao so totally rejected the co-operation of the Soviet Union that he even tried to stop Soviet military supplies getting to the North Vietnamese, whom he was supporting in the **Vietnam War**. Though a brilliant, if idiosyncratic leader, it is unclear whether his leadership, so opposed in style and ideology to European communism, helped or hindered China. Even with the reforms and slow changes in Chinese political life in the last quarter of the 20th century, Mao remained a potent symbol legitimating contemporary Chinese governments for some time. Whether this influence will long survive the gradual spread of capitalism into China is improbable.

Maoism

Maoism, largely a matter of following the ideas set forth in *The Little Red Book*, technically *The Thoughts of Chairman Mao*, is a radical version of **communism**, owing rather less than might be expected to the **Marxist-Leninism** which held sway, on and off, in China during his years in office. It also caught the attention of radicals world-wide, and much of the French, German and even American far left are still influenced by it. The crucial point of Maoism is the total rejection of the immunity of the official communist party to criticism, and the need directly to work with and listen to 'the people'. As a doctrine it is completely anti-élitist, rejecting not only hierarchy in organization, but even the authority of technical expertise. Thus Maoism represents a sort of populist **Marxism**, a direct opposition to **democratic centralism**, and urges a permanent rejection of **authority**. It also stresses communalism (see **commune**) and the small-scale organization of social and economic units, rather than large-scale organization with more 'privatized' individual life. It is a doctrine attractive to the impatient and anarchist, rather than the gradualist and ordered aspects of revolutionary expectations, which was why it was so popular, for example, among the student revolutionaries in Paris in 1968. To orthodox communism Maoism is an extremely dangerous doctrine, and the post-Mao Chinese leadership and the leaders of Western and Eastern communist parties have all sought to eradicate it. Technically it can only be described as utopian, but its form of expression, by a man who wrote naturally in the classic aphorisms of Chinese culture, makes it eminently more readable than the turgid jargon of much modern Marxism. Because Mao organized his revolution, and directed his thought to communism in predominantly agrarian and non-industrialized societies, Maoism has heavily influenced communist movements in the Third World, and especially in Asia. With the rejection of Marxism in the former Soviet bloc, and the popular rejection there of the heroes of the 1917 revolution and of orthodox communism, the influence of Maoism is likely to increase within surviving communist movements.

Marcuse

Herbert Marcuse (1898–1979) was one of the German émigré intellectuals who came to the USA between the two World Wars, settling ultimately in California where he taught and wrote political and social theory. Although his scholarly reputation was founded at least as early as the 1941 publication of his major study of Hegel, *Reason and Revolution*, his real fame came in the 1960s when he was taken up as an intellectual leader by the radical student movement in the USA.

Working within **Marxism**, Marcuse was always more interested in the 'humanist' or 'early' **Marx**, whose concern for the **alienation** of modern society was much nearer Marcuse's interests than the 'economist' Marx of *Das Kapital*. The books that earned Marcuse his role in the American radical movement were those like *One-Dimensional Man* and *Eros and Civilization* which concentrated more on the emotional and ideological constraints of modern mass society than the straightforward analysis of class struggle and economic exploitation.

In fact Marcuse quickly realized the great difficulty of fitting a Marxist class model to American society, where the relative affluence of blue-collar workers, especially if they were white and northern, and their conservative and racist social views made them, for him, poor material for a proletarian uprising. He was concerned for such status groups, but more because he felt they were suffering a **false consciousness** in striving to satisfy needs implanted by the media and advertising agencies in the interests of an inhuman and over-materialist economy. Marcuse's own hopes were for a new form of revolutionary class forged out of those, blacks, students, ecologists, anyone who was cut loose from the basic acquisitive economic structure, who would fight for human liberation from both capitalist and state socialist systems. His own work on Russia, *Soviet Communism and Russian Marxism*, had convinced him that the Marxist revolution as practised in Eastern Europe was every bit as dehumanizing as capitalism, and this semi-anarchist position was perfectly fitting for the Vietnam-anxious radicals of the period. In some ways his work is almost closer to **libertarianism** than to Marxism and, despite the death of the cause that made him famous, still stands close reading as an alternative radical critique of high-technology society.

Marshall Plan

The Marshall Plan was the economic aid plan for the recovery of European economies instituted by George Marshall when he was secretary of state in the Truman administration in the USA. He first suggested the plan in a famous speech at Harvard in June 1947. The idea was that a very large dollar programme of aid would be provided for post-war reconstruction on condition that the European powers first started by indicating a serious intent to collaborate rather than compete against each other. Warmly welcomed by France and Britain the plan was bitterly opposed by the Soviet Union, which saw it as an attempt to exert American influence on post-war Europe, and thus as a threat to their own control. The Western European nations rapidly set up the Organization for European Economic Co-operation (OEEC, which later became the OECD) to allocate the funds, and by 1948 the dollars started flowing in. In the four years between 1948 and 1952 over US $17,000 million were given, with the United Kingdom and France, along with West Germany, being the main beneficiaries. Though Marshall would have been prepared to seek congressional approval for aid to Eastern European nations, Soviet opposition precluded even this possibility.

As well as being the major single cause of the rapid economic recovery of Europe, the supply of these funds during the early days of the **cold war** (the Berlin Blockade, for example, coincided with the first payments) helped cement the alliances that later became **NATO** and the **Warsaw Pact**. The UK would certainly have found the recovery even harder had it not been for Marshall aid, especially as the initial post-war defence cuts had to be reversed with the increasing political tension, especially over the **Korean War**. Other countries, notably France, were able to take advantage of the dollars and the dislocation of social patterns arising from the war not just to repair, but massively to modernize their economies; by the late 1950s the French economy was no longer recognizable as a development of the **Third Republic** economy. The Marshall Plan lives in American political memory as their most generous effort to help democracy, and has become a catchword, so that plans to aid the post-communist Eastern European economies were often referred to as 'a new Marshall Plan'. It has not escaped critics that the Marshall Plan was, in the long term, both politically and economically helpful for the USA. It not only strengthened pro-American governments threatened by domestic communist parties, as in France, but ensured useful markets for American exports. Doubtless similar observations could be made about the Eastern European countries receiving aid 40 years later.

Martial Law

Martial law is a state of affairs declared by a civilian government in which the military forces are empowered to rule, govern and control an area, which can be a small locality or the entire nation, in a way involving direct force, and without the usual constraints of democratic decision-making or the acceptance of **civil rights**. It is always seen as a temporary state of affairs and, unlike a **military regime**, has **legitimacy**, because it has been decided upon and granted by the civilian government. Martial law is, without doubt, both draconian and unpopular; there have been no instances of martial law being declared in a major Western democracy since the Second World War, though Poland was subjected to martial law in 1981–83. It can only be either useful or acceptable given the complete breakdown of law and order—a situation where the civilian government authorizing it has probably lost all legitimacy anyway. In international law the term refers to the rule of a military commander over a foreign, typically colonial, territory.

Marx

Karl Marx (1818–83) is the most famous of all socialist or communist figures. More has been said and done in the name of **Marxism** than in the name of the work of any other social thinker in history. By origin he was a German academic and journalist, heavily influenced by the German philosophy of idealism, and particularly by **Hegel**. His political beliefs curtailed his career in Germany, and Marx moved to Paris in 1843 and to London in 1849, thereafter working as a writer and revolutionary activist, in close association with Friedrich **Engels**, whose contribution to the Marxist canon is considerable. As befitted one of his theories, that there was a need for a close connection between political practice and political theorizing, Marx was always closely connected with communist and other revolutionary movements, and much of his more evocative writing consisted either of journalistic analyses of such movements, or historical accounts of would-be revolutions. Modern scholarship has suggested that there are at least two distinct phases in his writing: early Marx, which includes at least the rather humanistic ideas of the *Economic and Philosophical Manuscripts* (1844) and *The Communist Manifesto* (1848); and later Marx, which has the much more technical and 'scientific' economics of *Das Kapital*, the first volume of which was published in 1867. (However, it should be noted that some scholars of Marx deny that his work was characterized by this epistemological break, and cite some works discovered relatively recently, notably the *Grundrisse*, from between these periods, as evidence for continuity.)

The most crucial part of his rich and complex theories is the doctrine that man, as a physical being, must be explained in materialistic terms. To Marx, a man was a being whose identity and nature arose out of his purely practical attempts to make his livelihood in what amounted almost to a struggle against a hostile physical environment. As a result, what man did determined what he became. In practical terms this meant that the conditions under which he earned his living, as owner or proprietor, wage labourer or peasant, formed his **ideology** and consciousness. But as Marx also argued that man existed only as a member of an economic **class**, and that all classes were always in competition with others below or above them in an economically-supported power hierarchy, he saw human civilization as characterized by class warfare. That this warfare had an economically-determined course, leading to an ultimate communist society in which there would be no further class antagonisms, and therefore no inequality, was an absolute article of faith. From it derived all the later communist hopes for **revolution** from the **proletariat** and the socialist belief in the need to abolish private ownership of property, because, for Marxists, control of property is the very definition of a class system. Marx, in his voluminous writings, touched on endless aspects of social life, but all were ultimately linked to a simple formula: the essence of man is determined by labour in pursuit of material ends; control of material both creates upper and lower classes and gives the upper class control over politics, including the construction of ideologies and social consciousness. Beyond this there are implacable economic rules which ultimately determine economic development. These economic laws make it inevitable that, ultimately, **capitalism** will collapse because of its own inherent contradictions, and **communism** will emerge. It is sometimes mistakenly argued today that the collapse of self-styled

Marxist regimes in Russia and Eastern Europe has invalidated Marxism—the fact that no Marxist had accepted these self-descriptions for a generation before the collapse rendering the argument invalid.

Marxism

Marxism is a general label to attach to any social theory that can claim a vague philosophical derivation from the works of Karl **Marx**. In fact Marxism as a general position has become so broad that there is often little serious connection, even in theory. When Marxism is taken to refer also to the operating policies of so-called Marxist or communist states, as with the Soviet Union before about 1990, the philosophical gap becomes enormous. This is not to suggest that the various branches of Marxism are themselves theoretically incoherent, nor that they have little in common, but that their connections can best be described as involving 'family resemblances' rather than a minimal set of necessary common postulates. The Marxism associated with the Second International (see **international socialism**), for example, is rigorously deterministic in an economic way, while that associated with the French school inspired by Althusser has distinct undertones of **functionalism** and that of the other French Marxist leader in the post-war years, Poulantzas, allows considerable autonomous political power to the state. Other brands of Marxist-derived theory may not even have 'Marx' as part of the title—**Trotskyism** and **Maoism**, while they are 'deviations' from what many would regard as proper Marxism, have much in common with original writings by Karl Marx that modern developments of his insights lack. When considering the actual doctrines of communist societies it is probably better, for the former Soviet Union and its Eastern European allies, to talk of **Marxist-Leninism**, because **Lenin**, and to some extent **Stalin**, left major impacts in the process of turning a general theory into a practical doctrine for revolutionaries and subsequent post-revolutionary governments.

The most that could be demanded as a common thread to all forms of modern Marxism would be the following tenets: that economic matters ultimately control political and cultural phenomena; that abolition of private property is necessary to ensure equality and an end to exploitation; and that such a society must be achieved by the **proletariat**, or its (not necessarily proletarian) leaders, developing a revolutionary consciousness, grasping power, and acting as a vanguard to usher in the communist society (see **vanguard of the proletariat**). Of particular importance in explaining the various splits is the whole question of leadership, and the extent to which there has got to be what Marx called a **dictatorship of the proletariat** before true democratic **communism** can flourish. A second distinction can be made between those who argue for the abolition of **capitalism** through **revolution**, and those, for example **Gramsci** and **Eurocommunism** in general, who favour **gradualism**.

Marxist-Leninism

Although it is traditional to describe the political system set up after the **Bolshevik** coup d'état of October 1917 in Russia as a **Marxist** society, it should, more properly, be described as Marxist-Leninist. Marxist-Leninism was the phrase coined by **Stalin** to describe the conflation of basic Marxist theory with the ideas of **Lenin**, the founder of the Soviet state, which guided the revolution and became the justifying creed of the post-revolutionary state. The need for additions to the Marxist canon primarily came from the fact that Marx had little to say of a concrete nature about the post-revolutionary society, or, indeed, about how the revolution itself should be organized and guided. His thoughts stressed the very long term, and what he described was essentially an **anarchist** society with little need for politics or the state, arrived at after the inevitability of history had run its course. Lenin, in his long career as an exiled revolutionary leader, had written at length on the conduct of the revolution and on the immediate post-revolutionary society. His contribution to the theories centred on the role of the communist party as the **vanguard of the proletariat**, which would not only lead the revolution but also control society during the intermediate phase while true socialism was being built. It was this justification for the rule of the party that was particularly valuable to the Bolsheviks, because it legitimated their rule. The concept of the **dictatorship of the proletariat** ultimately allowed Stalin and his successors a way of refusing to grant either basic democratic rights, or even basic consumer satisfaction, on the grounds that the mass could not be ready for freedom until the Soviet state had fully rescued them from the **false consciousness** they had been trained into by the previous regimes. As **Marx** himself had viewed Russia as a very unlikely place in which to have a proletarian revolution, because the industrial revolution there had hardly started, Lenin's additions were all the more necessary. The role of the party has been so central to communist politics that it would be fair to say that most of the Western communist parties have also been Marxist-Leninist rather than purely Marxist, unless they have taken the route of Lenin's rival, and become **Trotskyist**, or of Stalin's rival and become **Maoist**.

Mass Media

The media are the methods of mass communication and entertainment, which have developed into vital political forces with the advent of virtual total adult literacy and extensive ownership of television and radio sets in the developed world; in the countries of the European Union, for example, more than 95% of households have televisions. It might appear that literacy, with its concomitant development of large circulation newspapers, ought to have had a major impact on political attitudes, but it is possible that the greatest impact has been on the conduct of election campaigns. The spread of broadcasting, above all of news and current affairs, has given an immediacy to distant events that can also influence political opinions. Serious concern has developed over the ability of such media to be used as methods of social control and political influence. There is, however, little firm evidence that, for example, election broadcasts have much direct effect upon political choice in liberal democracies. In the 1979 British general election it was estimated that only 5% of voters read even the free party literature delivered to each household. The mass readership, and the mass television audience, are not especially interested in political information or debate, and their greater availability do not seem to have increased the demand.

Most countries have set up controls, of varying seriousness and severity, on the political bias of the broadcast media, though any extensive control of the print media is usually interpreted as unfair interference, or even as a denial of freedom of speech. Left-wing parties in some countries have argued for a greater control of newspapers because they are seen as tools of the ownership. For example, the British Labour Party claimed that the mass circulation newspapers, almost exclusively controlled by pro-Conservative Party interests, had an undue influence over the result of the 1992 general election. Such arguments are seldom heard in systems, for example in countries like Sweden, where direct party ownership of the press is common. Italy used to be a similar case, but now demonstrates, if anything the opposite since the media millionaire Silvio Berlusconi has used his dominant media position to create an entire personal political party which has twice lead him to the prime ministership.

Enormous power is at times attributed to the media and, when they can, politicians eagerly spend very large advertising budgets on print space and air time, but it is unclear that this, or the editorial content of newspapers and broadcasts in a relatively free mass media system that is free of **censorship**, has any significant effect on political behaviour. Most research on the topic shows that people select a newspaper because it generally supports the political line they already favour, or for apolitical reasons. None the less, the ability of the media to 'frame' an issue, by selective concentration on certain aspects and by following or creating stereotypes may have considerable impact. However, the wise politician will always seek to keep the media content, particularly at the local level and where there is a strong tradition of investigative journalism.

Massive Retaliation

Massive retaliation became the official policy of the administration of US President Dwight D. Eisenhower after 1954, in the wake of the USA's involvement in the **Korean War**. It was, very simply, the idea that any aggression by the Soviet Union in Europe or elsewhere would be met by a huge nuclear onslaught on the Soviet homeland. This was only plausible because, at that stage, there was neither a convincing alternative for the West, given comparative figures for conventional capacity, nor any danger of the East launching any sort of nuclear counter-strike. As the Soviet Union's nuclear arsenal grew in the late 1950s and early 1960s US strategic theory developed doctrines of **escalation** and **flexible response**, leading ultimately to **mutual assured destruction**, in order to preserve the goal of **deterrence**.

Materialism

According to the philosophical or sociological doctrine of materialism only the material, or physical, world need be or can be used in the explanation of social processes and institutions. Most commonly associated with theories of **Marxism** (though by no means limited to them), materialism, *inter alia*, denies the meaningfulness of, for example, religious experience or consciousness except as projections by people of their physical experience. In one of its forms, **dialectical materialism**, it is the quasi-Marxist doctrine that only technical changes in the modes and means of production cause development and change in societies and economies. Materialism thus insists that social consciousness is the product of the material conditions of life, and therefore that all other human institutions, whether legal and political systems, ideologies, religions, kinship patterns or even art forms are ultimately dependent on the economic infrastructure. **Engels**, rather than **Marx** himself, is largely responsible for the 'materialist conception of history' which, inverting **Hegel**, insists on the physical world and man's struggle with it for survival being basic, rather than human ideas, reason and spirit. It is materialism, whether in Marxism, socialism or other ideologies, that **Christianity**, and especially **Roman Catholicism**, has always sought to combat in politics. The term itself is less often used today, being frequently replaced by the more general idea of 'reductionism', the material world being only one of many possible things to which ideas can be 'reduced' when seeking to invalidate them.

Menshevik

Mensheviks were members of a faction inside the All-Russian Social Democratic Labour Party (RSDLP), the **Marxist** party which provided the ideas and leadership for the Russian Revolution and subsequent Soviet state. In 1903, only five years after its founding congress, the RSDLP split at a crucial party congress held in London (at that time the vast bulk of the party leadership was in exile), as a result of political manipulation by **Lenin**; some unity was restored to the RSDLP in 1906. The Mensheviks, the name means simply 'minority' in Russian, believed that a Marxist revolution was impossible in Russia because it was so underdeveloped economically, and favoured a period of reform and economic progress before anything like **socialism** or **communism** could be introduced. After the February revolution of 1917 they formed a party of their own, opposed to Lenin's **Bolsheviks**, and indeed were initially more popular than the latter in most parts of Russia. They were overthrown, along with the bourgeois parties, in the October revolution (or, as some would describe it, **coup d'état**) organized by the Bolsheviks, and the party was gradually suppressed.

Mercantilism

Mercantilism has not been an acceptable economic theory anywhere in the capitalist international arena for several centuries, and it is unlikely that one will find someone who admits to supporting mercantilism. One will, however, not infrequently find others being accused of blatant mercantilism. Mercantilist economic theories technically depend on a complete identification of wealth with some special commodity, historically usually gold or silver. The idea was that it was the essential policy of the state to be as wealthy as possible to facilitate an aggressive external relations policy, and it should therefore maximize national holdings of wealth of the precious commodity. This led in turn to highly protectionist policies, and in the extreme, to an autarkic economic system, completely closed to all external influence.

As international interdependence under a consensually liberal capitalist framework has become universal, the idea of a self-contained economy can be shown to be in no-one's interest, at least in the long term. Protectionist policies are no longer openly acceptable anywhere. At the same time, the idea that wealth comprised any one commodity has vanished. Even countries that seek to maximize, say, foreign-currency holdings, are aware that they are only using units of account, and that wealth is not, in fact, a zero sum matter. Nevertheless, the urge to protect one's national economy, to prefer one's own producers and to protect one's own labour force from unemployment has not vanished. Few governments find it comfortable to explain to their electorate that, in the long term it is in everyone's interests that their automobile industry collapse, or that cheap imports should be allowed from countries with lower labour costs causing unemployment at home. Hence, there develops a perpetual tendency to avoid the theoretical capitalist solution towards protectionism. Similarly, a desire to continue counter-competitive policies of state intervention in the economy, perhaps to have a large public sector running state-controlled industries, as required by traditional social democratic theory, can lead to such governments being described as essentially mercantilist by their critics.

Middle East

The Middle East is a term of European, chiefly British, origin, with a wide and rather inexact scope. Its maximum definition comprises the countries along the southern and eastern coastlines of the Mediterranean Sea, from Morocco to Turkey, plus Sudan, the countries of the Arabian peninsula, Jordan, Iraq and Iran. The terminology itself is not universally accepted: the description 'Near East' is often preferred in continental Europe and sometimes on the American continent, while some seek to maintain a distinction between the Asian and African components. Still others consider the term insufficiently specific, and indeed the countries included in any of these definitions have no particular sense of forming a geo-political unity (although all, with the exception of Israel, Turkey and Iran, are members of the League of Arab States, and, with the notable exception of Israel, **Islam** is the dominant religion throughout the region). The terminology is driven by strategic considerations which, in the European context, go back to the days of colonial expansion. The Middle East was of tremendous strategic importance to Western powers even before the development of oilfields in the 1920s and 1930s. This was primarily because it was, particularly after the opening of the Suez canal in 1869, the route to Asia, and because expansion through Turkey or Iran was the best hope for Russia to achieve year-round access to the high seas. Consequently the decline of the Ottoman Empire, which had controlled most of the southern Mediterranean littoral, led to major intrusions of political control, mainly by Britain and France, from the late 19th century onwards. One result of this was the creation of a series of national states with little natural cultural homogeneity or genuine national identity, a prime example being Iraq. After 1945 the tensions in the area grew enormously because of three factors: the increasing dependence of Europe on Middle Eastern oil reserves; the anti-colonial movement, combined with periodic upsurges of pan-Arabism; and the creation of the State of Israel from Palestinian territory (see **Arab–Israeli Conflict**). As these problems interacted over the post-war years two further elements entered. Firstly, the Israeli–Arab conflict came to be partially a surrogate theatre for Soviet–American **cold war** antagonisms, with each side rivalling each other to develop client states. Secondly, and rather later, the rise of Islamic **fundamentalism**, also tied to the Israel/Palestine problem, exacerbated the existing set of tensions, but also presented both sides in the cold war with a serious threat, either to the oil reserves, in the case of the West, or to its own territorial integrity, in the case of the Soviet Union. The end of the cold war was thought to offer some hope for a more peaceful future in the region, and some progress was indeed made, but the region's internal sources of conflict proved sufficiently enduring for the Middle East to remain the world's principal source of insecurity. Indeed, this would be likely to remain so even were there to be some sort of solution to the endemic Israeli–Arab problems.

Militant

Militant is, of course, a perfectly ordinary English word which means someone who is very strongly committed to, and very active in support of, some cause or other. It could be, and sometimes still is, applied to almost any active supporter of a creed. Perhaps the first common usage like this is, after all, the idea of 'The Church Militant'. In British politics during the 1970s the word became almost exclusively the property of the far left. The 'Militant Tendency' was a splinter group of extreme left-wing **Marxists** who penetrated the **Labour Party**, especially powerfully in a few economically depressed areas such as Liverpool, so named after their weekly paper *Militant*. This particular group was finally crushed by the more reformist minded national leadership, under Neil Kinnock, but only after bruising internal party fights. In more general contexts, referring to anyone as politically militant in contemporary Britain would inevitably imply a political position that was extreme judged by a consensus, but also, importantly, more prepared to use unorthodox measures to get its message across.

Militarism

Militarism is a concept that applies to the whole of a society, rather than a description of a government's policy, although the two are interwoven. A militarist society is one in which the values, ideologies and interests of the military are very widely shared. It is not just a matter of abstract approval of classic military virtues like heroism, honour and self-sacrifice, nor is it a matter of approving high defence expenditure to protect national interest. A militarist society values the military as a way of life, and its activities are not merely for pragmatic ends. Indeed, to the extent that militarism supports high expenditure on military institutions, a desire for the nation to be militarily mighty is as likely to be an end in itself as a clear cut consequentialist justification. The highly militarist German society before the First World War wanted a navy to rival the British Royal Navy as an end in itself, as a source of national pride, rather than to facilitate the building of an empire or because of national insecurity about invasion. The latter fear had much more to do with the provision of a large standing army to protect against French invasion than with the provision of a navy which had little obvious purpose.

Militaristic societies are likely to spread some degree of military activity widely among the civilian population; men will eagerly join volunteer military units and enjoy being seen training at weekends; rifle clubs will flourish; youth organizations will stress drills as much as hobbies; and anyone who can, will wear a uniform whenever possible. The military will provide spectacles—parades and tattoos will be highly popular entertainments. In fact, in such a context, as was true of Germany before the First World War, there may be more pressure from civilian support leagues for the military than even the military want, and certainly more than the government, which must also fund other less popular expenditures, can easily afford. Inevitably, militaristic societies are more likely to engage in war than those of more pacifistic or civilian temperament, but as much by accident as by design.

Military

As a noun, 'The Military' refers to the whole organization of defensive and offensive armed force in a society. Its typical political use is in some compound, such as the military-industrial complex, where it means the armed forces, weapons manufacturers and the civil service and political direction of them. The main point of describing this unitary element, in political analysis, is to suggest that they occupy a special set of homogeneous related interests opposed to the civil interests of the society, and, in most societies, an illegitimate set of interests, or an illegitimate use of power and influence in their pursuit. It is worth noting that the word almost never carries, in modern usage, the technical original meaning which related to land rather than sea forces (see also **armies**). Military is not distinct from Naval or Air, but rather includes all three branches of the modern armed forces. As such it obscures vital historical and political differences in most countries, producing a false sense of the uniformity of these aspects of social organization.

Military Regimes

Military regimes are usually autocratic governments where the **military** controls the country's political system—usually following a **coup d'état**. In military regimes the **civil liberties** of citizens, and normal political and constitutional arrangements, may be suspended. Thus, it is unlikely that opposition parties will be allowed to operate freely in a military regime. Although military regimes are frequently dictatorial it is not necessarily the case that they will be **totalitarian**. If they occur because of a national crisis or political emergency (see **emergency powers**) such regimes may have a degree of political **legitimacy**. Such is probably the case with the regime in power in Pakistan at the beginning of the 21st century. In some cases the leaders of the regime may intend to restore the democratic system of government as soon as it is deemed safe to do so, although the restoration of normal political life is often difficult. In fact, military regimes may be a thing of the past, as there are now far fewer than at some periods in the 20th century. Military regimes have been such a common form of government in part because military organizations often have more administrative and technical skills than civilian governments in less developed societies. Categorization may be increasingly difficult, however. It is unclear, for example, whether to treat Iraq as a military regime or not, given that it is kept in place by the loyalty of some parts of the military forces, but has civilian elements in the government, and was originally a one-party state.

Military coups and military regimes are most often associated with Third World countries, although Greece, Poland, Portugal and Turkey have all experienced periods of military government in the post-war period. In Latin America military regimes have frequently brought experiments with democratic government to an end, although their supporters would claim that military intervention was necessary to end the spiral of hyperinflation, urban **terrorism** and disorder which the troubled democracies were experiencing. In some countries the existence of a military regime is associated with extreme repression such as the so-called 'death squads' and torture units, found in El Salvador, Somoza's Nicaragua and in Argentina before civilian rule was restored after the Falkland Islands conflict.

Militias

The huge professional or conscript standing **armies** of the post-Second World War period, intended to fight a major war with little supplementation from the civilian population, are historically anomalous. More typically nations have relied mainly on part-time military forces of civilians (see **citizen soldier**) who meet regularly but infrequently to train together, and who can be called on by the government in emergencies. Only when called on do they become completely under national governmental control, only then are they paid properly, and there are often severe restrictions on how long they can be mobilized and where they can be sent to fight. One common constraint is that militias are seldom used outside their home country, as they are justified almost entirely on the grounds of national defence, with small professional standing armies being used for external adventures. Thus although Britain had a large militia system throughout the 19th century, it was not until 1914 that the militia, by then transformed into the Territorial Army, was used abroad. As modern high-technology warfare requires very rapid responses and advanced training, part-time soldiers are unlikely to be relied upon except in limited roles. The most important militia in a modern country is the National Guard in the USA, the successor to the militias raised by the colonial governments to fight the War of Independence and which, in the form of forces raised by the states, formed the backbone of US military force until 1916. Each state has its own National Guard force, under the control of its governor, though they can be 'nationalized' by the president in an emergency. National Guard units have been used in foreign wars, but presidents are reluctant to do this, and no militia forces were used, for example, in the **Vietnam War**.

Reserves are the stock of people in the population who have some experience of full-time military service, and who retain an obligation to rejoin the **military** in a national emergency. Typically ex-soldiers have an obligation to report to their units once or twice a year, possibly to undergo refresher training, and hold themselves available for emergency full-time service for a period of several years after their initial enlistment has ended. Reserves were the primary source of military personnel for large continental armies up to 1945, and two or three years of full-time conscript service was intended primarily as a training school for a very large force, most of whom at any one time would be in productive employment in civilian life. Reserves have not often been called up by Western countries in the post-war years, though they played a major role in the **Korean War** and in the Anglo-French invasion of Suez in 1956 (see **Arab–Israeli Conflict**), and limited numbers were summoned during the **Gulf War**. Israel, however, has frequently called up large reserve forces to fight in its conflicts with its neighbours. Towards the end of the **cold war** many military theorists were urging much greater reliance on reserves, partly for economic reasons but also as they could act as a restraint on offensive ambitions by governments. Both the USA and the United Kingdom needed to mobilize special reserve categories in the aftermath of the terrorist attacks on the USA on 11 September tragedy of 2001 and the ensuing conflict in Afghanistan.

Mill, James

James Mill (1773–1836), along with Jeremy **Bentham**, was one of the founders of the **utilitarian** social theories that came to dominate British, and to a lesser extent American, social thought during the 19th century. Though less influential than his close friend Bentham, and philosophically much less important than his son John Stuart **Mill**, James Mill's writings were probably more accessible than those of the other early founders. In particular he wrote more directly about political theory than did Bentham. He advocated an extension of electoral democracy rather before this became generally accepted among even radical middle class intellectuals. His theory of democracy was somewhat limited, however, because his distrust of the working class was almost as profound as his contempt for the traditional **aristocracy**. In a very Aristotelian manner he supported the extra influence for the middle classes, whom he saw as naturally balancing all interests in the state. In many ways he was a brilliant propagandist for selling utilitarian ideals to the rising professional and commercial **bourgeoisie**, rather than an original or creative developer of utilitarianism.

Mill, John Stuart

John Stuart Mill (1806–73) was the son of James **Mill** who, with his close friend and collaborator Jeremy **Bentham**, entirely controlled his education, with the more or less explicit intention of producing a brilliant successor as an exponent of **utilitarianism**. In this they succeeded, although he was to go far beyond them in some respects, and certainly produced a version of utilitarianism more sophisticated and more suited to British **liberalism** than that of his elders. Through a long career as a writer, though he also had much practical experience, including parliamentary, J. S. Mill worked on a variety of topics. His most famous works are the three essays, *On Liberty* (1859), *Considerations on Representative Government* (1861) and *Utilitarianism* (1863), though his purely philosophical work, especially the *System of Logic*, is also of continuing academic interest.

In *Utilitarianism* he tries to reduce the harshness and hedonism of Bentham's approach, accepting, for example, what Bentham denied, that not all sources of pleasure were equally valid. (He rejected, for example, Bentham's notion that it was better to be a pig satisfied than Socrates dissatisfied.) The essay *On Liberty* is probably the most read of all his works, arguing for a system of **libertarianism** in which the only justification allowable for government interference in anyone's life was to prevent them from harming others, and never the claim that a government might know a person's true interests better than the individual. Indeed his great fear, against which the whole essay is directed, was the **tyranny of the majority**, the fear of popular pressure against the non-conformist individual. His justification for such maximum individual liberty, however, is a brilliant thesis about human progress through the discovery of new truths only possible, according to Mill, in a society where no interference in personal belief, or the expression of belief, is tolerated. A beautiful stylist, with a wide-ranging scholarship, his major essays remain vital elements in curricula throughout departments of politics and philosophy, and much of the accepted values of Western society still conforms better to his vision than to that of almost any other thinker of his period.

Mills

C. Wright Mills (1916–62) was an American sociologist, one of few who dominated the field in the 1940s and early 1950s, and unusual, in the American context, for being considerably to the left, though he was never a convinced **Marxist**. Though much of his work, for example *The Sociological Imagination*, is of interest only to academics, he produced one of the first, and arguably still the best, radical critique of American politics and the changes in the system that threatened its democratic claims. This, *The Power Elite,* centres on the development from the Second World War onwards of the huge and influential military machine in the USA, an institution that had hardly existed before 1942. By demonstrating the connections between the military and the major industrial corporations, and linking this 'military-industrial complex' to the rising executive power of the presidency and the top civil service appointments, he painted, early in the 1950s, a picture of decision-making in America that was not to become commonly believed until the days of the **Vietnam War** and **Watergate**. His work has been an inspiration for authors of various political persuasions in the study of American politics, and though he perhaps exaggerated and selected his evidence rather carefully, few deny his perception, or would deny that he mounts a very powerful and persuasive argument. In particular his attack on the **mass media** for turning a once highly articulate and argumentative citizen body into passive receivers of others' views fits all too well with more 'scientific' research on opinion formation, and seems to prophesy the later development of political consultants and the huge impact of media techniques in grooming and selling electoral candidates. It is worth noting, in Mills' support, that his book starts with a quotation by the far from radical President Dwight D. Eisenhower, warning Congress against the dangers of 'the military-industrial complex'.

Minorities

Technically minorities are, obviously, those who are not, in some sense, in a majority in a particular area of a political system. In most usages minorities are thought of as having a common positive identity, rather than being united only in their opposition to the majority. Although it is perfectly proper to refer to a minority existing on only one issue, or by virtue of one single characteristic, this is not usually the most important meaning. The politically important sense of 'minority' is that a group in society has a set of common interests and beliefs over a wide set of issues, which marks it out as needing, deserving or even being given special treatment that the majority of citizens do not. Furthermore minorities are thought of usually as having a permanence, or at least a very long-term existence, and requiring the establishment of institutional or structural methods for helping them.

The most common politically-important minorities are racial, religious, ethnic or linguistic groups in a society who are seen as suffering across a broad spectrum of disadvantages and needing special legal protection and positive discrimination or **affirmative action**. In many societies sexual minorities have become increasingly vocal, particularly since the 1960s (see **homosexuality**). In all these cases what is at stake is not so much the actual arithmetical minority status, but the fact that the group in question is cut off from, and usually subordinate to, a dominant set of interests against which it needs protection. Indeed it would be only partially absurd to regard a group which was, as it happened, in a majority in the population as being nevertheless, a minority in this sense. Occasionally one finds women in general described as a political minority, even though they may be statistically in a majority, because of the way in which they have been historically treated as subordinate to males or lacking full rights.

A related use of minority is to refer to a minority party, or minority public opinion, where the difference with the overall culture is a major ideological contrast, and not merely a set of specific and contingent policy disagreements. In terms of debates about **voting systems**, for example, such political minorities are also often thought of as deserving special legal protection to ensure their views are represented in legislatures.

Mitterrand

François Mitterrand became president of France in 1981, and was re-elected to a second seven-year term in 1988. He was the first socialist to hold the presidency in the **Fifth Republic**. Born in 1916, Mitterrand was captured during the early stages of the Second World War, but escaped and returned to France where he worked in the resistance and prisoner of war movements, for which he was later decorated. He served in various junior ministerial posts during some of the **Fourth Republic** governments, but the creation of the Fifth Republic, initially under the firm control of the **Gaullists**, removed him from office for many years. Mitterrand spent this time working to overcome the main barrier to political success for the left in France, which was its fragmentation. The **Parti Communiste Français (PCF)** was bitterly opposed to the non-communist left, and was generally the most **Stalinist** of the Western European communist parties, and the non-communist left was itself divided into a set of rival groups. Mitterrand's major achievement was welding these groups into one **social democratic** party, the **Parti Socialiste (PS)** in 1971, though he had earlier been the candidate for the presidency of an all-party left-wing coalition. After that he pioneered an alliance with the PCF, in which the PS rapidly became the dominant member, leading to their success in the legislative elections following his election to the presidency in 1981. For a long time Mitterrand had been dismissed as a permanent loser, partly because of his association with the Fourth Republic, but he was eventually able to frame the French left in at least a semi-permanent way. As president he, inevitably, disappointed much of the left, being at most a reformer rather than a radical or revolutionary, and because he, unlike many socialists, did not want to reduce the power of the presidency as an office. In foreign policy he largely continued the Gaullist policy of French autonomy, and the effort to be the dominant power in the **European Union**. In economic policy the world recessions of the 1980s forced France, as much as any country, into the economic orthodoxy of the period—**monetarism**. Constitutionally Mitterrand succumbed to the attractions of a powerful office, and has ended up being seen as just as autocratic as his predecessors. Nevertheless, he did break the right-wing hold on effective power in France that had lasted, with few exceptions, for most of the Third and Fourth Republics and all of the Fifth Republic. It maybe that the office of the French Presidency forces on its incumbents certain characteristics, because Mitterrand's successor, Jacques Chirac, though from a right-wing party, has been criticized in much the same way as both Mitterrand and his predecessor Giscard d'Estaing.

Modernity

So much is made of 'post' modernity, and with phrases like 'the crisis of modernity' abounding; it seems necessary to have some sense of what is actually meant by modernity or the modern age itself. In its most trivial sense, of course, the modern is simply the new or the recent. Alternatively, in phrases like 'Modern European history', the reference is relatively arbitrary, and 'the modern' turns out to have started rather a long time ago. The question is whether there are characteristics of the social life, consciousness and structure of contemporary societies which still usefully distinguish the early 21st century and, for instance, the 17th century from what went before. Whether the 17th century is the relevant marker-point does not really matter—modernity appears to have begun at some stage during or after the concatenation of the Enlightenment, the Renaissance and the Protestant Reformation—different analysts will chose their favourite point to make their detailed explication. Furthermore, whenever it started, modernity clearly accelerated in the 19th century with the Industrial Revolution and the urbanization of Western society. Modernity is also clearly a Western concept both because it is Western societies that are seen as the originator of things modern, and also in as much as they seem to value modernity very much more.

Part of the test of whether one has a truly modern consciousness seems to be whether the idea of progress itself is highly valued. If the recent is more or less automatically to be preferred to the past, in ideas, fashion and cultural habit, then one is fully modern. If this is so, then we may indeed be seeing an end to modernity. Increasingly the recent is not automatically well-evaluated, and increasingly doubts are cast on both the possibility and desirability of endless progress. Sociologically it is probably safe to say, therefore, that a modern society is one with a high degree of individualism; a high regard for autonomy and privacy; a near sacredness attached to human rational endeavor and rational economic planning; a faith in science and the human capacity to control the environment and; master our own fates. A modern society is secular, free from the restraints of tradition and essentially utilitarian in ethics. The idea that the height of human civilization was at some stage in the past—the Greeks, the Italian Renaissance, a religious golden age, or any other option—is simply ridiculous to the modern mind. This modern mind appears to be increasingly perturbed, however, and there are signs in contemporary politics of conservative attempts to return to so-called 'traditional values'. Much of the argument of ecological groups, after all, suggest the non-sustainability of technical progress. Furthermore, modern science is increasingly raises issues where an ill-developed but resilient moral sense, widely if inchoately felt, suggests real caution. Certainly the bio-sciences now cause worry as the idea of experimentation with genetic structures becomes more and more plausible. Modernity has often enough been declared as something that is tautologically impossible, and many more people might find themselves drawn to **post-modernism**, were it less theoretically impenetrable, than at any stage in the recent past.

Modernization

Modernization entered political science and political discourse from sociology, and refers generally to the capacity of countries from outside the European/North American/Old **Commonwealth** countries, (the **First World**, in other words), to develop the economic and political capacity, and the social institutions, needed to support a **liberal democracy** such as is found in parts of the First World (see **political development**). While this approach in political science is obviously at risk of being biased in terms of Western values, there is a strong tradition in social and political theory of studying change in this way, much of it derived from Max **Weber**. In fact all the classic sociological theorists of development, **Marx** as much as **Durkheim**, conceive of something like 'modernity' as a stage all societies have to go through. The main thesis is that a form of political **division of labour** is needed, in which the political system moves from having only a few, all-embracing, authoritative posts, a tribal chieftain, perhaps, to highly specific and task-specialized roles in a modern bureaucratic and governmental system. At the same time changes in social conditions, especially communications and education, are seen as steadily increasing the capacity of a system to maintain and apply complex modern politics oriented to satisfying as many different political interests as possible. So much is modernization seen as a stage of historical development that it is not absurd to talk of 'post-modern' societies, those which have passed through the primary industrial stage on to something else—though what that something else might be is usually unclear.

Monarchy

A monarchy is a state ruled by an individual who has a position at the apex of an aristocratic pyramid of honour and **authority** which is generally inherited through a family connection. Monarchy is a very ancient system of government (it was, indeed, one of **Aristotle's** three basic forms of good government, along with **aristocracy** and **democracy**) which developed independently in various continents; many monarchial systems seem to have started with some form of election, with the succession later becoming hereditary by primogeniture and, until recent decades, usually male primogeniture. Now that we have elected rulers of other types, the notion of an elected monarch would seem superfluous. In many cases the monarch would be endowed with some form of religious significance, for example as the person chosen by God to head and protect the church in their nation (see **divine right**), or even with a form of godhead themself.

The most common form of monarchy today is constitutional monarchy, where the monarch has strictly limited powers and must accept the role and power of other bodies, such as **parliaments** and **cabinets**. Constitutional monarchies are found particularly in Northern Europe, where there are seven (Belgium, Denmark, Luxembourg, the Netherlands, Norway, Sweden and the United Kingdom; in addition, the British monarch is head of state of 16 other **Commonwealth** members). A constitutional monarchy was reintroduced in Spain after the death of **Franco** in 1975. The constitutional monarch typically has a residual role to play in helping the formation of new governments after an election, or in granting to the government the authority to dissolve parliament and call an election, much as have many presidents in systems where the president is **head of state**. In some countries, Sweden being the best example, even these residual powers have been stripped away. It would be wrong to dismiss entirely the potential political significance of monarchy. In some countries, the UK, Norway and the Netherlands being good examples, the symbolic authority is very high among certain sectors. Few military officers, for example, take entirely lightly the idea that their commissions come from the monarch, and might show much more loyalty to a king or queen than to a government, given the military distaste for politics, were a clash to arise. More generally monarchs as heads of state serve as a more clearly neutral symbol of national unity, and a focus for citizen loyalty, than do presidents. Monarchist tendencies have not entirely died out among ultra-traditionalist and conservative elements in European countries that have dispensed with them; in particular, there has been a monarchist resurgence in some Eastern European countries since the collapse of communism there in the late 1980s. The monarchies which have survived in Europe look likely to continue, if only because they provide a convenient way to separate the head of state role from the **head of government**, and because they remain popular with their subjects; in such countries the royal families regularly gain extremely high support in public opinion polls. However, especially in the United Kingdom, the public standing of royal families is vulnerable to their private behaviour, because the values society feels it needs them to espouse are in fact very different from the values by which much of society lives. The more 'ordinary' a monarchy becomes, the less support it gets in practice, although at the same time, egalitarian views in society run against the idea of a distant and superior monarchy.

Monetarism

Monetarism, as used in ordinary political discourse rather than in technical economics studies, refers to a general understanding of certain economic theories, usually associated with Milton Friedman or the **Chicago School** of economics. It rapidly became popular with politicians on the right in the USA and United Kingdom as an apparent alternative to **Keynesianism** in capitalist societies. The Conservative government of Margaret Thatcher elected in 1979 was perhaps the first avowedly 'monetarist' government in the UK, although many would argue that the economic policies of most governments since the late 1960s, including the Labour governments, have used monetarist policies. Certainly during the 1980s monetarism gained the same sort of consensus position that Keynesianism used to hold, and few politicians could honestly deny they were not, to some extent, monetarist.

The dominant concern of monetarism is the reduction of inflation at all costs, and its name derives from claims that the **money supply** in the economy is virtually the only factor affecting the inflation rate. However, in practice definitions of money are various, and under some of them money turns out to be extremely difficult to control. One implication of the theory is that inflation is itself the prime evil, and the prime cause of all other economic ills, especially unemployment. At the same time the theory, certainly as understood by most right-wing politicians, argues for a virtual return to **laissez-faire** economics and an abandonment of government control in any direct way, in favour of operating almost entirely through the money market and the rate of interest. As taxation increases are eschewed by monetarists their preferred means of reducing the money supply will inevitably be high interest rates and/or reducing public expenditure. In many ways the theory is not so much new, as a return to what was commonly understood as economic orthodoxy before Keynesian 'demand management' became politically acceptable. One political consequence of the popularity of monetarism has been that the concentration on interest rate mechanisms for economic policy has increased the importance of **central banks** at the expense of government economic departments, with attendant calls for them to be independent of central government as in the US or German models. Thus the first important announcement of the incoming Labour government in the UK in 1997 was a return to independence for the Bank of England. Since the creation of the **Third Way**, as espoused by the British **Labour Party**, the victory of monetarist thought over British politics has become complete.

Money Supply

Money supply, which can be measured in various ways, is the account of how much money in its several forms is circulating in an economy at any given time. The simplest definition of money supply, referred to by economists as M_0, is simply notes and coins in circulation. Other definitions may include some or all balances in various kinds of bank accounts, bank overdraft facilities, spending power cumulated over the population's credit cards, etc. It is easiest to think of it as aggregate spending power, because this is why it is thought to be vital in controlling economic factors like inflation. Changes in the money supply also act as good predictors of underlying currents in an economy. In the United Kingdom, for example, sharp growth in the money supply (and the accompanying expansion of consumer expenditure) in 1987 and early 1988 heralded an increase in inflation and deterioration in the balance of payments position that started in late 1988. Because of the close link between money supply and inflation, controlling the former has become a major weapon for governments wanting to control price rises without recourse to interventionist strategies like direct price and income restraint. However, the money supply is itself largely determined by government expenditure plans. When these exceed tax income to the government, the **deficit** has to be supported by borrowing, usually from the banking sector, and these loans to the government are effectively 'new money', thus increasing the money supply. Consequently **monetarist** strategies of interest rate increases in order to restrict the money supply have to be accompanied by progressive reductions in government borrowing forcing cuts in public expenditure. However, it is not at all clear that there *is* a simple causal connection between money supply and inflation, while other techniques to cut money supply, principally raising interest rates, have deflationary effects on the economy. An economy undergoing deflation produces less tax revenues, forcing further expenditure cuts if government borrowing, and thence money supply, is not to increase yet further. Nevertheless, since the near complete conversion of Western governments to quasi-monetarist policies from the late 1970s, attempts to control the money supply have been widespread.

Monroe Doctrine

The Monroe Doctrine is to some extent the major juridical basis for US policy in Latin America, and after decades of irrelevance has become important again in recent years, though it is essentially a unilateral declaration of what America intends to do, rather than a multilateral agreement about how nations on the American continent should collectively act. Announced by President Monroe in his State of the Union message to Congress in 1823, it states effectively that the USA will not allow interference in any country of the American continent by any European power, and that any such involvement will be regarded as a danger to the peace and security of the USA itself.

Originally intended to warn off the Holy Alliance powers (principally Austria, Prussia and Russia) from any attempt to help Spain regain control of its disintegrating South American empire, it was also directed against Tsarist Russia itself, which appeared to have colonial ambitions towards the Pacific coast of America. The doctrine was invoked on several occasions during the 19th century, and indeed expanded to mean that any vital interest of the USA anywhere on the continent could and would be protected. As US relations with most Latin American powers grew increasingly cordial during the 20th century the doctrine came to seem both less unilateral and more legalistic, with much of its meaning enshrined in inter-American treaties such as the Bogotá Pact which set up the **Organization of American States** in 1948.

However, the increase in radical opposition to the right-wing and often corrupt governments of Latin America led, after the Second World War, to a situation in which the Soviet Union directly or otherwise came to confront the USA as they supported different sides in the civil wars. The doctrine was used to justify the 1962 American action in blockading Cuba to force Soviet withdrawal of missiles (see **Cuban missile crisis**), and to justify the intervention by US Marines in the Dominican Republic in 1965 to prevent the election of a communist government. As the guerrilla campaigns against the traditional ruling classes, especially in Central America, grew, with increasing support from a Cuba more and more firmly in the Soviet camp, the importance of the Doctrine, and its clear nature as a declaration by the USA of what it would not tolerate, became more vital. Although there is no doubt that Cuban aid to left-wing movements in Latin America was both financed and encouraged by the Soviet Union, it remains true that the doctrine is actually being used to allow the USA to intervene in purely regional and national political and social disputes. The USA will not readily allow the establishment of any government of a communist nature anywhere in its hemisphere, whether or not this is actually the result of interference from a European power, and this is what the Monroe Doctrine has come to mean. In 1983 US forces intervened in Grenada after a coup threatened to place the island's government even more firmly in the Cuban and Soviet camp, and aid was channelled to the Contra guerrillas fighting the left-wing Sandinista government in Nicaragua through much of the 1980s.

Ironically the doctrine was also the first statement of American **isolationism**, and indeed part of the justification of the unilateral declaration of hegemony over the American continent was a promise not to intervene or have any interest in matters on the European continent. As the isolationist aspect of the doctrine has now completely disappeared with US membership of **NATO**, and its recent world leadership in **United Nations** activities, there is no good reason except **realpolitik** for other countries to accept their exclusion, even when invited to help a local state, from the southern half of the American continent. Effectively the Doctrine is an attempt to expand the rights of national sovereignty outside national boundaries, but in an age where national sovereignty itself is coming into question, any extension must be dubious.

Montesquieu

The French nobleman Charles-Louis de Secondat Montesquieu (1689–1755) is often seen, along with **Machiavelli**, as one of the founding fathers of modern political science. His major work, *The Spirit of the Laws* (1748), is an attempt to provide what would now be seen as a cultural and environmental explanation for the legitimacy of different forms of government in different contexts. He held, for example, that climate, geographical location and history had great influence over the nature of social relations, and therefore of political bonds. He tried to identify, at the same time, a particular ideological prop to different forms of government, such as a high value attached to the idea of 'honour' in a monarchial society.

Although his work was influential in helping to develop a more empirical aspect to political studies, influencing future writers as diverse as **Burke** and **Engels**, it is his constitutional theory that has been most important in retrospect. Montesquieu, along with **Locke**, developed the concept of the **separation of powers**, whereby the executive, legislative and judicial branches of government are independent of each other, and have the power to act as checks and balances over each other's actions. This, which he held to be a basic constitutional need if liberty was to be preserved from tyrannical governments, has its most famous expression in the US Constitution, the writers of which were acutely conscious of Montesquieu's ideas on the subject.

Moral Majority

The Moral Majority entered into the political vocabulary as the name of an American pressure group, founded in 1979, which formed an important part of the **new right**. Its purpose was to campaign for the election of morally conservative politicians and to alter public policy in a number of areas where it was thought that either the legislature or the Supreme Court had adopted standards that were not consonant with the views of the majority of Americans. Particular issues of concern to the Moral Majority included school prayer, **abortion** and the tolerance of **homosexuality**. The Moral Majority became identified in particular with two developments in the American political system in the late 1970s, becoming even more powerful in the 1980s after the presidential election victories of Ronald Reagan, which provoked controversy and in some cases the organization of groups to resist the Moral Majority's ambitions. The first was the growing involvement of the religious and the political right in the USA through the mobilization of Christian **fundamentalism**—mostly independent Baptists in the Moral Majority—in particular around a set of themes known as social issues or family issues. The second was the growth in popularity of a number of television and radio preachers who used their media spots to promote not merely a religious but also a political message. The Moral Majority's leader was Rev. Jerry Falwell—a leading television evangelist—although it is clear that much of the initiative for founding the group came from more political new right leaders such as Paul Weyrich, Richard Viguerie and Howard Phillips. The financial and sex scandals attached to many such television preachers in the late 1980s did not stem the general political influence of the movement immediately, although a decline in donations forced the organization to close in 1989. Similar groups continued, the term moral majority often being applied to them generally, although many observers sensed a decline in their influence during the Clinton presidency in the 1990s—it was instructive that even the more outrageous allegations against President Clinton for sexual impropriety damaged neither his standing nor his party in the subsequent presidential election. Despite the length of time passed since the dissolution of the organization bearing the name, the term remains closely associated with groups on the religious right. (See also **neo-conservatism**).

Moral Philosophy

As students of philosophy rapidly find out, often to their disappointment, moral philosophy does not consist of the teaching of moral truths, or even the study of moral codes. Moral philosophy is, largely, a metaphysical subject, that is, it is the study of the logical structure and philosophical nature of moral statements. How do we come to have moral beliefs? Can they be proven and disproven? What does it actually mean when someone says 'X is bad' or 'Y is desirable'? How is a moral argument made? Are there any moral beliefs that can be shown to be untenable? Admittedly moral philosophy in the Anglo-American world has moved away from the extreme **positivist** position it took up in the 1960s, and admittedly continental European philosophy tends to be more concerned with actual values, but these are only relative differences and the essence of moral philosophy remains the understanding of the nature of moral discourse, rather than making substantive moral arguments. In this it contrasts oddly with political philosophy. Even though the questions in political philosophy, such as 'what is the best form of the state?' and 'is private property necessary or even acceptable?', are just as much matters of value rather than fact, political philosophers try to give actual answers, rather than just discussing the process of thinking about the philosophy. The difference perhaps comes because political philosophers are usually able to take for granted human desires, and consider what political arrangements will best satisfy them, whereas a substantive moral philosophy would have to begin by defining what were acceptable desires in the first place. Of course, a study of moral philosophy can make one a better person, by sharpening one's understanding of moral argument, making one aware of inconsistencies and the implications of one's desires. But in the end moral philosophy can only work by assuming rationality of argument and compatibility of views to be prime values, and while they may be to philosophers, it is not always clear that they are qualities of any great interest to the rest of the population. Moral philosophy is in fact a slightly outdated term—it is now much more likely to described as 'ethics', and its philosophical practitioners as 'ethicists'. Whether or not this is connected to a growing tendency for it to be more substantive—actually to argue for specific moral goods rather than concentrate entirely on the form of moral argument—is unclear.

Mouvement Républicaine Populaire (MRP)

The Mouvement Républicaine Populaire was an important but relatively short-lived French political party. It was, in essence, a Catholic-based **Christian socialist** party, built on the Catholic part of the Resistance movement in the Second World War, and was electorally very popular throughout the **Fourth Republic**. This was particularly significant because the preceding

Third Republic had not entirely accepted Roman Catholics as having a legitimate place in politics, and it was in part the Resistance activity of Catholic groups that made them legitimate, just as happened to the communist parties in France and Italy. The MRP represented a moderate social democratic position which at the same time tried to deny the significance of class factors, and stressed Christian duty to others and traditional moral values, as in protection of family life. As France modernized and urbanized its social structure during the 1950s this position became less attractive, and once **de Gaulle** took power and created the **Fifth Republic** the party all but vanished, though it had been a major coalition partner during most of the Fourth Republic. MRP voters moved, on the whole, to the Gaullist parties, the chief representative of which is now the Rassemblement pour la République, and what religious voting still exists in France has continued to benefit either these parties or the Independent Republicans, now part of the Union pour la Démocratie Française (see **French party system**).

Multinationals

Since the 1970s national boundaries have come to be increasingly unimportant in the structure of large industrial and financial corporations. A multinational is such a corporation where the head office of the overall holding company, which probably produces nothing at all itself, is in one country, but the producing companies may be scattered over literally dozens of other countries. Where any particular branch of a multinational is located will depend on matters such as tax policy, governmental regulations on registering a company, laws on shareholder rights and so on. For example a large number of multinational companies are registered in the state of Delaware in the USA because its laws make it particularly easy to register a corporation, and tend to give boards of directors much more authority, and shareholders much less power, than other jurisdictions.

The problem multinationals present to political systems is that no government can really control them, and by shifting their reserves around they can seriously destabilize weak economies. For example, it is difficult to enforce labour-relations laws when a corporation can shift production from a factory in a country about to introduce a minimum wage standard to other factories it owns elsewhere. Similarly a successful branch of a multinational may be of little benefit to the economy where it is situated if its profits are mainly transmitted for investment elsewhere. The problem has grown worse as the general movement towards international free markets, especially financial markets, has grown stronger. Controls on the repatriation of profits, or on capital movements, have become increasingly less popular with economists and business professionals, yet some sort of control *is* needed when the interests of a company are not achieved mainly in one economy. For this reason the **European Union (EU)** is seen by many as a necessary device—a multinational government to counter multinational companies. The European Company Statute of 1990, for example, outlining uniform standards of accountability and so on, was intended to make for greater control of business practice, at least within the EU boundaries. Nothing obvious can be done, however, to protect those countries, the economically very weak **Third World** nations, who are most often seen as vulnerable to the power of huge multinational companies, whose annual budgets can be nearly as large as those of the countries in which they do business. This is in part the explanation for the fierce opposition from many groups, including anarchists, to the summits of the leading economic powers which characterized the beginning of the 21st century. (See also **globalization**.)

Multi-Party Systems

Party systems tend to be categorized by students of **comparative government** using a slightly unusual arithmetic. Obviously a multi-party system is a political system in which there is more than one political party contesting elections, but at which particular number a system becomes 'multi' is less clear. The original divisions were between one-party states, **two-party systems**, and 'multi'. Even with this simple counting system odd results would emerge. The United Kingdom, for example, in most early political science work was seen as a two-party system, despite the fact that in the 20th century there have always been at least three political parties represented in Parliament. There have always been candidates of several political parties contesting the US presidential elections, yet usually only the Republican and Democratic parties have been seen as sufficiently important to be counted. Even with recent 'third-party' candidates winning significant levels of support, the USA probably remains a two-party system, at least at the federal level. However, whether the UK, with a third party, the Liberal Democrats, getting up to one-quarter of total votes, though usually being unable to alter the balance of power, can be studied as a two-party system is less clear. This has led some commentators to regard Britain as a 'two-and-a-half' party system. West Germany, on the other hand, though it had, between the 1950s and 1983, only three parties in the Bundestag, was seen as a full multi-party system because the small Free Democratic Party (FDP) became a permanent coalition partner after 1969. Since 1983, when the Green Party first gained representation in the Bundestag, and 1990, when the first post-reunification general election was held, the number of German parties has increased, although only the Greens have yet played a part in coalition formation (see **German party system**). At its most full-blooded a multi-party system is one with at least three and usually more, often many more, political parties, each of them significant.

Therefore, some criteria need specifying for the significance of a party before it gets counted. The best test of this significance is that the inclusion or exclusion of a party from government coalitions makes a real difference, and is a real possibility. However, even this definition is inadequate where there is a party, the **Parti Communiste Français (PCF)** in the 1950s, for example, which has no chance of winning an election by itself, and is excluded as a possible coalition partner by all parties likely to be forming a government, but is nevertheless sizeable (see **French party system**). Much of this would be pedantry, were it not that the characteristics of party systems, among which, clearly, the 'multi-partyness' or otherwise of them is important, have major consequences for the nature of politics, policy and government. What is most important is to realize that there is a spectrum from true **single-party systems** to true multi-party systems, with no sharp divisions. Even apparent one-party systems can vary in the extent to which the single party is actually a coalition of competing interests, as opposed to being a monolithic and disciplined entity. In some multi-party systems the links between certain parties are so intense as to make it absurd to count them both as separate entities; in Germany the Christian Democratic Union (CDU) and the Christian Social Union (CSU) are effectively one party, and are counted as such. Political scientists have, in fact, developed complex counting rules to take account not only of the number, but also of the relative political power, of parties in any system.

Mussolini

Benito Mussolini (1883–1945) was the forerunner of European **fascism**, becoming prime minister of Italy in 1922, assuming dictatorial powers as *Il Duce* ('the leader'—**Hitler's** official title of *Der Führer* meant the same thing) from 1926. He died in 1945 when captured by the Italian partisans, though he had been out of power, except as a puppet ruler in German-occupied northern Italy, from 1943. Originally a socialist, indeed an influential agitator and left-wing journalist, he left the socialists in the First World War because he supported Italy's joining the allied powers against Austria. From then on he created and led the Italian fascist movement which, like the German Nazi party (see **national socialism**), was a curious mixture of right and left attitudes, amounting, in theory at least, to a radical and **populist** movement. Like the German equivalent, however, very little in the way of redistribution of wealth, or any other socialist policies, was attempted, and the capitalist system functioned perfectly happily under him. His fascist movement was even more corrupt, but considerably less violent, than Hitler's, and the worst excrescences, such as **anti-Semitism**, were very much milder. He came to power largely because a civil war between communists and conservatives seemed imminent, the King, Victor Emanuel III, appointing him prime minister to avoid this. (Hitler's first steps to power came in fairly similar circumstances, and were also more or less legitimate, being based on success in parliamentary elections.) His aggressive expansionist foreign policy, and the similarity of creed and practice made an alliance (the Axis) with Nazi Germany more or less inevitable. His fascist movement reconstructed Italian politics along **corporatist** lines, and produced a formal one-party state in which only members of the party could stand for office. At no stage, however, did the fascists very successfully permeate the basic culture of Italy, and they were never, for example, able to defy the Roman Catholic Church, with which, indeed, Mussolini signed the Lateran Treaty, giving to the **papacy** more security than it had enjoyed under the previous regime.

Mutual Assured Destruction (MAD)

Mutual assured destruction is a basic concept in nuclear **strategy**. It refers to a situation where the forces of opposed countries are so great and invulnerable to such an extent that neither can possibly hope to inflict damage on the other, however great, which would prevent the other imposing an unbearable cost on the aggressor. As such it is a vital element in calculating the requirements for **second strike capacity**. It should be noted that forces do not need to be equal for mutual assured destruction to exist, as long as the stronger power cannot hope to remove enough of the power of the weaker in a **first strike** to save itself from prohibitive damage. It should also be noted that unless 'destruction' is taken as very literal and very total, the concept involves an unavoidably subjective element, because how much damage country x is prepared to risk for the chance of a successful pre-emptive strike against country y is a matter for the judgement of the rulers of country x. Introduced as US strategic policy by Robert McNamara under the Kennedy administration during the early 1960s, it was crudely quantified as requiring the capacity to destroy, in retaliation, one-third of the enemy's population and two-thirds of its industrial capacity. It is sometimes argued that only the threat of mutual assured destruction prevented war in the period from the late 1960s, when the Soviet Union reached effective **nuclear parity** with the USA, until the essential demise of the nuclear threat with the end of the **cold war**. However, the strategy was perhaps less significant than has been claimed, particularly as the Soviet Union continued to believe that there were conditions under which a nuclear war could be meaningfully 'won', and even more so after the Americans moved, in the 1980s, towards a war-fighting doctrine with their Strategic Defense Initiative. (See also **Son of Star Wars**.)

N

Nation

Nation has come to be important in political terms largely either through the idea of **nationalism**, or as part of the **nation state** concept. No obvious technical definition exists, but any working definition in the social sciences would include most of the following criteria. A nation is a body of people who possess some sense of a single communal identity, with a shared historical tradition, with major elements of common culture, and with a substantial proportion of them inhabiting an identifiable geographical unit (see **ethnicity**). The difficulty of definition arises from the way in which all of these criteria may be false in any set of examples. For example, while Belgium is clearly a nation, the sharp, and historically long-term, religious and linguistic **cleavages** between the Flemish (largely Catholic Dutch-speaking) and Walloon (largely **anti-clerical** French-speaking) peoples, and the fact that Belgium only existed in its present form from the 1830s, seem to counter the definition. An even clearer example of historical discontinuity which has not prevented a very intense national identity would be Poland, which has not existed as an independent state for much of the last 1,000 years, and whose territory has shifted across much of central Europe. Similarly nations can exist despite extensive dispersion geographically: the identification of the Jewish diaspora with its traditional Palestinian homeland, both before and after the creation of the state of Israel in 1948, is a good example of this (see **Zionism**). Although the political usage of the term does generally denote something approximating to the nation state, as in the 'British nation' (which might more appropriately be seen as a union of three or four separate nations), the example of the Jewish nation, as well as the affinity felt for an ancestral homeland among Africans, Chinese and many other peoples now dispersed through much of the world, indicates that a deep human sentiment of 'belonging' is involved. Despite this, a school of social scientists argues that the idea of a nation is often largely 'constructed' by élites to raise support for a socio-economic system they dominate.

Nation State

Nation state describes a context in which the whole of a geographical area that is the homeland for people who identify themselves as a community because of shared culture, history, and probably language and ethnic character, is governed by one political system. Such contexts are the common experience today, but are not necessarily any more natural than other forms that have been common in history. There were, after all, no nation states in classical Greece, though there was clearly a Greek **nation**, which sensed that all Greeks had more in common than a Greek could have with a barbarian, and shared language, religion, culture and historical identity. Instead there were a number of, often warring, city states (see **polis**), and no sense of what we mean by 'civil war' attached to, for example, the Sparta–Athens conflicts.

Historically the growth of the nation state, and its developing legitimacy, came after the collapse of the Roman Empire and only when its successor in the West, the Germanic Holy Roman Empire, could no longer pretend to rule an international collection of separate sub-states. To some extent the growth of the earliest nation-states, especially France and England, were historical accidents, for the seeds of national identity, especially the linguistic and cultural homogeneity, actually came after rather than preceded the political hegemony of the national governments. Later important nation states, for example Italy and Germany, although clearly possessing many of the characteristics of nationhood, only united into nation states late in the 19th century. Even more to the point, a large number of nation states in the modern world are the arbitrary result of external power. Thus Pakistan, as it existed from 1947 to 1971, was almost entirely the creation of the British on leaving the Indian sub-continent, while Czechoslovakia was the creation of the victorious powers after the First World War. One of the underlying problems in conflicts in the **Middle East** has been the artificial creation of nation states such as Iraq by external powers early in the 20th century. Indeed the idea of 'nation-building' has been an important topic in the study of **political development**, where it has been expressly recognized that **Third World** states, once they have come into existence (frequently as a result of actions by departing colonial powers), have to create a sense of national identity before they can become sufficiently politically stable to hope for socio-economic progress.

Movements for regional autonomy or actual independence have continued to grow in political importance even in what might be seen as the historical leaders in nationhood, as well as being major problems for many new states, thus weakening the assumption that it is natural for large states to rule the populations of geographically-identifiable 'nations'. Nation states have been seen as desirable largely for the assumed benefits of the large scale in political systems, and a key element here has been the perceived threats to political and economic interests from other nation states. Ironically, while the significance of the concept appears to be weakening in Western Europe, where those nation states previously to be regarded as the most established are moving towards integration through the **European Union**, in other parts of the world, and particularly in Eastern Europe and the former Soviet Union, new nation states have been born or historic ones re-established. There can be no better example than the former Yugoslavia that geography does not always coincide with national and cultural identity. In the long term the increasing internationalization of world society may prove the nation state to have been historically artificial and relatively short-lived, with global interests and concerns coming to be seen as more important than localized cultural and ethnic identities.

National Socialism

National socialism was the doctrine of the German Nazi party (the full title of which was the Nationalsozialistische Deutsche Arbeiterpartei), a blend of intense nationalist, even xenophobic, policy with some pretences to be socialist, in at least the sense of representing the workers (hence the Arbeit in the full German title). It could never in fact be socialist, because it denied the reality of classes and class conflict, arguing instead that there was one true German nation, whose natural unity was threatened only by 'non-German' elements inside the country, and by external enemies. National socialism was closely allied with the wave of **fascism** which swept much of Europe in the 1920s and 1930s, although it had its roots in ideas already circulating in 19th-century Germany, and its **racism**, and particularly **anti-Semitism**, was far more pronounced than other fascist parties. However, as is usually true in fascist movements, opportunism was rampant, and any symbol that could be invoked to get support was used.

Nationalism

Nationalism is the political belief that some group of people represents a natural community which should live under one political system, be independent of others and, often, has the right to demand an equal standing in the world order with others. Although sometimes a genuine and widespread belief, especially under conditions of foreign rule, it is equally often a symbolic tool used by political leaders to control their citizens. Some political leaders have made use of nationalism by stressing national unity and focusing on threats from those who are clearly 'foreign' or 'different' to disguise or to execute otherwise unpopular policies. At its simplest nationalism contrasts with internationalist movements or creeds, and means a stress on local, at times almost tribal, identities and loyalties. Whether one sees nationalism as natural and desirable, or as a threat to world peace or rational organization, is almost entirely a subjective value. In fact the doctrine of nationalism, although widely acknowledged, cannot be very clearly defined (see **nation** and **nation state**). The racial, cultural and historical affinities normally associated with nationality might better be ascribed to **ethnicity**, as the structure of nations and nationality has frequently been artificially, or at least deliberately, created by politicians and governments.

Nationalization

Nationalization or, as it is sometimes referred to, particularly in the USA, socialization, is the policy of taking firms, enterprises or whole industries into public ownership. In clause IV of its constitution, adopted in 1918, the British **Labour Party** pledged to nationalize the means of production, distribution and exchange. However, the actual amount of nationalization promised in Labour manifestos varied from almost none to a massive part of the economy at different elections. Nevertheless, Tony Blair made the abandonment of this commitment a central part of his '**New Labour**' reforms following his election to the party leadership in 1994, his aim being to distance the party from its past ideology, and thereby broaden its appeal among the electorate.

The theoretical backing for nationalization was originally **Marxist**, and stems from the idea that ownership of the means of production defines **class** structures. Hence in an egalitarian and classless society industry should be held in trust for all the people by the state, rather than being privately owned. A secondary rationale, and one much more important in the Labour Party after the Second World War, is that government control and planning of the national economy is vital, and that this requires state ownership of at least the 'commanding heights' of the economy. Yet a third rationale is that some industries, and particularly service industries like transport, are too strategically vital to be run under the conditions of competitive profit maximization, and have to be state-owned and run. This latter argument makes nationalization of industry essentially no different from the widespread tendency, at least until recently, for vital services like public utilities to be taken out of the usual market conditions, or for some, like the postal service, to be almost everywhere a government monopoly.

In practice there has been a fourth rationale, and one that ironically has often led to Conservative governments nationalizing industries, which is to prevent the total collapse of a major firm that has failed to compete on the open market. Thus it was, for example, that the 1970–74 Conservative government nationalized part of Rolls-Royce in Britain, and the US federal government created AMTRAK in 1970 to keep at least some semblance of a passenger railway network going in the USA.

Forms of nationalization vary considerably, but they usually involve the creation of a monopoly run as much as possible on ordinary commercial lines, and with the structure and hierarchy of a commercial enterprise, but with the controlling body (the equivalent to a board of directors) being appointed directly by the government. The extent of direct governmental influence and control on day-to-day matters also varies, as does the general remit given to the management. This latter is usually to attempt to break even, although governments are usually prepared to subsidize public enterprises which make losses, which are sometimes substantial.

The first wave of major nationalizations in Europe took place after the Second World War. In the United Kingdom this was a direct intention of the 1945 Labour government, but similar or even greater nationalization policies were applied in France and Italy, mainly to facilitate industrial reconstruction after the war. In France, for example, both car manufacture and banking were extensively nationalized by post-war governments, whereas in Britain, while the central bank, the Bank of England, was nationalized (and, ironically, not returned to independence until the 1997 victory of a Labour government), the main focus was on utilities and natural monopoly industries.

Since the 1980s there has been a world-wide trend towards denationalization, or **privatization**. In the UK this was central to the policies of **Thatcherism**, and not only nationalized industries, such as steel, but public utilities such as water, gas and electricity, were sold either to institutions or through sales of shares to individual citizens. Although privatization was generally opposed by the Labour Party, and even by some figures on the right (Harold Macmillan, a previous Conservative prime minister, likened it to selling off the family silver), the Blair government's belief in the **Third Way** appeared to exclude the possibility of any renationalizations. Indeed, the prospect of the privatization of the postal service was raised on a number of occasions. However, the belief that the British rail system (nationalized in the late 1940s and privatized by the Conservatives in the 1990s) should be renationalized became increasingly popular in the early 2000s following a series of accidents and the insolvency of the company established to own and manage the system's infrastructure.

European socialism in general became somewhat disillusioned with nationalization in the 1990s and 2000s, as its form has tended not to affect the work conditions or financial rewards of ordinary workers at all; thus the alienating impact attributed to private ownership is in no way reduced. This in part is why more radical socialists have tended to stress worker participation, or **industrial democracy**. Following the collapse of **communism** in Eastern Europe and the former Soviet Union many of these countries embarked on rapid programmes of privatization, sometimes involving the allocation of vouchers to all citizens, regardless of their individual financial resources, to ensure that all had a share in the ownership of the economy.

NATO

NATO (North Atlantic Treaty Organization) is by far the most important of a set of politico-military organizations of co-operating Western states set up after the Second World War, during the early part of the **cold war**, to protect non-communist states from a perceived threat from the Eastern bloc. Similar bodies, like the South-East Asia Treaty Organization (SEATO) and the Central Treaty Organization (CENTO) used to cover military threats elsewhere in the world, but it was NATO that survived and remained at the forefront of East–West relations. NATO's membership includes the USA, Canada and most Western European countries, although some, such as Sweden, Ireland and Switzerland, have remained neutral states. France is only partially a member, having withdrawn from the integrated military structure in 1966. Although France has preferred to maintain a large degree of independence in defence policies, the French military have continued to co-operate and liaise with NATO, and could have been expected to play a full part in any war on the central front involving the **Warsaw Pact**. NATO works by co-ordinating the military capacities of its member states and allotting specific peacetime and wartime tasks. Under war conditions units of all the member states would come under a unified international command-structure, the head of which has always been a US general in recognition of the huge and disproportionate cost to the USA of NATO membership.

Much progress was made in the area of **arms control** during the 1980s not only in reducing the numbers of long-range nuclear missiles controlled by the USA and the then Soviet Union, but also in the withdrawal of intermediate and short-range nuclear weapons from the European continent itself. Furthermore, the members of NATO and the Warsaw Pact, in November 1990, signed the **Conventional Forces in Europe (CFE) Treaty**, which was to reduce levels of conventional force in Europe and effectively confirmed the end of the cold war. With these developments, and the final dissolution of the Warsaw Pact in 1991, NATO was left to seek a new justification for its existence; there was little support from member governments for the abolition of NATO, crucially because it provides a means of keeping the USA involved in European security. Militarily NATO was restructured to emphasize smaller and lighter forces which can be deployed easily to any trouble spot in Europe, and to reduce costs by relying much more heavily on reserves for the heavy battle formations that were previously its characteristic mode. NATO forces supported the UN operations in Bonsian and Herzegovina in the mid-1990s, and a NATO-led force assumed responsibility for peace-keeping in that country in December 1995. Two developments of great significance for NATO took place in March 1999. Firstly, full membership was accorded to the Czech Republic, Hungary and Poland, three former member countries of the Warsaw Pact, despite Russian opposition. Secondly, a NATO force carried out air-raids on Yugoslavia in response to the conflict in Kosovo.

At the beginning of the 21st century the debate over the future of NATO had become complex, particularly as the **European Union** was eager to field its own military force which would necessarily draw on the same units that its member states dedicated to NATO. It was likely that the **Organization for Security and Co-operation in Europe** would also have a role in the development of a multinational mutual-security arrangement for the whole of Europe.

Natural Justice

By natural justice is meant the ideas that there are some qualities and values inherent in the very concept of **law**, as opposed to arbitrary decision-making, and that individuals should be able to claim certain basic protections in the legal system regardless of whether they are specifically given those protections by statute. The two most common tenets of natural justice in the British legal system are *audi alteram partem* (that each party has a right to be heard in any dispute) and *nemo judex in parte sua* (that the judge of a case should have no personal interest in its outcome). In the United Kingdom in the 1960s these quite specific principles of natural justice were applied to a large number of administrative as well as judicial decision-making situations, and as a result the British judiciary both expanded its own jurisdiction and developed something which it had previously lacked—a coherent corpus of **administrative law** This was further enhanced at the end of the 20th century by the passing of the **Human Rights Act** 1998. (See **administrative courts** and **judicial review**).

Natural Law

Natural law has been a crucial idea in political, social and legal theory from early medieval times throughout Europe and, later, North America. Nearly all the most famous political theorists have had something to say on the matter, starting at the latest with **Aquinas**, probably influenced by the rediscovery of analysis of **Aristotle**, and arguably as early as **Augustine**. By no means all those who have used or discussed the concept have seen natural law in even remotely the same way. The contrast between **Hobbes'** view of natural law and **Locke's**, though they wrote in the same country and only a few years apart, could hardly be more sharp. Natural law is seen, variously, as God's will for the world, moral principles innate in the structure of the universe, the principles of rational self-interest, or the necessary elements logically underlying any legal system. In the last of these senses, especially, it is contrasted with **positive law**, those laws actually promulgated by the state.

Natural law began to become really important when the European **Enlightenment**, with its faith in the capacity of human reason to solve social problems, and its debunking of the right of the church to teach by authority of its special connection to God's will, simultaneously challenged the legitimacy of both secular and temporal powers. The very thinkers who did this needed some basis for their own views on right and wrong; for them moral intuition was seen as not rational enough, reliance on positive law was useless as they were, on the whole, opposed to most of the political authorities, and something had to take the place of these traditional sources of authority. Partly by analogy to what we would today call 'the laws of nature' in their scientific sense, natural law in politics and morals was seen as fixed in the universe by its very principles, and amenable to discovery by rational thought and analysis. Just as there could only be one physical law determining, for example, the rate of fall of an object from a tower, there could only be one correct way of organizing a political system, or of acting in a case of moral doubt. To believe anything else would be to accept a randomness about the universe which, in the days long before relativistic and probabilistic models in the physical sciences, was unthinkable. However, what these natural laws that governed political society—which should give answers to all the stock questions of political theory, determine the grounds of political obligation, the balance of power between the state and the individual and so on—actually were was rather harder to discover.

The natural law tradition in political theory was not, perhaps, all that long-lived before it fell victim, in English political thinking anyway, to attacks by sceptics like David **Hume**, and the philosophical radicals like Jeremy **Bentham**. Their inability to discover a foundation for natural law led them to resort to human psychological drives as the foundation of political principles, culminating in the **utilitarianism** so pervasive today. The tradition never completely died out, even in England, and, often under other names, continues to have some importance. In law it has never been possible to operate only by positive law, and, though they seldom use the language, leading jurists and judges in both America and Britain have to fall back at times on some conception of **natural rights** to fill gaps and handle problems of discretion, as with the English legal doctrine of **natural justice**. In continental Europe the continued importance of the philosophical tradition of **Kant** and **Hegel** has kept the idea alive more obviously, but in a rather changed state. The alternative home of natural law thinking in contemporary society is that of the Roman Catholic Church, but the inevitable conservatism of such ideas has made it hard for those of other political persuasions to continue accepting what might otherwise be an intellectually attractive position.

Natural Rights

Natural rights are those human rights or entitlements which are held to stem from **natural law**, whatever definition may be given to the latter concept. One can probably divide natural rights into two broad categories, as they are encountered in legal and political theory. One group consists of those rights, seldom specified, that a person would hold, even if not enforce, in the theoretical **state of nature**—rights, that is, that are fixed by divine law or by the very nature of man and the universe. These have often been incorporated into various declarations of **human rights**, and include those such as the right to life, to property, to family life, and in general to do anything, in total freedom, so long as the similar rights or person of others are not damaged (see **libertarianism**). The second group would consist of the more procedural rights that most legal systems find logically necessary if they are to be fair and efficient, as characterized by, for example, the English doctrine of **natural justice** or, in America, **due process** of law. What is definitional about natural rights is the contrast between their absolute and extra-governmental nature, and other rights which depend only on state policy, as, for example, with welfare rights stemming only from social policy legislation. Whatever natural rights are, they are held to exist independently of what any government does or says, and not to be capable of being legitimately over-ridden by any government, however often they may be ignored in practice. (See also **civil liberties**.)

Neo

A wide range of political and philosophical concepts are prefaced by the word 'neo'. This can either be to give an idea or theory respectability by tracing its roots back historically, or to discredit it by linking it to some previous theory which is now consensually disapproved of. Thus, for example, **neo-corporatism** is a label given to the modern tendency for government, industry and **trade unions** to come to common understandings about running a sector of industry. But this label is used mainly by those who disapprove of the tendency, the aim being to link it with the unfashionable **corporatist** policies of **Franco's** Spain and **Mussolini's** Italy. Family resemblances between concepts or theories are often more misleading than helpful, and the addition of a 'neo' prefix gives an often spurious sense of temporal development. Usually the base concept, **conservatism**, for example, was never homogenous, and the particular ideas enshrined in its 'neo' development are likely to have been part of the original. Where the preface does seem to be useful is the relatively rare case of the rebirth of an idea which has, over time, lost nearly all support and then comes back into popularity, modified for new circumstances, but not fundamentally changed.

Neo-Colonialism

The enormous economic and political influence that rich northern hemisphere countries often have over **Third World** nations is often bitterly resented in the latter. Neo-colonialism is the argument that the conditions of poor countries are often no better, and their peoples no freer, than when they were actually governed by the European colonial powers in the period up to the mid-20th century. There are several elements to this theory, all of them involving the impact of strong economies on less developed ones, but outright attempts at political control are also often suspected.

There are three main forms of trade between a major northern hemisphere industrial economy and a Third World country. The most important is, probably, where the Third World country is a primary producer, either of agricultural products or raw resources from extractive industry. It is argued that price levels for such products are largely dictated by the rich countries, the producers being effectively powerless unless they can organize into a semi-cartel, as with the Organization of the Petroleum Exporting Countries (OPEC). A second form is where a Third World country is a provider of cheap labour for the production of components in consumer goods assembled elsewhere. Often the poorer countries lack the expertise or investment capital to benefit from the marketing of finished products, but they can produce the labour for factories owned and built by companies based in richer countries. Thirdly there is the role of the Third World in providing mass markets for products experiencing market saturation or interruption in richer countries, often in cases where the consumer protection standards that would be imposed in the manufacturing country cannot realistically be imposed by a Third World government.

The reason why it seems appropriate to add the prefix **neo** to **colonialism** is that, especially in the first and third cases, these were precisely the motives for the 19th century colonial movements. If the same economic aims can be achieved without the expense of governing and garrisoning a country, so much the better. The suspicions of those who see **First World/Third World** relations as essentially colonial are intensified when it comes to the question of direct interference in the politics of the weaker countries. For whatever reasons, and however justified, there is no doubt that powerful nations, and especially the USA, have intervened repeatedly, overtly and covertly, particularly to oppose revolutionary movements and to prop up right-wing regimes. Even if the governments of the rich countries are not motivated by a need to protect their corporations operating in the Third World, the effect is often just that.

Other aspects can be seen as part of neo-colonialism but, whether they refer to the terms on which development aid is provided, to the role of banks in funding development or to the impact of multilateral trade agreements such as those overseen by the **World Trade Organization**, in all cases the weaker economies are totally dependent on decisions made elsewhere.

Neo-Conservatism

The term neo-conservatism was first coined by Michael Harrington in the USA to refer to a tendency in that country to reject some of the underlying assumptions of American liberalism, most notably, perhaps, the optimistic beliefs that progress is inevitable and that the government can ameliorate various social problems. It has come to be used of a disparate group of writers and academics such as Irving Kristol, Norman Podhoretz, Daniel Patrick Moynihan, Jeane Kirkpatrick, Nathan Glazer and Daniel Bell, although both Bell and Moynihan have rejected the label. Most of the major figures of American neo-conservatism are former Democrats and some, such as Moynihan, remained active in Democratic politics. Kirkpatrick, although the author of an article explaining why she could not become a Republican, joined President Reagan's administration as Permanent Representative to the United Nations.

Neo-conservatism is not so much a coherent theory as a set of reactions to contemporary politics, and especially reactions to the politics of the USA in the 1960s. While it is difficult to summarize the writings of such a diverse and prolific group, four themes seem central to neo-conservatism. Firstly, neo-conservatives support Western values and are hostile to communism. Such a position is only surprising in the context of a country severely shaken by the experiences of the **Vietnam War** and because the neo-conservatives have been concerned to make a clear intellectual defence of both capitalism and the policies of the USA.

Secondly, the neo-conservatives have, since the 1960s, expressed sustained scepticism about the role of government, and especially the federal government, in American life. The magazine co-edited by Kristol, first with Bell and then with Glazer, *The Public Interest*, prides itself on its unbiased assessment of public policy questions, and neo-conservatives have been leading advocates of such policies as deregulation and welfare reform.

Thirdly, neo-conservatism has a strongly traditional approach to matters of religion and morality and rejects the trends associated with the 1960s youth movement—especially sexual liberation and the counter-culture of an alternative society. It fears the destruction of the family and in this respect its arguments coincide with those of the **new right** groups such as the **Moral Majority** which became active in American politics in the 1970s.

Finally, neo-conservatism is hostile to utopias and to attempts to promote broad visions of equality. It is wedded to the notion of **equality of opportunity** and as a consequence has opposed such policies as **affirmative action** and quotas.

The neo-conservative movement changed the intellectual climate of the USA and provided a justification and explanation of trends which were already apparent in its politics. Although its impulses mesh well with those of other forces on the American right, including the new right and the **Republican Party**, it is, however, a distinct tendency and not to be confused with them. Ultimately, however, it had little influence on the administrations of Reagan and the elder Bush because the rightwards swing in the American electorate proved to be very much more a matter of basic economic rationality than of any theoretical disillusionment with liberalism. Furthermore the decline and eventual collapse of communism in Eastern Europe and the former Soviet Union deprived neo-conservatives of their favourite target. Its views regained a certain amount of support during the Clinton presidency, when the administration's policies were diametrically opposed to the neo-conservatives' aims, and questions as to Clinton's fitness for office amid allegations of sexual and financial impropriety brought the debate onto their territory. George W. Bush has frequently been seen as heavily influenced by neo-conservatism, and his first budget contained significant reductions in taxation and government spending on perceived 'liberal' projects.

Neo-Corporatism

Neo-corporatism is a political theory created in the 1970s as part of a radical critique of the nature of the state in capitalist societies, though some of its ideas would be accepted by less than radical political scientists. The 'neo' in the title is there simply to distinguish it from the **corporatist** theories of inter-war European **fascism**, and is sometimes omitted. The essence of the theory is that major industrial institutions, and especially **multinational** firms, have now entered into a very close alliance with the state, especially with the civil service. Instead of the state controlling and organizing industry as though the corporations were passive, they are seen as being necessary partners. Thus economic and industrial policy is worked out, according to this theory, jointly between industrial institutions and the civil service. Part of the explanation for this move is that the control of information and technical expertise needed for regulating industry is only available to civil services from the corporations themselves. To some extent the theory is not only true, but not particularly new, surprising or radical. It has always been the case that governments have relied on interest groups for the information they needed to construct policy. In the United Kingdom, for example, assistance from the National Farmers' Union has long been vital to the ministry responsible for agriculture in working out the yearly agricultural subsidy plans. But in this case there are many who feel that the power actually lies with the ministry, and the Union is forced to co-operate. A better example might be the various **regulatory agencies** in the USA, such as, for example, the Federal Communications Commission, or the Food and Drug Administration, where interchange between staff in the regulated industry and the agencies has tended to make the regulation organized more around the interests of the regulated than some notion of the public interest. The implication for those who use the idea as a criticism of modern political systems is that the spirit of Italian fascism, where industry was directly represented in a legislative chamber, is rising again, with the state becoming no more than a servant to sectional industrial interests. The trend to deregulate industry in North America and Western Europe has, to some extent, reduced the applicability of the theory, as has the collapse of organized trade union power in many countries, especially the UK.

Neo-Fascism

The increased popularity of far-right parties in a number of European countries in the late 1990s and early 2000s has caused many observers to contemplate a return to real political influence of **fascism** on the continent. One reason that it is very difficult to define 'neo-fascism' is that **fascism** itself never had much intellectual coherence or ideological core. Furthermore, some of the policies that were originally central, notably **racism** and **anti-Semitism**, are now much harder to express legally than in the past, so much of the common identity of current movements with those of the 1930s has to be made oblique. However, there is a neo-fascist current in most European countries, and it does focus on the traditional fascist values of racial purity, national identity, social discipline, **militarism** and **authoritarianism**.

The defeats of **Hitler** and **Mussolini** during the Second World War reduced fascism to a negligible political force across most of Europe, and the death of **Franco** in 1975 definitively removed it from power. However, by this time a number of small fascist parties had emerged.

The only overtly neo-fascist party which was of real importance in the 1970s and 1980s was the Movimento Sociale Italiano (MSI—which effectively became the Alleanza Nationale in 1995, and dropped virtually all of its actual fascist doctrine). Some parties in Germany, particularly Die Republikaner (REP) are, in fact, neo-fascist, but local political culture prevents them from saying so openly. Neo-fascist movements like the British National Front exist in many countries, but in recent decades most have been of only peripheral significance. The electoral success of neo-fascist movements fluctuates, largely with economic conditions, because fascism is a political reaction of the disenchanted lower-middle and working classes, allied through a **populist** streak. The Front National (FN) in France, for example, experienced a modicum of electoral success in the 1990s, quite overtly playing on the racist attitudes of the unemployed and poor of the French working class against the North African immigrant population, and on the discontent of the business sector after a lengthy period of socialist economic policy. The FN's previous modest successes were surpassed by its performance in the French presidential election held in April/May 2002, in which its leader, Jean-Marie Le Pen, received some 17% of the votes cast in the first round, advancing to oppose the incumbent president, Jacques Chirac, in the second ballot (amid opposition to Le Pen from nearly all the defeated first-round candidates, Chirac was re-elected with a comfortable majority). Le Pen focused his campaign on crime and immigration, suggesting a link between the two.

In Germany the strains of integrating the former East German state with the Federal Republic, combined with problems of **immigration** from Eastern Europe, have encouraged what was previously an insignificant neo-fascist movement. The successes of Le Pen, the Freedom Party of Jörg Haider in Austria and the Vlaams Blok in Belgium, together with strong electoral performances from far-right and anti-immigration groups in Denmark, the Netherlands, Norway and a number of other European countries, illustrated a trend towards increased sympathy for the far-right. While relatively few of these groups or their leaders could be properly described as neo-fascist —the label is much too widely and easily used, and none possess the militarist focus of fascism itself—there is no doubt that a complex of attitudes that lay behind the success of parties such as the German **National Socialist** (Nazi) party and the Italian Fascist Party of Mussolini has been rejuvenated because of analogous social and economic conditions which arose in a period starting some time in the late 1980s and developing in the late 1990s.

Neutralism

Neutralism, which is not to be confused with **neutrality**, is the status of many if not most of the **Third World** countries who have decided not to be formally involved in alliances with the world's major economic and military powers, and which remain free to accept aid and support from wherever it is offered. The conditions attached to aid by donor nations, frequently involving some level of commitment to democracy or stipulation of what should be purchased with money given, tend to result in informal alliances and relationships, and mean that neutralism in a pure form is seldom practised. Essentially neutralism is the same as 'non-alignment', and the Non-aligned Movement has over 100 members. Unlike the actual status of formal neutrality, which is a breach of the general duty all **United Nations** members have to support a UN mandate against an aggressor, it is perfectly compatible with active participation in international affairs and with full membership of the UN.

Neutralism need not involve total neutrality, because membership of regional alliances and defence pacts which do not involve relations with external major powers is perfectly possible. India, for example, is one of the leaders of the non-aligned nations, and yet there is no question of it being neutral in any conflict between, for example, Bangladesh and Pakistan, both of which countries are also practitioners of neutralism.

It is important to differentiate not only between neutrality and neutralism, but also between neutralism and **isolationism**. The latter, famous as the official US policy towards all international affairs outside its own hemisphere from the declaration of the **Monroe Doctrine** in 1823 until its entry in the Second World War in 1941 (with a brief break from 1917–20), involves a total abdication from international affairs, and a complete lack of interest in the outcome of any conflict. Isolationism was taken by the Americans, for example, to preclude membership of the **League of Nations**, yet many neutralist countries (and Sweden, a neutral country) have contributed to UN peace-keeping forces.

Neutrality

Neutrality does not just refer to a state of non-involvement in international conflict, and there is in fact a fairly precise meaning in international law. If a state wishes to assume a position of neutrality between countries who are at war with each other, it has an obligation under **international law** to refrain from aiding either party, or from allowing either to use its territory for any warlike purpose at all. In return for this it is to be allowed to continue trading with either or both of the war-making powers, although the latter have the right to blockade and prevent any prohibited trading, exercising care to protect the nationals and ships of the neutral country. None of the war-making powers may, within international law, attack the neutral state.

Although the idea of neutrality was at one time, during the era of **limited war**, perfectly sensible and minimized the impact of war on the rest of the international community, it did not, in the context of the two world wars, make a great deal of sense. In both wars, for example, protestations of neutrality did not save Belgium from invasion. In the First World War it was to a large extent Germany's refusal to avoid attacking neutral American merchant ships that brought the USA into the war on the side of Britain and France. Only Switzerland, which has been recognized internationally as permanently neutral since 1815, was fully able to avoid favouring or being used by one side or another. (Even Switzerland has accepted a limitation to its neutrality since voting to join the **United Nations** in 2002.) Even the most bitterly hostile of enemies can see the mutual benefit of having some genuinely neutral inter-mediary to deal with, for example, negotiations over prisoners of war.

Legally, in fact, not all nations even have the right to announce a general neutrality. All members of the United Nations, for example, share a common duty to defend each other and to aid in the punishment of an aggressor under certain conditions, and could not claim that their neutrality required or allowed them to be impartial between two parties if one had UN sanction. In practice the only effective neutrality is what has come to be known as 'armed neutrality'. This state of affairs, and modern Sweden may be the best example, involves not just the general intention not to be involved in any war, but a manifest ability, at some cost, to defend its own frontiers effectively. The Swedes in fact have an efficient armaments industry, and a very effective military capacity based on a large reserve and more or less total liability to conscription for military training. Being able to defend oneself actually comes close to a legal definition of neutrality, because it is always open to a combatant nation to claim the need to occupy a neutral to prevent its enemy from so doing, if it cannot trust the neutral itself to be able to honour its legal obligation not to allow any other party to benefit from its weakness.

Considering the readiness of aggressors to invade neutral countries in the potentially limited wars of the 20th century, the notion of neutrality in any third world war is largely imaginary. Not only was the sort of major war that used to be feared in Europe inherently likely to be nuclear, but the strategic position of a country like Sweden would make it extremely difficult for **NATO** or any likely enemy to respect the neutrality of at least its airspace. Neutrality is, of course, entirely possible in limited and small wars not involving a major power or alliance, but this is largely the neutrality of those who do not care to be involved, rather than the neutrality of a small nation which fears to be involved. Effectively it is only possible for a country to be neutral if it is sufficiently independent of both sides in a conflict. The position of Iran during the **Gulf War** of 1991 is a particularly interesting example of neutrality in a conflict not only involving close neighbours, but also a UN alliance spearheaded by the USA. Iran had not only been a bitter enemy of Iraq in the recent past, but had also been forced to be independent from most Western powers ever since the Iranian revolution in 1979. In contrast Jordan displayed a clear tendency to support Iraq, upon which it was economically dependent. Furthermore, there are very few potential conflicts that are not at least on the margins of the interests of major powers, and neutrality in the full sense of giving no aid or preference at all was not practised by the Soviet Union or the USA in any important post-war 20th century conflict.

New Class

New class refers to a theory, usually associated with the Yugoslav politician and dissident Milovan **Djilas**, to the effect that the supposed **egalitarianism** and classlessness of communist Soviet Union and Eastern Europe nevertheless did have **class** systems. The argument is that, although major private property holdings had been abolished, and a great degree of equality introduced for the mass of the citizenry, those who held senior positions in the state administration, and even more, in the Communist Party apparatus (the **apparatchik**), had enormous privileges that made them effectively a new ruling class. The control of power, as well as the material rewards, enjoyed by such people was indeed incompatible with a fully egalitarian and democratic society, but it is dubious that they actually constituted anything that could sensibly be called a 'class', mainly because their position was dependent on holding specified offices, and because there could be little or no direct inheritance of such privileged positions.

New Deal

The New Deal was the name given to the peacetime policies of Franklin Delano Roosevelt, President of the USA from 1933–45. These policies Roosevelt hoped would end or ameliorate the Great Depression in the USA which followed the stock market crash of 1929 and which threw millions of Americans out of work and into poverty. The phrase was first used in his speech accepting the Democratic presidential nomination in 1932 and it consciously echoed the call by his relative Theodore Roosevelt (US president from 1901–09) for a 'square deal' for the American people. Since the New Deal other American presidents have tried to coin similarly resonant terms for their policies so that there has been President Truman's Fair Deal, President Kennedy's New Frontier and President Johnson's Great Society.

The individual programmes contained in the New Deal were very much *ad hoc* responses to the problems of unemployment and social dislocation experienced in the USA of the 1930s. Only in retrospect did they seem to embrace any coherent political philosophy or underlying economic doctrine. The policies did, however, introduce a significant amount of government intervention to the economy and greatly expanded the role of the federal government generally. As a result the New Deal proved to be extremely controversial and met with substantial opposition both from businessmen wedded to traditional ideas of **laissez-faire** and from the Supreme Court, which ruled many of the key items of Roosevelt's legislative programme (for example, the National Industrial Recovery Act) unconstitutional. However, the policies were popular with the electorate as a whole and the New Deal is usually seen as a crucial period in American political history both because it precipitated a party **realignment** and because it greatly changed the nature of the US federal system (see **federalism**). As a result of the party realignment key groups in American society such as blacks, labour unions and the poor became linked to the **Democratic Party**, which used this coalition to retain the presidency from 1933–52 and to dominate congressional elections thereafter. Only with the rise of the new politics of the 1960s did the Democratic coalition seem in danger of losing its majority status, and even then the evidence of its break-up is ambiguous.

The New Deal is sometimes divided into two periods. In the first period, which lasted from 1933–35, the measures were generally exploratory and moderate. In the second period President Roosevelt, assured of electoral support after his re-election in 1936, felt able to act more radically and to confront the Supreme Court over its attempts to challenge his legislative programme.

New Economic Policy (NEP)

The New Economic Policy was introduced by **Lenin** at the 10th Congress of the Russian Communist Party (Bolsheviks), later the **Communist Party of the Soviet Union**, in March 1921. It represented a considerable relaxation of the strict 'war communist' economic policy introduced immediately after the second (**Bolshevik**) revolution of 1917. The banking system, which had been completely abolished, was reintroduced (though as state, nationalized banks), internal trading was allowed much more freely and without state planning controls on the movement and distribution of goods, and limited private trading for profit was allowed. In other words, it allowed a slight movement back towards a capitalist form of economics, and made sense to many who felt that Russia had to go through the equivalent of a bourgeois capitalist revolution before **communism** proper would have a foundation to build on. It was largely forced on Lenin anyway, because of riots over food shortages and a fear that the economy, and especially the agricultural economy, would collapse, and with it would vanish revolutionary control over the country. It had always been feared by many revolutionaries that, unless the rest of Europe went communist almost immediately, the revolution would not be able to survive alone in Russia. To doctrinaire Marxists, who had wanted to create total communism overnight, abolishing even money, the policy was unacceptable. But it was not until **Stalin** introduced the first of his five-year plans in 1929, using force and violence to suppress the opposition Lenin had tried to buy off, that the NEP was abolished.

New Labour

New Labour began as an unofficial label for Tony Blair's attempt to modernize the ideological appeal of the British **Labour Party** in the 1990s, in order to make it electorally competitive with the Thatcherite **Conservative Party**. It rapidly became so popular that the leadership adopted it, and by the early 21st century 'New Labour' had all but become the official name of the party. The Labour Party had been distinctly moderate or centre-left throughout the 1960s and 1970s, when it was in office for a total of 11 years. The defeat by the Conservatives in 1979 encouraged the activists, always more politically extreme, to drag the party considerably further to the left. From this position it was defeated again both in 1983 and 1987. Newer generations of leaders tried to remedy this by some movement back towards the centre, particularly under Neil Kinnock in the prelude to the general election of 1992. However, even this was not enough, with the electorate still seeing the party as too extreme for office, even though Thatcher had now been replaced by a less charismatic leader. After 1992 steady moves to radically transform the Party's constitution and official ideological goals were more successful, especially when a young leader, Tony Blair, took over in 1994. He and his allies fought an intense campaign to, in their own words, 'modernize' the party, and to develop a new doctrine for **social democratic** parties, the **Third Way**, even going so far as to abolish the party's historic commitment to nationalization of the means of production, hitherto enshrined in Clause IV of its constitution. The result was a convincing defeat of a tired Conservative administration in 1997, and an historically unprecedented full, second parliamentary term at the beginning of the 21st century.

The 'new' Labour party bears little resemblance to the old one. It has entirely accepted the free market and **monetarism** of its opponent, has accepted the need for severe fiscal orthodoxy and low tax rates, and was, at the beginning of the century, largely losing its ties to organized labour. It competes now mainly on managerial competence, with only a slight preferential option for the poorer or, in the modern language, the 'socially excluded'.

There have been few such major transformations of what a party stands for, at least without a split. A similar attempt after the 1979 defeat created a rival **Social Democratic Party**, which was rapidly swallowed up by the Liberal Party. What facilitated, as well as required, this later transformation was the major sociological change that the country had undergone since the founding of the Party. Effectively the old working class has diminished in size and new, less class-conscious voters are immune to the rhetoric of the old socialist position.

New Right

The description new right is usually applied to the ultra-**conservative** movement in the USA which came to political prominence around the time of Ronald Reagan's election to the presidency in 1980, and was partially responsible for his electoral success. The intellectual origins of the new right are rather curious, because many of its leading thinkers were former extreme liberals, some even having been **radical** activists in the 1960s and early 1970s. The new right has also never had a very coherent set of beliefs. One reason for this is that one of its major aspects has been **libertarian**, while another has been the demand for a return to 'traditional morality'. Many of the supporters of new right thinking have also been prominent in the upsurge of **fundamentalist** religious involvement in politics.

Despite this the new right was influential because it provided the politicians of the **Republican Party**, or some of them at least, with a semi-official ideology differentiating them from the **Democratic Party** on grounds other than simply being the party of the richer and whiter. Right-wing think-tanks such as the Hoover Institution and the American Enterprise Institute developed policy options in considerable detail, especially in economic, foreign affairs and defence areas. In practice the new right was a product of the forces that swept Reagan into power, and was more symptomatic of the **Yuppie**-dominated self-interest politics of the 1980s than a cause of it. Even Reagan never fully satisfied the new right, though many exponents of such attitudes were given government positions. Eventually the inevitable **pragmatic** nature of American politics defeated the movement. A number of new right candidates, most notably Patrick Buchanan, have attempted to win the Republican nomination for the US presidential elections of the 1990s and 2000s, with no success, and although President George W. Bush embraced some policies which found favour with new right commentators, the movement was effectively marginalized within the US system.

New Social Movements

New social movements, often referred to simply as NSMs, have been an increasingly important topic in political sociology over the last 20 years. The label refers to loosely organized popular groups, usually of a protest nature, like British CND, various European anti-nuclear movements, or the more mass-based environmental and ecological protest organizations that now abound. The title is very widely used however, and movements as diverse as those for

animal welfare or gay rights have often been studied alongside more traditionally political movements. The importance of NSMs is that they appear to
be thriving at a time when orthodox political participation as measured by
membership in political parties and trade unions, or even voting, is declining in
most Western democracies. Social movements have always existed, of course,
and indeed the origins of many parties and unions lie in early social movements. Their new incarnations exhibit a number of differences from the earlier
versions, however. To start with, NSMs recruit those expressly disenchanted
with ordinary politics; they recruit predominantly from the educated and
affluent (often called the 'new middle classes'). They also espouse some
ideological characteristics in common, despite their various aims. They tend
to be more participatory, wishing to avoid the rise of bureaucratic élites within
their own organizations; they are all prepared to take, and many prefer, radical
action to further their aims, the preference is for street demonstrations, sit-ins,
occupations, even some degree of violence, rather than routine pressure-group
activities. They nearly all eschew parliamentary ambitions, seeking only to
force the state to adopt their specific policies, rather than to take power
themselves. It is almost part of the definition that an NSM will concentrate
on a single issue (although the issue may be broadly defined, as with environmental protest groups) rather than try to produce an overall ideology or
programme, as must be done by those wishing to be elected to government.

NSMs vary enormously in their influence and always risk having their
policies 'stolen' by orthodox parties who then weave solutions into their overall
programmes. In general there is a connection, albeit ill-defined, between the
rise of NSMs and the development of a post-materialist culture in Western
democracies.

New Thinking

'New thinking' was Soviet leader Mikhail **Gorbachev's** own label for his fresh
approach to the Soviet Union's foreign policy, which became particularly
apparent in his speech to the United Nations in December 1988, when he also
announced unilateral troop withdrawals from **Eastern Europe**. New thinking
had several applications, and was as much a carefully calculated diplomatic tool
as it was an extension of his internal reforming zeal to international politics. To
the West the most important aspect was the new willingness to be involved in
very far-reaching conventional **arms control** talks whereas, due to the
complexities of the nuclear weapons issue, the **Intermediate Nuclear Forces
(INF) Treaty**, signed almost exactly a year before, had made little effective
difference to the balance of force in Europe. For 15 unproductive years the
West had been looking for a serious preparedness by the Soviet Union to
reduce its conventional troops, and to do so disproportionately to make up for

the existing imbalance, through the Mutual and Balanced Force Reduction (MBFR) talks. By stressing the need to look completely anew at all East–West relationships, and to abandon stereotypical fears and expectations, Gorbachev was offering something really significant. By linking this speech to a surprise and unilateral troop reduction, he won considerable support in the West. His initiative led to swiftly concluded negotiations and the conclusion of the **Conventional Forces in Europe (CFE) Treaty** in 1990.

A second aspect of new thinking was equally attractive to the West, though it was primarily aimed at the Eastern European socialist states. This involved the abdication of the **Brezhnev** doctrine, propounded in 1968 to justify the Soviet invasion of Czechoslovakia, which asserted that national sovereignty was less important than socialist solidarity, and that other socialist states had the right to intervene and prevent one of their allies overthrowing communism. Gorbachev recognized the right of each Eastern European country to determine its own policy, and kept to this. Not only did he not try to stop liberalizing movements in countries like Poland, Czechoslovakia and Hungary, but he also did not attempt to force his own domestic policies of **perestroika** and **glasnost** on the more **Stalinist** states like East Germany. New thinking was without doubt the most successful area of Gorbachev's reforms and much facilitated, if it did not actually cause, the end both of the Soviet empire in Europe and of the **cold war** itself.

Nomenclatura

The nomenclatura, literally just a list of names, was a vital technique for ensuring the control of the **Communist Party of the Soviet Union (CPSU)** over all aspects of industry, administration and other branches of the state. At every level, from the town through the regions and republics to the Central Committee of the CPSU in Moscow, there was a series of posts which could only be filled with the approval of the equivalent level branch of the Communist Party. Only candidates whose names were on the nomenclatura for that level could be appointed to such posts. Although it was not necessary to be a party member to have one's name on the list, it was extremely unusual for any appointment above the most junior, at the most local level, not to be a party member in good standing. It was by no means easy to become a member of the party in the last few decades of communist rule, following a tightening of membership requirements after **Khrushchev's** laxer policies. Thus the party officials could rely on obedience from managers and administrators appointed to nomenclatura posts. Good party behaviour, as well as technical efficiency, was required to get on to the nomenclatura for the next rung in a professional career, ensuring tighter and tighter control by the party the more senior the post. Nomenclatura came to be a shorthand way of referring to a privileged élite network, to which counterparts could certainly be found in Western countries. One lasting consequence of the nomenclatura system will be that the vast bulk of those experienced enough to hold any demanding post in Russia, or other previously Soviet republics, will have been members of the party; even though the power of the CPSU had been broken almost everywhere, the new rulers were not able to dispense with the services of its past members. (See also **apparatchik**.)

Non-Governmental Organizations

Non-Governmental Organizations (NGOs) are typically thought to be entities like Oxfam or Amnesty International, but the term can also cover the National Society for the Prevention of Cruelty to Children (NSPCC, a major British NGO) or the American League of Women Voters. NGOs are private bodies, usually of a charitable nature and legal status, operating on a 'not for profit' basis to provide wide-ranging benefits for individuals or societies. They are sometimes seen as pressure groups, and indeed part of their activity will involve bringing public pressure on governments and international organizations to adopt their preferred policy. They are, however, much more than pressure groups because they take it upon themselves to achieve ends rather than merely try to influence the governmental provision of goods. The really large and international NGOs, such as Oxfam, have quite considerable budgets, almost entirely donated by the public; complex bureaucracies; and deep reservoirs of public support and trust. Indeed, NGOs are often are trusted more than governments and invariably more than any commercial organization because of public faith in altruism as their only motivation. The title, Non-Governmental Organization, comes from the **United Nations**, which needed some way of recognizing and giving access to a range of bodies other than the nation states which comprise its official membership. As a title, it is too broad, but it confers some legitimacy, and makes it easier for an NGO to operate in several different countries where there might be considerable resentment at the intrusion of an agency formally tied to another state. It is, for example, easier for a country to allow a team from Amnesty International to inspect conditions in its prisons than to allow another state, or even the UN itself, to do so. Because the NGO is, precisely, non-governmental, no precedent is set which allows future incursions on national sovereignty. There is a problem arising from the public's faith in the motives of NGOs, namely that they also seem to take on an authority that may not be appropriate. If an environmental lobby organization denounces government policy on pollution control, it is very hard for the government in question to establish its own credentials, because whatever it says it is always seen as suspect when compared with the apparently impartial and 'innocent' views of the NGO. Furthermore, NGOs inevitably concentrate on a single issue, with no responsibility for the impact that their undoubtedly good work in one policy area may have to resources or even policy plans in another area.

Many NGOs operate in a national, as opposed to the international, arena and are often partially involved with government. The NSPCC, for example, not only provides its own children's homes and child-care investigation activities, but it has statutory authority in some contexts. The rise to prominence of NGOs is in part due to the failure of governments to mobilize resources, but it goes also to the widespread distrust of the state in civil society, and to the inherently suspect nature of individual states acting at the international level. It is notable that many large NGOs have less trouble recruiting young professionals for their services than the national civil services, even though the financial rewards are very much less.

Non-Proliferation Treaty (NPT)

One of the early fruits of international attempts to limit the danger of nuclear warfare was the signing in 1968 of the Non-Proliferation Treaty. This was signed at the time by only three of the five then known nuclear powers, the United Kingdom, the USA and the Soviet Union, who undertook not to provide the technology for making nuclear weapons to those countries who had not already acquired it. The idea seems to have been that international instability was particularly likely to arise if a country not locked into the **superpower** strategic deterrence game was able to make such weapons. It seems also to have been thought that such a new nuclear power, especially if its principal adversary had not yet become nuclear, would be much more tempted to use the weapons than were the existing nuclear powers. The treaty was also available for signing by those non-nuclear powers who wished publicly to state that they would never seek to develop or purchase such technology.

It is unclear whether the treaty has or could have any effect. Not only did France and the People's Republic of China refuse, until 1992, to accord to the treaty, theoretically on the grounds that it discriminated too much in favour of those powers who were already nuclear, but the technology cannot easily be constrained. Apart from a real difficulty in distinguishing between peaceful, energy-producing nuclear technology and potentially warlike usage, the scientific mysteries are not so great, nor the secrecy so well enforced, that a medium-sized nation cannot develop a weapon quite unaided. Entirely non-alarmist estimates suggest, for example, that at least seven nations which were non-nuclear in 1968 are now nuclear, or could develop such weapons within five years of so deciding. These include Argentina, India, Pakistan, Brazil and Egypt, as well as Iraq, which is now known to have such a programme. Israel is, of course, a nuclear power and managed this with no overt help from any other nuclear power, although it is strongly believed that covert, and actually illegal, help was provided by citizens of at least one other nuclear state. Whether any breach of the treaty has been involved in this process is unknown. South Africa signed the NPT in 1991, thus effectively giving up its nuclear, or near-nuclear, capability. Unlike the test ban treaties of 1963 and 1974, and the **SALT** and Strategic Arms Reduction Talks (START) processes, the NPT can hardly be seen as demonstrating international goodwill, but seems instead to function almost entirely in the self-interest of the originating nations. Interestingly it has been generally accepted by experts, including Americans, that the Soviet Union had a better record for carrying out its obligations under the NPT than the USA. The entire idea of non-proliferation has changed its focus now that the primary fear is the acquisition of nuclear weapons by so called 'rogue nations' like Iraq, or by terrorist organizations. While established nation states may find it easier to agree to non-proliferation regimes under these circumstances, the widespread availability of redundant nuclear technology in the aftermath of the **cold war** makes the situation much harder to police.

Nozick

Robert Nozick (1938–2002), along with John **Rawls**, did more than anyone else to re-create and revive political theory in the Western post-war world. Like Rawls he based his approach on **liberalism** and a trenchant defence of inalienable rights which governments may not take away just because to do so might be for the aggregate public good (see **natural rights**). Also like Rawls, and inevitably for someone who takes this position, he was a vehement opponent of **utilitarianism** and its subdued but definite acceptance by nearly all political actors in the West.

Nozick, however, was very much more firm than Rawls in holding these positions and, because of the particular rights he holds most dear, was much more critical of the legitimacy of modern government and of typical Western **welfare state**/mixed economy policy. His main work, *Anarchy, State and Utopia* (1974), is still hotly debated and much written about. Nozick's theory had three main strands to it. The first was that it was totally individual-based, rejecting any idea that societies, states or collectives of any form could be the bearers of rights or owe duties; these could be legitimate only in so far that they were voluntary aggregations of individuals, and not just because they may, as a matter of fact, have made most or all members better off. The second, consequent on the first strand, was its approach to the political system, which was semi-anarchist in that Nozick regarded as legitimate only the very minimum state power necessary to uphold the prior existing rights of the individual citizens. The state should, for Nozick, be not much more than a police force, and he did, indeed, go to some length to explain why even this was necessary, and why private enterprise policing was not enough, in a society of free individuals. The third main strand was that Nozick's prime human right was the right to property; not only did he take an absolute line on the inviolability of property rights, but his actual theory of how they arose was a strict and limited one. Nozick's theory of property is often taken to be a reworking of John **Locke's** theory, without, as it were, God, because Locke used a theological justification in part. For Nozick, if somebody has a right to property, this can have come about in two ways: the property may have been acquired legitimately as an original act, or it may have been transferred by a legitimate process from someone else who had a legitimate entitlement. As long as any distribution of property is entirely covered by such rules, then the distribution is just, however inegalitarian it may be. Nozick stressed that the justice in a particular distribution of property rights arises from the historical processes that have given people entitlements, not from the consequences of monetary distribution.

One of the principal features of Nozick's theories was their rejection of most elements of the modern **welfare state**, on the basis that they contravened his belief in the absolute nature of property rights, no matter how inegalitarian. Nozick regarded the taxation inherent in redistributive societies, that is, any taxation above that needed to pay for the minimal state, as a form of forced labour. Perhaps few people outside of radical **libertarians** actually agreed with Nozick, but his arguments were mounted with such massive skill, and his analyses are so penetrating, that he commanded enormous influence and respect in the development of modern political theory, and he was certainly the foremost modern exponent of the libertarian position.

Nuclear Parity

Negotiations and treaties associated with processes such as **SALT** and Strategic Arms Reduction Talks (START) made necessary means of assessing the relative strengths of the strategic nuclear forces of the USA and the Soviet Union. No one measure can be very satisfactory, but taking the various measures together, it was clear by the early 1980s that the Soviet Union had redressed America's historic advantage, and achieved, at least, a state of parity. In terms of launchers, missiles, total equivalent megatonnage and throw-weight, the Soviet Union was probably ahead, though the USA retained a lead in actual number of warheads, and probably in the technology of targeting. The main fear of the USA was that the combination of accuracy and explosive power achieved by the Soviet Union might have given it the ability to destroy 90% of the land-based US **ICBMs**, while the USA could not do the same to the Soviet forces. The concern that nuclear forces were moving out of parity, exposing the USA to a 'window of vulnerability', threw doubt on much orthodox strategic thinking and policy-making in the USA. In particular, the long-established policy of backing **NATO's** weak conventional defence in Germany with the threat of central strategic nuclear warfare came to seem highly non-credible. This was one of the reasons why NATO began to make real, and ultimately successful, attempts to negotiate conventional force reductions from the mid-1980s, through the Conference on Security and Co-operation in Europe, now the **Organziation for Security and Co-operation in Europe (OSCE)**, culminating in the **Conventional Forces in Europe (CFE)** Treaty of 1990.

O

Official Secrets Act

The Official Secrets Act, originally passed by Parliament in 1911, is the main source of state control over secrecy and espionage in Britain. Compared with many Western nations it is very powerful, and can be used to protect sensitive information that the government of the day does not want disclosed, even though the information hardly challenges the security of the state. Once one has signed the Act, and this can be required before quite trivial information is disclosed, one is permanently bound by it. Lengthy prison sentences can be, and have been, handed down under the Act, and from time to time journalists engaged in quite proper investigative reporting are restricted by it. Since the 1970s it has become increasingly unpopular and discredited, and several parliamentary attempts have been made, unsuccessfully, to abolish or amend it. By contrast the USA not only has no equivalent of the Official Secrets Act, but in 1966 passed the Freedom of Information Act. Access to information in the USA is so much more open than in the UK that British journalists sometimes find it easier to discover what their own government is doing by reading American government documents. The UK's equivalent of a freedom of information act, legislated at the beginning of the 21st century is nowhere near as far-reaching as the American equivalent, and no liberalization of the Official Secrets Act is probable.

Oligarchy

Oligarchy is one of **Aristotle's** basic forms of government. His theory, the first ever, of **comparative government** distinguished forms of government along two dimensions, one dealing with how many people ruled a society, and the other with whether they acted in the public interest or in their own interest. Oligarchy, according to this schema, is the rule of a few, in their own interests. It contrasts on one dimension with **monarchy** (literally the rule of one) and **democracy**, and on the other with **aristocracy**, also referring to the rule of a few, but where the few are the best of the society ruling in the public interest. In general it connotes any level of political system ruled undemocratically, and primarily to serve their own interests, by a small group.

Ombudsman

An ombudsman is an officer of state appointed to provide an extra check on the rights of citizens against governmental action. The system, Scandinavian in origin, is not widely utilized, and in many places where versions have been introduced, has proved somewhat of a disappointment. In principle it enables a citizen who feels that they have been the victim of **maladministration** to make a complaint to the ombudsman's office. This office will, after ensuring the complaint is not malicious or trivial, call for evidence and files on the matter and investigate the fairness and justice of the administrative action complained against. Where evidence of maladministration is found to be convincing, a variety of remedies is provided. Sometimes no more can be done than the publication of a judgment to the effect of maladministration, though it is more likely that at least some form of financial redress will be given. Whether or not disciplinary or even legal proceedings will be taken against the offending administrator is not usually at the ombudsman's discretion.

Compared with some European countries, notably in Scandinavia, the United Kingdom has only relatively recent experience of such a system, and the USA none, at least at the federal level. In the UK the Parliamentary Commissioner for Administration, the equivalent officer, is not entitled to accept complaints direct from members of the public, but only on referral from a member of parliament, which represents a severe restriction of powers. More recently similar offices have been set up for complaints against local government administration, and very specific schemes operate inside, for example, the health service and the banking industry. Some countries have also experimented with ombudsmen for more circumscribed roles, especially to represent complaints by members of the military, where it is felt that there are serious inbuilt difficulties about appealing through normal military justice channels. Versions of these institutional ombudsmen now common in the UK are relatively more effective than is the national office. Eastern European countries have found them to be particularly useful during the initial stages of **democratic transition**.

Though there are clear advantages to the system, there is also a serious query about why traditional avenues of complaint, either through the courts or through elected representatives, should not be adequate. If in fact it is possible for an institutional check to be made on the activities of administrators and policy-makers, it is unclear why the older methods of so doing should fail. The biggest weakness of the generalized ombudsman is that of selecting a suitable incumbent. If an outsider to the institution being checked, they are unlikely to have adequate knowledge genuinely to assess the merits of a complaint, and if an insider, they are likely to be over-sympathetic to former colleagues.

One-Party State (see Single-Party System)

Opinion Poll

Opinion polls are measures of public attitude, on any sort of issue, carried out by professional polling organizations whose main business is usually in market research. In the **mass media** a typical opinion poll is a measure of the **voting** intention of the electorate, of how the voters rank politicians and parties, and of what preferences the electorate has among various policy alternatives; these polls are taken with increasing frequency and assume greater importance as an election approaches. The techniques of such polling are complex; essentially there are two aspects, sampling and questionnaire design. The most accurate and reliable sampling designs are seldom used for the sort of political opinion polls published in the media both because they are expensive, and because they cannot produce results as quickly as is often required. A typical opinion poll will have a sample of between 800 and 1,200 voters selected by a system known as 'quota sampling'. With this method interviewers are sent to perhaps 50 locations, usually parliamentary constituencies, which are chosen randomly. They are each required to interview a sample constructed according to gender, age and class to provide a cross-section of the population. Although accuracy increases with larger samples, it does not do so proportionately, so that doubling the size of a sample does not halve the margin of error. Any answer in a sample of 1,000 is liable to a margin of error of plus or minus 3%.

Questionnaire design is both more complex, and less calculable in its effects. It is known that the wording of a question can affect the probability of a particular answer being given considerably, but so can something as unpredictable as the ordering of questions. Great efforts are made to make the questionnaires as neutral as possible, but it is hard to be sure this has been achieved. During the last decades of the 20th century it began to be clear that election-time polls in the UK systematically under-measured Conservative strength in ways that could not be accounted for by sample design; instead there appeared to be a need further to refine question wording. It needs to be remembered that, although during an election the polls will be entirely about politics, regular monthly polls are often added to lengthy consumer attitude questionnaires designed for the advertising industry, with possible effects on responses.

As well as the question of accuracy, concern is often expressed about the possibility of the publication of polls actually changing voters' attitudes. There is some evidence that the publication of poll results does affect attitudes, through a variety of psychological factors. For example some people have a tendency to want to be on the winning side, and will shift their preference to a party, or policy position, which seems to be gaining support. Meanwhile, others polled may give misleading answers, for a variety of reasons. Academic surveys taken after elections regularly find more people claiming to have voted for whichever party won the election than can have been the case given the actual result. Because of this concern about artificially creating a result France has banned the publication of electoral polls during election campaigns, and similar demands have been made elsewhere. Despite these problems media public opinion polls have a fairly good record of reliability, especially when investigating clear cut issues, such as predicting the proportion of the vote which is likely to go to each party or candidate. What they are less good at predicting is the way regional variations, or the vagaries of **voting systems**, might affect the final result of an election. Political parties make increasingly extensive use of an alternative way of measuring public opinion, the use of 'focus groups'. These are small groups of selected voters who are invited to discuss issues at some length and depth. Although the results cannot be generalized to the whole population with the statistical accuracy that a large representative sample allows, they provide far more of an insight into why opinions are held and how they might be changed.

Opposition

An opposition is a political grouping, party or loose association of individuals who wish to change the government and its policies. In some democratic states the opposition has a formal position and is expected to present itself as an alternative government both by challenging the government's measures between elections and by offering itself as a potential governing party at an election. However, this really only makes much sense in a clear **two–party system**. In the United Kingdom the leader and some whips of the largest opposition party in both houses of parliament are given formal recognition by the granting of salaries; the role of the opposition is further acknowledged by its right to reply to major government statements both in parliament and through the media. Even systems which have no formal recognition of an opposition leader find it necessary at times to treat some politician as holding that post *de facto*; for example, after the US president's annual 'State of the Union' message, someone has to be given television time to reply, in the interests of political fair play. (It is usually the Senate leader of the opposition party, even though his party may have a majority in Congress). There have always been problems about the way the opposition should comport itself— cries are sometimes heard for the opposition to be 'responsible', that is, not to attack the government over some particular policy. Probably the famous Tory leader of the 19th century, Lord Randolph Churchill, had it right when he asserted, simply, that 'the duty of her majesty's opposition is to oppose.'

In **single-party systems** the opposition may exist as an underground movement, as in the past in the Soviet Union where no formal opposition to the **Communist Party of the Soviet Union (CPSU)** was permitted but dissidents continued to exist. Alternatively an opposition may engage in armed struggle as, for example, in El Salvador during the 1980s. Despite the high level of repression in many states it is rare to find no traces of opposition, albeit from individuals acting clandestinely.

Organization for Security and Co-operation in Europe (OSCE)

The OSCE opened, as the Conference on Security and Co-operation in Europe (CSCE), at the invitation of the Finnish government, in Helsinki in July 1973, producing the Helsinki Final Act signed by all participants in 1975. The original members included every European nation (except Albania) as well as the USA and Canada. With the increasing complexity of central and Eastern Europe, there were, by mid-1992, 53 member states, and the number could grow still further. The **Helsinki process** continued with follow-up meetings in Belgrade (1977–78), Madrid (1980–83) and Vienna (1986–89). In addition there have been several summit meetings of representatives of the member states. The CSCE originated in the **cold war** era, during which it produced largely meaningless agreements on civil rights and economic co-operation, became a vital part of the **arms control** process at the end of that period (see **Stockholm Declaration**), and emerged as a body of potentially great influence for the post-cold war world.

Although the CSCE had developed a very complex infrastructure, with commissions, permanent secretariats, regular meetings at different governmental levels and so on, the depth of its institutionalization was still at an early stage at the beginning of the 1990s; however, in 1991 a secretariat was established in Prague. The CSCE had ambitions to become the peace-keeping establishment for post-Soviet Europe. However, its doctrine was based on collective security, much as with the failed **League of Nations**, and it had neither military nor economic force of its own. Indeed, as it was most popular with the weaker European states, especially the former members of the **Warsaw Pact** and the newly-independent states of the former Soviet Union, it was peculiarly ill-adapted to exercise any serious control. The powerful European states preferred either to develop the Western European Union, to retain **NATO**, or to create new, Western-dominated institutions. Furthermore, there were alternative but much longer-established forums, such as the Council of Europe or essentially economic groupings like the **European Union (EU)**. The CSCE negotiated an agreement with NATO for the latter to provide forces for peace-keeping, but that was unlikely to be implemented except in circumstances where the latter's own Council would already be prepared to deploy force. In December 1994 the summit conference adopted the new name of OSCE in order to reflect the organization's changing political role and strengthened secretariat. The OSCE has been quite successful in providing a negotiating forum for all European countries while they are steadily absorbed into the longer-existing economic and military structures, and is particularly relied on by the Baltic states. However the possibility of a greatly enlarged EU and a similarly enlarged NATO seem likely to make the organization redundant.

Organization of African Unity (OAU)

The Organization of African Unity (OAU) was founded in 1963 to promote organized and coherent policies among the non-aligned African nations (see **neutralism**), and to help eradicate the remaining colonial traces in Africa. As a result its principal concerns have been with South Africa, and with Rhodesia (now Zimbabwe) between the Unilateral Declaration of Independence (UDI) in 1965 and independence in 1980. In neither of these areas, nor in dealing with conflicts between African states or inside them, has the OAU been particularly effective, although its record improved somewhat in the 1990s and early 2000s. The OAU was, for example, severely split over both the Angolan civil war and the secessionist Biafran civil war in Nigeria. The reliance of many African states on external powers, for example Angola and Ethiopia on the Soviet Union, and some previous French colonies on France, has been a major factor in restricting the effectiveness of the OAU. The termination of Soviet influence in the continent, together with the achievement of majority rule in South Africa, allowed the OAU a fresh start. For example, in 1991 a treaty on the creation of an African Economic Community was signed, and efforts to transform the Organization into an African Union, following the model of the **European Union** were renewed (the African Union was constituted in July 2001 and was expected to enter into effect one year later). Despite its increased political importance and improved performance as a regional arbiter, it remained ineffectual in some important respects—for example, when electoral fraud in Zimbabwe became a serious issue in 2002, it was the Commonwealth, not the OAU, which took the lead.

Organization of American States (OAS)

The Organization of American States is a regional association founded in 1948, but building on earlier pan-American associations dating from the 19th century, to foster peace, security and mutual understanding and co-operation among the nations of the western hemisphere. The overwhelming economic, political and military dominance of the USA in the western hemisphere limits the utility of the OAS as a vehicle for genuine regional co-operation, and this imbalance was not significantly altered by Canada becoming a member in 1990. While the USA has tended to view the OAS as a means of preserving security, in terms of US interests, in Latin America (see **Monroe Doctrine**), many of the other members would prefer to concentrate on regional economic and technical development. Most regional political initiatives of the OAS have probably had little influence on the behaviour of members, and that has been particularly true in the case of the USA. Although the US actions during the **Cuban missile crisis** in 1962 (Cuba's membership has subsequently been in suspension) and in the Dominican Republic in 1965 were genuinely supported by most OAS members, on other occasions the USA has acted in defiance of the OAS. For example, in 1982 while the OAS was urging a negotiated settlement between Argentina and the United Kingdom of the Falkland Islands dispute, the USA and Chile gave moderate logistical support to the UK; while the OAS was supporting the Contadora Group initiative for peace in Central America during the mid-1980s, the USA was continuing to provide the Contra guerrillas fighting the Sandinista government in Nicaragua with covert aid; and in 1989 the OAS criticized the US military intervention in Panama.

Original Position

There are two meanings to the idea of the original position, compatible with each other, but of different derivation. The original position is sometimes used by political theorists, especially those committed to a **social contract** approach, with the same meaning as the **state of nature** which existed before the creation of deliberate political institutions. More recently the term has become of considerable importance in US constitutional law, particularly associated with the arguments of Judge Robert Bork, the rejection of whose nomination to the Supreme Court by the Senate in 1987 highlighted the controversy over the original position thesis. In this context the thesis basically states that the words in the US Constitution, agreed upon during 1787, and understood as they would have been at the time, are the binding law of the USA unless specifically altered by a full constitutional amendment subsequently passed. If the words in the 1787 document are not clear enough, they must be interpreted 'restrictively', to import as little judicial initiative as possible.

The intention of the original position theorists is to reduce judicial activism, to prohibit the creation of citizen rights or governmental duties unless very clearly authorized by Congress or a constitutional amending process. Although it is obviously democratic to insist that non-elected judges do not have the right to invent law, original position theorists are obviously inherently conservative in saying that courts cannot interpret liberally to bring an 18th-century document up to date. Thus with a majority of original position adherents **abortion** would probably be banned, overturning the 1973 *Roe v. Wade* case. This would not be argued on the grounds that the 1787 document prohibited abortion, but that pro-abortion law is based on the 'right to privacy', and there is nothing in the US Constitution that overtly guarantees the right to privacy. Similarly capital punishment would be seen as legitimate because the operative clause in the constitution, which prohibits 'cruel and unusual punishments', could not have been meant to ban the death penalty because, at the time, it was very usual, and not seen as cruel. Few commentators think the original position to be anything more than a cover for nakedly right-wing policy preferences, but constitutional lawyers nevertheless have difficulty denying the force of some of its theoretical basis. It remains an important position in American judicial thought, and the slow move of the Supreme Court towards the right with a succession of Republican nominations may return it to the front line of constitutional politics.

Overkill

Overkill is a concept in strategic theory, relating to nuclear warfare. It means a situation where one or more nations have so much nuclear weaponry that, whatever the enemy may do, they can guarantee to destroy the enemy's country totally and still have unused capacity. Alternatively it can mean that the combined nuclear capacity of the major states would serve to destroy the entire world and still not be used up. More figuratively it has come to mean using or threatening any force or political option which is stronger than is necessary or appropriate in the context. One might thus use 'overkill' in threatening an irritating neighbour more dramatically than was necessary to stop them doing something you dislike. It arises as an important concept because of the way **arms races** can lead to further and further build-up of forces beyond any rationally-needed level.

P

Pacifism

Pacifism is not a particular political doctrine, but the general belief that all war is morally unacceptable, and that there are no adequate justifications for using violence or physical force in pursuit of any end, political or otherwise. Although such beliefs obviously have existed throughout history, it is probable that only in the current and two previous centuries have they been at all widespread, organized, or come to be associated particularly with certain political positions. In part the reasons for this are historically accidental, because warfare for most of the post-medieval period, until especially the world wars, was largely confined to small and professional military forces. Conscription, practised extensively in continental European armies in the 19th century, and by all important nations during one or both of the world wars, made it hard for those with pacifist beliefs to avoid military service. Hence it became both necessary and possible for the collective exposition of the doctrine to develop.

Various other factors have been influential, for example the abandonment by Christian Churches, for example, of theological arguments that made the notion of a **just war** easy to promulgate, and the sheer horror of the First World War which persuaded many who experienced it afterwards to support the various peace movements that were formed. An important political reason for the wider spreading of pacifism was the analysis of the causes of war suggested by much anarchist and left-wing thought, and especially by **Marxism**. From this political position wars between nations are entirely prompted by the selfish economic aspirations of the ruling capitalist élites, but the only people to suffer in them are the exploited proletariats of both sides. Thus international communism, with the notion of fraternal bonding between workers of all countries, produces both the idea that the proletariat should unite against warmongering capitalists and an atmosphere conducive to pacifism.

The increasingly liberal politics of Western democratic nations, with an emphasis on **civil liberties**, has provided a context in which a genuine pacifist claim cannot be ignored. So, for example, the conscription laws in Germany allow those with an objection to war to serve in a non-combatant role. An additional factor that has increased the attraction of pacifism for many has been the threat that nuclear war, and perhaps any war fought with modern technology, threatens the ecological safety of the entire world. Despite this, pacifism occupies an unusual political position as an idea respected and protected but almost completely ignored by governments. Were pacifism ever to become sufficiently popular actually to restrict war-making capacity, it is likely that it would also cease to be a protected minority view.

Papacy

The papacy is not only the Pope himself, but also the administrative organization, the *curia*, through which the Roman Catholic Church both directs its operations for its estimated 1,100 million members world-wide, and conducts political and diplomatic business with governments and non-religious institutions. For the latter the papacy relies on the fact that the small precinct of inner Rome where the church has its headquarters, the Vatican City, is recognized universally as an independent state with full diplomatic status. The current existence of this papal state is a product of a long and complicated historical process in Italy. From medieval times until the 18th century the papacy had controlled large areas scattered throughout Italy, and run them just as any other local feudal lord. Indeed the revenues from these papal states were the main income for the church. With the rise of the various city states of northern Italy, the impact of the Napoleonic invasions and the creation of small monarchies in other, mainly southern, parts of the peninsula, the papal states were steadily diminished. The *Risorgimento*, the process which eventually led to the unification of Italy under a single monarchy in 1870, finally forced the papacy back to part of Rome and a few small holdings in neighbouring territories. It was under the fascist dictator Benito **Mussolini** that the position of the Vatican City was formalized. Mussolini, though opposed to the church, needed its acquiescence to his rule because of the powerful hold **Roman Catholicism** still retained over the population. The Lateran Treaty of 1929 recognized the sovereignty of the papacy over the Vatican City and paid compensation to the Church for the lands it had lost in the Risorgimento. The Concordat of the same year made Roman Catholicism the state religion of Italy, and awarded it various other privileges. Although in some ways it is absurd to treat the Vatican City as a real state, it has proved extremely useful to many nations to behave as though it were one. Over 60 nations have diplomatic missions to the papacy, and the Vatican appoints its own ambassadors (apostolic pro-nuncios) to many. From time to time the papacy can act in an international political context by assisting in negotiations where normal governmental and diplomatic contacts would be mistrusted. As the central directing organization of by far the largest

Christian denomination in the world, especially large (and growing) in the **Third World**, the Vatican and its various bureaucracies is in some ways an enormously powerful international body, as well as being an extremely rich one, despite past problems with its own merchant bank. To have such an organization headquartered in the capital of any one country without formal political independence would be potentially extremely dangerous, hence the general preparedness to treat the Vatican as a genuine state.

Paramilitary Forces

Paramilitary forces are those uniformed, armed and disciplined bodies that exist in most countries to carry out internal security and policing functions which are beyond the capacity of ordinary **police** forces. Frequently the boundaries between what would be considered an ordinary police force and a paramilitary force are very blurred. Nevertheless, most countries have found it necessary to retain a force to cope with, for example, serious rioting and disorderly demonstrations, equipped for and allowed to use greater force than even police forces that are normally armed. Such forces are usually trained in a very different way, have no responsibility for the day-to-day police work that requires some degree of acceptability by the citizens, and are often under a different political command structure than the civilian police. In France, for example, the *gendarmerie* is the nation-wide paramilitary police and quite separate from either the local or national police, and comes under the authority of the minister of defence, rather than the ministers of justice or the interior; in Germany the police function is constitutionally the responsibility of the *Länder*, but the federal government has created a paramilitary border police force under the authority of the federal interior ministry which not only does that job, but acts as a mobile and heavily-armed riot police. Theoretically at least, the United Kingdom has no such force, but this would not invariably be seen, even by liberals, as necessarily a protection against the use of undue force; either the police force would have to jeopardize its relationship with the public by using greater than usual force, or the regular army would have to be deployed, to control widespread outbreaks of disorder (see **aid to the civil power**). As the traditional role of the military in the West declines with the ending of the **cold war**, the armed forces in many countries are, in fact, trying to stress their own utility in such situations, so the distinction between paramilitary and military may well become eroded.

The political/constitutional heritage of a country has much to do with the presence or absence of such forces. In the UK, Canada, the USA and Australasia there has always been a very considerable fear of centralized police authority, indeed of police power at all, and a heavily armed and centrally controlled paramilitary force would never have been accepted because of the power it would give to the executive. Nevertheless this constitutional position has not entirely removed the need for the function to be fulfilled, and there are those who would wish to argue that the Royal Canadian Mounted Police, the National Guard in the USA and perhaps the Special Patrol Groups of British police authorities are little different, and scarcely preferable, to fully-fledged paramilitary forces. Whatever institutional arrangement is made to cope with it, the problem of public order policing is endemic, and as both police and public dislike the role being fulfilled by ordinary police forces, the argument for a special force is very powerful.

Pareto

Vilfredo Pareto (1848–1923) was the most important of the Italian political sociologists called the 'New Machiavellians' who started the power **élitism** school of analysis of modern societies, which developed, via the work of people like **Schumpeter** and **Dahl**, into modern **pluralism**. Pareto, who was at least as famous as an economist, attached especial importance to the fact, as he saw it, that the bulk of human behaviour was essentially non-rational, though justified and explained by rationalizations, myths and ideologies stemming from instinctual drives. These basic drives, common to all societies and all times, which he called 'residues', are masked by the justifying myths, 'derivations', but are the real source of social patterns, rather than the apparent **ideology** of a society.

In a theoretically complex way Pareto links this general proposition about human behaviour to a thesis about the structure of power in a society. According to him all societies have been, and always will be, ruled by a small élite governing in their own interest (see **oligarchy**), and keeping the masses in order either, depending on the nature of their 'residues', by force or by guile. These élites arise originally because political talents, just as much as intellectual or musical talents, are unequally distributed in a population. However, a governing élite naturally wishes to bequeath its position to its offspring, and élites regularly erect entry barriers against those who, though from the masses, have the capacity to govern. Over time the natural inequalities of talent in the population produce a revolutionary leadership among the lower classes of greater capacity (and greater preparedness to use force) than the ailing ruling class, and the latter is overthrown. It is replaced though by the new 'élite', which will eventually suffer the fate of its victims. This theory, which has surface resemblances to the views of **Marxism** on the class struggle, has been termed the 'circulation of élites'.

Although no one would accept the often curious details of Pareto's theory nowadays, the basic ideas, and the need to combine both a theory of ideology

367

and a theory of social structure to explain power distribution, are common to most subsequent work in the field.

Parliament

A parliament is in general a consultative assembly whose permission may or may not constitutionally be required for the formal passage of binding legislation. The word itself is mainly of English usage, where other languages are liable to use a version of the word simply meaning **assembly**. Most parliaments are nowadays elected assemblies with the duty of checking, controlling and sometimes electing the **executive** power. Their structures can vary, the essential choice being either bicameral or unicameral. A bicameral parliament (the norm in the Anglo-American world) will often have a separate basis for selection for the two 'houses' or chambers of parliament, and will usually have somewhat different powers for the two. A very common difference, for example, is the sole right of the 'lower' house to initiate bills that result in taxation. The selection procedure for the lower house (in the United Kingdom the House of Commons, in the USA the House of Representatives, in Germany the Bundestag) is usually the more clearly democratic. Thus the upper house in the UK, beginning a process of reform at the start of the 21st century, is the House of Lords, entirely unelected. The US Senate is elected on a basis of equal representation for each state, rather than of equally populated electoral districts, and Canadian senators are appointed by the governor-general on the recommendation of the prime minister (see **second chambers**).

Historically in Europe the development of democracy over the centuries has been largely the growth of power of parliament over the **monarchy**, and of the lower house over the upper. One can still see similar processes at work in other institutional contexts, an obvious one being the striving for power of the European Parliament over other institutions of the **European Union**. When the Eastern European countries started the process of **democratic transition** after the collapse of communism, they all opted for powerful parliaments rather than strong presidencies.

Parliamentary Government

Parliamentary government is a system of government in which the **executive** is responsible to an **assembly** or **parliament** which may be constituted by **election**—as has increasingly been the case in the 20th century—or by nomination by some wider body. These parliaments perform many functions, but in most their primary purpose is to legislate both in the sense of scrutinizing the detail of laws and in that of authorizing or legitimizing the passage of laws. Much attention is also given to parliament's right to supervise and control public expenditure; indeed, the powers of the original parliaments stemmed from the right to grant the executive money. Out of this power has developed the more general parliamentary functions of oversight of the executive, the role of representing individuals, groups and classes in any conflicts with the executive, and the use of parliament as a forum in which issues of the day may be debated. Most versions of parliamentary government make use of a **committee** system to consider the details of legislation and of the budgetary process.

The balance between these functions varies between countries just as the effectiveness of parliamentary government varies between political systems. Implicit in the very idea of parliamentary government, however, is the notion that the executive will not exercise power arbitrarily and will take parliament's views into account as being representative of the views of the people (see **accountability**). In most systems of parliamentary government the elections to the **legislature** determine the political character of the government, but in some systems where the **voting system** frequently produces no clear parliamentary majority there may be scope for discretion on the part of the monarch or **president** in forming a government to reflect the composition of the parliament. Normally governments must maintain the **confidence** of parliament to stay in power, although how this is interpreted varies from system to system.

In most parliamentary systems the members of the executive or ministers sit in parliament, thus making their accountability more direct; in France, however, a curious hybrid system operates so that, while ministers may run for parliamentary seats, if they become members of the government they do not sit within the National Assembly or Senate but are replaced by deputies nominated to substitute for them in the event of their appointment as a minister or member of the Constitutional Council, or of their death.

Parliamentary Socialism

The doctrine of parliamentary socialism, that radical reform of capitalist societies, along socialist lines, could be achieved only by legitimate power gained through electoral victory is linked with ideas like **gradualism**, and was seen by many socialist and Marxist thinkers as **revisionism**, as selling out to the capitalist powers. In the United Kingdom parliamentary socialism, though effectively always part of the **Labour Party's** assumptions, was most effectively argued by the **Fabians**, and opposed by left-wing elements of the trade unions and radical groups such as the Independent Labour Party. The radical argument against parliamentary socialism is, roughly, that taking part in the ordinary process of electoral politics perverts the socialist drive of activists. Putting too much energy into moderate policy-making in order to win a few more votes from non-radical voters means that the party ceases to be a real representative of the working classes. It is also often claimed that a process of 'co-option' takes place, in which the socialist leaders are taken to the heart of the ruling class, given authority and privilege, and cease to understand, or really care for, their working-class constituents. Once a socialist becomes a member of a parliament or government they tend to have more in common with fellow parliamentarians and government members than with their party's mass support; in technical political science this thesis is known as the **iron law of oligarchy**. Another line of argument against parliamentary socialism is that the problems of capitalist economies simply cannot be solved by legislation, which can only tinker symptomatically with problems, and that what is required is a total **revolution**. Some socialists have assumed an intermediary position of supporting parliamentary activity, but urging that as soon as a socialist majority took power it should pass an enabling act, abolishing the entire system and giving the government authority to make all necessary law. Supporters of parliamentary socialism rely on the argument that in a democracy there is no choice but to follow the established rules, because the masses will otherwise not give their support. They believe that the process of fighting elections, even if it means a long series of defeats, is the only effective way of educating the electorate out of their **false consciousness**. A version of this thesis, derived by **Gramsci**, was responsible for transforming the Italian Communist Party from a revolutionary movement into a reformist parliamentary party. The effective collapse of more moderate socialism in Western politics may, ironically, renew interest in this more extreme version which has no need to be electorally competitive with centrist parties and can attract all those who despair of consensual politics.

Parti Communiste Français (PCF)

The Parti Communiste Français was formed in 1920 when the majority of the SFIO, the French Socialist Party (see **Parti Socialiste**), left to form a communist party modelled on the **Communist Party of the Soviet Union (CPSU)**. For most of its history, and certainly well into the **Fifth Republic**, it was one of the most **Stalinist** communist parties in the West (see **Eurocommunism**). It was, however, electorally very popular until the mid-1970s. During the **Third Republic** it joined in the **popular front** electoral alliance that won the general elections in 1936, thus preventing a collapse of the republic into what had threatened to be a bitter clash between French fascists and the left. Significantly it only entered this alliance because **Stalin**, hoping to divert the threat from Nazi Germany away from the Soviet Union, had called for communists everywhere to unite with other left-wing groups. During the war the PCF went underground and formed a vital part of the resistance movement, though as often as not fighting the other, **de Gaulle**-inspired or Catholic, wings as well as the Germans. After the allied invasion in 1944 elements of the party tried to seize power in the south of France. Though invited into the post-war government under de Gaulle it rapidly withdrew rather than be tarnished with helping the US-backed French bourgeoisie. In the immediate post-war elections the PCF received over 25% of the vote, later settling to a level between 20% and 25%. Also during this period the party started to cast off some of its Stalinism and to lose its revolutionary fervour; at the time of the 1968 disturbances in Paris it exercised tight control on its members and refused to see the situation as having any revolutionary potential. This increasing moderation, however, culminating in 1976 when the party officially abandoned the doctrine of the **dictatorship of the proletariat**, did it no electoral good. Steadily its votes slipped away to the newly united Parti Socialiste which had developed out of a mess of small splinter groups fighting an internecine war. Though the PCF tried to counter this by alliances with the socialists, they could not quite accept the degree of policy modification required, and their best hope for power, the common programme between the two parties, collapsed just before the 1978 National Assembly elections, allowing the right to win yet again. By the 1981 presidential elections the PCF had come to see a possible victory for the socialists as their biggest danger, but the trend continued, and both the presidential election and the ensuing Assembly election were won by the Socialists. Although they were given four places in the Fifth Republic's first left-wing coalition government, formed after the general election held in the wake of François **Mitterrand's** presidential election victory, this arrangement lasted only until 1984, and even then was often characterized by acrimony. Subsequently their decline accelerated, so that by the late 1980s they had been surpassed as a force in French politics by the far-right Front National, and their level of public support had generally fallen beneath 10%. In the 2002 presidential election the PCF candidate received just 3.4% of the first-round votes cast, less than several other far-left candidates. The collapse of communism in Eastern Europe and the Soviet Union effectively removed the PCF's last source of legitimacy and there seemed little prospect of its being able to arrest its decline and exert significant political influence in the future.

Parti Socialiste

The French Socialist Party is, in its current form, a relatively new creation. Originally created in 1905 by a merger of two socialist parties, and inspired by the Second International (see **international socialism**), it was called simply the Section Française de l'Internationale Ouvrière (SFIO—French Section of the Workers' International). In 1920 the majority of the SFIO left the organization to form the **Parti Communiste Français (PCF)**, and for most of the next 50 years the latter was the dominant left-wing party in France, although it only participated in government in the immediate post-war period. The SFIO formed a part of the government much more often, and one of its leaders, Guy Mollet, was actually prime minister, in 1956–57, of the longest-lived **Fourth Republic** government.

The electoral dominance of the **Gaullists** and Independent Republicans, on the right and in the centre, during the first two decades of the **Fifth Republic** made clear the need for a **realignment** of the left (see **French party system**). First, in 1965, the SFIO joined with Radical Socialists and the Convention of Republican Institutions (CIR), whose leader was François **Mitterrand**, to form the Federation of the Democratic and Socialist Left (FGDS); Mitterrand became its president. In the 1965 presidential elections, when Mitterrand was the candidate of the FGDS, and at National Assembly elections in 1967, the new alliance appeared to be making electoral progress, before the Paris uprising of students and workers in May 1968 led to a set-back in the following month. Certainly the intention of the SFIO was to create a new and united democratic socialist party, but when the new Parti Socialiste was actually established, in 1969, Mitterrand's CIR did not join. Eventually, however, in 1971, the CIR became part of the Parti Socialiste, and Mitterrand became its first secretary. The new party spent most of the 1970s engaged in electoral co-operation with the PCF, even signing a common programme with them in 1972, and this alignment very nearly gave Mitterrand, as candidate for virtually the whole of the French left, victory over Valéry Giscard d'Estaing in the 1974 presidential election. By the mid-1970s the Parti Socialiste had clearly overtaken the PCF in popularity, and the stresses caused by this contributed to the communists breaking off co-operation just before the assembly elections of 1978, almost certainly preventing the left from gaining an assembly majority.

The Parti Socialiste continued to grow, and increasingly has come to resemble a party from the tradition of European **social democracy**. Meanwhile the electoral popularity of the PCF plummeted. In 1981 and 1988 Mitterrand won presidential election victories, and during the 1980s the Parti Socialiste was only out of government for the two years of the socialist president's **cohabitation** with a centre-right government. In the early 1990s, with the Parti Socialiste under threat from renewed electoral co-operation between the Gaullist Rassemblement pour la République and the Giscardian Union pour la Démocratie Française, much interest within the party focused on the succession to the ageing Mitterrand. The party did return to power later in the 1990s, but existed in a system of 'cohabitation' with a Gaullist president, Jacques Chirac. In what was seen by many as a humiliation, its candidate in the presidential election of 2002, the incumbent prime minister, Lionel Jospin, was beaten into third place in the first ballot by Chirac and the candidate of the far-right Front National, Jean-Marie Le Pen. In the early years of the 21st century, the party was suffering from the problem of all European left-wing parties —how much of its past ideology must it shed to compete in a world where social democracy seems to have had its day? The problem is particularly acute in France which is culturally much less willing to give up high levels of public investment and an economically powerful centralizing state than Europe's more successful economies.

Participatory Democracy

Participatory democracy is really an alternative label for **direct democracy**, although it does also involve a slight element of what is normally regarded as an opposite of the latter, that is **representative democracy**. The point is that participation need not necessarily carry the implication of ultimate decision-making power. Thus one can argue for a much greater degree of citizen participation in a political system while accepting that the ultimate decision-making and law-creating functions must be handled by a small body of elected representatives. Widespread use of public enquiries, advisory referendums, consultative bodies and similar devices can increase the degree to which ordinary people participate in the forming of policy. (See also **industrial democracy**.)

Party

A party, in political terms, is an organized group of people sharing common policy preferences and usually a general ideological position. Simply to have such a common view does not make the group a party—it is necessary also that it seeks, or has, political power. The historical derivation of the concept is complex, and 'party' has not always had the innocent sense it has now. Originally, to say of a group that it was a party was to suggest that it selfishly pursued its own collective interest, and that by existing and working towards power it destroyed a true latent unity of interest and opinion in society. Political parties in the sense we know them now did not become important until the extension of the **franchise** to large sections of the population. A typical development was for a party, previously existing merely as a group of like-minded men in parliament, to organize nationally in the hope of attracting the newly enfranchised voters and keeping their elective power; in the United Kingdom, to give a much simplified example, the Tories developed into the **Conservative Party** and Whigs into the **Liberal Party**. Alternatively a party may have been organized from the grass roots to seek the election of representatives of the newly enfranchised interests to the legislature (for example, the British **Labour Party**). These two basic modes of parliamentary party are often distinguished as 'cadre' parties and 'mass' parties. They represent no more than ideal types, and there are still examples of competitive parties with virtually no mass organization at all—just as there are mass parties which are really only loose coalitions of separate interests, groups or regions with no central agreement on policy.

The fighting of elections is not the only reason for the organization of political parties—the idea of a revolutionary party is an obvious example. Here, though, the aim is still to seek power, if by different means, just as in a **single-party system** a party, while not competing for power, still exists to wield it. Some parties form with little real expectation of winning power or even gaining seats because fighting elections, with the attendant publicity, is a good way of promoting a cause. If their advocacy of the cause through political channels proves popular, an existing and successful party may adopt similar policies; this has clearly happened in several countries where Green parties exist (see **environmentalism**). Such single issue campaigns, however, can only be regarded as belonging to a party, rather than a **pressure group**, if they are accompanied by a general **programme** for government.

Party List System

By far the simplest method of ensuring that parties in an elected body receive **proportional representation** is to count votes for them on a national or regional basis. Either the entire country can be treated as one constituency (as in Israel and the Netherlands), or large multi-member constituencies can be used (as used to be the case in Italy until its political reforms in 1992—see **Italian Second Republic**). In the simplest terms, the number of votes cast for a party is divided by the total number of votes cast, and this proportion of the seats to be filled is allocated to the party from a list of candidates submitted by the party and ranked in the order that the party wishes them to be elected. However, as the mathematics of this procedure will not produce precise numbers of seats, various methods of dividing up the total vote and allocating the remainder may be used. A variety of sequences of divisors exist, the object being to ensure that each candidate elected receives as nearly as is possible the same number of votes. However, it will always be true that the greater the number of seats in the constituency, and the higher the number by which the parties' votes are being divided, the more proportional the representation will be, and the more likely it will be that candidates of smaller parties will be elected. Alternatively a quota may be set, again using a variety of rules, and seats be allocated according to the multiples of that quota achieved by each party; the seats which are left after this procedure can be allocated according to the remainder votes, which may mean seats going to small parties which did not even reach the quota for a single seat. While approaching entire proportionality for the parties, the method can give undue power to the party élite which controls the ordering on the list, and removes the ability of voters to express any preference for particular candidates. Also, a major aspect of **representative democracy** is weakened the further away from single-member constituencies the system moves. Variations of the list system can ameliorate these problems, and allow some degree of voter choice for individual candidates.

Perestroika

Perestroika was one of the two main elements of Soviet leader Mikhail **Gorbachev's** original plans for wide-ranging reform in the then Soviet Union, along with **glasnost**. Technically perestroika simply means 'restructuring', but it rapidly took on extra ideological meaning. The proposal for perestroika was made in January 1987 at a meeting of the **Communist Party of the Soviet Union (CPSU)** Central Committee, and combined plans for both economic reorganization and some limited democratization, mainly in local government. These were linked, because the **politburo** had been convinced by Gorbachev that the reason earlier attempts at economic reform had not worked was the absence of grass roots level democracy. Thus even at the industrial level perestroika was essentially political, requiring, for example, the election of factory managers by the workers. More directly political, a limited degree of choice was to be allowed to voters in local elections, where they would now be given a choice of candidates, though they would all still be nominated by the CPSU. The important point is that perestroika was, initially, a plan to reform the existing economic system of state control, and not to replace it, so policies were aimed at increasing the incentives to operate the current system more efficiently. Perestroika was extended, in theory, to all state organizations. The Soviet military, for example, was called upon to apply perestroika, though as democracy is incompatible with military authority it was never very clear what they were supposed to do. In general, perestroika was what a Western manager would think of as an efficiency drive. The CPSU itself was supposed to become more democratic, although this did not mean, even to Gorbachev, that it should cease to be an all-pervading controlling force. Even these very moderate reforms were hotly contested by many inside the Politburo and the Central Committee, and it is unclear how effective they were, or ever could have been, in the industrial and administrative structures. It is hard to know how far the coverage of the term perestroika should be stretched, but it was certainly not originally intended to imply the much more far-reaching democratization of the political system that finally led to the disintegration of the Soviet Union. In contrast to glasnost, which proved unstoppable, perestroika achieved very little. The modernizations to the Soviet industrial and institutional systems with which perestroika sought to solve the problems which had allowed its own acceptance were proved to have been too little, and to have been introduced too late.

Plato

Plato (*c.*427–347 BC) is one of the earliest great philosophers and political thinkers in the Western tradition, and his works represent the major inheritance by Western political thought from the classical period. In some ways this is ironic; the usual image of classical Greek politics, or certainly the image of what was best about it, is of Athenian **participatory democracy**. Plato, however, was fiercely opposed to **democracy**, and his most important political writing, known to us as the *Republic*, is in part a vicious attack on it and a lengthy and subtle philosophical justification for rule by a small intellectual élite (see **aristocracy**). Other important works, notably *The Laws*, are blueprints for just such a society, which he hoped would stimulate the founding of new non-democratic Greek colonies. Indeed the Greek society Plato most admired was Sparta, the traditional authoritarian enemy of Athens.

Plato's reasons for opposing Athenian democracy can be analysed on at least two levels. For one thing he came himself from an aristocratic family. More important, certainly in his own eyes, was a distaste for the excesses of demagogically influenced masses arising from the execution by the democratic assembly of his friend and hero, Socrates, on a fallacious charge (according to Plato, anyway) of corrupting public morals. At the more theoretical level Plato opposed democracy because of certain conclusions he drew about the capacity of humanity to understand, and therefore follow, the good life. Briefly, human intellectual capacity is not at all equally distributed; knowledge of moral good is just as much dependent on this capacity as knowledge of any skill; indeed 'ruling' is just another skill or trade, as only the very most able are capable of seeing moral and political truth properly, and hence only they (Plato called them 'philosopher kings') should have political power. The theory is subtle and rich, and argues for the rule of the philosopher kings on many dimensions, all infused with very complex general philosophical views. He has been seen by some modern critics as tremendously right wing, even as some sort of precursor to **fascism** or other forms of **totalitarianism**, but this is crudely to abstract a powerful and complicated thinker from his context in a quite meaningless way. Plato is now among the most studied of political thinkers, and certainly is nowadays more influential than his successor, **Aristotle**, though this was not always so, for the medieval rediscovery of classical civilization really started with Aristotle, whose views were powerfully formative on the political thought of medieval Christianity (see **Aquinas**).

Perhaps the most alien element in Plato's thought is not the undemocratic constitution he advocates, but the way he sees the whole role of the state. To Plato (and here Aristotle followed him) the purpose of the state is to enforce decent living, actively to encourage a morality and religion, rather than to satisfy the demands of the population or even just to keep law and order to allow freedom. For this reason his philosophical arguments about the nature of goodness and our capacity to perceive it are not so much dismissed, as simply not seen as relevant when a modern thinker of almost any political persuasion considers his constitutional arguments.

Plebiscitory Democracy

Plebiscites are **referendums**, a system for allowing the whole of an electorate directly to give their opinion on some political question. The most successful and long-term experience is that of Switzerland, where a host of ordinary policy questions are routinely put to the electorate, following a tradition dating to the 16th century. They have been used in a variety of contexts in modern politics. One quite common use has been to hold a plebiscite for the population of a territory over which two countries have rival claims to sovereignty. Alternatively referendums are used to discover public attitudes to constitutional changes, as in the United Kingdom in 1975 (over retaining membership of the European Communities—EC, now the **European Union, EU**), and twice (in 1979 and 1997) in Wales and Scotland over **devolution**. It is generally agreed still that the UK cannot undertake constitutional reform without such action. Not only were referendums held to legitimize Scottish and Welsh devolution, but the proposal to join the EU's common currency is thought to require a referendum. Some countries, including Australia, Denmark and Ireland, require a referendum to be held on any constitutional amendment; in the cases of the last two, this quite frequently entails a referendum being held to endorse EU legislation. Many issues of policy at local or state levels are frequently decided in this way in the USA. The idea that a country might be governed extensively by the use of plebiscites on ordinary policy issues is attractive to some, because it seems to be a way of avoiding the disadvantages of **representative democracy** without the impracticalities of **direct democracy**.

To others, however, plebiscitory democracy has often seemed extremely dangerous. A principal argument against extensive use of referendums is that much depends on the specific framing of the question. The proportion of an electorate supporting some proposal can be crucially dependent on exactly what alternative they are offered on a ballot paper. An experiment carried out in the UK in 1975 by a public **opinion poll**, using a variety of questions about staying in the EC on different samples, produced very widely varying proportions supporting retention of membership. This appears to give far too much power to the political leaders who set the options, and leads on to a fear of manipulation of an electorate by an unscrupulously demagogic political leadership. The most recent serious example of the use (or misuse) of frequent referendums to support a political leadership was President Charles **de Gaulle's** tendency to put carefully structured options to the French electorate, backing his own preference with threats to resign were the country not to support him. Some countries have tried to protect the referendum as a tool by making some neutral body—in the Italian case the **constitutional court**, responsible for authorizing the use of a referendum and the wording of the options given.

A refinement of plebiscitory democracy which carries fewer dangers is the **initiative**, whereby a certain proportion of the electorate may trigger a referendum on a certain issue. This mechanism is most used at the local and regional levels, almost half of the US states make provision for it, and it may also be used at the national level in, for example, Italy and Switzerland. General demands for increased popular participation in government seem likely to extend the use of all forms of plebiscitory democracy.

PLO

The Palestine Liberation Organization was originally one of a series of political and activist groups that arose from the plight of the Palestinians expelled from their land when the State of Israel was formed. These refugees settled in UN-organized camps in most neighbouring countries, but especially in Jordan and Lebanon. Originally the hopes of the Palestinians were either for resettlement in Arab countries, or for the Arab League to win back for them their original homeland. After the Israeli defeat of Arab, and especially Syrian and Egyptian, forces in the **Arab–Israeli conflicts** of 1956 and 1967 they lost all such hope. Various groups were created to try, in their different ways, either through political negotiation or through **terrorist** tactics, to find a solution. The two most important were the Fatah organization (the Palestine National Liberation Movement), founded in 1957, and the PLO itself, founded in 1964. Fatah, as a militant terrorist organization, insisted on violent means, especially through trying to make alliances with the left-wing Muslim co-religionists in Lebanon against the richer urban Christians. It appears that the revolutionary and terrorist tactics of Fatah were influenced by the way the Algerian anti-colonial fighters had forced out the French in the early 1960s. The PLO, led by Ahmad Shukairi, a diplomat who had worked in Syria, took a much more peaceful line. As the diplomatic solution systematically failed to win the West away from supporting Israel, it lost credibility, and the masses of Palestinians in the camps swung behind Yasser Arafat, who combined Fatah and other extremist organizations with the PLO itself, under his own leadership, in 1968.

Following a series of bitter reverses, in particular the loss of Jordanian territory on the West Bank (of the River Jordan, regarded as an important part of the Palestinian 'homeland') during the Six-Day War of 1967, the PLO effectively sought to take over the Jordanian state. Jordan had welcomed, and indeed benefited, from Palestinian refugees, and it seemed a suitable society to become the new Palestinian homeland. King Hussein, however, finally lost patience with the demands of the PLO, and unleashed his army, which had become more and more disenchanted with having to put up with a 'foreign' power inside its own boundaries, especially when terrorist attacks on Israel regularly brought retaliation against Jordanian settlements. With an incredible fury they expelled the Palestinians in 1971, some 10,000 being killed, and Lebanon again became the potential homeland. From the mid-1970s, particularly after Arafat addressed the UN General Assembly in 1974, the PLO, and Arafat himself, generally gained international recognition and sympathy—the Arab League recognized it as the sole legitimate representative of the Palestinian people in that year. However, to counter persistent Palestinian attacks on Israeli targets, in 1982 Israel launched a massive military invasion of the southern half of Lebanon effectively controlled by the Palestinians, and drove them out. By late 1983 infighting between Palestinian factions, particularly the Syrian-backed forces of 'Abu Musa' and 'Abu Saleh', led to the complete withdrawal of forces loyal to Arafat from northern Lebanon. For some time thereafter the PLO was based in Tunis, although Arafat had also maintained particularly close links with Iraq. By 1987, when the series of demonstrations known as the *intifada* (uprising) began in the Israeli occupied territories of the Gaza Strip and the West Bank, the PLO had become more united and appeared to have accepted even more the need for a negotiated settlement. Indeed, in 1988 Arafat stated that the PLO was prepared to accept Israel's right to security in return for Israel's recognition of an independent Palestinian state. The PLO was, ironically, forced into political and diplomatic initiatives by the success of the Israeli war tactics which destroyed the military potential of the PLO, but also increased the international prestige of the Palestinians at the expense of the Israelis. The end of the **cold war** allowed the USA and the former Soviet Union to co-operate on the **Middle East**, and one consequence was increased pressure on Israel to accept the PLO as legitimate negotiating partners in the endless search for a peaceful solution; in November 1991 a Middle East peace conference opened in Madrid, with Israeli, Syrian, Egyptian, Lebanese and Palestinian-Jordanian delegations. Although the PLO lost some credibility by backing Iraq during the **Gulf War**, international impatience with Israel's policies on the West Bank, and the continued publicity surrounding the *intifada* movement, allowed the PLO's standing to continue its improvement. Following series of agreements on autonomy for some of the Occupied Territories in the mid-1990s Arafat became President of the Palestinian National Authority. Divisions within the movement began to re-emerge soon after, however, and as conflict with Israel resumed at the beginning of the 21st century, with an apparently impossible impasse over Israel's refusal to remove its settlers from areas the Palestinians regard as crucial to their further development towards statehood, the dominance of Fatah over the PLO, faced with both Islamist and secular opposition within Palestine, and reduced credibility abroad following the resumption of violence, appeared tenuous.

Pluralism

Pluralism is both a technical term in political science, and an evaluative word for a form of government, often used as a defence of what might otherwise be called **liberal democracy** or **representative democracy**. Technically a pluralist political system is one that has several centres of **power** and **authority**, rather than one in which the state is the sole controller of people's actions. Thus medieval society in Europe, where the **monarchy** and the church were co-equal rulers in their different spheres, and where craft corporations and feudal landlords also had a claim to the obedience of citizens, was truly pluralist. Nowadays, although the doctrine is slightly more complicated because a modern state will not accept formally that there are rival but equal sources of power and foci of legitimacy, it can be argued that societies like those of the USA, the United Kingdom and Western European countries in general are effectively pluralist. So, for example, trade unions and industrial associations, along with political parties and perhaps the administrative bureaucracy, effectively share power with the official government and legislature. One version of the pluralist thesis wants to attach major significance to the multiple and cross-cutting **interest groups** and **pressure groups** that exist in a modern society, or even to the multiplicity of social and ethnic **cleavages**, to argue that power and authority are widely dispersed in a pluralist Western democracy. In its modern form the theory of pluralism is rooted in the **group theory** approach of **Bentley** to the nature of society, but it was mainly developed by American political scientists after the Second World War, during the growth of the **behavioural** movement. Such writers as Robert **Dahl** undertook studies of power in local communities, and when they were unable to show that effective **participatory democracy** controlled affairs, argued instead that societies such as the USA were controlled by alternating and rival élites representing different interests. As power was disaggregated in this way, and, according to the theory, all legitimate groups got some say in decision-making, the essentially 'democratic' nature of the societies was claimed to be upheld. One version of this theory has come to be known as **polyarchy**, and later writers have tried to show that the realities of power in most societies, including supposedly **totalitarian** states like the Soviet Union before the collapse of communist power, are essentially pluralist. The most important rival theory of power in capitalist societies, apart from the **Marxist** theory, is that rather broad set of theories described as 'power élite' theories, often associated with writers such as C. Wright **Mills** and Ralph Miliband. Pluralism seems to be a development from the earlier **élitism**, and is connected with a parallel development in the theory of elections associated with political economists such as **Schumpeter** and **Downs**.

Police

The police are the specialist corps recruited to enforce the law, especially the **criminal law**, in a state. Most European countries began to develop such forces at the beginning of the 19th century, and their precise role in any political system naturally varies with the character of that system. Two political issues have always been controversial with respect to the role of the police. The first relates to police **accountability** and to the level of government which is thought to be appropriate to control the operations of a police force. In the United Kingdom, where the political role of the police has been relatively minor, it has always been thought preferable to place responsibility for the police in local authorities, although since 1964 the number of police authorities has been reduced, and the British central government subsequently acquired additional responsibilities for training and recruitment which to some extent balance the local nature of policing.

By contrast European systems have generally assumed that a centrally-organized police force would be more efficient. As a result the police in such countries as France have been seen as much as an arm of the state as a neutral instrument for upholding the laws and protecting the individual citizen.

The second issue which recurs in any discussion of the police is the extent to which they may use force or are constrained by the rules of law or **civil liberties**. In the UK, for example, the police are generally unarmed, although the experience of street riots in the 1980s forced them to experiment with new techniques of crowd control. (In Northern Ireland, of course, policing is on a quite different basis.) By comparison the USA, France and many other countries allow their police to be armed and to use a variety of modern methods approaching those of **paramilitary forces**. However, in the serious rioting in Los Angeles of 1992 police, and indeed the National Guard, were unable to restore order even with this level of force, and President Bush was obliged to summon the federal army.

Police State

A police state is a political system where those in power use naked force by police, secret police, the military and even private armies to control and dominate the population. Essentially a police state is identified by its contempt for ordinary notions of the **rule of law**, as well as by totally ignoring any idea of **civil liberties**. It is the immediate power of the executive, or whomever controls the repressive forces, to inflict punishment, even death, on particular individuals or groups, without having to show them guilty of breaking formally constituted law, that characterizes such a state. As an inevitable consequence of such political behaviour, the police themselves come to wield unchecked power on their own behalf, as well as on behalf of their political masters, with consequential corruption and an even wider spreading of terror.

The two best known and most fully developed police states in modern times have been Nazi Germany and the Soviet Union under Stalin, where the Gestapo and the NKVD (later known as the KGB), respectively, exercised direct power over anyone even suspected of opposing or even disapproving of the political system. Often in these examples the external forms of judicial process were held to, but using courts which would not have dared to do anything but support the police. Equally, however, often not even a sham of legal respectability was made. The whole concept of a police state refers, of course, to a technique of ruling, and neither to the structure of a state nor its justifying political ideology. It is not impossible that a majoritarian democracy could operate, at least against some unpopular minority, by police-state tactics, and both the United Kingdom in its governing of Northern Ireland and some southern states of the USA on questions of racial politics have been accused of such behaviour. In general, though, only a dictatorship of some form will be likely to be a thorough-going police state. The converse is not, of course, true—dictatorships, totalitarian systems and so on do not have to be police states.

Polis

Polis is a concept central to classical political theory, and is vital for understanding the politics of that period. It provides the etymological root for politics and related words. Usually inadequately translated into English as 'city state', a 'polis' was the basic unit of political organization throughout the Graeco-Roman world, but was especially important in Greece from the Dark Ages until the Hellenistic period at least. For the leading Greek political theorists like **Plato** and **Aristotle**, living in a polis was a constituent of being human, hence Aristotle's famous definition of man as a 'political animal', where political actually meant the inhabitant of a polis. The polis was a relatively small self-contained state focused on a city, though the agricultural hinterland was seen as equally a part. Citizenship of this unit was the principal political identity, and was vastly more important than the much less formal notion of being a Greek, or even of being part of the various federations of city states that existed from time to time. It was to the small, almost neighbourhood community of the polis that loyalty went, and from which protection and benefit could be hoped for. Theorists varied in their accounts of the reason for the vital nature of the polis, but, especially during democratic periods, the main idea was that participation in the life of the polis gave moral development to the citizen, organized their religion, provided their culture, and was the overriding duty of the citizen or even the metic (non-citizen but legally resident alien). The polis concept is particularly important when contrasted with the **state of nature** or **social contract** thinkers of the **Enlightenment**, because few Greeks would have thought that someone living in a state of nature was even truly human, so important was the collective bond and shared identity of fellow members of a city state. This was more powerful, both in theory and practice, than the patriotism expected later of a subject in a European **nation state**, in part because of the difference in scale and the impossibility of genuine participation. Indeed later, not only during the Roman Empire when lip service at least was paid to the importance of Roman citizenship, but in, for example, medieval Italian city states, this focus on very local loyalty was to prove a major barrier to building national communities. Even during periods of what the Greeks called 'tyranny', when actual participation in decision-making was denied, the sense of collective interest and identity was stronger than under similar but more recent regimes.

Politburo

Technically the Politburo, the Political Bureau of the **Communist Party of the Soviet Union (CPSU)**—or other communist party organized along Soviet lines—was just a committee in permanent session of the irregularly meeting Party Congress, no more than, for example, the National Executive Committee of the British **Labour Party**. In practice the Politburo was as near as the Soviet Union came to having a **cabinet**, a body continuously directing policy and making all urgent, and many day-to-day, decisions. Its exact role and power, as well as its membership, varied enormously over the period from 1917 to 1991. Under **Stalin** it hardly met, while under **Khrushchev** it was more or less a rubber stamp for his decisions, being packed with his men. (When Khrushchev was overthrown, this was achieved by a majority forming against him not in the Politburo, but in the Central Committee of the party, a much larger and less controllable body.) After Khrushchev's time it became more representative of the various forces and interests in the Soviet Union, and subsequent leaders had to make sure they had a majority in the Politburo for any policy. It was by winning the fight for control of the Politburo that Yuri Andropov became undisputed leader of the country in 1982, and it was Mikhail **Gorbachev's** power base in the Politburo that enabled him to launch the political restructuring (see **glasnost** and **perestroika**) that ultimately caused the demise of the entire CPSU. Although officially a party body rather than a constitutional organ of state, the party and the state were so intertwined that the distinction was largely without meaning. Those who headed the vital state ministries (and who were, of course, senior party members) were also on the Politburo, thus linking the two pillars of the political system in one decision-making body. It was a small body, usually with only about 16 full members, somewhat smaller than the British cabinet but about the same size as the US federal cabinet, making it relatively easy to agree upon and then enforce policies. Its membership in a typical year during the 1980s consisted of perhaps half a dozen people there purely through holding high central party office, four or five who held vital regional party leaderships, as well as representatives of the most important state organs, principally the ministers of defence and foreign affairs, and the head of the KGB.

Political-Business Cycle

The political-business cycle is a political science concept thought to be applicable in different ways in most **liberal democracies**, although the research in this area applies most obviously to the USA and the United Kingdom. The basic idea is that government intervention in the economy is inevitably influenced in part by electoral considerations. Depending on how near a government is to facing a general election, its attitude to economic decisions changes. At its simplest, it has long been thought in the UK that governments are prepared to be fairly tough in economic decision making for the first two or three years after an election but much less prepared to make decisions that may lead to short-term unpopularity as the parliamentary term, a maximum of five years, nears its end. Decisions on interest rates, for example, or on government expenditure and tax changes, may be made even though they could lead to inflationary pressure in the last year or so before an election, when the same government might have been more financially conservative shortly after winning an election. In popular language, this is often referred to as a Chancellor of the Exchequer being pressured by his cabinet colleagues into a 'give-away' budget six months or so before a likely election date.

There is some evidence for this, as there is for a political-business cycle in the US, tied to the fixed two-yearly congressional elections and, to a much greater extent, to the four-yearly presidential election cycle. The problems of such a cycle are often alluded to in electoral rhetoric when one party will blame the other for causing 'stop-go' or 'boom-bust' trends in the economy by their predilection for mass electoral bribery of this form. It may have been a more serious problem in the days when Keynesian economic policies, which stressed demand management by tax and expenditure policies, were in vogue. However any such political imposition on the inherent cyclic nature of the capitalist economy is clearly best avoided. This is one of the reasons highly independent **central banks** along the US and German models are often recommended. Nothing, however, can prevent a government from tailoring its expenditure plans to an election cycle, except the fear of gaining a reputation for fiscal irresponsibility. The memories of the electorate, and their general preference for short- rather than long-term satisfaction probably makes it more dangerous not to run a generous budget before an election than to risk such a reputation.

Political Culture

Political culture was a popular technical term in political science during the **behavioural** revolution, and, though it suffered a decline in academic popularity for some time, had re-emerged as a vital analytic concept by the end of the 20th century. Basically a 'political culture' is the totality of ideas and attitudes towards authority, discipline, governmental responsibilities and entitlements, and associated patterns of cultural transmission such as the education system and even family life. The importance of all these factors, and the reason for linking them together into one portmanteau concept, is that they give an overall profile of how people are likely to react to political matters. Thus a classic study into political culture across several countries, *The Civic Culture*, showed that some societies seemed to transmit a general distrust for authority, and to create very low levels of political hopefulness in their citizens, while others, rightly or wrongly, bred citizens who felt they could trust politicians and that they themselves had a fair say in determining policy and political decisions. All sorts of matters can be relevant in applying this concept, from the discipline systems in schools to, in one perhaps extreme case, child-rearing patterns in Myanmar (Burma). While no one, arguably, has ever managed to define or measure the concept sufficiently precisely to make it theoretically testable, it is clear that some general set of views about the nature and utility of government and authority can plausibly be seen as prevailing in all societies, and may well be a more important determinant of the decisions and shape of government than more obviously contemporary events. In particular 'cultural' explanations are seen as a necessary complement to rational choice explanations. The latter are quite effective at explaining why political institutions chose particular options and policies from those deemed conceivable—

although it takes a cultural explanation to uncover why that was the preference set in the first place.

Political Development

Political development was a major research topic in political science in the 1950s and 1960s, but has of late become somewhat less fashionable. The basic idea, operating by analogy with economic development, was that there existed a fairly objective path of political progress through which societies moved towards further political sophistication, just as there is, arguably, a trend towards greater economic capacity which all economies can at least hope to take. Political development had obvious serious problems in avoiding a purely ideological bias in which nations were seen as more developed the more they came to resemble Western **liberal democracies**, or whatever else was taken as the ideal. Particularly in the USA, a great deal of effort was put into **comparative government** studies with a developmental approach, and much of this was organized around the popular sociological theories of the day, which were all forms of **functionalism**. The idea that there is a developmental path towards greater political complexity and more efficient problem-solving is not new, however. All of the major social theorists of the 19th and early 20th centuries, **Comte**, **Marx**, Herbert Spencer (1820–1903), **Durkheim**, **Weber** and, arguably, the philosophers of the English tradition of **utilitarianism**, believed in some sort of regular developmental sequence in the changes that political systems underwent. In a less theoretical mode the policies of the powers of European **colonialism** often implied such a notion too, with the idea that the local inhabitants of, for example, India had to be led slowly towards a capacity for independence by stages of taking more and more responsibility as their economic and educational systems improved. In a similar way many non-democratic nations of the **Third World** claim to be on a path of gradual development of political capacity, usually going hand in hand with economic development. Thus the ideas of **directed democracy** and justifications for one-party states often start from the argument that fully-fledged liberal democracy is incompatible with the stresses arising from the need to build national unity and to organize a productive economy. Too much importance, however, tends to be placed on the fact that Western democracies followed a roughly similar path from **feudalism** to **democracy**, and that newer nations should therefore be expected to follow a similar developmental sequence.

Political Machine

The great days of the party machine are probably long gone in modern liberal democracies, but it may well become a feature of states in the process of

democratic transition. A classic example of the 19th and early 20th centuries is the **Democratic Party** machine in the US city of Chicago, which continued to be very influential in the city's politics until the 1960s. A 'party machine' implies a highly efficient group of party activists, some at least full-time paid party agents, who organize the vote of the party faithful and deliver it reliably to candidates approved by the party leaders. Clearly there has to be some incentive for voters loyally to follow the instructions of their party organizers (typically the party 'precinct captain' in the major US cities). The big US machines thrived on the mass immigration of the Industrial Revolution. Thousands of European immigrants would arrive in the cities to be met by the party workers who would help organize their accommodation and jobs in return for political support. As the machines became established, their control over patronage, ensuring the control of thousands of civil-service employees in the city governments, helped further ensure their power. Ultimately it became impossible to have a political career without the support of the leading party officials who inevitably demanded favours, either personal, or in terms of legislative and executive decisions made by those they arranged to have elected.

Once a city administration was controlled by nominees of the party, there was little to stop it from increasing its power. Anyone who wanted a licence to run a bar, sell newspapers, or almost anything else would end up owing the party loyalty. A very similar process occurred in Italy in the post-1945 period when internal immigration from the south provided supporters either for the Communist Party or the Christian Democrats in the northern industrial centres. In fact the Christian Democrat party machine was equally strong in the south, sometimes acting extremely crudely. (A notorious example involves a mayor of Naples who distributed left-foot shoes to poor, potential voters before an election, with the matching right shoes not to be delivered until after the election, should he win.) Party machines depend on an ignorant and economically vulnerable population and on the possibility, through a patronage system, of political control of civil-service appointments. All three factors have largely disappeared from modern political systems.

Political Obligation

Political obligation is the theory of why, and when, a person is morally obliged to obey a government. There is a series of alternative theories to account for the requirement to obey governments. Probably the most commonly referred to is the idea of **consent**, but arguments ranging from **divine right** to *force majeure* have also been presented. Political obligation is at the heart of **social contract** political philosophies, in which its exact form depends upon the description of the hypothetical **state of nature**. There is, of course, no general argument that can satisfy everyone, but there seems to be a widespread acceptance that obedience of a state's laws is preferable to anarchy; it is only where laws restrict very personal liberties, such as racial integration in South Africa during the **apartheid** regime, or **abortion** in Ireland, that the citizen's obligation to obey the state might be regarded as having been nullified in international circles.

Political Participation

Political participation is usually defined as the extent to which citizens avail themselves of those ordinary democratic rights of political activity to which they are constitutionally entitled, and the measure is held by political sociologists to indicate the nature of the country's **political culture**. Participation rates vary enormously according to the measure chosen. If electoral turn-out is used, most Western democracies seem to be highly participatory, although the USA, with turn-outs as low as 50% even in presidential elections, is an exception. In the United Kingdom 70% or more of the electorate vote regularly, although, and in common with most of Europe, turn-out in British elections is tending to decline. Far fewer are regarded as being politically active in the sense of belonging to a political party (about 2%) or attending political rallies, demonstrations and so on (perhaps another 2%). There is no reason to apply the concept only to **liberal democracies**. Participation can be usefully measured in other contexts, and can reveal much about the political nature of that society. Thus varying rates of attendance at party meetings or rallies in various states where a **single–party system** operates, when this activity is genuinely voluntary, might give an indication of the **legitimacy** and popularity of the state. Participation is clearly partly dependant on the overall strength of the civil society, of which it also, in a circular manner, a measure. *Non*-participation is rather more difficult to analyse; it may be an indicator either that citizens are satisfied with their lives, or that they are apathetic and believe that participation will achieve nothing.

Political Science

Political science is one of a number of titles for the academic study of politics and political behaviour. As an academic discipline the subject is very old. In the 4th century BC **Aristotle** referred to it as the 'Queen' of sciences, but for many centuries thereafter it lost a separate identity. Until perhaps the 19th century such intellectual work as was carried out on politics was by political philosophers, theologians or journalists, but seldom by full-time professional political analysts. (Although the first professorship in the subject was, in fact, set up in Sweden in the 17th century.) Gradually, by a process of intellectual separation of powers, a separate discipline emerged from the previous conglomeration of law, economics and philosophy, so that by the end of the 19th century most American and many German universities had professors and departments of politics or political science. Britain was relatively late to develop this trend, and despite the creation earlier of the London School of Economics and Political Science, any widespread study and teaching of the subject is a post-1945 phenomenon. Political science as such has no collective corpus of knowledge, or even commonly agreed methodology, but is somewhat of a portmanteau for a series of subdisciplines, the workers in which do not necessarily accept others as really sharing a common discipline except in terms of subject matter. Thus **political theory**, **comparative government**, **political sociology**, international relations and, perhaps, political history are rather separated subdisciplines (and indeed contain further often incompatible subdivisions within themselves). Broadly, though, political science is the study of the nature, distribution and dynamics of **power**, usually at the national or international level, but sometimes at a very 'micro' level. The techniques of the discipline range from highly mathematical and statistical analyses of objective data (most commonly found in political sociology), via rather journalistic descriptive accounts of political institutions, or almost ethnographical accounts of foreign political cultures, to logical and conceptual analysis of political morality. Increasingly the rather artificial distinction between the subdisciplines is being eroded, as empirical researchers realize the need to be 'guided by' theory, and as theorists see that they must seek to explain and generalize about real political phenomena as well as worry about moral implications. At the same time the technical training of the profession, especially in terms of quantitive techniques, is getting steadily better, and considerable progress is being made in developing empirically-founded generalizations, and powerful analytic models, as exist in, for example, economics.

Political Sociology

Political sociology is a subdiscipline of **political science** and, as its name suggests, resembles sociology both in terms of its subject matter and research techniques. Political sociologists tend to concentrate very much more on the behaviour, beliefs and formation of the masses, while other branches of political science look much more to the behaviour and attitudes of political élites. Thus a major area of political sociology (and perhaps the best developed area in the whole of political science) is the study, by survey research and statistical analysis, of electoral behaviour in Western democracies. Apart from those who specialize in political theory itself, political sociologists are also probably the most 'theoretical' of the political scientists conducting empirical research, mainly because of the influence of the great founding fathers of sociological theory, **Marx**, **Weber** and **Durkheim**, all of whom made serious attempts at theoretical explanation of political phenomena.

Political Theory

Political theory really falls into two broad alternative disciplines, though many of the past practitioners of the subject would have to be seen as belonging on both sides of the divide. On the one hand it tends nowadays to connote a philosophical examination of the meaning and logic of political values, to concern itself with the 'ought' questions at the heart of political belief, as, for example, with the perennial topic of the basis of a citizen's **political obligation** to obey the state. On the other hand political theory increasingly is coming to bear the same relationship to empirical political research as does, for example, theoretical physics to applied physics. That is, political theory is trying to weld together the insights, data and understandings of those who study the actuality of political life into a coherent, explanatory theory or theories of political behaviour capable, even, of generating predictions. Traditionally the classic political theorists like **Plato** or **Hobbes** in fact covered both alternatives. Ideally political theory should probably be defined as trying to combine the empirical truths about human political reactions with the moral truths of what is politically desirable by designing institutions and constitutions which will generate the desirable by harnessing human political nature. That is clearly a massive undertaking, perhaps never capable of more than limited achievement, but it is increasingly the goal of a united and coherent **political science**.

Political Union

Even though the **European Union (EU)** was founded as a set of predominantly economic bodies in the 1950s, there have always been ambitions that a political unity of some sort would grow as the member states increasingly integrated their economies. Indeed the original impetus for a Western European movement after 1945 was essentially political, because it was seen as a way of preventing future European wars. In recent years enthusiasm for some degree of institutionalized political union has grown in some circles, especially the European Commission—the EU's civil service. Initially the demand was just for much closer co-operation on foreign policy, to be achieved by agreement between **heads of government** or in the Council of Ministers. But as economic integration approached, culminating in the establishment of a European **central bank** to administer the new single currency, the euro, in 1999 and the entry into circulation of its notes and coins in 2002, the demands for political union increased. Much of the debate has focused on the concept of

federalism. Unfortunately, the word federalism translates very badly among the languages of Europe, carrying very different implications according to different national experiences and political cultures. There is a general agreement that some degree of further political integration is desirable, but how great and of what sort is not only controversial between member states, but inside most of them as well. The proponents of political union, apart from the Commission, are mainly the smaller countries at the heart of the original European Economic Community (EEC), Belgium, Luxembourg and the Netherlands, who have little political impact in the world individually, and can only become more influential as part of a greater political union. The United Kingdom, as in most cases involving greater European co-operation, is clearly the least enthusiastic, although the degree of genuine enthusiasm in France and Germany is also suspect in the minds of most analysts. In many ways the debate is redundant, because the EU already has a range of powers to decide and enforce policy, and it is not clear that political union really means much more than recognizing these powers and bringing them under more obvious public control. Also, there already exists a political union in the sense that the European Parliament, directly elected from constituencies in the member states, could, if granted more powers to oversee the Commission, function as a democratic **legislature** in those many and extensive areas where the Treaty of Rome authorizes Community Law. Indeed, reform treaties from Maastricht onwards have all incrementally increased the Parliament's powers in an attempt to eradicate the 'democratic deficit'. The main obstacle to political union is probably not the attitudes of the current members, but the pressing question of the future expansion of the EU and, in particular, the problem of how, and how far, to integrate Central and Eastern European economies into the system.

Politically Correct

It is not clear whether the idea of 'politically correct' speech and thought as a standard increasingly imposed by public opinion in Western societies is real, or a journalistic exaggeration of a very minor tendency. Furthermore, if there *is* a real pressure for people to be politically correct, it is unclear that this is particularly new. Political correctness as it is understood in the USA refers to a set of attitudes about **discrimination**, mainly in the fields of race and sex. It is politically incorrect to speak in any way that can be seen as differentiating between people in a way that could conceivably be detrimental to them. It is even more incorrect to give credence to any empirical data, however scientific, that might support a comparative judgment about any group *vis-à-vis* another. Thus researchers trying to establish even a basic physiological difference between racial groups have been found to be politically incorrect, just as a suggestion that men might be better suited to some forms of work and women to others would be banned. One way of defining politically correct language is that it avoids utterances which might be described as one of a large number of 'isms', such as ageism, **racism**, physicalism (people are not crippled or disabled, but 'physically challenged'), sexism, ethnicism (accepting that ethnic divisions in society have any relevance), creedism (making allowance for the fact that different faiths hold profoundly different beliefs and attitudes), and so on. It must be noted immediately that if political correctness is an issue, it is an issue only for the minority of the population in universities or the educated professions. One is not going to find anyone attacked for politically incorrect thinking in a diner on Main Street, Hicksville, though one would in a bistro on Broadway, New York. This last sentence is an example of politically incorrect writing, committing several sins involving social classism and metropolitanism.

Though on the whole the politically correct are somewhat of a joke, the tendency to intolerance of incorrectness found in some US intellectual establishments has meant that great injustice can be, and perhaps has been, done to unfashionable thinkers. An even greater problem is the insidious effect of promoting blandness in language, and requiring enormous circumlocution to express many views safely.

Polyarchy

Polyarchy is a concept invented by Robert **Dahl**, and taken up by other **pluralists**, to define modern self-described democratic states. In this theory society is controlled by a set of competing interest groups, roughly as in Bentley's **group theory**, with the government as little more than an honest broker in the middle. The derivation is, of course, from the Greek, along Aristotelian lines, meaning the rule of the many, although not **democracy**, the rule of the people. The best description and analyses of polyarchy are found in the **community power** studies, where details of influence and power in small social settings are shown to involve this sort of group competition.

Popular Front

Popular fronts in general are alliances, either just for electoral tactics or as would-be governing conventions, between all left-wing (and sometimes liberal-centrist) parties in a political system. Typically they involve some form of co-operation with a communist party which would otherwise be confined to the fringe of political life. The most famous popular front, and the one usually meant by the phrase, was the alliance formed in France in the mid-

1930s between the socialists and the left-radicals (who were in fact a centrist party of the lower-middle classes and richer peasants). In 1936 this coalition took office, supported by the **Parti Communiste Français**, which had received orders from the Third International (see **international socialism**) to co-operate, though it refused actually to enter office. It was the first left-wing government that France had experienced in the 20th century, and was brought to power partly because of the international economic depression, which took effect in France later than in the United Kingdom or the USA. The second reason for its success was that both the centre and the far left in France had become badly frightened by an upsurge of extreme right-wing, at times openly fascist, strength and agitation inspired by Hitler's Germany. Thus an alliance that might plausibly have occurred much earlier, and solved many of the problems and deep divisions in French society, was delayed until much too late.

The government, which lasted until 1938, made a brave attempt at social reform. Its most important reforms were increasing industrial wages, shortening working hours and carrying out long needed welfare programmes. But by then the economy, which had long needed modernization, could not sustain the demands made on it, and French financiers deserted the franc forcing the government to moderate much of its programme. External threats and the whole problem of defence added to burdens that were exacerbated by the hostility of the trade unions who felt the pace of change was much too slow and staged crippling strikes. The popular front coalition fell as a direct result of its leader, Daladier's, appeasement of Hitler at Munich, which the more left-wing members could not accept. Had the **Third Republic** not been destroyed soon after by the Second World War, some revived form of the government would probably have returned to office, but nothing quite like it was to reappear on the French political scene, unless the periodic co-operation between the **Parti Socialiste** and the increasingly minor PCF is regarded as such.

Popular fronts appeared at roughly the same time in Spain (losing the civil war to Franco) and Chile. The first Chilean popular front government, elected in 1938 (although the communist party was outlawed in 1948, while the front itself continued in government until 1952), certainly achieved lasting social reform. However, Chile's second popular front, elected in 1970 under the leadership of Salvador Allende, was too far to the left to allow the centre and right parties to help it against the brutal **coup d'état** of General Augusto Pinochet, and led straight to military dictatorship. Popular fronts are less and less likely to emerge as the non-communist left in most developed countries increasingly gains ground over the communists, and becomes electorally popular in its own right through presenting an efficient and united alternative to the centre and right.

Populism

Populism is a political tradition especially prevalent in Latin America, though various European and North American movements (**National Socialism**, McCarthyism) have been described as populist. Its essence is that it mobilizes masses of the poorer sectors of society against the existing institutions of the state, but under the very firm psychological control of a charismatic leader (see **charisma**). Populism tends to have no precise or logically consistent ideology, but to be a rag-bag of attitudes and values chosen, perhaps cynically, to appeal to alienated and deprived members of a mass society and to direct their fury and energy against existing rulers, without actually committing the populist leaders to any very concrete promises about the likely reforms. It attacks traditional symbols of prestige, in the name of popular equality, but not usually by promising the creation of a normal **liberal democracy**. Thus populist rhetoric tends to be a collection of strands of both left- and right-wing thought, with a heavy stress on leadership on the one hand, and popular equality on the other, often with a highly illiberal and intolerant position on traditional civic liberties. The most famous post-war populist is probably Juan Perón of Argentina. Typically, he was among the leaders of a military **coup d'état** in 1943, before cultivating sufficient mass support to have himself elected president in 1946, and characteristically of populist movements in general, he studied and admired Italian **fascism** in practice. Perhaps the closest to an example in the last two decades is the French Front National leader, Jean-Marie Le Pen, who advanced to the second round of voting in the presidential election of 2002, although most far right movements have some element of populism.

Populism tends to be over-used, being applied to almost any unorganized mass protest movement whose leadership comes from a higher social class than most of its membership, and it is doubtful whether it has, as a concept, enough analytic capacity to be useful. Those who fear populism as a danger to the stability of the democratic state, such as W. Kornhauser in his *The Politics of Mass Society*, make much of the alienated and drifting marginality of the followers of typical populist leaders, and advocate social systems where multiple ties to class, family, ethnicity and ordinary organized political groups can give a sense of identity and meaning to the individual, thus making them immune to the often irrational and emotive forces that populism both uses and inspires. In another sense populism simply means having mass popular backing, or acting in the interests of the people, hence the derivation from the Latin 'populus'. In this decreasingly common usage 'popular' or 'populist' democracy carries none of the sinister overtones of the main definition. In a much looser way a politician in a functioning democracy who appeals deliberately to attitudes in the mass public which are not much found among the governing classes is sometimes referred to as a populist. Margaret Thatcher was often described as populist because she voiced traditional moral outrage in areas like law and order or the family, or stressed patriotism and British national sovereignty, in ways which were much more popular with working-class voters than with the more liberal attitudes of most Conservative members of parliament.

Positive Law

Positive law is a term found at least as early as Thomas **Hobbes**, and used to describe a concept apparent much earlier. Basically it is often necessary to distinguish, when talking about laws, between those that exist in some theoretical or moral sense, as with **natural law**, and those which exist in a practical sense. The latter are considered as 'positive' laws, and the term refers to legislated rules that are observed and enforced in a particular society. There may, but need not be, overlap: a particular statute (or diktat of a ruling élite) may also be seen as morally or theoretically desirable or necessary, but equally the two realms may be totally opposed. Whether or not some rule is a positive law is an empirical question. There is no inconsistency, for example, in holding that Hitler's laws depriving German Jews of their property were certainly laws in the positive sense, but were 'illegal' in terms of moral or natural law.

The more extremely pragmatic of legal theorists, especially the school founded in Britain by John Austin (1790–1859) and called 'legal positivists', wanted to restrict the whole of legal study, and the whole legitimacy of law, to positive law. A law, for Austin, was simply the command of a sovereign (that is, anyone powerful enough to enforce it), and no other sort of law was anything more than metaphysical speculation. Until fairly recently a modified version of this doctrine was probably the majority view in Britain and in some American law schools, but increasingly it is losing out to a revivified 'natural law' school. The distinction is, nevertheless, intellectually useful, though also much harder to apply than was once thought. The main problem lies in identifying the sociological evidence required to establish that some rule indeed exists as a positive law. Most modern legal philosophers would rely on something rather like the ideas of one of Austin's successors, H. L. A. Hart (1907–92), who argued that there was in any legal system a primary 'rule of recognition' which identified what were the positive laws, and that this rule of recognition could be observed in the behaviour of those who were involved with law, such as judges, police, parliamentarians and so on. The main theoretical difficulty with the positive law/moral law distinction is that any legal system leaves a large amount of room for discretion by judges, and it is difficult to differentiate between a judge who feels bound by a natural or moral law higher than positive law, and one who is simply finding the positive law obscure and exercising such discretion.

Positivism

Positivism is a term found generally in the social sciences to indicate a particular approach to the methodology of study. Broadly it indicates a 'scientific' approach in which human behaviour is to be treated as an objective phenomenon to be studied in conditions of **value freedom**. At its crudest this means that beliefs, attitudes and values of human actors are to be dismissed as insufficiently concrete or objective to become data for scientific study. Thus **Durkheim**, the leading exponent of positivist social science, would not accept that what an actor thought he was doing was a relevant part of any social science description. Even so personal an act as suicide could only be measured 'externally', and suicide rates, as statistics, rather than the accounts of would-be suicides, were the appropriate subject matter. Although there is no logical necessity, positivism tends to go hand-in-hand with a preference for statistical and mathematical techniques, and with theories which stress the 'system' rather than the individual in explaining political phenomena. Positivism sees as its enemy those who would study political values, either as political philosophers or as, say, political psychologists, the first because their approach is 'metaphysical', the second because they are concerned with individuals and their perceptions, rather than with systems and the externally measurable. Though very popular in the immediate post-war development of political science, few today hold to such an extreme position, and the label is increasingly a vague and general way of indicating the main thrust, rather than the detailed methodology, of a social scientist. This is partly because the naïve view of what it is to be a 'scientist', or the attraction of being one, has declined considerably with the development of more subtle philosophies and sociologies of scientific activity, and partly because anyone interested in empiricism and its related theoretical and research techniques has had a more obvious refuge in identifying with **Marxists** in the fundamental split with non-Marxists which at one time seemed to dominate social science.

Post-Industrial Society

This was a term popular, though with widely varying connotations, during the second half of the 20th century. The variance was particularly marked when comparing North American to European usages, though in both cases the aim was the same. Post-industrial, never an apposite label, was an attempt to grasp the fundamental differences between the societies of the classic industrial age, (from the Industrial Revolution to the middle of the 20th century) and later

Western technologically developed societies. Apart from the non-obvious assumption that there is a fundamental distinction, this is clearly an area of speculation that can go in any of a variety of directions. The relatively benign American usage has focused on the shift from industrial production to the service economy, and the production of knowledge and information as the main activities of modern economies. In Europe the term has been more deeply sociological and has tended to suggest an extensive alienation caused by an ever deeper penetration of social forces into people's lives.

In practice the deep sociological differences between service economics and industrial economics are probably more apparent than real. Hierarchy still commands in people's work lives, and the relative affluence between social classes has not changed much. The idea that people are less individual, less psychologically free, since the arrival of mass society, is almost certainly based on a false conception of a golden age. It is very strange to think that the more affluent modern worker, freed from many risks of health and much better educated, is somehow or other more alienated than his unskilled industrial working grandfather living before an extensive welfare society.

Post-Materialism

Post-materialism is the central idea in a political science approach developed in the 1970s to explain changing voting behaviour, and also a general change in political action and attitudes in Western Europe and North America. In a modified version, the theory still attracts many political scientists, and has almost become a paradigm in political sociology. The facts that led to the theory largely concerned increased voter volatility—changing one's vote from election to election—and declining degrees of strong identification with, or loyalty to, traditional political parties. In addition **new social movements** were attracting thousands of members, and sometimes seemed the preferred mode of political action for those who felt that they were left of the political centre. The core of the theory, and hence its name, was that traditional 'materialistic' concerns for economic welfare and security, both against private disasters and international threats were no longer the main motivations for political action. Supporters of the theory argued that the political generations born after the Second World War had experienced no real poverty, economic insecurity, housing problems, or any of the terror of war and impending war that preceding generations had taken for granted. Welfare schemes, governmental acceptance of social duties and relative success in managing the capitalist economic systems had made the old concerns of political parties much less pressing. Similarly, although the world was frozen in the cold war, the bipolar hegemonies of the USA and the Soviet Union actually produced much greater international stability than had been known for generations.

Though the old motivation for political behaviour had lapsed, the parties and other major institutions like trade unions had not adapted. Thus, new concerns were ill catered for in the post-materialist world by institutions that were still largely materialist. These new concerns were identified largely by a social psychological theory that claimed that people have hierarchies of needs. Once the most basic need for physical security is satisfied, higher order needs for personal development and moral growth take precedence. In political terms these were identified above all with a desire for a more democratic, egalitarian and non-authoritarian society. Moral concerns for the environment, for First World duties to the Third World and for maximum personal freedom came to the fore. This led to voting for ecological parties; old parties losing their loyal voting blocks as they were assessed more rationally and individually; and to the rise of non-party organizations like anti-war movements, gay-rights groups, and environmental pressure groups.

Not surprisingly, such post-materialist tendencies were found to be stronger among the young. But they were also much more common in the middle class, and above all, amongst the well educated. Thus critics suggest that what was really happening was simply the disproportionate growth of a 'new middle class', and that the old concerns remained strong among the bulk of the population.

Post-Modernism

Post-modernism, often called by its detractors 'PoMo', is one of the widest-ranging intellectual fashions seen in the last 150 years. Like many of its predecessors this self-consciously radical generalized social commentary and theory originated in France and has recruited extensively amongst the American intelligentsia. Its range of influence is remarkable, because post-modernism is seen not only in academic and cultural activities from sociological theory to art criticism, but also in architectural style. It is so often and viciously derided by those who have not fallen to its fashionable influence, that those who are simply neutral tend to an instinctive sympathy, even if they neither pretend to understand or apply post-modern theory.

Post-modernism's core conception can be guessed from its name. By describing the mode of thought as 'post' and 'modern', its advocates are claiming to reject the consensus in Western though that sees the **Enlightenment**, with its break with medieval thought and its celebration of rationality, as heralding an unstoppable progress in human life, understanding and experience. It is not conservative in claiming that things were somehow better before the Enlightenment, simply asserting that enlightenment rationality is as time-bound and relativist in its truths as any preceding period. The universalistic claims of rationality, and the hubris of thinking society on the way to real truth rather than local belief, are the objects of post-modern scorn. A central concept of post-modern thinking, the idea of a 'metanarrative' can best display what it is all about. The modern age, post-modernists claim, thinks in terms of a great narrative or explanatory story which applies to us all, and gives us universally valid truth. Post-modernists argue that we are all prisoners of our conditions, our characteristics, our communities, and that only local narratives, no longer presented as 'meta' can tell us our own partial truths. Clearly this can produce what seem like very reactionary arguments. Post-modernists have very little time for grand debates about human rights, for example, and positively loathe **Marxism**, because both are based on claims to absolute and unvarying truths. At the same time, the typical causes espoused by post-modernism are, by those old enlightenment standards, rather radical. Gender and sexual identity, and racial and ecological concerns all figure strongly in approval and explication by post-modern thought, its proponents suggesting, with some merit, that classic liberalism and classic Marxist thought alike, were deficient in their concern for gays, transsexuals, blacks, and those who set the global ecological status higher than scientific progress, whether capitalist or Marxist.

Whether post-modernism, which is already ageing at the beginning of the 21st century, will fade away and be no more important in the long term of intellectual progress than, for example, Dadaism is yet to be seen. But as post-modernists do not believe in the concept of progress, it may matter less to them.

Power

Power, by which is meant here social, economic or political power, is at the heart both of actual political conflict, and of the discipline of **political science**. Despite this it is extremely hard to give any useful definition, and not only are most definitions contentious, but some theorists hold that **value freedom** cannot exist in accounts either of what power is or when it exists. The safest definitions are, typically, formal, and perhaps vacuous. Thus one very common definition of power in modern political science is 'the ability of A to make B do something B would not choose to do'. The trouble is that such definitions raise almost more questions than they answer. For example, if I get B to want something they 'would not otherwise want', which I want, am I not exercising power? Or, suppose two people both try to get B to do (different) unwanted things, which is to be seen as the more powerful? How does one deal with 'potential' power, the power I might well have, but choose not to use, to make someone do something? What are the sources of power? Above all, there is a problem of measuring power. This is not simply an erudite quibble, because important modern theories about the nature of politics, especially **élitism** and **pluralism**, depend on answers to these questions. It is held against pluralism, especially in the version represented by the **community power** studies, that only open conflicts between identified interests are taken as evidence for the theories of power distribution, while a secret élite who managed to ensure that no one ever got the chance of attacking them would be regarded as powerless. Clearly no one definition can be satisfactory to all needs, and no use of the concept of power can guarantee to be value free.

Notwithstanding all this, we have an intuitive understanding of power as something that may indeed, as in the words of **Mao Zedong**, come out of the mouths of guns, but also out of the mouths of people, as with 'powerful' orators, which can be wielded evilly, but also for good, and which does ultimately depend on the ability to change peoples' preferences. The preferences may be between obeying or dying, or they may be much more trivial preferences, perhaps for one toothpaste over another. To use 'power' as a concept at all involves assuming some basic possible human autonomy, some set of preferences that would 'naturally' exist. While this is obviously sometimes no problem (we would naturally prefer not to tell robbers where our valuables are, and pulling our fingernails out is an effective use of power to change our preferences), sometimes the arguments become highly metaphysical. It is the belief that power relations are endemic to all human interaction and largely determine the quality of human life that makes the concept central, and justifies political science as an academic discipline, because politics is, ultimately, the exercise of power. What has, perhaps, emerged in political science over the last generation is an increasing tendency to see power as arising from relationships, rather than being wielded consciously by individuals. This has partly been helped by the radical thinking of power as endemic, even in the language and discourse of thinkers associated with the French **post-modernists**.

Pragmatic

Pragmatic has been used almost as often in a pejorative sense of politicians as in a commendatory way by politicians of themselves. Whatever its technical dictionary meaning, the best way of characterizing its use in political argument is to say that in its commendatory usage it is the political equivalent of 'common sense', and when used as opprobrium it means 'lacking in ideas', or possibly 'just muddling through'. Usually it is the conservative side in politics who wish to think of themselves as pragmatic, and in so doing they are seeking to draw a distinction between 'ideologues', those who are committed to some social theory which they feel will solve everything and to which they will stick at any cost, and the 'practical' or common-sense approach of those who consider each problem separately and all solutions 'on their merits'. Despite the almost 'knock-about' way the term and its opposites are used, there is a serious point of rival political theory underlying it. It has been an article of conservative faith in most Western countries since the **Enlightenment** that human reason is not powerful enough fully to understand the complexity of politics and society. As a result conservatives distrust all general theories which purport to give blueprints for policy or social reconstruction. The argument, as put classically by **Burke**, is that given our incapacity to theorize and understand, we should, on the whole, change little, and change only slowly. Instead we should generally accept that any institution which has lasted for some time should stay much as it is, and opt for what a later philosopher, Karl Popper (1902–94), called 'social engineering'. This entails a gradual, piecemeal and 'practical' orientation to reform, guided at least as much by precedent, instinct and above all caution as by any theory. It is this concatenation of values that 'pragmatism' is meant to convey, and thus 'pragmatic' suits the conservative temperament. The opposition is from those who are committed to a general theory, who believe in the possibility of **radical** and systematic reform and change. To this position pragmatism all too easily slips into opportunism, and is a synonym for mindless short-term expediency. The distinction, in fact, between pragmatists and ideologues is probably false, if only because pragmatism, with its dogmatic insistence on the impossibility of far-seeing deliberate reform, is itself a deliberate 'ideological' standpoint on human nature. But taken at face value, from the point of view of political science, the distinction between those who would welcome the two labels may well be more useful than the more conventional **left** versus **right** characterizations.

Pre-Strategic

The initial use of the concept 'préstratégique' was in French defence policy in the late 1980s, but it has come to be an accepted term among all defence analysts. A pre-strategic weapon is a nuclear weapon, most likely a short-range missile or aircraft delivered device, with a small yield intended for attacks on troops, bridges, marshalling yards or anything with a fairly immediate impact on a battlefield war. It was intended, conceptually, to clear away a mass of overlapping distinctions and to identify those nuclear weapons which were not intended for the major destruction of civilian population or economic capacity. As the possibility of superpower nuclear warfare at the strategic level has faded, so the particular distinction has lost its power. Nevertheless, pre-strategic weapons are likely to be the growth area in nuclear armaments. The need for a quick, cheap and devastating, but limited, attack may actually grow as the threat of countries (indeed, even of non-national revolutionary forces) outside the 'nuclear club' getting nuclear weapons is likely to increase. Originally these weapons would have taken a position in the **escalation** ladder before a full nuclear strategic strike—a warning shot. However, with the end of the **cold war** this idea of nuclear escalation has now become quite outmoded.

President

A president is a **head of state** in a **republic**, who can represent, legally and symbolically, the entire state. Usually the presidency carries only the symbolic and emotional powers of a modern constitutional monarchy, with the added limitation that they must in some sense be elected and do not achieve their position by family inheritance. Some, and the US president is the leading example, are also powerful political figures as heads of the **executive**. Still more complex is a situation like that in the French **Fifth Republic** where the president has somewhat usurped direct **head of government** powers from the **prime minister**, while the constitutional position might be argued to restrict the president to the role of head of state.

Like monarchial heads of state, the ultimate power that nearly all presidents still have is to be influential, and possibly determining, in the selection of who should be the head of government after any election where the results are unclear. They usually have, in addition, emergency powers, though these are very seldom used. Presidents are by no means confined to electoral democracies; the need to identify an individual as at least the symbolic leader of the people has meant that most dictatorships and one-party systems also have a presidential role. Modern democracies have to choose directly between having a parliamentary or a powerful presidential constitution. There is clearly no one correct solution. At the same time that the newly democratized Eastern European countries all chose not to have powerful presidencies because they thought parliaments better at building consensus, Italy considered adopting one because the divided nature of its society makes parliamentary government so unstable (see **Italian Second Republic**).

Presidential Government

A **head of state**, whether bearing the title president, king or queen, or some other, may carry a wide variety of powers. Presidential government is a system which gives a strong role to the head of the **executive** who participates fully in its actual decision-making processes. It is therefore to be contrasted with systems where the head of state has purely ceremonial duties, or merely has the function of appointing a **prime minister** or other official to head the government. Forms of presidential government vary but in many countries, including the USA and France, the president is elected separately from the legislature.

In systems which are marked by a **separation of powers**, such as the USA, presidential government is sometimes seen as a constitutional distortion because power is meant to be balanced between the various institutions. In the USA such terms as 'imperial presidency' became common after the period of the **Vietnam War** and **Watergate**. Because of concern over excessive presidential power there was a major reassertion of congressional authority, particularly during the administration of President Jimmy Carter. From 1981–92, however, the US government was under the firm leadership of presidents from the **Republican Party**; although they did not always have their own way, Congress, controlled by the **Democratic Party**, was able only to limit and block their initiatives, and not to enforce a different agenda. France, where President François **Mitterrand** also had to contend with a resurgent parliament for two years when the Gaullists held a majority (see **cohabitation**) may be the only other genuinely presidential system in the developed democratic world, but some **cabinet government** systems, especially the United Kingdom's and arguably Germany's, give the prime minister so much individual power that they are often accused of being 'presidential'.

Pressure Group

Pressure groups are voluntary organizations formed to defend a particular **interest group** in a society or to promote a cause or political position. These groups can operate in a number of different ways and seek to exert pressure at a number of different points in the political system, but normally they do not themselves directly seek elective office nor put forward a **programme** covering the whole range of governmental activities. The sanctions which pressure groups have vary from the **strike**, which is used by trade unions, and direct action, frequently used by movements which feel marginal to the political system as a whole, to the withdrawal of co-operation by citizens' groups. Typically the pressure applied by these groups derives more from the publicity generated than from any direct effect of the action. (See also **civil disobedience** and **new social movements**).

Primaries

The primary election is a way of allowing the electors themselves to select who shall run for office under a particular party label. As a device it became extremely popular in the USA in the early years of the 20th century, when the Progressive Movement was seeking to break the hold on the political process of what were often seen as corrupt party machines. The growth of the **initiative** and **recall** also dates from this period, but the primary election has become the most common form of determining who should be a candidate. Because many US states are extremely 'safe' for either the **Democratic Party** or the **Republican Party** the primary can often effectively be the election. In Maryland, for example, it is highly unlikely that a Republican could be elected to a major state or congressional office, so the winner of the primary is, *de facto*, the overall winner. Primaries vary in form but a distinction is usually drawn between the so-called open primary, where any qualified elector can vote in any party primary, and the closed primary where there has to be some formal evidence of party affiliation before an elector can participate in a party's selection of its candidate. In more recent years the parties have taken steps, which the courts have generally upheld, to abolish the open primary, and the number of states using the primary to express their preference in relation to the presidential nomination has grown so that the primaries now virtually determine the outcome of the candidate selection process well in advance of the party conventions. This development has been criticized as costly, because the candidates have to campaign across the states, and inflexible, because it may mean that a party will find itself bound to a candidate who has become inappropriate or unpopular after the primaries but before the presidential election. The primaries for the presidential candidature nominations are held in most states during the first six months of the year in which the election is to be held. The earliest primaries, starting with New Hampshire, are of particular importance, as a strong performance by one of the candidates can often establish an invincible lead. Due to the very high costs of primary campaigns, conducted mainly by television advertising and direct mail, a poor performance can quickly lead to a candidate having to withdraw from the race. Thus the arithmetically larger primaries in the states of California and New York can, in fact, be relatively unimportant, as unassailable leads may already have been established. Even a 'winning' performance, such as that of George Bush as incumbent president, in 1992, when he was receiving only about 70% of the primary votes cast against 30% for an extreme right-winger, Patrick Buchanan, can damage positions within a party.

The idea of introducing a primary system into the United Kingdom has often been mooted, but it would be resisted as a transfer of power from the activists to the ordinary electors who in theory are less knowledgeable than the party workers about the merits of individual candidates. In favour of such a move is the fact that in some constituencies selection as a Labour or Conservative candidate is tantamount to election, and that it is undemocratic to allow a very small group of perhaps unrepresentative partisans to make such an important choice.

Prime Minister

The prime minister emerged as a distinct figure in Britain in the early 18th century and Sir Robert Walpole is generally credited with having been the first prime minister. Originally the term was one of abuse since it carried the connotation that the politician in question was in some sense arrogating power that ought properly to belong to the monarch. As the 18th century passed the office became more defined and the prime minister became accepted as the channel for the communication of advice from the cabinet to the monarch, as the chairman of cabinet meetings and, in the 19th century as parties developed, as the leader of the government party.

In Britain the office of prime minister remained almost informal until 1937 when a Ministers of the Crown Act recognized the term in law for the first time. Otherwise the official style of the prime minister was 'First Lord of the Treasury'. The older Commonwealth countries which modelled their constitutions on Britain's—for example Australia, Canada and New Zealand—had little difficulty adapting the office to their own political systems. Some countries such as the first two of these, however, have allowed the office to develop slightly differently and in Australia, for example, there is a prime minister's department which serves the prime minister alone and gives support in the central policy-making process. In the United Kingdom such a department, although suggested from time to time, is thought to be a dangerous step towards the personalization of power and to undermine **collective responsibility**; indeed, confrontations occurred between cabinet ministers and prime minister Margaret Thatcher owing to her extensive reliance on personal advisers. In a genuine system of **cabinet government** like that of the UK the prime minister can, ultimately, only wield power with the acquiesence of their cabinet colleagues, and even the strongest individuals can, quite suddenly, lose their power and their office if they stretch the loyalty of those colleagues and of their party's members of parliament, or even members in general, too hard, as was demonstrated by Thatcher's sudden fall from power in 1990. The governments headed by the Labour leader Tony Blair from 1997 were regarded as suffering from too much detailed intervention by the prime minister and his immediate circle in the day-to-day running of the separate departments; the problem was not so much a clash between the prime minister and the ministers, who were largely Blair loyalists, but a clash between Blair's political appointees and the established civil service.

Many countries in continental Europe adopted the term during the 19th century. Here, however, the powers of the prime minister have sometimes been at odds with the claims of the **president**. In France, for example, where the office of prime minister emerged after the restoration of the monarchy, the balance of power between prime minister and head of state has fluctuated. In the present French polity (see **Fifth Republic**) it is clear that the prime minister is subordinate to the president who is the real determinant of government policy, as became apparent during the period of **cohabitation**. In earlier republics, however, the president had occupied a much weaker role, akin to that of a constitutional monarch, and the prime minister had accordingly been the true head of the **executive**.

Privatization

Privatization is particularly identified with the brand of conservatism favoured by the former British prime minister, Margaret Thatcher (see **Thatcherism**). However, during the 1980s similar policies were adopted in many countries throughout the world, and were even accepted, although sometimes reluctantly, by **social democratic** parties. In many ways privatization is simply a new word for de-nationalization, the removal from government control of monopolies both in the service sector and in manufacturing industry. However, whereas the de-nationalization that previous Conservative governments had undertaken, such as the reversal, in 1953, of the **nationalization** of the iron and steel industry, was carried out by selling the assets of the state company to industry at fixed prices, and was virtually a reflex reversal of the previous **Labour Party** government's legislation, Thatcher saw privatization as desirable for two reasons. Firstly, by making the new private companies responsible to shareholders, and therefore profit oriented, they ought to become more efficient. Secondly, and at least as important, it was a way of spreading shareholding widely among the population, and bringing Britain back to the traditional **Conservative Party** aim of 'a property-owning democracy', a 1950s slogan which was reintroduced. Shares in several large state monopolies were offered for sale to institutions and members of the public, using merchant banks and obeying both the legal and practical rules of issuing shares to raise capital, with the government taking the profit from the sales. Special regulations were introduced and what amounted to a lottery run to ensure that thousands of minor shareholders could afford to buy at least a few shares. Although it was initially seen as rather a gimmick, by the end of the Thatcher era a very large minority of people who would never have thought of owning shares in publicly quoted companies held anything from a few hundred to several thousand shares in electricity, gas, water and telecommunications companies. By expanding the shareholding base the Conservative Party made it virtually impossible for its political opponents to reverse privatizations, unless the shares became worthless (see below); indeed, many voters who would otherwise regard themselves as firm Labour supporters are among those who have purchased shares. The trend towards privatizations outlasted Thatcher, with the Conservative governments of her successor, John Major, undertaking a complex privatization of the country's railway system.

The major criticism of privatization has been that these industries were nearly all natural monopolies, and there is no way to arrange genuine consumer choice among, for example, water or electricity suppliers. Consequently it is far from clear that the need to satisfy the profit demands of shareholders, which has been done most successfully, is any more in the consumer's interests than the previous system. Privatization has come to mean, by analogy, any structural reforms which give financial accountability and management authority to small units of a state system. The move to allow individual schools to control their own finances by 'opting out' of local education authority control, or to allow National Health Service (NHS) hospitals to become self-managing trusts, is seen by some as an attempt to 'privatize' something that should clearly be a state responsibility. While managerial efficiency may be improved by many of these reforms, the emphasis on market forces and profitability introduces serious doubts about whether these services will continue to be run in the **public interest**, although independent regulatory authorities, for example in the gas, water and telecommunications industries, have been established. By the beginning of the 21st century at least one of these privatizations, that of the erstwhile British Rail, was widely held to be a total failure. Indeed the major privatized element, Railtrack, which owned and operated the infrastructure, but not the trains, was forced into receivership with the assent of the Labour government, and the Conservatives, who had carried out the privatization, were unable convincingly to attack the government on the issue. Other similar privatized utilities, notably the air-traffic control system (itself privatized by Labour), were also clearly in real difficulties.

Programme

A party's programme is its list of goals for achievement if elected to office. Often this programme will be enshrined in a document like a party **manifesto**, or in a keynote speech at the beginning of a campaign by the party leader. There is, however, a wider meaning for programme. The very idea of a programme involves the assumption that governments ought to have detailed, systematic and coherent plans, and that the electorate has the job of choosing between alternative complete plans. It further suggests that a government should be rewarded or punished in the following election according to how much of their programme has been fulfilled. The problem with this is that it ignores two basic facts about politics. Firstly, the unpredictability of economic and political factors which most often force a government to react to circumstances, rather than to carry out its pre-planned programme. Indeed many public-policy theorists argue that government can never take more than incremental steps, so that each year's policy in an area has to consist of doing more or less what was done in the previous year, with only minor modifications, which can be tested out in practice and either dropped or developed depending on their success (see **pragmatism**). Secondly, programmatic politics ignores the crucial role of personality and personal competence in electoral choice. This is widely recognized in the USA, for example, where each party produces a lengthy statement, its platform, at every election, the content of which is vigorously debated at the party conventions. However, the platform is binding neither to the party nor to individual candidates, and often completely ignored by presidential candidates, who tend to fight on idiosyncratic matters to do with their personal characteristics. Similarly, in countries where **coalition** government is the norm, the manifestos produced by the separate parties cannot be anything more than a very loose guide to what an ensuing government might do. Programmes are only useful to the extent that they particularize general party **ideology**, because sound voting decisions need to involve an assessment of what a party or its leader might do about an unforeseen situation.

Proletariat

Proletariat, a term popularized but not invented by **Marx**, refers to the propertyless working class in a capitalist society, those at the bottom of the power and wealth distribution and exploited by the **bourgeoisie**. The origin is from ancient Rome where the unpropertied mass, the 'proles' (literally 'offspring'), sent their children for military service to the state in lieu of taxes. This element of service is taken up in **Marxism** which has the proletariat's labour as their only economic asset. In Marxist theory the proletariat will be the last class in history, because the revolution they will raise, under the leadership of the **vanguard of the proletariat** (as which communist parties traditionally identified themselves) will neither wish nor be able to exploit anyone. There is, in Marxism, an exact technical definition of the proletariat, as those who neither own nor control the means of production. More loosely, though, it is used simply to mean the poor, and often with the implication that it is the urban or industrial poor, because those employed in agriculture are seldom seen as being part of the proletariat. One often finds the adjectival form 'proletarian' used by those on the left as a very general commendatory modifier, not infrequently in usages that are mildly ludicrous as in 'proletarian theatre'. In such cases it is neither that the theatre is run by, nor attended by, actual members of the industrial working class, but that it enshrines values the Marxist intelligentsia believe are in the interest of the proletariat (see **dictatorship of the proletariat**).

Proportional Representation

Some **voting systems**, but in particular the plurality system, can have the effect of distributing electoral gains in a very uneven fashion. Proportional representation refers to any method of election which seeks to ensure that minorities as well as majorities and pluralities are adequately represented in the legislature, and which distributes seats or units of legislative representation in accordance with the proportion of the vote recorded in the whole electoral division. There are many different methods of translating votes into such units and indeed an infinite variety of redistributional formulae. Two major distinctions, however, may be made. In some countries (for example Ireland) the voting and allocation of seats is done on a constituency basis with individual candidates. In others (for example Israel and the Netherlands) voting occurs on the basis of a **party list system**. In elections to the Israeli legislature a voter may not indicate a preference for an individual candidate since the voting is entirely on a list system, and indeed there are no constituencies since the whole country is treated as a single entity. Proportional representation of one form or another is the norm in Western democracies, except for the Anglo-American systems of North America, the United Kingdom and the Commonwealth. While it is undoubtedly 'fairer' in some sense, there is a strong tradition that holds that proportional representation produces weak governments by giving representation to too many small political parties, requiring complex and vulnerable coalitions. Certainly constitutions drawn up expressly to strengthen government stability, such as those of post-war Germany and the French **Fifth Republic**, have sought to limit the full effect of proportionality, and have performed favourably compared to more fully proportional systems, such as that of pre-1993 Italy. It is also widely considered that, by granting representation to such small parties, proportional systems permit groups and individuals from the extremes of the political spectrum to receive publicity and thereby improve their standing—the increasingly strong electoral performances of far-right groups in continental Europe in the 1990s and early 2000s were cited in support of this view.

Public Choice Theory

Public choice theory is little more than a detailed application of **rational choice theory** to a wide area of political decision making. It self-consciously applies economic analysis to, for example, the design of constitutions, the behaviour of bureaucrats, or the strategies of pressure groups. It very frequently employs the intricate mathematics of economic analysis, especially that branch known as 'comparative statics' in micro-economics. The difference between self-styled public choice theorists and other social scientists applying rational choice theory, is largely one of the analyst's values. Public choice theorists are wedded to the idea that capitalist economics is indeed the best possible way of arranging our economic life. From this position they arrive at the premise that behaviour which would be considered less than optimal in an economic system, must also be judged so in a political system. Not surprisingly the public choice industry is almost entirely to be found in American academe, although its founding fathers, who had rather more modest aims and more tolerant moral preferences, were in fact British.

One characteristic of public choice theory is that it has to assume that the motivations of important political actors, whether they be cabinet members, party leaders or civil servants, are the same as those of leading businessmen. Or rather, that they are the same as leading businessmen who are operating by strict, perfect competition motives. Thus, a party leader is thought to be only interested in getting elected; a bureaucrat who tries to enlarge the influence of his department is compared unfavourably with the businessman, forgetting that company growth is often more of an incentive to a corporate CEO than profit maximization. Very little of interest to mainline political scientists has ever come out of public choice theory, but the public choice theorists, with greater mathematical training than most social scientists, are usually content to dismiss this fact on the grounds that their colleagues cannot understand them.

Public Interest

Public interest is one of a family of related terms, with **common good** and **general will**, which are used to distinguish the selfish or personal interests or cares of individuals or groups from the best interests of society as a whole. The public interest refers to some policy or goal in which every member of a society shares equally, regardless of wealth, position, status or power. Most political theorists today are sceptical of the existence of more than a very few goals that might, in the long term, really be seen as 'in the public interest'. Partly this is because there is almost always the possibility of arguing that, were society reformed or changed in some fundamental way, then it would be obvious that most people would not benefit from the relevant policy, or that the policy was only solving a problem that need not exist at all were such reform to be carried out. Thus a major campaign against crime, for example, otherwise a fairly obvious example of a public interest (we are probably all equally likely to be mugged), is not in the public interest in the long term if one takes the view that violent crime is the result of **alienation** caused by an exploitative society. Even military defence, often used as the single clearest example of a public interest, can be attacked on the grounds that it is not in the interest of those badly treated by society that the political system should be protected from its enemies. However, the basic distinction between policies that are equally useful to all citizens, and those that are only for the good of a few, is clearly analytically useful. Part of the logic of the argument depends on being able to strip away the particular details of an individual's life and position, and treat them simply as a member of 'the public'. So legislation to protect the environment might be claimed to be in the public interest even though there are some, the shareholders in a factory, perhaps, who will lose money by having to pay for pollution controls. The argument is that X may lose money as a shareholder, but as an ordinary member of the public walking down a street and having to breathe, will gain equally with all other oxygen breathers.

Public and Private Spheres

The distinction between the public and private spheres of life has for some time been overtly important in political theory, although of course the distinction has always been in existence and has had latent implications for political theory since its inception. That being said, it does not follow that the distinction has always been seen as legitimate or relevant to state action. At its simplest, the private sphere can be defined negatively as those areas of life in which the state either does not or should not take an interest. The private sphere is the area of social life not constrained by formal rules and regulations, the area within which individuals make up their own rules and patterns of interaction. The private sphere is maximized in **liberal** thought and minimized in **conservative** and **socialist** thought, although for different reasons.

For a liberal, minimum governmental interference with individual freedom is highly prized, so the greatest possible amount of decision making should be left to individuals in their arrangements and agreements. For a conservative, the state may have few duties, but it has an inevitable right to legislate for morality. On the one hand, the state cannot be neutral over any matter if individual decisions in that area may weaken it. Simultaneously the state may well see itself as the moral guardian of the people, following a tradition as old as Plato and Aristotle. In either case, and they are likely to be inseparable in practice, the state may well intervene in very private matters. It might, for example, ban birth control, both because it is wedded to some theology that is opposed to artificial contraception, and because it believes that population growth is necessary for the greatness of the nation. In the opposing case, a socialist state may interfere just as much because it is committed to building a new human nature, and it may involve itself in the details of private life to eradicate, for example, 'bourgeoisie morality'.

The public/private divide has come to be of interest particularly to **feminist** social scientists who are concerned that one reason women have seldom been important in politics is that culturally they are seen as more naturally occupied with the private sphere, whereas the public sphere is seen as a male arena. Such an analytic usage is descriptive and carries no moral or ideological implications.

411

The distinction is, inevitably, arbitrary. There is no obvious distinction between human interactions that are seen at some time and place as properly the concern of the public, and those which are not. It may be that the very distinction is ideological, and simply plays into the hands of those who wish to ban some, and urge other, government actions.

R

Racism

Racism is any political or social belief that justifies treating people differently according to their racial origins. In fact, since the adoption of **affirmative action** policies in many countries to redress historical patterns of **discrimination** by giving special advantages to people of certain races, **ethnicity**, gender or other distinguishing characteristic, this definition cannot be taken literally. Racist doctrines have existed in world history since the earliest evidence, and have only been thought of as inherently wrong and scientifically absurd since the second half of the 20th century. There is no reliable scientific evidence at all for any form of inherent inferiority of any racial group, though from time to time apparent evidence emerges. Thus in the 1970s some psychologists claimed to be able to show that certain racial groups, for example blacks in the USA and the Irish, systematically scored less well than other groups in intelligence quotient (IQ) tests. Apart from other unreliabilities in the testing, it is generally accepted that environmental factors, and the possible cultural bias, of such tests can account for any apparent racial differences.

In fact, not only is there no evidence of racial inferiority, but the very notion of racial types is scientifically at best obscure and at worst entire fiction. It is sometimes hard to grasp just how crude the tests used for racial stereotyping in those countries, notably South Africa (see **apartheid**), which have operated a formal racial segregation policy can be, and how much of the pseudo-science that characterized Hitler's theory of racial types (see **anti-Semitism**) is still taken seriously. Babies whose parentage is unknown can be characterized into race categories on no more evidence than a microscopic examination of whether a head-hair curls more than 'normal' for a white person.

There are really two different aspects to racism. One is a theory of innate differences between racial types which is used or advocated by those who the scale would show as superior in order to justify economic and political inequality. The other, and much more common, is based on cultural differentiation, and simply asserts that people of such and such a background are 'different', and should not be allowed equal competition for jobs or other rewards with the indigenous members of the nation's culture. Without doubt this is still a potent force in the mass cultures of Western societies, and from all available evidence racism of this type is at least as strong in the former Soviet Union and Eastern Europe.

Why and how particular groups become the targets of racial hatred and discriminatory behaviour from time to time is unclear. The social science theories that attempt to deal with it, often as a subcategory of a general problem of ethnicity in politics, are unsatisfactory. It is a natural problem for **Marxism**, as racial groupings seldom fit neatly into the expected lines of class conflict, and the tendency is for Marxists to see racism as a **false consciousness** deliberately or otherwise implanted into the masses to divert them from seeing their common brotherhood as workers facing the true class enemy. But non-Marxist social scientists have no more convincing an approach, and ultimately tend to assume that racism, as a form of xenophobia, rises from social strains, especially in contexts where there is considerable status-anxiety.

The extent of the hatred of others because of surface and visible physical differences is hard to estimate, but is certainly surprisingly widespread. The idea that there is some natural antipathy between white and non-white, or that only 'caucasians' indulge in racist feelings, is palpably false. Much of the **caste** system in India, for example, rests on the racial distinction between the original Tamil inhabitants and the 'Aryan' invaders from the north over 3,000 years ago. The Chinese are often reported to be clearly racist in their attitudes to whites in a way that transcends mere ideological opposition to capitalists. A form of reciprocal racism has developed in some societies where racial minorities discriminated against by whites not only develop a defensive racist intolerance of the oppressors, but also of other minorities. Thus, for example, some American black leaders are openly anti-Semitic.

Radical

Radical, as a political epithet, has two general meanings, though purists may wish to insist only on its primary derivation. This, from the Latin *radix* (root), means anyone who advocates far reaching and fundamental change in a political system. Literally, a radical is one who proposes to attack some political or social problem by going deep into the socio-economic fabric to get at the fundamental or root cause and alter this basic social weakness. As such it can be contrasted with a more 'symptomatic' policy cure. For example, the problem of crime could be dealt with by a reform of policing tactics, or it could be seen as resulting from very basic economic and socializing forces. To attack crime rates by changing the latter would be a 'radical' approach; to try to deal with crime either by severe penal sanctions, or by intensive 'community policing', might be more or less politically extreme, but would not be radical. It is important to keep this distinction clear. Extremeness of policy is highly relative. To deal with a crime wave by increasing the number of offences for which the state might execute someone would not have been extreme in the early 19th century, but to introduce a probation service would have been. Neither policy would have been 'radical', though reacting to a crime wave in 1825 by introducing unemployment benefit would have been both radical and extreme.

A secondary meaning of radical as signifying someone on the **left** of the political spectrum has developed. It makes perfect sense, however, to talk of the radical centre or even the radical right. In some political cultures the word does not have the rather emotive connotations it has in English: the French Radical Party of the **Third Republic** was a moderate and traditional liberal party.

Raison d'état

Raison d'état is used to describe an overwhelmingly important general social or state motive for an action. There may be, it is argued, problems of such utter importance to the entire well-being of a state, or interests so vital to the entire population, taken as a whole, that all ordinary moral or political restrictions on government actions must be dropped. It derives from debates on **international law** in the 17th century, and has become somewhat discredited. It is not so much that the general idea has been discarded, but rather that the way of stating the claim creates unease.

In a sense, of course, it is only an extreme version of the idea that some policy or other is in the **public interest**, or is for the **common good**. But there are two differences between public interests and *raisons d'état*. Firstly, most liberal political theory maintains that there are some **natural rights** or freedoms that cannot be curtailed for the common good. The doctrine of *raison d'état*, if adopted, would deny this. It might, for example, be held that in general an absolute right to **due process** of law existed, yet **martial law** might be declared on the grounds that the threat to security was so intense that, for *raison d'état*, the right had to be abrogated.

Secondly, the 'state' itself is very much to the forefront when a *raison d'état* argument is invoked—it is the continued existence of the very basic structure of authority and legitimacy that is at stake. This argument has arisen, even if the language has not been used, when the restoration of the death penalty has been urged in Britain for terrorist crimes only.

By its nature the argument is more often used and found in international politics than in domestic politics, and its slight discredited feeling probably has to do with the undue ease that nations have experienced in finding *raisons d'état* for abrogating international agreements (for example, President George W. Bush's desire to abandon US participation in nuclear proliferation treaties in order to enable the development of the National Missile Defence scheme). Nevertheless, 'realist' international relations theory, in which *raison d'état* is a vital concept, is still a common predisposition among many international relations intellectuals and practitioners.

Raison de guerre

The idea of *raison de guerre* first developed in the 17th century, at the time that **international law** was beginning to be a serious intellectual activity in the works of writers like **Grotius**. *Raison de guerre* is essentially a derogation from the rules of international law, and especially from the theory of **just war**. All it amounts to is the acceptance that armies will ultimately do whatever they have to do to win. The concept is linked closely to the more general doctrine of *raison d'état*, that the protection of a state and the furtherance of its interest will always dominate in foreign policy. There is a weaker version of *raison de guerre* which does not allow a breach of the laws of war, but does allow acts which would normally be considered immoral and uncivilized. For example the allied bombing of Monte Cassino in the Second World War, and the consequent destruction of one of Europe's finest monasteries and libraries, was justified by the doctrine of *raison de guerre*.

Ratification

The process of ratification is the formal approval required by many constitutions which set up elaborate systems of checks and balances and which seeks to make certain kinds of constitutional change difficult to achieve without a substantial measure of political unanimity. Thus in the USA, for example, treaties negotiated by the president must be ratified by a two-thirds vote of the Senate—in some cases, such as the Treaty of Versailles after the First World War and the SALT II treaty on arms control, Senate support was not forthcoming. Constitutional amendments in the USA need to be ratified by a vote in each of the state legislatures. Similarly, acts and treaties which amend the founding treaties of the **European Union** require ratification by the legislature of each member state and, since the Single European Act came into force in 1987, by the European Parliament. Even where such a treaty does not require parliamentary ratification, an analogous process may exist where it is tested for compatibility with the constitution by some body like a **constitutional court**, which is the applicable doctrine in France and Germany.

Rational Choice Theory

Rational choice theory came to the other social sciences, especially political science and, more belatedly sociology, from economics, in the second half of the 20th century. The essence of the approach is very simple. It maintains that the primary explanation for an action is that the actor calculated said action to be the most efficient way of acquiring a desired goal. Obvious as this must seem to anyone from outside the social sciences or philosophy, it is in fact neither obvious, simple, or even necessarily often true. Rational choice theory is the best, indeed usually the only, approach available to economists, but it is controversial as to whether or not our economic behaviour is typical of our more general social behaviour. When buying or selling it is a rare person who deliberately acts other than to maximize a relatively measurable utility. (Though even in economics phenomena like brand loyalty or 'retail-therapy' can decidedly blur the edges of rational strategic calculation.)

Voting behaviour was the first area to which political scientists applied rational choice theory, because it is relatively easy to see the act of voting as akin to making a purchase. The voter trades in his vote by giving it to the party whose political programme he thinks will most likely benefit him. Even here there are alternative theories, the most common being that voters have a psychological tie to a party like that of a sports fan to a football team, and voting is no more rational than automatically supporting Manchester City FC because one was born in Manchester. Equally a protest vote, given to a party of which one does not particularly approve in order to signal disaffection with the one that might be the 'rational' choice, is problematic. The problem then is that almost any action can be shown to be rational, if one sufficiently widens the meaning of the rational connection. Thus, a protest vote is rational if one aims to send a signal; voting for a party because one identifies with it psychologically, is rational if propping up one's self-image is a target that can be realized through rational achievement. The economists' use of rationality works because they can readily dispense with ideas like altruism or mood, and because they are more concerned about predicting aggregate behaviour rather than individual behaviour. Thus, even if quite a lot of people buy soap powder because the colour of the package attracts them, these individual non-rational behaviours are likely to cancel out in the aggregate, leaving a result that looks price-and-cost rational.

Much of social behaviour has not traditionally been seen as means–end related, but rather as the result of acting out values, social expectations, or sheer habit (traditional ways are preferred simply because they are traditional). Nevertheless, rational choice theory has been applied, sometimes with surprisingly successful results, even to such areas as church attendance, participation in hopeless political protest, and the lower rate of female participation in politics. The main criticism of it is more to do with how full an explanation rational choice theory can provide. It may be that given an actor's set of values, much of what he chooses can be shown to follow a rational choice paradigm. Typically though, we want to know why he or she held the values in the first place. Again it is because there seems to be no need to explain *why* people prefer to buy cheaper goods that rational choice theory works in economics.

Rawls

John Rawls (b. 1921), a Harvard professor of philosophy, is without doubt one of the very few creative and influential writers of political theory in the contemporary West. His most important work, *A Theory of Justice*, published in 1971, was a major attack on the prevailing **utilitarianism** of theories of **political obligation** and social order, and constituted a brilliant attempt to revivify the **social contract** approach to political and social theory. His work started a rethinking of accepted positions in many related subjects, especially jurisprudence, where legal philosophers have followed him in attacking the **positive law** theories which were the legal counterpart of utilitarianism. The essential points of Rawls' work are twofold. He wants to re-establish the pre-eminence of **natural rights** arguments, so that there will be some values we hold as absolute, principally the right to liberty, and secondly, but only secondly, a right to equality. He also wishes to change the methodology from the sort of cost-accounting approach held dear by utilitarians, to a more absolute form of argument. In pursuit of the latter he relies heavily on what he calls the 'justice as fairness' argument. One technique for making these points is the 'veil of ignorance'. Essentially this calls on us to try to pretend that we do not know certain basic social facts about ourselves. Thus we are to imagine a person who is ignorant of his sex, age, class or period of history. What social institutions would such a person think were fair? The point is that if you do not know whether you are to be a slave or ruler, man or woman, living in the 10th or 20th century, you could not opt for 'unfair' rules, lest you ended up on the wrong side of the bargain. Once stated, it is a very simple test of whether an institution is 'fair' or not, but no one before Rawls had thought of this way of modernizing the traditional social contract methodology. Rawls has reinstated a particular form of liberal political theory and, whether it lasts or not, he is one of the very few creative and original contemporary thinkers in the field.

Reactionary

Reactionary is one of those political terms invariably used pejoratively, though there is nothing in its basic meaning that requires this. A reactionary is, literally, one who reacts against some development or change, or opposes some proposed change in society. It is normally used in association with, or almost in place of, **conservatism**, though it is highly relative. Thus propaganda inside communist societies often refers to 'reactionary' forces, those who are holding up true socialist progress, though even the propagandists would not seriously hold that those they are attacking are actually conservative. The term came into popular usage through liberal thinkers in the 19th century, whose idea of the inevitability and desirability of progress was so strong that they felt it was possible to identify groups or institutions who were clearly attempting to hold back an unarguably good process. In as much as conservatism does imply a resistance to rapid change, and a doubt that there is necessarily any particular path of social progress for humanity to follow, the connection between reaction and conservatism has a surface plausibility. The implication however is that a reactionary has nothing but a negative opposition to trends or ideas, or a desire for traditional values and structures, and as such is politically anachronistic. Outside some theory that tells its exponents what progress really is the term reactionary has little use, because most policy-making is a matter of reacting to circumstances, and from any political perspective there will be many trends in a society which clearly should be resisted.

Realignment

Realignment is a concept in political science usually referring to the change of basic voting loyalties by groups in the electorate. **Political sociology** has demonstrated that most electorates consist of socio-demographic groups with strong long-term identifications with a particular political party. Although not everyone who is, for example, a young, urban, northern, working-class male will always vote for the Labour Party in Britain, the odds are strongly in favour of him doing so. Similarly nearly all blacks in the USA will vote Democrat. These loyalties, often inherited in a fairly automatic way from parents, and reinforced by peer-group pressure, last for decades and result in a high predictability in electoral behaviour.

From time to time, however, social change, major events like wars or economic disruption cause sudden breaks in these semi-automatic electoral regularities. When this happens a realignment may occur, shifting the bulk of whole socio-demographic groups to new party loyalties. It is often argued, for example, that the economic collapse in the USA after the Wall Street crash, and Franklin Roosevelt's recovery policies, made the 1932 presidential election a realigning election in which new voting loyalties, known as the **New Deal** coalition, were formed and which lasted until at least the 1960s. Similarly the elections after the First World War in Britain, when the Labour Party was first able to present itself as a viable socialist alternative party, set up new working-class loyalties, taking voters from the Liberals and realigning electoral politics in Britain in a way which lasted at least until the 1970s. Realignment should not be confused with dealignment, a similar process, but one which sees voters being cut loose from any stable ties to parties, so that their vote loses long-term predictability.

Realpolitik

Realpolitik is a German political concept dating from the mid-19th century and often thought to be especially characteristic of Karl Otto von Bismarck's policies, both domestic and foreign. Literally it means nothing more than the politics of realism, an injunction not to allow wishful thinking or sentimentality to cloud one's judgement. It has taken on more sinister overtones, particularly in modern usage. At its most moderate 'realpolitik' is used to describe an over-cynical approach, one that allows little room for human altruism, or that always seeks an ulterior motive behind another actor's statements or justifications. At its strongest it suggests that no moral values should be allowed to affect the single-minded pursuit of one's own, or one's country's, self-interest, and an absolute assumption that any opponent will certainly behave in this way.

While realpolitik in either of its current meanings is clearly characteristic of much modern political behaviour, the fixed assumption that people do only act in this way is probably itself an illusion that would not be acceptable to a practitioner of realpolitik under its original meaning. Perhaps a more useful modern definition of realpolitik is that it is, in **game theory** terms, a loss-minimizing strategy or 'fail-safe'—a way of conducting politics which, though it may occasionally mean getting a sub-optimal result, will minimize the catastrophes that would happen were a 'best-case scenario' regularly to be relied on. A more modern version of realpolitik is the, largely American, development of 'realist' theory in international relations in which a state's own interests are assumed to be supreme both as a justification for and a predictor of action, leading, for example, to a widespread contempt for concepts such as **international law**.

Recall

Recall is a method for securing greater **accountability** of officials and elected personnel by providing a procedure by which the electorate may vote to terminate an appointment before the normal retirement date or before the normal date on which the need for re-election would occur. This device became popular in the USA in the Progressive era (1890–1920) and it now exists in a number of the states, usually alongside two other methods for producing **direct democracy**, the **initiative** and **referendum**. Because it can be abused by parties, factions and single-issue groups, US state constitutions tend to put severe restrictions on access to the ballot—normally by requiring a large percentage of the eligible electorate to petition for recall prior to the question being placed before the electorate as a whole. Recent developments in the USA suggest, however, that direct mail soliciting may have made such restrictions less effective than in the past by easing the process of acquiring the necessary signatures. In the USA recall is generally used for elected officials, but there is no theoretical reason why it could not also be used for appointed ones.

Referendum

The referendum is a method of referring a question or set of questions to the electorate directly rather than allowing them to be settled by the people's representatives in the legislature (see **direct democracy** and **representative democracy**). It was used frequently in the USA from the revolutionary period at the state level and was used even earlier, and frequently since, in Switzerland. The policy question may originate from a group of electors directly via an **initiative** or from an official body such as a state government, legislature or constitutional council. It has been used to determine basic constitutional questions, for example in Greece to decide whether to retain the monarchy after the restoration of democracy, and in France in 1962 to decide whether the president should be directly elected. The referendum is also often used to determine issues of morality which divide a government or party (as with the questions of legalizing divorce and **abortion** in Italy or Ireland) and to settle local matters which it is thought are best left to individual areas to decide (for example the sale of alcohol on the Sabbath in Wales). Referendums have also been manipulated and exploited to enhance the personal power of an autocratic ruler as occurred in France in 1851 after Napoleon III's coup d'état and in Germany after Adolf **Hitler** obtained full political power in 1934. In these cases the referendum is seen as conferring **legitimacy** and popular approval on an individual, and sanctions unconstitutional or extra-legal activity. The development of the **European Union (EU)** has seen an increase in the frequency of referendums in its member states, as many are constitutionally obliged to submit major EU treaties directly to the electorate.

The form which the referendum takes and its legal effect varies with political systems. The referendum may be purely advisory, or it may be binding in the sense that either a measure requires **ratification** in a referendum to enter into force or that a referendum result places an obligation on the executive or legislature to act in conformity with the popular decision within a specified period (see **plebiscitory democracy**). In this latter case, as with the use of citizen-inspired propositions in California, enormous problems may arise when a state government and legislature finds itself obliged to legislate a proposal which it either thinks absurd or literally cannot achieve. For example, in the 1980s Californian referendum results on intiatives proposing the control of insurance companies led to many companies simply refusing to do business in California.

Regulation

Regulations are very detailed rules created by authoritative bodies and applicable to specific areas of life. Very often 'regulation' will apply to rules inside organizations and public bodies. It is relatively rare to talk about a parliament passing a regulation, as opposed to a law, though a parliament may well pass a law which bestows on some other agency the right to make detailed regulations in some specific area. Thus a corporation may have regulations governing employment practices and a college may have fire safety regulations, but the college is also likely to have some higher and broader level of rules, called something like statutes or by-laws.

In contemporary usage a vital example of regulation is in **European Union** legislation, where the European Commission has the right to pass regulations. These, unlike their more normal legislation, called **directives**, have the quality of direct applicability. This means that a Deregulation has immediately the full force of law in each member country, and can be called upon by citizens in legal cases. A regulation might, for example, cover the labelling of food products or the safety standards for electrical appliances. In such cases individual countries are being treated as essentially non-existent, because the need for standardization is seen as supra-national. More usually a directive will be issued, instructing member governments to pass their own laws for achieving some common end.

Regulatory Agencies

Regulatory agencies are institutions created by governments and given quasi-legislative powers to oversee some area of policy. The best known agencies are those created by the US Congress, particularly the agencies that came out of Roosevelt's **New Deal** era. The greatest of the New Deal agencies, at least in terms of its long-term impact, was almost certainly the Securities and Exchange Commission, which regulates in great detail both the trading of stocks and shares, and matters like the amalgamation and floating of corporations. This was a response to the Wall Street crash of 1929 and the ensuing depression. Another New Deal agency which continues to be of great importance is the National Labor Relations Board, introduced to guarantee the recognition rights of **trade unions**, to mediate between employers and unions and to protect the right to **strike**, which had come under severe pressure from unscrupulous employers presented with a weak labour force during the Depression. There are dozens of others, among the most important of which are the Environmental Protection Agency, the Federal Communications Commission and the Federal Trade Commission. The structure of most agencies is that the president appoints the members, who serve for fixed terms, but cannot dismiss them. Thus although any particular commissioner may owe political loyalty to a particular president, the commission as a whole will reflect a variety of political views. The agencies can make detailed regulations without coming under electoral pressure to look after particular interests, unlike members of Congress, and, because of their expertise, can deal with complex detail. They are charged with regulating the industry in question, giving due consideration both to the public interest and to the long-term interest of the industry itself, so they can gain the confidence of employers, investors, consumers and workers, rather than being partisan. A curious feature is that in some ways they breach the distinction, sharply felt in the USA, between administrative, legislative and judicial activities (see **separation of powers**). Not only do they make regulations, but they assess penalties for breaching them and hear their own appeals against their judgments. Other countries have similar bodies. In the United Kingdom, for example, a number of regulatory agencies have been introduced to oversee the activities of formerly nationalized monopolies (see **privatization**). However, these seldom have as much independent power as the US agencies; the roles performed by the US regulatory agencies are elsewhere more likely to be handled by the mainstream **civil service**.

Representation

Representation is a political concept that arises in a variety of contexts, with subtly but importantly shifting meanings. Technically it means simply a system in which the interests or beliefs of many are 'represented' before some decision-making body by only one or a few people working on behalf of the many. In parliamentary terms representation refers to the constitutional system for electing members of the legislative body who will work for the interests of those who elected them, for whom they are 'representative'. In other political contexts representation may mean the mass *or* some governing élite choosing a few people from the many not normally allowed access to decision-making to come to meetings to pass on the views of those they 'represent'. It does not follow, either in theory or practice, that representatives have any share in the making of decisions. Anyone can 'make representations' to a decision-maker, and may or may not seriously be listened to. So, for example, as a result of student activism in the 1960s, many universities have elaborate systems to provide student representation on university senates, but very few have allowed students an equal, if any, voice in policy-making.

Representative Democracy

Representative democracy is a form of indirect rule by the majority of the electorate. In this system (the only widespread form of democracy in actual practice), political decision-making is done by a small number of people elected by the whole electorate. Typically the elected representatives in a national **legislature** will number only a few hundred, regardless of whether the electorate is a few million or hundreds of million. The usual system is to divide the nation into geographical constituencies, each sending one or more representatives to the legislative assembly. In each constituency several will compete to be elected, and, depending on the details of the electoral laws, the person or persons most popular with the voters will be elected. It may also be the case that the political executive is elected by the people, especially as in a presidential system like that of France or the USA.

There are two problems that lead critics sometimes to challenge the 'democracy' claim of representative democracy. The first is that the vagaries of **voting systems** and voting patterns may well result in the control of the legislative assembly lying in the hands of a group representing very much less than a majority of the population. It is common in the United Kingdom, for example, for a government to be formed by a party which, though having a majority of members of the House of Commons, was supported at the polls by perhaps only a third of the total electorate. Nevertheless, this highly 'unrepresentative' group may be able to force the passage of laws bitterly disliked by a majority of the population for the whole term of a parliament; furthermore, each member of the ruling party would claim to be representing all of their constituents, whichever candidate they had voted for. The second point relates to the whole doctrine of representation. There are really only two models of how the mass of the individuals can be represented by a few people. One, **delegation**, involves elected members being instructed by those they represent exactly how they should vote in the legislative assembly. In this way the majority of preferences of each constituency are directly transmitted to the assembly, and the mass of the population can be said, in some sense, to have their views turned into law. The other model, most ably and famously defended by Edmund **Burke** in his addresses to his own constituents in 18th-century Britain, rejects the idea of binding delegation. Instead the representative is seen as chosen for their qualities, and perhaps for the general principles on which they stand for election. Once chosen, however, they become a free agent, entitled to cast their legislative vote as they believe best, regardless of the opinions of their constituents. At *best* this latter model is what is practised in actual representative democracies. In fact the usual system does not even give the voter the chance of selecting someone who will at least stand by their own convictions. Instead most electoral systems operate so that only those nominated by major political parties can be elected, and most parliamentary systems with tight party discipline controlling how 'representatives' vote. Thus the voters are in fact choosing among rival party-teams, and the character of the person they elect is largely irrelevant, except perhaps in parochial matters. Exactly who is being represented, and exactly how democratic representative democracy actually is, can therefore be placed in substantial doubt. There has also emerged, in the last decades of the 20th century, an argument that bodies with authority, whether parliaments, courts or any élite, should be representative of the people they rule in the sense of having approximately the same gender, ethnic and socio-economic make-up. Politically this has been most obvious in the demand that positive discrimination (or 'affirmative action' steps should be taken to ensure that women are equally represented in parliaments. The demand is hard to satisfy without clashing with other values such as the right for anyone to stand for election, and the absolute freedom of choice guaranteed to the electorate. Thus the French Conseil d'État struck down part of a bill passed through the National Assembly in 1984 which would have required parties to have quotas amongst their candidates for women. This was regarded as unconstitutional; similar quota systems proposed for the British Labour Party were held to be illegal.

Republic

Republic is unusual among political terms in being one that is actually very easy to give an ostensive definition to, but of which it is rather hard to explain the history. A republic is, very simply, a system of government that does not entail **monarchy**, nor, at least officially, aristocratic or oligarchical rule. But this does not necessarily mean that republican government must be democratic, because there is a large gap between abolishing **oligarchy** and insisting on universal suffrage. The Roman Republic was, for example, the original precedent for republicanism, but had a clear class structure where only the higher orders of the society had any rights to participate in government. Despite this the ordinary working definition of a republic nowadays is any society that is both democratic and non-monarchial, and a huge number of the states in the world have 'Republic' somewhere in their official title. The fight over monarchy is long dead—the title means little, and the political questions it used to raise are now pointless.

Republican Party

The US Republican Party was founded in 1854 as a coalition of anti-slavery groups. (An earlier Republican Party, founded in 1791, eventually evolved into the **Democratic Party**.) In 1860 Abraham Lincoln was elected as the first

Republican president. The Republican Party is generally recognized as the more conservative of the two main American parties, though this is a difficult judgement to make, and ignores the areas, **civil rights** for example, in which parts of the Democratic Party have often been to the right of most Republicans. It was not really until the latter third of the 19th century that this case could seriously be made. As the Democrats became the party of the cities, of the immigrants and the industrial working class, the Republicans became the party of the big corporations and of the rural élite. It was quite common to find a state, Illinois was a good example, where large cities like Chicago were entirely Democratic, and all the small towns and rural areas were entirely Republican. It was Republican support for the emerging huge economic conglomerates, called 'Trusts', the pioneers of the rail-roads or steel production, for example, which finally gave the Republicans this image of supporting 'corporate America', but it has never been a simple middle and upper class/ Republican versus working class/Democrat split, in parallel to much of Europe. Indeed, the Progressive era, lasting roughly from 1890–20, was partly Republican-inspired. Not until the economic depression which led to the Democrats' introduction of the **New Deal** in 1933 were the parties policies very clearly distinguishable. In the post-war world the Republicans have been identified with a more straightforward conservative programme—low taxes, low welfare provision, concern over **law and order**, pressure for **laissez-faire** economics and a general dislike of government interference. Historically, the Republicans tended to do well in elections at the personal, but not legislative level, controlling few state **legislatures** and effectively being in a permanent minority in the federal Congress, but holding the presidency for most of the post-war period and consistently winning many state governorships. The difference in voter behaviour appeared to be explained by the belief that Democrats make good representatives of the people, charged with looking after local interests, whereas Republicans are better at controlling an **executive**. However, during the 1990s this pattern was broken, as the Republicans won majorities in both houses of the federal Congress during a Democratic presidency, and gained control of numerous state legislatures.

Responsibility

An officer of the state, whether elected or appointed, whether from the civil service, cabinet or police, has responsibilities. These may be clear-cut and precise, directly involving their own acts, or very diffuse and relating to a duty to oversee or share blame with others. In the first of these senses there is clearly no definitional problem at all. The difficulty with the political notion of responsibility is in the latter area. Here a person may be held responsible for something done, or not done, by someone else for whom they have 'responsibility', but whom they may never have met and whose actions they could not, in practice, conceivably have controlled.

The political need for **accountability** means that there must be some clearly identifiable individual who can be held responsible for an abuse or failure of power, or a mistake or casualness in policy-making. Hence, at least according to orthodox British constitutional law, a civil servant's mistake is answered for before parliament by the member of parliament who, as a minister of the crown, is their nominal superior, and that minister may have to resign to atone for that mistake, however little an ordinary judgement of guilt could be directed at them. In practice it is very unlikely that a minister will nowadays resign when some mistake is made by a subordinate official, which would not have happened had the rules, for which the minister clearly *is* responsible, been followed. Thus, though the opposition demanded the resignation of Kenneth Baker as Home Secretary when incompetence in a British prison led to the escape of suspected terrorists in 1991, it was clear that he felt no obligation to do so. Subsequent Home Secretaries have been equally trenchant in their refusal to be held personally responsible for their department's errors. In contrast, the Foreign Secretary, Lord Carrington, resigned in 1982 when the Argentine invasion of the Falkland Islands took the British government by surprise, because he felt that the advice tendered to the cabinet was more clearly something for which he had actual, as opposed to merely formal, responsibility. Though the consequences for individuals can sometimes appear unduly harsh, the doctrine would be worth retaining not only to ensure accountability but also to prevent those who are elected from hiding behind the anonymity of the public bureaucracy. However, it must be treated now as a defunct part of the constitution because the reality of political careers clearly makes it impossible for anyone to emulate Carrington.

A related, though nowadays seldom important, doctrine is that of 'responsible government'. This, which used to be paired with the idea of 'representative government', referred to stages in the development of self-government in colonies. As a first stage on the road to independence local citizens would be invited or selected to form a government under the general supervision of the colonial power, that government to be given gradual responsibility for increasing areas of public affairs. This would usually, however, come some time before they were allowed representative government, that is, before the population would be allowed themselves to choose and sanction which of their number would be given these responsibilities.

Revisionism

Revisionism is usually a term in **Marxist** or **socialist** debate, indicating a falling-away from a previous and 'purer' form of a theory. Thus left-wing thinkers like Rosa **Luxemburg** or, for that matter, Leon **Trotsky** were accused of revisionism for suggesting methods alternative to **Lenin's** for communist revolution. Most modern forms of Marxism might be accused of revisionism in this way, and it remains a highly selective and value-laden concept. Non-Marxist writers have taken over the concept to describe any later, and alternative, theory or account where there had previously been a generally-accepted version. So now there are, for example, revisionist theories about the **cold war** by Americans who are less convinced than previous writers of the purity of US foreign policy in the 1950s. However, the most important 'revisionism' in the late 20th and early 21st centuries is that concerning the treatment of Jews in Nazi Germany, a number of historians having sought to deny the existence, or deprecate the importance, of the Holocaust. This indicates the way in which revisionism is used not only to indicate later alternative theories, but especially those which serve to pour doubt on comforting original certainties.

Revolution

The early use of the term revolution referred to the 'turning around' of political power and was applied to restorations of monarchies as well as to their overthrowals; analogies could be made to astrology's revolution of the stars and to the turning of the wheel of fortune. The common feature, however, is clearly a process of change. Revolution is, of course, often used allegorically to refer to any wide-ranging change in society, one instituted, perhaps, by scientific or technological change, but in political science the primary meaning must be the deliberate, intentional, and most probably violent overthrow of one ruling class by another which leads the mobilized masses against the existing system, not only vastly altering the distribution of power in the society, but also resulting in major changes in the whole social structure. As such it is quite different from a **coup d'état** which simply replaces one set of rulers with another, with no crucial ensuing alteration of the overall political and social scene. This full-blooded form of revolution (which also excludes similarly great socio-political change as a result of defeat in war or success in an anti-colonial uprising) is, almost by definition, a result of class conflict. It is also very rare. The great revolutions in world history are few: the French Revolution, which led to the creation of a middle-class controlled republic instead of an aristocratically-controlled monarchy; the Russian Revolution, replacing a tyrannical monarchy with an authoritarian and even more totalitarian populist élite; the Chinese Revolution which replaced a corrupt oligarchical republic with a dictatorship; and only a handful of others. There are periods in history, however, when several countries collectively go through so sudden and dramatic a change in both their actual governmental forms, and the publicly accepted ideology that, whether planned or not, whether violent or not, revolution seems the only term. Thus it was common to talk about the revolutions in Eastern Europe between 1989 and 1991 which swept away communist regimes which had, only months before, seemed unmovable. It is interesting that such language seems to have been dropped in favour of the more technical idea of a '**democratic transition**', largely because of the continued presence of the old ruling parties within the politics of the new nations, and the lack of mass violence involved in the changes.

Right

Right, or right-wing, like **left**, derives as a term of political description from the French Estates General which sat immediately before the French Revolution. Those who were neither aristocratic nor clerical, and therefore most prone to be **radical**, were traditionally seated on the left of the chamber, the others on the right. Hence right-wing has come to stand for forces of privilege and traditional authority. The term has absolutely no fixed semantic content, and can only ever be used relatively. It would be a mistake to see 'right' as a synonym for **conservative**, and, indeed, in many contexts conservatives themselves will protest against the label. The nearest one can come to a definition is that the 'right' are those least in favour of socio-political change in any context, unless that change be regressive to an (often imaginary) past age (see **reactionary**) Even this minimalist definition can be problematic. The changes desired by the Berlusconi government elected in Italy in 2001 are far-reaching, and are not a return to a past, imagined or otherwise. Nevertheless, the changes involve undoing policies precious to previous left-wing parties, and will have the consequence of producing a society nearer to an overall image of a conservative free-market system. In that sense then they are right-wing, somewhat in the sense that it has always been possible to talk of the 'radical right'.

Further aspects of being right-wing, which really follow from that definition, are that the right tends to believe in authority and obedience rather than participation and liberty, to stick to values that fit well with their contemporary societies and to defend whatever system of privilege exists in their society. (Sociologically, it is of course also the case that the more one benefits from the existing system, the more likely one is to be right-wing.) It is not at all uncommon, for example, to hear analysts of communist politics talk of the 'right wing' of the party, by which they have not meant those whose ideology is more pro-Western, but rather those who wished to retain the pertaining Soviet or other communist system, rather than risk experiments with a more liberal socialism. During the revolutions against communism in the Soviet Union and its eastern bloc in the period 1989–91 right-wing invariably meant orthodox communists dedicated to Marxism, and the left were understood to be in favour of liberal values and a capitalist system. The relativity must be stressed, but the utility of the labels cannot be denied for this reason.

Roman Catholicism

Roman Catholicism, one of the largest of all world religious sects, and with more adherents than any other Christian denomination, has in the past been enormously important in Western politics. As the original faith of medieval Europe the Roman Catholic Church was built deeply into the developing political systems of the **First World**, and though the Reformation led to a considerable diminution in its importance in those areas, mainly Britain and Northern Europe, where Protestantism prevailed, the politics of countries where the Counter-Reformation succeeded remain deeply imbued with Roman Catholic influences. Latin America, settled by the most determined of the Counter-Reformation states, Spain and Portugal, is almost entirely Roman Catholic, and the church has frequently played a crucial role in the unstable political systems of the region.

Although there can be no doubt that Roman Catholicism is politically most influential, the nature and direction of its influence differs greatly as the actual history of Roman Catholicism varies. In those societies (Latin America, Italy, Poland and Ireland, for example) where it is unrivalled by Protestant or non-Christian religions, the Church has often been closely allied either with governing parties and classes, or has been the major opposition to governing secular élites. Elsewhere Roman Catholicism has tended to correlate with social class and reinforce voting patterns. In the USA and the United Kingdom, for example, Roman Catholics have tended to be of lower social class, and to have voted strongly for left-wing parties, although religion *per se* has not been the basis for social **cleavages**. Yet in the Netherlands Roman Catholics have been of great political importance as one of three basic political sectors which cut across class lines, the others representing, respectively, the Protestants and the 'secular' (basically socialist) sectors. Religious cleavages of this form, however, tend to become less important over time. The proportion of Roman Catholics voting for the Labour party in the UK is now not much different from the proportion of members of the Church of England doing so, while the Roman Catholic Church has more or less vanished as a political force in French politics (see **Mouvement Républicaine Populaire**), and in the Netherlands the two Protestant parties have allied with the Roman Catholic party to become a predominantly middle-class non-denominational Christian party like the German Christian Democratic Union. In those countries where Roman Catholicism is not only the dominant religion but also has special ties with, or influence over, the state, Ireland being one of the most obvious cases, many details of policy are affected, especially those, like **abortion**, and birth control, which relate to family life and private morality.

The sheer size of the Roman Catholic congregation world-wide, combined with the highly authoritarian and hierarchical nature of the church, has at times made its leader, the Pope, a major figure in world politics, with little power but with the sort of influence seldom held by heads of even the biggest states. As reforming movements such as that in Dutch Roman Catholicism reduce the political power of the Roman hierarchy within the Church, and as church members privately or publicly act in defiance of church teaching, this role may well decline. At the same time the influence of **liberation theology** has made the Roman Catholic Church in areas of the Third World positively radical, often to the consternation of the authorities in Rome.

Rousseau

Jean Jacques Rousseau (1712–78) was the leading French political thinker of the 18th century, a man often credited, though by then dead, with inspiring the French Revolution, and still perhaps the principal inspiration for the whole **participatory democracy** movement. His work, which covered many areas, as was typical of the **Enlightenment** *philosophes*, who were happy to number him among them, is best portrayed in three works. Of these the *Social Contract* is by far the best known, if only by its title, but the *Discourse on the Origin of Inequality* certainly and, arguably, *Émile* (his treatise on education) are equally important for an understanding of his political theory. In the *Social Contract* Rousseau argued that democracy was only possible, and could only guarantee freedom (his principal concern), when people lived in small 'face-to-face' communities where all citizens could and would fully join in the making of all laws in some form of participatory assembly. For Rousseau, **representative democracy** as usually practised in the West was meaningless, making citizens free only for a few minutes every few years when they went to the polls. He insisted that freedom involved being subject only to those rules one had intentionally 'willed', hence his concept of the **general will**, a joint and communal intention which came about only when the whole society met together, ignored their private desires and voted for what they felt was in the **public interest**. Rousseau, though obviously a champion of an extreme if impracticable democratic freedom, has also been seen as a dangerously author-itarian writer, whose views anticipate **fascism**. This opposition comes about because of his very great concern for equality, and his belief in mass meetings and mass influence, both of which seem to threaten liberal individualism. What is usually forgotten in such attacks is that Rousseau himself was so aware of the social conditions necessary for his theories to apply, especially that they could only work in very small communities where everyone knew each other, that he despaired of them ever being implemented in his contemporary Europe. Although his major book is called the *Social Contract,* and although he is usually considered along with **Hobbes** and **Locke** as a **social contract** thinker, his own views are much closer to the classical Greek political philosophers, in that he regarded mankind as essentially social in nature, and dismissed the idea of man living in a **state of nature**, except, perhaps, as a 'noble savage', one without the hallmark of humanity, the use of language.

Rule of Law

The meaning of the rule of law is fairly simple, but its application can often lead to considerable problems: decision-makers of a society express their decisions in terms of general rules or principles, which are then applied automatically and indiscriminately by courts, police and administrators to anyone who comes within their ambit. The stress is on the neutrality and generality of such decision-making. **Aristotle's** *Politics* was perhaps the first recognition that individual human judgment on each and every case of social conflict that came before a judge was not likely to produce fairness and equity, and thus recommended that judges should be no more than appliers of previously fixed rules to factual cases. Following this idea, the rule of law has come to be seen as a major contribution to equality and liberty. It requires legislatures to look only at the abstract feature of a problem, and to promulgate a general rule, and judges to look only at relevant characteristics, under the immediate rule, in deciding cases. The 'judge' can be anyone with decision-making powers on particular cases—for example, an employee of the Department of Employment deciding on an unemployment compensation case, or even a librarian deciding the fine someone should pay on an overdue book. The essence is that they should decide only according to the rule laid down, not according to their own sense of justice or personal preference. This can sometimes lead to largely similar cases being judged very differently due to marginal circumstantial variations. The rule of law is contrasted with arbitrary power, as happens in a **police state**, or the personal whim of a dictator, however enlightened. It is celebrated in the US Constitution which specifically calls for 'the rule of law and not of men'.

S

SALT (Strategic Arms Limitation Talks)

A period of **détente** between the USA and the Soviet Union (formally, the Union of Soviet Socialist Republics—USSR) allowed for the first serious negotiations on **arms control** between the **superpowers** to commence in 1969. A coincidence of different motives made for relatively easy and rapid progress. The USA wished to avoid an expensive **arms race** with the USSR, in part because it was heavily involved in the financially ruinous **Vietnam War**. Furthermore it was very much in the USA's interest to have the USSR remain relatively passive while it was so heavily engaged in South-East Asia. The USSR had been seeking **nuclear parity** with the USA ever since the **Cuban missile crisis** of 1962, and could not hope to achieve this if the USA was to continue increasing its missile stock. Even given this no agreement could have been achieved but for a specific fact about strategic nuclear war. At least according to the US theory of **mutual assured destruction**, nuclear weapons were unlike **conventional arms** because there was an upper limit to the number of warheads that could possibly be needed. The USA believed that its nuclear inventory had already reached such a level, and that adding to it would not give any added security, so were prepared to agree to some form of parity with the USSR. The SALT I Treaty (technically the Interim Agreement on Strategic Offensive Arms), signed in 1972, was, however, very limited because of verification problems. Neither country was prepared to allow on-site inspection, so verification had to be limited to what are known as 'national technical means'. This essentially meant reconnaissance satellites, which could do little more than count the total numbers of missile silos or, as SALT I's critics put it, 'holes in the ground'. Very little could be ascertained about the technology installed in the missiles, and even less about submarine-launched ballistic missiles (SLBMs). Nevertheless, SALT I brought a degree of stability by putting an upper limit on the total number of missiles each country could have, based roughly on existing US force levels. SALT I was always intended as a temporary holding operation, to be completed in a more ambitious way by a second treaty, on which negotiations started immediately. The **Anti-Ballistic**

Missile (ABM) Treaty was negotiated and signed as part of the same procedure.

A second treaty, SALT II, was ready for signing by 1979, and dealt more specifically with the total numbers and explosive power of warheads, rather than with the mere delivery systems limited under SALT I. It took account of the new technology of MIRV (multiple independently-targeted re-entry vehicle) warheads that SALT I had ignored. Since the development of this technology in the late 1960s the number of missiles had become much less important because each missile could carry up to a dozen, or even more, separate warheads. Little could be done to control the total number of these precisely, and negotiations proceeded obliquely by calculating the maximum number of warheads a missile of a given thrust and size could theoretically carry, and assuming that all missiles *would* carry this maximum. At the same time as the SALT II negotiations were taking place deployment of another new technology, the slow, low-flying, but very sophisticated, cruise missile, was being planned. Although outside the remit of the SALT procedure, as they were non-strategic, cruise missiles could not be ignored as they could be launched from ground, air, ship or submarine, and travel several thousand miles; although their main purpose was against battlefield targets, they could also theoretically be used against strategic targets. (Ground-launched cruise missiles only came under control later in the politically very different context of the **Intermediate Nuclear Forces (INF) Treaty**.)

The SALT II Treaty was successfully negotiated despite these difficulties, although the limits agreed on allowed the number and sophistication of weapons on both sides to increase considerably. It was, however, never ratified because the USSR's invasion of Afghanistan, combined with unrelated political opposition to the USSR in domestic US politics, forced President Jimmy Carter to withdraw it from Senate consideration. Despite this both sides agreed to abide by it and, to a very large extent its limits were followed, despite a collapse of détente after Ronald Reagan's accession to the presidency in 1981, past its proposed expiry date of the end of 1985 and until the whole atmosphere of superpower arms control negotiations had changed in the late 1980s.

Sanctions

When sanctions are referred to in politics, it is almost always as a shorthand for the supposed application of non-violent sanctions in international relations. A sanction, of course, is simply a punishment applied by a stronger to a weaker actor to persuade him to stop doing something, as opposed to a pure punishment which may have an entirely retributive intent. The apparent attraction of sanctions in this sense in the international arena is that they are seen, very simply, as an alternative to going to war against a state which is behaving against the interests or moral preferences of other actor states. It is characteristic of sanctions in practice that they involve international co-operation, while straightforward war-making can be unilateral. Although countries have always made threats to other countries, the actual application of a sanction is a complicated matter and relatively recent as a concept in international politics.

Probably the first important appearance of the idea of sanctions was the policy of the **League of Nations**, between the two world wars, to oppose expansionist policies by aggressor states not by international or military action but by international economic action. Sanctions typically take the form of a trade embargo such that the offending nation is allowed neither to export or import some or all goods, and it may be completely isolated financially and economically. For most of the last decade of the 20th century, for example, Iraq was subject to **United Nations**-legitimated trade sanctions which concentrated on preventing it earning any international currency through oil exports. These were enforced because Iraq refused fully to co-operate with the UN attempt to prevent them from developing weapons of mass destruction.

Two important points have to be made about sanctions. The first is that there is little evidence of them ever having worked. Countries can endure great hardship if they are politically united, and the external application of sanctions is a very effective way of building internal cohesion and hatred of the sanction imposing external world. Secondly, sanctions are seldom as 'peaceful' or non-violent as they appear. Typically, great hardship is created in the poorest sectors of a sanctioned society, while the intransigent political élites remain relatively immune.

In the end the direct application of force by those nations who feel entitled to prevent another state from doing something is probably not only the more efficient means, but the more humane policy. It is, of course, much harder to get an alliance together to take military action than to carry out a trade boycott. If this means that it is less easy to gain approval for direct force than for sanctions, then that may indicate that there are relatively few examples of genuinely justified international coercive actions.

Satire

Satire has been a vital political weapon at some time or other in most societies. There are elements of intentional political satire in Aristophanes' play *The Wasps,* Voltaire's novel *Candide* lampoons political doctrines of his day and English literature is full of satire in plays, poetry and novels, particularly during the 18th and early 19th centuries—*Gulliver's Travels* by Jonathan Swift is certainly one of the best known examples. In the 1960s television satire came of age in most Western countries, and especially in the United Kingdom and the USA, with programmes such as *That Was the Week That Was*. Similarly, satirical political periodicals like the British *Private Eye* and the French *Le Canard Enchaîné* have long been important. The essence of satire is to exaggerate grossly characteristics of the political targets—visually exemplified, for example, in the British television series of the 1980s, *Spitting Image*, and its numerous European counterparts, with their puppets' distorted ears and over-large noses.

At its simplest level satire works by making a political opponent look ridiculous, pricking pomposity, reducing authority by encouraging laughter, or by reminding readers or audience of a politician's less pleasant aspects. More deeply, satire can work by taking an argument literally, and encouraging people to think much more clearly about the logical implications of initially acceptable stances. Swift's essay *Modest Proposal*, encouraging the eating of Irish babies to avoid famine, by extension from the territorial swallowing of Ireland by England, is such an example. Perhaps George Orwell's *Animal Farm* is a combination of both styles: it makes egalitarian doctrines seem ridiculous by extending them to absurdity, and at the same time it makes the leaders of communist societies seem less than human by the animal analogy. Satire tends to flourish for brief periods in societies, and then fade away as the ever present forces that encourage deference to those in **authority** re-emerge.

Scenario

A scenario is any imaginary description of a possible future problem, which can be used by the potential actors to plan policy and **strategy**. As such it is closely related to **game theory**. Scenarios have been extensively used in defence, with a large number of models of potential conflicts being set up to enable conventional and nuclear force requirements to be calculated, and to study the political, diplomatic and military consequences of a variety of postures that might be adopted. At its most technical, a scenario can be the basis for extremely complicated and even computerized simulations. An example of a purely domestic British political scenario might be the result of an election in which no party held a majority in parliament, and where the previous prime minister, though now the leader of a minority party, refused to resign. The scenario, especially if built with sufficient realistic detail, would allow examination of the adequacy of our understanding of, for example, the constitutional position of the monarch, and perhaps help in the development of theories about the need for a written constitution. It is no different in principle from a technique sometimes used by physical scientists called a 'thought-experiment'. Increasingly university departments, under pressure to modernize their teaching techniques, are using scenario-building along with simulation games to help students grasp the dynamics of politics.

Schumpeter

Joseph Alois Schumpeter (1883–1950) was born and educated in Vienna, later emigrating to the USA, in 1932, to take up a professorship at Harvard. His principal academic discipline was as an economist, in which role he gained great prestige, but his work is probably now most important in political science. Schumpeter's great work, *Capitalism, Socialism and Democracy* (1942) mainly concerns an analysis, similar to the approach of **Weber**, of how the sheer scale of modern industry is likely to force a convergence between **capitalism** and **socialism** as modes of production, because of the tendency towards a bureaucratic form of management in both societies (see **convergence thesis**). At the same time he argued that the scale of industrial units might well require some form of **nationalization** if they were to be controlled at all.

The part of his theory that is still vitally important to political sociology is his discussion of democracy, where he developed aspects of the earlier theories of power **élitism**, and where his arguments form the basis both for later American **pluralism**, and for the important work of Anthony **Downs**, *An Economic Theory of Democracy*. As rational choice theory gains ever increasing strength in the social sciences, Schumpeter's early efforts to apply economic thought processes to other topics is seen as foundational. 'Schumpeter's main contention was that democracy could only sensibly be seen as a procedure for government, a decision-making mechanism, and did not entail specific values in itself, thus setting him apart from the classical tradition of democratic theory descended from **Rousseau** and John Stuart **Mill**. To Schumpeter democracy was no more than the periodic elections during which voters chose one or other of a set of teams of competing leaders, the political parties. That done, he felt that the ordinary citizen not only could not, but should not, have any further role in the shaping of policy.

In part this latter aspect flows from his very pessimistic assessment of human rational capacity, and his belief, borrowed from earlier works on crowd psychology, that people, in the mass, lost whatever rational capacity they had and became subject to mass hysteria, and to manipulation by political demagogues. It is noticeable that Schumpeter's own life, lived mainly in Austria and Germany until he was nearly 50, made him acutely conscious of the dangers of unstable mass democracy. His experience, however brief, in government (he was minister of finance for the Austrian Republic in 1919) clearly also contributed to his view of economics and policy-making.

Secession

Secession means the attempt by some region in a political system to become independent of the rest of the state and rule itself as an autonomous nation. Numerous civil wars have been fought over attempted secession moves, for example the American Civil War when the southern states declared themselves a new nation as the Confederate States of America and fought for their independence. More recently secessionist moves in the largely artificial post-colonial countries of Africa have led to civil war, most notoriously in the horn of Africa, the former Belgian Congo (now the Democratic Republic of the Congo) and Nigeria. Secessionist movements are much more likely in federal or confederal states, partly because by their very nature they keep alive the idea and symbolism of autonomy, partly because their very existence as a federation is precisely because of the existence of internal ethnic or social divisions, and partly because they seldom have a lengthy history of unity sufficient to overcome separatist tendencies.

Though attractive, where a region has a strong sense of local identity or of shared interests that conflict with the rest of the society, secession seldom succeeds. Almost nowhere is the idea of secession seen as legitimate, though there are exceptions, notably in the 1936 'Stalin' constitution of the Soviet Union where the right to secede was formally granted to all constituent republics. Ironically this right was not carried over into the more liberal 1977 constitution, so that the genuine desire to secede expressed by the constituent republics in the early 1990s was technically no longer legal, and rapidly led to the complete break-up of the Union. Secession demands have been, and may be expected to continue to be, intense in much of Eastern Europe, because the national boundaries drawn up after the two world wars, as for example in Yugoslavia and Czechoslovakia, both of which fragmented in the 1990s, largely imposed unity on disparate historical and cultural entities, and in parts of the former Soviet Union, where republican boundaries often bore little relevance to demographic realities, particularly after the often forced movements of population during the tsarist and communist periods. It may not technically be correct to refer to the split of Czechoslovakia into the Czech and the Slovak Republics in this way because it was done by agreement, but it is clear that the alternative would have been outright secession by the Slovaks.

Second Ballot

The second ballot **voting system** is a modification of the simple plurality method and requires that candidates secure an overall majority of votes (that is, 50% + 1) before they can be elected. Thus in France, for example, after a first ballot for the National Assembly a second ballot is held in those constituencies where no candidate had achieved an overall majority, and in which candidates with less than 12.5% of the votes withdraw, thereby freeing their supporters to vote for a candidate more likely to be elected. (For the 1986 legislative elections only a system of **proportional representation** was used.) At presidential elections in, for example, Austria, France and Poland there is, if necessary, a run-off between the top two candidates remaining in contention after the first ballot. The candidate gaining most votes in the second ballot, whether or not they have achieved a majority, is duly elected. The advantage of this system is that it does give voters who have supported unsuccessful candidates in the first ballot the chance to express a second choice. It also encourages alliances and less formal arrangements between parties, as those with broadly similar ideologies will often agree that the less successful of their candidates will withdraw from the contest in each constituency and encourage their supporters to vote for the other. Minor parties, or parties with no obvious alliance partners, tend to do much less well in second ballots.

Second Chamber

Second chambers are legislative bodies which are composed on a different principle to that of the first or most important chamber of a country's parliament (see **assembly**). In many instances the existence of a bicameral **parliament** has its origins in the medieval period, when representation of different social classes was thought to require separate chambers. Thus the second chamber may be an appointive or hereditary chamber, as with the United Kingdom's House of Lords until the beginning of the 21st century giving representation to political and social elders. In federal systems, for example the US or Australian **Senates**, the second chamber is especially likely to be representative of states or regions rather than of individual voters *per se*. The German second chamber, the Bundesrat, represents the Länder, with each German state sending a **delegation** to the chamber which casts its vote *en bloc*. The powers of the second chamber will usually differ from those of the lower and more politically representative chamber, although—as in the USA—it is not always the case that the second chamber will see itself as politically subordinate. Typically, lower chambers regard themselves as paramount in financial matters; second chambers often concentrate on the revising of legislation or the conduct of foreign policy. In some countries the boundaries of power between the two chambers remains unclear. Second chambers have frequently been seen as conservative bodies which could check the excesses of the more popular chamber: while sometimes true it need not be so. The French Senate in the early years of the **Fifth Republic** was a liberal force critical of the government and the US Senate has often been more liberal than the House of Representatives. The theoretical constitutional problems of designing and justifying a second chamber are well illustrated by attempts to reform the British House of Lords. The Labour government elected in 1997 found little problem in expelling most of the hereditary peers, but then came across serious and insoluble problems in obtaining political agreement as to the nature and composition of a new chamber and what powers the resulting body should have.

Second Strike Capacity

Second strike capacity is one of the many technical terms developed by strategic theorists after the development of nuclear weapons, and as part of the overall doctrine of nuclear **deterrence**. It means that a country must have sufficient nuclear weapons, or weapons sufficiently well hidden and protected that, even if an enemy successfully launched a nuclear attack with total surprise, the defenders can guarantee to have, after bearing the attack, enough nuclear capacity to inflict guaranteed damage on the attacker. This level of guaranteed damage must be enough to make the original attack not worth the inevitable cost (see **mutual assured destruction**). Typically, second strike capacity involves the special protection of the defender's nuclear weapons, either by siting them in virtually invulnerable silos, or in nuclear submarines. The problem with the doctrine is that it refers not to a static concept but to a dynamic one, because what was at one time an invulnerable silo, or an undetectable location, can cease to be if the potential enemy improves the power of its weapons, or the sophistication of its reconnaissance. Thus the search for the, essentially defensive, second strike capacity can in itself lead to an **arms race**.

Secular State

A secular state is one which has no official ties to any religious movement. The United Kingdom, therefore, cannot technically be regarded as secular because there is an officially **established church**, the Church of England, just as the Scandinavian countries have established Lutheran churches whose ministers are very nearly civil servants, and Greece establishes the Greek Orthodox Church. The USA, however, with the First Amendment to its constitution expressly forbidding the creation of an established church, is a secular state. In practice the term has more to do with the extent to which governing parties are really independent of religious affiliation. With this alternative definition, the UK, the USA and Scandinavia are essentially secular. In contrast, Italy could not be so regarded, even though **Roman Catholicism** ceased to be the official state religion in 1985, because the major party of government from the Second World War until the collapse of the 'Old Republic' in the early 1990s, the Christian Democrats, had vital and close ties to the church. Some states, the Netherlands being a good example, are ambiguous on the issue, having clearly identified parties with close religious connections (often in government), but a general acceptance of the need to ensure religious freedom Germany demonstrates how complex the idea of secularism can be. Like the USA the German constitution actually contains a clause saying, in so many words, that no church can be established. The constitution also, however, protects religious freedom in a way that allows considerable influence over, for example education, if one of the provincial governments wishes to do so. Furthermore the German government collects funds for churches by the application of a church tax which, though voluntary, is paid by the majority of the population. Away from **Christianity**, Iran is an important example of a non-secular state; its government is suffused by clerics and the prevailing ideology of the state itself is the religious ethic of **Islam** (see **theocracy**). In this context Israel is another ambiguous case because of the special position given in some ways to Rabbinic law; there is no direct involvement, however, of the government in religious matters, and non-religious Jews are not deprived of any civil rights. (See also **secularization**.)

Secularization

Although it is common to spell this concept out fully as 'religious secularization', the extra word is redundant. Secularization means becoming secular, that is non-spiritual, non-religious, with the contrast being the sacred. Secularization usually refers, as a shorthand, to the long historical process by which all manifestations of religion have become less and less important in Western societies. There are many strands to secularization, just as there are many rival explanations for it. There are also those who still resolutely deny that secularization has really taken place, and certainly deny any inevitability to the process. Those who do deny, or wish to minimize, the extent of secularization have two recourses. They can either deny that past societies were influenced as much by religion as many like to think, or deny that the data that seem to show an inexorable process of secularization really implies that at all.

The core sociological finding that supports the idea of secularization is that formal religious observance, either in attendance at organized worship or in any other measure of membership of churches, has declined steadily throughout the last century, and particularly rapidly in the second half of the 20th century, in nearly all Western societies. Other measurements support this apparent trend—thus civil rather than religious marriage has become more popular, smaller percentages of children are baptized and vocations to the priesthood and ministry have sharply declined. It will be noted that most of the references above are to Christianity. There is far less evidence of secularization among most non-Christian faiths, although Jewish communities in most

Western societies seem also to have experienced secularization. Furthermore, all religions, including Christianity, seem to have at least withstood secularizing tendencies, if not actually to have increased in popularity, in many non-Western societies. The main criticism, is that other measurements, such as the percentage of people in surveys claiming to believe in God, do not show the near collapse of traditional religion that external and objective measures indicate. An apparent glaring exception to secularization as a pervasive trend apparently endemic to modern industrial society is the continuing high rate of religious observance in the USA. As most of the sociological theory that predicted secularization links it to the nature of advanced industrial society, American 'exceptionalism' requires an explanation that has not been consensually forthcoming.

Senates

Senates are **second chambers** of a legislature. Originally senates, deriving from ideas about the Roman Senate in republican times, were seen as bodies especially constituted of the oldest, ablest and wisest people able to transcend the petty and partisan strife of ordinary politics and look more directly to the public interest. Partly for this reason they are, or were, often indirectly elected by an electoral college. There is still often a sense of the Senate being more distanced from partisanship. They are usually much smaller bodies than the lower house, and a sense of collegiality can prevail to make something real out of an otherwise anachronistic ideal. In most cases senates are elected on a different franchise from the lower house and have different powers within the legislative process. In Italy and France the role of the Senate is secondary to the more important lower house which is seen as the embodiment of the popular political will.

Senates are frequently used in federal systems (see **federalism**), where it is thought constitutionally desirable to ensure that the territorial units of the federation are represented as well as the individual citizens, and where safeguards against simple majority rule need to be built into the system. In the USA the Senate represents the 50 states equally and has frequently been seen as the more important legislative body. Certainly the US Senate has retained formidable powers in such areas as foreign policy and the confirmation of major presidential appointments, and its members have much more political prominence than the 435 members of the House of Representatives. A US senator is elected for a six-year term and thus enjoys more security of tenure than a counterpart in the House.

Separation of Powers

Separation of powers, a classic doctrine of liberal politics, is associated with both **Locke** and **Montesquieu**, and is supposed to typify, above that of all other countries, the structure of the US Constitution. The idea is that the dangers of political power overcoming the public interest will be minimized if the different sorts of legal power are distinguished and handed to separate bodies for exercise. The three forms of power that are usually identified are the rule-making power (**legislature**), the power to apply rules and policies (**executive**) and the power to try alleged offenders against these rules (**judiciary**).

If these three types of power are rigorously separated, with checks against the usurpation of one type of power by another agency, it is thought that the utilization of power will be kept under control. Furthermore it is seen as inherently likely that abuse of power will arise if, for example, the same body both makes a rule and decides if someone has broken it. Few political systems operate, even in theory, by a strict separation of power—the role of judicial power in the United Kingdom, for example, is less than clear, and both parliament, the legislative body, and the cabinet, as the executive, interpenetrate each other's area. (This has begun to be politically controversial at the beginning of the 21st century because of the role of the Lord Chancellor, who is the head of the judiciary, the presiding officer of the House of Lords, and a cabinet member heading an executive department. Even the senior judiciary have called for an end to this anomaly.) However, the distinction between legislature and executive is valid, and keeping at least roughly to it not only reduces the dangers of abuse of power, but probably makes for more efficient government. One of the major problems with totalitarian political systems, or with one-party states and military dictatorships, is that the desires of one major group are not only politically dominant, but are exercised in all three fields. The doctrine is closely linked to the idea of the **rule of law**, which absolutely requires a separation between at least the executive and judiciary.

Sexism

Sexism, after **racism**, was one of the first of the negative '-isms' to come into the public consciousness as a result of the general rethinking of roles, reactions and obligations in modern society that started in the 1960s (see also **politically correct**). Other, later, examples would include, for example, ageism, which has now achieved almost equal legal status in some constitutions, such as that of Canada. In theory sexism is a difference in treatment between genders where none is merited (many -people would only allow such distinction where purely physical characteristics are concerned, and some even look for **affirmative action** in those areas), or the behaviour of members of one gender which is likely to demean the other. In practice it is nearly always the preferential treatment of men over women, or behaviour by men which is degrading to women. Unequal pay for women doing equivalent jobs to men, unequal promotion prospects and governmental or institutional policies which discriminate against women (intentionally or otherwise) are sexist, as are attitudes which belittle the potential contribution of women in society, generally by treating them as domestic and sexual commodities of men. Many areas where sexist **discrimination** has been prevalent have begun to be taken care of by, for example, **equality of opportunity** legislation in employment matters, which is at least partially effective in most Western democracies. Even there, however, government inertia and administrative incompetence continues. For example the 1990 tax reform in the United Kingdom was non-sexist in legislating that married men and women should be taxed separately, but still retained a special tax allowance for married men which was not granted to married women—the assumption being that a husband would earn more than a wife (this tax allowance was subsequently made transferable between husband and wife, and then abolished). In private life, and in the areas of employment not covered by legislation, sexism is still very common as a pattern of behaviour. Early apparent evidence that legislation was making a major inroad on sex discrimination is now doubted. What seems to have happened is that women initially made great progress but then came up against what has been termed the 'glass ceiling' in terms of promotions. Thus though a majority of graduates into the legal profession are now women, the number of women partners in major law firms is seriously unrepresentative of that fact. Similarly in nearly all professions there remains evidence of underpayment of women compared with men.

Shari'a

Shari'a is a general term for Islamic law, referring, as near as it is possible to make an analogy, to the body of precedent and interpretation which makes up common law in the Anglo-American conception of law. As such it is not just abstract legal philosophy, but neither is it concrete statutes legislated by Islamic governments. It derives, in theory at least, from the Koran, but more practically from a long tradition of interpretation and intellectual development by legal scholars and practising Shari'a lawyers. Until relatively recently, the absence of any state overtly and fully dedicated to the application of Islamic law had restricted the area in which Shari'a developed; it had come to apply mainly in areas outside major state interest, particularly family and inheritance law. In the last 30 years, Islamic political fundamentalism has given impetus to a much broader development of Shari'a law because of a need for a well-developed legal code for those countries, notably Pakistan, which have set themselves the goal of running a society entirely based on Islamic principles. Inevitably the Iranian Revolution played a major part in this impetus towards application to states' legal codes, and the work of the religious-legal experts who ran the Iranian state has been crucial in the development of a fully embracing Islamic law. The two most important branches of this development have also been the intellectually and politically most challenging. On one hand what Western countries would call public law, or **constitutional law**, had to be developed if the goal of truly Islamic states was to be achieved. **Islam**, however, has never recognized the autonomy of the state from general moral and religious rule as Western countries have, and the idea of a public law governing individual and state interactions separately from the law governing individual to individual relations is necessarily difficult to establish. It would have been much the same situation had Western European society decided to make itself an entirely Roman Catholic society to be governed completely by canon law. The other area has been the need to develop a working commercial law.

This second area of banking and investment law has been even more complicated in some ways, because the heart of banking and investment is the process of raising funds by charging interest on loans. Even more vehemently than in medieval canon law, usury is forbidden by Shari'a, thus the development of laws allowing a banking sector which can cope with Western economic pressures has been a considerable challenge.

Single-Party Systems

A single-party system is usually one where there is an actual constitutional ban, or an effectively enforced unofficial ban, on the number of parties allowed to stand in elections. Alternatively, there may not even be elections at all, and the party is deemed permanently to be in power. However, single-party systems often in fact hide considerable degrees of internal conflict, with power struggles capable of resulting in major changes of policy within the party. In other cases legal alternative parties may be tolerated by the ruling party, but have no chance of election, or several theoretically separate parties be welded into one tightly-controlled organization. The latter was the case in communist East Germany, for example, while in Mexico the Partido Revolucionario Institucional, in office from 1929–2000, took care to arrange the election of a token handful of members from opposition parties to give a safety valve to public feelings, until elections began to become more genuinely democratic in the 1980s. Finally, effective single-party systems can come about by the sheer preponderance of public opinion in some areas. Until recently many of the southern states in the USA were effectively single-party systems because there was absolutely no chance of a representative of the **Republican Party** winning office. In such a situation the **primary** of the **Democratic Party**, where the choice of who should be the Democratic candidate was at issue, was the only effective election. (Many of the states concerned are now more balanced, even tending towards support for the Republicans, partly as a result of the strong links between that party and influential Christian groups.) The counting of how many parties there are, in any meaningful sense, in a party system is in fact more complicated than it seems (see **multi-party systems**).

Single Transferable Vote (STV)

Many methods of **proportional representation**, but particularly the **party list system**, require a legal and constitutional recognition of political parties, and indeed are centred upon fairness to the parties, but diminish the ability of voters to express their preferences for individual candidates, and weaken the links of **representative democracy** between elected and electors. In some political cultures, notably Anglo-American, these tendencies are disliked and have met with resistance. There the desire is fully to reflect the preferences of individual voters for individual candidates. The most usual method of proportional representation which takes into account these views is the single transferable vote, used, for example, in elections in the Republic of Ireland. Here the notion of a 'wasted vote' is taken even more seriously than in other methods. Multi-member constituencies are required, and a quota of votes is calculated by dividing the total number of votes cast by the number of candidates to be elected. Not only can second and subsequent preferences of the least successful candidates be redistributed (as in the **alternative vote** system), but also a proportionally-adjusted number of alternative preferences from the 'excess' votes of candidates who have achieved the necessary quota. STV is probably the voting system which allows the vote of an individual to have its maximum effect in achieving the election of their most favoured candidates, and guarantees a close approximation to proportionality.

Social Capital

Social capital is a concept that has been known in the social sciences for decades, but it has recently changed its meaning and become freshly significant. Originally social capital was mostly applied to the sociology of education. It referred to the many connections and experiences of the more fortunate in society which had aided their successes, in addition to their more straightforward financial or 'economic capital' advantages. There is no connection whatsoever between this meaning and the current usage of social capital in political science and development studies. It now refers to a set of rather intangible social or collective attributes that make for stable and effective political systems. It is allied to the renewed interest in **trust**, and to other more recent usages such as **civil society**, as well as the older idea of a **civic culture**.

Basically social capital is that set of expectations, almost of social habits, which make it possible for governments to rely on public support at times of stress, or to call forth great public effort or periods of stoicism. Traditions of mutual help and neighbourliness, for example, a strong commitment to public service on the part of educated élites, even extensive collection for charity can turn into vital social capital in this way. The problem with the concept is that its advocates seem to think that the government or state should, and could, act to create or increase the 'stock' of social capital. Not only is it unclear how this could be done, but it is arguable that any such artificially created social patterns are both invasions on privacy and unlikely to be very effective. When all is said and done, social capital is little more than an attempt to describe in political science terms the characteristics of a tight-knit community. There is also the analytic point that such patterns of loyalties are indeed social, and appertain more frequently to sub-cultures rather than to states, which may not easily utilize them even where they exist. For example, it may be that in both the United Kingdom and Germany during the Second World War huge reserves of social capital existed and helped the inhabitants of heavily bombed cities to continue working and living. But in both countries these tended to be attributes of tight working-class communities existing more despite of rather than because of the state.

Social Contract

Social contract theory was especially important around the time of the European **Enlightenment**, the most famous exponents being **Hobbes**, **Locke** and **Rousseau**. The main purpose of these theories was to provide a sound logical base for the particular polity most favoured by the individual theorists on the basis of an appeal to the rational self-interest of ordinary people. Historically the tradition arose because, with the Enlightenment, the possibility of justifying a political system by reference to tradition or to some theological argument in terms of God's will or the **divine right** of kings vanished. The basic argument always took the same form: assume that people are living without any government at all. That is, they are free and autonomous individuals, but also subject to all the difficulties and dangers of living in a state of anarchy. Would such free people wish to have a government? What sort of government would they wish to see set up, and under what conditions would they give up just what proportion of their independence for the benefits of such a government? The answers which come out of this particular thought-experiment depend very much on the description of the anarchical set-up (usually called the **state of nature**) put in. Hobbes, for example, painted the state of nature as so awful that he thought it likely that consent would freely be given to the most authoritarian and draconian of governments. Locke, however, argued that the state of nature was only mildly awkward, and thus derived a very liberal and weak state from his social contract. It was not necessarily assumed that the social contract had ever been an actual historical event; the emphasis was much more on a logical defence of a hypothetical state by suggesting what would happen were people free to make such a choice. The method of theorizing became unfashionable for a long time, being replaced by **utilitarian** arguments which tended to get to much the same conclusions from a different approach. Since the 1960s modified versions of social contract theories have reappeared, especially in the work of the most important of all modern political philosophers, John **Rawls**.

Social Democracy

Social democracy is a label used to indicate a reformist and non-Marxist left-of-centre party, one which differs from moderate **conservatism** only in relatively marginal ways. A typical social democrat party, for example, will probably espouse some degree of **nationalization**, but do so more in terms of the capacity for organized planning of the economy, or the guaranteed production of public utilities, than from any theoretical opposition to private property *per se*. Again, a social democrat party is likely to opt for higher and more proportional direct taxation, and for taxes on industry and commerce, on the grounds of social justice. Such a party will, in general, seek some redistribution of wealth, especially through an organized **welfare state**, but will not make equality a primary goal in its own right. The Social Democratic Party of Germany (SPD) and the French **Parti Socialiste** are all social democrat parties, whether or not the words appear in their titles. The British **Labour Party**, was formerly social democrat, but since the rise to power of Tony Blair and his reformists who re-branded the party **'New Labour'**, it is difficult to claim that the label is still valid. The other parties mentioned have either begun, or appear likely to begin, to move the same way as an international consensus forms around the commitment to a more **laissez-faire** economic policy and a monetarist fiscal policy.

The prototypes, or paradigms, of social democracy are the more or less identical and so-named social democrat parties of the Scandinavian countries, which presided over a mixed (that is, capitalist but partly nationalized and highly planned) economy, and a tax-expensive welfare state, for most of the period between the end of the First World War and the early 1970s and, in the case of Sweden into the 1990s . Occasionally, as in the German constitution (*Grundgesetz*—the Basic Law), the phrase 'social democracy' is used to identify an entire system of government. If this usage means anything at all, it is a combination of the political theory concept of a **liberal democracy** combined with some general sense of a semi-legal right to the protection of a welfare state. In most cases where a party actually calls itself 'social democrat', the explicit use of the title is an attempt to establish a special identity to a more right-wing version of what is in fact a generally unrevolutionary and unradical form of **socialism**, and does not usually connote any specific theoretical or ideological position.

Social Market Economy

The social market economy is unique to modern Germany, and it is the result of a set of political and economic principles imposed by the first governments of the new Federal Republic in the 1950s. Much of the credit for the supposed German economic miracle occurring in the middle of the 20th century, is given to this socio-economic philosophy, enshrined in the German constitution and applied, at least in theory, to this day. Although the major external characteristics of the social market philosophy are easy enough to describe, it is extremely difficult to go into depth. At its simplest, the social market economy is one that combines a deep commitment to free-market economics with an equally deep commitment to very generous state **welfare** and educational policies. The extra ingredient, which other countries who try to balance both market economies and decent welfare provision sometimes omit, is a commitment on the part of the state to ensure the conditions for effective and non-distorted economic competition. A good example is the deliberate depoliticization of the interest rate mechanism by entrusting the exchange rates to a completely independent **central bank**, which cannot be politically coerced. As a result, a minimal inflation rate has always been a hallmark of the German economy; the associated risk of high unemployment has been acceptable because of the generous welfare provisions.

Other aspects would include writing into law quite complex worker representation in the operation of even large private companies; legislatively balancing funds to minimize income discrepancies between the states in the federation; a counter-cyclical fund for government expenditure, equally legislatively protected; and well established government support for private savings schemes.

In truth elements of the social market mechanisms are found in many countries; The USA, for example, has always had tough anti-trust laws, and France has always had a highly independent central bank and high welfare expenditure. What differentiates Germany is the explicitness of the philosophy and the complete consensus in politics that such an approach is vital. It is all part of the way the post-war German political system set itself to avoid the excesses of both the left and right during the inter-war years. Similarly, it is part of the historical tendency among the German political class to believe that, with regard to matters of economic organization or constitutional structure it is the duty and the right of a strong central state to impose and nourish a values consensus, rather than allow them to be treated as mere procedure.

Social Mobility

Social mobility is a measure of the extent to which individuals in a society can as adults find themselves in a different social class to that of their parents. Although it may seem a dry sociological index, it is in fact crucial to many sociological theories and impacts on an individual's chances in life more than most macro-characteristics of modern society. In an entirely meritocratic society—to use the jargon—one's class of origin would have no bearing on which class one ended up in. In practice, social mobility is severely limited in most societies; the higher one's family class, the more likely one will spend one's adult life in that or a higher social location. The reasons for this restrictiveness are complex and not fully understood. In older societies, not wedded to doctrines of equal opportunity, there was little mystery—social mobility was neither expected nor encouraged, and the prevailing ideology often held strongly to the idea that people had a 'natural', that is, inherited, class position. (In **caste** societies, of course, this is even more the case—caste cannot, *de jure* and not just *de facto*, be overcome.) However, in the latter half of the 20th century, most **liberal democracies** have officially accepted the Napoleonic idea of *carrière ouvert aux talents*. Yet the chances of the son of a professional or businessman achieving the same status as his father are still very much higher than the chance that a coal miner's son will become a doctor or an executive. To a large extent this is a matter of education; despite full, free, public education many factors restrict the educational success of those whose parents are not themselves educated and relatively affluent.

There is some degree of implicit value judgement in most social mobility research, however, because the idea that people might not want to 'improve themselves', and might feel that following their father in a trade or even a manual labouring job is a fully admirable and satisfactory life, is never countenanced. In part this is because much of the research is influenced by a theory of society which requires that, by the 'logic of industrialization', efficient societies will ensure that the better jobs, because they are more demanding, are always filled by the most able. The other half of the research is influenced by a pervasive left-wing orientation, by which it is taken for granted that low levels of recruitment to upper-class jobs from the lower class must be against the interests and desires of those with low-status family experiences.

There has, in fact, been considerable gross social mobility in modern societies; this is because the shrinkage of first the agricultural sector and then the unskilled working-class sectors of the economy have inevitably meant a growth in the middle classes, particularly in lower professional and managerial employment. However, social mobility researchers concentrate on the idea of 'relative' social mobility—how much greater is the probability of a bank manager's son gaining a similar job compared to the son of a manual worker? It is the continued low rates of relative mobility, despite high rates of gross or absolute mobility, that is thought to be problematic. The use of a male example is intentional. The biggest single problem with social mobility research is that it has concentrated excessively on father and sons, in part because of technical problems in calculating class positions for married women.

Socialism

As with communism, socialism can mean a variety of different things, not because of ambiguity or vagueness, but because it is a concept that operates in several different ideological vocabularies. Within **Marxism**, socialism has a very technical meaning, referring to a phase before the establishment of true **communism**. Outside that debate, socialism does become extremely vague, and is best differentiated into a number of versions, such as **Christian socialism**, **social democracy** and so on. At its simplest, the core meaning of socialism is that it is a politico-economic system where the state controls, either through planning or more directly, and may legally own, the basic means of production. In so controlling industrial, and sometimes agricultural, assets the aim is to produce what is needed by the society without regard to what may be most profitable to produce.

At the same time all versions of socialism expect to produce an egalitarian society, one in which all are cared for by society, with no need either for poverty, or the relief of poverty by private charity. The famous words 'From each according to his abilities, to each according to his needs', first used by the French socialist Louis Blanc (1811–82) in *The Organization of Work* (1840), may summarize socialism at its best. Socialism has gone through many variations, and dating its origin is next to impossible. Certainly it stems most seriously from the industrial revolution, and many who are not Marxists would probably agree that socialism arose as a reaction to **capitalism**, and could not become a popular theory until the development of extensive industrial private property with a society based on contractual relations rather than semi-feudal status relations. Nevertheless, the essential ideas of equality and the effective abolition of private property, combined with the need for social protection against the chances of fate, can be found much earlier in political theory, not least notably in early Christianity. The basic varieties of socialism today can be arranged fairly easily on a spectrum according to just how much control of the economy, and just how much equality, are seen as necessary or desirable. To some extent this coincides with the more broadly used **left/right** spectrum, on which, for example, the British **Labour Party** used to be seen as only mildly left or socialist, and the **Parti Communiste Français** very far to the left, and very socialist. An alternative principle for differentiation would be the extent to which a basically Marxist 'economic determinist' view is taken, as opposed simply to a fairly untheoretical demand for a more just and equal society, with more state impact on the economy. In this sense, for example, the Social Democratic Party of Germany (SPD), the earliest socialist party in Europe, started far to the left, and became less socialist, more right wing, in the late 1950s when it officially gave up Marxism and became a 'reformist' party acceptable even to the conservative CDU/CSU in the grand coalition government of 1966–69.

With the collapse of a genuine revolutionary left after the **democratic transitions** in Eastern Europe and the Soviet Union, and the dominance in the West of **monetarist** economic theory, even in nominally socialist and **social democrat** parties, there seems no way for a European socialist party to be more than reformist, nor for it to have a theoretically sharply distinguishable position.

Socialist International

The Socialist International is one of the inheritors of the internationalist movement among **communist** and **socialist** parties in the late 19th and early 20th centuries (see **international socialism**). Before the October 1917 Russian Revolution there was no very clear-cut distinction between socialist and communist movements, with varying degrees of revolutionary consciousness to be found under both labels. Common to both movements was a commitment to international working-class solidarity, with a general acceptance that the nation-state was a bourgeois contrivance to manipulate the proletariat. However, after 1917 the revolutionary element became dominant and the international movement was re-created as the Communist International (also known as Comintern or the Third International, which existed only until 1943) in 1919, with very strict membership rules designed to ensure that all national member parties supported revolution rather than **parliamentary socialism**. In Western Europe this resulted in many splits in formerly united socialist or communist parties, and a rival, **gradualist** or parliamentary, movement was created in 1923, initially called the Labour and Socialist International, which traced its origin through the Second International back to the creation of the First International in 1864. Suspended during the war, the movement was refounded in 1951 as the Socialist International. Its membership includes most of the moderate socialist and **social democratic** parties in Europe and elsewhere, such as the British **Labour Party**.

Son of Star Wars

Son of Star Wars is a nickname which has been widely accepted for something the USA originally called the National Missile Defence Programme, and now simply calls the Missile Defence Programme (MDP). The name change demonstrates part of the problem—the word 'national' indicated too clearly the extent to which this amounted to a 'go-it-alone' policy on the part of the USA, one of the principal causes of the intense international objections. The MDP is called the Son of Star Wars because it is the second generation of an attempt by the USA to put up an anti-ballistic missile shield. In scope it is far more modest than President Reagan's famous Star Wars programme (technically the Strategic Defence Initiative). Son of Star Wars proposes radar and communication systems, some based in the United Kingdom and Greenland, in combination with satellites in space, which would provide early warnings of a nuclear attack. The first plan involved space-based interceptor systems, and it was intended to protect the USA from a full-scale strategic attack by the Soviet Union. The attempt by the USA to overcome international opposition to MDP involves proposing a multi-national defence system covering the territory of countries wishing to take part. Inevitably, the larger the area to be defended, the greater the technical challenge. The system is primarily being designed to defend the USA from small-scale attacks by countries such as the Democratic People's Republic of Korea (North Korea), Iran, and so-called 'rogue states' elsewhere in the world. The technologies are still highly imprecise, and several tests have already failed or been delayed. Russia's initial complete opposition to the amendment of the ruling 1972 **Anti-Ballistic Missile (ABM) Treaty** meant that the US policy would require an outright breach of a treaty obligation and thus, a defiance of international law. However, the treaty reducing strategic nuclear capability signed by the US and Russian presidents in May 2002 was perceived to supersede the ABM Treaty.

Whether the plan is really plausible is difficult to say. Certainly any 'rogue state' that launched an attack on the USA would effectively be committing suicide, but strategic planners have long contemplated such a threat where a country feels itself pushed to an extreme limit. In the past, Israel has been seen as possibly capable of such action, but it is unclear how most countries, however radically disenchanted by American world power, could be persuaded to launch such a strike. The probability than any highly reliable scheme can be developed, at least at a cost that even the USA can easily pay, must be remote. Even under a distinctly right-wing administration, the USA was already trimming its defence expenditure and redefining its strategic goals in 2001, before the attacks on the World Trade Center and Pentagon and the subsequent 'War on Terrorism' forced a further reassessment. The main enemies of the MDP may well be the US Army and Navy, who would lose yet further in competition for defence funding were this programme to go ahead. The 'War on Terrorism', in which both these forces were heavily involved, forced MDP down, but not off, the Bush administration's agenda in late 2001 and 2002.

Sovereignty

Sovereignty means the right to own and control some area of the world. It has, nowadays, nothing to do with **monarchy**, which might seem to be implied by the connotation of sovereign, but entirely refers to the idea of independent rule by a country or institution over a certain territory or set of political concerns. Thus a country might dispute the sovereignty of an island over which another country had established control, claiming that they had the right to rule. It is a curiously important concept which is applicable to the ideology of **colonialism**, but can, at the same time, be used inside one country. Thus it is possible, for example, to talk about the sovereignty of the people, as against *de facto* rule by an élite. Its basic meaning is **legitimacy** of rule, as opposed to actual **power**. As a result, those who actually control a country, even though they may have done so for a long time, may face denial of their sovereignty over that area. A secondary meaning that has become important more recently focuses on the idea of national independence, the sole right of the authorities of a particular country to take decisions affecting its citizens. So, especially in the United Kingdom, debates about extending the powers of the **European Union** become entangled in the language of sovereignty; those opposed to an extension insist that the UK would be giving up its sovereignty were it to adopt the common European currency, the euro, controlled by the European Central Bank. Similarly, verification of arms control agreements has required intrusive inspection of countries' military facilities, requiring a relaxation of sovereignty. A rival concept has been developed to deal with some of these issues—the idea of 'pooled sovereignty'. Thus in the case of Europe, instead of seeing anyone giving up sovereignty, all member states 'pool' their sovereignty together. Whether this is anything more than verbal gymnastics will only become clear if issues arise in which the outcome is different from what it would have been had sovereignty actually been abandoned.

Soviet Bloc

The Soviet bloc is a shorthand for those Eastern European states which were under the more or less firm control of the Union of Soviet Socialist Republics

(USSR, known as the Soviet Union), and governed by communist parties, from the late 1940s until the wave of anti-communist revolutions between 1989 and 1991 (see **democratic transitions**). It included for certain the major Central and South-Eastern European countries of Hungary, Poland, Czechoslovakia, Bulgaria and Romania, and what was the German Democratic Republic, or 'East Germany', until German reunification in 1990. It could more loosely be used to cover Albania and Yugoslavia; however, Albania in time became more of a Chinese satellite, particularly between 1960 and 1972, while Yugoslavia followed a very independent line under Tito; these two countries were not guaranteed to side with the USSR on many issues, this being the effective test of membership of the bloc. In particular Yugoslavia played no role in the USSR's war plans for the **Warsaw Pact**. An alternative definition might be to take membership of **COMECON** (technically the Council for Mutual Economic Assistance—CMEA), set up by Moscow in 1949 and which developed into the Soviet bloc's version of the **European Union**. Such a definition would also place Cuba in the bloc which, though geographically odd, makes quite good political sense. As COMECON was originally intended by **Stalin** to be used as a force to bring the over-independent Yugoslavs to heel, this definition would exclude the most autonomous of Soviet wartime acquisitions.

It was Mikhail **Gorbachev's** renunciation of the **Brezhnev** doctrine, which had justified Soviet interventions in domestic politics to prop up orthodox communist rule, such as in Hungary in 1956 and Czechoslovakia in 1968, that opened the first major cracks in the bloc. As the USSR was forced to agree to major conventional force cuts in Europe for economic and diplomatic reasons, the long-held hatred of the populations of these countries boiled over into amazingly rapid, and largely non-violent, **revolutions** which swept away all the trappings of communist rule in a period of little more than two years.

Stalin

Joseph Stalin (1879–1953), born Iosif Vissarionovich Dzhugashvili, was a Georgian peasant by origin who rapidly rose to power in the **Bolshevik** movement before and after the Russian Revolution. By the early 1920s he was close to the centre of power, then wielded by **Lenin**, and benefited from Lenin's suspicion of other communist leaders, including **Trotsky**, so that he was able to use his 1922 appointment as general secretary of the communist party to gradually take ultimate power after Lenin's death in 1924. Stalin ruled the Soviet Union, his power increasing all the time, from then until his death in 1953. For the latter part of his reign, especially after the mid-1930s, he was a total dictator, whose paranoia led to a huge bloodletting in countless purges of party, military and administrative leaders. The estimates of death resulting from his reign have been put as high as 20 million, and the major source of his power was his use of the secret police, especially the NKVD, later renamed as the KGB (see **police state**). His main policies were to force the **collectivization** of agriculture, this itself meaning the forced mass migration of millions of peasants, and death for many of those who resisted, and the development of heavy industry at the expense of immediate living standards. He controlled the whole social, economic and cultural world in the Soviet Union brutally and totally. His major motivation seems to have been a desperate fear for the security of the revolutionary society once it became apparent that other Western societies were not likely to follow the revolutionary path; indeed he transformed the originally internationalist orientation of Soviet theory, enunciating his own doctrine of 'socialism in one country' as early as 1924. This led to his trying to arrange an anti-capitalist mutual protection treaty with **Hitler**, though on Germany's invasion of the Soviet Union in 1941 Stalin's energies and efforts led to a costly but ultimately successful war effort, and the acquisition of most of Eastern Europe as a Soviet 'empire'.

Stalinism

Stalinism is a word used to describe a particular brand of **communism**, often used of European communists or communist parties. It means the most hard-line, inflexible and undemocratic version of **Marxist–Leninism**, and is associated with the style of policy and practice adopted by the Soviet ruler Joseph **Stalin** in the 1930s and 1940s. Stalinism places particularly heavy stress on the duty of rank-and-file members of communist movements to obey the hierarchy, denounces internal debate and, until the 1980s, demanded the strictest adherence to the Soviet line in any policy. Unquestioning support for the leadership, and the total denial of the possibility of a non-revolutionary road to socialism, were parts of the Stalinist's position. For most of the post-war period the **Parti Communiste Français** was seen as especially Stalinist, in contrast, for example, to the **Eurocommunism** of the Italian communist party. The concept is also used of the formerly Soviet-dominated Eastern European states, where relatively 'liberal' societies like, for example, Yugoslavia or Czechoslovakia (before 1968), were contrasted with the more 'Stalinist' regimes in East Germany and, at one time, Poland. The term is sometimes used as a figurative description for anyone who wields political authority in a particularly heavy-handed way, with intolerance of debate or dissension.

State

'State', though a very commonly-used word in the political vocabulary, is surprisingly opaque. Even the derivation of the term is obscure, and in many cultures (including early medieval European society, to take one example) it would be hard to specify what word should be translated as 'state'. It is easier to define it negatively; the state is, for example, not equivalent to the mere **government**. Governments come and go, at least in democracies, without changing the state. In a different way the state is often contrasted, by political theorists, to what they call **civil society**, the whole range of organized and permanent institutions and behavioural practices, like the economy, churches, schools and family patterns, that make up our ordinary life under the ultimate control of the coercive force of politics. The state means, essentially, the whole fixed political system, the set-up of authoritative and legitimately powerful roles by which we are finally controlled, ordered, and organized. Thus the **police**, the **army** and the **civil service** are aspects of the state, as is **parliament** and perhaps local authorities. But many institutions with a great deal of actual power, **trade unions** for example, are not part of the state, because they are voluntary organizations which could, at least hypothetically, be dispensed with, and especially because they directly represent one section of society against another. (In contrast trade unions clearly *were* part of the state in the Soviet Union under communist rule, because they were controlled by the party to exercise discipline over workers. In the original Italian theory of fascism it was bodies like unions and employers federations which became the state.) At least in theory, state organizations are neutral in any such sectional conflict. For this reason political parties are not part of the state (and in most constitutions are totally ignored), and the governments formed and supported by them are not quite seen as part of the state. The offices of, for example, **prime minister** or **president**, however, which depend entirely on parties for their filling and operation, are state offices, even though neither the parties that compete for them, nor the actual individuals filling them, are in their own right part of the state, but are rather aspects of civil society. As a concept the state was somewhat overlooked in political theory and research for much of the 20th century, especially in the Anglo-Saxon world, and still creates considerable confusion and uncertainty. The easiest way to think of it is as the set of fixed roles and institutions that make up the generally legitimate political institutions within which partisan conflict takes place. A state can even survive a revolution if the new rulers continue to use state bodies such as courts and the pre-revolutionary personnel to control the society, as happened, for example, in Germany when there were many such continuities between the **Weimar Republic** and **Hitler** regimes. Without doubt there is a cultural difference in attitude to the state between some European countries, notably France and

Italy where it is distrusted and feared, and others like the UK where it is largely ignored by the public.

State Capitalism

State capitalism was a phrase coined by **Lenin**, and used by him to describe the nature of **Bolshevik** economic policy during the brief period between the Russian Revolution and the creation of the **New Economic Policy (NEP)**. What he meant by it was that Russia had not fully experienced the transformation from feudal to capitalist society, which **Marx** had seen as a necessary stage in social progress, and which he saw as being carried out by the **bourgeoisie**. This point was generally accepted by all parts of the Russian left, but the moderate **Menshevik** party and their centrist allies felt that it meant the revolution should go no further than the abolition of Tsarist **feudalism**, and that true **socialism** would have to wait for the ultimate breakdown of bourgeois **capitalism**. Instead, Lenin argued, the building of a developed industrial infrastructure could be carried out directly by the state under the control of the leaders of the proletarian revolution. This still implied a period, perhaps a lengthy one, before the 'withering away of the state' and the arrival of true egalitarian socialism, but at least one where exploitation was minimal and socialist goals expressly sought. Even after Lenin had dropped the idea (or the phrase, at least) it continued in common left-wing parlance. Later in the 20th century it was used, usually pejoratively, by Western left-wing groups anxious to stress the irrelevance of comparisons with Soviet policies in criticisms of **Marxism**, because the Soviet Union was not practising **communism** but 'merely' state capitalism.

State of Nature

The state of nature is a powerful concept in many brands of political theory, but especially **social contract** theory and its modern versions such as that developed by John **Rawls**. The state of nature is an imaginative reconstruction of how human life and interpersonal relations might have been before the creation of organized political society. Theoretically such an image is used to deduce what the major drawbacks of living in a pre-political environment would be, and thereby to decide what rules for organized political life would recommend themselves to those in a position to make such a choice. Naturally much depends on the original description of how people unconstrained by political authority behave. Taking a very pessimistic view of human nature, as did Thomas **Hobbes**, then the recommendations for the best form of political organization are going to be very different from those given by a political theorist like John **Locke**, who thinks that people would be able to co-operate fairly well without government, and would thus only agree to a rather limited form of political control. The obvious problem is the lack of any evidence about non-political social systems, and the arguments about the form of the state of nature are entirely hypothetical. Nevertheless, given some basic views about human nature, it can be a theoretical technique of great analytic power, even though it is now accepted that man has never lived outside of at least a rudimentary state.

Status

All known societies have had some form of hierarchical ordering in their population, an awareness that some people are, in one way or another, 'higher' on a scale than others. Status is a general way of referring to this phenomenon, and of measuring it. Some of the forms of relative standing are well known and accounted for by specific social theories; economic **class** and **caste**, for example, are well defined. Status is more ambiguous, both because many different factors can enter into the **stratification**, and because it is inherently more subjective. Essentially status is a measure of social respect, of how the value system of a society appraises individuals as more or less worthy of deference, admiration, or honour. It *is* often highly correlated with economic class, and certainly with wealth, but the connection is not automatic. Indeed in some contexts wealth follows from status, rather than endowing it.

A status hierarchy is likely to have evolved over a lengthy period, and to be preserved by those at its head—in their own interest. As such it can often involve the prevention of those lower in the hierarchy from making full use, and receiving full benefit from, their talents (see **discrimination**). This is particularly so when the characteristics that give social status are relatively fixed and out of an individual's control. Attempts to disguise the characteristics of racial or ethnic origin (for example by blacks, particularly in the USA, cosmetically to lighten skin colour and straighten hair) confirm the existence of such hierarchies and the difficulty of countering their social influences. Other status characteristics, such as educational attainment, earning more or being awarded a title or decoration, can be achieved through individual effort, although even here coming from a background of high non-achieved status can be of assistance. The most basic status determinant in modern Western societies is a person's job. Research has shown that there is a fairly high degree of consensus among the population on how to rank occupations, though rankings vary from country to country, and any particular ranking will represent a number of different evaluations. In most societies airline pilots and medical doctors rank high on status scales, whereas coal-miners and nurses rank very much lower. Skill, responsibility and high academic qualifications seem to lead to higher rankings than the danger, unpleasantness and social utility of an occupation. Once established, the status stratification can affect decisions made by, for example bank managers or traffic police, in favour of those with higher status where the realities of a situation, such as income or driving offence, are equal. Status rankings are never uniform throughout a society, and there usually exist subcultures with markedly different evaluations of status from the dominant culture of the society. For example, the most successful or violent criminal might head their own status ranking. But some form of social stratification, interweaving income, class, traditional values from the past, religious affiliation and many other factors seems to exist everywhere, even in relatively egalitarian societies. Even republics, which have overtly overthrown aristocratic classes, often feel the need to invent their own honours systems with complex orders of decorations and medals.

Stockholm Declaration

The Helsinki Final Act of 1975 (see **Helsinki process**) had included, as a suggestion for confidence-building measures, the idea of extensive exchanges of information on military exercises and movements by the participating members. The Madrid follow-up conference of 1980–83 recommended the creation of a parallel negotiating forum, the Conference on Security and Confidence-Building Measures and Disarmament in Europe, usually abbreviated to CDE. This conference began to meet in Stockholm in 1984, and by 1986 had produced a far-reaching agreement, the Stockholm Declaration, on confidence-building measures. The agreement introduced quite severe restrictions on the numbers of troops which could be deployed in an exercise, on the numbers of troops which could be moved out of barracks at any one time and, most importantly, on advance notice periods that had to be given for any such movements or exercises. Above all rights of inspection were provided for, including unannounced 'challenge inspections' and flights by observers over the area of an exercise to monitor the movement of troops. These agreements were immediately and scrupulously observed by all signatory states (the USA, Canada and all European states, with the exception of Albania). The impetus for these confidence-building measures was based on an old theory, much influenced by reflections on the origin of the first world war, that wars are often the result of an automatic process of mobilization triggered by nervousness on the part of one country in the face of apparently sudden and threatening troop movements by another. At the time very significant, it is unclear whether this agreement will hold and help control the risk of pre-emptive war in the new European order. (See also **Organization for Security and Co-operation in Europe**.)

Strategic Arms Limitation Talks (see SALT)

Strategy

Strategy, as opposed to tactics, involves longer-term, and farther-reaching preparations and planning. Primarily strategy and tactics are military terms, though they can be and are applied in any conflict situation. Thus it is possible to contrast politicians who are concerned only with electoral tactics (how best to win the imminent general election), with those who have a political strategy (for example, how to restructure the economy).

In contemporary defence terminology it is probably best to think of strategy as inherently political, and tactics as the purely technical decisions of the military about how best to achieve the strategic goals set by their political superiors. Thus vital questions on the nature of **NATO's** overall policy for the use of nuclear weapons, or whether Britain should retain a military capacity to intervene in conflicts outside Europe, are strategic questions. What exact forces to deploy, armed with what, and with which precise orders, are tactics.

In terms of nuclear warfare there is a slightly different distinction. Strategic nuclear forces consist of major intercontinental missile systems intended to massively destroy the homeland of the enemy. Tactical weapons (sometimes called 'battlefield' or short-range nuclear weapons) are intended for use against enemy military formations, and have much lower yield warheads. NATO systematically refused to promise never to be the first to use tactical nuclear weapons, but always allowed it to be thought that it would only use strategic missile forces in defence against a Soviet **first strike**. Strategy has increasingly taken on an alternate meaning with no direct reference to conflict, as in industrial strategy or the idea of strategic planning, to mean very little more than long-term and broadly-cast plans and analysis. Thus the United Kingdom, for example, has a something known as the 'Strategic Rail Authority' to guide long-term transportation policy, and every public institution is urged to carry out 'strategic reviews'.

Stratification

Stratification, usually more fully 'social' stratification, refers to the way in which a social system is hierarchically ordered. The most common and obvious form of stratification is a **class** system, but race, and, at times, religion or even language, can be forms of stratification. Because political parties tend to form around layers in a stratification system, the basics of social stratification have much to do with the nature of politics and partisanship in a society. Stratification involves more than just social **cleavages**: a society divided between Protestants and Catholics could not be said to be stratified on religious terms unless some elements of social **status** went with religion (as they often do) so that, as for example in parts of the USA at times, Protestants were in some ways socially superior to the more recently arrived Catholic population. However, as such evaluations tend to be derived from income and employment attributes, stratification often collapses back into a crude class system. This is only untrue where the overall culture positively elevates some values associated with the stratification over and above socio-economic matters.

Strike

Trade union organization developed in many countries during the 19th century in an attempt to achieve better terms and conditions for industrial and agricultural workers. They were successors to, rather than developments from, the **corporatism** of the medieval craft guilds, as the agrarian and industrial revolutions led to the creation of much larger bodies of subservient labourers. The ultimate weapon of these workers when bargaining with employers was to withdraw their labour—to go on strike. For two main reasons this weapon was not immediately an easy one to use. Firstly, the legal position of a group collectively refusing to work for an employer was very dubious in most countries, and even where it was not illegal employers could often use threats and coercion to break strikes with impunity. Secondly, the existing **socialist** doctrine on strikes was far too radical to suit the pragmatic needs of workers simply trying to improve their working conditions. This doctrine, usually called **syndicalism**, called for a general strike to destroy the **capitalist** economy and replace it with a form of worker control. Not only did ordinary trade unionists not want this, but when they did go on strike it was easy to portray them as having revolutionary intent. Although unions had been organized and carried out small strikes for some time, the first mass strike in the United Kingdom was the 1889 dock workers strike. Although the law oscillated in many countries, especially over the right of strikers to picket their place of work (indeed the details of the right to picket remain controversial in the UK to this day), gradually the right to strike was granted in most jurisdictions. The key date in the UK was 1906 when the Trades Disputes Act was passed by a Liberal government, taking away the legal liability that strike leaders had previously risked. By the inter-war years the basic idea that a union could call a strike, and could unite with other unions to extend the strike, was accepted in most of the Western world.

In practice the use of the strike as a weapon in industrial disputes has varied widely. In the USA major unions tend to negotiate contracts lasting for several years, during which no strikes are called, though there is frequently a lengthy strike during the renegotiating phase of each contract. In much of Europe, especially France and Italy, strikes have most often been political actions called to highlight the unions' opposition to general government policies rather than being pragmatic negotiating tools. In the UK, particularly during the Conservative government of Margaret Thatcher in 1979, labour-relations laws have tended to put constraints on trade-union activities. Complex issues such as the conducting of ballots of trade union members before the leadership may call a strike, the right of striking union members preventing other workers (union members or not) from working, and the legality of strikes called by local or factory leadership, but without support from the central union leadership, have been difficult to resolve. There are many conflicting elements at play: should balloting and 'cooling off' periods be compulsory before a strike can legitimately commence?; the validity of ballot results has been questioned when they are largely supervised by the union itself, and continued membership of the union is sometimes necessary for employment in the industry because of the 'closed shop'; far from opposing the closed shop for the power it gives to unions, some employers actually favour it as it simplifies the negotiating procedure. In general labour-relations law in the UK has weakened unions, and made strikes much less common, and less effective when held. The 1984–85 miners' strike was a particularly heavy symbolic defeat for the trade union movement. As trade unions became increasingly unpopular it was inevitable that they would be less willing to risk major strike action. But the real cause of the general decline of strikes throughout the Western economies has been the decline in the size of the industrial working class, and the even faster decline in the proportion of that class which is unionized. Similarly, the huge increase in the importance of part-time work in the Western economies has made the strike weapon largely anachronistic. Where strikes continue to be frequent, for example Italy, it is because they have always had more of a political and symbolic role than their pragmatic effect on employers justified. Italy may be the only country, for example, where self-employed taxi drivers have gone on strike. Nevertheless, the right to strike, if limited in law, is by now one of the basic **civil liberties** any modern society would be expected to guarantee.

Structural Functionalism

Structural functionalism is one variant of a general theoretical approach to the analysis of political systems, and is not easily distinguishable from **functionalism** or **systems theory**. It has principally been used by students of **comparative government** to make intelligent comparisons between very different societies at different levels of socio-economic or **political development**. Essentially the theory consists of identifying a set of necessary functions or 'tasks' that any social system must fulfil for survival, and then researching what institutions or structures seem capable of satisfying these needs. Thus it may be possible to show that, for example, tasks carried out by political parties in a developed Western democracy are still carried out in a primitive tribal society, but by other structures. At this stage important questions of relative efficiency, and of the fit between **political culture** and political institutions, can be asked. Though increasingly abandoned, the theory seemed at one time to hold great hope for an exact, generalized, and perhaps even quantified, science of comparative politics.

Subsidiarity

The doctrine of subsidiarity, which sprang to prominence in the politics of the **European Union (EU)** in the early 1990s, was first used by Pope Pius XI in 1931. What it essentially means is that government should take place at the lowest level possible. In its usage by Pius XI, the co-signator of the Lateran Treaty with Mussolini (see **papacy**) and author of the encyclical *Quadragesimo anno* which pronounced on the incompatibility of Christianity and true socialism, the intention of the doctrine was in favour of both **federalism** and **decentralization**. This, indeed, was also the interpretation of most of the member governments of the EU who were in favour of a tiered structure of government with the European level at the apex, and national and regional levels beneath it, with decisions being taken and implemented at the appropriate level: which level actually was appropriate would always have to be determined by the European Parliament or other EU institution (see **directive** and **regulation**). The British and Danish governments, however, sought to use subsidiarity as a concealment for their attempts to increase the number of policy areas which rested at the national level, allowing them to claim victories for their respective national **sovereignties**, which in turn would increase their chances of gaining national approval for the Maastricht Treaty's economic and **political union** objectives.

Superpower

Superpowers in the modern world are those few nation states with huge economic resources far transcending the next division in such a league table. The exact number varies with different analyses. The most common view until the beginning of the 1990s allowed only two superpowers, the USA and the Soviet Union, with the possible addition of the People's Republic of China. Since the near collapse of the Soviet/Russian economy, the accompanying enforced military retrenchment and the ending of the Soviet Union's imperial rule in Eastern Europe, many analysts insist that the USA is now the sole superpower. However, this definition combines a series of variables together—

actual economic wealth, population size and, above all, the extent to which these qualities have been used to produce military strength, especially in the possession of sophisticated nuclear armaments. Ignoring the nuclear aspect might more easily allow China into the club, although its actual economic strength is much less. Alternatively, taking merely economic capacity and wealth would certainly entitle Japan, with no nuclear capacity and very limited conventional forces, a position as a superpower. (Although even this judgment requires a certain blindness to possible fragility in the Japanese economy which does not rest on population size or domestic raw-material possession.) Perhaps more than anything else superpower status depends on a desire actually to use the power resources available. Thus the **European Union** has all the ingredients, including nuclear forces, to be a superpower, but clearly lacks the political will to be one. What has often been noted by historians is that being a superpower (or in the older language, an imperial power) is on the whole expensive and unrewarding.

Supply-Side Economics

Supply-side economics is usually seen as the 'invention' of the US right-wing economist Arthur Laffer, who so influenced Ronald Reagan when he was campaigning for the presidency in 1980 that the economic policy approach that came to be called Reaganomics was largely based on Laffer's theories. The basic idea of supply-side economics, which still has influential supporters on the American right, is the advocacy of relatively low taxation on high incomes, and especially on marginal income (essentially industry's profits). The argument is that releasing this income from taxation will produce extra invested funds, which will, in turn, produce more jobs, increased productivity and higher profitability. Consequently, reducing tax for those whose surplus income is likely to be invested is good for the whole economy—a version of the 'trickle-down' thesis. In contrast, reducing taxes for lower earners simply increases consumption, which has only a short-term impact on the economy and one which, if the economy is not in recession, may be inflationary. The theory has never been taken seriously by most professional economists, and there is no evidence from Reagan's experiment with **fiscal policy** based on Laffer's ideas that trickle-down does work. Nevertheless, the supply-side approach was, and to some extent still is, important politically in presenting an apparent justification for reducing the level of taxation on high incomes.

Syndicalism

Syndicalism is a version of trade unionism which was mainly important in the years before the First World War, though it remains a potentially explosive strand in the thinking of organized labour everywhere. Inspired largely by the writings of Georges Sorel (1847–1922), and especially his *Reflections on Violence* (1908), syndicalism seeks control of society by direct **strike** action leading to co-operative worker control of industry. Strikes, and especially the strategy of the general strike, supposed to be able to collapse a capitalist industry in just a few days, were seen as the only useful and legitimate tactic for organized labour to take in pursuit of **socialism**. The main country affected by syndicalism was France, and even today the French union movement has traces of syndicalism in its make-up.

There were two important consequences of **trade unions** accepting a syndicalist position, one tactical and one theoretical. The tactical impact was that the highly syndicalist French union movement refused to make political alliances with socialist parties, or to form their own parliamentary party. Electoral reform was seen as a dangerous **revisionism**, and thus the path that socialism took in Britain, where the unions formed the **Labour Party** specifically to get representatives of workers elected, was ignored. As a result no broadly-based working-class political alliance was possible, and none of the funding and organizing experience of the unions was available to French parliamentary socialists. This contributed to the inability, save briefly during the **popular front** period, of a socialist government to take office in France until 1981. The second consequence, more theoretical, was to force a breach with orthodox **communist** parties, because syndicalist insistence on worker control and ownership of their own factories and workplaces clashed with the ideas of **democratic centralism** and the **vanguard of the proletariat** that Lenin used to build modern international communism. There was always far more of an **anarchist** flavour about the syndicalists, not only in France but in Italy and during its brief periods of importance in Britain, during the period 1911–14, and in inter-war America. A shorter-term and more practical implication on French trade unionism is that because of this aspect of its past it has tended to use its efforts much more in pursuit of often symbolic political goals, rather than in more mundane bargaining for wage and work condition improvements.

Systems Theory

Systems theory is a version of **functionalism**, popular in the 1950s and 1960s, and especially associated in political studies with the works of the American academic David Easton (b. 1917). It concentrated on the idea of a political system as being a mechanism by which popular demands and popular support for the state were combined to produce those policy outputs that best ensured the long-term stability of the political system (or the **state** itself). Along with functionalist and **structural functionalist** theories, systems theory was often seen as unduly conservative because of its stress on stability rather than change. The basic idea, that political systems could be seen as analogous to operating mechanical systems, with feedback loops and clear goals, has continued to be useful in some areas of political science.

T

Tactical Nuclear Weapons

In one sense tactical nuclear weapons, or 'battlefield' weapons as they are sometimes misleadingly called, are not easily distinguishable from other 'conventional' munitions, except in power. They are, or were originally, intended for short-range use against purely military targets such as troop concentrations, vital supply or communications centres and so on, rather than against civilian or industrial targets. The 'yield' measured in the standard units of megatonnage is small (it can be as little as one kiloton, though 10 kilotons would be more usual). Originally they were deployed mainly by **NATO** forces in Western Europe, and NATO doctrine had come to rely increasingly on a first and early use (perhaps within two or three days of hostilities beginning) in order to offset the supposed **Warsaw Pact** superiority in **conventional arms**. However, this **scenario**, which made tactical nuclear weapons simply more devastating versions of ordinary warfare mechanisms became increasingly inaccurate. For several reasons the Soviet Union started, in the late 1970s, to deploy its own version of short-range nuclear missiles, the SS-20. As these could be fired from inside Soviet borders, effective counter-attacks by Western powers, especially with their own new generation of such weapons, the land-based cruise missiles and the Pershing II ballistic missile, could not easily be distinguished from more purposive and deliberate strategic strikes against the Soviet homeland. This would have considerably increased the risk of **escalation** to all-out nuclear war. In addition, what is known as the 'collateral' damage to civilian centres in the vicinity of the military targets could not be limited. As a result much of NATO doctrine came to be seen as faulty, and began to weaken political unity in the Western alliance. This **arms race** at the **pre-strategic** level, triggered when NATO announced in 1977 that it would emplace its new missiles, led, after Mikhail Gorbachev's rise to power and Ronald Reagan's mid-term conversion to arms control, to urgent and ultimately successful negotiations. The result was the first **arms control** treaty actually to abolish a category of weapons when these missiles, which had come to be labelled 'intermediate', were subject to the **Intermediate Nuclear Forces (INF) Treaty** of 1987.

Initially NATO continued to rely on a tactical nuclear strategy through other weapons, either airborne short-range missiles and bombs or artillery shells. The collapse of the Warsaw Pact by the end of 1990, however, led to a decision to remove all short-range weapons from Germany. The British armed forces scrapped virtually all of their pre-strategic forces, relying almost exclusively on their submarine-carried missiles for **deterrence**. Meanwhile the USA abandoned plans for a new tactical air-to-surface missile

There has always been serious concern about problems of command and control in the theory of tactical use of nuclear weaponry; much of the fear, even at the height of the **cold war**, came from doubts about the actual political situations under which they would be used, and the degree of central control by Washington, London and Paris that could be maintained. The end of the cold war and the concentration of Western defence planning on very different security scenarios has removed any remaining justification for such weapons.

Tactical Voting

Although most people cast their vote for the candidate they would prefer to win the election, there are situations when it may be rational not to do so. This is often the case where voters not only have a preference for one party, but a strong distaste for another. Where this happens it becomes a matter of tactics whether to vote for the preferred party, or in the way which might most harm the disliked party. In a hypothetical British constituency where the distribution of votes at the previous election was Conservative 45%, Liberal Democrat 42% and Labour 13%, a committed Labour supporter who desperately wants to see the Conservative candidate defeated might choose to transfer their vote to the Liberal Democrats, reasoning that they have a chance of defeating the Conservatives whereas Labour does not. The same Labour supporter might rationally decide to do the same thing even though they disliked the Liberal Democrats even more than the Conservatives, concluding that the Liberal Democrats had no chance of gaining an overall majority in parliament, whereas Labour did, and that each Conservative candidate defeated was a step towards the ultimate goal of a national Labour victory. It is, however, uncertain whether, before 1997, tactical voting had more than a minimal effect at British general elections, although the results of by-elections often suggest that many voters have changed their traditional support to make a protest, with the candidate of the party in government the usual victim. Many other motivating factors are probably more important in arriving at the **voting** decision. A firm supporter of a party may refuse to vote for a candidate of any other party for ideological reasons, or may favour other forms of tactics, such as maximizing the national vote for their party. The parties themselves tend not to overtly encourage tactical voting, as the practice could easily do them more harm than good if applied nation-wide. For similar reasons parties resist suggestions to refrain from nominating candidates in constituencies where they have no chance of winning, thereby perhaps aiding the chances of another party defeating the incumbent candidate, because of the symbolic defeatist message this would convey to party workers and supporters. Centre parties, such as the Liberal Democrats, which are most often going to be in the position of benefiting from tactical voting are also particularly at risk: they cannot let their own voters act tactically precisely because they need to maximize their total vote to show potential supporters that a vote for them would not be wasted. The British general elections of 1997 and 2001, however, certainly saw an increase in the impact of tactical voting, as an the number of voters determined to deprive the Conservatives of parliamentary seats increased, the principal benificiaries being the Liberal Democrats (see **Liberal Party**).

There are some electoral systems where tactical voting certainly exists, and has a strong impact. Typical is the French case where elections are often held in two stages. In presidential elections only two candidates may proceed from the first to the **second ballot**, and in National Assembly elections only those with more than 12.5% of the votes in the first round may proceed (in practice candidates with more votes than this often withdraw, acknowledging that they cannot win). The unsuccessful candidates from the first round may then urge their supporters to vote for the candidate among those who remain that they most favour. Although this sometimes rebounds and their voters go elsewhere, it allows for tactical alliances either at the constituency level or nation-wide which can have a profound electoral impact. Tactical voting is mainly restricted to simple plurality systems, because it has no obvious analogue in an effective **proportional representation** system. There are halfway houses, however, the he obvious case being Germany where voters cast two votes, one for a party list in an overall national count, and one for a single member in plurality-counted constituencies. Casting both votes for the same party is only one option a voter may exercise to maximize his interests.

Taliban

The Taliban were, from the mid-1990s until late 2001, the ruling force in Afghanistan, having defeated the *Mujahidin* warriors who had fought Soviet occupation, although at no time did they succeed in controlling all of the country. Although their power in the parts of Afghanistan they control was absolute, by no means all the population, or even a large majority, were necessarily strong supporters. Relatively few people were actually members of the movement, which saw itself as a religious, military and revolutionary élite. The Taliban's members were also ethnically distinct from many Afghans, being mostly Pashtuns, from Kandahar in the south, observing the Sunni branch of **Islam** (hence their support in Pakistan and Saudi Arabia), rather than Shi'a: members of this latter Muslim minority provided the most durable resistance to the Taliban in northern Afghanistan.

The movement takes its name, sometimes translated as 'the seekers', from the fact that they were originally students at various Pakistani Islamic colleges (madrassas) run by the fundamentalist Jamiat-e-Ulema, on the border with Afghanistan. When in power it was almost completely dominated by its original theological and political leader, a Mullah Mohammad Omar. A much larger body of religious leaders, the inner shura (council), based in Kandahar, was required to be consulted on policy matters (its opinion was usually accepted). Mullah Omar, who had previously assumed the religious title of Emir of the Faithful, was formally head of state.

It is widely accepted that the Taliban were encouraged and helped in their ascendancy, some would say entirely created, by one of the Pakistani military intelligence services, the Inter Service Intelligence (ISI). The motivations for this seem mixed: the ISI represents a distinctly fundamentalist faction amongst the increasingly Islamicized Pakistani military. It was also very much in Pakistan's interest to have Afghanistan controlled by forces indebted to Pakistan, given the complexities of international politics in the area. The idea common among critics in the West of Western policy towards Afghanistan, that the USA itself created the Taliban to fight the Soviet Union, is simply false, as should be obvious from the way the Taliban have persecuted the *Mujahidin*, whom the West did indeed support. If **fundamentalism**, a much misused word, ever has a valid descriptive role, it is to describe movements like the Taliban. They were interested not just in Islamic purity, but they also essentially rejected any intellectual or moral compromise with modernity and wished to create a medieval Islamic society: they renamed Afghanistan the Islamic Emirate of Afghanistan, as the basis for what they themselves described as Caliphate, ultimately to stretch over the whole region and totally opposed to the secular West. The repression of women under the Taliban was almost complete—they were forced to wear the restrictive traditional dress (the burka), forbidden to work or to be educated, or to appear in public unless accompanied by a male relative. The counterpart to this is that men are forced to wear beards under penalty of imprisonment. The full-blooded version of **Shari'a** criminal law, complete with mutilations and blinding for non-capital offences, runs throughout the society, and a body of religious police enforce even minor moral teachings with street beatings or worse.

Inevitably Afghanistan became home to other groups of Islamic political fundamentalists, and it was believed by Western governments to be deeply implicated in international terrorism. Taliban Afghanistan was treated to a large extent as outside decent international society, being recognized by only a handful of states, and by no means by most other Islamic states. Its removal from power by a combination of US-led and ex-*Mujahidin* forces during the 'War Against Terrorism' in November 2001 proved popular within Afghanistan and internationally (see **Afghan War**).

Terrorism

Following the end of the **Cold War**, the threat of 'international terrorism' was widely seen as the greatest affecting Western society. This sentiment increased following the attacks on the World Trade Center and Pentagon in September 2001. The USA proclaimed a 'War on Terrorism' in response, although this term itself provoked questions—critics asked whether it was desirable or indeed possible to declare war on a concept, particularly one so ill-defined as terrorism.

It is probably impossible to give a general definition of terrorism that would not be too general to be useful. The best that can be said is that terrorism includes any use of violence towards political, moral or religious ends which is not carried out by the official military institutions of a state. Because the concept is, too often, used with an implicitly evaluative undertone, it is, as political theorists say, 'inherently contestable'. Simply put, one person's terrorist is another's 'freedom fighter'. Merely to say that terrorists use terror as a weapon, which is why it has the evaluative tone, is to say nothing—even orthodox military strategy has relied at times on simply terrifying civilian populations. It is thus better to concentrate on the distinction between actions of an official uniformed military and other actors lacking the international recognition of statehood.

That being said, terrorist operations differ from most orthodox military strategy in two ways. First terrorists do, very frequently, strike at unarmed civilian groups with no direct responsibility for state policy. In part they do this because such civilians are easier targets than those offered by a nation's military, or its well-guarded political élite. The main reason for such targeting, however, relates to the second difference from military **strategy**. The actual aim of a terrorist campaign is to influence the civilian population, rather than to damage the military capacity of the enemy. Even when military personnel are attacked, as with the IRA attacks on the British army in Ulster, the aim is still to influence civilian attitudes, not seriously to reduce the strength of the army, which would be well beyond a terrorist group's capacity. Terrorist activity aims to hurt the general population of the enemy state so much that out of fear, impatience with inconvenience, or unwillingness to take the economic and human consequences of the attacks, they withdraw public support for the government policies objected to by the terrorists. Something like this is true even when dealing with such groups as extreme Islamic fundamentalists whose aim is to drive the USA out of all influence and presence in the Muslim world. Even terrorist leaders like the Saudi Arabian Islamist leader Osama bin Laden, who openly calls for a *Jihad* against the USA because of a detestation of all of secular Western culture, do not expect actually to kill enough Americans to reduce their potential world power. Rather they hope to make the projection of such power and influence something the American voter will not risk. It must be admitted, however, that analyses like these probably over-rationalize the actual thought processes of terrorists, certainly of the lower ranks, if not of the leadership. Frustration, hatred and despair probably lead to terrorism, from a simple desire for revenge against wrongs, imagined or otherwise.

In practice, terrorists often seem to combine a massively exaggerated estimate of how easy it is to change public support for a government with a very considerable desire to hurt for its own sake. A secondary motivation for terrorism has been said to be that of drawing world attention to the plight and cause of the terrorists' community; as such it again largely underestimates the reaction of the public when attacked by terrorist campaigns. The problem for terrorism is the same as that faced by orthodox military strategy when it attempts to destroy civilian morale by, for example, mass bombing raids on cities. Most historical evidence suggests that such attacks are counter-produc-tive—populations refuse to be cowed, and actually become more supportive of the governments the terrorists are trying to undermine.

Finally, it must be stressed that terrorism is not a product of late 20th century society. At the very least, organized political groups using terrorists techniques to attack civilian morale, go back to the 19th century, becoming more widespread in the early 20th century. The IRA, for example, ran a bombing campaign in mainland Britain in the 1920s. For that matter, the assassination of Archduke Franz Ferdinand of Austria, which triggered the First World War, was only one of a series of terrorist attacks by independence movements in the Austro-Hungarian Empire. What has changed is that the nature of 21st-century society and the easy availability of technological means of killing, has enormously increased the scale at which terrorists can destroy life.

Thatcherism

Margaret Thatcher became leader of the British **Conservative Party** in 1975, and prime minister in 1979, holding both positions until 1990. It was after the Conservative defeat in 1974 that she rose to prominence as the standard bearer of the right wing of the party, which accused their former leader Edward Heath of causing the electoral failure by taking the party too much into a centrist position. Thatcher, advocating what she described as 'the politics of conviction', quite deliberately broke the **consensual** approach which had dominated British party politics since the era of **Butskellism**. Her political philosophy, though always eclectic, had two main thrusts. The first was an economic policy of **monetarism**, in contrast to the prevailing **Keynesian** orthodoxy. (It should be noted, however, that monetarism was beginning to be accepted even by the Labour government of 1974–79, and has since become almost as much of an orthodoxy as Keynesianism had been.)

The second thrust was the idea of 'rolling back the state', of creating private opportunity and personal responsibility in all areas of life. This took many forms. Perhaps the most representative was the **privatization** of nationalized industries, as in the selling to the public and to industry shares in the water, electricity, gas and telecommunications utilities. Thatcherism also encompassed the reduction of the role of central or local government in many traditional areas such as council housing, and was extended to decentralization of functions which had to stay in the state domain. Thus the National Health Service and the schools system were reformed, with hospitals and schools encouraged to take more direct control over their own budgets and practices.

Thatcherism was so pervasive that it is difficult to put any bounds on its reach. Thatcher was opposed to the power of large institutions, especially if they had aspects of a monopoly position. For example the exclusive rights of opticians to sell reading glasses, or of solicitors to conveyance in the sale of houses, were taken away, and even the privileges of barristers over ordinary solicitors were eroded. The first target of this approach, however, was the **trade union** movement, and a series of pieces of legislation massively reduced the ability of unions to call **strikes** and generally restricted their practices.

Naturally there were many other aspects to Thatcher's policies. She was right-wing in a conventional way across the policy spectrum: tough on **law and order** issues, close to the USA in foreign policy and dubious of the European Communities (now the **European Union**) less moved by social injustice than some, but none of these are specifically 'Thatcherite' attitudes. Thatcherism, were it to be analysed by a political theorist, would concentrate on her notion of freedom and responsibility of the individual in a way that links her far more with **libertarianism** and 19th century **liberalism** than with the traditional 'Tory' philosophy of the Conservative Party. Her influence on the Conservative Party began to wane shortly after she was removed from power, and by the beginning of the 21st century very few Conservative politicians were comfortable with a Thatcherite label.

Theocracy

A theocracy is any political system run by clerics, or by and along the tenets of any organized religion. There are few modern examples, though the state of

Iran since the overthrow of the Shah could be an example, and **Taliban** Afghanistan another. Sometimes the term is used extravagantly to indicate a state where religious ideas, or religious institutions, have what is seen as an undue influence. Thus a political system such as modern Italy, where **Roman Catholicism** carries considerable political influence, having a privileged position in the constitution, and with the dominant political party being church-oriented and led, could be seen by some as verging on theocracy.

Theocratic values were in the past more important, and more common, than in the present world. Medieval political society, for example, was suffused by political doctrines supporting the rule of established religious order, because the political authorities relied on **Christianity** as a justifying **ideology**. Even earlier societies, classical Athens for example, could have made little sense of theocracy because it assumes a distinction between political and religious rule and obligation. Yet these societies were so structured that the functions of the priesthood were connected to those of political leadership. In much later primitive societies this pattern can still be seen. In European terms it was the Reformation which forced a division between politics and religion by establishing the principle of religious toleration. Thus the constitution of the USA actually carries a prohibition on the 'establishment' of any religion as a guard against any theocratic tendencies (see **secular state**). There are still countries in the developed world, including the United Kingdom and the Scandinavian countries, where an **established church** exists.

Third Republic

The French Third Republic lasted from its creation in 1870, after the defeat of the Second Empire during the Franco–Prussian War, until France's defeat by Germany in 1940. Although it was permanently troubled by political unrest and apparent instability, its 70-year rule is in fact the longest of any French regime since the 1789 Revolution, and the Republic's ability to withstand the shock of the First World War testifies to its strength. It was very much a parliamentary regime, with a president who never dared use even what few powers he constitutionally had. Originally intended only as a provisional government, a majority of the deputies in the first elected assembly were actually monarchists, the deep divisions in French society, exacerbated by a fragmented and irresponsible party system, prevented it from ever developing powerful political institutions. From the start a vital sector of the traditional French ruling class, the Catholic and aristocratic right wing, was excluded from real participation, partly because they still could not easily accept the original republican notions of the French Revolution. At the same time the parties of the centre, who formed most of the coalitions, were almost as hostile to the emerging working-class organizations. As a result the republic was very much run by, and for, the middle classes and the peasantry, with the result that the frequently changing governments had neither the ability nor the incentive to help modernize what was probably one of the most backward economies in Europe. Scandal after scandal rocked the Republic, starting perhaps with the infamous Dreyfus case, which led to deep suspicion and conflict between the military and the republican forces at a time when France's need to avenge its 1870 defeat was symbolically vital. Not until after the First World War were any efforts made to ameliorate the conditions of industrial workers, and even then the opposition to serious income tax by the supporters of the ruling centrist parties forced the governments into relying on state borrowing rather than more efficient means of raising revenue. The republic might have fallen earlier, under the combined threat of German-inspired fascist movements from the right and hostility from the developing and Moscow-inspired communist party on the left. It was saved, temporarily, by the formation of a **popular front** government in the late 1930s, resulting from a switch to a leftwards orientation by the Radical party. With the German invasion of 1940 the regime which had done so little for so many in France fell, largely because there was no reserve of **legitimacy** left to a state that had started almost by accident. Few were prepared to die for the protection of a small élite of politicians who had followed each other in and out of office, acting as little more than delegates for conservative entrenched interests in, largely rural, constituencies.

Third Way

The Third Way is one of a series of attempts by the British **Labour Party** to characterize what they now stand for since they have overtly abandoned the principles of **social democracy**. Social democracy, however often it disappointed its own left wing, at least theoretically stood for a discernibly different approach to running an industrial society from **liberalism** or laissez-faire **capitalism**. Above all it implied considerable state control of the economy, at least at the level of regulation, and sometimes in terms of nationalization. The British Labour Party and, more or less, all other European social democratic parties, have become complete converts to a deregulated market economy, the fine tuning of which is made long-range through **central bank** manipulation of interest rates. This leaves only expenditure and tax policy as mechanisms for economic control; social democratic parties are now electorally unable to advocate high tax rates, and they find themselves committed to fiscal orthodoxy to make good their commitment to a competitive capitalist economy.

What then differentiates a social democratic party from parties to its right on the political spectrum? The concept of the third way, for which there is no generally agreed and precise definition, operates by trying to insist that such parties are still 'progressive'—a term they do not define. The third way is supposed to be a method by which the traditional values of social democracy can be protected while *carrying out* the economic policies of its traditional conservative enemies (see also **Conservative Party**). To the extent that it has any content, four tenets are cited frequently. These are *opportunity, responsibility, community* and *democracy*. Opportunity is to be increased so that no sector of the population is excluded from the minimum educational and financial base needed for successful competition in the capitalist economy, and no vestiges of discrimination are to remain. Responsibility is more of an appeal to the citizenry to play their part than a set of policies for them; it comprises stressing the need to be wise investors for their own future and being good parents who make plans for their children's futures—these are particularly important because the third way is no longer able to guarantee extensive cradle to grave welfare.

Community, again is largely rhetorical, but may be used to justify legislation such as tax breaks for married couples, which may shore up what are seen as traditionally valuable social mechanisms. Finally, democracy implies ever more extensive consultative mechanisms to make those in power fully accountable to those they rule. There appears to be absolutely nothing in the third way that an intelligent and decent Conservative Party member would not regard him or herself as committed to.

Third World

The Third World is most easily defined negatively, in that it consists of those countries not in the **First World** or Second World. The First World consists of the leading Western industrialized countries of Europe, North America, Japan and the old British colonies which are of the same level of economic development; it is, in fact, the world of the industrially developed **capitalist** economy. The Second World (a term very seldom used, if not now extinct) covers the industrialized nations of the former **Soviet bloc**. Thus the Third World is the less industrialized, non- or under-developed world, much of it consisting of ex-colonies of the European powers.

Despite its popularity as a media label, the Third World has very little homogeneity, exhibits vast social and economic differences, and has little in the way of common political or economic interests and policies. It is not even certain whether any particular country not in the first two worlds will always automatically qualify for membership of the Third World. Is India, for example, a Third World country? Despite its poverty and its status as an ex-colony, it is a nuclear power in terms of energy and weapons, and manages to run a political system not always very different from a Western parliamentary democracy. Other countries, notably the oil-producing states of the Middle

East, have enormous international political influence while otherwise being obvious candidate members. The economically highly productive but politically backward countries of the Pacific rim, notably South Korea and Taiwan, similarly defy categorization. Some would introduce a further category, the Fourth World, for those underdeveloped countries which also lack any significant exploitable natural resources. The label Third World is probably too deeply entrenched to be avoided, but in fact very few statements using it can be made with any reliability (as, increasingly, with the other two worlds), and any degree of precision requires so many qualifications as to render the tripartite categorization largely useless.

Thought Reform

Thought reform is the idea that a person's political and social attitudes and views can be radically altered to fit in with a particular ideology with which they lack sympathy. Indeed, so thorough is the idea of thought reform that not only evaluations, but supposedly factual beliefs, are seen as alterable. The exact history of the concept is hard to trace, and its use in political discourse is confused by its extensive discussion in fictional literature, and especially in science fiction. Probably the first systematic non-fictional usage arose from treatment by the Chinese of American and British prisoners during the **Korean War**. It seems that some of these prisoners were subjected to intensive conditioning, partly by torture but mainly by psychological means, to persuade them of the entire truth of the Chinese Marxist interpretation of the war and of the relative merits of the East rather than the West in international conflict. It is entirely unclear how successful, and if successful how long-lasting, these conversions were. Similar attempts to condition French and later US prisoners during the wars in Indochina seem to have been failures. Certainly the Chinese later, during the **cultural revolution**, adopted intensive processes of political re-education to persuade those whom the Red Guard saw as 'deviationists' to adopt the more radical views and to confess and seek absolution from their sins and failings. By talking of thought 'reform', rather than of 'change', one is of course accepting a premise buried deep in the process itself, that deviating views are actually not only wrong but a species almost of mental illness, which can be cured, the victim being brought to see reality properly rather than in a distorted way. In the same way the Soviet Union used psychiatric medicine and mental health clinics on leading dissidents, to alter their beliefs and attitudes towards what was regarded as a correct ideologically, and therefore 'normal', political position. Certainly a comparison can be made with the Roman Catholic Inquisition, where the leading inquisitors were genuinely concerned to re-convert heretics, even if by brutal means, and not simply to kill them to stop the spread of a heresy.

Threat Assessment

Military **strategy**, and the designing and equipping of a nation's defence posture, requires some assessment of the dangers which need defending against. Part of this process is a purely political decision by a government's foreign-affairs experts—ultimately only politicians can tell the **military** who are to be seen as the potential enemies. But even when the potential enemies have been identified for them, the military planners have to decide how real the potential threats from these countries are, how strong the threat is, and the particular form which the threat may take. The total process is usually called 'threat assessment'. Some aspects of threat assessment are objective and even simple, because they deal with the basic economic capacity of a potential enemy to build and operate military hardware with which the threat might be made. Other aspects involve very difficult matters of intelligence gathering. An enemy may be capable of several different kinds of threat, and some assessment has to be made about the most likely strategy for them to adopt, as it is unlikely that it will be possible to defend against all forms of attack. By far the hardest calculation is the likelihood that a potential enemy will, in fact, do any of the things they are capable of. This was particularly important in strategic nuclear planning when the whole question of the credibility of nuclear strategy was vital. There was never any doubt that the Soviet Union had the capacity to launch a huge strategic nuclear strike against the USA (and vice versa), but just how credible was it, given all the consequences of nuclear warfare, that they would ever do so? Military planners avoid, at all cost, getting into this area of psychological analysis. For them what a country *could* do becomes what they *will* do in terms of threat assessment. This is obviously too simple, and it can be problematic even in the simpler case of assessing the level of conventional hardware. For example, a combat aircraft may be 'nuclear capable', but mainly designed for a conventional war role. Because of the doctrine that the threat is what the enemy could do, the dual capability is going to increase the nuclear threat estimate, without any good reason based on enemy intentions. Similarly questions of the reliability of the enemy's troops will be ignored, because threat assessment is always made from a 'worst case' **scenario**. The problem with such threat assessments is that they force up the assessors concept of what is needed, thus boosting defence expenditure. Worse, because the enemy is making the same sort of assessment, perhaps from the position of knowing that they intend no threat, your extra expenditure itself becomes evidence of a threat and contributes to an expensive and futile **arms race**. Threat assessment has become even harder at the beginning of the 21st century because the general nature of the threat to Western societies is much more vague. Even where a government, concerned principally about **terrorism**, identifies certain states as potential supporters of this threat, it is much harder to calculate how to deter them. Indeed President George W. Bush in his 2002 declaration of 'war on terrorism' would clearly prefer to be able simply to attack the nation states he identified as supporters of terrorism, but he could not get his allies to see them as 'threats', even though they agreed with the USA about the more general terrorist threat.

Totalitarianism

Totalitarianism is a political concept often either combined with, or even confused with, others such as **authoritarianism** or **dictatorship**. The confusion arises because there tends to be an empirical connection so that authoritarian or dictatorial societies are often also totalitarian. There is, however, no necessary connection. To call a society totalitarian means that the political rulers control every aspect of private and social life in the society, as well as having so extensive a political **power** that virtually no liberty or autonomy in decision-making is left to individuals or groups outside the political power system. Thus the Soviet Union was often described as being totalitarian, particularly under **Stalin**, but this was not because it operated a **single-party system** where only the **Communist Party of the Soviet Union (CPSU)** wielded power. The Soviet Union was totalitarian because of the way it *used* power. The whole of the media, educational system, and social, sporting and other leisure activities, were controlled by, and used to propagate the ideology of, the CPSU. All industrial decisions, including activities of **trade unions**, were under direct control of party-appointed officials. Even the military organizations were controlled and ideologized directly by the party, via the system of making the deputy commander of each unit, of whatever level, a party 'political commissar'. It is this character of complete permeation of a society by the personnel and ideas of the ruling group that makes for totalitarianism. Other forms of society could, and at times have been, equally totalitarian. A thorough-going **theocracy**, for example, where the church had the ability to penetrate and organize all aspects of life, would be totalitarian. Some writers have even tried to claim that the exponents of radically **participatory democracy**, like, for example, **Rousseau** in his *Social Contract,* were 'totalitarian democrats'. This latter example arises from the way that Rousseau insists on as much communal activity, and as much homogeneity, as possible among citizens in order to minimize conflict and to aid the production of a publicly-spirited **general will** among all citizens. It is similar to the fears of writers like John Stuart **Mill** and **de Tocqueville** about the **tyranny of the majority**. In practice few political systems can wholly penetrate a society, and some form of underground **libertarianism** usually flourishes, as with the dissident movement in the Soviet Union, or the capacity to combat some aspects of Nazism by the churches in the Third Reich.

Trade Unions

Trade unions are organized groups of working people, usually but not invariably in industrial and commercial rather than agricultural concerns. Until relatively recently they have been predominantly of working class, that is, skilled and unskilled manual worker, membership. Since the 1970s, however, certainly in the United Kingdom and to some extent elsewhere, traditional middle-class professions have become unionized. The UK and Germany have the oldest trade-union organizations of a legal nature, though in both countries the fight for legal recognition was prolonged. In the UK it was not until legislation following industrial unrest and violent state coercion at the beginning of the 20th century that modern legal protection for the rights to **strike** and to picket (absolutely essential ingredients of union activity) were granted, in 1906. German unions gained similar protection at roughly the same time, and, except for a period of repression during the Nazi regime, the two union movements have been very similar.

The main set-back for British unions came with the failure of the only-once-attempted general strike in 1926, but in the immediate post-war decades unions were strong, and usually accepted by governments. The attempted legal restriction of union activities through the Industrial Relations Court set up by the 1970–74 Conservative government was so violently rejected by the unions that it was quickly abolished by the 1974–79 Labour government. (Indeed it was the Conservatives' conflict with the unions that effectively lost them power.) A slower, more subtle and more complex attack on trade-union rights under the Thatcher administration met with greater success. By the 1980s public attitudes to the unions had shifted independently (accelerated by the unions' activities during the 'Winter of Discontent' which contributed to Labour's losing the 1979 general election), the more moderate white-collar unions had assumed a more important position and there was an increasing acceptance of **laissez-faire** policies in general. The British trade-union movement has always been closely tied to the **Labour Party**, which it helped set up, far more closely than unions elsewhere in the Western world are linked to their left-wing parties. Unions tend to be divided among themselves as much as they present a common front to the government or industrial leadership, and Britain's highly organized and powerful Trades Union Congress (TUC), organized since 1868, may be unique. Even this body has weakened with the dwindling membership of many unions, splits leading to the creation of new non-affiliated unions and the disaffiliation of other existing unions. By the 1990s union membership in the UK had fallen significantly beneath 40% of the total work-force; although this level remained high by international standards, it must be remembered that most members are passive, joining either as a condition of holding their job, or out of social pressure, and take almost no part in union politics. In the USA, in contrast, as few as 15% of workers are still in unions.

Unionism in France, though existing as an underground force from around 1830, was never strong until the post–Second World War years, if then. In part this was due to the low degree of industrialization in France, but also to the **syndicalist** political views that led them both to eschew formal parliamentary links or co-operation, and to advocate direct general strike action to force social revolution. As in Italy, the split between a communist party-dominated majority and a Catholic-dominated minority wing further weakened French unions. In the USA the union movement was split into two bodies, the American Federation of Labour (AFL) and the Congress of Industrial Organizations (CIO) until the mid-1950s, and although individual unions are important in their own industries, the federal level joint union organizations are of little political importance. The other Western nations with important union movements are mainly the 'Old Commonwealth' countries, where Australia and New Zealand follow the British, and Canada the US, patterns.

At least since the late 1970s the phenomenon of trade unionism has been unpopular in British public opinion, with regularly 70% of opinion poll samples thinking they have too much power. (A figure that is not notably different among members themselves.) Unionism tends to be strongest everywhere either in craft or large-scale industry, and weak in distributive, white collar or very unskilled trades. Various attempts are made by governments from time to time (and of all political colours) to restrain union power, but the whole principle of unionization, to establish somewhat more equal bargaining power between employers and employees, is so well-established that, despite the surface unpopularity of unions, little can be done to curtail their major privileges under law. Unions existed, with compulsory membership, in all **Soviet bloc** countries, but the right to strike was usually withheld, and, with the exception of the Polish Solidarity movement of the 1980s, these unions were so totally controlled by the local communist parties as to be mere façades. Perhaps the most important theoretical, as well as practical, question about union membership is the problem of what is known, in the UK, as 'the closed shop'. This is a system where no one is allowed to keep a job in a factory or other workplace unless they join the relevant union. Although a constant target of criticism by conservatives in both the USA and the UK, it is a practice that employers themselves quite often approve of, if only because it simplifies their own negotiating strategies. The union's argument is quite simple—the benefits they gain by concerted action should not be enjoyed by those unprepared to share the effort, and it is certainly true that unions operating in a non-closed shop environment tend to be less effective. This, again, is not a phenomenon restricted to working-class movements—some university libraries in the UK, for example, operate a closed shop rule even for academic level staff.

Treaty

'*Pacta serva sunt*'—promises must be kept to—is one of the oldest maxims, perhaps the very corner stone, of **international law**, and is what underlies the significance of the idea of a treaty in both public international law and the academic study of international relations. A treaty is a formal agreement between two or more states or other accepted international actors. It is important that the actors be recognized by international law before an agreement between them can be seen as a treaty, because treaties both depend on international law for their validity and at the same time serve to develop international law further. Thus a government might, to get out of a crisis, sign an agreement with a terrorist group to release hostages, but that group could not rely on the agreement in international law arbitration, or if the treaty were upheld, the effect would be to transform the terrorists from an illegal band into a legitimate state actor.

Essentially treaties can be either bilateral or multilateral. A bilateral treaty is like a private contract in civil law—merely a negotiated interest between two actors who have struck a bargain that both think is in their best interest. More important and theoretically interesting are multilateral treaties, agreements between several countries to act towards each other in particular ways, or to set up international mechanisms and institutions to achieve goals co-operatively. These types of treaties can be essentially negative, a multilateral arms control treaty, for example, restricting or banning nuclear testing. Positive treaties, the best single example being the Treaty of Rome (see **European Union**), can create complex webs of rights and duties and set up supranational institutions with their own legitimacy which may even transcend, intentionally or otherwise, the legitimacy of those who sign the treaty in the first place.

Treaties are themselves, as noted above, sources of international law—not only because they set out rules binding the signatories, but because international law works in part by generalizing principles from specifics. Thus, a well established treaty which, for instance, establishes territorial limits on national waters between its signatories may be used as a form of precedent to bind other countries that have never negotiated such an agreement. It is important to see that treaties are creatures of international, rather than domestic, law: while treaties are binding between the states that sign them, they may have no legal impact within those states. It is a matter that differs across national legal cultures as to whether a citizen inside a state may claim that his state is bound by something in a treaty it has signed. There are numerous other words used to describe international agreements; about the only thing that makes treaties stand out is that they usually require ratification within each signing country by the country's constitutional mechanisms. Thus, for example, the US President cannot make a treaty valid by signing it—it requires ratification by the Senate as well. He can, however, in more limited ways, bind the USA to behave in a certain way by signing an executive agreement with another head of state.

Tribunals

In French law a tribunal is a lower court, roughly equivalent to an English Crown Court, whereas in the United Kingdom it is usually a quasi-judicial institution. A British tribunal decides conflicts between individuals or between individuals and institutions, governmental or otherwise. It will have some of the powers of a court, and its proceedings can be almost as formal, though they are usually less so. One of the most common uses of tribunals is in complex areas of **administrative law** dealing with issues like employment, rent assessment, social security benefits and **immigration** matters. The reasons for using tribunals in these cases are twofold. Firstly there is a massive number of cases in these areas, many of them quite simple but nevertheless requiring rapid settlement. To put them into the main courts system would either involve its huge expansion, with attendant problems of providing qualified judges, or inordinate delays. Secondly, although the law in such cases is usually clear, the facts are often not. Indeed there may be a dearth of hard facts, and discretion based on a deep experience of the problem area is required. Such decisions are much better made by experienced lay people (presided over by someone legally qualified) who can swiftly adjudicate on the matter at issue without being too hampered by legal procedure. Hence the use of tribunals, which began to be written into legislation in the 1950s, has expanded enormously.

Of course tribunals can wrongly apply law, or may exercise their discretion unjustifiably, so there are appeals tribunals, more heavily weighted towards formal legal decisions. In special cases appeals can be taken into the full court system, but this happens only rarely, when legislation is so unclear or contradictory that a full legal interpretation, or reinterpretation, is required. There has often been considerable objection to the courts hearing appeals from tribunals, and efforts have been made to prevent the courts from intervening. These have never been successful because the judges regard themselves as the ultimate controllers of all judicial and quasi-judicial establishments, and always find a way of allowing the courts to intervene in special cases.

The term tribunal is also used to describe disciplinary bodies within private institutions, such as **trade unions** or professional associations, and which operate almost like courts, though with their **authority** only deriving from the voluntary membership of individuals. Even these bodies can find themselves appealed from to the courts if they are seen as having broken the rules of **natural justice**. The existence of tribunals in various areas highlights the enormous amount of conflict resolution needed in any modern society, and the extent to which the formal law courts are only part of the adjudication and decision-making system.

Trotsky

Leon Trotsky (1879–1940) changed his name from Lev Davidovich Bronstein after escaping from exile in Siberia in 1902. He, along with **Lenin**, was one of the great leaders of the Russian revolutionary forces both before and after the 1917 Revolution. Also like Lenin, he was a revolutionary before he was a **Marxist**. Trotsky was arrested and exiled when only 19, for trying to foment revolution among industrial workers, though his own family was relatively prosperous. On his escape he fled to London where he met and worked with Lenin and rapidly became a leading member, especially as a propagandist, of the then more or less united All-Russian Social Democratic Labour Party (RSDLP), most of which was similarly in exile. During the period from the turn of the century to 1917 the RSDLP was badly split between factions with very different interpretations of how **socialism** could be achieved in Russia. One wing, later to be known as **Mensheviks**, took a version of Marxism which required Russia to go through a full industrial revolution of a **capitalist** nature, and thus felt that, even if a revolution set up a democracy, a lengthy period of co-operation with liberal **bourgeois** parties would be necessary. The other wing, Lenin's **Bolsheviks**, argued instead that an alliance between what there was of an industrial proletariat and the peasantry could force the pace of industrial transformation, making it unnecessary to endure the transition phase of liberal capitalism. Trotsky, however, could never quite make up his mind about this split, floated back and forth in the endless congresses of the exiles, and thus created ill will and suspicion on both sides. He returned to Russia briefly in 1905 to help the abortive revolution of that year, and he was back in Russia much earlier in 1917 than Lenin, playing a vital role in organizing the extreme communist opposition to the original moderate government.

His own analysis was, in fact, even more revolutionary than Lenin's, when he worked it out, because he denied that the support of the peasantry was needed, and argued for what he called 'permanent revolution'. This was a strategy in which the first revolution, to overthrow the autocratic Tsarist regime, should be immediately followed by a purely proletarian revolution, and one which should be 'exported' to all Western countries, as he believed that underdeveloped Russia could not long sustain a socialist society. Though he co-operated ultimately with Lenin, he was always unhappy with the latter's stress of the leadership of the party. He held a variety of vital posts in the Bolshevik government set up in October 1917, the most important of which was the creation and running of the Red Army with which he successfully, though brutally, won the civil war against the traditionalist 'White' Russian army. He lost power, after Lenin's death, to **Stalin** and his faction, who advocated 'socialism in one country', and because he opposed the central authority and the ignoring of the Russian masses which Stalin took to even greater lengths than had Lenin. Expelled from the party, he was exiled yet again, this time permanently, in 1929, and ultimately murdered, supposedly on Stalin's orders, in 1940. He spent the last few years of his life in propaganda against what he saw as the corruption of the revolution, even attempting, with no real success, to create a rival international communist movement (the so-called Fourth International). Trotsky perhaps remains theoretically the most interesting character of the whole Russian revolutionary movement, but the one whose ideas were least acceptable to orthodox communists on either side of the **iron curtain**.

Trotskyism

Because **Trotsky** had disagreed with **Lenin**, and even more with the followers of **Stalin**, in Russia after 1917, and was exiled and ultimately murdered by the Stalinists, he has been a vitally emotive symbol for extreme left-wing **Marxist** groups who wished to distance themselves from what they saw as the discredited **state capitalism** of the 'communist' Soviet Union. In recent years self-styled 'Trotskyist' political groups have proliferated on the left in many Western countries. All that is meant by this appellation is that these movements deny the acceptability of any non-revolutionary strategy, or of any compromise with other parties. Two aspects of Trotsky's thought particularly appeal to these groups. First, Trotsky had a belief in what he called 'permanent revolution'. In fact this doctrine is usually misunderstood by these self-styled groups, who tend to see it as a semi-anarchist call never to accept or support authority at all, seeing it as similar to some of the elements in the Maoist **cultural revolution**. All Trotsky meant by it was that, in contrast to the Russian social democrats, he did not believe that there would have to be a lengthy period of **bourgeois** capitalist rule in Russia after the revolution against semi-feudal Tsarist autocracy. Instead he felt the first, anti-Tsarist revolution could immediately be followed by a full-scale revolution by the urban proletariat against the new reformist bourgeois government. (In fact, many would prefer to describe the second, October, revolution of 1917 as a **coup d'état** or *putsch* by the **Bolsheviks**.) The second point is Trotsky's opposition to Lenin's stress on the need for a highly disciplined and author-itarian party organized on the principles of **democratic centralism**. This, of course, is highly attractive to far-left splinter groups in Western political systems, because their major enemy is as likely to be an orthodox communist party as a conservative party. Whether Trotsky would particularly have approved of such groups is somewhat unclear. At the end of his life he was working for the creation of international and national co-operation by all left-wing parties in **popular front** governments. In any case plenty of other Marxist leaders, notably Rosa **Luxemburg**, were equally opposed to Lenin's views on centralized party authority. Trotskyism has enjoyed a something of a rebirth with the far-left as Marxist critics of society seek a new rallying point after the collapse of Soviet communism.

Trust

It may seem odd that such an ordinary and apparently non-technical word as trust could be an important social science concept, but it is rapidly coming to be seriously studied, especially by advocates of **social capital** as an analytic framework. Trust does not mean anything more to a political scientist that it does to a layman, but it is the recognition by academe of the importance of trust that is new. It is a blunt fact that societies differ enormously in the extent to which individuals typically trust each other. It has always been recognized that trust in social institutions varies considerably. Much of the early work on **political culture** was largely taken up by measuring the extent to which citizens trusted their political leaders and institutions. Several Western countries scored very poorly on such indicators, but it was the beginning of the **democratic transitions** in Eastern Europe that made social scientists look again at the phenomenon. Not only the old communist institutions, but even the new ones, particularly the parties and parliaments, seem to engender very little trust in the citizenry.

Although there are, in some countries, fairly good reasons for distrusting the new political élites, it has become obvious that this pervasive mistrust is often just a reflection of a generalized distrust in 'others'. Anthropologists have long realized that cultures vary enormously on this basic question. Some societies, not only primitive societies but also advanced ones such as modern Italy, display an intense 'familialism' such that only those to whom one can trace a family connection can ever really be trusted to be honest and reliable. In other societies there may be high levels of trust within subcultures, but intense distrust of other groups, especially, and inevitably, of immigrants. Where there is such a deep distrust of the stranger, it is almost impossible to develop distant political institutions that are trusted. This has very serious implications for the legitimacy of states, and for their capacity to extract social effort in crisis situations. The theoretical problem is that of the direction of causation: does unwillingness by the individual to trust others cause, or stem from, distrust of social and political institutions? It is often pointed out, for example, that societies in the **Balkans** have very low levels of trust, arguably because they were governed for so long by the corrupt and alien Ottoman Empire. The secondary problem for social science is to design social institutions that can help foster trust at both individual and societal levels.

Two-Party Systems

Genuine two-party systems are actually very rare. The classic examples have always been held to be the Anglo-American democracies, and the USA, at least at the federal level, is as near as exists to a genuine two-party system. Even US presidential elections usually have several more candidates, and in the 1980 election the third party candidate, John Anderson, though ultimately getting a very poor vote, was seen by some commentators as a serious threat earlier in the campaign. Ross Perot, who eventually won the highest 'third party' vote since Theodore Roosevelt in 1912 presented an even greater threat in the elections of the 1990s. Moreover, in the 2000 election it was considered that Ralph Nader, the Green Party candidate, attracted sufficient votes from the Democrat, Al Gore, to deprive him of victory in least one additional state, and thereby of the presidency. Britain has never been a true two-party system since the early years of the 20th century (and even then, only if pre-independence Irish representation is discounted); there have always been members of parliament from several parties, and always, especially, some sort of parliamentary Liberal party. As the dealignment of voters from the traditional two-class, two-party model has developed, especially with a modest Liberal (now Liberal Democrat) revival from its post-war nadir and the rise of the Scottish and Welsh nationalists, the House of Commons cannot be described as bipartisan. Generally, as is the case with the one party in a **single-party system**, the 'two' parties in a two-party system tend to be so broadly based as to be almost portmanteaus for a set of ideologically conflictual elements. The point is that unless the social **cleavage** structure of a society is very simple indeed, there will always be more points of view, and more sectional interests, than can properly be represented by one or two united and homogeneous parties. The existence, or apparent existence, of two-party systems owes more to a combination of the greater salience of one cleavage than of the others and an election system that is, as in the Anglo-American polities, extremely unproportional in its representative effects.

Tyranny of the Majority

The tyranny of the majority is a phrase found in John Stuart **Mill's** essay *On Liberty*, but is representative of a general fear found among many liberal political thinkers in the 19th century, notably in the works of **de Tocqueville**. The idea is that liberal values, especially values of freedom of expression and the freedom to exercise a life style of one's own, however unconventional, as long as it hurts no one, will be seriously at risk in majoritarian democracy. For Mill the uneducated working-class majority was seen as peculiarly prone to intolerance of opinion and behaviour, and likely to persecute, at least informally if not legally, anyone who did not 'fit in' with common trends. He certainly believed in at least restricted democracy, but held to such a strong notion of the limitations on rightful government interference with private liberty that he had reason to doubt that freedom would be protected as well in a popular democracy as in some forms of enlightened despotism. A similar though somewhat more pragmatic view was held by de Tocqueville, mainly in his classic work on the emerging political system of the USA, *Democracy in America*. Here his argument was that there were tremendous pressures towards conformity, and therefore mediocrity, at work through the combination of egalitarianism and popular democracy, and furthermore that the mass of ill-educated citizens were prone to exploitation and being misled by talented but corrupt demagogues. He was hardly alone in this view, as the authors of the *Federalist Papers*, and the founding fathers of the US Constitution had argued for intervening layers of electoral colleges to insulate the presidency and the Senate from direct influence by the masses. Much later a version of this fear of intolerance to minorities on the part of masses, whipped up to fury by unscrupulous demagogues, formed part of the **pluralist** thesis common to most American post-war political scientists. In particular Kornhauser's *The Politics of Mass Society* argued that vicious dictatorships of the Nazi type could easily arise unless the social structure prevented direct access of leading political figures to the emotions of the masses. In many ways the tyranny of the majority is a version of the standing tension between the two halves of the prime Western goal of creating **liberal democracy**.

U

Underclass

The idea of an underclass, which has entered sociology theory from the USA, is a politically charged and controversial concept. If it has a valid application even in the USA, its application in the United Kingdom is even more problematic. An underclass is not just another class, at the bottom of the class hierarchy; it is not simply like the working class but even less affluent. Rather, an underclass is seen as almost outside the usual institutions and mechanisms of society, cut off from the working class almost as much as from the middle class. An underclass is defined by a multiplicity of indicators, involving a breakdown of normal relations to society. For example, permanent and intergenerationally inherited unemployment is a crucial part of the definition. Anyone can become unemployed; some are unemployed for very long periods, and if unemployment strikes when one is old enough, it may be unlikely that one will succeed in ever getting a job again. Such unemployment is, of course, much more common the further down a class hierarchy one is. But unemployment of an underclass is different. The second generation of an underclass probably has never had, and can never expect to have, a job; he or she comes from a family unit where possibly no one has ever worked in their own life experience. Welfare is the expected and permanent source of income. Education is minimal, with no parental expectations of it being taken seriously, or having any useful function in life. The family structure itself is negligible—almost inevitably a (female) one-parent family background, probably with several half-siblings, with the fathers all absent and having played no part in one's life. The consequences of all these factors, along with the inevitable deep poverty are to produce a class of people with no emotional or ideological commitment to society, with no sense of a valid role, with no expectations of mutuality of duties and rights, emotionally incapable of self-organization and efforts at 'betterment', either for the individual or the group.

This is an ideal stereotype, naturally. Any particular individual of the underclass may lack some of the aforementioned characteristics. Similarly some characteristics, particularly bad employment histories, may be experienced by people who, none the less, occupy more traditional and socially integrated class locations. The concept is criticized both theoretically and empirically, but it has a certain robustness so that it continues to be taken seriously even by those sociologists who denounce it. At core, it is based on the urban black experience in the USA and translates badly to the UK and Western Europe. In part the theoretical problem is that it is too early to be sure whether such a phenomenon has developed, because it depends largely on the inheritance over generations of these characteristics, and outside of the USA there has not been time for a second generation to mature and risk passing on its own inheritance. (See also **Welfarism**.)

Unilateralism

Unilateralism is the removal by one side in a potential armed conflict of an entire class, or at least a significant proportion of one, of weapons, whether of not any other country agrees to do so. It first came to prominence in the British anti-nuclear movement of the 1950s, led by the Campaign for Nuclear Disarmament (CND) after its foundation in 1958, which had the specific objective of persuading the government of the United Kingdom to abandon all of its nuclear weapons, irrespective of the actions of other countries (see **pressure groups**). During the late 1950s and early 1960s CND attracted considerable mass support for its unilateralist campaign, as was especially demonstrated during its annual symbolic march from the town of Aldermaston (the site of the nuclear weapons research establishment) to London. It also attracted politically important support from within the **Labour Party** and certain trade unions. The Labour Party adopted a motion advocating unilateral nuclear disarmament in 1960, but has always veered away from unilateralism when in government. CND and unilateralism experienced a revival of support during the late 1970s and 1980s, initially associated with the decision to base US ground-launched cruise missiles on British soil. This class of missile was multilaterally abandoned under the **Intermediate Nuclear Forces (INF) Treaty** of 1987, but the public opposition to the missiles in the UK and other Western European countries was of less significance here than the new impetus to general disarmament which accompanied the **Gorbachev** era in the Soviet Union.

The unilateralist position is not, in principle, restricted to nuclear weapons. Clearly any fully-fledged pacifist, who holds that it is wrong in any and all circumstances to use force, would logically be required to be in favour of total unilateral disarmament. British advocates of disarmament in the 1930s had also used the term, but not in such a strictly pacifist sense. What makes unilateralism special is that it is *not* necessary to be pacifist to adopt it, and many unilateralists insist that they support at least the current, and possibly a considerably increased, level of defence spending on **conventional arms**. The arguments of unilateralism are diverse, as is the motivation of its supporters. They break down roughly into two aspects. The first, more often prominent in the 1950s than in the later period, is that it is wrong in general to use weapons of such power, and which can only cause massive destruction to non-combatants. The second is that the proliferation of nuclear weaponry makes all-out nuclear war more rather than less likely. It is thus held that abandoning Britain's nuclear weapons is, among other things, a policy most likely to protect the UK from attack. It was further argued, in this direction, that abandoning nuclear weaponry and removing US nuclear forces from UK territory would ensure that the 'enemy', traditionally the Soviet Union, had no reason to use similar weapons on the UK. As such the unilateralist argument essentially conflicts with the general **deterrence** theory behind much nuclear **strategy**. There is no doubt that the unilateralist argument commanded considerable public support up to the mid-1980s. It was again the official policy of the British Labour Party for most of the 1980s. However, there was at least equally strong opposition to unilateralism, and its place in the Labour **manifestos** for the 1983 and 1987 general elections undoubtedly contributed to the party's heavy defeats. There was substantial sympathy for unilateralism in other parts of the political spectrum, especially the Liberal (now Liberal Democrat) Party, whose leaders, however, prevented unilateralism ever becoming official policy. The arguments for unilateralism have now become much weaker with the end of any serious nuclear threat from the successors to the Soviet Union. In fact, the nuclear threat is now widely perceived to be from minor powers desperate enough to try to blackmail a country like the UK. Here the argument for a credible deterrent may, in fact, be stronger than it ever was against the vastly more powerful **Soviet bloc**. It is noteworthy that by 2002 both the USA and the UK found it worthwhile explicitly to state that they would have no hesitation in using nuclear weapons against such a state, though the British Secretary of State for Defence went on, curiously, to state that he was not at all sure this threat would work as a deterrent.

United Nations (UN)

The United Nations replaced the inter-war **League of Nations** in an attempt to ensure world peace and secure the economic, social and political conditions under which this can be achieved. It started as an agreement between the allies fighting Hitler's axis powers in the Second World War, and much of its structure and subsequent problems follow from this. Its charter originated from discussions held at Dumbarton Oaks (Washington, DC) in 1944, between the USA, the United Kingdom, the Soviet Union and later China, and the Charter was signed in June 1945, with an initial membership of 51 countries. By 1992 the total number of members had reached 179, following a sudden increase in the total number of internationally-recognized states after the dissolution of the Soviet Union and the former Yugoslavia. Paradoxically, two of the then Soviet republics, Belarus and Ukraine, became full and independent members of the UN from its inception as part of a political compromise made to retain the joint membership of both the USA and the Soviet Union. Given that the vital first few years of the UN coincided with the worst of the early **cold war** days the continued membership of both **superpowers** was quite an achievement. By contrast, until 1971 the 'China' that occupied a seat at the UN was not the communist People's Republic of China (PRC), the major world power led by **Mao Zedong**, but the island Republic of China (Taiwan), as the USA refused to recognize the mainland government.

The UN's wartime origins show also in its basic organization. The most important organ of the UN is the Security Council, in permanent session and charged with maintenance of international peace and security, including calling on the member states to put together peace-keeping forces to monitor cease-fires or conflicts in specific disputes. Peace-keeping forces are allowed to use their weapons only in self-defence, but ultimately the Security Council may sanction a full military operation. The body has 15 members, of which five are permanent. They are, in effect, the main victorious allies of the Second World War, the USA, Russia (having inherited the seat of the Soviet Union upon its dissolution in 1991) the UK, France and the PRC. Until the PRC replaced Taiwan in 1971, therefore, this insignificant island was actually a permanent member of the Security Council. Even since then the second-tier powers of the UK and France have retained permanent membership, while equal or superior powers, at least in economic terms, such as Germany and Japan, only serve for two-year periods as and when elected. As the five permanent members each have an absolute veto on Security Council resolutions, the international power balance has been effectively freeze-framed at 1945, and any one of them has been able to block effective UN action, and frequently has. Since the collapse of the superpower status of the Soviet Union there has been evidence of a new world order, in which the greater recognition of global common interests has greatly reduced the tendency for one or other of the permanent members to use their veto. The first mark of this was the Council's ability to recruit a force, under US leadership, to fight the **Gulf War** after Iraq's invasion of Kuwait. As the USA involved itself in a self-declared 'war on terrorism' after the attacks on its territory in September 2001, it spared no effort to ensure UN support for as much of its activity as possible. It was quite clear, however, that both the USA and its main ally the UK would not be deterred from acting without a UN mandate were that unavailable.

The other main organ, the General Assembly, consists of all members and can debate and pass resolutions on any matter covered by the Charter, except for disputes already on the agenda of the Security Council. However, it is largely a propaganda arena and ideological battlefield to which few nations in conflict pay any attention. The most important work of the UN, other than the peace-keeping of the Security Council, is done by the specialized agencies, and by the direct personal diplomacy of the administrative head, the secretary-general. The secretaries-general have nearly all been extremely-widely respected international statespeople whose personal interventions have often been of great help. The specialized agencies like the World Health Organization and the International Labour Organization (which actually began under the League of Nations) have, along with other agencies affiliated to the UN such as the regional commissions, made major contributions to international social welfare and economic development. Others, like the United Nations High Commissioner for Refugees, or the International Court of Justice, though dependent on political consensus for their work, have often been able to minimize the human suffering that would have been consequent on political conflict that the UN has not actually been able to avoid. The internal budget of the UN has frequently been the subject of controversy, however, largely because major contributors, particularly the USA (liable for 25% of the budget in the years 1989–91) and the former Soviet Union (liable for 11.6%), objected to the level of their financial burden compared to the weight of their voice in the General Assembly, where **Third World** nations tend to dominate.

The greater effectiveness of the UN compared with the League of Nations is shown mainly in its ability on several occasions to put military forces in the field which have either stopped international aggression (as eventually in the **Korean War**, and more swiftly in the Gulf War) or minimized it, as with the peace-keeping forces in Cyprus and the Belgian Congo. This competence, and its general ability to function as an international safety valve, is due to the fact that while the League of Nations lacked two of the most important powers, the USA and, from 1933, Germany, the UN has had both the USA and the Soviet Union/Russia firmly entrenched in the Security Council. (Though it must be noted that UN action against the communist North Korean forces invading South Korea was only possible because the Soviet Union was, at that time, boycotting the UN. It would otherwise undoubtedly have used its veto in support of North Korea.) Already the longest lasting and most universal international political body, its new found strength in the post-**cold war** era has already revitalized the UN, and it may play an ever increasing role.

Utilitarianism

Utilitarianism is the moral, social and political theory originated by Jeremy **Bentham** and James **Mill**, and further developed by John Stuart **Mill**. At its core is a simple equation between 'the good', and 'happiness' or pleasure. The basic thesis states that whatever measure, policy, choice or decision maximizes the positive balance of pleasure over pain across a population, or for a single individual if only they are concerned, is what is 'good' and therefore 'right'. The theory expressly denies, in its earlier versions, any ordering, moral or otherwise, of the sources of pleasure. In Bentham's own words, 'pushpin is as good as poetry'. Except for the distribution principle, 'that each man should count as one, and none for more than one', utilitarianism allows no other moral or political criteria of decision. Bentham argued that it ought, in principle, to be possible directly to quantify and sum the positive and negative consequences, in terms of pleasure, of any act by what he called the 'felicific calculus'. Policy-making for a society, as much as private moral decision-making for an individual, would then become essentially an automatic process. Naturally there have been many adjustments and refinements to this basic utilitarian theory over the years. Two may be identified as of particular importance.

John Stuart Mill attempted to get away from the over-hedonistic emphasis by suggesting that there were, in fact, hierarchies of desirability. He argued that those who had experienced both of what he defined as 'gross' and 'refined' pleasures would always opt for the less basic or gross. He also attempted, though somewhat unconvincingly, to demonstrate how our other basic politico-moral values, for example a desire for justice or a high value on freedom, could be derived from the utility principle. The other broad area of development, mainly the work of modern moral philosophers, can produce some unfortunate consequences of utilitarian argument when applied as a public political philosophy as well as a private moral code. The problem has tended to be that what maximizes the interests or happiness of a single individual might, were everyone to act in the same way, be disastrous as a public policy. Thus there has come about a distinction between 'rule' versus 'act' utilitarianism. An 'act' utilitarian requires that each individual ensures that their every act maximizes their own utility, whereas the more plausible 'rule' utilitarian requires that laws and regulations be decided so that, on balance across the population, the rule maximizes the sum of individual utilities, even though in particular cases individuals would not, as selfish utility maximizers, choose to act as the rule requires. The whole aim of utilitarianism is to escape, as much as possible, from reliance on any source of moral authority, whether it be religion, another metaphysic or appeal to such abstractions as **natural law**. Although it is not immediately obvious, nearly all modern parties and governments in the Western world have in fact operated according to a utilitarian approach. Most of economic theory, and the whole of 'welfare economics' (see **welfarism**), and many of the theoretical models and justifications for democracy, are frankly utilitarian. Policy analysis, especially as developed by civil servants and academic specialists in the 1960s, is equally based on a utility calculus, and until recently the prevailing theories of law and jurisprudence were derived from utilitarianism. Only in the 1970s did political theorists of a non-Marxist kind even begin to develop non-utilitarian general political philosophies, so total was the hold of the Benthamite tradition over Western intellectuals. Even then it is instructive to note that the new approaches, by thinkers like **Rawls**, **Nozick** and Dworkin, were based on a return to a tradition of political theory, mainly that of John **Locke**, which was the original competitor to the thinkers from whom utilitarianism itself derived, such as **Hobbes** and David **Hume**. In a secular society, and one without the intellectual armoury of 'scientific socialism', which has to operate with a minimum of coercion and in a more or less democratic manner, there is really little alternative to an appeal to rational self-interest, which is what utilitarianism amounts to.

Utopianism

Utopianism is an approach to social or political theory based upon the design of a perfect society (a 'utopia', after the title of Sir Thomas More's example of the genre, from 1516, using an imaginary island of that name). Earlier writers had, of course, had elements of utopianism in their work. The most obvious are the political systems designed in **Plato's** *Republic* and *The Laws*. The point of difference though is that Plato, and most political theorists, either expect that their systems could actually be put into operation, or admit that they are second best precisely because of the impossibility of carrying out an ideal design in reality. More's *Utopia* and subsequent works of utopian writing stress the ideal as a measuring tool for reality, rather than as an empirical possibility. Utopias, if intended as such, are really thought experiments, political theory's equivalent to the perfect frictionless bearing, or perhaps an economist's perfect competition model.

The idea that utopias are impossible, and that some recognized writings on utopias may never have been intended as blueprints, is stressed because the concept of utopianism has largely become derogatory. **Marx** was one of the earliest writers to use the concept as a criticism, when writing of some early **socialist** blueprints. Marx thought that, by not taking sufficient note of the brutal facts of material restrictions and **class** warfare, these socialist writers were being purely utopian, operating in a fantasy land. Thomas More did not believe that his island political paradise could ever exist; later Jean Jacques **Rousseau** was to stress in his writings, especially the *Social Contract,* that hardly any existing society could be transformed to his specifications. This is why, indeed, the conditions of political life are so much more pleasant on the island of Utopia than in, for example, **Hobbes'** *Leviathan*. The latter is, if anything, the opposite of a utopia, a dystopia, a system designed to fit with the worst possible realities of human nature and political incompetence, and thus practicable but hardly desirable. At the same time, while Hobbes might help us set up a state that could work, as might **Machiavelli**, it requires a Thomas More or a Rousseau to inspire our political judgements and ambitions.

V

Value Freedom

Value freedom is a methodological requirement of a useful social science, and would be treated as one of the primary requisites in judging most **political science**, though not **political theory**, writing. It consists of the effort to carry out analyses in the most impartial manner possible, and in not allowing individual preferences to bias the research, data collection or conclusions drawn. The model being invoked is, of course, that of the natural sciences. It is believed by the advocates of value freedom that a physicist, for example, has no private preference for any one theory of nuclear particles rather than another, and therefore produces unbiased work. Similarly, it ought to be possible to study the causes of social stability, or of voting behaviour, or of the efficiency of presidential rather than prime-ministerial governments without any bias resulting from personal conviction. As such it is a goal both long established as ideal (**Weber** wrote extensively on the problem and **Comte** thought he had achieved it), and hotly contested by various schools of the philosophy of science. There are two major points that raise doubt about the possibility of such value freedom in social science research. The first is the general argument that all people are subject to the dominant **ideology** of their society. As a result truth, and especially truth about social reality, is inevitably relative. A Marxist like Georg Lukács (1885–1971), for example, would argue that an economist working inside the framework of a capitalist society simply cannot grasp that **capitalism** is doomed to collapse through its internal contradictions and because of its exploitative nature, because to accept this would be incompatible with their entire outlook. A second, more subtle argument denies the utility of analogy with the physical sciences because they too are seen as less than impartial. A physicist, because of training, career expectations and individual creative limitations, is stuck inside a 'paradigm' in which there is indeed a preference for one theory over another. A theory that fits into the overall received view, rather than one which would force a general rethinking, will be preferred. Thus political sociologists may be forced into working towards, for example, a **rational choice theory** of voting both because such a theory defends the **liberal democracy** they have been socialized to believe in, and because the intellectual apparatus they have been trained in is only efficient given such assumptions. There is no ultimate solution, and perhaps it does not really matter. What is important is not so much that values do not enter into the choice of theory or research method, but that they be explicit and open, so that those who oppose them can criticize the work. Some political theories of **liberalism**, like **utilitarianism**, seek for value freedom in a different sense; they seek to create a constitutional framework in which as wide a variety of human values as possible can be achieved. This sense of value freedom could be said to pervade most justifications for democracy.

Vanguard of the Proletariat

The vanguard of the proletariat is a **Marxist** notion made more famous, and relied upon heavily, by **Leninism**. It refers to the **communist** party in any society, and especially in a **revolution** or a post-revolutionary period. The basic Leninist thesis is that the ordinary mass of the industrial **proletariat** cannot come to a true consciousness of their situation, and cannot develop a fully revolutionary spirit, spontaneously and without leadership. Consequently a party of professional revolutionaries must be formed from those who do have the capacity to escape from **false consciousness** and ideological manipulation. This party will raise the revolutionary consciousness of the masses, and lead them in the revolution, hence being the 'vanguard'. The more important extension of this doctrine, in itself plausible, is that, after the revolution, there will still be a need for direction and control of the efforts of the proletariat in building the truly socialist society. Thus the initial revolutionary leadership becomes institutionalized into a **dictatorship of the proletariat** via the rule of a single dominant communist party. Here there is a considerable strain between the original thought of **Marx** and **Engels** and the subsequent interpretation of how a post-revolutionary society should be run, as developed by Lenin and taken to extremes by **Stalin**. Inside the Marxist tradition **Trotsky's** theory of 'permanent revolution' avoids at least this institutionalization, as did **Mao Zedong's** doctrine of how communism should develop in China, as best exemplified by his **cultural revolution** in the 1960s.

Vatican II

The second Vatican Council in the modern history of the Roman Catholic Church sat from 1961–65, involving nearly 3,000 delegates from all sectors and regions of the church. It was called for largely spiritual reasons, to help find the church a stance in an increasingly **secularized** and politically divided world, and it differed enormously in tone from much of the Roman Catholic

Church's orientation to such problems in the previous century. Above all it involved a liberalization of the control of the hierarchy over individual Catholics, and a much needed affirmation of the importance of individual conscience in spiritual matters. Given how severely the loyalty of the laity was to be challenged by conservative teachings on birth control immediately after the council and throughout the reign of Pope John Paul II, this liberalization was necessary. Without Vatican II the Roman Catholic Church might well have collapsed in developed Western societies. It is hard to exaggerate the importance to the faithful of the decrees of this Council, or to make them comprehensible to non-Roman Catholics. Indeed, most living Roman Catholics, having gown up since the Council, can often barely imagine how illiberal and restrictive the Church was beforehand. Simple matters of liturgical reform, such as the priest celebrating mass facing the congregation rather than with his back to them, as though involved in a secret rite, symbolize but cannot really convey the changes. Quite specific teachings may also be misunderstood. The result of Vatican II has been a commitment to ecumenicalism and a declaration of the validity of religious freedom—such values seem self-evidently correct, yet were not part of orthodox teaching before the early 1960s.

Politically, Vatican II has often been seen as necessary to prevent a split between the Roman Catholic Church in America and in Western Europe, because American Roman Catholics had already adopted or clearly made their preferences known for the more relaxed and liberal interpretations. It must be admitted, however, that much of the Church has never lived up to the spirit of Vatican II; papal authority still oppresses that of local bishops, and the role of the clergy *vis-à-vis* the laity has not been transformed as much as was envisaged. Furthermore, in the last 20 years serious 'counter-revolutionary' and reactionary forces, some deep inside the Vatican bureaucracy, have systematically attempted to reverse many of the changes. The Roman Catholic Church's usual response, historically, to challenges from political society and from intellectual development has been to throw up walls and try to order its faithful to turn away from modernity and progress. These conservative forces, claiming that Christianity is in danger of moral decay from secular society, would like to repeat these previous attempts at avoidance. Most probably though, inadequate as it was, the liberalization brought about by the council, will make such a retreat into a religious and intellectual ghetto impossible to enforce.

Vichy

The Vichy regime (named after the town in central France where it was set up in 1940) was the collaborationist civilian French government of unoccupied France, set up with German support after their invasion of northern and western France. The assembly of the **Third Republic** gave full power to the emergency prime minister, Henri Pétain, who had been perhaps France's greatest military leader in the First World War. However, he rapidly declared himself head of the French state, and organized, or acquiesced in the organization of, a semi-**fascist** state along authoritarian lines. The Vichy regime was by no means as unpopular as post-war French propaganda has suggested. There had always been a strong element of distaste on the right for the Third Republic, and indeed, among many sectors, a refusal quite to accept the principles of the French Revolution and its democratic republican spirit. Pétain himself, and he was old and feeble before the war even started, came under the influence of deliberately pro-Nazi leaders, especially Laval, a third republican politician, and Admiral Darlan. These men and their followers co-operated actively with the Germans, even when, in 1944, the German army occupied the area of France officially under Vichy control. Their police force, the Milice, was hardly less enthusiastic than the Gestapo in carrying out anti-resistance, and at times **anti-Semitic** measures. To many industrialists Vichy, unhampered by free trade unions and supported by a strong and resourceful administration and civil service, was a positive improvement on the semi-anarchy of industry under the Third Republic. The essence of the Vichy regime, with its authoritarian and reactionary ideology, is well represented by the symbolic replacement of the traditional revolutionary slogan of the Republic (Liberty, Equality and Fraternity) with one of Pétain's devising, 'Work, Family and Country'. The Vichy regime was entirely discredited once France had been liberated, and its leading members tried for treason. However, their counter-argument, that they were trying to preserve at least some vestige of French autonomy and were essentially patriots forced to accept and moderate the consequences of a military defeat for which they were not responsible, cannot entirely be dismissed.

Vietnam War

The Vietnam War was a struggle between North and South Vietnam in which the USA was directly involved in the defence of the South, and which had severe repercussions both on the politics of South-East Asia and on US domestic politics. Civil war in Vietnam had been developing since the French withdrawal from Indo-China in 1954 following the humiliating military defeat of the French forces at Dien Bien Phu. The ensuing peace settlement set up two states, North and South Vietnam, with the North governed by the nationalist leaders of the anti-French campaign who were also, but incidentally, **communist**. The South was theoretically democratic, though corruption was rife, much of the population indifferent to who ruled and from the outset reliant on US economic and military aid. Military aggression by the communist North led to President John F. Kennedy's decision in 1961 to allow US military advisers to fight with the troops they were training, and the involvement continued to escalate through the remainder of his presidency and into the Johnson and Nixon presidencies. The point at which the US effort shifted from aid to outright warfare was in 1965, when an alleged attack on US naval units by the North Vietnamese allowed Johnson to persuade Congress to pass a resolution, the 'Gulf of Tonkin Resolution', authorizing a major troop deployment. At first the war appeared to be going well for the USA, but the sudden outbreak of unsuspected Northern forces throughout South Vietnam in 1968, the Tet Offensive, which very nearly took control of all urban centres, shook American self-confidence. Widespread opposition to the war in the late 1960s and the polarization of opinion on the issue weakened American commitment. The deterioration of the military situation in favour of the North Vietnamese and mounting congressional opposition to the war forced President Nixon to commence withdrawal of US troops in 1969. By August 1972 the last US combat troops were withdrawn and in January 1973 a cease-fire was implemented. In 1975 the North Vietnamese army successfully invaded the South and captured its capital, Saigon, requiring the evacuation of remaining US personnel.

Apart from the tragedy of the war for the Vietnamese themselves, the war dominated American political life for nearly a decade and cast doubt on the willingness of the USA to intervene again in a military confrontation with communist forces. Indeed as late as the Gulf War there was a clear hesitancy on the part of the Pentagon to risk involvement. The USA clearly had in mind the analogy between the Soviet Union's failure in Afghanistan and its own Vietnam failure when forced to make war in Afghanistan as part of President George W. Bush's 'war on terrorism' of 2002. The ease with which US-supported forces did prevail may have finally laid the Vietnam Ghost to rest.

The Vietnam War also contributed to the abuses of executive power which culminated in the **Watergate** crisis. The long-term consequence was to weaken American morale and self-image so much that President Ronald Reagan was able to be elected in 1980, and re-elected in 1984, on a programme that deliberately set out to build up US military might and restore to the USA a sense of being an invulnerable **superpower**. The resulting **arms race** contributed to the demise of the Soviet Union through the pressure exerted on its economy. It is, therefore, arguable that precisely because the USA 'lost' the war in Vietnam, it ultimately 'won' the **cold war**.

Voting

Voting is an act of choice among a set of alternatives, by a free individual, and is at the heart of modern **democracy**. People have, of course, voted for candidates for office, or for policy alternatives, in every social system ever experienced. The recorded history of voting goes back, at least, to the Greek **polis**. The modern word for the study of voting behaviour, psephology, derives from the classical Greek 'psephos', the piece of pottery on which certain votes, mainly about the banishment of those seen as dangerous to the state, were inscribed. Voting is no more than the voicing of individual opinions—the problems arise in counting the votes (see **voting systems**), and in deciding for whom, or for what alternative, the votes have been cast.

When the voting is in an election to choose a candidate among others, the most important requisites are the secret and individual ballots, which allow the impartial measurement of opinion. The use of these is actually quite recent, at least in their fullest form; the secret ballot was not used for parliamentary elections in the United Kingdom until the late 19th century. Allowing candidates to put party labels on the ballot slips, the minimum necessary to avoid wasted votes, did not happen until the late 1960s.

The vote has been restricted, throughout history, for a variety of reasons. Probably the most common qualification, in national politics, has been a wealth or property qualification. Since the late 19th century there has been a series of developments on the **franchise**, each slightly extending voting rights, firstly among men and later to women. The typical modern standard in the late 20th century is that all citizens over the age of 18 should be allowed to vote.

Voting Systems

There are two broad families of voting systems used in modern democracies. Historically the earliest is that called the simple plurality or, more colloquially, the 'first-past-the-post' system. Here the candidate with more votes than any other is elected, and elections are carried out in a series of single-member constituencies. This method is used in the United Kingdom, the USA, Canada and in many non-governmental contexts world-wide. It is not only possible, but very common, for a candidate, or an entire government, to be elected without gaining a majority of the votes cast, because the combined votes of two or more opposing candidates, or parties, total more than those for the one elected. In fact no British government has been formed having received a majority of the votes cast in a general election since 1935; however, most of these governments held a majority, sometimes large, of seats in the House of Commons.

A modification of simple plurality, the **second ballot** system, is used in France. A candidate is only declared elected on the first ballot if they receive a majority of votes cast (that is, 50% + 1). In constituencies where this does not occur (in practice, about two-thirds of all constituencies) a second ballot is held a week later, in which only candidates gaining more than 12.5% in the first ballot, less any voluntary withdrawals, participate. Another modification of the simple plurality is the **alternative vote**, where voters indicate not only their first choice among candidates, but also their subsequent choices in numeric order. When no candidate achieves a majority of first preferences, the second preferences of the weaker candidates are reallocated until an overall majority is obtained.

The alternative approach to elections is to attempt to achieve **proportional representation** of voter preferences in the elected body. There is a wide variety of such systems. The three most common are the **party list system**, the **single transferable vote** and the **additional member**. There are many elements to the argument on voting systems. One major concern is the idea of fairness. In the 2001 British general election, for example, the Liberal Democrats gained 18.3% of the national vote, but only won 52 seats, 7.9% of the total, in the House of Commons; a proportionate or 'fair' result would have given them 121 seats (indeed, this represented the Liberal Democrats' best performance in terms of seats for some years, in part as a result of **tactical voting**. In 1992 they won just 20 seats, with only a slightly smaller share of the total votes cast). Another concern is that non-proportional systems 'waste' many votes. Not only does someone who votes for a candidate not receiving a plurality in their constituency fail to gain any representation for their vote, but also someone who votes for a winning candidate with a massive majority (in the USA and the United Kingdom up to 60% of seats can be regarded as 'safe' in this sense) might think of their vote as wasted. If those perceiving of their intended votes as likely to be wasted either decide to cast them for a candidate on whom they might not be wasted, or not to vote at all, then the genuine democratic intent of the electorate is distorted. It is difficult to deny that some form of proportional representation would be fairer to parties and candidates than the plurality system. However, it is often claimed that proportional representation may lead to unstable and shifting **coalition** government. Though coalitions *are* more likely in proportional systems, it is neither inevitable that they will occur, nor that they will be weak and unstable. West Germany, and now Germany, has had a form of proportional representation since 1947, and has always been ruled by a coalition, but the coalitions have been as stable as those produced by most simple plurality systems. Furthermore votes can still be 'wasted' in a **multi-party system** with near perfect proportionality if the political culture makes the admission of one party to a coalition impossible. Between the 1960s and 1980s the Italian communist party regularly gained about one-third of total votes cast, but was never admitted to government, while most coalitions contained some parties with support of 5% or lower. A stronger argument against the coalition governments often produced under proportional representation is that the compromise and bargaining between parties can result in necessary decisions not being taken, and that therefore government by the biggest minority is indeed preferable to a coalition.

War Crimes Tribunals

Until recently, the attempt to prosecute and punish individuals guilty of crimes against humanity during wars was an *ad hoc* business, and largely a matter of the winners in a war punishing some of the leading members of the defeated enemy society. Alternatively, it was a matter of domestic courts trying people from defeated countries or even, in the case of Germany, from their own population, under a patchwork of domestic and **international law**. The Nuremberg War Crimes Tribunal was such a matter of victors punishing losers, and it set the precedent for the legitimacy of international action against those guilty of war crimes. In the 1990s the gradual shift away from the classic doctrine of national sovereignty and a greater acceptance of the rights of the international community to police itself, combined with several shocking returns to barbarism, especially in the former Yugoslavia, led to the creation of new tribunals. The most important is the tribunal created by the UN in 1993 to deal with crimes against 'international humanitarian law' in the countries of the former Yugoslavia. This tribunal is still sitting, and in 2001 was successful in arranging the deportation of the former political leader of Yugoslavia, Slobodan Milošević to face trial. Another such tribunal was created in 1994 to prosecute those guilty of offences in Rwanda. This, though doubtless equally necessary, has the slightly unusual character of being effectively an external punishment of those guilty of horror during an internal ethnic conflict. As a precedent it may indeed be more important, as it signals an even greater breach of the doctrine of national **sovereignty**.

Clearly such *ad hoc* tribunals, however effective and impartial, will always risk the appearance of being unsystematic and *post hoc* responses to specific events. What is needed, and this has now been accepted internationally, is a criminal version of the permanent international court, the International Court of Justice (see also **international law**). Thus, in 1998, an international conference in Rome under UN auspices finalized the statute of an International Criminal Court, which will have jurisdiction over war crimes, crimes against humanity and genocide. It is also supposed to have jurisdiction over the rather vague crime of aggression, but it is unclear whether this will ever be defined in a way acceptable to powerful members of the international system. The court lacks full support, especially from the USA (which indicated its refusal to participate in 2002), but it is scheduled to come into effective existence in July 2002. Exactly how powerful a body it will be remains to be seen. Although *ad hoc* tribunals have their problems, they are at least well supported by the states who create them; a permanent court would have to rely on a longer-term legitimacy, even in situations where it did not have backing from a few powerful and closely concerned powers. The really important element in modern war crimes tribunals, whether they be *ad hoc* or the permanent court, is that there must be a guarantee that they will come into operation after conflicts. The successes of the tribunal dealing with the former Yugoslavia mean that there is now a possible deterrent effect. Previously trials like those at Nuremberg were justified largely as retribution, as the making of a moral point. But if it comes to be expected that losers in any conflict will be punished for crimes against humanity, international criminal law may come to function as domestic criminal law is intended.

Warsaw Pact

The Warsaw Pact was the treaty setting up the Soviet-dominated opposition grouping to **NATO**, signed in 1955, and theoretically initiated as a response to West Germany joining NATO in the same year. The military structure was known as the Warsaw Treaty Organization. Its membership included most of the **Soviet bloc**, though Albania, which had come more and more under Chinese influence, ceased to participate in 1961 and formally left in 1968, and both Hungary and Czechoslovakia tried to leave, unsuccessfully, at the times of their anti-Soviet risings in 1956 and 1968 respectively. The Warsaw Pact set up a unified military command structure under the control of Moscow, and was largely armed by the Soviet Union. In practice it was nothing more than an extension of the Soviet military forces, whereby the Eastern European countries provided perhaps 20 of the 70 or more divisions stationed in non-Soviet Eastern Europe. Towards the end of its history (it was formally abolished in July 1991, but had effectively ceased to function after the beginning of the Eastern European revolutions in 1989) many doubts existed among Western defence analysts about the reliability of the armies of most members of the Pact. Furthermore, as the Soviet Union made a practice of always equipping these forces with less-modern weapons systems, they would have been largely ineffective even if politically reliable. The only time the Pact actually engaged in military operations was the crushing of the Czech uprising in 1968. Even this, however, was mainly a propaganda exercise to demonstrate a spurious East European solidarity, with the real offensive entirely carried out by troops from the Soviet Union. No non–Soviet member had any access to nuclear weapons, and the only seriously effective other member was believed to be the quite small East German army. Western analysts believed the Soviet Union's real interest in the Pact was, in fact, to help control its satellites and, particularly in the early days, to protect against any renewed threat from Germany, which the Soviet regimes never ceased to fear.

Watergate

The Watergate is a complex of residential, office and hotel accommodation in Washington, DC, where a suite of rooms had been rented by the Democratic Party National Committee for the presidential election campaign of 1972. These rooms were burgled by a group of people working under the orders of senior members of the Republican Party, including some holding important positions on President Richard Nixon's White House staff. The aim of the burglars appears to have been to gain information about Democratic campaign plans. The discovery of the burglars and their subsequent trials unleashed a massive burst of investigative reporting which ended by incriminating a host of major and minor figures, not so much for having been involved in the initial crime, but for attempting to cover up the White House connections, and generally to impede the course of justice. Among these were officers as senior as the Attorney-General and the president's Chief of Staff.

At that level the scandal would have been serious but, as most of it became public only after Nixon had won the 1972 election, it would not have prevented his continuing in the presidency. It became increasingly clear, however, that the president himself had been involved in the cover-up, and members of the House of Representatives began to move for his impeachment. At the same time secret tape recordings the president had made of conversations in the White House came to be revealed, and court proceedings were instigated to force him to disclose them as vital evidence. Nixon's attempts to prevent this move, claiming that the tapes were covered by a doctrine of executive privilege, were finally overthrown by the Supreme Court. The culmination of these developments led, as impeachment began to seem inevitable, to Nixon's resignation in 1974; he was succeeded by the Vice-President, Gerald Ford, who shortly after gave him a presidential pardon. The crisis shook US politics; faith in executive leadership, already weakened by Nixon's style of government (sometimes called 'imperial presidency') and his secret extension of the **Vietnam War** into Cambodia, collapsed. The following years saw Congress increase in power, relative to the presidency, and a series of attempts to curtail presidential prerogatives (see **presidential government**) and control financial corruption in electoral campaigns. The name Watergate has lingered and become a journalistic cliché, so that almost any political scandal, especially if it involves the theft of documents or the leaking and/or concealment of confidential information, has '-gate' tagged to the end of it. A notorious example was the 'Irangate' scandal towards the end of Ronald Reagan's presidency.

Weber

Max Weber (1864–1920) was a German academic and politician and one of the three or four founding fathers of sociology. In contrast to **Durkheim** and **Marx** he argued for a sociological position in which the inner feelings and self-perceptions of the actors themselves were part of the explanation of human behaviour. His most famous sociological work is *The Protestant Ethic and the Spirit of Capitalism* (1904–05), in which he argued for a natural affinity between certain views of how heavenly salvation was to be earned and the technical requirements of **capitalist** economic development. As far as politics is concerned he is important for two major doctrines. The most important is probably his theory of **bureaucracy**, which has been widely copied and developed, and still inspires most social science research on this vital phenomenon. But he was also the creator of a developmental theory of political change which suggested a move from charismatic authority (see **charisma**), via traditional authority to rational-legal authority, which has informed much of subsequent studies in social and **political development**.

Weimar Republic

The Weimar Republic was the official name for the German political system formed in the aftermath of the First World War in 1919, and lasting until the coming to power of **Hitler** with his 'Third Reich' in 1933. It was quite unstable, attempting to operate a competitive party-based democracy in a country which had not only no tradition of such politics, but was also deeply divided by internal social and political **cleavages**, especially between the communists and the fascists. The period, though short-lived, has remained one of great importance and fascination to social scientists, historians, and indeed novelists, because it was the breeding ground for Nazi politics, and because it represents one of the best cases for theories of revolutionary activity and democratic stability.

Welfare State

Welfare state is a term that came into general use during the Second World War coalition government in Britain, largely as a result of the influential Beveridge Report of 1942. This set up a plan for a comprehensive set of services, financed largely out of national insurance contributions levied both on workers and employers. The scheme was to ensure not only the previously acquired right to an old-age pension, but to put unemployment pay, sickness and injury benefit, and a variety of other financial protections against hardship, on to a regularized basis. In the past such matters had either not been attended to at all, or were covered by *ad hoc* and usually inadequate legislation. The welfare state, while having no detailed content, is the general idea that misfortunes that have financial consequences to those unable to manage should all be dealt with by the state, through its taxing power. Arguments raged, and still do, about how extensive welfare should be. Should it cover only the small number of the almost destitute, or should it be a safety net for many, or should everyone in society be granted an automatic protection against potential disaster? In some cases, as with the British National Health Service (NHS), the entire population is covered by a system of free, or highly subsidized, medicine. In other cases means tests are used to direct special benefit payments, for example to families with low incomes and several children, and to those particularly in need. The spirit, if not the content, of the welfare state has never been seriously challenged in Britain since the 1945–51 Labour governments implemented the basis of the Beveridge Report. No one need now rely on private charity to sustain a basic, if low standard of living, whatever ill fortune in terms of unemployment, illness, industrial injury, family breakdown or whatever may happen. At times, though probably misleadingly, the idea of the welfare state is extended to cover the social services, so that the general principle outlined above is coupled with the rather less unanimously popular existence of a large bureaucracy of social workers of various kinds.

In recent years the proportion of gross national product spent on the various social services has caused concern in a number of Western political systems, and ways have been sought to curb expenditure on these services. Although the Thatcher administration in Britain (1979–90) made considerable efforts to cut back the range of welfare services, and often talked of the need for private charity to play a more important role, little real impact was made to the structure of the system. General cuts in public expenditure, however, seriously reduced the actual value of benefits and services. The need for cut-backs in the welfare state continued to dominate domestic policy throughout Western Europe, and even more in the previously communist East where a huge percentage of GDP was dedicated to welfare benefits. No government has so far found a way radically to cut the expenditure burden in these areas. Some areas, like the British NHS, actually require huge additional resources because of historic underfunding. In others, especially the payment of support to one-parent families and the long-term unemployed, trends in both society and the economy have arguably increased the funding required. As these trends have coincided with a political position throughout the West which makes tax increases politically unacceptable, there seems considerable likelihood of continued crisis in this policy domain.

Welfarism

Welfarism is a vague, and often pejorative, political reference to the principles behind the **welfare state**. It does no more than indicate that the beliefs so characterized hold that the state should take responsibility for the financial security of those in society unable to manage on their own resources. As a result it is perhaps more often used by conservative politicians, especially in the USA, who themselves adopt a much more **laissez-faire** approach, to attack others who they feel are over-solicitous to the poor. Alternatively it is a general statement that society should take such responsibility, and a denial of the **reactionary** 'let them stand on their own feet' position.

World Trade Organization

The World Trade Organization (WTO) was set up by the meeting in Marrakesh of its predecessor organization, the General Agreement on Tariffs and Trade (**GATT**), and came into existence in 1995. GATT itself had been created in 1947 as part of the post-war attempt to build institutions to control and develop world economic activity. The other two institutions founded in 1947, the International Monetary Fund (**IMF**) and the International Fund for Reconstruction and Development (better known as the World Bank) have been remarkably successful. GATT, however, had always been much weaker, because its general aim, the abolition of all barriers to free trade and the creation of a world with no local tariffs protecting national economies, was much more difficult to achieve. Much progress had been made by regular rounds of negotiations in lowering trade barriers, but inevitably these reductions had largely been in the interest of the more powerful economies, as GATT had no enforcement mechanisms, and only a very weak conflict resolution system.

The WTO was created in the hope that as a result of increasing **globalization** in the latter half of the 20th century, the ultimate goal of complete freedom of trade would now be more attainable. Nothing could be, or was done, about the fundamental problem, the lack of an enforcement system. The IMF and the World Bank can enforce their policy preferences by financial coercion—any country which wants a loan or other international aid has no choice but to agree to their analyses of its economy. The WTO however, like GATT, lacks any powerful central policy-making directorate, ultimately it is a mechanism for multilateral negotiations. Whatever enforcement comes about is enforcement by the general drift of international self-interests. Where the

WTO is clearly more effective than GATT is in its conflict-resolution system. It is not enough simply to get some general agreement on, say, the terms under which bananas will be produced and traded; because even if a satisfactory general agreement can be reached at one of the periodic international meetings, individual countries may disobey. Under GATT such acts of disobedience were adjudged by a panel of experts who not only had to be unanimous in their decision, but the offending country also had to agree to be tried. The WTO allows majority decisions, and the consent of countries to being judged is not required. Thus, it is now worthwhile for a country suffering from another's discrimination against its product, to make a complaint. The WTO heard over 300 cases in the first five years of its existence, roughly as many as GATT had dealt with in its entire existence.

The problems that face the WTO in fact are of a different nature. It is increasingly seen, somewhat unfairly, as the main body responsible for economic globalization in a world where globalization has become deeply suspect to many radical political movements. This became apparent when the first international meeting of the WTO, held in Seattle (USA) in 1999, had to be broken off because of the sometimes violent protests taking place throughout the city. Subsequent meetings of international organizations, including the G-8, the World Economic Forum and the **European Union**, attracted similar protests, with varying degrees of violence, ostensibly in protest at the trade policies of the developed world.

Y

Yuppie

Yuppie is an acronym for 'Young, Upwardly-mobile, Professional', although some would give the 'u' as standing for 'Urban'. It was the first of a series of acronyms coined by American journalists to describe the social groups that emerged, or became prominent as electoral target groups, during the 1980s. Others include 'Dinks' ('Dual Income, No Kids') and variations on the idea of comfortably-off middle-aged people whose children are no longer financial burdens. What all these groups have in common is that they were ideal electoral audiences for policies aimed at reducing both taxes and social expenditure , as such groups had no direct personal need for state-provided education, health services, public transport and so on (see **welfarism**). It was precisely these groups that US President Ronald Reagan's first federal budgets, in 1981 and 1982, were aimed at, and the strategy was extremely successful. The brash arrogance of the Yuppies and the self-satisfied attitudes of the other acronymic groups soon began to appal Americans, however, particularly when some were revealed to have participated in illegal trading in the stock-markets and other abuses of their, already very extensive, freedoms. It was not a purely American phenomenon, of course. Many other Western societies experienced the politics of Yuppiedom, though no other country gave the favoured groups the respectability that they briefly enjoyed in the USA. In the United Kingdom, for example, similar tax and economic policies were targeted successfully at particular voter groups by the **Conservative Party**, not only the City of London-based Yuppies, but also their down-market cousin, 'Essex Man'. Although Essex Man and, eventually, Yuppie were recognized as terms of scorn, this has not stopped those who might be so described from enjoying their prosperity, nor prevented governments from reaping the electoral benefits of having encouraged these groups. The phrase was seldom heard by the early 21st century, but it played so large a part in characterizing the politics of the last two decades of the 20th that historians will long have recourse to it. The word was the most obvious symbol of a shift towards egocentric politics arising from the removal of much of the socio-economic security Western societies had built for themselves after 1945.

Z

Zionism

Zionism is the political creed, dating from early in the diaspora, that the old Jewish national homeland of Palestine should be regained by Jews and run as a national home and centre for world-wide Jewish solidarity. Although Zionism grew with increasing fervour from the early 20th century, the rise of vicious **anti-Semitism** in Europe during the 1930s greatly increased its support. For a long time the area demanded, Palestine, was governed under a mandate from the **League of Nations**, and then the **United Nations**, by the United Kingdom, because, whatever international Judaism might argue historically, it was a fully populated Arab country which could not be evacuated or suddenly flooded with European Jews, and tight immigration controls were applied. After the European Holocaust, however, it became both morally and practically difficult for Western powers to maintain their protection of the area and, after a terrorist campaign and the withdrawal of British troops, militant Jewish groups founded the State of Israel as the official Zionist homeland.

While the general doctrine of Zionism has remained vitally important to most Jews, world-wide, the problem of the Palestinian people, especially in the areas which Israel added to its control after its defensive wars against Arab states, has diminished external support, and even produced political strains inside Israel. Nowadays Zionism principally refers to a **hawks and doves** orientation towards Israeli policy. Zionists support at least the retention of the land gained in the various **Arab–Israeli conflicts** since 1947, and possibly a further integration of these areas by the settlement of Jewish immigrants, mainly from the former Soviet Union. Zionism still retains considerable support, often among financially and politically powerful Jewish lobbies in Western countries, and especially in the USA. Non-Zionists, whether Jewish, Israeli or neither, increasingly believe that some sort of accommodation, almost certainly involving the creation of a Palestinian state somewhere inside the current *de facto* Israeli borders, is both right and politically necessary.

At a UN conference on **racism** in September 2001, a number of Arab states, led by Syria, proposed a that the conference equate Zionism with racism, claiming that in its contemporary sense the suppression of the Palestinian people was a necessary constituent of the Zionist programme. Israel and the USA stated that the proposals amounted to an attempt to impose an anti-Israel agenda on the conference, and withdrew in protest; the motion to have such wording included in the conference's declaration was defeated.

A secondary meaning sometimes given to Zionism refers to the internal politics of Israel, and especially to the extent to which the theological, rather than purely ethnic and cultural aspects of Judaism, should be enforced or encouraged by the state.

2338 016